FRANK LLOYD WRIGHT'S MONONA TERRACE

# FRANK LLOYD WRIGHT'S MONONA TERRACE

## THE ENDURING POWER OF A CIVIC VISION

David V. Mollenhoff and Mary Jane Hamilton

The University of Wisconsin Press

The University of Wisconsin Press
2537 Daniels Street
Madison, Wisconsin 53718

3 Henrietta Street
London WC2E 8LU, England

5   4   3   2   1

Printed in the United States of America

Library of Congress Cataloging-in-Publication Data
Mollenhoff, David V.
    Frank Lloyd Wright's Monona Terrace: the enduring
power of a civic vision / David V. Mollenhoff and
Mary Jane Hamilton.
    336 pp.    cm.
    Includes bibliographical references and index.
    ISBN 0-299-15500-5 (cloth: alk. paper)
    1. Monona Terrace (Madison, Wis.). 2. Wright,
Frank Lloyd, 1867–1959—Criticism and interpretation.
3. Convention facilities — Wisconsin — Madison.
4. Madison (Wis.) — Buildings, structures, etc.
I. Hamilton, Mary Jane. II. Title.
NA6880.5.U62M335    1999
725'.13'092 — dc21    98-29148

Publication of this book has been made possible in part by a
grant from the Warren G. Moon Fund.

THIS BOOK IS DEDICATED TO MARSHALL ERDMAN, 1922–1995

## CHAPTER 1
### A STAGE FOR THE DRAMA
#### 1837 – 1938

**A New Temple of Democracy**
**That Glorious Link between Capitol and Lake**
**Nolen's Vision Takes Shape — Slowly**
**The Pursuit of Community, Culture,**
   **and Commerce**
**Quiet! Civic Impresario at Work**
**The Great Crescendo, October 1938**

Beginning in 1837, the year Madison is designated
Wisconsin's territorial capital, leaders try to realize
the extraordinary potential of the city's unique
isthmus site between two lakes and especially the
thousand-foot link between the state capitol and
Lake Monona. The quest spawns a spectrum of
plans. John Nolen, a famous urban planner, urges
that the lake end of the link be kept free of
buildings. Later a powerful business organization
says this is the best location for a new civic
auditorium, a building the city needs for concerts,
conventions, and civic events. The Great Depression
halts the battle about how to develop the premiere
sweet spot on the isthmus, but resumes when New
Deal programs encourage local leaders to seek
grants for both a civic auditorium and a city-county
office building. Joseph Jackson, the new head
of a revitalized business organization, has strong
ideas about where these buildings should be
located, but his solution sets the stage for an
epic civic battle with Frank Lloyd Wright.

## CHAPTER 2
### AN OLD MADISON BOY
#### 1878 – 1938

**The Madison Years**
**The Chicago Years**
**The Early Taliesin Years**

Frank Lloyd Wright's family moves to Madison
in 1878, and until he dies eighty years later
he maintains a strong but often tempestuous
relationship with his hometown. He spends his
formative years in Madison, where he secures
his only academic training at the University of
Wisconsin and receives a remarkably thorough,
life-changing immersion in architecture from
Professor Allan Conover. Even after Wright moves
to Chicago in 1887, he often returns to Madison
to supervise commissions, visit friends, and
prospect for new business. After he builds Taliesin
just forty miles from Madison in 1911, the city
becomes the center of his social and business
network, but by then the famous architect is
thumbing his nose at traditional morality and
merchants' bills. No one sees Wright at closer
range and for a longer period than Madisonians,
and what they see reveals much about the
controversial man.

## CHAPTER 3
### THE DREAM CIVIC CENTER
#### 1938 – 1949

**The Conception**
**Counterattack**
**The War Interlude**
**A Noble Enterprise for a Noble Purpose**

Just when Joseph Jackson and other civic leaders
think they have the votes and federal money to
build the civic auditorium on Lake Mendota and
a new city-county building in downtown Madison,
Paul Harloff, a retired electrical contractor,
commissions Wright to design a single building to
serve these functions and more. The architect's
huge semicircular complex, called a "Dream Civic
Center" by local papers, is sited on the Lake
Monona shore, exactly where Nolen proposed a
view-preserving esplanade. Many blame Wright's
eleventh hour initiative for derailing the plan for
the city-county building. Jackson counterattacks
with a nationally known urban planner, Ladislas
Segoe, who proposes an update of Nolen's plan.
After World War II, Jackson again tries to preempt
Wright's plan by promoting what he calls a War
Memorial auditorium on Lake Mendota, less than a
mile from the site of Wright's dream civic center.
The effort fails, but it transforms the definition
of a civic center and presages the auditorium
crusade of the 1950s.

## CHAPTER 4
### THE CIVIC AUDITORIUM CRUSADE
#### 1953 – 1965

**The Citizen Crusade**
**The Honeymoon**
**A Gauntlet of Generals**
**The Countercrusade**
**A Truce with Hope**

By 1953, as Madison leaders resume their planning
for a civic auditorium and a city-county building,
a controversial local politician persuades Wright
to reintroduce the dream civic center. Leadership
of the Wright initiative shifts to two talented
Madisonians, Helen Groves and Mary Lescohier.
They organize a citizen army and conduct a
remarkable grassroots campaign that persuades
voters to approve Wright as the architect for a
new civic auditorium. Despite the support of
Mayor Ivan Nestingen, the project encounters
intense opposition. After Wright dies in 1959,
Madison sends the project out for bids but learns
the cost is nearly triple the amount available. This
crisis catapults Henry Reynolds, a strong Terrace
opponent, into the mayor's office. Nevertheless,
the fight to build Monona Terrace continues, and
the project is transformed into a home for culture
and conventions.

## CHAPTER 5
### SALVAGING THE DREAM
### 1965 – 1980

**The Monona Basin Plan**
**Metro Square**
**The State Street Civic Center**

Van Potter, a well-known University of Wisconsin cancer researcher and Wright aficionado, reignites the Monona Terrace controversy by proposing that cultural and civic facilities be located along the entire Monona Basin, a three-mile sweep of lakeshore that includes the old Terrace site. He also proposes that William Wesley Peters, the head of Wright's successor architectural firm, be hired to prepare such a plan. City leaders agree and even adopt Peters' master plan. Under the leadership of Mayor Otto Festge, the first phase of the plan, a civic auditorium, proceeds to the bid-letting stage, but once again its cost exceeds the budget. Then in 1973 Paul Soglin, a University of Wisconsin student radical, is elected mayor, and he tries to get voters to approve additional money for the Peters auditorium. When voters refuse, a downtown business organization persuades Madison to restore a 1928 movie palace as a cultural arts complex. When it opens in 1980, everyone thinks Wright's grand plan on the lake is irretrievably dead.

## CHAPTER 6
### THE CONVENTION CENTER CRUSADE
### 1985 – 1997

**The Crash Course**
**The Quiet Crescendo of Wright Thinking**
**The Monona Terrace Commission**
**The 1992 Referendum: Yes Means Build It!**
**Final Ingredients**
**The Fleischli Fusillade**
**Pile Drivers in the Park**
**The Grand Opening**

In the late 1980s city leaders try to persuade voters to build a locally designed convention center near Wright's original Monona Terrace site, but voters refuse to endorse the $47 million project. During this debate several wonder whether Wright's Monona Terrace plan could be adapted as a convention center, but no one officially explores the idea until Paul Soglin begins his second stint as mayor in 1989. Armed with a preliminary feasibility study, Soglin proposes to adapt the Terrace as a convention center, and he creates a commission to work with Tony Puttnam, a senior architect at Taliesin Architects, and assigns a city staff team and others to finalize plans and costs. Experts determine the center will cost $67 million, but this time the State of Wisconsin, Dane County, and the private sector step forward to pay a large share. Even after citizens approve the plan in 1992, opponents attack the project with an unprecedented fusillade of lawsuits but to no avail. Finally, in July 1997, fifty-nine years after Wright proposed his first design, his enduring vision becomes a reality.

## CHAPTER 7
### TRIUMPH OF THE VISION
### 1938 – 1997

**Why Monona Terrace Took So Long**
**Evolution of Wright's Three Basic Designs**
**Limitations of Wright's Designs**
**But Is It Really Wright?**
**The Place of Monona Terrace**
**in Wright's Lifework**
**The Power of Wright's Vision**

Many questions swirl around Monona Terrace, Wright's most controversial project. Why did it take so long? How did the footprint and cross-section change as the design evolved? What limitations were inherent in Wright's iterations? Should the convention center be regarded as an authentic Wright design? What place should the Terrace have in the context of Wright's lifework, a body of more than seven hundred building designs? And, finally, what explains the six-decade appeal of Wright's civic vision?

### AFTERWORD
### FUTURE SYNERGY

Madison should take additional steps to more fully develop Wright's hometown legacy, including the construction of several other never-built designs.

## CONTENTS

# PREFACE

Why would an internationally famous architect work on a project for twenty-one years, prepare eight versions of the design, wine and dine prospective supporters, publicly debate its merits, commit his staff to work tens of thousands of hours, write tracts extolling its virtues, create thousands of drawings, renderings, and specifications, and direct the construction of a huge, extraordinarily detailed model — all in exchange for fees totaling $250? How could an architectural project generate five referenda, ten lawsuits, ten pieces of state legislation, and four thousand newspaper articles? How could an architect's civic vision lead to the formation of three very different coalitions of supporters and detractors in three decades? What would cause residents to *elect* an architect twice, once during his lifetime and once posthumously? Why would residents vote to build an architect's project thirty-three years after his death? These questions about Frank Lloyd Wright's Monona Terrace intrigued us.

When we began to research this story, we knew its general twists and turns, but we did not realize how extraordinary it was in Wright's career or in the annals of architecture. Wright practiced architecture for sixty-six years and designed more than seven hundred buildings, but only for Monona Terrace did he manifest so much enthusiasm, commitment, and even passion. We gradually realized that no novelist could concoct a story half as good as what really happened with Monona Terrace.

Yet, with the exception of one essay, a handful of articles, and several paragraphs in Wright biographies and books, the story of Monona Terrace remained untold. Moreover, much that had been written about the project suffered from factual errors, incorrect interpretations, and faulty assumptions. These realizations and the beginning of construction in late 1994 led us to conclude that the story deserved a fully researched and generously illustrated book that answered two questions: Why was Monona Terrace so important to Frank Lloyd Wright, and why did the project cause such a strong and sustained reaction from his client community, Madison, Wisconsin?

We determined that the book would have to serve two primary audiences: general readers who are interested in Wright, Monona Terrace, and local and state history; and specialists, including architects, urban planners, historians, and Wright scholars. To satisfy the needs of these diverse audiences, we designed the book so that it could be read on two levels. General readers could extract the story from text and graphics — or even from graphics alone — whereas specialists could secure additional information from appendixes, the bibliography, detailed endnotes, and an index that covers captions and endnotes as well as text.

Graphics constitute nearly half this book and for good reason: this story is profoundly visual. From thousands of choices we selected more than 250 images that capture the drama — cartoons, bumper stickers, original renderings, and several rare and previously unpublished photographs. To create the all-important sense of place, we commissioned the University of Wisconsin Cartographic Laboratory to make twenty special maps. To show the evolution of Wright's designs we had an architect in his successor firm prepare detailed footprint and cross-section drawings of key versions.

The book's organization is straightforward. Chapter 1 sets the stage by providing the history and geography of the city and site through 1938, the year that Wright introduced his grand civic center. Chapter 2 is a minibiography of Wright and his complex relationship with Madison, his hometown, through 1938. Chapters 3 through 6 chronicle the seven attempts to build Wright's vision, whereas Chapter 7 analyzes the entire project and compares designs, and an afterword suggests future actions.

All too often stories like this slip into the mists because documents are lost or destroyed. Happily, this was not the case with Monona Terrace. The Frank Lloyd Wright Archives contain a rich collection of documents, including original drawings, letters, and project files. Thousands of Madison newspaper articles provide a veritable project diary. In dusty corners of the City-County Building we found a remarkably complete record of local governments' actions. From personal papers of key participants we obtained rare insider perspectives. To supplement these paper sources, we interviewed more than fifty people, including governors, civic leaders, opponents and proponents, former Wright associates, consultants, and a sharp ninety-two-year-old man who was a Dane County supervisor in 1938 when Wright made his first public presentation of the project.

Like most books, this one took longer to complete than we planned, but the research was replete with surprises, and the amount of documentation exceeded our estimates. We hope the pleasure we derived from researching and writing the story of Wright's great civic vision is evident to you, the reader.

*David V. Mollenhoff and Mary Jane Hamilton*
*Madison, Wisconsin, 1998*

## DONORS

The authors gratefully acknowledge financial support from the following individuals, corporations, and foundations.

AIA Wisconsin/Wisconsin Architects Foundation

Dorothy L. Ballantyne

CUNA Mutual Group Foundation, Inc.

The Erdman Family

The Evjue Foundation, Inc.

W. Jerome Frautschi

Garver Memorial Trust

Hooper Corporation

Irwin and Robert Goodman Fund

J. H. Findorff & Son, Inc.

M&I Madison Bank

Madison Dairy Produce Company

Madison Gas and Electric Foundation

Madison Trust of the Brittingham Fund, Inc.

Thomas J. and Nancy S. Mohs

Norman Bassett Foundation

Oscar Mayer Foods Corporation

Potter Lawson, Inc.

R. J. Nickles, Inc.

James K. and Carol C. Ruhly

Steve Brown Apartments

Straus Printing Company

Sub-Zero Freezer Company, Inc.

Thompson, Plumb & Associates, Inc.

Webcrafters, Inc.

Wingra Stone

## ACKNOWLEDGMENTS

What splendid support and encouragement we received in writing this book! To recall the many who helped us along the way is a source of joy; to acknowledge their huge role is humbling. Our thanks go to

- Eric Lloyd Wright, Neil Levine, Edgar Tafel, and Sam Diman who at the beginning of our journey pronounced the concept good and urged us to do it.

- The twenty-six individuals, corporations, and foundations listed on the donor acknowledgment page who underwrote the cost of researching, writing, and publishing this book and without whose support this book would have remained a mere idea.

- Katie Benton, David Chang, Mark Koerner, Katy Magee, Beth Miller, Honor Sachs, Karen Spierling, and Barb Wyatt, our eight outstanding research assistants, who found needles in haystacks, imposed pattern on complexity, slogged though daunting terrain, and returned with a jaunty "what's next?"

- Allen Fitchen, now-retired director of the University of Wisconsin Press, who buoyed our spirits by expressing a strong interest in the book when it was scarcely more than an idea, to Elizabeth Steinberg, assistant director, and to their many helpful colleagues, including Diana Cook, Terry Emmrich, Charles Evenson, Raphael Kadushin, Sheila Leary, Scott Lenz, Carol Olsen, Joan Strasbaugh, and Margaret Walsh.

- Bruce Brooks Pfeiffer, director of the Frank Lloyd Wright Archives, and staff members Indira Berndtson, Penny Fowler, Sara Hammond, Oscar Munoz, and Margo Stipe, who made our research trips so productive and pleasant.

- Elizabeth Dawsari, director of the William Wesley Peters Library, and her colleagues, Molly Clark and Helen Hynes, and to Elke Vormfelde for photographing drawings from the Taliesin Architects Archives.

- Taliesin Architects, Ltd., and especially to Tony Puttnam, chief architect for Monona Terrace, for many clarifying explanations; to his colleagues, including Denise Weiland for the preparation of footprints and cross-sections of key project iterations, and Peter Rött; to former Wright apprentices, including Charles Montooth, Thomas Casey, Joe Fabris, John Rattenbury, and Roy Arnold for their informative recollections of their work on the Terrace.

- Julie Aulik, Julie Steele, and Beth Mylander at the Taliesin Preservation Commission, for assisting with special photography.

- The Getty Research Center staff members, for providing copies of correspondence housed in the Frank Lloyd Wright Archives.

- H. Nicholas Muller III, former director of the State Historical Society of Wisconsin, for his help in so many areas, and to his resourceful staff, including Loraine Adkins, David Benjamin, Lori Bessler, Nicolette Bomberg, Joan Burke, Andrea Christofferson, Jim Draeger, Delores Ducklow, Michael Edmonds, Dee Grimsrud, Jim Hansen, Laura Hemming, Jack Holzhueter, Andy Kraushaar, Carolyn Mattern, Harry Miller, Marie North, Rick Pifer, Scott Portman, Keith Rabiola, Gene Spindler, and Tracy Will.

- Frank Cook, director of the University of Wisconsin Archives, and his helpful staff, including Kathy Jacob and Bernie Schermetzler.

- Madison Newspapers, Inc., the holding corporation for the *Wisconsin State Journal* and *Capital Times*, for help in compiling newspaper accounts and photos, and especially to Ron Larson, Dennis McCormick, Carol Schmitt, and Meg Theno.

- Linda Baldwin, advertising director for *Isthmus*, and Marc Eisen, editor, for making newspaper archives and photos available.

- Peter Canon and Jack Stark, staff members at the State of Wisconsin Legislative Reference Bureau, for help in untangling long-forgotten bill histories.

- Staffers at the City of Madison and Dane County, including George Austin, Ted Ballweg, Bill Bauer, Sharon Christensen, Bob D'Angelo, Larry Nelson, Archie Nicolette, Katherine Rankin, Paul Reilly, John Rothschild, John Urich, Ann Waidelich, and Si Widstrand, all of whom helped provide the complex city and county perspectives.

- A small group with special expertise, including Madison historian Frank Custer, whose legendary files included heretofore unknown newspaper stories on Wright, Cord historian Stan Gilliland, Madison historic preservation consultant Tim Heggland, WHA-TV producer Diane Kostecke, and State of Wisconsin architect and capitol restoration specialist Charles Quagliana.

- Descendants and friends of Monona Terrace proponents and opponents, including Agnes Blair, Ruth Boyle, Marshall Browne, Jr., Susan Groves, Crystal Harloff, Barbara Harloff Karmann, James Harloff, and Dorothy Haines, whose family documents and recollections greatly enriched this story.

- More than fifty key participants who shared their recollections with us, including George Harb, who was a member of the county board when Wright first presented his idea in 1938, and Lynette Swenson, Carol Troyer-Shank, and Jill Olson, for transcribing these interviews.

- Deborah Archer, president of the Greater Madison Convention and Visitors Bureau, and her staff, who helped us reconstruct the history of the Madison hospitality industry.

- Joan LeMahieu, director of the Monona Terrace Community and Convention Center, and her staff, including Jean Benzine, Barbara Brink, and Bill Zeinemann.

- Arnold Alanen, Anne Biebel, Paul Boyer, Stan Cravens, William Cronon, Max Gaebler, Jack Holzhueter, Katherine Rankin, Steve Schur, Paul Sprague, and Bill Thompson, a spectrum of experts who read portions of or the entire manuscript and provided invaluable comments.

- A large group of people, including Art Hove, Mark LeFebvre, Bill Martinelli, Dick Munz, George Talbot, Carol Toussaint, and Ann Waidelich, whose important contributions spanned several categories or fell into still others.

- Onno Brouwer, director of the University of Wisconsin Cartographic Laboratory, and Kathy Sopa and Wendy Zareczny.

- The wonderfully competent team of Steve Agard and Kathy Schoenick at Hyperion Studios, and Thom Straus at Straus Printing Company, who transformed the manuscript and more than two hundred graphics into the book you now hold in your hand.

- And, finally, our spouses, who provided patience and support during our long journey.

To all of these people and, in truth, to many more, we offer our heartfelt thanks for all you did to make this book possible.

# ORIENTATION MAPS

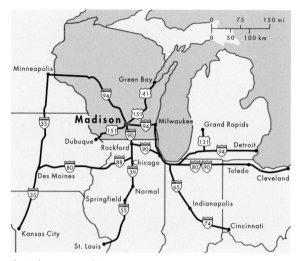

The Midwestern United States

*U.W.–Madison Cartographic Laboratory*

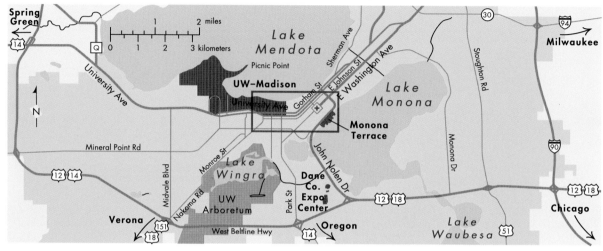

The Madison, Wisconsin, Area

*U.W.–Madison Cartographic Laboratory*

## Capitol Square and Western Isthmus

① Camp Randall Stadium
② Bascom Hill
③ Memorial Union
④ State Historical Society
⑤ Memorial Library
⑥ State Street Mall
⑦ Elvehjem Museum of Art
⑧ Kohl Center
⑨ Federal Courthouse
⑩ Madison Civic Center
⑪ Wisconsin Veterans Museum
⑫ Children's Museum
⑬ State Historical Museum
⑭ Travel Information Center
⑮ State Capitol Building
⑯ Greater Madison Convention & Visitors Bureau
⑰ Madison Municipal Building
⑱ City–County Building
⑲ Olin Terrace
⑳ State Office Building
㉑ Monona Terrace
㉒ Law Park

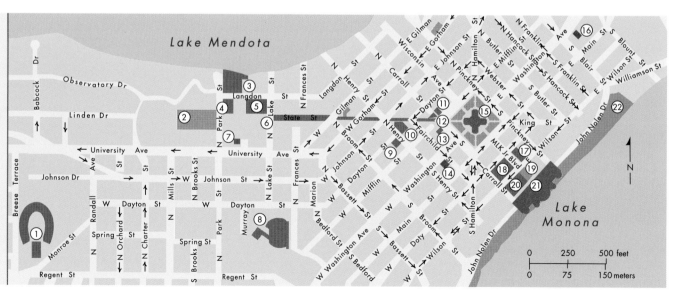

The Madison Isthmus

*U.W.–Madison Cartographic Laboratory*

FRANK LLOYD WRIGHT'S MONONA TERRACE

FIGURE 1.1

A Stage for the Drama: The View
down Monona Avenue, 1914

*SHSW. WHi(X3)51104*

Monona Avenue—two blocks long,
broad, and dramatic—appears in the
center of this 1914 photograph. It was
designed by James Duane Doty,
founder of Madison, to link the capitol
to Lake Monona. At the end of this
important street, later renamed Martin
Luther King Jr. Boulevard, was an
abrupt fifty-foot drop to filled land
along the lakeshore where railroads
had built four tracks. The avenue, the
lake bed at its end, and the six blocks
on each side were the stage for a
great civic battle.

This photograph, taken from the new
capitol building while it was under
construction, captures a quiet weekday
afternoon, probably in the fall, when
only a few wagons and cars were
parked in front of stores, and only a
few pedestrians can be seen on the
sidewalks. That's the way the Capitol
Square was on most weekdays. But
on Friday and Saturday nights, when
farmers came to town and joined the
city folk, the square bustled. Commercial
development was mostly limited to the
one block surrounding the square, and
a prestigious residential neighborhood
occupied the lakefront.

Madison was then in the midst of a
growth spurt and its downtown was
becoming more densely populated
with the first wave of apartment
buildings. One such building, the
massive, four-story Bellevue Apartments
built the year before, is plainly visible
to the left of Monona Avenue and
dominates the smaller frame homes
around it. In the 1990s this building
became the epicenter of opposition
to the convention center.

# CHAPTER 1

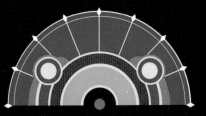

# A STAGE FOR THE DRAMA

FIGURE 1.2

**The 1904 Wisconsin Capitol Fire**

*Courtesy Ann Waidelich*

Clanging fire bells awakened Madisonians in the early morning hours of February 27, 1904. As word spread that the capitol was afire, residents flocked to see the conflagration, shown here in a famous postcard photo. Many did more than watch. Governor Robert Marion La Follette flitted through the burning building barking orders, and hundreds of citizens and students worked to save nearly all the contents. It was a day that became etched in the minds of those who saw what happened. But, above all, the fire launched a great debate about what kind of new capitol the state should build and the immediate surroundings it should have.

In this photo the south end of the capitol is on the left, the dome and assembly chamber in the center, and the north wing on the right. The fire-damaged building had been built in two stages, the central domed building (1857–1869) and two wings, begun in 1882. In 1883 a terrible construction accident that occurred while extending the south wing (see Fig. 2.15) left an indelible impression on sixteen-year-old Frank Lloyd Wright.

At 2:45 A.M. on February 27, 1904, a Saturday, a watchman at Wisconsin's capitol smelled fire and found that the ceiling of a small room adjoining the assembly chamber had been set ablaze by a wall-mounted gas lamp. Unable to douse the fire with a bucket of water, the watchman called the Madison Fire Department, which arrived promptly. Firefighters hooked up hoses to special capitol hydrants and turned on the water. Nothing came out. By the time they connected to city hydrants, they could do little but limit the spread of the spectacular conflagration (see Fig. 1.2). When the blaze was finally extinguished

a day later, both the assembly and senate chambers were totally destroyed and adjacent areas extensively damaged. The day after that, state officials learned that the insurance policy on the capitol had lapsed and that the state would have to cover the fire damage, estimated at $1 million. It was not an auspicious day in Wisconsin's history.[1]

## A NEW TEMPLE OF DEMOCRACY

The stunning capitol fire provoked sober statements, recriminations, and nostalgia but few tears. Just nine months earlier the legislature had created the Capitol Improvement Commission to develop a plan to tastefully enlarge the building. In fact, the commission had already picked three well-known architects to participate in a design competition. Although the fire required changing the instructions for the three architects, the commission's intent was to use the structure "as far as practicable." Most legislators thought the old building could be tastefully expanded to serve the state's needs in the future.[2]

In December 1904, just ten months after the fire, the commission selected a capitol enlargement plan submitted by Cass Gilbert, the well-known New York architect, but the decision triggered an acrimonious political debate that raged during much of 1905. A prominent Wisconsin architect whose entry was rejected in favor of the New York architect's persuaded many legislators that the selection process was unfair. Other legislators opposed Gilbert's design because it practically touched the sidewalks of the Capitol Square, Madison's downtown business district. Still others were concerned about its huge price tag, estimated at $5 million. Gilbert was so angered by the controversy and criticism that he refused to have anything more to do with the project.[3]

The controversy over the Gilbert design came at a buoyant and effervescent time in Wisconsin history — the economy was robust, and state leaders were earning a national reputation for progressive reforms. Like their counterparts elsewhere, Wisconsin progressives were reacting to the unpleasant and unacceptable consequences of the simultaneous urbanization and industrialization of the late nineteenth century. Progressives were appalled that so many people lived in squalid conditions and by the rampant corruption, ominous concentration of wealth, exploitation of workers, governments that served special interest groups, and political power concentrated in the hands of a few. In reaction, the progressives, a broad coalition of urban, well-educated, largely Republican, and Protestant Americans, spearheaded one of the most remarkable reform movements in American history. They demanded reforms based on the highest moral standards; asserted every citizen's obligation to improve the community and the world; demanded stronger, more accountable, and much more accessible government; expressed confidence in experts to solve the increasingly complex urban problems; and, above all, manifested an intense concern for the public interest, the common good, and the popular will.[4]

No state was more often or more flatteringly associated with the new progressive movement than Wisconsin, and no one in Wisconsin was more directly affiliated with it than Governor Robert Marion La Follette (see Fig. 1.3). During his three terms as governor (1901–1907) La Follette initiated the direct primary (the first in the nation), implemented a tough railroad regulation program, and began the practice of meeting with University of Wisconsin professors to help solve state problems, one of the first "brain trusts" in the country, which became known as the Wisconsin Idea. He also broke the back of machine politics by inaugurating a civil service, heavily taxed railroads

No name is more quickly and properly associated with Wisconsin than La Follette's. Indeed, the name is still nearly a household word, although the man who made it legendary died in 1925.

La Follette, a Republican, was elected district attorney for Dane County in 1880, just one year after he was graduated from the University of Wisconsin. He handled the office with such skill that he was elected to Congress in 1884. Although at twenty-nine he was the youngest member of the House of Representatives, he nevertheless received attention for his brilliant speeches and soon began his attack on the Republican "Wisconsin machine." La Follette lost his seat in a Democratic landslide in 1890 and resumed his law practice in Madison, remaining active in state and local politics. He was elected governor in 1900 and pushed through the legislature a remarkable mix of legislation that established his reputation as a crusading progressive.

When he was elected to the U.S. Senate in 1906 for the first of three terms, La Follette was viewed as an extreme radical, and he often addressed empty chairs. Gradually, however, he formed coalitions with a few like-minded reformers who tried to change the structure of the Senate to eliminate the power of big business, an initiative that led to the formation of the national Progressive Party. La Follette hoped to get the new party's nomination for president in 1912, but Theodore Roosevelt won the prize. La Follette ran for president as a Progressive in 1924 but lost to Calvin Coolidge.

When "Fighting Bob" died, his sons continued the dynasty. Robert, Jr., took his father's seat in the Senate, and in 1930 Philip was elected governor. The La Follette name is still greatly admired for his transformation of Wisconsin politics from a boss-ridden machine to a national model of progressivism.

to provide revenue for the state, and instituted the personal income tax. A veritable parade of journalists and reformers arrived in Wisconsin to see what writers called the "laboratory of democracy." La Follette won a seat in the U.S. Senate in 1906, and his successors in the governor's mansion advanced and strengthened Wisconsin's image as a progressive state with an impressive list of first-time national legislation, including workers' compensation, a state income tax, comprehensive regulation of child labor, campaign expense disclosure requirements, a state vocational education program, and an extraordinarily popular program for transmitting the latest agricultural research to farmers through county extension agents.[5]

The combination of a flourishing state economy and the national attention that Wisconsin was receiving from the passage of so much pioneering progressive legislation boosted confidence and pride among state legislators and made them eager to have a splendid new monument to democracy. As Governor James Davidson, La Follette's successor, later put it, "The resources of Wisconsin are so ample, the income of the state so abundant, and the spirit of the people ... so high and liberal, that anything less in the character of this chief of all state buildings ... would result in reproach." To no one's surprise the Wisconsin Legislature in December 1905 voted to hold a second architectural competition to secure a design for a truly grand new centerpiece for the state.[6]

The new national architectural competition got underway in early 1906, and in June the capitol commissioners hired the world-famous Chicago architect Daniel Burnham to judge the entries. Burnham was best known for his pioneering skyscrapers and for his layout of the inspiring "White City" for the Columbian Exposition held in Chicago in 1893. Burnham recommended the elegant plan developed by George B. Post and Sons (see Fig. 1.4), a large, highly regarded New York firm best known for its design of the New York Stock Exchange building. The commission concurred, and a few months later so did the legislature. Construction began in 1907 and was completed ten years later.[7]

## THAT GLORIOUS LINK BETWEEN CAPITOL AND LAKE

Significantly, the footprint of Post's spectacular new capitol was nearly twice as large as the fire-damaged capitol's. This caused Post and a group of state and local leaders to conclude that the fourteen-acre Capitol Park was too small for such a huge new building (see Fig. 1.5). It was a classic case of buying a new suit and needing new accessories to properly set it off. What was remarkable was that critics of the undersized Capitol Park agreed on the accessories that would give the new capitol the dignity they sought. What we must do, they argued, is increase the size of the park along Monona Avenue, a street that ran for just one thousand feet between the square and Lake Monona (see Fig. 1.1, p. 2). (Monona Avenue became Martin Luther King Jr. Boulevard in 1987.)

### THE STOUT CRUSADE

Curiously, concern about the big footprint disappeared almost as quickly as it had been raised—but not for long. On February 27, 1907, a front-page story in the *Madison Democrat* disclosed that real estate agents had been working secretly for weeks to secure options on properties located between the capitol and the lake and between South Carroll and South Pinckney—property that experts said was worth about $2 million. The story disclosed that agents had acquired options totaling $1.7 million and that once all parcels had been optioned, the state would

FIGURE 1.4

**1906 Rendering of
New Capitol Building**

*Courtesy Wisconsin Department of Administration,
photo by Eric Oxendorf*

This 5-by-6-foot ink and watercolor rendering executed by the New York architectural firm of George B. Post in 1906 wowed nearly all who saw it. People were enchanted by its vivid detail, delicate pink-brown palette, and breathtaking beauty, as well as the palpable grandeur of its neoclassical design.

Daniel Burnham, the famous Chicago architect hired to critique the architectural competition for the Wisconsin capitol, urged the commissioners to select the Post plan. Burnham applauded the dignity of the broad terrace surrounding the building, the "ideal proportion" of the interior, and the "impressive and beautiful" mass of the dome. Burnham was not without suggestions for improving the design, however. For example, he said that the four slender tourelles at the base of the dome (three are visible in the rendering) were too large, and Post replaced them with statuary groups.

Construction began in 1907 and was completed in 1917 at a cost of $7.2 million, substantially more than the original $6 million estimate. Everything about the building was first class, from the white Vermont granite exterior to the specially cast hardware for the doors. Tours of the building have been popular since it opened, and visitors always thrill to the panoramic view of the city from the promenade at the base of the dome. Figures 1.5, 1.7, and 1.16 show the location of the capitol.

buy the property, raze the buildings, and build a spectacular park so that Wisconsin's grand new capitol would enjoy two blocks of lake frontage. Madisonians were stunned to read that something so big had been done behind their back.[8]

The *Democrat*'s story—and a flurry of others that appeared in the days that followed—suggested that James Huff Stout, a wealthy lumberman from Menomonie, Wisconsin, was behind the scheme and would underwrite a large part of the project. Stout had been a state senator since 1894 and enjoyed widespread acclaim for his philanthropic support of the Stout Institute, the first U.S. school to specialize in the training of manual and domestic arts teachers. (Today the school is the University of Wisconsin–Stout.) By 1907 he had spearheaded and underwritten large-scale civic improvements and beautification programs in Menomonie, several of which bore similarities to what Stout wanted to do for Madison. (Significantly, Stout was not the only person who favored a large park between the capitol

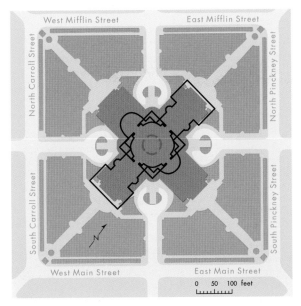

FIGURE 1.5

**The Small Lot and Skyscraper Problems**

*U.W.–Madison Cartographic Laboratory*

While state and local leaders were discussing the new Post-designed capitol, two factors caused many to conclude that the grounds were too small. First, the footprint for the new building was twice as large as that of the fire-damaged capitol's. This diagram shows the footprint of the old building in black and the new building in brown. The second factor was the threat posed by the new urban icon, the skyscraper. Although Madison had none in 1906, almost everyone assumed that as the city grew, the capitol would be surrounded by a wall of tall buildings. These two perceptions produced remarkable agreement on the need to give the new capitol an unobstructed view of Lake Monona. The diagram also shows the alignment of the new building relative to the old capitol.

and the lake, although he was the most outspoken proponent at the state level. As the caption to Figure 1.6 notes, a prominent Madisonian also embraced the idea.)[9]

As chair of the Senate Committee on Capitol and Grounds, Stout had begun to lobby for an expanded park when the 1905 Gilbert plan was presented. Unlike many of his legislative colleagues, who thought the building was too big, Stout said the building was just fine and that the solution was to enlarge the grounds. As Stout told a senate colleague in 1905, an expanded Capitol Park "may cost a million or more but it will be money wisely spent. It will give room for the future."[10]

Stout's outspoken views on the need to expand Capitol Park led reporters to conclude that the rich lumberman would be underwriting the project. But that was only a rumor; Stout's real role was to introduce a bill in May 1907 that authorized the state to spend up to $1.75 million to buy the six blocks between the capitol and the lake. However, few legislators had an appetite for such a large appropriation on top of the $6 million already appropriated for the new capitol.[11]

## THE OLIN CRUSADE

Stout's 1907 call for a greatly expanded Capitol Park came at an ideal time in Madison history. Considerable public attention was focused on beautification—an old and dominant theme in the city's history. Indeed, the natural beauty of the slender isthmus site was a main reason that James Duane Doty, founder of the town called Madison City, had been able to persuade the first Wisconsin Territorial Legislature to choose the city as the site for the capital in 1836 (see Figs. 1.7, 1.8, and 1.9). For many years Madisonians routinely heard national celebrities make superlative comments about the city's beauty. For example, in 1854 Horace Greeley, the famous editor of the *New York Tribune*, spent a few days in the city and reported in his nationally read column that "Madison has the most magnificent site of any inland town I ever saw."[12]

Madison leaders were naturally delighted with such testimonials and made them the standard menu for city promotions for the next four decades. By 1892,

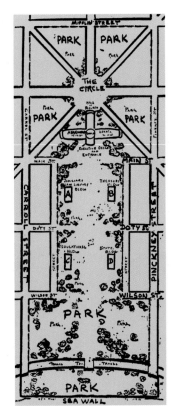

FIGURE 1.6

**1907 Gapen Plan**

*Courtesy Wisconsin State Journal, enhanced by W. J. Martinelli*

Although the debate about expanding Capitol Park had been raging for weeks, this drawing did not appear in the *Wisconsin State Journal* until April 30, 1907, and marked the first time anyone had seen the plan. It was the brainchild of Dr. Clarke Gapen, a Madison physician, lawyer, and civic leader. Gapen urged city and state leaders to substantially widen Monona Avenue so the grand new capitol building could front on Lake Monona and be freed from its cramped setting surrounded by commercial buildings. The outspoken civic leader also recommended that the lake be filled at the foot of Monona Avenue for a small park and that a platform be built over the railroad tracks to allow people to get to the park. Finally, Gapen said, the city should hire someone like Daniel Burnham to design this great civic center. Burnham, a Chicago architect, had done visionary downtown plans for Cleveland, San Francisco, and Washington, D.C. (Although the Post design had already been selected, this drawing shows a capitol design that Gapen apparently preferred.)

Six weeks earlier the *State Journal* had published a sizzling article in which Gapen had accused Madison's leaders of having no imagination, courage, or appreciation of the rare beauty that nature bequeathed the city and of sleeping through one of the greatest opportunities the city ever had. Yes, the cost would be high, Gapen allowed, but "Wisconsin is a great and rich state and becoming greater and richer."

however, civic leaders realized that touting the city's beauty was not enough. In that year leaders urged a concerted cleanup of the lakeshore (see Fig. 1.10) and opened a privately sponsored carriage drive along the shore of Lake Mendota just west of the University of Wisconsin. City leaders filled seventy

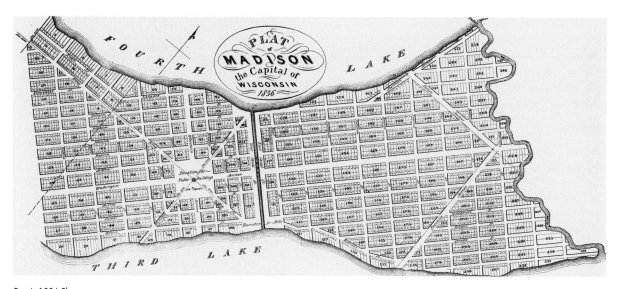

Doty's 1836 Plat

*Courtesy SHSW and Historic Urban Plans, Inc.*

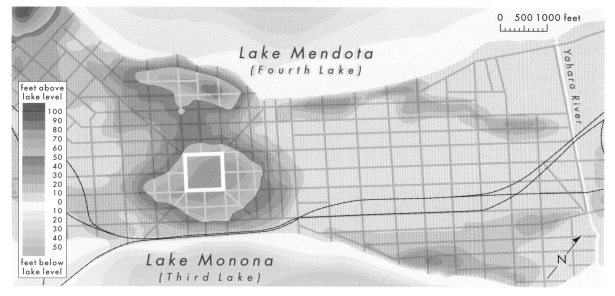

Isthmus Topography

*U.W.–Madison Cartographic Laboratory*

FIGURE 1.7

### Doty's City on an Isthmus: The Original Plat of Madison

What James Duane Doty thought when he first saw the slender isthmus between two lakes in 1829 is not known, but it left an indelible impression in his mind. Seven years later he presented his paper plan for Madison City to the Wisconsin Territorial Legislature as a location for the capital. Why Madison was chosen over eighteen other locations still provokes debate, but one fact has never been disputed: the site was beautiful.

Doty and his surveyor arrived at the town site in late October 1836 and spent two days there on their way to Belmont where the territorial legislature was meeting to select a capital. This gave the surveyor time to establish the exterior lines of the plat and Doty time to think about how he would take advantage of the unique site and its natural beauty. The first thing the two men did was locate the oak stake that federal surveyors had pounded into the earth at a point in the isthmus where the corners of four sections came together. (A section is a square mile in area.) By extraordinary coincidence this section corner lay close to the narrow point of the isthmus and close to the top of a seventy-five-foot hill that dominated the center of the isthmus. The serendipitous location of the surveyor's stake appears as a red dot on the plat map. Surely the experience of standing at this surveyor's stake persuaded Doty that this would be the logical center of his city. He would create a city upon a hill.

Next, Doty had to decide how to lay out streets. By now Doty had platted several Wisconsin cities, including Green Bay and Fond du Lac, and had used the familiar grid system for all. But for Madison City Doty wanted something more distinctive, so he selected a radial street plan rarely used in the United States but common in Europe. According to the radial plan, streets focus on a central feature like spokes on a wheel. Doty had seen the idea in Detroit in 1818, and a few years later he saw the most elegant example in the United States, Washington, D.C., laid out by the French surveyor Pierre L'Enfant. Doty proposed as the hub of the radial street system a fourteen-acre square reserved for the capitol. The map shows Doty's original plat and its radial street layout.

Doty's final design decision was street widths. According to the baroque European radial system, width denotes relative importance. Put yourself in Doty's shoes. From the surveyor's section corner stake most of the isthmus was a prairie in 1836, with only a few small oaks to block views. To the north Doty could see Lake Mendota. To the east, southeast, and south he enjoyed the panoramic views of Lake Monona. Of these, the most dramatic was the view to the southeast, where the lake was just sixteen hundred feet from the surveyor's stake. The land sloped gradually downward until it reached the edge of an abrupt hill at water's edge. There, fifty feet below, was the lake, sparkling in the morning sun. Surely this explains why Doty positioned a street along this southeasterly axis and gave it maximum importance by making it 132 feet wide. This pivotal perception by a frontier promoter set the stage for a great debate about how the drama and beauty of this area could best be developed.

The plat map also shows several other important features. The dark line at the narrow point of the isthmus on the original plat was Doty's proposed location for a canal, a concept that was later abandoned because of the extensive excavation it required. Instead, as the topographic map shows, city leaders straightened the meandering stream and renamed it the Yahara River. The hill shown at the upper left of the topographic map towers one hundred feet over Lake Mendota and was Doty's proposed location for the University of Wisconsin. A decade later the site was purchased for this purpose.

The original names of the lakes, Third Lake and Fourth Lake, which appear on the original plat, were later changed to Lake Monona and Lake Mendota, respectively. Federal surveyors gave the lakes their numbered names to reflect the sequence in which they encountered them. Two other lakes lie to the south of the two that form the Madison isthmus and caused Madison to be known for many years as the City of the Four Lakes.

Doty originally named the street between the square and the lake "Wisconsin Avenue." In the 1880s Madison changed the name to Monona Avenue, and in 1987 to Martin Luther King Jr. Boulevard.

FIGURE 1.8

**Olin Terrace — a Site Sacred to Native Americans?**

Wisconsin Archeologist 1, no. 4 (1922)

James Duane Doty, the man who platted Madison, was hardly the first to declare the importance of the hilltop adjacent to Lake Monona (now a part of the entrance plaza to Monona Terrace and known as Olin Terrace). That honor is enjoyed by the Native Americans who built distinctive earthen mounds on this site at least three thousand years ago.

The two conical mounds were built as early as 1000 B.C. by peoples of the Woodland (Hopewellian) tradition. Excavations of other Madison-area conical mounds show that they were used for burial purposes and that they contained seashells from both the Atlantic and Gulf coasts, which suggests that these people were involved in a continental trading network. The third mound, a stylized turtle, is known as an *effigy* and was built by another Indian civilization between 400 and 1300 A.D. More than one thousand effigy mounds were built in the Madison area, the greatest concentration in the world. Almost all were erected on hills that provided water-oriented views. This extraordinary concentration strongly suggests that Madison was special, if not sacred, to this native culture. An early surveyor reported that the two conical mounds were forty-two feet in diameter and that the turtle effigy was 318 feet long and 40 feet wide. (For an 1880s photo of this mound site, see Fig. 1.23.)

In 1818 when James Duane Doty was just eighteen, he said good-bye to his family in upper New York State and boarded a steamer for Detroit, a frontier village of just seven hundred people. The tall, good-looking, articulate, and incredibly ambitious young man met the attorney general of Michigan Territory, a man who was so impressed by Doty's intellect and abilities that he asked the young man to be his clerk. Doty accepted and one year later was admitted to the bar, appointed clerk of the Michigan Supreme Court, and made secretary of the village of Detroit. At twenty-one Doty made two trips to Washington, D.C. — once to be admitted to practice before the Supreme Court and the second time to lobby for the creation of a judgeship in what is now Wisconsin, Iowa, and Minnesota. When Doty was only twenty-five, President James Monroe appointed him to a federal judgeship in Western Michigan Territory.

During most of the next nine years Doty adjudicated federal cases in Mackinac, Michigan, and Green Bay and Prairie du Chien, Wisconsin, a rigorous 1,360-mile circuit he made each year by canoe. During this time he developed a unique "native code," based on Native American, not American values, and learned to speak French, Chippewa, Winnebago, and Sioux. When President Andrew Jackson appointed another man to Doty's judgeship in 1832, Doty, then only thirty-two, secured two federal commissions to lay out military roads between Chicago and Green Bay and between Green Bay and Prairie du Chien.

In 1834 Doty won a seat in the Michigan Legislature and got that body to pass a bill to create the Wisconsin Territory, no mean feat for a first-term legislator, and at the same time became the Wisconsin agent for John Jacob Astor, then the richest man in the country. During this period Doty began to gain experience in laying out cities, including Green Bay, Fond du Lac, and Madison (see Fig. 1.7).

In 1838 Doty won a term in Congress as the delegate from Wisconsin Territory, and in 1841 he began the first of two two-year terms as territorial governor. While governor, Doty

lived in a modest home on what is now called Doty Street, just one block from what would become the Monona Terrace Community and Convention Center.

Four years after he left the governorship, Doty was elected to the U.S. House of Representatives and served two terms (1849–1853). One final fling at national politics awaited Doty. In 1861, soon after Doty turned sixty-two, President Abraham Lincoln appointed him superintendent of Indian affairs at Salt Lake City; two years later Lincoln made Doty the governor of Utah Territory. During the Utah years the restless Doty traveled to Los Angeles, enjoying the climate and tropical fruits. He died in June 1865.

Boathouses near the Madison Depot
*SHSW. WHi(X3)50729*

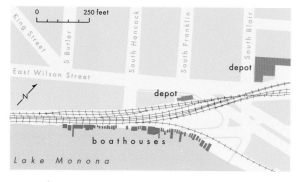

Location of Boathouses
*U.W.–Madison Cartographic Laboratory*

FIGURE 1.10

**Welcome to Beautiful Madison! Lakeshore Eyesores**

Trains carried thousands of people to Madison, steaming into town from the south and crossing a corner of Lake Monona on a trestle. The tracks then followed the shoreline beside the downtown area and into the depot. But as the train pulled into the station, passengers got an eyeful — not of Madison's vaunted beauty but of rundown shacks along the lakeshore.

Madison boat owners began building the illegal shacks in the nineteenth century. This diagram shows the more than forty boathouses that blighted the lake in the early 1930s. If their location had been less central, probably no one would have said anything, but the shacks stood directly across the street from the passenger depots of the two major railroads serving Madison. And the shanties were littered with tin cans and trash, roofed with tar paper, untouched by paint, and loved by hobos in cold and rainy weather.

Madison leaders hated these boathouses and did just about everything they could to banish them. That was why they hired the young Frank Lloyd Wright to design a big, handsome public boathouse in 1893 (see Figs. 2.25 and A.1); it was one of Wright's first commissions. That was also why Nolen's 1909 plan proposed a union depot (so called because it served both railroads) there with direct access to the esplanade and the lake (see Fig. 1.18). The shacks remained until the 1930s, when the city finally secured legislation to force their removal.

carriages for the drive's festive opening and waxed enthusiasm about opening other drives so that more people could appreciate Madison's natural beauty. Then, in 1893, the president of the city's largest bank issued the sternest warning anyone had ever heard about protecting Madison's beauty: "We have about destroyed the original beauty and the approaches to our lake borders.... Could the distinguished men for whom our principal streets were named but rise and look upon the unfortunate change wrought by ourselves, destroying nature's loveliness, they would exclaim, ' 'twas bright, 'twas heavenly bright, but 'tis past.'" Suddenly, Madison business leaders were demanding flowers, fountains, boulevards, trees, and public lake access. It was the year that beautification became popular in Madison.[13]

Madison business leaders moved aggressively on several fronts. They hired Olaf Benson, the Chicago landscape architect whose firm had laid out the Windy City's lakefront Lincoln Park, to design boulevards and parks at several locations, including the end of Monona Avenue. They hired Frank Lloyd Wright, who had grown up in Madison and had just opened an architectural office in Chicago, to design elegant public boathouses for Lakes Monona and Mendota. (See Chapter 2 and Figs. 2.1, 2.25, and A.1 for photographs and drawings of these buildings.)[14]

Madison's beautifiers got a boost from the Columbian Exposition in Chicago in 1893. Twenty-one million Americans strolled through the sprawling grounds on Chicago's lakeshore, marveling at the spectacular mélange of classical buildings artfully arranged around a large central basin. To Americans long accustomed to dirty, ugly, poorly laid-out, park-deficient cities, the exposition was a revelation that fueled expectations. Hundreds of Madisonians attended the exposition and realized that cities could be beautiful, orderly,

clean, and even inspiring. The exposition was largely responsible for what became known as the City Beautiful movement in the United States, a paradigmatic shift that fueled interest in city planning and, especially in large-scale enclaves of classical buildings, broad boulevards, large fountains, ornamental sculpture, and formal landscaping.[15]

In 1894 Madison leaders announced the formation of what would become one of the most remarkable organizations in city history, the Madison Park and Pleasure Drive Association. Its members concentrated their initial energies on creating rustic drives around Madison lakes. Then in 1899 the association used a grant from wealthy businessman Daniel K. Tenney to begin developing public parks within the city's limits. Association leaders tried to get the city to develop the parks, but it refused to do much, which forced the association to function as a private parks department for many years.[16]

The president of the association from its formation in 1894 until 1909 was John Myers Olin, arguably the most extraordinary civic leader in Madison's history (see Fig. 1.11). Olin's profession was law, but his passion was parks. He was the force behind the creation of Madison's pleasure drives and the precedent-setting development of Tenney Park in 1899. In 1903 Olin organized the most powerful men in the city behind his plan to create a park on both sides of the Yahara River where it cut through the isthmus (see Fig. 1.7). Connecting the two pieces of the park required that the city raise eight vehicular and railroad bridges by eight feet so that powerboats could pass between the two lakes. Olin raised the money singlehandedly, persuaded the railroads to assume their share of the costs, and got the project underway in just six months. These achievements were but a prelude to a remarkable period of park development in Madison.[17]

ohn Myers Olin was a cold and austere man who seldom smiled or laughed, but his civic achievements and lofty visions for the city earned him a spot in the hearts of his contemporaries.

Olin came to Madison in 1874 when he was just twenty-three, with a job offer from University of Wisconsin president John Bascom. Olin had studied under Bascom when the two were at Williams College several years earlier, and Bascom was so impressed with Olin's ability that he wanted the young man to teach oratory and rhetoric at the U.W. Olin accepted and worked in this capacity for four years before entering the U.W. Law School. Olin finished the two-year program in just one year and in 1879 opened a solo practice in Madison; in 1885 he began teaching at the law school.

Although Olin was an outstanding professor and lawyer, most Madisonians remember him for his civic achievements. For fifteen years (1894 – 1909) Olin was president and the driving force behind the Madison Park and Pleasure Drive Association. When he began, the city had fewer than four acres of public parks, but when he turned the reins over to others in 1909 the city had 269 acres of parkland and had raised more than $250,000 in donations for the acquisition, development, and maintenance of parks. Furthermore, he did most of this fund-raising by sending out penny postcards to association members, reminding them to send in their annual five-dollar contributions. Nearly one in ten Madison households belonged to the organization.

Olin also persuaded city leaders that Madison required a comprehensive city plan at a time when few had even heard of urban planning. It was Olin who made the imaginative arrangements to inveigle John Nolen, then the most highly regarded planner in the country, to work for Madison.

Olin must be counted among a rare fraternity of visionaries; he spent much of his life teaching leaders to demand things they did not know the city needed. His achievements constitute a benchmark for urban citizenship that few can ever hope to match, much less surpass.

Olin's secret was his focus. Just as he used words with consummate skill, so too did he focus his energy on the one point where his effort would bear the most fruit. As Olin told association members at their annual meeting in 1902, his job was the "creation of an intelligent public sentiment and the promotion of correct opinions." When he began his park crusade in 1894, most Madison leaders thought parks were frills, but when Olin was finished, parks had become necessities.

After he died in 1924 at seventy-three city leaders honored Olin by naming two parks after him: Olin Park in 1927 (see Fig. 3.12) and Olin Terrace in 1934 (Fig. 3.3). In 1938 Frank Lloyd Wright honored Olin's memory by naming his project Olin Terraces, making it plural to distinguish it from Olin Terrace.

The Yahara project established Olin as a civic impresario and ushered in an era in which some of Madison's richest men gave large amounts of money to buy and develop new city parks. By 1905 Madison had 154 acres of public parks and 4.6 miles of public water frontage. Because this was accomplished almost entirely by a privately run and funded organization, the Madison Park and Pleasure Drive Association, the group drew national and even international praise. The mayor of Wellington, New Zealand, approvingly noted in his inaugural address what Madison had achieved, and French and Swedish officials asked for copies of the association's annual report so that they might emulate this private-sector solution to the need for open space. Even Madisonians were awed by what Olin had done in only a few years.[18]

Olin's commitment to park development made him a natural ally of state senator Stout and his plans to greatly expand Capitol Park. Both men were comfortable with big visionary ideas and sought the same end. For example, in June 1907 Olin was the principal speaker in support of Stout's bill to have the state buy the six blocks of land between Capitol Park and Lake Monona. In his vivid testimony Olin said that the plan would give Madison the most beautiful capitol in the United States and would cost Wisconsin taxpayers only five cents for every $1,000 of assessed valuation. Olin also scheduled the headline-generating annual association meeting to coincide with the introduction of the park expansion bills.[19]

When Stout failed to get the 1907 state legislature to buy six of the most expensive blocks in downtown Madison for the capitol, Olin decided to try an equally audacious but different strategy. He would try to get an outstanding representative of the new discipline of city planning to do a comprehensive

FIGURE 1.12

**Madison as a Factory Town**

SHSW. WHi(X3)38099

Many Madison leaders in the late nineteenth and early twentieth centuries admired few things more than sooty coal smoke pouring from a factory chimney. That was why the artist gave the chimney and coal smoke such a prominent place in this 1880s chromolithograph. Black smoke meant jobs, prosperity, and paychecks, and Madison, the palaver went, desperately needed manufacturing jobs in order to increase the city's population. But with few exceptions, factory proponents seldom prevailed in Madison in the nineteenth century.

One exception was breweries. After the Civil War, Madison's large German population supported five breweries, and each helped give Madison the look and feel of a factory town.

When this relatively large (nearly 2-by-3-foot) advertisement was printed, it was distributed to Madison-area saloons that sold Fauerbach beer. The brewery was located on a Lake Monona site now occupied by a condominium project.

plan for Madison. Olin was confident that any good city planner would recommend enlarging Capitol Park.

Olin's interest in city planning and his conviction that Madison must have a plan had been growing for years. Madison rarely boomed, but it did grow steadily. From 1880 to 1900 the city's population nearly doubled to twenty thousand, and in 1900 a group of prominent business leaders formed the Forty Thousand Club, which would work to double the city's population again by 1910. Olin was not alarmed by the population growth; what worried him was the clamor to make Madison grow by encouraging *factories* (see Fig. 1.12).

Before the Civil War, Madison was second only to Milwaukee in population. By 1895, however, Madison had dropped to ninth place, which many business leaders found disgraceful and embarrassing. That was why so many sought to lure factories: they thought factories were the best way to make the city grow fast. As one factory proponent put it, "Let us see the smoke from factory chimneys, let us hear the music of rattling machinery and thrift and prosperity will reverberate through every street in this now quiet peninsula." It was a popular refrain from the end of the Civil War until well into the twentieth century.[20]

Olin was hardly alone in his opposition to factories. Dozens of other members of Madison's intellectual, professional, and salaried classes shared his view. Their goal was to keep Madison a sophisticated, cultured, clean, beautiful college town and state capital. They took great pride that Madison had more residents listed in *Who's Who* than Milwaukee did with ten times the population. They ridiculed as a "profanation" the claim that bigger was better and that growth was always good, even as the rest of the country was marching to the brassy din of industrialization.[21]

FIGURE 1.13

**Madison as Athens of the West**

*SHSW. WHi(X3)2319*

Before kites, balloons, and airplanes took cameras aloft, the task fell to a remarkable breed of artists who specialized in what were called bird's-eye drawings. This 1907 bird's-eye captured the University of Wisconsin campus in the midst of a great boom that began in the late 1880s when a new president transformed the small liberal arts college into a university and persuaded the State of Wisconsin to provide generous support. From 1887 to 1900 student enrollment zoomed from five hundred to more than two thousand, and by 1920 more than seven thousand students were enrolled. New buildings were being erected on a dramatically expanded campus at an unprecedented rate. This rapid new growth caused business leaders to think of the university as a powerful source of economic growth and not just as a prestigious city ornament.

The boom significantly increased the university's influence in Madison and gave the city a more intellectual, cultural, and literary flavor. Some even began to tout the city as the "Athens of the West." Professors were elected to the common council, and one even became mayor. Other professors used their expertise to solve city problems, a pattern that may have been the inspiration for what later became known as the Wisconsin Idea. For example, in 1901 professors helped Madison get one of the most sophisticated sewerage systems in the country. Although university values seldom dominated Madison, they profoundly shaped the city. University leaders ridiculed the gospel of growth, the idea that growth for the sake of growth is good. They vigorously opposed efforts to turn Madison into a factory town and championed beautification. Still others supported efforts to reform city government and stifle the saloon.

The bird's-eye portrays many campus landmarks. The turreted building at the extreme right is known as the Red Gym and was sometimes used for cultural events and conventions. The large white building in the foreground is the home of the State Historical Society of Wisconsin. The large building partly concealed behind the historical society is Science Hall. Bascom Hall, still bearing the dome it sported until 1916, graces the top of a hill overlooking Lake Mendota, and major campus buildings form a sloping mall. The spired building at the bottom of the mall is Assembly Hall.

They feared industrialization would destroy Madison's beauty. This point of view had been eloquently captured by a *Harper's Weekly* writer who noted that Madison, like other cities in 1889, "is at intervals seized with the wish to become a great manufacturing center. To my mind this is a mistake. Any town that has railroads and pluck and enterprise ... can grow into a manufacturing center; few towns, however, can become beautiful and learned, or can achieve social distinction.... Madison can of course darken her skies with the smoke of countless furnaces, and cover her vacant lots with long rows of tenement houses if she so wills it.... It would be a great pity if she did so, however. The industrial West can ill afford to sacrifice those shining qualities that have made Madison famous for the paltry sake of a larger census return.... Madison ought to be content as well as proud of her present. She is rich and prosperous and cultured; let her exist for the sake of being beautiful."[22]

However, Olin and the antifactory group were not opposed to growth. For example, they considered university-related growth not only acceptable but desirable (see Fig. 1.13). The group also welcomed growth from resorts, conventions, and meetings (see Fig. 1.14).

As a lawyer John Olin was a great believer in due diligence, and he used this skill to find the best urban planner in the country. Throughout his search one name kept coming up: John Nolen (see Fig. 1.15). Nolen's highly regarded practice was based in Cambridge, Massachusetts. Although his firm was just two years old in 1908, Nolen had already contracted to do plans for San Diego, Savannah, Roanoke, and Charlotte, North Carolina, and was

VIEW OF MADISON THE CAPITAL OF WISCONSIN.
TAKEN FROM THE WATER CURE,
SOUTH SIDE OF LAKE MENONA, 1855.

FIGURE 1.14

**Madison as a Northern Resort, 1855 Currier Print**

*Courtesy Mariners' Museum, Newport News, Va.*

The two well-dressed couples in the center foreground of this 1855 Currier print represent what many civic leaders hoped Madison would become: a famous northern resort. The four are standing on the observation deck of a posh health resort in what is now Olin Park. Completed one year earlier, it was the first lakeshore resort to be built in the city. Guests at the sixty-room facility enjoyed hydrotherapy, a healthful diet, horseback riding, billiard tables, a well-stocked bar, and a panoramic view of Madison, then a city of about ten thousand, across the lake.

Civic leaders sought resorts because they would attract rich cultured people and allow Madison to enhance its image as a center of culture, learning, and legislation. Resort promoters were adamantly opposed to making Madison a factory town with soot-belching chimneys and "grimy workers," a phrase that everyone knew meant *immigrants.*

The glory years for Madison's resort industry began immediately after the Civil War when thousands thronged to the city each summer to enjoy its cool breezes, clean air, beautiful lakes, and healthful recreation. Many guests came from southern cities such as St. Louis and New Orleans to escape summer diseases caused by poor sanitation. Prominent guests included the St. Louis beer barons Everhard Anheuser and Adolphus Busch; Robert Lincoln, the president's son; and William T. Sherman, the famous Civil War general.

Unfortunately, those who wanted Madison to become a famous northern resort failed to understand that the short summer season was seldom long enough to permit investors to recoup their initial construction and high annual operating costs. Although business was good in some years, it was never enough to cause Madison to boom as a resort town — at least when tourists were dependent upon railroads. In fact, not until after World War I did the combination of good roads and affordable automobiles elevate tourism from an anemic affectation to a genuine industry.

The Currier lithograph was a direct result of Horace Greeley's visit to Madison in 1855. In a column describing his Madison visit, Greeley, the editor of the *New York Tribune,* wrote that "Madison has the most magnificent site of any inland town I ever saw." Greeley was a good friend of the famous printmakers Nathaniel and Charles Currier, and their New York offices were near Greeley's paper. Charles Currier concluded that Greeley's superlative-laden account created a market for a Madison print, so he commissioned an artist to prepare this scene.

regarded by close observers as the rising young star in the field. Olin wanted Nolen not only to do a plan for Madison but to move his practice and work full time there. The astute Madison lawyer almost succeeded by promising Nolen he could start the first university department of urban planning in the country, do the plans for several state agencies, and be Madison's first city planner. Although Olin failed to get Nolen to move to Madison, Olin did get the planner to make Madison a preferred client, a distinction that meant that he would spend more time in the city and charge a lower fee.[23]

Next, Olin worked to sell Nolen and his brand-new specialty to Madison's leaders. Despite the effect of the Columbian Exposition, most Madisonians had never heard of city planning, hardly surprising because the discipline was in its infancy and only a few cities had commissioned plans. City planning

was embraced by progressives like Olin who saw it as a strategy to create better cities. They believed comprehensive city plans would increase public parks and open space; provide zoning that would prevent neighborhoods from being ruined by factories and other nuisances; and establish building codes, which offered safer and more sanitary structures.[24]

NOLEN'S GRAND PLAN: A "PRACTICABLE IDEAL"

Nolen made his first public presentation at the gala annual meeting of the Madison Park and Pleasure Drive Association in April 1908, but because he had spent only two days in Madison before the meeting, he limited his talk to generalities. Nevertheless, he made a good first impression on people. However, later that year he spent several weeks in Madison, and in December 1908 he began to criticize the congested site for the new capitol, the lack of public access to the lake frontage (see Fig. 1.16),

FIGURE 1.15

**JOHN NOLEN**
*PIONEER URBAN PLANNER*

*Courtesy Terrence Conlon*

When John Nolen agreed to prepare a comprehensive plan for Madison in 1908, the sandy-haired man with the walrus mustache was just thirty-eight but already regarded as one of the best urban planners in the fledgling profession. At fifteen Nolen was graduated first in his class from an elite private Philadelphia high school where he demonstrated an unusual facility for public speaking, an avid interest in public issues, and a voracious appetite for books. Nolen went on to get a degree with high honors from the Wharton School of Business and then spent ten years directing an adult education program known as the People's University at the University of Pennsylvania. The program provided Nolen with stimulating personal contacts with many leading thinkers of the day. By 1897 Nolen was convinced that the great problems of his age were "not so much national as municipal" and that the true leaders of the era were those who worked to make urban ideals a reality.

In 1904, then thirty-four, he resigned his post at the People's University and set sail for Europe to study the design and management of its cities. He returned to the United States intent upon becoming an urban planner. At that time no academic institution offered an urban planning program, but Harvard had just begun a graduate program in landscape architecture, a discipline whose curriculum included components of what later became urban planning. Consequently, Nolen moved his family to Cambridge, Massachusetts, entered the new Harvard program, and studied under Frederick Law Olmsted. Six months before he finished the program with highest honors, Nolen opened a planning office in Cambridge and began a whirlwind practice that required him to travel thirty thousand miles and spend six months in the field each year. Nolen had hit the market when a few farsighted civic leaders were seeking plans for their cities.

Nolen was the keynote speaker at the first meeting of the National Conference on City Planning in 1909 and was one of the first presidents of the American Institute of Planners (AIP). His Cambridge-based practice was quickly recognized as one of the best in the United States. When Nolen died in 1937, he had completed 450 projects, written six books and one hundred papers, worked to establish urban planning programs at major universities, provided farsighted leadership to his new profession, and was widely regarded as the dean of American urban planning.

the clutter of boathouses (see Fig. 1.10), the absence of playgrounds, and the narrow streets. All these things, Nolen asserted, were normal products of "haphazard" growth, and the only way to correct them was to prepare a city plan. If you care about Madison, you *must* prepare a comprehensive plan, the planner said.[25]

Nolen's plea for a plan was really a warm-up for the main act, a familiar Olin tour de force. In January 1909 Olin assembled three hundred top state and local leaders and delivered one of his characteristically long but brilliant speeches, arguing that a city plan was not just an opportunity but an obligation. Prominent in Olin's oration was a plea for bigger capitol grounds. "And what will be the effect of ... the $6 million new capitol?" he asked. "Do you think that it will feel as though it has been imprisoned and will mourn its inability to escape by way of Lake Monona?" At the end of the meeting Olin organized the Committee of Fifty to guide the planning process and sent almost everyone home that night excited about Madison's future.[26]

Finally, in April 1909 nearly five hundred civic leaders jammed into the new Central High School cafeteria to hear Nolen's comprehensive recommendations for Madison. The occasion was the annual meeting of the Madison Park and Pleasure Drive Association. Curiously, Olin prefaced his introduction of Nolen with a rare twinge of timidity: "I shall be surprised if some of this audience shall not pass from this room convinced that Mr. Nolen is a visionary dreamer and that the reputation of myself and others for conservatism has been severely impaired." Surely, this was Olin's oblique attempt at humor, and the audience probably laughed. But Olin clearly was alerting the governor, the mayor, a major railroad president, state and local legislators, and the local luminaries in the room that night that they were

about to hear proposals far bigger and more visionary they had ever heard before.[27]

"My main appeal tonight is to ask you — the state, the city, the railroads, the citizens — to unite in saving Madison from becoming a mediocre capital," Nolen began. Then he turned on the lantern slide projector and showed examples of "fine city streets, orderly railroad approaches and surroundings, magnificent public buildings, open green squares and plazas, refreshing waterfronts, ennobling statuary, convenient and ample playgrounds, large parks, parkways and boulevards, art museums, theaters, opera and concert halls," as one reporter put it. All the slides were of European cityscapes, and Nolen used them to show his audience that the poorest worker in Europe had opportunities that the wealthiest citizens of Madison could not command. It was the preface for an even more important point that the Boston planner wanted to make: Madison will never become a great city and Wisconsin will not become a great state until its leaders demonstrate a willingness to subordinate private to public, quantity to quality, property rights to people rights, and laissez faire to comprehensive plans. It was a message designed to warm progressives' hearts.[28]

Then Nolen turned to the most radical components of his plan, "the great Capitol Mall," the six blocks between the Capitol Square and Lake Monona, and the esplanade along the lake (see Figs. 1.17 and 1.18). This "Lake Monona approach to the capitol," he said, "is certainly unexcelled and probably unequaled in any American commonwealth, and is as good in relation to state needs as the capitol at Washington is to those of the national." Then, discussing the esplanade along the lakefront, Nolen predicted that it "might be better than anything that has so far been done in this country; in fact, when the situation of the capitol ... and the beauty

of Lake Monona are considered, this esplanade might equal the best that has been done in Europe." He said that "if properly done and carried out," the capitol mall and esplanade "would contribute more than any other one thing to the making of Madison, and, in a measure, to Wisconsin."[29]

Nolen's final point was directed at the many progressives in the audience. Consider making the creation of model cities "one of the principal features of the new Wisconsin idea," and think about making Madison the first model city in the state. The salutary influence of this simple step would be incalculable, he argued. The planner could scarcely contain his enthusiasm for Madison's future and was offering his plan as a "practicable ideal" (see Fig. 1.19). Do this, Nolen told his audience, and you will "establish a new standard for city-making in the United States."[30]

The April 1909 annual meeting of the association and the speech by Nolen were obviously intended as a pep rally for a new Stout initiative to enlarge Capitol Park. Two days after the association's meeting the Menomonie senator introduced a bill directing the governor to appoint a commission to

FIGURE 1.16

**1908 Bird's-Eye of Madison, before Nolen**

SHSW. WHi(X3)51518

This 1908 drawing was the last bird's-eye done for Madison, and the only one ever done in color. Bird's-eyes were popular with booster groups and chambers of commerce because they allowed people to see and understand cities at a glance and because artists could take liberties a camera would not. For example, in this drawing the artist has shown the new capitol as a completed building, even though its construction had barely gotten underway.

This bird's-eye shows the slender isthmus on which the city was built, the location of the Capitol Square, then the city's dominant business district, and the location of the University of Wisconsin campus, adjoining Lake Mendota in the upper left. The wide street in the center is Monona Avenue, flanked on the left by South Carroll Street and on the right by South Pinckney Street.

The bird's-eye also reveals some of the reasons that Nolen wanted to beautify the lake frontage. Note the deep erosion immediately behind the railroad tracks on what people called a steep embankment, a bluff, an escarpment, or a cliff. Although the practice was hardly safe, thousands of people used the tracks as a promenade on nice days year 'round. Note too the row of boathouses at the lakeshore in the lower right. How Nolen proposed to transform this area is shown in Figures 1.17 and 1.18.

report on "an adequate and appropriate setting for the new capitol and its approaches." The 1909 bill cut back the amount of land the state would buy to a two-block strip between Wilson and the lake, South Carroll, and South Pinckney. The bill also required the railroads to build a platform over their tracks so that pedestrians could walk safely from the square to the lakeshore, and authorized the filling of the lake for a park. Because Stout sought the broadest support possible, he used the most general words and made no reference to money.[31]

Just when enthusiasm appeared to be at its peak in 1909, just when everything seemed poised to proceed, the bold Olin-Nolen-Stout scheme began to unravel. In May the legislature refused to

FIGURE 1.17

**The 1909 Nolen Plan, a Bird's-Eye View**

© The Architectural Archives of the University of Pennsylvania

This "Monona Lake Front improvement," shown here in a dramatic bird's-eye drawing, was the most radical and controversial component of Nolen's 1909 plan and the part that most excited the Boston-based city planner. As Nolen wrote in *Madison: A Model City*, this improvement "might ... be better than anything of its kind ... in this country. In fact, ... it is not too much to say that this waterfront esplanade ... might equal any similar development anywhere in the world." The planner hoped that the concept would give Madison some "dignity and even some restrained splendor."

Nolen's goal was to use design to strengthen the "organic relation between the new capitol and Lake Monona," which he proposed to achieve with three components: a "waterfront esplanade," a terrace, and a "great Capitol Mall." The esplanade dominates the foreground, but the drawing shows only the center two thousand feet. As noted in the plan (see Fig. 1.18), the esplanade actually extends for more than a mile along the lakeshore. The terrace, a broad pedestrian promenade extending for two blocks immediately behind the four rectangular towers, is actually a platform bridging the four

railroad tracks. Receding into the distance at the center of the drawing and behind the terrace is Nolen's thousand-foot tree-lined mall, flanked by six large buildings rendered in the Classical Style.

To allow people to move from the terrace to the lakeshore, Nolen proposed six flights of stairs. Greeting people when they arrived — indeed, beckoning them from the terrace — was a glorious fountain, three hundred feet long and forty feet wide, whose jets sent plumes of water seventy feet into the air.

Although Nolen's lakefront improvement was never fully implemented, it continued to play a large role in Madison history. For example, when the Wright plan was announced in 1938, and again in the fifties, almost all who opposed it said they wanted Nolen's plan instead because it did not block the view of the lake from Monona Avenue. However, those who opposed the Wright plan sometimes conveniently ignored key elements of the Nolen plan. They often portrayed the Nolen plan as free of buildings; in fact, Nolen proposed two relatively large semicircular buildings, each about four hundred feet long and about forty feet tall.

Nolen first presented the "lakefront improvement" to the public in April 1909, but the plan was not published in book form until March 1911.

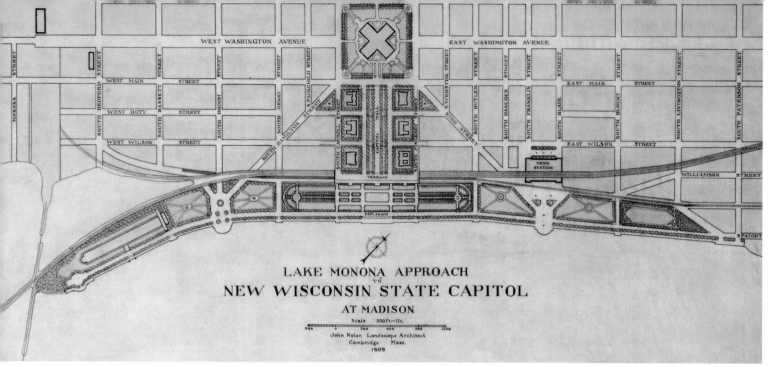

LAKE MONONA APPROACH
TO
NEW WISCONSIN STATE CAPITOL
AT MADISON

Scale   300Ft.=1In.

John Nolen Landscape Architect
Cambridge   Mass.
1909

FIGURE 1.18

**The 1909 Nolen Plan**

© The Architectural Archives of the University of Pennsylvania

When Nolen first showed his lakefront plan to the public in April 1909, people were stunned by its size, scale, and beauty; even today it evokes oohs and ahs from first-time viewers. Nolen was an observant world traveler, and he wanted something outstanding for Madison, a city he enthusiastically believed had the potential to rank with some of the world's most beautiful cities, including Lucerne, Geneva, Weimar, Oxford, Versailles, and Rio de Janeiro.

Nolen proposed that nearly twenty acres — the six blocks between Doty's Capitol Square and the lake — be purchased, razed, and rebuilt as a "great Capitol Mall." The planner also proposed that about sixty acres of Lake Monona be filled for an esplanade more than one mile long and extending about six hundred feet out into the lake.

As the plan clearly shows, Nolen wanted to develop the mall and esplanade in the City Beautiful tradition that emphasized large-scale symmetrical plans, broad boulevards and malls, and a preference for geometric shapes, formal landscaping, large fountains, the classical architectural style, and deep building setbacks. Such plans were made popular by the 1893 Columbian Exposition in Chicago.

Nolen proposed specific uses for each of the six blocks on the mall. He said the four closest to the capitol should be reserved for state office buildings and that the two overlooking Lake Monona should be devoted "to the pleasure interests of the people." One should be "a really fine theater and opera house," to be operated by the state as "an educational feature of the new Wisconsin Idea," and the other should be "a much needed hotel with a character and situation scarcely equaled elsewhere in Wisconsin and comparable in many ways to the Chateau Frontenac at Quebec" (see Fig. 1.19).

Although Nolen was critical of Doty's failure to provide wider streets for major thoroughfares, he obviously approved of Doty's decision to create a strong axial link between the capitol and the lake.

Finally, note the suggested location of the union railroad depot near the right end of the esplanade. In that location passengers could enjoy the beauty of the esplanade, a dramatic contrast to the shabby row of shanties that then lined this shore (see Fig. 1.10.)

---

endorse Stout's bill. In September Olin resigned as president of the Madison Park and Pleasure Drive Association, a post he had held for sixteen years. Then in December 1910 Stout died.[32]

The push for the expanded Capitol Park that began in 1905 and its estimated price tag of $2 million still seemed outrageous to most legislators, coming as it did on top of the unprecedented $6 million commitment for the new capitol building. (The price of the new capitol later increased to $7.2 million.) If anything, the crusade to create the expanded park fanned latent anti-Madison sentiment. Olin did not resign until after the Committee of Fifty had approved Nolen's final draft for the plan, but by then this extraordinary civic leader was physically and emotionally exhausted. Although he had accomplished far more than he ever dreamed, he was experiencing growing opposition from the Madison Common Council to the renewal of Nolen's part-time salary, adding a half mill to the park tax first levied in 1909, and even a growing reaction to his own leadership.[33]

Two of the most capable leaders in the state, Stout and Olin, augmented by one of the best planners in the country, Nolen, had given this grand plan their best shot and failed. In the end they had the vision but not the votes. Their vision was indisputably wonderful, desirable, and timely, but, alas, it was also indisputably dead. Or was it?

## NOLEN'S VISION TAKES SHAPE—SLOWLY

When Nolen's plan was finally published in March 1911 as a 168-page heavily illustrated book called *Madison: A Model City*, it appeared to be a complete failure. No one was crusading for the big ideas packed into this thin volume. But slowly, incrementally, and in surprising places the yeast of the great Nolen vision began to work, first on the mall and then on the esplanade.

Nolen's mall got its first vote of confidence in 1914 several weeks after a long-awaited statue of a tall gilded lady arrived in Madison aboard a railroad flatcar. The elegant figure known as *Wisconsin* (see Fig. 1.20) had been designed by the famous sculptor Daniel Chester French to crown the dome of the new capitol. The question posed by its arrival was in what direction the statue should face. Once the dilemma became known, the commissioners were inundated with advice. Some said it should face west, toward the University of Wisconsin campus.

Some said it should face east, toward the rising sun and the symbolic dawn of a new day for humanity embodied in Wisconsin's progressive legislation. No one said it should face the cold northern winds.

George Post, the capitol architect, strongly recommended that *Wisconsin* be oriented toward Monona Avenue because this "was the most interesting view" and because he always thought of the Nolen mall as the front entrance to the capitol. French agreed but for different reasons; he said that southeast would provide the "most favorable light and shade."[34]

The completion of the capitol in 1917 and the end of World War I the following year renewed interest in the Nolen plan.

In 1922 the federal government bought one of the six blocks of Nolen's mall for a new post office and

FIGURE 1.19
**Dufferin Terrace, Origin of the Term *Terrace***

*John Nolen, Madison: A Model City*

When John Nolen stood at the end of Monona Avenue in 1908 and looked out over Lake Monona, he was reminded of Dufferin Terrace, a broad pedestrian promenade he had seen during a visit to Quebec City. Nolen included this photograph of Dufferin Terrace in *Madison: A Model City*. The popular promenade lies below the dramatic hilltop on which Quebec City is located and gives pedestrians a panoramic view of the St. Lawrence River and the old (lower) city on the right. The distinctive conical turrets of the Chateau Frontenac, the landmark downtown hotel, are visible in the upper left. Nolen enthusiastically urged Madisonians to create a similar terrace over the railroad tracks, as shown in Figures 1.17 and 1.18, and predicted that it could equal or even exceed the beauty of the splendid Dufferin.

This was the origin of the term *terrace* as it was used in Madison. In 1934 local leaders, taking their cue from Nolen's plan, named Monona Avenue's street-end park "Olin Terrace," and in 1938 Wright named his civic center "Olin Terraces" because his plan was an extension of Olin Terrace. Then, in the early 1950s, Wright and his followers began calling the project "Monona Terrace."

FIGURE 1.20
**Daniel Chester French's *Wisconsin***

*Photo by Craig Wilson, Kite Aerial Photography*

Crowning the top of the capitol's distinctive white granite dome is a 15-foot, 4-inch, two-ton gold-leafed female figure known as *Wisconsin*. The figure was designed by Daniel Chester French, the famous American sculptor probably best known for his seated figure of Lincoln at the Lincoln Memorial in Washington, D.C. This photograph was taken in 1995, after the famous statue was restored; thus it appears here just as it did on July 20, 1914, when it was hoisted to its lofty pedestal. The capitol commissioners' decision to face *Wisconsin* on Monona Avenue was the first official affirmation of Nolen's mall and esplanade.

FIGURE 1.21
**1929 Federal Building, Precedent for the Nolen Mall**

*SHSW. WHi(D487)6948*

Madison's neoclassical Federal Building, shown here in a 1930s photograph, is not exactly a head-turning design, but its significance as a precedent can hardly be exaggerated. The Federal Building was the first to be positioned on Nolen's mall, as envisioned in his 1909 plan. A bill calling for the building's construction was first introduced in 1912, but several additional bills were required to appropriate more than $1 million to acquire the site and build it. Construction began in 1927, and the building was officially opened in February 1929. The start of its construction also prompted the city to declare the six blocks along Monona Avenue to be the official civic center. The Federal Building was set back fifty feet from the property line, much less than what Nolen wanted but a big improvement over the practice of building out to the property line, then common in downtown commercial areas. Next to follow the federal precedent of locating on Nolen's mall was the State of Wisconsin, with a large office building designed in 1929 (see Fig. 1.22). Madison and Dane County followed with a joint building completed in 1957 (see Fig. 4.31).

The building served as a federal courthouse until 1984, when a new downtown facility was completed, and as the city's main post office until 1976, when a much larger suburban complex was built. In 1978 Madison bought the building for additional office space; it is now known as the Madison Municipal Building.

federal courthouse. When the $1 million building opened in 1929, it became the first of several government buildings that would eventually grace Nolen's mall (see Fig. 1.21).[35]

Groundbreaking for the Federal Building in 1927 prompted the common council to designate the six-block Nolen mall as the official civic center. The history-making decision had been recommended by a blue-ribbon committee appointed by the mayor to study Madison's "future development." To build support for this initiative and stimulate greater interest in city planning, the *Wisconsin State Journal* serialized the full 1909 Nolen plan for the second time. (The first was in 1921.) Once again the graphic centerpiece was the mall-esplanade, which kept the dramatic plan feature fresh in readers' minds. The wording of the official resolution made it clear that the civic center was to be an enclave of government buildings. However, Nolen envisioned the mall as a complex of state buildings; the city expanded the definition to include city, county, and federal governments. The expanded definition reflected the federal fait accompli but also that city leaders were already thinking about this area as a future home for local government offices.[36]

The final step taken during the 1920s to realize the Nolen mall was the decision to build the first state office building, construction of which began in 1930 (see Fig. 1.22) but not where the Boston planner had proposed. The building occupied one of the two choice lakefront blocks that Nolen had thought would be better used for an opera house or a grand hotel (see Fig. 1.23).

Also in 1927 Madison took one absolutely critical step to establish the Nolen esplanade or something similar: it secured permission from the state to fill in the shore of Lake Monona out to a prescribed

FIGURE 1.22

**The 1932 State Office Building**

SHSW. WHi(W6)23987

The granite-faced State Office Building, known as the Capitol Annex, was the second government facility to be added to Nolen's mall; unfortunately, Arthur Peabody, the state architect, refused to follow Nolen's recommendations for a gracious setback. This photograph, taken sometime soon after completion of the building in 1932, shows the Art Deco–Style ornamentation designed by staff architect Karl Sheldon in 1929. The center section was added in 1938 and the west wing in 1956. To keep costs low, state authorities used prison labor to cut the stone, and a federal grant covered 45 percent of the cost of the original structure.

In 1936 Sheldon went into private practice and soon thereafter prepared a design for a city-county building across the street (to the right of the photo).

Before the state began this building, the entire block was occupied by a single-family home, the Fairchild mansion (see Fig. 1.23).

point called a *dock line* (see Fig. 1.24). Unfortunately, the 1927 law failed to specify the purposes for which the lake could be filled, an oversight that required the city to secure an amendment in 1931 that permitted "parks, playgrounds, bathing beaches, municipal boathouses, piers, wharves, public buildings, highways, streets, pleasure drives and boulevards." The amendment covered all the functions envisioned by the 1909 Nolen plan plus highways, which were receiving growing attention as car ownership increased. (In the 1950s the question of what

FIGURE 1.23

**The Fairchild Mansion**

SHSW. WHi(X3)17064

It is hard to imagine that a single home once occupied the entire block where the huge State Office Building now stands. Shown here in an 1880s photo is the Fairchild mansion, the home that once occupied the site. Built in 1849 by Jairus Fairchild, a prominent civic leader who was elected Madison's first mayor in 1856, the house was later occupied by Fairchild's son, Lucius, who served as Wisconsin's governor from 1866 to 1871. When this photograph was taken, the area was dominated by large elegant homes and was one of the city's most prestigious neighborhoods. The Fairchild home was a social center for Madison's elite, and its grounds were exceedingly popular with little boys because they could pick the sweetest and best grapes in town from the Fairchild vineyards — that is, when Mrs. Fairchild wasn't looking. The vineyard was located near the main entrance of today's State Office Building. The house was torn down to make way for the State Office Building in 1929.

In the mid-1930s the area to the left of the Fairchild house was developed as Olin Terrace (see Fig. 3.3) and still later as the entrance to the Monona Terrace Community and Convention Center. But when this photo was taken the area had just been planted with grass and landscaped by owners of nearby houses. During the nineteenth century the city did not believe it had any responsibility to buy, develop, or maintain parks; consequently, private property owners had to take the initiative. In this case they petitioned the city for permission to remove rubbish and unsightly undergrowth and plant grass. The city allowed them to proceed, but only if they did all the work and paid all costs.

The photo also shows the site of two of the three Indian mounds shown in Figure 1.8. The conical mound stood near the corner of the Fairchild house closest to the camera. The effigy mound ran from the lower left corner of the photograph to a point near the large tree to the left of the house. All three mounds were removed when the right-of-way for Wilson Street was graded and the street-end park was created.

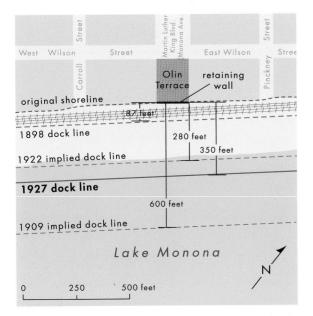

F I G U R E   1 . 2 4

**The 1927 Dock Line: Authorization to Fill Lake Monona Shore**

*U.W.–Madison Cartographic Laboratory*

State law authorizes cities to give lakeshore property owners the right to fill the edges of navigable bodies of water. Whenever a city does this, it establishes a limit known as a *dock line*, that is, a vertical plane beyond which the waterway cannot be filled. This map shows the location of two dock lines requested by Madison and approved by the state, one in 1898 and another in 1927. The 1898 dock line, shown as a heavy dotted red line, was actually used to gain retroactive approval of a four-track right-of-way that ran along the shore of Lake Monona for more than a mile.

The 1927 dock line, shown in solid red, authorized Madison to fill Lake Monona out to 350 feet from the Olin Terrace retaining wall. Contemporary sources suggest that Madison asked for this dock line so that it could build a lakeshore drive, but the width of the fill requested suggests that the city envisioned much more than a road.

In the 1950s Monona Terrace opponents argued that the intent of the 1927 law was to authorize the Nolen plan and nothing more. That claim appears to be false. As this map shows, the dock line that the Nolen esplanade needed would have required filling 250 feet more, which suggests that the Nolen plan was not the basis for the 1927 law. The source may have been a 1922 transportation and zoning plan prepared by Harland Bartholomew, a St. Louis city planner. Bartholomew recommended that Madison build a union railroad depot at the foot of Monona Avenue and a highway along the lakeshore, a plan that called for eleven railroad tracks and a four-lane highway. As denoted by the light dotted line on the map, this would have required a dock line 280 feet from the original shoreline.

The most likely basis for the 1927 law was the 1925 plan of the Association of Commerce to build a civic auditorium at the foot of Monona Avenue.

Association representatives said that the auditorium would require filling the lake almost exactly where the official dock line was located.

Unfortunately, the 1927 law suffered from several flaws, one of which was the failure to specify functions for which the filled land could be used. A 1931 amendment provided the full range of functions envisioned by Nolen in his 1909 plan, including public buildings. In the 1950s opponents of Wright's Monona Terrace argued that "public buildings" did not mean *large* public buildings.

legislators intended that the city do on this filled land became a major issue in regard to Monona Terrace.)

Thus, by the end of 1929, twenty years after the Nolen mall and esplanade were first presented to the public, key components had been implemented. Nolen's original six-block site had been designated as the official civic center, the Federal Building had opened, plans for a large state office building had been approved, and the state had given Madison permission to fill in Lake Monona where Nolen proposed a lakefront esplanade. The Nolen plan was hardly setting speed records for implementation, but it had proved a powerful template for guiding development in this area.

## THE PURSUIT OF COMMUNITY, CULTURE, AND COMMERCE: THE EARLY AUDITORIUM CRUSADE

During the first three decades of the twentieth century Madison leaders also eagerly tried to construct a new category of building: a publicly owned and operated multipurpose civic auditorium. Although some communities, including Madison, had constructed such a building in the midnineteenth century (Fig. 1.25), the concept fell from favor and was not revived until the Progressive era. During this period the civic auditorium was portrayed as essential for modern government, and for nearly half a century its shimmy and siren song proved almost irresistible to Madison leaders. The idea hit Madison with such force that all mayors from 1917 to 1930 used at least one of their addresses to new

council members to urge them to secure one of these benefit-laden buildings for the people. The quest was complicated because three groups concurrently sought different versions of the building: progressives sought an auditorium to restore an inclusive sense of community; music, drama, and art lovers wanted a first-rate cultural arts facility; and business leaders tried to get an auditorium that would boost commerce.[37]

### THE SEARCH FOR COMMUNITY

In the beginning Madison society was small and simple. Just about everybody in Madison was a refugee, direct or indirect, from New England and therefore shared many of the same values. People worked, played, and even worshipped together. However, this blissful picture did not last long. The cumulative effects of immigration, population growth, and specialization fragmented Madison into dozens of ethnic, economic, religious, and social groups. Madison became pluralistic, impersonal, and complex.[38]

These developments deeply troubled Madison progressives who wanted to restore a genuine feeling of community in Madison, to make democracy more than a buzzword. Progressives were especially eager to create inclusive organizations to overcome the mosaic of groups and stereotypes that then fragmented, stratified, and segregated Madison society. That was why they were so enthusiastic about municipal clubs whose clubhouses offered reading rooms, gymnasiums, swimming pools, and social rooms. In Madison this concept got plenty of attention, but no one — least of all the city — was willing to underwrite the cost of the clubhouse.[39]

The successor to the municipal club was the "social center," a nationwide movement whose backers proposed to use schools as clubhouses. The concept had great appeal because schools were publicly owned and were available in evenings and on

FIGURE 1.25

**Madison's First Civic Auditorium and Convention Center**

*Courtesy Ann Waidelich*

The urge to build a civic auditorium and convention center was first expressed when Madison became a city in 1856. In his inaugural address to the first common council, Mayor Jairus Fairchild said that "no city can be complete without some convenient and capacious hall for public use." Madison was in the midst of a great economic boom, and city leaders were so confident that they borrowed $100,000 to build fire stations, schools, and an elegant city hall and civic auditorium, shown in this postcard ca. 1905. Architects modeled the building after a Venetian palace.

The first two floors contained city offices, and the third floor held the civic auditorium. At its grand opening in 1858 reporters paid particular attention to the "spacious and splendid" auditorium, "an ornament to the city and an object of public pride." The 100-by-50-foot room boasted 24-foot ceilings, huge arched windows, and two 12-burner gas chandeliers. The room could seat nine hundred people for what an 1858 city report described as "conventions and other public assemblies including concerts, lectures, and reputable exhibitions."

The first city auditorium hosted a cavalcade of famous people, including Ralph Waldo Emerson, and a remarkable array of popular entertainment, but its use declined after 1871 when a larger, privately owned theater was built. In the 1920s the third floor was remodeled for city offices and council chambers; in 1954 the picturesque old sandstone structure was razed and replaced by a new building at another location (see Fig. 4.31).

The old City Hall stood at the corner of Wisconsin Avenue and West Mifflin Street, directly across the street from the capitol; a second government building, the post office, occupied the opposite corner. The red brick building next to City Hall was the Fuller Opera House, an elegant 1890 theater.

weekends. Madison embraced the social center as early as 1907 when Madison schools began building "assembly rooms" to provide a place for neighborhood social and civic meetings. In 1910 the national leader of the social center movement, Edward J. Ward, accepted a faculty position at the University of Wisconsin. In 1911 Ward brought the first National Conference on Social and Civic Centers to Madison with big-name guest speakers, including New Jersey governor Woodrow Wilson, to endorse the concept. Following this conference and further agitation by local social center backers, the Madison school board made schools available for Boy Scouts, girls' clubs, adult musical groups, and adult night-school classes. To the great disappointment of center backers, the expanding use of schools provoked a backlash from teachers who objected to having their rooms disrupted; consequently, by the end of World War I the idea of using schools to achieve a more perfect community had been virtually abandoned.[40]

After World War I the progressive ideal of a community center was reintroduced in an even more attractive form known as "liberty buildings." The concept was promoted by *American City*, a monthly magazine widely read by city officials, as an alternative to the traditional stone and bronze monuments used to honor war veterans. Instead, *American City* in 1918–1919 urged cities to create "living" memorials, that is, buildings that could be used to foster liberty and democracy, the two ideals for which the war had been fought. As envisioned by the magazine editors, the building would be a community center consisting of a large auditorium and many smaller rooms in which the entire community could come together to experience "community fellowship and unity." As envisioned by national leaders, the auditorium would be open for large public meetings and entertainment, whereas the smaller rooms would serve as permanent headquarters for nonsectarian and nonpartisan civic groups such as the Boy Scouts, women's clubs, musical and literary societies, the Red Cross, and others. Still other rooms in the community center would be available for adult education, dances, and dining.[41]

Although the idea of a liberty building–community center delighted Madison progressives and received the strong support of the Madison Association of Commerce, a local booster organization, the common council refused to submit the issue to referendum.[42]

Unlike many progressive ideals, the community center did not evaporate in the 1920s. In fact, in 1926 another version known as the town hall, or public auditorium, swept the country, and the Madison Association of Commerce was quick to embrace the idea. Like the liberty building, the new incarnation was to be owned and operated by the city and would contain both an auditorium for public meetings and many smaller rooms for civic organizations. As the concept was explained to readers of the association's *Bulletin*, dozens of cities across the country had built town halls and had found them to be "an absolute necessity" and a "tremendous force for welding the community into a contented unit."[43]

For nearly thirty years progressives sought a building that could create a more perfect community. Their long and vigorous pursuit of the idea showed that it exerted a deep and enduring appeal, so great that it would continue into the 1950s and the Monona Terrace crusade. Several times from 1900 to 1929 seekers of community thought they had their building in sight, but it eluded their grasp, partly because two other groups were also seeking civic salvation with an auditorium.

THE DESIRE FOR CULTURE

During the last two decades of the nineteenth century, Madison leaders had portrayed the city as having "a large and cultured audience" for Shakespearean plays and touring classical musicians. In fact, such talk was unbridled boosterism; most Madisonians preferred vaudeville and minstrel shows, and can-can girls were the all-time favorite among the men. Not until the 1890 opening of the Fuller Opera House, an ornate, privately owned theater with a sloped floor, did Madison have a first-class hall for drama and music. By this time the national market for drama and classical music had matured, and dozens of companies were touring the country. Because Madison lies between Chicago and Minneapolis, the Fuller's managers could book one-night stands for the New York Philharmonic, the Chicago Symphony Orchestra, and many others. By 1900 tiny Madison, Wisconsin, with a population of twenty thousand, was enjoying a reputation as a sophisticated consumer of culture.[44]

These developments delighted the growing arts community but also posed troubling questions for progressives who believed that music and drama had the power to improve human character. John Nolen used this argument in his *Madison: A Model City*, noting that "the influence of our theaters is a colossal, national influence in forming the taste, the moral will, and mental capacity of our people. Whether we know it or not, our theaters are supplied in passion, imagination, and delight with means of appeal far more potent than any possessed by our schools and colleges; and whether you like it or not, night after night, year after year, our theaters are educating our people, by the millions.... The question is, Shall the theaters educate these millions right or wrong?"

Nolen's hope was that Madison would recognize the power of the arts to educate people and that "art is not only the flowering of civilization, it is also its seed."[45]

Madison progressives agreed with Nolen's assessment of the arts and therefore joined forces with the local arts community to secure a superior performing arts facility. They did not, however, promote a public theater on the site Nolen recommended. The Boston planner had proposed "a really fine theater and opera house" on one of the two blocks flanking the lake end of Monona Avenue. However, by 1917 the Madison Club, a private organization for the business elite, had begun construction on the eastern block, and in 1929 the state purchased the Fairchild property, which occupied the western block, for the state office building.

The crusade for a city-owned cultural arts facility during the first three decades of the twentieth century was a direct result of the University of Wisconsin's growing role in providing cultural entertainment in Madison. The rapid growth of the university, which began in the 1890s, increased the size of the "gown" audience for drama and music and the role of the Music Department. The department regularly sponsored faculty and student recitals and in 1912 began to bring artists not affiliated with the university to the city whenever possible. However, these concerts were often arranged at the last minute, poorly publicized, and sparsely attended, especially by students. Leaders of the Student Union, the dominant campuswide social organization, reasoned that if students were given the responsibility for managing cultural events — and especially if they scheduled an annual concert series — more students would attend.[46]

The first Student Union Concert Series was held in 1920 and was a great success; it attracted a large and appreciative student audience but hundreds of local residents as well. In the late 1920s student managers began to book some of the best talent in the world, artists such as Ignace Paderewski, Sergei

Stock Pavilion Exterior

*Courtesy Ann Waidelich*

Stock Pavilion Interior

*SHSW. WHi(X3)40728*

FIGURE 1.26

## The U.W. Stock Pavilion, Madison's Unique Concert Hall

When this handsomely proportioned Tudor Revival building opened its doors in 1909, it was the largest building of its kind in the country. Christened the Stock Pavilion, it was designed as a combination barn, show ring, and classroom for the University of Wisconsin School of Agriculture. For fourteen years the building accommodated cattle shows, sheep shearings, horse sales, and demonstrations of the latest animal husbandry techniques for Wisconsin farmers. Then, in 1923 and continuing through the 1960s, it began serving a function its architects never anticipated: the Stock Pavilion became Madison's premiere concert hall.

That was because the building had two redeeming qualities. First, it could seat more than three thousand people — about half on the concrete bleachers shown in the interior photo, and fifteen hundred more on folding chairs on the dirt floor in the center. Madison's other auditoriums could seat less than half this number, far too few to attract nationally known artists and orchestras. Second, it had great acoustics, thanks to its long, narrow, cathedral shape and the reverberation-dampening sawdust on the arena floor.

But it had a long list of shortcomings too. Large columns blocked views for many, and patrons seated on the arena floor opposite the temporary stage rarely glimpsed the performers. Freight trains on a track next to the building would sometimes rumble by in the middle of a contralto's *Ave Maria,* radiators hissed, and steam pipes chugged. Cold drafts wafted about the barn, and artists' dressing rooms were three hundred feet away in another building. Then there was the smell. Before concerts, crews with shovels would pick up anything obvious and then cover the dirt floor with a thick blanket of sawdust. Even so, as one writer put it, there remained a "faint, dull cattle smell." And the sawdust created additional problems. Chairs would sink in several inches as the audience sat down, most would list a little to one side, and patrons would often go home with sawdust in their shoes. Some Madisonians referred to this unique concert hall as the "cowliseum," but most called it "the cow barn" with a mixture of embarrassment and humor. Of course, those terms never appeared on promotional flyers for a performance to be given in this rustic arena. Instead, the flyers announced that the concert would be held at the "University Pavilion."

The Stock Pavilion represented a syndrome peculiar to Madison: the tendency of city leaders to use the existence of public assembly buildings at the University of Wisconsin and others owned by state government — even if they were retrograde — to put off the development of city facilities. The logic was both simple and compelling: why buy a ladder when your neighbor has one you can borrow any time you like?

Rachmaninoff, and Fritz Kreisler. But to keep ticket prices at an affordable level, a hall seating three thousand people was essential. With just one exception, no hall was big enough. Assembly Hall, whose name was later changed to Music Hall, was a handsome 1879 sandstone building on campus, but it held only eight hundred (see Fig. 1.13). The 1893 University of Wisconsin Armory and Gymnasium, commonly known in Madison as the Red Gym, could seat as many as five thousand but was fundamentally a gymnasium and had bad acoustics. Even the Memorial Union, completed in 1928 with its multipurpose Great Hall, could seat only five hundred. And downtown Madison's Fuller Opera House was not an option because it could hold but fifteen hundred.[47]

The only public building in Madison that could hold three thousand was the University of Wisconsin Stock Pavilion (see Fig. 1.26), but patrons of classical music ridiculed its smells, drafts, unwanted noises, and concrete bleachers. Rarely did a concert by an internationally famous musician occur in the "cow barn" without an outpouring of indignation and embarrassment by civic leaders and editorial writers. Indeed, from a cultural standpoint no factor generated more clamor for a decent concert hall than the use of the Stock Pavilion.[48]

## THE QUEST FOR COMMERCE

Madison business leaders also hungered for an auditorium. The decision of the Wisconsin Republican Party, headed by Governor La Follette, to hold its statewide convention in Madison in July 1902 was no accident; it was the first fruit of a conscious strategy devised by the strong new booster organization known as the Forty Thousand Club, the forerunner of the Association of Commerce. Its members saw the meeting industry as an effective way to achieve their goal. Forty Thousand Club leaders said Madison was a natural meeting city.

After all, nine railroad lines entered the city from nearly every direction, conventioneers could visit state officials at the capitol, the University of Wisconsin's prestigious campus beckoned, and the lakes offered recreational opportunities.[49]

Madisonians put on a memorable display of hospitality for the Republican delegates. Shopkeepers filled their windows with welcome signs, streetcars maintained five-minute headways, official greeters roamed the streets to help badge-bedecked delegates find their way, and residents opened up their homes because hotels didn't have enough rooms. The Republicans were impressed and said so. The 1902 state Republican convention gave Madisonians an exciting glimpse of the future. Conventions brought to town well-heeled people who sprinkled their money on hotels, restaurants, theaters, stores, steamboats, and streetcars. Conventions enhanced the city's intellectual atmosphere and added vitality. Madison business leaders began to see conventions as an industry.[50]

Naturally, Madisonians wanted more. The combination of Republican kudos and Forty Thousand Club invitations brought dozens of additional meetings to Madison. Hoteliers were quick to grasp this promising source of new business and in 1905 formed the city's first convention-promoting organization, the Hotelmen's Association, and adopted a catchy new slogan: "Madison the beautiful for conventions great and small, a benefit for all." This spurt of conventions caused hundreds of new and remodeled hotel rooms to be added to the city's inventory between 1905 and 1908. In 1910 a Milwaukee newspaper acknowledged that Madison had become the primary convention city in the state.[51]

In 1913 the Association of Commerce replaced the Forty Thousand Club. The association was much larger and more representative than any previous commerce-nurturing organization and for the first

time had full-time paid staff. Significantly, the association board adopted the theme "Madison, Ideal Convention City of the West" and directed its new executive director to function as a one-person convention bureau. No organization trumpeted the virtues of the convention industry more often, more loudly, or more effectively than the Association of Commerce, but it was hardly alone. Joining the association in this lusty cheerleading were Madison's two local papers, the *Wisconsin State Journal* and *Capital Times*.[52]

During these early years tiny convention-promotion budgets forced the association to find creative ways to market Madison. Techniques included distributing thousands of brochures and leaflets portraying Madison as "Wisconsin's Most Interesting Convention and Vacation City," using postcards to disseminate a pro-convention message to the world (see Fig. 1.27), and encouraging members to solicit their trade associations to hold conventions in Madison. The association even got its members to use their automobiles to give conventioneers tours of the city. The organization's weekly *Bulletin* functioned as a conveyor belt for industry-related exhortations, news, and solicitation tips.[53]

In 1918 the association began to focus much of its energy on securing a civic auditorium and was without a doubt the most outspoken proponent. Although association leaders acknowledged the importance of such a building for enhancing cultural and community life, their primary interest was boosting business and attracting conventions. The association's first big push for a civic auditorium came in 1918 just a few weeks after the World War I armistice and was a part of the "liberty building" initiative described earlier. Although the original idea was a building "dedicated to community fellowship and unity," the association proposed that Madison's

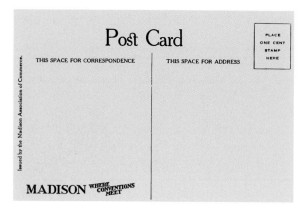

FIGURE 1.27

**The Postcard Convention-Marketing Strategy**

*Courtesy Vincent Freed Mollenhoff*

This penny postcard issued in the 1920s reflected the importance Madison business leaders gave to conventions. The cards were printed under the auspices of the Association of Commerce and sold to visitors in downtown hotels and stores. The strategy was simple: to get Madison visitors to broadcast a commercial message to the world. That message, "Madison, Where Conventions Meet," appears in the lower lefthand corner of the postcard. On the other side was a dramatic and popular bird's-eye view of the four Madison-area lakes.

liberty building be a combination convention hall, auditorium, city hall, and armory. The association further proposed that the auditorium be a large arena-like facility with a flat floor to accommodate conventions, auto shows, sporting events, and national speakers.

Association leaders tried to persuade the common council to hold a referendum in the spring of 1919 on a $500,000 bond issue for the building, but the council refused and for good reason. During the first two decades of the twentieth century, the population of Madison had nearly doubled, to 38,378, and the city was confronted with a long list of big-ticket, growth-necessitated items, including schools, roads, and a new sewage-processing system. Furthermore, the city's ability to borrow money for these improvements by

issuing bonds was limited by state law to 5 percent of total assessed valuation, and most elected city leaders did not think the remaining borrowing capacity was sufficient to do both the necessities and the auditorium.[54]

The association was disappointed, but its members did not give up. In 1922 they persuaded the city to form its first auditorium committee to explore the feasibility of the idea, an act that became a ritual for almost all mayors until 1973. Unfortunately for the association and other auditorium backers, the committee decided that an auditorium was "entirely out of the question" because of the city's already high debt load. The conclusion was a huge disappointment because the city was beginning to get national conventions, and large groups sometimes had to be accommodated in downtown warehouses.[55]

Then, in April 1925, Madison mayor Milo Kittleson made a history-making proposal (see Fig. 1.28). The mayor recognized the continuing need for an auditorium, as well as the need to accommodate the rapidly expanding number of boat owners, and urged the city to explore the feasibility of a combination auditorium and boathouse on filled land at the foot of Monona Avenue. This was the first time anyone had publicly suggested this location, and it triggered a flurry of actions. The council approved another auditorium committee composed of council members, citizens, and a representative from the Association of Commerce.[56]

The lakeshore civic auditorium appealed to the board of the Association of Commerce, which saw it as the capstone of Nolen's dream for a civic center. The site was big, inexpensive, close to the Capitol Square, and would not take any valuable land off the tax rolls. (Interestingly, these were the same arguments later used by proponents of the Frank Lloyd Wright Monona Terrace plan.) Business

leaders were thrilled because the filled lakeshore site would provide enough parking for about eighteen hundred cars. Given the serious shortage of parking in downtown Madison, few subjects more warmed the hearts of business leaders. The business community also was excited about the construction of two large new downtown hotels the previous year (see Fig. 1.29), which greatly increased the city's cachet as a convention venue. Now Madison could accommodate conventions as large as eighteen hundred persons and

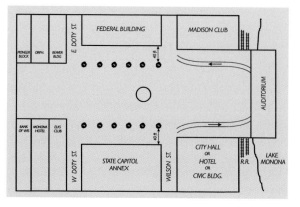

FIGURE 1.28

**1925 Precedent for Lakeshore Civic Auditorium**

*Courtesy Wisconsin State Journal, redrawn by W. J. Martinelli*

This precedent-setting plan was published by the *Wisconsin State Journal* on October 18, 1925. The diagram was prepared by the Association of Commerce, whose board had endorsed the plan. The concept was apparently first proposed in early 1925 by Thomas J. Ross, a Madison council member, and received the encouragement of Mayor Milo Kittleson in his address to the common council in April 1925. According to an association official, the plan would require about three hundred feet of the lake to be filled beyond the railroad tracks, a distance that almost perfectly correlates with the location of the 1927 dock line (see Fig. 1.24).

To Association of Commerce leaders the plan was a logical capstone to John Nolen's 1909 civic center plan. The association suggested that a "city hall or hotel or civic building" be built on the Fairchild property and that a state office building be located across the street from the Federal Building. Also shown is the Madison Club's new (1918) building. Members enjoyed an elegant dining room, billiard rooms, and a veranda with a lake view. The circle in the center of Monona Avenue represented a monument to Madison soldiers and sailors.

could compete for big state and national conventions — but only if Madison had a civic auditorium where all delegates could meet in one place. Thus, to association leaders, a civic auditorium was now essential for realizing Madison's convention potential.[57]

Because the business community had so much to gain from the lakeshore auditorium proposal, it took an aggressive leadership role. The Association of Commerce's board approached architects, who said that an auditorium big enough to accommodate five to six thousand people could be built on filled land for about $400,000. The association even held special informational meetings for its members, a practice reserved for the most important projects. Association leaders calculated they could get a majority of citizens to vote for the project if they tied it to making hundreds of convenient new parking spaces available downtown—and they knew they could get the spaces by filling in three hundred feet of the downtown lakeshore for about four thousand feet. But once again the city council refused to put the referendum on the ballot because it did not consider the auditorium to be essential or affordable.[58]

In 1927 the association made a fourth attempt to get the city to build an auditorium, this time by boldly asking the city to raise taxes, a rare stand for a business group. The decision was a direct response to the city's having nearly reached its legal borrowing limit. The association proposed that the city levy a tax of one mill on all property for five years, which the group calculated would bring in enough to build a first-class, $425,000 auditorium. Business leaders argued that in five years the auditorium would be paid for and the city could lower taxes. Meanwhile, the newly formed Madison Civic Music Association, exasperated by the lack of a large first-class hall for music and drama, decided to place the muscle of the city's cultural

Loraine Hotel

*Courtesy Ann Waidelich*

Belmont Hotel

*Courtesy Ann Waidelich*

FIGURE 1.29

**New Hotels: Attracting Conventions and Preserving the Capitol View**

Never in Madison's history were so many hotel rooms added in such a short time. In just four months in 1924 Madison's Capitol Square suddenly boasted 450 new hotel rooms.

The million-dollar 250-room Loraine Hotel opened in May, and the $300,000, 200-room Belmont Hotel opened in September. Business at the Loraine was so good that its owners added 150 rooms just a year after it opened. The completion of these hotels greatly increased Madison's capacity for conventions and caused the business community to demand an auditorium, a building it believed was essential to the growth of the convention industry.

For decades the Loraine was Madison's fanciest hotel and therefore enjoyed the patronage of such luminaries as Mae West, Ethel Barrymore, Harry Truman, and even Frank Lloyd Wright when he was stranded in town during a snowstorm in 1957. The Loraine was also where Wright first revealed his "Dream Civic Center" plan (as the newspapers dubbed it) to the Lions Club in 1938. The hotel featured the elegant Crystal Ballroom, so named for its huge chandeliers, and a multipurpose room that could seat one thousand conventioneers. The Belmont offered smaller rooms for traveling salesmen, conventioneers, and legislators who wanted "comfort at slight expense"; many rooms offered spectacular views of the capitol, the square, and the lakes.

The eleven-story Belmont and the ten-story Loraine became embroiled in a simmering Madison aesthetic controversy: should buildings around the square be allowed to block the view of the capitol dome? Nolen in his 1909 plan urged Madisonians to adopt a height-restriction law. When Madison's first skyscraper, an eight-story building, was announced in 1911, Nolen disciples asked the common council to stop it but were rebuffed. When the Belmont's owners announced their plan to build an eleven-story hotel, Madison leaders persuaded Wisconsin legislators to enact height restrictions. The attorney general declared the law unconstitutional, arguing that a municipality could regulate buildings only for safety and health, not aesthetics. Antiskyscraper forces appealed the case to the Wisconsin Supreme Court and won. Since 1924 all buildings have conformed to the height restrictions. Thanks to Nolen and his disciples, the dome of Wisconsin's capitol will forever dominate the Madison skyline, a rare but dramatic instance in which beauty triumphed over business.

Today, the Loraine is a state office building, and the Belmont is the YWCA.

FIGURE 1.30

**1929 Civic Auditorium Proposal**

*Courtesy The Capital Times*

On March 15, 1929, James R. Law, a partner in Madison's largest and most prestigious architectural firm, sent this drawing of a civic auditorium to Arthur Peabody, chair of the city's Plan Committee. Although Peabody was not on the Auditorium Committee, he was a close friend of Law's and, as the state architect, a well-connected and highly respected expert on public buildings. Law said he was submitting his proposal to help Peabody in "visualizing the possibilities of an auditorium," but the timing of Law's action was hardly coincidental. One week later the mayor's Auditorium Committee made its report to the common council, saying that Madison should have an auditorium.

Law's dramatic drawing with its roof-mounted searchlights appears to fit the committee's specifications perfectly. Law told Peabody that the main floor could be used for automobile shows, athletic events, dancing, and banquets and that for concerts and lectures the building could accommodate forty-five hundred people. Law estimated the cost at $450,000, almost exactly what the Auditorium Committee had in mind. Law's 1929 auditorium plan was a casualty of the Great Depression.

community behind the association's one-mill proposal. But even this united front of commerce and culture could not persuade the common council to increase property taxes.[59]

Four times the association had tried and failed to persuade the city to build a civic auditorium. Most organizations would give up but not Madison's business association; in 1928 it got the mayor, A. G. Schmedeman, to form a third city auditorium committee. The committee determined that a $500,000 "auditorium and exposition center" could be financed entirely with city bonds and would increase the city tax rate by only one-third of a mill. James Law, a prominent Madison architect, submitted a drawing of an auditorium and exposition center that featured a large flat floor and display booths around the sides, exactly what most business community leaders

dreamed about (see Fig. 1.30). But the committee inexplicably proposed that the auditorium be located on a marshy block in the center of the isthmus — six and eight blocks from the square. How could the committee make such a recommendation? wondered the association's exasperated director. No other city in the United States had the opportunity to put a civic auditorium "on a beautiful lake.... To pass up this opportunity ... and locate the auditorium somewhere on just ordinary property without a lake setting ... would be a great mistake," he said. But once again the council refused to proceed with even this tiny tax increase.[60]

The sixth, last, and in many ways the most remarkable attempt to build a civic auditorium during this decade came in August 1929 when a wealthy Madison real estate developer offered to finance and build a civic auditorium, lease it to the city at an amount that would cover interest and principal, and at the end of the lease term sell it to the city for one dollar. The proposal was an ingenious attempt to circumvent the city's inability to float bonds to finance the building, but it too failed, a victim of the Great Depression.[61]

The 1905 decision to build an elegant, breathtakingly expensive, and undeniably beautiful new Wisconsin capitol had triggered a remarkable chain of events. Expanding the capitol required bigger grounds, many said, and this perception focused attention on the sweet spot created by James Duane Doty at the axis of the capitol and Lake Monona when he laid out the city. Everyone liked John Nolen's plan for a great mall between the capitol and the lake and a shoreline esplanade. But Nolen's plan was as expensive as it was exciting, and state government had no appetite for such a huge outlay. Nevertheless, Nolen's plan proved remarkably durable, and by 1929 it had served as a template for the location of the Federal Building, State Office Building, and

dock line (though not exactly where Nolen said). Moreover, the blocks along Monona Avenue had been officially designated as Madison's civic center. Implementing key parts of the Nolen plan elevated expectations, and almost everyone assumed that when additional government offices were constructed, they would be built in the officially designated civic center. And when the civic auditorium was built, most assumed it would be there as well.

The ten-year effort to build a civic auditorium was singularly frustrating — six attempts without success. But civic leaders pursued the auditorium at a time when the city had too little borrowing capacity and most elected officials had little appetite for increasing property taxes to build something they saw as nice but hardly necessary. Most council members believed the city had many places for Madisonians to meet, several University of Wisconsin buildings that could accommodate cultural events, and plenty of downtown hotels for conventions. This perception of the civic auditorium as a desirable but expensive facility whose functions could be accommodated with existing buildings became a familiar refrain for decades.

The early auditorium crusade failed for a second reason: each of the three groups that said it wanted an auditorium meant something different. Those who sought to restore a feeling of community wanted a civic clubhouse with a big room where everybody could meet and plenty of smaller rooms for civic organizations and programs. Those who sought a cultural arts facility wanted a sloped-floor auditorium with good acoustics for music and drama. And those who wanted to boost commerce wanted an arena-like building with a large flat floor in the center for sporting events, conventions, and exhibitions. These disparate definitions and constituencies would complicate the auditorium quest.

But the stock market crash of October 1929 settled the argument: there would be no civic auditorium, at least for now.

## QUIET!
## CIVIC IMPRESARIO AT WORK

Madison never suffered the embarrassment of Great Depression bread lines, but it hardly escaped the pain of the nation's worst economic catastrophe. Between 1929 and 1933 annual new home starts skidded from nearly five hundred to just twenty-one, bank deposits dropped from $30 million to $17 million, building permits plummeted from $5.3 million to $303,000, and city property tax collections declined from $3.8 million to about $3.2 million. By early 1935, however, Madison's economic vital signs were beginning to point upward. Banks were making loans, 129 new dwellings were started, building permits climbed to more than $1 million worth, and bank deposits spurted to $27 million. Once again Madisonians heard the pleasing staccato of carpenters' hammers and smelled the smoke of steam shovels.[62]

After six years of struggling with the grinding effects of the depression, Madison's business leaders were sufficiently encouraged to plan for better times. "Prepare for prosperity!" That was the slogan adopted in April 1935 by the Association of Commerce. "We have been on the defensive for four years," said Alvin Gillette, the association's director, "and now we must go on the offensive."[63]

To plan for a better future with so many dark clouds swirling about took courage and faith, and to Mayor James Law (see Fig. 1.31) such planning made perfect sense. Law, a principal in Madison's largest architectural firm, had been appointed in December 1932 by the common council to fill the

FIGURE 1.31

## JAMES R. LAW
### *ARCHITECT-MAYOR*

SHSW. WHi(X3)51483

Law Park, the site of Frank Lloyd Wright's Monona Terrace, is probably Madison's best-known open space. But few know anything about the man after whom it was named.

James R. Law III was born on April 1, 1885, the son of a Madison stonemason. As a little boy, he would pore over architectural drawings that his father would lay out on the kitchen table. Someday, the little boy vowed, I will be an architect. When he was eighteen he began work as a draftsman for the Madison architectural firm of Claude and Starck, and six years later he entered the University of Pennsylvania School of Architecture, where he completed the two-year program. In 1913, after brief stints with Claude and Starck and, later, Arthur Peabody, the supervising architect of the State of Wisconsin, Law opened his own firm, which was later joined by Ellis Potter and Law's brother Ed. By the 1920s Law, Law and Potter had become Madison's preeminent firm.

Law never sought political office — it sought him. When Madison mayor A. G. Schmedeman was elected governor of Wisconsin in November 1932, a delegation of Madison leaders, impressed by Law's integrity and ability, urged him to place his name in nomination. Law consented, and to his great surprise the common council appointed him mayor in December 1932.

Three years into the depression was a terrible time to become mayor. The economy was still in free fall, the city was struggling to pay its bills, and nobody really knew what to do. Law skillfully guided the municipal corporation through one of its darkest periods. He reduced the city's debt by $4 million, established modern accounting practices, and gave all employees sick leave, paid vacations, and pensions. He was a great believer in parks and planning and never tired of pushing both. Law found not only that he enjoyed being mayor but that he was good at it. He was reelected four times, serving for eleven years, a record that stood until the 1990s.

Law was a close ally of Joe Jackson's and served a term as president of the Madison and Wisconsin Foundation while still the mayor. Like Jackson, Law admired Nolen's plan and worked to realize his esplanade along Lake Monona. Law was never a fan of Wright's architecture, although he kept those feelings to himself; Wright, by contrast, was outspokenly critical of Law's buildings.

Jim, as he was universally known, was appreciated for his ready smile, kindliness, unimpeachable integrity, broad vision, and practicality. When Law walked down the street, he chatted with plasterers and company presidents alike.

In 1943 Law was named to chair the state highway commission, a post he held until his death in 1952.

IGURE 1.32

## OSEPH W. JACKSON
### IVIC IMPRESARIO

HSW. WHi(X3)50321

or more than thirty years Joseph W. Jackson did everything he ould to thwart Frank Lloyd Wright's vision of a dream civic center — rom 1938, when Wright unveiled the project, until Jackson's death in 1969 at ninety (see Chapters 3–5). But Jackson was much nore than Wright's foe.

ackson was born on December 27, 1878, to a prominent Madison urgeon and his socialite wife. Three of Joe Jackson's four brothers grew up to become doctors and practiced at the Jackson Clinic ounded by their grandfather. But Joe was interested in sports. ackson attended the University of Wisconsin for nearly two years, bitching on the baseball team, but in 1900, when he was twenty-one, ne decided to escape the confining expectations of his parents. ackson became a cowboy in northwest North Dakota on the same ange where Theodore Roosevelt once had his ranch. Jackson's decision to follow in TR's footsteps was probably no accident. During he early 1890s TR made several trips to Madison to research his our-volume work, *The Winning of the West,* at the State Historical Society of Wisconsin. The teenaged Jackson would have had numerous opportunities to meet Roosevelt at social events in Madison, ncluding a gala reception at the home of Robert and Belle La Follette. Later in life a portrait of Teddy Roosevelt always adorned ackson's office wall.

During his North Dakota years Jackson led the rugged outdoor ife, married, moved to a small town on the high prairie, and got o involved in civic affairs that in 1910 he was elected mayor at hirty-one. When World War I was declared, Jackson enlisted in he army, earned the rank of colonel, and forever after practiced batriotism with pious zeal.

n 1919 Jackson moved his wife and six children back to Madison, where he became the business manager of the family-owned ackson Clinic. The hardscrabble life in small-town North Dakota nade him appreciate Madison's extraordinary beauty, wealth, and culture as never before. Sometime soon after his return to

Madison, he read Nolen's book and was profoundly influenced by it. As Jackson later put it in his memoirs, "my one ambition [was] to see Madison become that 'Model American City' which John Nolen visualized."

In 1937 Jackson abandoned the high salary and security of his clinic position to become executive director of the Madison and Wisconsin Foundation, a new type of chamber of commerce that he invented. From this bully pulpit Jackson never tired of telling Madisonians that civic service was "a duty and a privilege" and that Madison would become a great city only if unselfish citizens with compelling civic vision and unswerving determination provided leadership. Armed with these deeply held beliefs, this gritty idealist spearheaded efforts to secure hundreds of acres of public parks, thousands of feet of public lakeshore, a federal hospital, modern airport, dozens of new businesses providing thousands of jobs, a huge new downtown hotel, and much more.

unexpired mayoral term of A. G. Schmedeman, who had been elected governor in November 1932. Law had the unpopular task of cutting city expenses and paying off the city's high bonded indebtedness, but he performed the task with such skill that in 1934 he formed a citizens' committee to help him plan the city's future—a task that assumed that city bonds would fund major new projects. Although many years would pass before the city was out of danger, many thought safety was already in sight.[64]

But the slowly reviving local economy and the improvements in city finances were not all that emboldened Madison business leaders and the mayor. They had a third reason for their optimism: in April 1935 President Franklin Delano Roosevelt launched an array of economy-boosting programs, including a $4.8 billion appropriation for the Works Progress Administration (WPA). Anticipating congressional approval, Law worked with city leaders to identify high-priority public works projects, including schools, storm sewers, a sewage treatment plant, streets, bridges, parks, fire stations, municipal golf course, new city hall, and, most expensive of all, "an auditorium and armory." Law was confident that he could secure $1 million in federal grants for Madison.[65]

Law included an auditorium on his wish list for federal funding largely because business leaders regarded it as a necessity for boosting the city's relatively large convention industry. Law's inclusion of the armory and his reason for conjoining it with the auditorium had a much shorter history. In July 1934 the commander of Madison's naval reserve unit had written to Law to suggest that Madison could probably get a federal grant to build a naval armory if the city would donate a piece of lakeshore land. Naturally, Law was interested in any project that would generate a big federal grant, but what caught the mayor's eye was the commander's offer to make the drill hall available for civic purposes. In fact, the cavernous main floor of the 1893 campus armory known as the Red Gym (see Fig. 1.13) had served for years as an auditorium that could hold as many as five thousand people. And as an architect Law knew that an armory could easily be designed so that it could function as an effective municipal auditorium.[66]

To Law and prominent business leaders the auditorium-armory was almost irresistible. The naval reserve would pay rent for its use of the facility, and this income would help pay for the building. In addition, the city could charge rent for sporting events, conventions, and meetings. Best of all, the New Deal would pay 45 percent of the cost. Exactly where the auditorium-armory would be located was not specified, but city leaders assumed that it would be "on the lake shore near the center of the city."[67]

No one was more excited by these developments than Colonel Joseph W. Jackson, the business administrator for the Jackson Clinic, the preeminent medical practice in Madison founded by his grandfather. (Jackson was always pleased when people used his World War I military title, but his closest friends called him Bud.) He was one of those men who could do his job in his sleep and who sought fulfillment in other channels. He was immensely talented, a blend of doer, dreamer, builder, researcher, planner, skilled writer, and persuasive speaker (see Fig. 1.32). He had the rare ability to write the scripts, produce the play, and market the production. And he loved Madison.

Jackson had been a major player among Madison leaders since the late 1920s; in 1933 he was elected to the board of the Association of Commerce, and in 1934 he became its vice president. During the 1930s Jackson compiled a glistening résumé as a civic leader. He was probably best known for his almost heroic work in acquiring six hundred acres for the

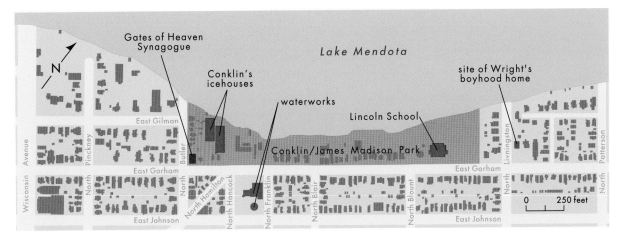

FIGURE 1.33

### The Conklin Site: Auditorium Battleground

*U.W.–Madison Cartographic Laboratory and W. J. Martinelli*

One of the most fiercely contested civic battlegrounds in Madison was the Lake Mendota frontage at the end of North Hamilton Street (the diagonal street on the left). The area is shown as it appeared in the 1930s, with two exceptions: Gates of Heaven Synagogue, which was moved to the site in 1971, and the green area, a reminder that the area was gradually converted to a city park and that nearly all structures except the synagogue and Lincoln School will eventually be removed.

In the 1930s the area was known as "the Conklin site," after the family that cut, stored, and distributed Lake Mendota ice from this location. The Conklins' hulking icehouses, set in an otherwise residential area, are shown in red. In the early 1930s inexpensive electric refrigerators made the Conklins' ice business obsolete, and it closed.

Jackson's great vision for the Mendota frontage from Wisconsin Avenue (at far left), to Livingston Street (on the right) was to make it into a great public park with a civic center complex at the foot of North Hamilton. He spent more than thirty years trying to make this dream a reality. In 1935 and 1938 he schemed to locate an auditorium-armory and marina there. In 1939 he got Ladislas Segoe, an urban planning consultant, to recommend this site as the best location for such a facility and persuaded the city to buy the site. During World War II he convinced the city to buy several adjacent parcels; by the end of the war the city owned 750 feet of frontage. From then on, people called it Conklin Park. From 1946 to 1949 Jackson worked to locate a war memorial there. During the 1950s, when Madisonians said they wanted Frank Lloyd Wright to design an auditorium at Monona Terrace, Jackson pushed the Conklin site, declaring it superior. In the early 1960s Jackson maneuvered to bring Segoe back to the city (see Chapter 4) and to recommend Conklin Park as the best auditorium site.

Although Jackson failed to get an auditorium built at the Conklin site, he continued to encourage the city to buy more lake frontage to the east. He was still at it in 1963, by then aged eighty-four, when he persuaded the city to change the name from Conklin Park to James Madison Park, after one of Jackson's great heroes, and to adopt a master plan that called for the acquisition of all properties between Franklin and Livingston. The current boundaries of James Madison Park are shown in green.

Directly across Johnson Street from the Conklin site was the city waterworks, an auditorium site strongly preferred by Mayor Henry Reynolds in the 1960s. The map also shows the locations of Wright's boyhood home and school.

University of Wisconsin Arboretum by persuading owners to sell at low prices and then raising the money to buy it. His highly visible work at the Association of Commerce included designing and launching the "Prepare for Prosperity Campaign" and leading a statewide effort to hold a celebration of Wisconsin's territorial centennial in Madison in July 1936.[68]

By virtue of his rich network of civic leaders and his personal friendship with Law, Jackson knew about the letter from the naval reserve commander; through his membership on the board of the Association of Commerce, Jackson almost surely helped formulate Law's list of projects that the city submitted for federal funding in February 1935.

Jackson saw the auditorium-armory as the chance of a lifetime to realize one of his great dreams for Madison: to create a great public park and civic complex on the shore of Lake Mendota, just three blocks north of the Capitol Square. The site was then occupied by hulking icehouses owned by the Conklin family. During this period Jackson took the first of several steps in a lifelong, unwavering crusade to realize his dream. But looking back, the importance of the precedent he was about to establish can hardly be exaggerated.

Jackson was a skilled strategist who believed in preemptive strikes and the incremental realization of one's goals. What he did to establish the Conklin site as the "official" location for the auditorium-armory is a case in point (see Fig. 1.33). In late June 1935 Jackson used his position as vice president of the Association of Commerce to appoint his good friend A. G. Gallistel, the University of Wisconsin's director of physical plant planning, to chair the association's Municipal Pier Committee. According to the association's *Bulletin*, this committee was created to accommodate the needs of the rapidly growing ranks of sailboat owners. Just one week later the committee concluded that a municipal pier "should be a part of a recreational center for Madison" and that it should be located "in the neighborhood of North Hamilton Street on the lake." In fact, Jackson had worked out a much more ambitious plan with Gallistel that was revealed in the committee's report: *"Eventually the municipal auditorium and convention hall should be placed at this* [the Conklin] *site"* (emphasis added). Jackson's cards were now face up on the table.[69]

But the Municipal Pier Committee did not stop there. Anticipating the need for a detailed plan in order to secure a federal grant, the committee persuaded the city engineer to prepare drawings and specifications for a "recreation center" at the Conklin site. Jackson and his committee members moved quickly to get the state legislature to authorize the construction of a breakwater that would create a harbor in Lake Mendota. This was the first of many times that Jackson would use the legislature to achieve his goals. Significantly, Jackson took all these steps while the Conklins still owned the property.[70]

Unfortunately for Jackson, the auditorium-armory concept failed to win a federal grant in 1935, but Jackson's efforts produced something much more valuable: he had persuaded opinion leaders that the Conklin site was the best place for a civic auditorium, armory, and municipal marina. Furthermore, Jackson had engineered this new consensus in just five months, after Law submitted his project list to the federal government. Meanwhile, Jackson's mind was working on another important feat.

REINVENTING THE ASSOCIATION OF COMMERCE

In the summer of 1936 the Association of Commerce's board appointed a special committee, composed of the mayor, the dean of the University of Wisconsin School of Commerce, the association's president, five past presidents, and Jackson, who described the other committee members as his "most intimate personal friends." It was the type of heavy-duty brain trust that organizations convene only at critical junctures in their history. The official charge to the committee was to determine what type of commercial organization was "best fitted to the unusual needs of Madison." This was a polite way of saying that the association faced serious problems that required immediate attention and, in this case, that Jackson had solutions.[71]

First, association membership and income had been hard hit by the depression. Between 1929 and 1936 association membership declined from nine hundred to about five hundred, and its $32,000 budget was cut in half. Second, the organization lacked a comprehensive, compelling, and entrepreneurial program. Yes, it pushed traditional chamber-of-commerce programs — promoting conventions, organizing banquets, trumpeting the big annual auto show, publishing promotional booklets, and compiling annual business statistics—but they seemed almost custodial. Third, association support for high-priority business-improvement schemes such as the auditorium was often just talk. Fourth, the association had failed to appeal to leaders of Madison's two huge public institutions, the University of Wisconsin and the State of Wisconsin.[72]

Jackson told the other special committee members that the association needed a dramatic makeover, including a new funding system, new vision, and new structure, and they agreed. He told them that whatever they did should appeal to the state and the university, two large components of the community, and not just the business community. He said the new organization should emphasize planning and the pursuit of prioritized goals. Once again they agreed. He urged them to find ways to allow people from all over the state to feel a stronger affinity for Madison because it was the capital and home of the university. Jackson's idea was to create a hybrid organization that was part chamber of commerce and part philanthropic foundation. Jackson was confident that if Madison set up the right type of community foundation, wealthy citizens from all over the state would make large grants for Madison's civic improvement. Unfortunately, Jackson could find no example of what he wanted to do anywhere in the country.[73]

More than anything else, Jackson wanted to brainstorm his idea with someone who had an extensive knowledge of U.S. cities, an entrepreneurial mind, and an understanding of the dynamics of local leadership. For Jackson that man was John Nolen, the highly regarded city planner who had done a master plan for Madison in 1909. Jackson was a devout believer in Nolen's plan and wanted to do everything he could to realize Nolen's government mall along Monona Avenue and the esplanade along the Monona lakeshore.[74]

Characteristically, Jackson found a way to befriend his hero. It came in 1934 when Madison leaders were planning the official opening of the arboretum. Because Nolen had made the arboretum one of his formal recommendations in his 1909 plan, Jackson thought Nolen should be invited back to Madison to speak at the opening and give the keynote address to the Association of Commerce's annual meeting. The association's directors asked Jackson to extend the invitation. Nolen and Jackson hit it off immediately. Jackson gave Nolen an astute update of what had happened since he last visited the city and helped the planner hone his remarks for his Madison audiences.[75]

In August 1936, after an almost two-year hiatus (because federal funding had not come through, nothing had happened), Jackson resumed his correspondence with Nolen with a warm "hello my good friend." "Things are moving along—never as rapidly as my restless spirit feels they should," he continued. Jackson closed his letter with his real purpose, his wish "that something would bring you back to Madison for at least a few days." Jackson was eager to pick Nolen's brain about the hybrid civic organization he wanted to create.[76]

A few days later, before Nolen could reply, Jackson wrote a second letter disclosing a stunning development: the association's special committee had asked Jackson to be executive director of the new association. Jackson had not sought the job; his goal was to recast the association in a vibrant new form and to continue serving on the board. Now Jackson really needed to talk to Nolen.

Nolen's promptly penned reply could not have been more supportive. "Nothing better could happen to Madison," Nolen began, "for it may still be the Model City of which we have dreamed, for which we have worked and which is already partly accomplished. You, my dear Jackson, are ready and ripe for the enterprise. It would be the crowning event of your life work." But Nolen was not finished. "In general my advice is don't hesitate, decide and act.... You should say 'yes' to the call. Two ends are at stake — the future of Madison and the fuller realization of your own highest life purpose. Go for it, Colonel!" Nolen also told Jackson that he had never heard of a hybrid organization such that his friend was considering, but he knew cities that had started community foundations. Once again Nolen encouraged Jackson to give the new organization a try.[77]

Jackson was fifty-seven, too old by most standards to change careers, and as business administrator of the Jackson Clinic he enjoyed a good salary and job security. On the other hand, after eighteen years in that position, the robustly healthy Jackson yearned for a new challenge, and nothing was more exciting than the prospect of shaping the city he loved.[78]

However, before Jackson said yes to the association directors, he wanted to confirm that Nolen was willing to do an update of his 1909 plan. Jackson believed that Nolen was the best person for the job and that an updated plan was essential for Madison to realize its potential. Nolen promised Jackson that he would do everything in his power to work Madison into his busy schedule and explained that the cost would be $10,000. Jackson found the prospect of working with his hero terribly exciting.[79]

Then came three momentous announcements in just three months. In November 1936 the executive secretary of the Association of Commerce announced his resignation (Jackson apparently had been offered the job before the incumbent was asked to leave). In December 1936 the association board voted unanimously to approve a "new program of work." And in January 1937 association members voted unanimously to create the Madison and Wisconsin Foundation. Immediately after the membership meeting the board appointed Jackson as the new executive director at a salary of $7,500 per year. This was half of what Jackson had earned at the Jackson Clinic, but that was all right with Jackson.[80]

From December 1937 to March 1938 Jackson used the *Bulletin* to dispense bite-sized pieces of his twenty-thousand-word "program statement" to foundation members. In this fashion members learned about the new mission and vision statement, new goals, the organization's history, the rationale for the new organization, and why a new master plan was the key to Madison's future. It was clear, compelling, comprehensive, tightly argued, and vintage Jackson. Madison had never seen anything like it. What most *Bulletin* readers did not realize was that a lot more was going on behind the scenes.[81]

A NEW MASTER PLAN FOR MADISON

On February 13, 1937, one month before the Madison and Wisconsin Foundation officially opened its doors, Joe Jackson had written to John Nolen and reported: "Well the evil deed is 'did.' The old Madison Association of Commerce is now the 'Madison and Wisconsin Foundation' and newspapers announced that J. W. Jackson was made executive director. Also, it is publicly stated that the No. 1 item of the program is to complete the city plan for the future physical development of Madison as the Capital City of the State of

Wisconsin." Jackson explained that he and Mayor Law had concluded that the best way to proceed would be for Nolen to come to Madison for "a preliminary survey" and cost estimate. "When can you come?"[82]

Six days later Jackson received a telegram from Nolen's son. "It is my sad duty to tell you that my father passed away peacefully yesterday and that it was impossible for us to read him your last letter which would have given him great pleasure and satisfaction. He talked with me several times in the last few weeks about Madison in which you know his interest was keen."[83]

Jackson was devastated. His hero, confidant, and the man he had hoped would be his colleague was dead. Nolen's updated Madison plan was to have been the centerpiece of Jackson's great campaign to realize the city's promise as a model city. Worst of all, Jackson had no one in reserve, and getting someone to fill Nolen's shoes would be tough. To Jackson's great surprise he found Nolen's replacement much faster than he thought.

In March 1937, the same month Jackson officially began his job as executive director, Clarence A. Dykstra was appointed president of the University of Wisconsin. Jackson must have been thrilled to read of Dykstra's background in Madison newspapers. Since 1930 Dykstra had been the city manager of Cincinnati, where he gained a reputation as an outstanding public administrator. At the beginning of his career Dykstra had held the top staff job at three civic development organizations in Cleveland, Chicago, and Los Angeles, and between Cincinnati and the civic development jobs Dykstra had been a professor of political science. Given the importance of the University of Wisconsin to the new Madison and Wisconsin Foundation, and the new president's

background in city development, Joe Jackson was assuredly one of Dykstra's first callers.[84]

Dykstra was almost certainly the person who urged Jackson to consider Ladislas Segoe as John Nolen's replacement. At the time Segoe was the principal of a Cincinnati city planning consultancy (see Fig. 1.34). Dykstra had a high regard for Segoe with whom he had just finished collaborating on a national research project and because he was familiar with Segoe's 1925 plan for Cincinnati.[85]

Segoe looked good on paper, but Jackson could not afford to take chances. Jackson decided to have the planner make a presentation to the Rotary Club of Madison, a tough-minded representative group of Madison's leaders. Segoe accepted Jackson's invitation and on July 11, 1937, Madison Rotarians were treated to an unusual program. The Rotary Club president introduced Mayor Law, who then introduced university president Dykstra, who gave a short talk that included praise for "the fine work being done by the Madison and Wisconsin Foundation." Dykstra then introduced the main speaker, his friend and former Cincinnati colleague. Ladislas Segoe gave a carefully tailored talk about how city planning could allow Madison to realize its great potential, so clearly seen by John Nolen. Jackson did not say a word at the meeting, but the impresario's fingerprints were everywhere. Jackson got good feedback on Segoe's talk, and the chemistry between the two men was superb.[86]

Jackson decided that Segoe was his man and that he wanted Segoe to do a comprehensive master plan for Madison. Comprehensive master plans then were the highest art form of the planning profession, and Jackson wanted the best. This meant that Segoe had to analyze Madison's economy, population, transportation systems, parks, zoning ordinances, schools, public buildings, and capital budgeting

program. From conversations with Segoe, Jackson learned that such a plan would cost at least $16,000.[87]

Getting this amount of money would not be easy, but the wily new foundation director had an idea. Jackson's campaign to hold a great celebration in Madison in 1936 to commemorate the one hundredth anniversary of the formation of Wisconsin Territory had been a great financial success; Wisconsin Centennial, Inc. (WCI), the sponsoring organization, had ended up with enough money in its treasury to pay for Segoe's work. Jackson, acting secretary of WCI, urged its board members to transfer this money to a new organization that would be known as the Madison Planning Trust and to have the trust administer Madison's new master plan. The trust was an independent semipublic organization empowered to employ and supervise Segoe. What better way to spend this windfall, Jackson asked, than to plan the growth of Wisconsin's capital city for the next century? The board agreed, and Jackson went off to persuade WCI sponsors, namely, the state, the City of Madison, and 190 individuals.[88]

Jackson sold the concept to every sponsor of the centennial, and WCI turned its money over to the Madison Planning Trust. Jackson made sure that his friends and colleagues served as the new entity's trustees. Thus, by February 1938, just seven months after Segoe became the heir to Nolen's hallowed place in Madison, Jackson had $16,000 dedicated to cover the costs of "the most complete and comprehensive city plan yet produced in America" and a pliant new trust run by his friends.[89]

In early March 1938 the trustees advised Segoe that he was their choice, and in early May the local newspapers announced that Segoe had been hired to write the plan. Jackson boasted that Segoe had been hired after a "careful country wide search,"

Ladislas Segoe was forty-four and a promising urban and regional planner when he was hired to do a comprehensive plan for Madison in 1938. Born and educated in Hungary, Segoe immigrated to New York City in 1921 where his civil engineering degree landed him a job with a consulting company that specialized in comprehensive city plans. After several years as an assistant to a senior planner, Segoe was given full responsibility for a master plan for Cincinnati. He did such a good job that the city hired him to be its chief planner. After two years Segoe resigned and opened a consulting business.

From 1928 to 1938 Segoe attracted national attention with an innovative method of comprehensive city planning. Segoe emphasized planning for the entire metropolitan area, avoiding the artificial distinction between physical and social planning, doing a sophisticated analysis of the local economy, and linking planning with capital budgeting. In 1935 Segoe presented a paper, "What City, Regional, State, and National Planning Can Do for the Future of America," to the National Planning Conference, which opened two career-boosting doors for him. He was invited to lecture at the Harvard School of City Planning and to serve as the technical director for a group that advised the federal government how to allocate grants to cities under New Deal programs. In this latter capacity Segoe worked for Clarence Dykstra, then the Cincinnati city manager, who in 1937 was appointed president of the University of Wisconsin. Dykstra recommended Segoe to Joe Jackson, then head of the Madison and Wisconsin Foundation.

In 1941, just a year after he completed Madison's comprehensive plan, Segoe wrote an urban planning textbook, *Principles and Practice of Urban Planning,* described in its introduction as "the most influential planning book in the United States during the first half of the twentieth century." During the 1950s and 1960s Segoe continued to do comprehensive community plans, but he also wrote extensively about the effect of interstate highways on regional development, the perverse tendency of urban renewal to concentrate social problems, and the importance of maintaining professionalism as citizens sought greater participation in community planning.

Late in his life Segoe compiled a list of sixteen U.S. cities where he felt he had made a major contribution. They included New York, San Francisco, Toronto, Chicago, Cincinnati, Detroit, Philadelphia, and Madison, Wisconsin. In the 1960s, in recognition of Segoe's work on behalf of the city, the Madison Common Council named a major artery on the West Side of the city "Segoe Road." This decision, and another in the 1960s to name the artery in Law Park "John Nolen Drive," may make Madison the only city in the country to name two major streets after city planners. Segoe retired in 1968 and died in 1983.

but all evidentiary arrows point to the simple referral from Dykstra. Jackson often exaggerated to add dignity and heft to his cause.[90]

## A New Auditorium-Armory-Marina Complex at Conklin Park

Every year Mayor Law and civic leaders like Joe Jackson scrutinized President Roosevelt's latest public works program because it created opportunities for major community improvements. Roosevelt's 1938 public works bill seemed almost too good to be true. It encouraged cities to build large public buildings and offered to pay 45 percent of the costs. Law and Jackson saw the bill as a rare opportunity to pursue two long-sought public projects: the municipal auditorium and a new city-county building. Law, Jackson, and other city leaders linked arms and tried to get in step with this invigorating New Deal music.

Officers in the local naval reserve unit saw the same opportunity and again formally requested Law's help in getting a grant for an auditorium-armory. In retrospect, the earlier attempt to secure such a facility in 1934–1935 looked as if had been the perfect homework assignment. A mayoral committee endorsed the Conklin site, said that such a building could hold six thousand people, and calculated that Madison could recover its share of the cost from rent paid by the navy, fees from conventioneers and event promoters, and boat-mooring and -storage fees. To get the initial capital the city would sell revenue bonds, a special form of municipal borrowing that repays bond holders from revenue generated by the project and not from real estate taxes. In August 1938 the city sought a federal grant of $356,000 for the auditorium-armory and the Lake Mendota breakwater project (see Fig. 1.35). Jackson was thrilled.[91]

FIGURE 1.35

**1938 Auditorium-Armory-Marina Proposal for Conklin Park**

*Courtesy* Wisconsin State Journal

This 1938 perspective, labeled "Naval Armory Community Building," by Madison architect William V. Kaeser, was one of several schemes devised by Joe Jackson, the executive director of the Madison and Wisconsin Foundation, to locate public facilities at the Conklin site. This project was to include an auditorium for Madison-area residents, an armory serving the Madison unit of the U.S. Naval Reserve, and a marina serving Lake Mendota boaters. The sketch was done to help the city secure a federal grant for the project. The complex, which was to occupy the two blocks bounded by North Butler on the west, North Franklin on the east, East Gorham on the south, and Lake Mendota on the north (see Fig. 1.33), was rejected by the federal government.

## THE NEW JOINT CITY-COUNTY BUILDING

Just about everyone agreed that the 1858 city hall and the 1886 county courthouse were too small to handle government business in 1938. Madison had tried to replace its city hall for decades, and the county began to explore an "annex" in the 1920s. Both governments suffered from the same problem: too little money and too many projects with higher priority. However, Roosevelt's generous public works program prompted Madison and Dane County to apply for money.[92]

At first the two governments walked separate paths. Dane County applied for a grant for an annex to solve its overcrowding problem, and it was approved

in June 1938. To the surprise of most county supervisors, the newspaper announcement provoked a vigorous debate. Wouldn't it be better, wondered city leaders, instead of creating two structures, to build just one? The announcement of the county grant came at a time when the city was taking its first steps toward building a new, separate city hall under the same public works program. As an architect, Law well understood the savings that both governments could enjoy if they did a joint building. As a result of the 1927 city decision to make the six blocks along Monona Avenue the official civic center (exactly what Nolen had recommended in 1909), almost all civic leaders thought the best location for the city-county

building was the block across the street from the Federal Building.[93] (As the orientation maps at the front of the book show, the City-County Building was built where many civic leaders wanted it in 1938, but it was not completed until 1957. See also Fig. 4.31.)

To get the two governments working together Mayor Law called a rare special meeting of the common council on the evening of July 5 and persuaded the council to approve the formation of a city-county committee to explore a joint building. At their regularly scheduled meeting just two days later, county supervisors agreed to go along with the city's suggestion. Both governments moved with unprecedented speed to meet a stern federal deadline. All projects receiving New Deal grants had to begin construction by December 31, 1938, which was just six months away.[94]

The city-county committee members pronounced the joint concept feasible and urged their respective governments to move forward with the plan. The common council authorized the mayor to submit an application to the federal government for the city hall component and to borrow up to $530,000 in general obligation bonds on top of the federal grant. Madison voters approved the plan by 2-to-1 at a special election in September 1938; now the question was whether the federal government would approve the $900,000 grant that would allow the nearly $2 million joint building to go forward (see Fig. 1.36).[95]

## THE GREAT CRESCENDO, OCTOBER 1938

Progress on the city-county building and auditorium-armory was remarkable. Federal officials approved the county's grant for its part of the new dual building on September 27 and Madison's grant for the new

The publication of this architect's elevation on the front page of the *Capital Times* on July 21, 1938, may have triggered the fifty-nine-year battle to build an auditorium on filled land at the foot of Monona Avenue. Wright had little tolerance for mundane buildings like this, and he probably viewed it as an opportunity to demonstrate that he could do something better. The site of this proposed building was a city block fronting on Monona Avenue exactly where the City-County Building is located today (see orientation map on page xii).

This elevation was done by Karl Sheldon, a principal in Starck, Sheldon and Schneider, a Madison architectural firm, to help the city and county secure a federal grant. As a staff architect for the State of Wisconsin, Sheldon had prepared plans for the State Office Building just across the street (see Fig. 1.22). The building was to be located in the heart of John Nolen's civic center, exactly where the City-County Building is located today. Even Joe Jackson, who was rarely restrained in his praise of a project he supported, said its style was "plain but handsome."

city hall on October 28. Approval of a $56,000 federal grant for the Conklin site breakwater was announced on October 23. The only federal grant that had not been approved by the end of the month was the $300,000 auditorium-armory, but federal feedback on it was encouraging.[96]

While the auditorium-armory and the city-county building were cruising along, the city was making progress on another Nolen front. Beginning in 1934 under Law's leadership the city had begun to

fill the Lake Monona shoreline where Nolen had proposed his esplanade. So significant was Law's leadership on this that the common council took the unusual step of naming the park after him in 1934. Like Nolen, Law wanted to create a lakefront park and eliminate the row of boathouse shacks that marred the shoreline. In 1937 newspapers reported that the last boathouse had been removed.[97]

Jackson had played large roles in these and many other projects, sometimes behind the scenes and sometimes on the front page. After he took over as executive director of the Madison and Wisconsin Foundation in March 1937, Jackson's professional life resembled a nineteen-month version of Ravel's *Bolero*. It began slowly, methodically, distinctively. Gradually, the pace quickened. Now, at the end of October 1938, the cymbals were crashing and the climax was near. Everything looked promising.[98]

FIGURE 2.1

**1893 Lake Mendota Boathouse**

*Courtesy Ann Waidelich*

Frank Lloyd Wright's Lake Mendota boathouse, shown here in an 1890s postcard, was located on a steep hillside at the end of North Carroll Street in what is now the U.W.–Madison fraternity and sorority row. The brown-shingled and cream stucco structure was built for $4,600 and opened in April 1894. An arched entrance and two flanking pavilions capped by low-pitched roofs dominate the waterfront elevation. For a street view of the building, see Figure 2.25. Unfortunately, the building was razed in 1926.

**CHAPTER 2**

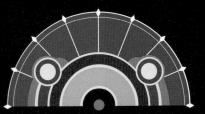

**AN OLD MADISON BOY**

William C. Wright was a brilliant man who spent much of his life trying to find a remunerative career and satisfying family relationships. Born in 1825 in Massachusetts, the precocious young man published his first two musical compositions when he was twenty-two. After graduation from college, he taught music at a women's preparatory school in Utica, New York, and there met his first wife, Permelia Holcomb. Soon after their marriage in 1851 Wright moved his family to East Hartford, Connecticut, where he taught music, was organist for a local church, and studied law. While in Connecticut he was admitted to the bar, published his first book, *The Piano Forte Manual*, and the couple had two of their three children. In 1859 Wright moved his family to Lone Rock, a small Wisconsin town, where he practiced law and was appointed commissioner of the Richland County Circuit Court. In 1863 he was elected superintendent of the Richland County school system and in the same year was ordained a Baptist minister. Tragically, his wife died in childbirth in 1864, leaving him with three young children.

Anna Lloyd Jones was born in Wales in 1838, immigrated with her family to the United States when she was six, and lived with her family on several farms in southern Wisconsin. In the early 1860s her parents and siblings bought farms in the rural Township of Wyoming near Spring Green. Anna and her siblings were raised in the liberal, free-thinking religious tradition that became Unitarianism in the midnineteenth century. When she finished her schooling, she taught in several rural schools. During her stint as a teacher in Richland County, she met her future husband, William C. Wright, then the county commissioner of schools. Anna had naturally curly brown hair, brown eyes, and was five-foot-eight, tall for a woman of that time.

In this 1883 photograph William was fifty-eight and Anna was forty-five. The Wrights had three children, Frank in 1867, Mary Jane in 1869, and Maginel in 1877.

According to William's divorce papers, filed in 1885, his eighteen-year marriage to Anna Lloyd Wright was an almost unrelieved failure. After he left Madison, the nearly penniless sixty-year-old lived in the same town as his son George — first in Nebraska, then later in Missouri and Iowa. Before he died in 1904, Wright had published three books, several scholarly articles, and nearly one hundred musical compositions.

Anna doted on her only son, Frank. She moved to Chicago before his marriage and lived next door to his Oak Park home and studio. During this period she helped found the Nineteenth Century Club, the preeminent Oak Park women's organization. Club members remember her scholarly lectures on Emerson and Browning and her attention-getting report on women's right to vote and own property. She died in 1923.

In October 1877 the fifty-two-year-old William C. Wright lost his job. For the last three years he had served as pastor of the First Baptist Church in Weymouth, Massachusetts, a small town ten miles southeast of Boston. There he gave stirring erudite sermons, increased membership, persuaded a wealthy member to donate money for a new pipe organ, established a church-sponsored singing school, and held Sunday evening musical programs. To casual observers the diminutive, finely featured man was a successful professional (see Fig. 2.2), but doctrinaire church members thought their talented pastor was leading his flock in the wrong direction. The new organ was fine for Sunday services, but the singing school and Sunday evening programs veered alarmingly in the direction of entertainment, even fun. Their liberal pastor, they concluded, would have to go. Just six months earlier Wright's thirty-nine-year-old wife, Anna, had given birth prematurely to a girl, Maginel, who was sickly and required extraordinary care. The couple also had two other children, Frank, ten, and Mary Jane, eight; William had three other children by his first wife, the youngest of whom, sixteen-year-old Elizabeth (Lizzie), also lived in the household. Where the family should go and what he should do after he was fired was anything but clear.[1]

The Wrights had met in Wisconsin in the mid-1860s while he was superintendent of schools for Richland County, a hilly rural area north of the Wisconsin River and forty miles west of Madison, and she was a teacher in one of the county schools. Anna Lloyd Jones was one of ten children of a clannish Welsh family that had settled in the picturesque Wyoming Valley just south of the meandering Wisconsin River toward the end of the Civil War. William had been a widower for a year and the single father of three children younger than six. In 1863 he decided to follow his father's footsteps and become a Baptist minister. When he and Anna were married in

August 1866, he had two small congregations, both in Richland County. He was forty-one and she was twenty-eight. Their first child, Frank Lincoln, was born on June 8, 1867 (see Fig. 2.3).[2]

William Wright was conspicuously brilliant. He had entered college at fourteen and received a degree from what is now Colgate University. By the time he met Anna, he had been admitted to the bar, been ordained a Baptist minister, and published one book and several musical compositions. He was a spellbinding orator and knew how to modulate his bass voice for greatest effect. He was a gifted singer, violinist, pianist, organist, and composer. His library included many of the great books of Western civilization. Almost everyone was drawn to his convivial personality, intrigued by his knowledge, and awed by his abilities. Anna undoubtedly thought he was quite a catch.[3]

However, William struggled as a breadwinner because his professional qualifications — with the exception of law, which he seldom chose to practice — doomed him to low-paying, precarious, and often thankless positions. For example, because the Central Baptist Society in Richland Center could not afford to pay their pastor, William Wright had to move his family to McGregor, Iowa, a small town on the Mississippi River where he co-owned a music store and preached part time. After trying for two years to eke out a living in McGregor, and the birth of a daughter, Mary Jane, William moved his growing family to Pawtucket, Rhode Island, where he served as minister of the High Street Baptist Church. After three years in Pawtucket, William became minister of the First Baptist Church in Weymouth.[4]

Even before he was dismissed by the Weymouth congregation, Wright had experienced an "irrepressible conflict" between his denomination's demand to preach "the Gospel" and his growing belief in "religious character." So great was this conflict

that Wright resolved to never preach again except upon "a free platform." Five months after he left his Baptist church, he delivered a sermon at the Weymouth Univeralist Church, a denomination that celebrated its freedom from creeds. William's conversion to liberal religion was surely a welcome development to Anna, whose family were Unitarians even before leaving Wales.[5]

At this critical juncture William resolved to move his family back to Wisconsin. He chose Madison partly because it offered outstanding educational opportunities for his children and partly because he hoped he could be hired as a Unitarian minister somewhere in the area. He had good reason to think he might attain his professional goal.

In 1875 Anna's brother, Jenkin, thirty-two, had been appointed missionary secretary by the Western Unitarian Conference, a position that made him responsible for spearheading the formation of Unitarian congregations between Ohio and Colorado. One of his most promising new church locations was Madison, the home of the University of Wisconsin. Anna was undoubtedly pleased by the prospect of returning to Wisconsin because she could be near her family. In the spring of 1878 the Wright family traveled to Wisconsin and lived with Anna's relatives in the Wyoming Valley. Sometime that fall they moved to Madison.[6]

## THE MADISON YEARS, 1878 TO 1887

When the Wrights arrived in Madison, the city had about ten thousand people, nearly two thousand fewer than at the height of a great boom before the Civil War. City leaders were trying to find ways to get the city growing again. One group insisted that building factories was the city's best bet, while another tried to make the city into a great northern

FIGURE 2.3

**Frank Lincoln Wright, Age Ten**

*Courtesy FLW FDN. 6001.0003*

This portrait of Frank in his Sunday best was taken just a few months before the Wright family's move to Madison in 1878 from Weymouth, Massachusetts. Weymouth was a small town ten miles southeast of Boston, where his father was a Baptist minister. Before Madison, Frank had lived in five cities in four states, but he would spend nine formative years in Wisconsin's capital. There he would attend public schools from the sixth through twelfth grades, take courses at the University of Wisconsin, secure his first training as an architect, and develop a rich network of friends and relatives. For these reasons he always considered Madison his hometown.

resort, a midwestern version of Saratoga and Newport. Although most Madisonians were immigrants or the children of immigrants, the city was run by refugees from New England known as "codfish aristocrats." Madison leaders were

FIGURE 2.4

**Wright's Madison, 1878 to 1887**

*SHSW. Angell and Hastreiter*

Highlighted on this extraordinarily detailed 1889 map are places that were important to Wright and his family during the Madison years. A red circle means the building has been demolished, a green circle that it still stands, and a yellow circle that it has been moved.

1. Wright family residence. Currently occupied by a 1901 home.

2. Doyon/Leitch residence (see also Fig. 2.5), home of Wright's childhood friend Charlie Doyon. Today the mansion is a Madison landmark.

3. Neighborhood (Second Ward) School (see also Fig. 2.7) where Wright attended seventh and eighth grades.

4. Gates of Heaven Synagogue (see also Fig. 2.9). From 1879 to 1886 Wright attended Unitarian services in this rented building. Its original location is shown as 4A and its current location as 4B.

5. Madison High School. Wright was in class when he heard the roar of the capitol collapse on November 8, 1883.

6. First Unitarian Church (see also Fig. 2.21), where Wright attended from 1886 to 1887.

7. 1858 City Hall (see also Fig. 1.25), which included the city library where Wright borrowed books.

8. Keyes Building, where Wright attended weekly fraternity meetings on Saturday nights in 1886. Currently occupied by the Mullins Building.

9. Ellsworth Block, a rented location of William C. Wright's music conservatory in 1885. The building is now called The Atrium.

10. Bruen's Block, site of the rented space in which William Wright's conservatory was located from 1880 to 1884. Now the site of Firstar Bank Madison.

11. State Bank (see also Fig. 2.22), where Wright worked as an "office assistant" for Allan Conover.

12. Perry's pawn shop, where Wright sold his father's books to get money for a train ticket to Chicago.

13. South Wing, state capitol. Wright stood for hours at the fence surrounding the capitol (near the current sidewalk), watching the rescue of workers from the collapsed south wing.

14. Dane County Courthouse (see also Fig. 2.12). Wright worked for Allan Conover when he was supervising architect for this building. The site is now a parking ramp.

15. Assembly Hall (see also Fig. 2.17), the scene of a gala class of '89 party where Wright stumbled through a date with an attractive classmate. Today the building is known as Music Hall.

16. Science Hall (see also Fig. 2.13). Wright worked for Conover when he was supervising architect and contractor for this building.

17. North Hall (see also Fig. 2.17), where Wright took mechanical drawing and descriptive geometry.

18. University Hall (see also Fig. 2.17), where Wright took French. The building is now known as Bascom Hall.

FIGURE 2.5

**The Mansion Next Door**

*SHSW. WHi(J2)11*

The contrast between two lakefront properties could hardly have been greater. This grand 1857 limestone-walled, slate-roofed, twenty-one-room Gothic revival mansion with nine fireplaces and the city's first indoor plumbing was separated from the Wrights' modest frame house only by a street that dead-ended at Lake Mendota. The mansion (no. 2. in Fig. 2.4) had cost about $14,000, whereas a house like the Wrights' probably was built for about $500. Unfortunately, no pictures of the Wright home have ever been found. In the 1880s the mansion was owned by Moses R. Doyon, a Madison mayor and prominent banker. Doyon's son, Charles, was involved in a boyhood printing business with Frank Wright and Robie Lamp.

The Doyon house was built by William Leitch, an immigrant from Scotland who later served four terms as Madison mayor. The mansion was added to the National Register of Historic Places in 1975; the Wright house was razed in about 1901 so that a much larger house could be built for Adolph Kayser, a Madison businessman who also served as mayor.

immensely proud of the city's singular qualities, its natural beauty, status as the state capital, and especially the University of Wisconsin. But Madison was still a small, sleepy midwestern town. Cows grazed in the streets during the day, oil lamps lit the streets at night, and mules pulled streetcars barely bigger than stagecoaches. City promoters tried to portray Madison as a cultural oasis of classical music and drama, but Wild West shows and can-can girls drew the biggest crowds.[7]

During their first year in Madison the Wrights lived in two locations, both rented, while William apparently tried to become the first minister of the new Unitarian congregation. Toward that end, he surely attended the November 1878 meeting of the Wisconsin Conference of Unitarian and Independent Churches at which his brother-in-law made a strong appeal for local support for a new Unitarian society in Madison. (Madison Unitarians referred to the member organization as a *society* and used *church* when speaking of the society's building.) Records show that Wright presided at a follow-up meeting in January 1879 to lay plans for the new society and that he was later elected secretary. However, Wright quickly learned that his recent departure from the more rigid Baptist denomination, his unfamiliarity with prospective local members, and his lack of support from national Unitarian leaders would prevent him from securing the Madison post. Although he could have practiced law, Madison already had dozens of lawyers, and that career apparently did not appeal to Wright. Similarly, his résumé qualified him to be a school administrator, but no such posts were available. Consequently, Wright decided to open what was then called a music conservatory, a studio where he gave voice and instrumental lessons (see no. 11 in Fig. 2.4). Although he possessed extraordinary musical talent, breaking into this business would not be easy because the city already had at least eighteen private music teachers. To supplement his income from the conservatory, William composed and sold popular music and preached to small rural Unitarian enclaves in southern Wisconsin.[8]

In October 1879 William Wright paid $2,000 for two large city lots and a house on East Gorham Street on the shore of Lake Mendota, just eight blocks from the capitol (see no. 1 in Fig. 2.4). Where Wright got the money for the property is not known, but all available evidence points to Anna's relatives. The house stood at the crown of a low narrow ridge that followed Lake Mendota for nearly half a mile on the north side of the Madison isthmus. The neighborhood, a curious mix of mansions (see Fig. 2.5) and modest homes, lay near the eastern edge of the city.[9]

The Wright house was clearly in the latter category. Both Frank and Maginel recalled the brown, one-and-a-half-story frame house surrounded by a fence. Woodbine wreathed the front porch columns, and smoke bushes grew in the half-acre yard. A great oak tree towered above the house and from it hung a vine whose bottom was shaped like the back of a horse. A grove of plum trees grew in the backyard, and behind it, near the lakeshore, was a barn for the family cow. Both children remembered the parlor with its newly laid waxed-maple floors, two Persian rugs with brilliant patterns over a white background, net curtains, maple and rattan furniture (including two unusual folding chairs covered with prickly Brussels carpeting), pots of geraniums on the window sills, and the much-used square piano. Both also remembered their father composing at the piano with a pen clenched in his teeth, its tip dripping black ink on his white beard (see Fig. 2.6). And everywhere, they recalled, there were books, books, books.[10]

That young Frank's upstairs room was off-limits to everyone was made clear by the handpainted sign on his door:

SANCTUM SANCTORUM
KEEP OUT

One day when her big brother was away, Maginel decided to trespass and found a long low room with dormers full of delicious smells from printer's ink, oil paints, shellac, and turpentine. She spied a printing press, piles of paper stock, calling cards bearing the names of Frank's girlfriends, colored inks and pencils, and oil paints. Finally, she noticed his scroll saw and several half-finished brackets he had made with it. Frank's recollections of the attic room included its sloped walls, artistically arranged clusters of dried leaves and pods, and several amateurish oil paintings he had done in Weymouth.[11]

Wright was a voracious reader. He borrowed books from his father's extensive library, checked out books from the public library (see no. 7 in Fig. 2.4), and received books from relatives. His favorite authors included Plutarch, Johann Wolfgang Goethe, John Greenleaf Whittier, Henry Wadsworth Longfellow, Jules Verne, and John Ruskin (*The Seven Lamps of Architecture*). But his all-time favorite was *Arabian Nights* and especially the story about Aladdin and his magic lamp. Aladdin enchanted Wright's creative soul, and in later life he used the story as a metaphor for human creativity.[12]

During his first two years at the house on the lake Wright attended the seventh and eighth grades at the Second Ward School (see Fig. 2.7 and no. 3 in Fig. 2.4), less than a block from home, and quickly acquired the nickname "Shaggy" because he wore his hair so long.[13]

On the school playground, probably in the fall of 1879, Wright, then twelve, came to the rescue of Robie (pronounced ROW-be) Lamp, who would become Wright's closest boyhood chum and lifelong friend. The freckle-faced thirteen-year-old had red hair and blue eyes; a childhood illness forced him to get around on crutches. Other boys at the Second Ward School called Robie a cripple and sometimes did cruel things. That day they grabbed Robie's crutches, threw him to the ground, and covered him with leaves. Frank chased the boys away, got Robie on his feet, and restored a smile to his face. Wright was almost in tears as he told his mother about the incident and asked whether he might bring Robie home. It was the beginning of a deep friendship that lasted until Robie's death in 1916.[14]

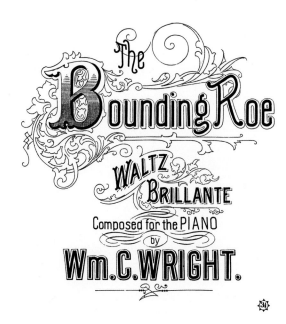

FIGURE 2.6

**William C. Wright, Composer**

*Collection of Mary Jane Hamilton*

This piece of sheet music for "The Bounding Roe" and another, "Floating by the Bay," were written while William ran his conservatory in Madison but were not published until 1886, after his divorce from Anna. The first, designed to capture the movements of a small Eurasian deer, was dedicated "to the young ladies of Stoughton," one of several small cities near Madison where Wright routinely traveled to teach music. "Floating by the Bay" is a dreamy piece that Wright probably conceived while out in the family rowboat somewhere on Lake Mendota. The piece was almost surely written while he was trying to escape the increasing hostility of his wife.

The two boys who happened to share the same birthday became practically inseparable. Robie was bright and creative and, like Wright, had a passion for inventing, drawing, and designing. Using their ingenuity, salvaged materials, Wright's scroll saw, and his father's lathe, the boys built a pedal-powered boat called a "water velocipede," a catamaran, fanciful colored kites with long tails, cross-bows, bows and arrows, a double-runnered bobsled, and

FIGURE 2.7

**Wright's Neighborhood School**

*Courtesy Theodora H. Kubly*

This is the Second Ward School, where Wright attended seventh and eighth grades. It stood less than five hundred feet west of Wright's home. During his seventh grade year (1879–80) the principal was his maternal aunt, Jane Lloyd Jones. The school's playground was where Wright rescued Robie Lamp from school bullies.

When this two-story cream brick Italianate-Style school was built in 1867 at a cost of $16,000, its design was considered state-of-the-art in part because it had indoor toilets, a first for a Madison school. The plumbing feat was relatively easy; all the plumbers had to do was run a sewage pipe from the school into adjacent Lake Mendota. That was the way sewage was processed in Madison at that time.

The building was replaced in 1915 with a much larger building and renamed Lincoln School. It has since been converted to apartments.

an iceboat (see Fig. 2.8). Much of their play focused on Lake Mendota and included rowing the family boat, swimming (sometimes all the way to Maple Bluff, now an elite Madison suburb), and ice skating.[15]

Perhaps their greatest love was printing. Like many boys of this era, Wright had a small printing press capable of producing work of professional quality, although only for small jobs such as business and

Iceboating and Skating on Lake Monona, 1878

*Collection of David Mollenhoff*

FIGURE 2.8

**Wright's Boyhood Activities**

In his *Autobiography* Wright reserves some of his most enthusiastic passages for descriptions of boyhood activities in Madison, three of which are shown here. "What play spaces!" the lake provided, he recalled. In 1878, the year the Wrights moved to Madison, the lakes were alive with the fast new-style iceboats that Madison men adapted from a prototype they had seen at the 1876 Centennial Exposition in Philadelphia. The thirteen thousand acres of ice on Madison lakes and the thrilling speed of the iceboat — then the fastest vehicle on earth — quickly made the city a national mecca for the sport. Frank Wright and Robie Lamp joined the craze and built an iceboat to use on Lake Mendota's ninety-seven hundred acres. The engraving from a March 1878 edition of *Harper's Weekly* shows the new-style iceboats on Lake Monona. Although Wright does not mention ice skating in his *Autobiography*, many of his apprentices later admired his exceptional skill on skates.

Wright also spent countless hours making ornate designs with his scroll saw, including whatnots for the family parlor and many others for sale. Wright was undoubtedly taught to use the saw by his father, who used it to make violins.

Recalling the joy of composing, typesetting, and printing with his small printing presses, Wright wrote, "Is there anything more pleasurable to the mind than unsullied paper?" With Robie and Charlie Doyon, Wright spent hours in the basement of the Gorham Street house where they printed business cards and even published a "new style newspaper — a scroll." This cut for "Charley's Printing Office," actually an ad for a business unrelated to Wright and Doyon's, was typical of advertisements that appeared in children's magazines at the time.

1880s Advertisement from *The Youth's Companion*

1880s Advertisement from *The Youth's Companion*

FIGURE 2.9

**Wright's Boyhood Unitarian Church**

*Courtesy City of Madison, photo by Katherine Rankin*

When the Unitarian Society was organized in Madison in early 1879, only fourteen people pledged financial support. Even so, organizers thought that prospects for the church were excellent because college towns attracted large numbers of religious liberals. With initial member pledges and a grant from the American Unitarian Association, leaders of the new organization rented the building shown here, Gates of Heaven Synagogue (see no. 4 in Fig. 2.4). The Wrights attended religious services there for seven years. Unitarians stopped renting the synagogue in 1886 when the First Unitarian Church was completed (see Fig. 2.21).

This handsome sandstone Victorian Romanesque structure was built in 1863 by liberal German Jews who had settled in Madison, but they used it only until 1871 when the congregation disbanded. It is the fourth-oldest extant synagogue in the United States and was placed on the National Register of Historic places in 1970. To save the landmark from destruction when a large office building was erected in 1971, it was moved from its original site at 214 West Washington Avenue to its current site in James Madison Park. This photo shows the building at its new site. Now fully restored, it has become a popular place for weddings and civic events.

FIGURE 2.10

**The God Almighty Lloyd Jones Clan**

*SHSW. WHi(X3)39465*

To many residents of the Wyoming Valley, Wright's maternal relatives were known as the "God Almighty Lloyd Joneses" because they were clannish and embraced high-minded principles. This 1883 photograph includes members of the Lloyd Jones family who played large roles in Frank Lloyd Wright's life. Seated in the center is Wright's grandfather, Richard Lloyd Jones, the patriarch; the empty chair symbolizes his deceased grandmother, Mary. Frank, sixteen, sits to the right of his grandfather with his sister Maginel, six, on his lap. To the right of Frank are Aunt Susan and Uncle Jenkin Lloyd Jones. When Wright moved to Chicago four years after this picture was taken, he lived with Susan and Jenkin until he could find a rooming house. Sitting in front of Susan and Jenkin is their son Richard Lloyd Jones, who later became publisher of the *Wisconsin State Journal*. To the left of Frank is his sister Mary Jane, fourteen; her hand rests on the shoulder of Aunt Jane. She and her sister, Ellen, seated behind and to the left of the senior Richard, later founded the Hillside Home School, a coeducational boarding school designed by Frank. Standing directly behind Mary Jane are Frank's parents, William Wright and Anna Lloyd Jones Wright. The bearded man holding the child (second from the left in the back row) is Frank's Uncle James Lloyd Jones, the owner of the farm on which Frank spent the late spring and summer months from his eleventh to his seventeenth year. To the right of James is Uncle John Lloyd Wright, who also owned a farm in the Wyoming Valley, including the land on which Taliesin was built. To the right of John is Uncle Thomas Lloyd Jones, a skilled carpenter who built most of the family's farm buildings and from whom Frank learned much.

calling cards. (The press was probably a gift from his paternal grandfather, who had once worked as a printer.) The two boys spent hours experimenting, composing, and typesetting and quickly got to the point where they needed a larger, more expensive press, additional fonts, and other equipment. That much money—$90 to $200—was a serious problem.

In his *Autobiography* Wright told how he got a playmate-neighbor's wealthy father to loan them $200. The man had one condition: make his son, Charlie Doyon, a principal in the firm. The boys accepted, bought their new equipment, and formed a new company, Wright, Doyon, and Lamp, Publishers and Printers. Wright does not say whether they

ever repaid the senior Doyon, the first of many wealthy patrons who sustained Wright's artistic endeavors during his long life.[16]

As Wright recalled, the first few years at the Madison house were happy. There were the wonderful times with Robie, the dreamy hours spent reading, tinkering, decorating, painting, and sketching. Finally, there was the large role that music played in the life of the family. William made Maginel a miniature violin to play when she was very young, and under his tutelage Frank became a skilled pianist and violist. Throughout his life Frank would refer to music as "an edifice of sound." Many nights Wright fell asleep listening to his father playing Bach and Beethoven on the parlor piano. During winter evenings, Wright recalled, the family engaged in "happy riots" in the parlor when "no one could tell where laughter left off and the singing began." Jane (Mary Jane), two years younger than Frank and a gifted piano player who loved to perform, would invite her girlfriends over and play rollicking Gilbert and Sullivan tunes from *The Mikado, Pirates of Penzance,* and several other shows. How Frank loved these songs! Anna would sit beside the piano with Maginel in her lap, and William would leave his study door open so that he could enjoy the festivities. At other times Wright and Jane would take turns playing classical pieces on the piano. From these experiences Wright developed a lifelong love of music. Later, in Oak Park with his family and still later with his apprentices at Taliesin, Wright sought to re-create these festive evenings.[17]

The Unitarian church also played a large part in family life during the Madison years. William continued as a circuit rider to Unitarian enclaves in southern Wisconsin, and from 1884 to 1886 Anna served as vice president of the Ladies Society, a largely social organization that met every Saturday. As a boy Frank attended Sunday school (see Fig. 2.9 and no. 4 in Fig. 2.4), which featured a new curriculum developed by his Uncle Jenkin. There the young man learned about the founders of world religions, including Jesus, Buddha, Zoroaster, Confucius, and Mohammed.[18]

FIGURE 2.11

# ALLAN CONOVER
## PROFESSOR, EMPLOYER, AND MENTOR

SHSW. WHi(X3)25698

Frank Wright was one of those people who seldom acknowledge that they have learned anything from anyone. But Wright made one exception. From Allan Darst Conover, the budding architect acknowledged, he "really learned the most." Wright had the good fortune to be hired by Conover as his "office man" and to work for him for at least eighteen and perhaps as long as twenty-four months.

Conover, a strikingly good-looking six-footer with reddish hair and piercing blue eyes, received one of the first two engineering degrees awarded by the University of Wisconsin in 1874; in 1879 he was made a full professor of engineering. Because of his highly regarded abilities as a civil engineer, Conover was appointed supervising architect for the new Dane County Courthouse in 1884 and contractor for the prestigious high-tech Science Hall for the University of Wisconsin in 1885. To take on these additional responsibilities, Conover turned over most of his teaching load to another instructor, established a downtown Madison office, and hired several employees, including Wright.

Wright learned so much from Conover for three reasons. First, Conover had a keen interest in cutting-edge technology. When most of his colleagues were teaching their students how to use iron as a structural material, Conover was pioneering the use of steel in Science Hall. Second, Conover developed methods to make engineering education more relevant, compelling, and fun. Whereas his predecessors drew their case studies from military textbooks, Conover looked for teaching opportunities in his backyard. He was especially fond of getting his students involved in the solution of pressing municipal problems, such as a sewerage system for Madison. Conover was also a great believer in taking students on field trips to inspect the latest bridges and buildings, always taking pains to analyze design and workmanship and to inspect the latest technologies long before they appeared in textbooks. Finally, Conover believed in delegating difficult, responsible assignments, even to his young employees. For

example, he sent Frank Wright clamoring to the top of Science Hall on a skeleton of steel girders to remove a faulty clip. He sent another employee, a recent engineering graduate, to the Pittsburgh mill of the Carnegie Steel Company to make sure that special beams being fabricated for Science Hall met all specifications before they were shipped.

In 1887 Conover formed an architectural firm with Lew Porter, a former U.W. engineering student, and with him designed nearly 150 buildings in Wisconsin, including several local and national landmarks, such as the University of Wisconsin's Red Gym.

FIGURE 2.12

## The 1886 Dane County Courthouse: On-the-Job Training

*Courtesy Frank Custer*

When Allan Conover hired Frank Wright in 1885, the civil engineer was overseeing the construction of the new red brick and terra cotta Dane County Courthouse shown here in this vintage postcard. Work on the Richardsonian Romanesque building began in 1884 and was completed in October 1886. The building was designed by Henry C. Koch, a well-known Milwaukee architect who also designed Science Hall. The Dane County Board of Supervisors hired Conover to be the supervising architect, that is, to make sure that the building was constructed exactly in accordance with the plans, because Koch's busy practice and Milwaukee location made it impossible for him to make frequent trips to Madison. The courthouse exposed Wright to a relatively new fireproof construction system, consisting of a cement attic floor, cast-iron roof joists, and a slate roof. It was in this building that Wright first unveiled his Madison civic center plans in 1938.

FIGURE 2.13

## Science Hall: More On-the-Job Training

*University of Wisconsin Archives. X25-898*

When the new Science Hall, shown here, was completed in 1887, the state-of-the-art building generated both pride and controversy, and Professor Allan Conover played a large role on both counts. In the late nineteenth century, confidence in science knew few bounds and the educational implication was clear: provide high-quality scientific education. Consequently, when the first Science Hall burned to the ground in 1884, the state moved quickly to replace it. Unfortunately, when the bids for the new building came back, they were much higher than the appropriation. That caused university regents to hire Allan Conover as the contractor; they hoped that he would reduce the building's cost.

The quality-oriented Conover visited more than a dozen of the best universities in the country to inspect their science buildings. The trip persuaded Conover that Science Hall needed upgrading from "slow burn" to "fireproof" and that instructional facilities should be greatly improved. Conover changed the design to accommodate these findings, but they caused building costs to soar to $286,000, more than double the initial estimates, and provoked legislators to conduct an investigation in early 1887.

Only one known document, Wright's *Autobiography*, provides any detail about what Wright did on Science Hall. In a celebrated passage Wright describes a dangerous winter climb to the top of the roof on steel trusses to replace a part.

In 1974 Science Hall was added to the National Register of Historic Places for its role in the history of scientific education, but curiously it was not until the 1990s that tests revealed an additional and compelling reason for its listing: Science Hall was one of the first buildings in the United States to use steel for structural framing. Experts now think it may be the oldest extant building with this distinction.

FIGURE 2.14

**Frank Lincoln Wright, Office Assistant**

SHSW. WHi(X3)50727

This heretofore unpublished portrait was taken by Madison photographer E. R. Curtiss. Exactly when it was taken is not known, but analysis suggests that it was probably in late 1885 after Wright had turned eighteen and secured a job in the office of Allan Conover. Wright is wearing the conservative but stylish clothing then common in the business community. During his high school years Wright had earned the nickname "Shaggy" for his long hair, but it appears that he stopped at the barber shop on his way to the portrait studio. No other formal portrait of Wright as an adult shows his hair so short.

From the time he was in the sixth grade (1878) until he was a junior in high school (1884), Frank spent the late spring and early summer months helping Uncle James on his farm in the Wyoming Valley (see Fig. 2.10 for a photograph of the Lloyd Jones clan). Frank complained bitterly about the excruciatingly hard work on the farm, "adding tired to tired," as he called it. But he also realized that he gained much from the experience. It was during this time that he drank deeply from the cup of nature and later expressed these perceptions in near poetry, came to appreciate the direct relationship

between function and design in farm buildings, and learned to value disciplined work.[19]

When Frank was fifteen, he noticed that the relationship between his parents had begun to sour. His father was spending more time in his study with the door closed, more time in the rowboat, more time with a campus professor studying Sanskrit, and more time with friends away from home. He recalled that his father's income declined and that the proud man was trying to deny the "pinch of poverty."[20]

Although the teenager claimed that he did not realize it, the marriage had been over for a long time. Anna had refused to sleep with William since 1883, repeatedly told him she hated him and wanted him out of the house, manifested an "ungovernable temper," and even physically attacked him. Whenever William would ask Anna to mend something, she would either refuse or throw the mended items in his face or on the floor. Anna's behavior was so alarming that William once asked her brothers whether the family had a history of mental illness. Although the brothers acknowledged that Anna had a temper, they denied any history of insanity. Even so, William had good reason to wonder.[21]

When William and Anna were first married, Lizzie, his youngest daughter by his first marriage, had become the target for Anna's physical and psychological abuse. She would beat the girl with a heavy wooden meat-tenderizing hammer until Lizzie was black and blue, and Anna would jerk her around by the hair so hard that big clumps would come out. Once she grabbed Lizzie by the hair, stuck a big carving fork in her face, and threatened to blind her. Still another time she told Lizzie that she would like to put her head on a chopping block and lop it off. After these rages Anna would sometimes stay in bed for several days. To protect Lizzie, William

would periodically send her off to live with relatives. However, Lizzie attended high school in Madison, and her father performed her wedding ceremony in the Gorham Street house in November 1881.[22]

Seeking a much-needed absence from his plummeting marriage, William spent Thanksgiving 1884 with his children from his first marriage in Nebraska. There William told his son George that things with Anna were getting "worse and worse." Elizabeth's husband told William that it was bad enough to run the risk of hell in the next world "without living in it in this one." When William returned to Madison in December, the profoundly frustrated man filed for divorce on the ground of desertion; Anna did not contest the divorce and did not appear for any of the court-appointed hearings. Under the terms of the April 1885 divorce decree, Anna, forty-six, got the house, nearly all its contents, and custody of the children; William, sixty, left with his clothes, his violins, some books, and a mahogany bookcase.[23]

The divorce was an epochal event for the family, especially for Frank, then seventeen and a senior in high school (see no. 5 in Fig. 2.4). As the elder son, he was obligated to become the breadwinner. Wright said his mother got him a job with Allan Conover, a highly regarded Madison consulting engineer (see Fig. 2.11, and no. 11 in Fig. 2.4), but the credit is probably one of the many examples of Wright's mother-gilding that peppers his *Autobiography*. In all likelihood, his father helped him get the job with Conover—in 1885 William's conservatory (see no. 9 in Fig. 2.4) was near Conover's office on Madison's Capitol Square. Exactly when Wright started work for Conover is not known, but it was probably soon after the divorce became final in April 1885 and William's support for the family stopped.[24]

Conover, a professor of engineering at the University of Wisconsin, had opened his civil engineering consulting practice that year to accommodate the growing number of well-paying freelance jobs that were coming his way. He received two large but very different jobs, one for Dane County and another for the University of Wisconsin. The county hired him to be supervising architect for the new Dane County Courthouse (see Fig. 2.12 and no. 14 in Fig. 2.4), and the university hired him to be the supervising architect and contractor for Science Hall (see Fig. 2.13 and no. 16 in Fig. 2.4). The courthouse project required Conover to certify that the building was constructed exactly according to the original drawings prepared by the Milwaukee architect. The Science Hall project required Conover to supervise workers, keep construction costs within the modest budget, make the building as fireproof as possible, and even to improve it if he could.[25]

Because these assignments required that he have an office, Conover rented space on the Capitol Square and hired several employees. Although Wright claimed he was a draftsman, records suggest he was really was "an office man" (see Fig. 2.14). After all, Wright was only eighteen and had no drafting experience, but he had other assets that quickly proved more important: a brilliant mind, a keen desire to learn, and some remarkably pertinent boyhood experience. From the construction accident at the capitol in 1883 (see Fig. 2.15 and no. 13 in Fig. 2.4), Wright learned that improper design and sloppy construction can be deadly. From the 1884 fire that destroyed the old Science Hall, he learned that fire could consume conventional wooden construction in minutes. In his "Sanctum Santorum," an embryonic architectural studio and workshop, Wright refined his drawing, painting, and design skills. From architecture books that he checked out from the public library and received as gifts from his aunts, he gleaned architectural principles and concepts [26]

FIGURE 2.15

**The 1883 Capitol Collapse**

*SHSW. WHi(X3)154*

At 1:40 P.M. on Thursday, November 8, 1883, almost everyone within a mile of the Capitol Square heard a loud rumble and then a crashing roar. Frank Wright, then sixteen and a junior, was in class at Madison High School (see Fig. 2.22), just a block away. Upon hearing the extraordinary noise, he rushed to the square and saw a scene so terrible that it remained in his memory for the rest of his life. As this photograph taken soon after the tragedy shows, the center of the new four-story south wing addition, then under construction, suddenly collapsed. Wright recalled in his *Autobiography* that when he arrived, he saw "a cloud of white lime dust blow from the windows of the outside walls" followed by "agonized human cries." Workers covered with lime dust and blood raced from the basement entrance, arms flailing to throw off chunks of masonry and beams. "Some," Wright reported, "fell dead on the grass under the clear sky and others fell insensible." One moaning lime-whitened worker hung upside down from a windowsill, his foot crushed and pinned by an iron beam. "A ghastly red stream ran from him down the stone wall." A crowd standing on a pile of brick rubble at the edge of the building suddenly broke up when someone noticed a man's hand sticking out from the bricks. Throwing the bricks aside, rescuers retrieved a crushed, lifeless body. Sobbing women ran about, looking for their husbands. Wright stood "for hours clinging to the iron fence that surrounded the (capitol) park." Finally, he went home ill and "dreamed of it that night and the next and the next."

Eight men were killed and sixteen were seriously injured. For months charges, countercharges, and accounts of the investigation coursed through local papers. Blame for the tragedy was distributed among the architect, for faulty design and inadequate supervision; the contractor, for weakening interior supporting columns; the iron supplier, for providing defective columns; and even the state building commission, for demanding that the cost of the building be reduced.

The tragedy profoundly affected Wright and may have galvanized his desire to be an architect. In his *Autobiography*, Wright noted that the capitol architect had designed the interior supporting columns "excessively large" but had failed to provide diligent supervision of the contractor. It was lesson a Wright never forgot. Indeed, a hallmark of his professional practice was making frequent, often unannounced visits to job sites and, whenever possible, keeping an apprentice on larger job sites at all times.

UNITY CHAPEL, HELENA, WIS.

*The earliest known published drawing by Frank Lloyd Wright. Drawing from* **Fourth Annual,** *All Souls Church.*

**Allan D. Conover**
**Civil Engineer**
**Madison, Wis.**

*August 22, 1885*

*Dear Uncle:*

*I have forwarded to you today my preliminary sketches for "Unity Chapel." I have simply made them in pencil on a piece of old paper but the idea is my own and I have copied from nothing. Any changes which you may think proper or anything to be taken off if you will let me know I will make it satisfactory to you. If however you think the designs not worthy of consideration please return them as I should like to keep them.... I have figured it up + it can be built for 10 to 12 hundred. If necessary I will furnish you with more detailed drawings and working plans. Please let me know the faults and shortcomings and whether you can make use of them or not, at your earliest convenience.*

*Affectionately,*
*your nephew*
*F. Wright*

On Sunday, August 16, 1885, Wright attended the Lloyd Joneses' annual "grove meeting" in the Wyoming Valley. Although most people there were Lloyd Joneses, it was really a gathering of area families who professed a belief in Unitarian principles. At the time they did not have a church, so they met in a grove of tall pines. On this day Jenkin Lloyd Jones, then missionary secretary for the Western Unitarian Conference and minister of Chicago's All Souls Church, exhorted the group to build a "Unity Chapel" in this grove, a building that could be used for religious services but also as a community meetinghouse. Frank Wright, then eighteen, was the office man for Allan Conover and was already beginning to think of himself as an architect. Six days after hearing his Uncle Jenkin's plea for Unity Chapel, Wright penned a letter (here slightly edited), his first attempt to secure an architectural commission. Note how the young man used his boss's letterhead and expressed confidence in his own ability to provide "more detailed drawings and working plans" — a suggestion that his architectural education or at least his assessment of it was further along than many thought.

What Wright did not realize was that his uncle had planned to have a prominent Chicago architect, J. L. Silsbee, design the chapel. Normally, Silsbee would not have accepted such a small project, but earlier that summer Jenkin had hired Silsbee to design his new Chicago church, and it appears that the architect agreed to do the chapel as a favor to his client. Silsbee's plan for the chapel was published in December 1885.

Unfortunately, no one knows what "preliminary sketches" Wright submitted to Jenkin or what he did with them. Jenkin may have shown them to Silsbee, and they may have played a role in Silsbee's decision about eighteen months later to hire Wright. When the chapel was completed in August 1886, a Unitarian journal that Jenkin edited said that Wright, "a boy architect belonging to the family looked after the interior." The rendering shown here was done by Wright sometime in 1887 when he was working for Silsbee.

The simple but pleasingly proportioned Unity Chapel still stands in the grove of pine trees within view of Taliesin. The chapel also served as a popular place for political meetings, Hillside Home School graduations, and later for Taliesin apprentice programs. Even before the chapel was completed, its grounds served as a family cemetery; Frank Lloyd Wright, members of the Fellowship, and a select group of others were later buried there. The grounds continue to function as a cemetery for the family and people connected with Taliesin.

Working for Conover was a dream job for Wright because it immersed him in the day-to-day world of architecture—reading plans, improving designs, and inspecting jobs. He had the good fortune to work on two large sophisticated buildings with a man who was intimately familiar with the latest construction technology and who apparently was willing to share it with Wright. The Science Hall project, for example, allowed Wright to work on one of the nation's first steel-frame buildings; steel was a great advance over cast iron and a material whose structural power delighted Wright for the rest of his life. Wright also paid close attention to Conover's innovations, such as suspending a large, sloped-floor demonstration auditorium from steel trusses in Science Hall to eliminate vision-obstructing columns. (Wright later adapted this concept for his 1893 Monona boathouse.) With both the courthouse and Science Hall, Wright learned how to design fire-resistant buildings. Wright benefited from Conover's willingness to give him and other young engineering graduates he had hired remarkably responsible assignments, a practice that Wright later used with his apprentices. Finally, the eager office man appreciated Conover's emphasis on field trips and site inspections, which allowed Wright to see the progress of what had existed on paper only a few weeks earlier. These hands-on teaching methods were still another aspect of the Conover experience that Wright would later make a prominent part of his Taliesin apprentice program.[27]

Interestingly, Wright may have learned practices from Conover and the Science Hall project that later exasperated workers, apprentices, and clients: changing a building's design during construction to increase its utility and emphasizing quality. The impressionable Wright may have thought these practices were standard.

No one can doubt that Wright's learning curve was nearly vertical during his time with Conover, an experience that helped him make two major decisions. First, he concluded that architecture would be his life's work. Significantly, he based this decision on his own experience and not, as he claimed in his *Autobiography*, on his mother's prenatal prediction. By August 1885 Wright was so secure in his architectural abilities that he tried to obtain his first independent commission (see Fig. 2.16). His second decision was to pursue formal training. Presumably, Wright discussed this with Conover, who must have urged his eighteen-year-old employee to enroll in the University of Wisconsin's Department of Engineering.[28]

In truth, Wright had no choice. Nowhere else could he get so much for so little (see Fig. 2.17). Tuition for Wisconsin residents was free — though students had to pay various fees — and he could avoid room and board by living at home. And the civil engineering curriculum was as close to an architectural school as Wright could get. On January 7, 1886, Wright was admitted as a special student because working on his Uncle James's farm in the late spring of his high school years prevented him from accumulating sufficient credits to graduate from high school.[29]

At the time the university year was divided into three terms: winter (January through March), spring (March through June), and fall (September through December). Wright took just one course, French, during the winter term but received no grade and took no courses in the spring term (see no. 18 in Fig. 2.4). For the fall term he enrolled in two courses, descriptive geometry and mechanical drawing (see Fig. 2.18 and no. 17 in Fig. 2.4), and received average grades in both. These courses were the only ones Wright took for credit at the University of Wisconsin, although he may have audited others.

FIGURE 2.17

**Wright's University of Wisconsin Experience**

*University of Wisconsin Archives. X25-2315*

This bird's-eye drawing shows the U.W. campus as it appeared when Wright entered as a special student in January 1886 and the buildings that were a part of his brief college career. He took French in University Hall (now Bascom Hall) at the top center of the drawing and mechanical drawing and descriptive geometry in North Hall (top right). Assembly Hall, the churchlike building at the lower left of the mall (now known as Music Hall), was the site of the campus dance at which the socially inept Wright embarrassed himself and his date. Science Hall, the large building at the lower right of the mall, was actually under construction while Wright was a student.

Although Wright attended the U.W. for only six months (January through March and September through December), he apparently intended to graduate with the class of 1889 because he wore the class mortarboard with its distinctive red tassel, attended class-sponsored events, and identified himself as a class member in the school yearbook. The distinctive logo of the class of '89 appears at right.

Few realize that Wright's step-brother George Irving Wright (see Fig. 2.22) received a law degree from the University of Wisconsin in 1880 while the family lived in Madison. In his *Autobiography* Wright never mentioned any of his three step-siblings.

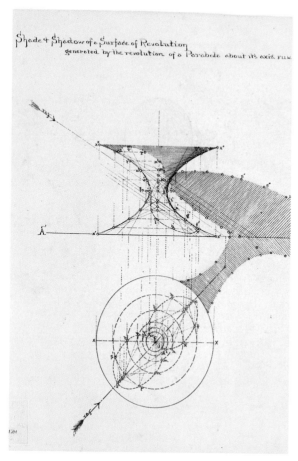

## FIGURE 2.18

**1886 Geometry Class Drawing**

© FLW FDN. 8501.001

"Shade and Shadow of a Surface ... generated by the revolution of a Parabola about its axis" is one of three extant drawings prepared by the nineteen-year-old Frank Wright for his "Descriptive Geometry" class sometime in the fall of 1886. Done in pencil and ink, the drawing reveals Wright's ability to produce complex shapes and delicate shading. This drawing and the other two in the series show that the young man was capable of doing sophisticated drafting-table work for Allan Conover. The geometry course was taught by Storm Bull, a fellow Unitarian who later became the first professor elected mayor of Madison. When Wright took the course, it was held in temporary space on an upper floor of North Hall because the old Science Hall had burned down and its replacement was not yet complete.

Note the extra *L* in Wright's initials at the end of the title at top right. This reflected his decision to drop his middle name, Lincoln, in favor of Lloyd, part of a self-reinvention process that Wright began before he left Madison.

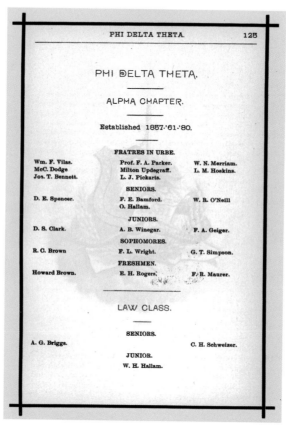

## FIGURE 2.19

**Phi Delta Theta Fraternity Man**

*University of Wisconsin Archives*

On November 13, 1886, Frank Lloyd Wright became the eighty-first member initiated into the Alpha Chapter of Phi Delta Theta, the oldest fraternity on the University of Wisconsin campus. The fraternity's emblem and membership roster appeared in the 1887 university yearbook. Wright is listed as a sophomore, but by the time the annual was published, Wright had settled in Chicago. Fraternity membership was extremely expensive then, probably enough to double his college costs, but Wright joined anyway.

*June 26, 1887*

*My dear Frank*

*It is two weeks since I wrote you but I think of you every day I have been very sad of late My gardens are all dried up and everything is very high I am afraid that I can not pay my debts by Fall I am glad you are doing so well I am sure you have everything to be hopeful about but — I hope you have cancels every debt before now. Oh Frank think now of being a wise Financier try and see how much you can do with your wages What can I do about your debt here I went to pay Jennie's bill at Stoltzes — and he gave me a seven dollar bill for your dancing gaiters if he had knocked me down, it would not have hurt me so much. You told me you got them in Chicago. What did you do with your money. Can you send me money to pay it Good by my precious boy. I am tired tonight.*

*Your Mother*

## FIGURE 2.20

**Can't You Be More Frugal, Frank?**

*Courtesy Wisconsin State Journal*
© FLW FDN.

Sometime before he left Madison for Chicago in early 1887, Wright demonstrated his lifelong propensity to live pretentiously without the means. As this letter from his mother makes clear, Wright had bought a pair of expensive dancing shoes, called gaiters, at Stoltze's, Madison's fanciest shoe store, left town without paying the $7 bill, and then lied to his mother about where he bought them. This excerpt is printed as his mother wrote it, including missing punctuation and other errors. Jennie is Wright's younger sister Mary Jane.

This light course load left plenty of time for his job and an increasingly crowded social life.[30]

Throughout 1886 Wright seemed far more interested in the social side of student life than the academic. Like other members of the class of 1889, Wright bought and wore a mortar board with the tassel in the class colors along with then-stylish "skin-tight pants ... and toothpick shoes." Wright plunged into extra-curricular activities; he sang bass in the University Choral Club, joined the U.W. Association of Engineers, and, most important, pledged Phi Delta Theta fraternity (see Fig. 2.19 and no. 8 in Fig. 2.4).[31]

While at the U.W., Wright first demonstrated his love of the grand gesture. For a class party he decked himself out in a black suit, white tie, and white gloves, bought an expensive pair of dancing shoes (see Fig. 2.20), and rented a carriage to take his date about two hundred feet from her dorm to Assembly Hall (no. 15 in Fig. 2.4), where the party was held. Unfortunately, the young man embarrassed himself by delivering his date to the men's entrance and then failed to retrieve her from the ladies' dressing room until after the first dances were over. Finally, she found him and they danced. Said Wright: "We're having a good time, aren't we?" "Are we?" she responded icily.[32]

During Wright's university year, his Unitarian friends and organizations opened doors and introduced him to leading thinkers (see Fig. 2.21). For example, he attended the bimonthly meetings of the Contemporary Club, whose members met to study current literary, scientific, political, economic, and social issues; among the speakers were leading university scholars such as Frederick Jackson Turner, who later developed the famous frontier interpretation of American history. Participation in the Channing Club, an organization for college students, may have been responsible for Wright's invitation to

pledge Phi Delta Theta because 20 percent of its members were Unitarians. Contact with Unitarians such as F. A. Parker, a U.W. music professor, may have been responsible for Wright's decision to join the Choral Club.[33]

Things were happening quickly in Wright's life. There was the chagrin of his parents' divorce, his desire to transcend his family's modest circumstances, the confidence-boosting Conover experience, and his love of extracurricular university activities. From all this the young man concluded that he needed a new persona, a shinier, more attractive image. His first act of self-reinvention was to change his middle name. By the fall of 1886 Wright was signing his geometry drawings "Frank Ll Wright" instead of Frank L. Wright. His middle name was Lincoln, probably his father's choice; but now, with the second *l*, Wright declared he would be the son of his mother, a Lloyd Jones.[34]

Wright later padded the Madison years of his résumé. He told the world in his *Autobiography* that he attended the University of Wisconsin for three and a half years, although he took only three class-es for credit in just two terms, all concentrated in 1886. He said the parlor piano at home was a Steinway; it was a much less expensive Emerson. Still later he told people he was born in 1869, not 1867. Wright's mentor in crafting these deceptions apparently was his mother. She told her children after the divorce that if anyone asked where their father was, they should "tell them he is dead." And she told everyone she was a widow. When they were newly married, Anna said her husband was seventeen years her senior, although he was only thirteen years older than she.[35]

As a result of his work for Conover, Wright was now certain he could be an outstanding architect, but he chafed at the dry teaching methods then common at the university. He yearned to be successful and

FIGURE 2.21

**Lessons from the New Unitarian Church**

*Courtesy Ann Waidelich*

Frank, his mother, and sisters were undoubtedly present on Sunday morning, March 7, 1886, when the First Unitarian Church was dedicated. The $17,000 Norman stone building, shown here in a color postcard, stood just one block off the Capitol Square (see no. 6 in Fig. 2.4) and was designed by the prestigious Boston firm of Peabody and Stearns.

Construction of the new church began in the spring of 1885, about the time that Wright began his work with Allan Conover; its progress surely received the scrutiny of the budding architect. Several features of the church auditorium apparently caught Wright's impressionable eye because they show up in several later buildings. For example, the barrel-vaulted ceiling appeared in the children's playroom in Wright's Oak Park house, and the olive and terra cotta color scheme used for the church auditorium may have inspired the colors Wright is credited with selecting for the interior of Unity Chapel, completed just five months after the Unitarian church.

important, to transcend his modest beginnings and demonstrate his prowess in a bigger, more prestigious pond. Then, in January 1887, the state began an investigation of cost overruns on Science Hall, which probably caused Wright to conclude that his days on the Conover payroll were numbered. He also owed money for his expensive party clothing and could not afford the high annual fraternity fees.[36]

Sometime in early 1887, against his mother's will and contrary to the advice of his Uncle Jenkin in Chicago, the indomitable nineteen-year-old secretly left the little brown house by the lake. He carried a suitcase and some of his father's most valuable books,

FIGURE 2.22

# THE EARLY AND MADISON YEARS
# 1867 - 1887

Frank Wright
About Age 2

SHSW. WHi (X3)50596

**1866**
William Wright marries Anna Lloyd Jones on August 17

**1867**
Frank Lincoln Wright born in or near Richland Center, Wisconsin, on June 8

William C. Wright
About Age 50

Courtesy
FLW FDN. 6301.0015

**1869**
Wrights move to McGregor, Iowa, and a daughter, Mary Jane, is born

**1871**
Wrights move to Central Falls, Rhode Island, and later to Pawtucket

**1874**
Wrights move to Weymouth, Massachusetts

**1877**
Wright is dismissed as Baptist pastor in October, just four months after a daughter, Maginel, is born

## MADISON

**1878**
Wrights move to Madison

**1879**
Wright helps found First Unitarian Society, buys house, preaches to rural Unitarians, and teaches music

George Wright

University of Wisconsin
Archives. X25-1460

**1880**
Frank's step-brother George receives degree from the U.W. Law School

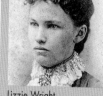

Lizzie Wright

State Historical Society of Iowa

**1881**
Frank's step-sister Lizzie is married in Madison home by William C. Wright

Madison High School

SHSW. WHi (X3)32023

**1883**
Frank witnesses collapse of capitol while attending Madison High School

State Bank Block

SHSW. Hanks Collection

**1884**
William sues Anna for divorce

**1885**
Divorce is granted, William leaves Madison, and Frank gets a job working for Allan Conover at this downtown Madison building

University of Wisconsin Pennant

Courtesy Frank Custer

**1886**
Frank takes engineering courses at the University of Wisconsin and changes middle name to Lloyd while continuing to work for Conover

Northwestern Railroad Depot

SHSW. Angell and Hastreiter

**1887**
Frank Lloyd Wright leaves Madison for Chicago from the Northwestern Depot

including a leather-bound copy of Plutarch's *Lives* and Gibbon's *Decline and Fall of the Roman Empire.* Wright walked to Benjamin Perry's pawn shop on King Street (no. 12 in Fig. 2.4), sold his father's books, continued down the hill to the Northwestern railroad depot, and used the proceeds from his father's books to buy a one-way ticket to Chicago.[37] (For a chronology of Wright's early life, see Fig. 2.22.)

As the train pulled out of the station, Wright's mind surely swirled with memories of nine momentous years, nearly half his life. Already he was experiencing an Aladdin-inspired reverie of a remarkable, magical life in Chicago where he would become great and famous. But try as he might, he could not leave one thing behind and that was a feeling he held throughout his life: that Madison was his hometown, the place where the boy became a man and where he received his incomparable immersion in architecture from Professor Conover.

## THE CHICAGO YEARS, 1887 TO 1911

Wright returned to Madison almost every year to visit friends and to attend weddings, funerals, the annual summer Lloyd Jones reunion, and other events. His visits usually went unnoticed but not in 1889. Indeed, a paid press agent could not have written a more favorable account. "Mr. Frank Wright and his wife passed through here today on their way back to Chicago from their wedding tour," began a squib in the *Wisconsin State Journal* on June 10, 1889. "Mr. Wright is an old Madison boy, and his friends were ... considerably surprised at his taking unto himself a better half. He is at present in business with Adler & Sullivan, architects, Chicago. At the end of his five years partnership he will go to Europe to study."[38]

Not exactly. The grand-sounding wedding tour was a train ride from Chicago to Madison to Spring Green and back again. "In business" with Adler and Sullivan? Not exactly. Wright was employed as a draftsman for the firm (see Fig. 2.23) and had a five-year loan from Sullivan. The forthcoming trip to Europe? Wright undoubtedly was already contemplating a Continental tour, but in 1889 it was little more than his image-enhancing invention for a friendly editor who knew Wright through Madison's First Unitarian Society. And the surprise that Wright had married? Well, that was real. Before he left Madison, Wright had demonstrated near total incompetence with the opposite sex.[39]

Indeed, since leaving Madison in early 1887 Wright had made remarkable progress both professionally and personally. Almost immediately upon arriving in Chicago he landed a job as a tracer, an entry-level job, with Joseph Lyman Silsbee, a well-established architect who specialized in elegant Queen Anne and Shingle-Style houses for the carriage trade. Wright insisted that he got the job because Silsbee was impressed by his portfolio of drawings, but Wright's uncle Jenkin Lloyd Jones, who had become well known as the minister of Chicago's All Souls Church, may have urged Silsbee to interview or even hire his nephew.[40]

Until he found a rooming house, Wright lived with Uncle Jenkin and his family in their southside neighborhood and enjoyed many good times with Jenkin's son, Richard, who later became the editor and publisher of Madison's *Wisconsin State Journal.* But Wright's closest friend was Cecil Corwin, a Silsbee draftsman. The two talked about everything far into the night, attended music and drama performances, and dined in restaurants. Wright also attended church at All Souls on Sunday, borrowed architecture

books from the church's lending library, and participated in its intellectual and literary groups.[41]

Although Wright would spend only one year with Silsbee, it was an enormously valuable experience. The twenty-year-old Wright was awed by the "amazing ease" with which Silsbee could draw and tried to emulate his "soft, deep black lead pencil strokes" and "remarkable free-hand sketches." It was Wright's first experience with an architectural firm and little escaped him. The impressionable Wright also learned to appreciate Japanese art from Silsbee, whose office and home displayed his collection of Japanese prints and sculpture. Finally, Silsbee had a talent for picking rising young architects and engineers, including George Elmslie and Paul Mueller. Elmslie followed Wright to the Sullivan firm and then opened a practice in Minneapolis where he designed dozens of outstanding Prairie-School buildings. Mueller, a brilliant engineer, later designed special foundations for Wright's famous earthquake-proof Imperial Hotel in Tokyo.[42]

Significantly, one of the first projects that Wright worked on after he joined the Silsbee firm was the original building for the Hillside Home School, a coeducational boarding school run by Wright's two maternal aunts, three-quarters of a mile from where he would later build Taliesin. (Hillside is widely regarded as Wright's first commission, even though it was done under Silsbee's employ.) His second and more elaborate Hillside building later became the nucleus for his apprentice program.[43]

Silsbee quickly saw Wright's promise, promoted him to draftsman, and raised his wages. Even so, Wright claimed he tired of Silsbee's architectural "sentimentality" and sought something more. In 1888 a colleague told him that partners in the prestigious firm of Adler and Sullivan needed a draftsman to complete interior drawings for the multifunction

megastructure known as the Auditorium Building on a premiere block of Michigan Avenue. It included a 4,200-seat auditorium (7,000-seat capacity), 400-room hotel, and 136 business offices. Wright was offered the job and quickly accepted.[44]

In Chicago Wright's social circle revolved around a few colleagues and his Uncle Jenkin's church. In fact, it was in the middle of the dance floor at a party sponsored by the church's book club that Wright crashed into a pretty girl in a pink dress. They collided with such force that she fell to the ground and he saw stars. She was Catherine Tobin, a high school student with blue eyes and curly red hair. Catherine, then sixteen, and the twenty-year-old Frank began to date almost immediately. They took long walks, went to church, and attended concerts. He became a regular at her family's Sunday dinner table.[45]

When Anna Wright heard that her son was thinking about marriage, she was horrified and promptly boarded a train for Chicago. First, she tried to talk him out of it, but it did no good. Then she secretly spoke with Cecil Corwin, who tried to steer Wright away from Catherine. That didn't work either. Anna could see that her task was going to be difficult, so she and her two daughters moved to Oak Park and shared a house with the female minister of that suburb's Universalist Unity Church. She picked the area because it reminded her of Madison and because it was about thirteen miles from Kenwood, where Catherine lived and Frank then roomed. Anna persuaded her son to move into her new Oak Park quarters and then persuaded the Tobins to send Catherine to visit relatives in northern Michigan for several months. Alas, distance made the lovebirds' hearts grow fonder. They were married on June 1, 1889, and a few days later arrived in Madison on their wedding "tour."[46]

With her son now settled in Chicago and with her brother Jenkin and his family there too, Anna decided to join the family enclave. Four months after the wedding Anna sold the Madison house for $4,000 to Adolph Kayser, a prominent Madison business leader who later razed the modest house and built the large residence that stands on the lot today. The sale gave Anna enough money to buy a house in suburban Chicago. But the question was where. That was resolved by an extraordinary deal that Wright had made with Sullivan before the wedding.[47]

Wright had approached Sullivan and told him he was about to be married and that he needed greater job security — he had been hired only to do final work on the auditorium project. Sullivan was eager to keep Wright because the young man could visualize three-dimensional space with rare and uncanny ease, speed, and accuracy; he could also draw with grace, style, and originality and could quickly conceive outstanding design solutions for clients' projects. As Wright gratuitously put it in his *Autobiography*, he had become a "good pencil in the Master's hand," and "at a time when he sorely needed one."[48]

The partners agreed to give Wright a five-year contract worth $5,000; Wright made an audacious counterproposal. Couldn't you lend me $5,000 now, Wright asked, and then deduct the loan payments from my salary each week? For some time Wright had had his eye on a large corner lot in Oak Park where he wanted to build a house. Sullivan inspected the lot and agreed. A thrilled Wright used the loan to buy the vacant half of the lot, and his equally thrilled mother used her money to buy the other half, on which stood a white clapboard house. Anna and her two daughters moved in immediately, and so did the newlyweds until their house was completed in early 1890 (see Fig. 2.24).[49]

What an impressive way to launch a career! Less than three years after arriving in Chicago, Wright had secured a well-paid job with one of the most highly regarded architectural firms in the country, married a beautiful woman, and designed and built a stylish new house in one of the city's toniest suburbs. He was only twenty-two.

The Wrights' first child arrived in 1890; five others followed in 1892, 1894, 1895, 1898, and 1903. These were challenging times for the young couple. They had the normal expenses of a growing family, the pinch of repaying the loan, and Wright's never-sated appetite for luxuries. Wright insisted on having the best of everything—Oriental rugs, sculpture, a state-of-the-art camera, elegant clothing, season tickets to the symphony, and even a horse, which he would ride out on the open prairie at the edge of town. To Wright, living this way was normal; as he put it in his *Autobiography*, "so long as we had the luxuries the necessities could pretty well take care of themselves." That delusion had been evident in Madison and soon became habitual in Chicago.[50]

Wright needed more money than his salary provided, and he thought he could get it by what he called "bootlegging." Adler and Sullivan rarely accepted residential work unless it was for a major client, but when they did, Wright designed the houses. Wright concluded that he could earn additional income by doing houses for people who were not Adler and Sullivan clients. Although such work violated the agreement with his employer, he did the jobs anyway (working from a studio at home), and when the designs were published, he attributed them to his good friend, Cecil Corwin. The houses were designed in the then-popular Queen Anne, Colonial Revival, and Dutch Colonial Styles and were apparently modeled after designs published by prominent eastern architects. However, none of the houses was a mere copy; in fact, Wright transformed each with a unique flair that demonstrated his ability to improve the designs of some of the best architects in the country. Not surprisingly, most of his clients were members of the All Souls Church in Oakwood or the Unity (Universalist) Church in Oak Park, which he and Catherine eventually joined. When Sullivan found out about the "bootlegged" homes,

Wright's Extended Family

*Courtesy FLW FDN. 6305.0048*

Oak Park Home and Studio

*Courtesy the Frank Lloyd Wright Home and Studio Foundation, photo by Don Kalec*

FIGURE 2.24

**The Good Life in the Suburbs**

Sometime in the summer of 1890 Wright assembled the Chicago Lloyd Jones clan on the front steps of his recently completed house. From left to right are Uncle Jenkin Lloyd Jones, minister of All Souls Church; Susan Lloyd Jones, wife of the minister; Wright's sister Jane; Catherine, holding Frank Lloyd Wright, Jr., known to the family as Lloyd; Anna Wright; Wright's sister Maginel; Wright (with a mustache); and Mary, the daughter of Jenkin and Susan. As a reminder that they were living the good life in the suburbs, Wright had his aunt hold a tennis racket and posed everyone on an Oriental carpet. The photographer was probably Richard Lloyd Jones, son of Jenkin and Susan and later editor of the *Wisconsin State Journal*. While Frank Lloyd Wright and his family lived in this Oak Park house (1890–1911), his mother lived next door in a white clapboard house.

The Shingle Style house was modeled after a design by Bruce Price, a famous Welsh architect, for Tuxedo Park, an exclusive enclave near New York City. When it was completed in 1890, the two-thousand-square-foot residence was adequate for a family of three, but the arrival of more children caused the architect to add a magnificent barrel-vaulted playroom on the back of the house in 1895.

Although Wright always maintained a downtown Chicago office where he could meet clients and contractors, he did most of his creative work in his home studio. In the original house Wright used the front room on the second floor, where he designed the "bootleg" houses. In 1898 his growing architectural practice required Wright to build a large studio addition, a portion of which is visible at the left of the house. By 1909 Wright's house and studio had become a sprawling complex of sixty-two hundred square feet.

he felt betrayed and angry. The apprentice and the master argued, and, according to Wright, "I ... threw my pencil down on my table ... and walked out of the Adler & Sullivan office ... never to return."[51]

If Wright's nearly two years in Madison with Conover and his year with Silsbee constituted his undergraduate education in architecture, his six-year stint with Sullivan was his graduate school. Sullivan obviously liked Wright, and the two men would talk for hours in the firm's aerie-like seventeenth-floor

offices after everyone else went home. Because of this close relationship Wright called Sullivan his *lieber meister*, German for 'beloved master', but it was because of Wright's extraordinary talent that Sullivan took Wright under his wing, made him his primary draftsman, and gave him supervisory responsibilities over the drafting room. Although Wright said little about Dankmar Adler in his *Autobiography*, there can be no doubt that the young man was dazzled by Adler's engineering prowess and that Wright absorbed his work with a keen and retentive eye.

Wright had the good fortune to be with Adler and Sullivan when the firm was doing some of its most prestigious commissions, including the famous Auditorium Building. When completed in 1890, it housed the largest auditorium — one of the most beautiful and acoustically perfect — in the United States. The room's outstanding sound was directly attributable to Adler's elliptical ceiling arches, which rippled out from the stage, an innovation duplicated in auditoriums all over the world. Forty-eight years later the Auditorium Building served as Wright's inspiration for the seven-thousand-seat auditorium in his civic center for Madison.[52]

The fledged but now jobless Wright was eager to try his architectural wings. At the time Illinois had no architectural licensing or even registration requirement, so there were no tests to take or forms to fill out. Sometime during the first half of 1893, Wright, now twenty-six, opened an office on the fifteenth floor of the Adler and Sullivan–designed Schiller Building in downtown Chicago. The gold leaf lettering on the plate-glass door to his office suite read simply, "Frank Lloyd Wright, Architect." Like any new professional, his big problem was finding clients. The strained circumstances under which he left Adler and Sullivan meant that he had to be scrupulously careful not to do anything that might be perceived as a client raid.[53]

As a new solo architect Wright desperately needed work, and he got one of his first commissions from Madison, his hometown. However, to get the job Wright was forced to enter an architectural competition — something he later opposed on principle and rarely did. Wright contended that competition jurors threw out the best and the worst and selected the mediocre. But this was not a time to quibble about

principles; in March he learned that prominent civic leaders had formed a new organization, the Madison Improvement Association, and were seeking an architect for two large public boathouses (see Figs. 2.1, and 2.25). In May he was delighted to hear that he had won the $7,000 commission.[54]

How Wright heard about this regional competition is not known, but how the winner was selected is clear: he was picked by the association's executive committee, several members of which knew Wright well. Moses R. Doyon, the committee chair, had lived next door to Wright, and Lucien S. Hanks was the father of a school chum of Wright's. Also on the committee was John M. Olin, the prominent lawyer who later became the driving force behind the Madison park and pleasure drive movement. After the selection of the up-and-coming young architect, these men functioned as his clients for the boathouse project, which was the basis for Wright's later description of Olin as "my client."[55]

In his quest for work Wright entered a second architectural competition in 1893 for a $500,000 library and museum for Milwaukee. Although Wright's Beaux Arts–inspired design failed to win this national competition, the following year he entered the drawings in an exhibition sponsored by the Chicago Architectural Club. There they reportedly caught the discerning eye of Daniel Burnham, the prominent Chicago architect and city planner, chief of construction for the World's Columbian Exposition of 1893, and newly elected president of the American Institute of Architects. Burnham was so impressed by Wright's facile grasp of classical conventions that he offered to underwrite all costs of the finest European architectural training program. The program included four years at the exclusive École des Beaux Arts in Paris, two years at the new American (architectural) Academy in Rome, and a

job with the Burnham firm when he returned. It was a stupendous offer, and for a time Wright could not think what to say. This was exactly what Wright had told the Madison newspaper editor he intended to do when he passed through the city with his new bride in 1889. But now, five years later, Wright told Burnham that he was unwilling to spend his career wrapping contemporary buildings in classical shrouds and that he saw the then-common architectural practice as "uncreative" and "untrue." Wright would follow his own rapidly developing muse.[56]

The Oak Park architect was part of a great wave of reform that swept through the United States in the late nineteenth and early twentieth centuries. What Robert Marion La Follette and his progressive friends would do to reform government, Wright would do for architecture. His ambitious, single-minded goal was to revitalize American architecture by ending its servile captivity to European and classical forms. What, Wright asked himself, were the qualities of *American* civilization that its architecture should express?[57]

Wright's first six years of solo practice (1893–1899) were an unrelenting experiment. Almost all his commissions were houses, and nearly all were drawn in then-popular styles — Queen Anne, Tudor, Dutch Colonial, and Shingle—but always with a unique twist. During this period Wright began to flatten, elongate, and increase the overhang of his roofs, group his windows in bands, and remove ornamentation, key elements of what would later become a coherent style.[58]

From 1900 to 1909 Wright released a burst of originality that took two different and distinctive forms, one for urban and another for suburban sites. The impetus for Wright's innovative urban style was an administration building for the Larkin Soap Company in Buffalo, New York, completed in 1906. From the first time he saw the ugly, noisy,

FIGURE 2.25

## 1893 Public Boathouses

One of the first commissions Wright received in private practice were these two Madison boathouses, one for Lake Mendota and one for Lake Monona. This photo shows the Mendota building at the foot of North Carroll Street as it looked in 1894, soon after it was completed. (For a lakeside view, see Fig. 2.1.) In this building and its Monona counterpart Wright artfully blended square and circular elements. For example, for the Mendota building Wright used a pleasing semicircular roofed promenade to guide pedestrians into two towers offering panoramic lake views. The cream-colored stucco and brown shingled building had space for twenty-eight rowboats on two levels. The Madison Improvement Association, a private organization, raised the $4,600 to build this public structure. Tragically, the building was razed in 1926 by the City of Madison, with virtually no public discussion and with no apparent awareness of who designed it. The site remains vacant.

Wright's elevation drawing for the much larger Monona boathouse, his first circular building, is shown at right. The central element, a cylinder sixty feet in diameter, incorporated an ingenious truss system in its conical roof. The trusses carry the weight of the roof down through the exterior walls and achieve column-free space on the first and second levels. Boat owners could row into the center of the building and pull their boats out of the water onto a ramped floor. With the help of an interior crane the building could store fifty-six boats. To increase usable space on the first floor, Wright added four corner pavilions. Dramatizing its circularity is a 360-degree band of arched openings on the second level. Not until the 1930s did the circle become a dominant form for Wright. Ironically, one building from that decade was the first Monona Terrace, a semicircular structure planned for a site just one thousand feet from the boathouse on the same shoreline.

The Monona boathouse, designed to replace a row of ugly private boathouses, was never built because of unexpectedly high costs and a sharp recession that killed donations. Figure A.1 shows how Wright's design would look if it were built.

The site for the Monona boathouse was the end of King Street, shown on the turn-of-the-century postcard. The tip of the cone-shaped roof rose seventy feet above the lake and the flagpole another twenty feet — the equivalent of a nine-story building, which suggests that Wright intended the building as a visual punctuation point for this radial street.

Note the conical-roofed building in the postcard. It belonged to the Christian Dick building and was designed in 1889 by Allan Conover, Wright's former employer. Wright may have wanted to echo this roof's shape with his boathouse.

Lake Mendota Boathouse from North Carroll Street

*SHSW. WHi(X3)43817*

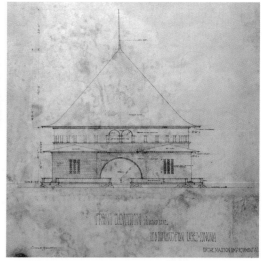

Lake Monona Boathouse Lakefront Elevation

*© FLW FDN. 9308.01*

View down King Street toward Monona Boathouse Site

*Courtesy Ann Waidelich*

sooty industrial site in 1902, Wright insisted that his design provide a pleasant, even inspiring, environment for the company's eighteen hundred employees. Wright's refusal to produce a conventional corporate headquarters reflected his deeply held belief that the fundamental job of the architect is to create a better world, one building at a time. His solution was to create a five-story brick building around a large central atrium. To keep industrial noise and dirt out, he sealed the structure, drew filtered air from the roof level, and distributed it throughout the building. The top floor contained an employee restaurant, a beautiful fern-filled conservatory, and a brick-paved recreational promenade. The building was so revolutionary that Wright had to prepare a model so that Larkin executives could understand it. Although some contemporary critics branded the building "hopelessly ugly," its unique blend of employee-focused design and technological break-throughs made it a landmark office design. Wright later used the atrium concept with even greater success for the 1936 S. C. Johnson Wax Admin-istration Building in Racine, Wisconsin, and for an unexecuted 1946 design for a Dallas hotel; if it had been built, it would have been America's first high-rise atrium hotel (see Fig. 3.21).[59]

In 1903, as he was preparing plans for the Larkin project, Wright received a commission from Robie Lamp, his childhood friend, for a residence within a fully developed residential block in downtown Madison. Wright's design (see Fig. 2.26) showed how a powerful urban template like the Larkin building could influence another design.[60]

Still another example of Wright's innovative urban template was his 1905 commission for the new Unity Temple in Oak Park, just four blocks from his house and studio. The site selected by the building committee was a corner lot at the intersection of

two increasingly busy streets, one of which already had noisy streetcars rolling by all day long. Wright prepared a bold, beautiful, and practical design, one of the first significant American architectural statements in poured concrete. The concrete construction made the building fireproof (its frame predecessor had burned a few months earlier), kept street noise out of the auditorium, and, Wright argued, would be less expensive than traditional brick. But many thought the decision to use concrete for a church was sacrilegious. (Thirty-three years later Wright's decision to use such a utilitarian material for Monona Terrace provoked great controversy.)

Inside, amber stained glass in a skylight and clerestory windows suffused the cube-shaped auditorium with a warm glow. Wright's design was so revolutionary that he had to take a page from his Larkin experience and prepare a model so that church members could visualize its unique shape and appreciate its many innovative features.[61]

During the fall of 1905, while Wright was preparing plans for the new Oak Park church, he received a commission from Cudworth Bye, the son of a prominent congregation member and longtime family friend, for a boathouse for the University of Wisconsin crew (Fig. 2.27). The boathouse, which shared conceptual genes with Unity Temple and the Larkin building, showed how far Wright's design philosophy had evolved in the dozen years since he did the 1893 boathouses for Madison.[62]

Although the Larkin building and Unity Temple made architectural history, the former for its atrium for a commercial office building and the latter for the use of concrete aggregate as the exterior finish, Wright was incubating something that would have even greater influence. It was a powerful new design philosophy with six principles:

- The thoughtful integration of building with nature—deference not dominance. Do not, he said, place a building on a hill, make it *of* the hill.

- Reliance on natural and indigenous materials such as wood and stone and using their color, texture, and beauty in the design. For example, Wright insisted that quarried stone be laid to simulate a natural outcrop, never cut into angular blocks. Wright also advocated staining, not painting, woods.

- Designing space so that it offers a sense of hearth and union with the natural world outdoors.

- Incorporation of site-determined, nature-inspired decorative details. For example, if Wright found sumac growing on the site, he would create a geometric abstraction of the plant and incorporate the design in art-glass windows.

- Strong emphasis on the flexible and open flow of space. Wright opposed the then-common practice of cutting up houses into boxes called rooms.

- Using machine-age materials such as steel beams, glass, and reinforced concrete to achieve design goals. He saw them as ways to liberate design from age-old constraints and to make space more interesting, inspiring, and beautiful.[63]

Wright translated these design principles into the now-famous Prairie Style and used it successfully for his suburban and rural houses. Salient exterior qualities included strong horizontal lines achieved by placing the first floor low to the ground (often by eliminating basements); using low-angled hipped roofs with generous eaves; grouping windows in horizontal bands; retaining uninterrupted horizontal sweeps of stucco and brick for house and terrace walls; seldom going above two stories in height; using low massive chimneys; and relying on the natural beauty of wood, brick, and stone. Salient

Rocky Roost
SHSW. WHi(X3)26370

Robert M. Lamp
Madison Past and Present

Lamp House
SHSW. WHi(X3)25960

interior qualities of Prairie houses included minimizing ornamentation and limiting it to natural motifs; vaulting ceilings and eliminating attics; locating fireplaces near the center of the house; removing walls between living and dining rooms to achieve a more open flow of space; and using custom-designed furniture, floor coverings, art-glass windows, and lighting fixtures to achieve a totally unified design.[64]

Wright was hardly the only member of the Prairie School, although he was the preeminent and, some would say, the dominant leader. Wright was a founding member of "the eighteen," a group of Chicago architects who met for lunch to share their enthusiasm for creating a new and uniquely American architecture. From this group and other architectural firms came dozens of skilled Prairie practitioners. For example, working in the office of Adler and Sullivan

FIGURE 2.27

**A Boathouse for Wright's Alma Mater**

Ausgeführte Bauten und Entwürfe, Plate LV

That Wright was eager to design a building for the University of Wisconsin was evident from a November 2, 1905, letter. "My dear Cudworth," Wright began. "We are always ready when 'Alma Mater' calls. We will desingn [sic] anything for the U.W. from a chicken coop to a cathedral, no matter how busy we may be. Yours truly, Frank Lloyd Wright." (© FLW FDN.; courtesy SHSW)

Cudworth Bye was commodore of the U.W. Boat Club, one of several student organizations then responsible for intervarsity athletic competition. Bye, an Oak Park native, had many Wright connections. Bye's older sister was the best friend of Wright's younger sister Maginel, and Bye's father was a prominent member of the Oak Park Unity Church, which had recently selected Wright to design its new church.

In December 1905 Wright sent Bye sketches of his boathouse proposal, which was similar to the plate shown here from the famous Wasmuth portfolio. The U.W. boathouse was one of several original designs in which Wright abandoned the hipped roof in favor of projecting slab roofs. The design for a building seventy-five feet long provided club and locker-room facilities for the men and storage for their eight-man sculls. Significantly, the boathouse was sited on the recently dredged and straightened Yahara River (see Fig. 1.7) rather than on Lake Mendota. In fact, the crew already had a boathouse on Lake Mendota, but the lake was either frozen or too rough to use during the spring. Thus, while eastern college crews — U.W.'s competitors — were practicing on open water, U.W. men were working out on indoor rowing machines. That was why Bye and his teammates wanted a boathouse on the Yahara; its flowing water stayed open nearly all year round and would allow open water practice in the spring.

Unfortunately, Bye was not able to raise enough money for Wright's boathouse, but its publicly owned site is still available on the Yahara Greenway.

was Louis Claude, who later set up an office in Madison and built dozens of Prairie School designs throughout southern Wisconsin. Other devotees did the same thing in other midwestern cities. Examples of Wright's mature Prairie designs can be seen all over the country. In the Chicago area, the Robie House is widely considered one of the best examples; in Madison, Wright's Prairie contribution is the Gilmore House (Fig. 2.28).[65]

One of the most fascinating aspects of Wright's practice during the Chicago years was how he obtained clients, never an easy task for an iconoclast who insisted on designing bold, path-breaking buildings. The problem was real: his 1894 house for William H. Winslow in River Forest, Illinois, was so advanced that the owner had to take the back way to the commuter train to avoid his neighbors' ridicule. Wright got clients through a winning combination of networking and salesmanship. He was especially successful in getting commissions from other members of the Oak Park Unity Church and the Caxton Club, an exclusive group of Chicago bibliophiles.

Wright even found that he could get commissions by getting to know other tenants of his office building. Former clients recall Wright's preacherlike fervor, forceful well-thought-out arguments, supreme confidence, and charming personality.[66]

Wright also demonstrated a remarkable ability to secure additional jobs and referrals from clients. For example, the Martin family was responsible for nine commissions in a single decade. Wright first designed a house in Oak Park and a Chicago factory for William Martin. William had a brother, Darwin, a highly paid executive with the Larkin Soap Company who was largely responsible for Wright's selection for that project. Darwin also commissioned a ten-thousand-square-foot residence, one of Wright's largest and finest Prairie houses, and helped Wright secure still other jobs from family members and other company executives. Such dynamics explain why Wright-designed houses are found in enclaves all over the country.[67]

Most of Wright's clients were highly educated, upper-middle-class professionals (predominantly business executives and engineers) who loved music and theater. As a group they found Wright's design philosophy compelling, were receptive to new ideas, and were willing to take the road less traveled.[68]

During his first sixteen years in private practice (1893–1909) Wright received about 430 commissions, about 130 of which were completed — a lifetime's production for many architects. Recognition of Wright's achievements came slowly at first but then with increasing frequency. At least forty-two articles appeared by 1900 and ninety-six by 1909. Some stories ran in popular household magazines such as *House Beautiful* and *Ladies Home Journal* and others in professional journals such as *Architectural Review* and *Architectural Record*. Many were written by magazine editors and admiring contemporaries, but some were prepared by Wright, based on his many lectures. Major museum exhibits also testified to Wright's growing fame. In 1902 and again in 1907 the Chicago Architectural Club devoted an entire gallery at the Art Institute of Chicago to the architect's work. In 1906 the museum displayed two hundred prints that Wright had collected during his 1905 trip to Japan, testimony to his growing role as a connoisseur of Asian art. Interestingly, as his reputation grew, so too did his impish iconoclasm. For example, when he addressed the newly formed Architectural League of America in 1900, he lambasted his colleagues for "peddling pre-packaged styles," described large firms as "plan factories," and asserted that Chicago's courthouse was "weak and servile."[69]

By 1909 Wright had become one of the best-known and most widely publicized architects in the United States and was about to become much better known to the world. In 1908 he learned that Ernst Wasmuth, a prestigious publishing company in Berlin, wanted to do a book devoted to his work. The same firm had done similar books for several of Europe's most famous architects, but never had the publisher devoted one to an American architect. The forty-two-year-old Wright was honored and managed to parlay the offer into a large portfolio and a smaller picture book.[70]

Wright appeared to be on a professional roll, but the truth was more complex. For sixteen years he had thrown himself into his work with an almost reckless intensity. Seven-day workweeks and long hours were common, and some projects required extensive travel. In his *Autobiography* he confessed, "I was losing my grip on my work and even my interest in it." He did not know what he wanted except to get away. He was bored by the production of formulaic designs — a classic case of burnout. Furthermore, no big, challenging projects were in the pipeline or even on the horizon.[71]

He was increasingly aware that he had been an inadequate father. The task of raising the six children had fallen almost entirely to Catherine. One Sunday a client-friend who was having dinner with the Wrights caught one of the children and said: "Quick now, Frank — what's the name of this one?" The surprised architect gave the name of another child. As he put it in his *Autobiography*, "The architect absorbed the father in me."[72]

Still another problem was that suburban life had become "too ritualized, too predictable, and too stifling" for Wright. People saw Wright speeding around Oak Park with other women in his yellow Stoddard-Dayton roadster. He let his hair grow longer, he wore more unusual clothing, his behavior became increasingly unorthodox and independent. In the summer of 1908 Wright told Catherine he wanted a divorce. His wife of nineteen years refused but said that if he still felt the same way after one year, she would agree to a divorce. The year passed,

FIGURE 2.28

**Prominent Chicago Architect Wins Madison Client**
*SHSW. WHi(X3)31320*

In March 1908 *Architectural Record* published Wright's essay, "In the Cause of Architecture." It was another reminder that Wright had become well known within the profession. Eugene Gilmore, a U.W. law professor, and his wife, Blanche, were greatly enthused by the article and decided to commission Wright to design a $10,000 Prairie Style house for their lot in Madison's University Heights. The Gilmores were hardly alone in hiring big-name architects to design houses in the increasingly prestigious suburb. In 1909 plumbing magnate Charles Crane commissioned Louis Sullivan to design a massive $70,000 Prairie Style house for his daughter and son-in-law. In 1911 John Olin hired Milwaukee architects Ferry and Clas to design a forty-three-room, $69,000 home.

What distinguished the Gilmore site was its superior location atop the highest hill in "the Heights" that offered panoramic views of Lake Mendota and the isthmus. Wright designed the classic Prairie Style house shown here. Because the house had symmetrical wings, huge overhanging eaves, and occupied a hilltop, it reminded people of an airplane about to take off. Consequently, in Madison the building is widely known as "the airplane house."

but Catherine could not bring herself to grant her husband's request.[73]

In September 1909 Wright left Oak Park, ostensibly to work with his German publishers on the two publications, but on November 7 the *Chicago Tribune* carried a prominent story detailing an additional agenda. A reporter had learned that a Mr. and Mrs. Wright had been staying at an elegant new Berlin hotel but had checked out three days earlier. With a journalistic thunderclap the *Tribune* reported that Catherine was still in Oak Park and

FIGURE 2.29

# THE CHICAGO YEARS

## 1 8 8 7 – 1 9 1 1

**1887**
Obtains job with J. L. Silsbee
Publishes first rendering in *Inland Architect*

**1888**
Secures position with
® Adler and Sullivan

**1889**
Marries Catherine Lee Tobin
Builds home in Oak Park

**1890**
First of six children born

Milwaukee Library and Museum Proposal
© FLW FDN. 9306.002

**1893**
Establishes independent architectural practice
Enters architectural competition for the Milwaukee Library and Museum

**1900**
First major article devoted to his work appears in *Architectural Review*

**1902**
Work displayed at the Art Institute of Chicago
Secures commission for the Larkin Company office building in Buffalo, New York

Larkin Building
Interior Atrium

*Courtesy*
*FLW FDN. 0403.046*

Unity Temple, Oak Park, Illinois
© FLW FDN. 0611.003

**1905**
Travels to Japan with Catherine
Secures commission for the Unity Temple in Oak Park, Illinois

**1906**
Displays over 200 Japanese prints at the Art Institute of Chicago

**1907**
Second one-person exhibit of Wright's work mounted at the Art Institute of Chicago

Robie House, Chicago, Illinois
*Courtesy Phil Hamilton*

**1908**
Secures commission for Robie House in Chicago, Illinois

Mamah Cheney
*Courtesy*
*FLW FDN. 6700.0006*

**1909**
Sails for Europe with Mamah Cheney where he oversees preparations for two German publications on his work

**1910**
Returns from Europe in the fall

**1911**
Takes brief second trip to Germany
Purchases land near Spring Green, Wisconsin, and begins construction of a new home on it

that the new "Mrs. Wright" was Mamah Borthwick Cheney (pronounced MAY-ma CHAY-nee), the wife of a former client. When the reporter finally caught up with Wright, the architect said he was on his way to Japan — which of course he was not — and that he was on a "spiritual hegira," surely one of the most creative terms for an affair ever conceived.[74]

Five years earlier Wright had designed a Prairie Style house for Edwin and Mamah Cheney just six blocks from his own house and studio. Catherine and Mamah were members of the same women's clubs, and the couples sometimes attended the same Oak Park social events. But the two women were quite different. Mamah held bachelor's and master's degrees from the University of Michigan, was fluent in several languages, had worked as a librarian and teacher until she married at thirty, advocated radical freedom for women, and was unhappily married. Catherine held no college degrees, could speak only English, had been a housewife since she married at eighteen, and thought monogamy was ordained by God.[75]

What the world was about to learn was that Wright and Mamah Cheney had fallen in love, probably years earlier, and had been planning their trip to Europe for some time. Mamah had left Oak Park in June with her two children to visit a friend in Colorado. She called her husband from there and told him to pick up the children. Anticipating a long European sojourn, Wright had arranged for colleagues to take over his architectural practice. Wright and Cheney apparently rendezvoused at New York's Plaza Hotel and then sailed to Europe together, probably under assumed names. The pair spent the fall and winter in Europe, sometimes together, sometimes apart. Wright rented a villa in Florence where he did final work for his portfolio and book, while Mamah translated a work by a Swedish feminist and taught languages at a German

FIGURE 2.30

**Taliesin, Wright's Wet Oil Canvas**

*Photo by Zane Williams*

Something about this hill caught Wright's eye when he was a boy working on his uncle's farm in the valley below. Perhaps, Wright speculated, it was the pasqueflowers. Perhaps it was the exhilarating feeling he got when he stood at the crown of the hill. Or perhaps it was because it overlooked the valley of his Lloyd Jones ancestors. Whatever the reasons, Wright selected this hill for his famous home, Taliesin (pronounced tally s in), Welsh for "shining brow."

Wright built the first Taliesin in 1911, then rebuilt it in 1914 after a tragic fire, and again in 1925 after still another fire, each time expanding and refining. From the time he formed the Fellowship in 1932 until he died in 1959, Wright made further, almost annual, changes to the famous building. The original Taliesin had just four thousand square feet, but by 1959 his sprawling country estate had grown to twenty-five thousand square feet. It was, as one writer put it, Wright's "wet oil canvas."

Taliesin is Wright's premiere but protean portrait of organic architecture. Rather than locate the house on top of the hill, he placed it below the top; its limestone walls looked more like a natural outcrop than a building foundation. Wright even measured the slope of surrounding hills so the pitch of the roofs would be in harmony, and upon their carefully calibrated surfaces he placed cedar shingles that soon resembled the gray bark of nearby oak trees. To achieve the golden yellow for the stucco's color, the sensitive architect used Wisconsin River sand. Today Taliesin is one of the world's most famous buildings, an autobiography covering forty-eight years of Wright's life, written in limestone, cedar, sand, steel, and glass.

FIGURE 2.31

**Frank Lloyd Wright, Age Forty-three**

*Courtesy FLW FDN. 6002.0008*

Wright was forty-four when he moved into Taliesin in the fall of 1911. This picture shows what he looked like about a year earlier, after his return from Europe. Friends noticed that his hair was starting to gray and hung just off his shoulders and that he had begun to wear a broad-brimmed hat and knee trousers with long stockings that made him look like the man on every box of Quaker Oats.

university. In March 1910 Wright rented a "little cream white villa" just outside Florence where he and Mamah spent a romantic summer.[76]

In October 1910 Wright returned to Oak Park, and Mamah remained in Europe. Wright had become a

pariah to most of his neighbors, but Catherine and the children welcomed him home and hoped that he would stay. For the next few months Wright's life was a skein of deceptions. He insisted that the Mamah affair was over and that he was going to resume his marriage and his practice; in fact, Wright was planning to leave Oak Park. Toward that end he subdivided the house and studio into two dwelling units so that Catherine could receive income from the rented side.[77] (For a chronology of the Chicago years, see Fig. 2.29.)

The question was where the forty-five-year-old architect could start a new life. To Wright the answer was clear and obvious. He would return to the Wisconsin valley where his grandfather had settled, where many of his relatives still lived, and where he had spent so much time as a young man. He loved this valley and could recall almost everything about it in vivid season-by-season detail. As he reflected on the picturesque valley, his mind kept returning to a hilltop that overlooked it, "one of my favorite places when I was a boy, for pasqueflowers grew there in March sun while the snow still streaked the hillsides. When you are on its crown you are out in mid-air as though swinging in a plane." This was the hilltop where Wright would resume his life.[78]

The Taliesin deception began in November 1910 when Wright persuaded Darwin Martin, his soft-hearted client and pliant patron, to lend him $25,000. Wright told Martin that he needed the money to restart his practice and for a second trip to Germany to complete arrangements for the publication of his books. Then, in early April 1911, Wright gave his patron several revealing updates. In a telegram he told Martin that he had "to help my mother out of a tight real estate situation," and a few days later he told the Buffalo executive that he had helped his mother "buy a small farm" and that he was going to see about building

"a small house for her." On April 10, 1911, Anna Wright purchased the thirty-one acres of land in the Wyoming Valley that included her son's favorite hilltop; soon thereafter he completed plans for a "Cottage for Mrs. Anna Lloyd Wright." But what the wily architect intended to build was anything but a cottage and certainly not for his mother. His real goal was to build an architectural studio, a nearly self-sufficient farm, and a country estate for himself and his lover.[79]

## THE EARLY TALIESIN YEARS, 1911 TO 1938

Construction of Taliesin (see Fig. 2.30) began in May and was nearly completed in late December 1911 when the *Chicago Tribune* reported that Frank Lloyd Wright (see Fig. 2.31) and Mamah Borthwick were living together at his new country estate. By this time Mamah had received her divorce and resumed her maiden name, but Wright was still legally married. Wright's decision to move his mistress into Taliesin embarrassed his Madison and Wyoming Valley relatives. By 1911 several of his cousins held prominent positions in Madison. Cousin Thomas Lloyd Jones was principal of the big new Madison High School, cousin Chester Lloyd Jones was a young professor of political science at the University of Wisconsin, and cousin Richard Lloyd Jones was the publisher of the *Wisconsin State Journal*. To Wright's aunts, Jane and Nell, who operated Hillside, the progressive hundred-student boarding school just three-quarters of a mile from Taliesin, the architect's adulterous arrangement was also a financial threat. That was because some Chicago-area parents who read about the scandal in local papers decided to withdraw their children from the school rather than expose them to this moral contagion.[80]

Wright felt the sting of his family's rebuke and was increasingly frustrated by the unrelenting press coverage of his defiant decision to live with Mamah at Taliesin. His plan was to remain silent and hope the storm would pass. When it did not, Wright retaliated with an audacious press conference on Christmas Day 1911. With the rectitude of a minister at the pulpit Wright asserted his principles of "honest" living in a signed statement that he passed out to reporters. Referring to his life with Mamah, Wright said, "We are living the life that truth dictates. Our hope is that we may benefit humanity. Our determination is to be true to our ideals at all cost." Wright's actions were tantamount to passing out cups of gasoline for his own immolation, but Wright did not care. To him it was just another case of the family motto, Truth Against the World. It was not an auspicious beginning for Taliesin, the place that would be his primary residence for forty-eight years.[81]

So strident was Wright's counterattack and so incendiary were its contents that his Wisconsin relatives were forced to practice damage control. The *Chicago Herald*'s headline said it all: "Wright Kin Gather to 'Try' Architect." The day the article appeared Richard Lloyd Jones (see Fig. 2.32) wrote his cousin a strongly worded personal letter, saying: "I am thoroughly sorry for you, Frank, ... but I also thoroughly disapprove of your manner of demonstrating your philosophy and particularly ... in the shadow of Hillside Home School and in the valley where the family has made its home for so many years."[82]

STARTING OVER:
WISCONSIN, JAPAN, CALIFORNIA, AND ARIZONA

By 1912 Wright had become an outcast. Even so, he had to get on with his life, and his first priority was restoring his architectural practice. Indeed, since running off to Europe with Mamah three years

earlier, and especially since his Taliesin "love nest" scandal, few would hire the controversial architect. In 1909, the last good year of his practice, Wright received twenty-seven commissions, twelve of which were built; in 1912, by contrast, the architect received eleven commissions, four of which were built. In the wake of the 1911 headlines in Wright's home state, few Wisconsinites were willing to risk opprobrium by hiring such a controversial man. Those who were included Arthur L. Richards, a Milwaukee businessman who commissioned Wright to do a high-rise, fireproof hotel in downtown Madison (see Fig. 2.33), and Frederick Kehl, the owner of a well-known Madison dancing school who commissioned a new dance academy. Neither was built. Even the members of his boyhood church, Madison's First Unitarian Society, hired local architects Claude and Starck instead of Wright to do their new parish house.[83]

To this modest portfolio there was one magnificent exception: Midway Gardens, a beautiful upscale city block–sized entertainment complex meant as an alternative to Chicago's "smoky dens ... and saloons." Wright's plans for Midway Gardens included an outdoor German-style beer garden and band shell and a spirit-lifting winter garden for dining, dancing, and drinking. For the ornately detailed "good time place," Wright even hired Alfonso Iannelli, a young Italian-born sculptor with whom he collaborated to produce more than one hundred cast-concrete figures to adorn the garden. (Iannelli would later play a cameo role in the Monona Terrace story.) Although the project opened in June 1914, so many finishing details remained that Wright had to work throughout the summer and even on weekends to finish it.[84]

On Saturday, August 15, 1914, Wright and his twenty-two-year-old son, John, who was serving as

FIGURE 2.32

**RICHARD LLOYD JONES**
*COUSIN AND NEWSPAPER PUBLISHER*

*Courtesy Jenkin Lloyd Jones*

For most of their early lives first cousins Richard Lloyd Jones and Frank Lloyd Wright saw each other frequently. When Wright lived in Madison, Jones lived in Janesville, just forty miles away, where his father, Jenkin Lloyd Jones, was a Unitarian minister. Even when Richard moved to Chicago in the early 1880s, the two boys would see each other at annual family reunions in the Wyoming Valley.

Jones enjoyed a brilliant career in journalism, first with newspapers and then as an editor of two national magazines, *Collier's* and *Cosmopolitan*. In 1911 Jones bought the *Wisconsin State Journal*, intending to make it a mouthpiece for Robert Marion La Follette and the burgeoning national Progressive movement. Just a few months after moving to Madison, Jones had the unenviable assignment of covering the sensational news that Wright had moved his new mistress into the just-completed Taliesin. Jones was much more comfortable championing his famous cousin. For example, in 1912 he gave front-page treatment to Wright's proposed design for a downtown Madison high-rise hotel (see Fig. 2.33). Although Jones sold his interest in the *Journal* in 1919 and moved to Tulsa, Oklahoma, where he bought another newspaper, he continued to promote his cousin's work, especially the Phi Gamma Delta fraternity house (see Fig. 2.37). In 1929 Jones had Wright design his new house in Tulsa.

FIGURE 2.33

"A Real Hotel," Wright's 1912 Design

© FLW FDN. 1110.001

In 1912 Madison's booming convention industry made hotel rooms scarce; that was why Arthur Richards, a Milwaukee businessman, commissioned Wright to prepare this design for an eight-story, 126-room, fireproof $250,000 hotel. Richards controlled an ideal location at the intersection of Monona Avenue and Doty Street in downtown Madison, just one block from Lake Monona and the capitol. Wright proposed an aggregate concrete exterior and a lobby decorated with copper and art glass.

Championing the project was Wright's cousin Richard Lloyd Jones, the editor and publisher of the *Wisconsin State Journal*. Lloyd Jones used his hotel crusade to put his cousin's name on the front page of his paper for the first time. Jones's breathy early March 1912 headline, "Hotel To Be Built This Year," proved false; the project was never built because Richards could not secure enough local financial support.

project construction superintendent, were having lunch at the nearly finished Midway project when a secretary appeared and told the senior Wright that he was wanted on the telephone. When he returned, the ashen-faced Wright groaned, grabbed a table to keep from falling, and told his son to get a taxi for Union Station. There had been a fire at Taliesin. Relatives picked Wright up at the Madison depot and whisked him to Spring Green by car. Visibly sagging as he approached the smoldering ruins, Wright learned what had happened. Julian Carlton,

a handyman and table waiter, had set Taliesin afire with gasoline while the residents and hired help were at lunch and then attacked with a hatchet those who tried to escape. When Carlton's rampage was over, seven lay dead, including Mamah and her two visiting children (see Fig. 2.34). Wright was devastated. Friends and relatives claimed all the bodies except Mamah's for burial. The following day his son John and two cousins helped Wright bury Mamah in the family cemetery next to Unity Chapel, and that evening the distraught architect conducted a tearful vigil beside her grave. He tried to get his mind off the tragedy by returning to Chicago, where he walked the streets for days, his mind befogged by sorrow.[85]

Wright was one of those people who seem to have a powerful steel spring that releases its energy only when they have been prostrated by life's worst blows. Mamah's death was one of those times for Wright. He resolved to rebuild the extensively damaged Taliesin and continue his architectural career, but the huge hole left by Mamah and the ache of her absence left Wright vulnerable. Less than four months after the tragedy, Wright received a condolence letter from a forty-five-year-old socialite-sculptress named Miriam Noel. Wright's acknowledgment produced a second letter from Noel that said, "If my friendship can serve you in any way, it is yours." Wright suggested she meet him at his Chicago office on Christmas Eve "so we can plan our evening as we will," and she agreed. Wright was obviously attracted to the red-haired, green-eyed woman who favored capes and turbans, wore a monocle, and smoked cigarettes. Within a few months of their first meeting, the woman Wright described as "brilliantly intellectual ... [and] sophisticated" was living at Taliesin. Later Wright said he felt sorry for Noel, but this was anything but a social worker–client relationship.[86]

When Miriam Noel moved into Taliesin, Wright had already begun work on the Imperial Hotel in downtown Tokyo, the largest project he had ever undertaken. Wright's 5 percent commission on the nearly $5 million building was a stupendous $250,000. Wright won this commission because a friend and fellow expert in Japanese art had recommended him to one of the hotel's developers in 1911 and because the architect made a good impression on the development team during his 1913 trip. Wright signed the final contract in 1916, but construction did not start until 1919.[87]

The project required Wright to make six trips to Japan and left precious little time to secure and complete U.S. commissions. For example, in the nearly four years from November 1918 through August 1922, Wright was in Japan for more than three. One of the few commissions he was able to nurture to completion during this period was a line of affordable houses known as "American System-Builts" (see Fig. 2.35).[88]

Wright used his years in Japan to increase his already large and highly regarded collection of Japanese art. Although Silsbee, his first Chicago boss, had exposed Wright to the genre when he was just twenty, he did not begin to seriously study Japanese prints for several years. What intrigued Wright was the way Japanese artists concentrated on "the elimination of the non-essential," a concept the young professional was striving to incorporate in his work during the early years of his career. Wright became so interested in this art form that he traveled to Japan in 1905 and returned with hundreds of prints. When he made his second trip to Japan in 1913 to meet with the developers of the Imperial Hotel, he returned to the United States with so much Japanese art that it required a railroad boxcar to transport it to Taliesin. During subsequent trips to Japan between 1916 and 1922 Wright claimed to have purchased $500,000 worth of art for himself and wealthy Chicago and New York collectors. Even New York's Metropolitan Museum of Art bought several hundred prints from Wright. As a result of his Imperial-related trips, Wright acquired one of the largest and most valuable collections of Japanese art in the country. (This collection would play a large role as collateral and a source of quick cash during the bad times that lay ahead; many of Wright's prints would end up in museums in New York, Chicago, Philadelphia, Kansas City, Minneapolis, Ann Arbor, and Madison.)[89]

When Wright returned from his last trip to Japan in August 1922, he was glad to be back in the United States but anxious about his future. He left Japan feeling the sting of mounting criticism about the Imperial's excessive ornamentation and being behind schedule and over budget. The long intense project had drained his energy and grayed his hair. But at fifty-five, Wright's greatest concern was his lack of work stemming from his long absence from the country.[90]

Precisely because he had almost no work, Wright accepted an invitation to practice with his son Lloyd, now thirty-two, who had opened an architectural practice in Hollywood, California. During this interlude Wright and his son developed the "textile block system," custom-poured concrete blocks that featured pattern and color and could be made on the job site in all shapes and sizes. Wright saw the textile block as a way to achieve great beauty and strength — even earthquake resistance — at low cost and began to use this new design technology, first with the Millard House in Pasadena. Because the textile block proved to be much more expensive and less watertight than Wright had hoped, he rarely used it outside California.[91]

FIGURE 2.34

**1914 Taliesin Tragedy**

One of the most grisly murders in Wisconsin's history took place at Taliesin on Saturday, August 15, 1914, when Julian Carlton, a handyman and table waiter, set the house ablaze with gasoline and then attacked with a hatchet anyone who tried to escape. The *Wisconsin State Journal* broke the story on Saturday, and on Sunday the *Chicago Tribune* made it a front-page story with a large photo of Mamah Borthwick Cheney. The tragedy received extensive newspaper coverage around the country.

FROM INTERNATIONAL HERO TO PARIAH

September 1, 1923, turned out to be one of the most important days of Wright's life. That was the day set for the grand opening of the Imperial Hotel. Wright had been back in the States for a year, practicing with his son in California, but a former associate had kept the architect apprised of completion details.

At noon that day a massive earthquake and firestorm hit Tokyo, leaving 140,000 people dead, 300,000 buildings burned, and 4,500 acres of the city reduced to smoldering ashes. Newspapers reported that the Imperial had been destroyed, which surely depressed the man who had invested nearly nine years of his life on this project. Then, on September 13, Wright received a cable from his associate: HOTEL STANDS UNDAMAGED AS MONUMENT OF YOUR GENIUS CONGRATULATIONS. What emotions ran through Wright's mind are not known, but they must have included profound relief and unrestrained joy. When the world learned that the hotel had withstood the cataclysm, criticism of the hotel stopped, and Wright was hailed as a hero and genius. People were especially interested in the quake-proof

FIGURE 2.35

**American System-Builts,
Wright's Affordable Housing Initiative**

*SHSW. WHi(X3)51138*

For much of his professional career Wright sought ways to make good housing available at affordable prices. This, and other advertisements that appeared in Madison, Milwaukee, and Chicago newspapers beginning in March 1917, marked the beginning of a national marketing campaign by Wright's client, Arthur L. Richards of Milwaukee, to sell what Wright called "system-built" or "ready-cut" homes. Wright and his staff prepared nine hundred drawings for Richards, enough for an entire line of single- and multifamily houses. All were designed on standard three-foot modules, and all components were precut at the factory and then shipped to the field for erection. Prices ranged from $2,000 to $15,000. Richards' plan was to set up franchised dealers all over the country, but his timing proved terrible. The same newspapers that carried this advertisement carried stories about the growing war in Europe and mobilization orders for American soldiers. Although several demonstration houses were built and sold, the company was a casualty of World War I. System-Builts, as they are now called, have recently been found in midwestern states, and many more undoubtedly await discovery. The Madison dealer was A. B. Groves.

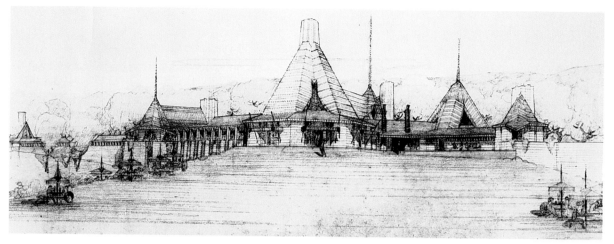

Perspective of Nakoma Country Club from Golf Course

© FLW FDN. 2403.036

Interior of Main Lounge

*Courtesy Alden Aust*

FIGURE 2.36

## A Tepee for the Country Club?

Wright's decision to live with a mistress at Taliesin beginning in 1912 and another beginning in 1915 made Madisonians so mad that with just one minor exception they refused to commission the man to do anything for nearly a decade. However, that changed almost overnight when the Imperial Hotel survived the devastating 1923 Tokyo earthquake. Suddenly, conservative Madison business leaders were once again willing to hire the now internationally famous hometown boy. Just a few weeks after the Imperial miracle, members of the Nakoma Country Club met with Wright to design a new clubhouse.

Taking a cue from the Indian name of the club and the subdivision around the golf course, Wright proposed one of the most unusual golf clubhouses ever designed, a rambling building that looked like an Indian village of connected tepees. For the main lounge Wright proposed a fifty-foot tepee with a four-sided "campfire" in the center. Flanking the lounge were locker rooms, a tea pavilion for the women, and a "nineteenth hole" for the men. Wright proposed to locate the building atop the highest hill on the grounds, from which members could see the state capitol in the distance and nearby Lake Wingra.

Unfortunately, the clubhouse was never built. Several months after it was presented to country club members, Madison newspapers began to carry stories about Wright's female and financial problems. The combination of Wright's plummeting reputation, ballooning clubhouse construction estimates, and members' growing concerns about the daring design caused club leaders to dump Wright in favor of a local architect.

floating foundations devised by Wright and his engineer, Paul Mueller. The Imperial's survival sent Wright's reputation soaring as never before — and at a time when he sorely needed it. That year Wright received a questionnaire from *Who's Who in America* for the first time. "What have you done that is worthy of special mention?" it asked. Wright replied: "The Imperial Hotel of Tokyo, Japan and 176 other Buildings of Note."[92]

In October, during one of Wright's periodic trips back to Wisconsin, William T. Evjue (pronounced EV-you), the editor and publisher of Madison's *Capital Times*, drove out to Taliesin for an interview. Evjue was eager to scoop his paper's rival, the *Wisconsin State Journal.* He had first met Wright in 1914 when Evjue was business manager of the *Journal* and Richard Lloyd Jones was its editor and publisher. Soon after the war in Europe broke out in 1914 Jones's *Journal* began attacking Senator Robert Marion La Follette's opposition to U.S. involvement in the conflict. These attacks from the very paper that had once championed the progressive politician were too much for Evjue. Sensing a market for a progressive, pro–La Follette, prolabor newspaper in southern Wisconsin, Evjue started the *Capital Times* in 1917. His instincts proved accurate, and the *Times* enjoyed rapidly growing circulation. Jones's *Journal* held its own, but the paper's growing debt forced Wright's cousin to sell it in 1919. Although Jones bought another newspaper in Tulsa, Oklahoma, he retained a strong interest in Madison affairs.[93]

The headline on Evjue's story declared: "Wright Now Being Proclaimed World Leader." In it the confidence-drunk architect announced that he was going to open offices in Chicago, Los Angeles, and Tokyo. Although this grand scheme was barroom bravado, it reflected the sharp upturn in Wright's fortunes, and the story marked the beginning of a warm friendship between the two men that would last for more than three decades.[94]

The Imperial miracle made Wright a trophy architect and caused his project portfolio to thicken as eager clients sought his services. For the first time in more than a decade Wright was even able to secure commissions in Madison, where people had been slow to forgive his scandalous behavior. For example, in the fall of 1923 Wright received a commission to design a clubhouse for the new Nakoma Country Club (see Fig. 2.36) and in the fall of 1924 agreed to design a house for the University of Wisconsin chapter of Phi Gamma Delta fraternity (see Fig. 2.37). Wright also had three houses underway in Los Angeles, a design for an insurance company skyscraper in downtown Chicago, and an unusual tourist destination featuring a planetarium and a rooftop restaurant on a Maryland mountaintop. The surge of commissions required Wright to hire extra draftsmen for the Taliesin studio. Further brightening his prospects were plans by two European publishers to release new books on Wright.[95]

In the midst of all this professional success, the architect made what would prove to be a disastrous personal decision. In November 1923, after waiting the obligatory year following the divorce from his first wife Catherine, Wright married Miriam Noel, his mistress of nine years. Why Wright married her is not clear. Wright knew that she was subject to "strange disturbances," and they appeared to worsen after the marriage. Today doctors would probably attribute her erratic behavior to morphine addiction and specifically to withdrawal from the terrible drug. In May 1924 Miriam walked out of Taliesin, and Wright breathed a sigh of relief.[96]

Wright, now nearly fifty-seven, thought of himself as a free man — but if history was any indication, he would not be without female companionship for

long. During the summer and early fall of 1924 Wright tried to fill what he called "an aching void" by becoming involved with twenty-two-year-old Mary Hurlbut, a striking, highly intelligent French major at the University of Wisconsin. Wright even made an aggressive if unsuccessful pass at Zona Gale, fifty, a University of Wisconsin regent and winner of the 1921 Pulitzer Prize for her drama *Miss Lulu Bett*.[97]

Then, on November 30, 1924, Wright and a male friend attended a matinee featuring Madame Karsavina, the famous Petrograd ballerina, at the Eighth Street Theater in Chicago. Just before the curtain rose, the usher showed a "dark slender gentlewoman" to an empty seat in the box occupied by Wright and his friend. From that moment on Wright paid scant attention to the stage so that he could secretly observe every detail of the aristocratic woman. At intermission they introduced themselves, and after the performance he invited her out for tea. Olgivanna Hinzenberg, twenty-six, had been born in Montenegro, educated in Russia, and had studied for several years near Paris under Georgi Gurdjieff, a philosopher-savant who taught that rhythmic dance, labor, and physical self-discipline integrated the body and mind. Olgivanna, who had a seven-year-old child, Svetlana, had come to Chicago to work out final divorce terms with her husband, an architect. Wright was enchanted by her beauty, intelligence, accent, and bearing — indeed, by her being. He was in love and he knew it.[98]

In February 1925, just three months after they met, Olgivanna moved into Taliesin and before the end of the year gave birth to a girl, Iovanna. That April lightning struck Taliesin, and the resulting fire destroyed $300,000 worth of Oriental tapestries, screens, sculpture, and some prints, none of which was insured. The good news was that almost all of

Wright's valuable Japanese print collection was spared because it had been stored in the Taliesin vault. The bad news was that the architect carried only $39,000 in insurance on the house, woefully insufficient to rebuild, which forced Wright to take out a $43,000 mortgage from Madison's Bank of Wisconsin.[99]

Meanwhile, Wright's attempt to divorce Miriam Noel was not going well. In August 1926 Noel refused to grant the divorce and demanded the right to live at Taliesin. When Noel heard that Olgivanna was living there, she was furious and sued Olga for alienating Wright's affections. When Olgivanna's estranged husband read about the scandal, he had attorneys begin legal proceedings to give him full custody of Svetlana, their daughter.[100]

Faced with the prospect that authorities might forcefully take Svetlana from them, Wright and Olga decided to flee, a decision that assured more days on the front pages of the nation's newspapers. But exactly where they went no one knew, that is, until someone tipped Minnesota law enforcement officials that the couple and the two girls were hiding out in a lakeside cabin twenty miles southwest of Minneapolis under the assumed name of Richardson. On October 21, 1926, Wright and Olga were jailed, and the two children were placed in police custody (see Fig. 2.38). After investigating, Minnesota officials decided not to prosecute Wright on Noel's latest charge (transporting a woman across state lines for immoral purposes), and Olga's husband dropped his charge (adultery) when she gave him generous visitation rights. Noel, angry that Minnesota authorities had not pressed charges, directed her lawyers to find clever new legal nooses for Wright's neck.[101]

If Wright was no longer a fugitive from the law, he was anything but a free man. The torrent of newspaper stories detailing the salacious saga of

FIGURE 2.37

**Bunking with the Brothers at Phi Gamma Delta**

© FLW FDN. 2504.041; courtesy Fiji Building Association and the Elvehjem Museum of Art

One dreary winter afternoon in early 1925 Ted Swanson answered the doorbell of the Phi Gamma Delta fraternity house, a stately 1850s mansion that stood along fraternity and sorority row near the University of Wisconsin campus. To his great surprise, he found Frank Lloyd Wright with suitcase in hand. Wright explained that he had been hired to design the new fraternity house two blocks away on Lake Mendota and that he was going to live at the old house for a few days to determine how the new one should be designed. The momentarily stymied Swanson met with several others and then gave Wright a bunk in the thirty-four-man dormitory, a desk in a room with one of the brothers, and a tour of the house.

Accounts of this remarkable incident agree that the famous architect fitted in wonderfully and that he especially enjoyed the evening bull sessions. To Swanson and several other brothers who happened to be engineering majors, Wright explained the intricacies of the Imperial Hotel foundation. Swanson reported that as the young men got to know their famous guest, one of them screwed up his courage and asked Wright about his views on women. The architect explained that he "required more than one woman to satisfy his soul." It was both a summary of his life that so far included one wife, one mistress, and one mistress-turned-wife and a thinly veiled announcement that Olgivanna, a woman he had met a few months earlier, was about to move into Taliesin.

What Wright learned during his sojourn with the brothers was embodied in the clean-slate design shown in this colored pencil rendering dated January 27, 1925. The architect proposed a Mayan-inspired design based on the "textile block" construction system he had used for several California houses. Wright concluded that the front of the building should be a gracious minihotel for returning alumni; the middle (the narrow part extending to the lake) should be used for studying, sleeping, and dining; and the large lakefront social hall should be reserved for chapter meetings and noisy parties. As Richard Lloyd Jones, the publisher of the *Wisconsin State Journal*, put it, it was the most scientific design ever done for a fraternity house. Although the design was innovative, even radical, Jones was somewhat biased — he was a gung-ho fraternity alum, had secured the commission for his cousin, and was co-owner of the new site. Unfortunately, Wright's personal and financial troubles and high initial bids caused fraternity leaders to give the commission to the Madison firm of Law, Law and Potter. Their modified Wright design still stands at 16 Langdon Street.

Frank and Olga and Miriam virtually destroyed his ability to secure commissions. Few would hire him, and some clients looked for ways to wiggle out of their contracts. Both the Nakoma Country Club and the Phi Gamma Delta fraternity dumped Wright and replaced him with Madison architects.[102]

Meanwhile, Wright was incurring huge bills from fighting Noel's legal actions and failing to make mortgage payments. In September 1926 the bank foreclosed on its mortgage, took several thousand Japanese prints, and in April 1927 sold off Wright's cattle.[103]

That Wright had devoted clients, friends, and relatives who were willing to take extraordinary steps on his behalf was clear from the formation in August 1927 of Frank Lloyd Wright, Inc., a "rescue" corporation. The premises of the corporation were that (1) the architect was incapable of handling his financial affairs; (2) a one-time infusion of money would pay off his debts and allow him to begin expressing his genius once again; and (3) future commissions would pay back contributors. Taking the lead role in creating the corporation was Philip La Follette, son of the famous Wisconsin governor and senator, Robert Marion La Follette. The well-known attorney and future governor secured contributions from several of Wright's longtime patrons, friends, and even family members to pay his mortgage and endow an anticipated divorce trust fund for Noel. In exchange, contributors stipulated stern ground rules. The board would receive all the architect's commissions, make all major financial decisions, and pay Wright a salary and expenses. At least, that was the theory.[104]

Soon after La Follette formed the rescue corporation, Wright reached a divorce agreement with Miriam Noel that required him to pay her $6,000 in cash and create a trust fund of $30,000. La Follette paid these amounts from the rescue corporation, and the divorce was finalized. Unfortunately for Wright, the rescue corporation then did not have enough money to pay off his Taliesin mortgage. In January 1928 the bank ordered Wright out of Taliesin, and in July the bank sold the house at sheriff's sale. The high bidder was the Bank of Wisconsin at $25,000, substantially less than the mortgage balance. La Follette then negotiated a deal with the bank to pay off Wright's mortgage and other bank costs for $40,000, but this forced the lawyer to go back to Wright's corporate supporters for more money.[105]

Fortunately for Wright, at the same time he was evicted from Taliesin, he accepted the invitation of an old family friend to become a consultant on the Arizona Biltmore, a grand new resort hotel planned for Phoenix. The family friend was especially interested in securing Wright's advice on how his textile block concept could be incorporated in the hotel's design.[106]

By late 1928 things were beginning to look up. In August, the requisite one year after his divorce from Noel, Wright married Olgivanna. A few weeks later La Follette worked out a financial settlement with the Bank of Wisconsin, using fresh funds from the rescue corporation and proceeds from the bank's sale of Wright's Japanese prints. In October a much happier man, Olga, and their two children moved back into Taliesin (see Fig. 2.39). Once again Wright was at one of those critical junctures. What was he going to do with the rest of his life?[107]

Wright decided to form a new venture known as the Hillside Home School of Allied Arts to be located at nearby Hillside, the country boarding school that Wright had acquired from his aunts in 1915. Wright's plan was to attract world-class sculptors, fabric designers, woodworkers, metalworkers, and, of

FIGURE 2.38

**Scandalous Headlines of 1926**

From 1925 to 1929 Wright's name frequently appeared in articles and even headlines of the nation's newspapers — often in unflattering ways. Triggering these racy stories was Wright's decision to move Olgivanna into Taliesin in February 1925 and to have an out-of-wedlock child with her; the discovery of these facts by his estranged wife, Miriam Noel; and her unrelenting attempts to evict Olga, move back into Taliesin, and punish Wright. These two headlines appeared in Madison newspapers on October 21, 1926, when Wright and Olga were captured in a Minnesota cabin after a month as fugitives trying to avoid arrest warrants. Newspapers were also avidly reporting Wright's financial problems that led to the architect's eviction in January 1928 and the sheriff's sale of Taliesin in July. These were national stories, but they got the most extensive coverage in Madison, where they irreparably tarnished the architect's image.

course, architects who would serve as academy faculty and who would work with students to create outstanding designs for industrial products. Wright proposed to secure start-up and operational costs from corporate underwriters who would then have first pick of outstanding product designs developed by students. Wright also wanted the academy to become affiliated with the University of Wisconsin so that university faculty could teach there.[108]

In late 1928 and early 1929 Wright sent letters to prospective underwriters and met with University of Wisconsin faculty members. The faculty encouraged Wright to secure the approval of the new university president, Glenn Frank, a man who actively encouraged departures from academic convention. Frank and a special university committee considered the cooperative venture during a half-dozen meetings

but deadlocked over the site and curriculum. The committee probably questioned the wisdom of entering a partnership with a man whose financial acumen was notoriously poor. Industrialists refused to underwrite Wright's proposal, and world-class artists such as Swedish sculptor Carl Milles were apparently put off by the poor condition of the property and by Wright's failure to obtain funding.[109]

Doors close, doors open. The architect focused his attention on two huge projects, both named "St. Mark's," although one name was in Spanish and the other in English. San Marcos-in-the-Desert was the brainchild of a wealthy Arizona real estate developer who owned thousands of acres of land south of Phoenix and wanted Wright to design an upscale resort hotel that could compete with the sumptuous Biltmore. In January 1929 Wright began working

FIGURE 2.39

**Picnic with the Family**

SHSW. WHi(X3)21623

This picture, taken sometime in the fall of 1928 or the spring of 1929, is a reminder that a new chapter in Wright's life was beginning. Behind him were his itinerant years in Japan, California, and Arizona, his storm-tossed years with Miriam Noel, and his trip to the edge of the financial brink. In this photo Wright, now sixty-one; Olgivanna, about thirty-one; Svetlana, about twelve; and Iovanna, about four, are picnicking somewhere along the Wisconsin River. Picnics were a tradition with the Lloyd Joneses; when Wright established the Fellowship, he planned festive picnics for the entire group on summer weekends.

drawings at a temporary desert camp known as Ocatilla, the conceptual forerunner of Taliesin West. Final bids for the project in November 1929 came in at $700,000.[110]

St. Mark's-in-the-Bouwerie was the idea of a liberal Episcopal priest who wanted to construct several high-rise New York apartment buildings on church property as a parish investment. Their unique design was based on the tree, a symbol Wright often used to explain organic architecture. Wright proposed to plunge a foundation deep into Manhattan bedrock (the taproot), send a postlike spine soaring skyward (the trunk), and hang cantilevered apartment modules (the branches) from the spine. Wright was enamored of this concept and later recycled it for projects in Washington, D.C., and Bartlesville, Oklahoma. One of Wright's biographers artfully described this recycling propensity: "No design that Wright believed in was ever truly abandoned, it was only postponed." Plans for the $700,000 high-rise project were completed in the summer of 1929.[111]

The two new St. Mark's projects, especially their initial fees, sent Wright's confidence soaring and tested the ability of his board to supervise its wily employee. One afternoon in the fall of 1929 Phil La Follette, who had devised Wright's corporate short leash and who at that point had not been paid a cent for his work, saw something that forced him to conclude that he and his rescue corporation colleagues had been outmaneuvered. Driving down a Madison street "proud as a potentate" was Frank Lloyd Wright in a brand new, bright orange L-29 Cord, one of fastest, sleekest, technologically advanced, and most expensive production automobiles in the world (see Fig. 2.40).[112]

When the stock market crashed in October 1929 so did the big St. Mark's jobs that would have produced huge fees for Wright. In fact, the only project that

moved forward that fall was the Tulsa residence for his cousin Richard Lloyd Jones. During 1930 Wright had just three commissions, a prototype YMCA camp cottage, a recycled version of the St. Mark's apartment tower for a Chicago client, and a gallery for a former client, none of which was built. This meant that Wright had almost no income to pay his rescue corporation investors. Because their loan was secured only by the architect's future income, they lost almost all their money.[113]

Wright's inability to get new commissions was not entirely his fault; after all, the entire economy was in a steep nose dive. Nevertheless, finding reasons not to hire the man was easy: his controversial lifestyle, financial incompetence, reputation as a lone ranger, and remote location 40 miles west of Madison, 130 miles west of Milwaukee, 150 miles northwest of Chicago, and 270 miles southeast of Minneapolis. Indeed, if Wright's goal had been to force potential clients to make a pilgrimage to his place of self-imposed exile, Taliesin was ideally located.[114]

If Taliesin's location was inconvenient for securing national business, it should have been ideal for landing Madison-area commissions — even during the Great Depression. But a combination of factors banished Wright from such work. For example, the federal government hired the Chicago firm of Holabird and Root to do its huge U.S. Forest Products Laboratory because Wright's reputation was so sullied. The University of Wisconsin built the Field House and the State of Wisconsin built the State Office Building, but Arthur Peabody, the state architect who controlled both state and university projects, refused to give Wright any work. He did not approve of Wright's unconventional style, preferred to have staff architects do his work, and was put off by Wright's unrelenting, gleeful criticism of his buildings.[115]

Wright's womanizing and financial problems — and the attendant headlines — also affected his ability to secure commercial and residential commissions in Madison. Indeed, nowhere in the country was this unflattering epoch of Wright's life more fully reported than in Madison. Local architectural firms, and especially Law, Law and Potter, were the primary beneficiaries of Wright's journey through the mud. It was Law, Law and Potter that took over the Phi Gamma Delta fraternity house project in 1926 and accepted a commission to remodel Wright's 1908 Prairie Style Gilmore House in 1930. When Wright heard that the Madison firm had taken the Gilmore job, he fired off a smoking letter to the managing partner, Jim Law, expressing his contempt for the firm and its willingness to "lay their awkward destructive hands upon work you could not possibly understand." These incidents were the basis for most of Wright's disdain for the Madison firm and especially for Jim Law when he became mayor in 1932. Being denied commissions by his hometown when he was so close, so talented, and needed work so badly left a festering wound that would later surface during Wright's efforts to build Monona Terrace.[116]

With virtually no commissions the proud Wright resolved to maintain his visibility by lecturing, writing, and exhibiting his work (see Figs. 2.41 and 2.42). In the spring of 1930, for example, he was invited to give the prestigious Kahn Lectures at Princeton University and the following year Princeton published the lectures as a book, *Modern Architecture*. In 1930 Wright was also invited to present his first lecture and exhibit in Madison, a practice that he repeated many times before he died. In 1932 the first edition of his *Autobiography* came out, and in the same year the Museum of Modern Art made Wright a prominent part of an exhibit on modern architecture.[117]

Wright's L-29

*Courtesy Laura Weiss Robinson*

Wright's 810

*Courtesy FLW FDN. 3803.2759*

FIGURE 2.40

### Oh, Those Gorgeous Cords!

Wright was an unabashed connoisseur of cars. During his Chicago years the rising young architect drove a bright yellow two-seater Stoddard-Dayton sports car. During the early 1920s he owned a custom-built Cadillac and a huge Packard. Then Wright fell in love with the L-29 Cord, an American classic. When the car was introduced in 1929, it was the first production automobile to feature front-wheel drive, a breakthrough that allowed the car to be nearly one foot lower than nearly all others. Stylists accentuated its low profile by giving the car a 138-inch wheel base (fifteen inches longer than today's S-class Mercedes sedans) and seven-foot swooping front fenders, sumptuous Spanish leather seats, and a hood as long as a dining room table with all the leaves in place.

It became instantly synonymous with technical sophistication, elegance, wealth, and prestige. Wright was among the first buyers and because of his fame prepared a testimonial at the request of E. L. Cord. Said Wright: "I became a Cord owner because I believe the principle of the front-drive to be logical and scientific, therefore inevitable for all cars. But the proportions and lines of the Cord, too, come nearer [to] expressing the beauty of both science and logic than any car I have ever seen." The photo at upper left shows Wright's restored L-29 cabriolet with the architect's original custom two-tone bright-orange-and-cream paint job.

In 1936 the L-29 was replaced with the 810 series that also sparkled with technical sophistication and style. Cord kept the front-wheel drive but added a nearly two-hundred-horsepower supercharged V-8 that could propel the car at 120 miles per hour, and for a time it was the fastest production car in the country. Once again the stylists wrapped this technically glistening platform in one of the most beguilingly beautiful automobile bodies ever crafted. Of course, Wright had to have one; the black-and-white photo of Wright's 810 convertible coupe was taken at Taliesin West during the winter of 1938–39.

For Madison car buffs, seeing one of Wright's vehicles was a special treat. One day in the early 1930s Grant O. Gale, a U.W. graduate, spotted the L-29 parked on a downtown street. As he stood admiring it, Wright returned and explained its uniqueness. The excited man rushed home to tell his wife about the marvelous car and the special privilege of meeting Wright.

Unfortunately, the honoraria from lectures, royalties from books, and publicity from exhibits produced little money and virtually no new work. In 1932 Wright hit a new low. That January he sent a shipment of valuable Japanese art books to a Chicago friend with instructions to sell them to a dealer to raise enough money to make two payments on his expensive Cord. In the spring things were so bad that Olgivanna wrote to Wright's sister Maginel begging for money (see

Fig. 2.43), and Wright wrote to Lucien M. Hanks, a longtime Madison friend and prominent banker, pleading with Hanks to dissuade a Madison merchant from repossessing the grand piano that stood in the Taliesin living room. Soon after his *Autobiography* was published, the Wrights drove into Madison to have dinner with some close Madison friends. Afterward Wright tried but failed to sell a copy of his new book to the host for $3 so he and Olgivanna could go to a movie. The final indignity in that awful year came when Wright was in Madison on business and got into a fistfight with C. R. Sechrest, a former Taliesin employee to whom Wright owed money. The irate man kicked Wright in the head and broke his nose.[118]

In June Wright turned sixty-five. Almost everybody thought Wright's career was over and for good reason. He had not had a sizable commission built since 1929, and most architects pigeon-holed Wright in the box labeled Elder Statesman Without Portfolio. But the remarkable Wright was anything but finished. At the depth of the worst depression in American history, Wright decided to start a school for architects to be known as the Taliesin Fellowship. Almost everyone was stunned by the audacious move. Where, people wondered, would he get the money?[119]

The Fellowship was unlike any school of architecture the world had ever seen. To the young men and women who read the 1932 prospectus, its primary cachet was the opportunity to become an "apprentice" to Frank Lloyd Wright. Recalling his vigorous learning experience as an employee of Allan Conover nearly a half-century earlier, Wright made learning by doing the Fellowship's modus operandi. Wright wanted his apprentices to have a rich blend of drafting room and field experience that included carpentry, masonry, and job supervision. His ultimate goal was to produce not just outstanding architects but "well correlated human beings" who appreciated and were proficient in at least one of the fine arts — sculpture, painting, pottery, dance, drama, and music. Finally, because Wright believed in the salutary effects of mixing intellectual and physical work, he expected nearly everyone to help maintain Taliesin as a working farm. That meant chopping wood, slopping pigs, milking cows, plowing fields, and repairing buildings. Tuition, room, and board for this unusual head-and-hands curriculum was

initially pegged at $675 per year but was raised the following year to $1,100.[120]

The yeast of Wright's idea worked much faster than he anticipated. William Wesley Peters, an engineering student at the Massachusetts Institute of Technology (MIT), was one of the first apprentices to arrive. Like many who came during the first few years, he was persuaded to join by reading Wright's *Autobiography*. After a short interview Wright admitted the tall man (Peters was six-foot-four) who would play such a large role in the Fellowship, Wright's life, and the architectural practice after Wright's death (see Fig. 2.44). When Wright told Peters he was accepted, the student wrote a check for $675 and handed it to a momentarily flabbergasted Wright. It was more money than he had seen for months. Others joined the Fellowship after reading copies of Wright's prospectus posted on bulletin boards of U.S. schools of architecture. Still others were inspired to join when Charles Morgan, a good friend of Wright's, gave talks at high schools. To get students' attention Morgan would enter auditorium stages doing cartwheels, enchant his audience with his facile artistic skills, and then close with a joy-of-architecture pitch. By December 1932 thirty young men and women from all over the United States and several foreign countries — some experienced architects, some high school graduates, and many in-between — had signed up as apprentices to Wright.[121]

Now that students were arriving, Wright had the formidable task of building the school he had advertised. Both Taliesin and the Hillside school were suffering from years of neglect and vandalism. Although the architect received substantial funds that autumn from the apprentices' tuition, the money was grossly insufficient to transform Taliesin and Hillside into an architecture school. However, he now

had something he had never had before, a small band of willing apprentices, and he supplemented their efforts with neighborhood workmen. Using every money-saving trick he could think of, Wright began to develop his new school, but the first few years were unrelentingly hardscrabble. Apprentices had to cut down trees, saw them into lumber, and keep lime-kiln fires going in winter when temperatures dipped to 20 degrees below zero. Dependent upon fireplaces and wood-fired boilers for heat, the apprentices joked that it took half the group to keep the other half warm. Commissions were both small and scarce, the work arduous, and the hours long.[122]

But ingenuity and sweat went only so far; Wright still needed glass, paint, mattresses, typewriters, lumber, hardware, and many other items that required cash or a willing merchant. He had almost no cash and had already exhausted the goodwill of Spring Green merchants, so Wright drove into Madison and made his pitch. I can put only a small amount down now, explained Wright, but we have projects in the pipeline. When we get our commissions, I will pay you the balance. This strategy persuaded Madison merchants to "sell" Wright what he needed. What the merchants did not realize was that Wright's slender portfolio contained only small-scale projects with tiny commissions (see Fig. 2.45). In effect, Wright was asking Madison merchants to finance his new school, which soon provoked a shameful blizzard of letters between increasingly angry merchants and their debtor (see Fig. 2.46). Wright's misrepresentations generated bad blood with the Madison business community that lingered for decades.[123]

Offsetting the ill will was a clever use of the Taliesin Playhouse, a small theater that Wright and his apprentices built in the old Hillside gymnasium. On Sunday afternoons the Fellowship invited

Then it happened. [The] L-29 Cord cabriolet whizzed up to the curb and slammed to a stop. There was no mistaking the gaunt-faced, white-haired man wearing that flat hat, gray cape, and the habitual flowing tie. He charged out of the Cord car and asked me who I was. I admitted [to] being the culprit who had arranged for the meeting. "Where's the dinner?" My apologies, but the refectory had closed more than an hour before.

"No matter. Where are the young men I am to talk to?" I led Maestro into Richardson House and on to its den. On the way, I told the first resident we passed to assemble everybody. HE is here! The den we entered was a rarely used common room. In the center was a long table which had two equally long sofas backed up to it. There were a half-dozen large chairs around the walls. Overhead was a chandelier — the kind with six bare lightbulbs standing upright around a wrought iron ring. Oh yes, there was a small, unused fireplace stuck into the light brownish gray outer wall.

Mr. Wright asked what we did in this dreadful room. "Well," I explained, "we sit around and read Time magazine or just talk. We really don't come here too much." His response was explosive: "I can see why you don't. This is an awful place, and I refuse to talk here if this is the way it's going to be." I was ready to die. What saved me was that some of the other residents had come into the den by that time. Immediately, Frank Lloyd Wright picked out several of the healthier-looking lads and began to direct furniture moving. "Put that ugly table against the far wall, turn these couches around so they face each other. Bring all those chairs over here and put them in a semicircle facing the fireplace."

"Does that fireplace work?" No one knew because no one had ever tried it. "Get some paper and let's try." We did. It worked. More newspaper plus a few other combustibles were contributed to make a feeble, wavering fire. Then he ordered, "Turn out those glaring overhead lights!" Just about everyone jumped to comply.

That room looked entirely different from the way any of us had seen it before. The six chairs and the two sofas were casually grouped facing the fireplace. The only light in the room came from the colorful, unsteady fire. The den was warm, softly lighted, and filled with young men standing around, eager to find out what would happen next. "Sit down. Sit down," he commanded. The available seats were filled immediately. The less lucky sat on the floor looking at the fire or over their shoulders at the world's greatest living architect who had just performed a miracle with our dingy den.

"What shall we talk about?" he asked, now softly. [All the subjects focused on architecture.] "No," he said, "We aren't going to talk about architecture tonight." His young audience couldn't imagine why not. "I would like to talk about some interesting ideas that I was introduced to in Japan. How many of you are acquainted with Lao Tse?" No response.

"Lao Tse," he began, "was the founder of Taoism." There followed a nearly two-hour discourse about the meaning of Taoism, which, Wright said, was as important in the Orient as Confucianism or Buddhism, even if we students didn't know about it.

Trying to remember that lengthy lecture, which took place more than fifty years ago, I may be wrong on some of the particulars. On one thing, though, I have total recall: Frank Lloyd Wright held two dozen undergraduates spellbound with his intensity about Oriental philosophy. All of us were so consumed by his performance that no one asked any questions when he finished. He was in complete control.

FIGURE 2.42

## Wright Wows U.W. Undergraduates

*Courtesy Reynolds Olsen Tjensvold*

Wright almost always relished the opportunity to speak at the University of Wisconsin and often lectured to SRO audiences at the thirteen-hundred-seat Memorial Union Theater. But sometimes he spoke to much smaller groups. Reynolds Olsen Tjensvold vividly recalls one such occasion when he was a sophomore in the U.W. Experimental College in 1931. All students at the Experimental College were required to arrange for a distinguished person to give an after-dinner talk in the refectory. When Olsen Tjensvold's turn came, he decided to stop the dull parade of professors, so he invited Frank Lloyd Wright. The young man agreed to meet Wright in front of the Adams Hall refectory, but the famous architect failed to show. Too embarrassed to go inside and face the taunts of his classmates, he sat out on "the curb getting colder and colder in that nearly dark, late fall evening," as he detailed in this (slightly edited) account that he wrote many years later.

FIGURE 2.43

**1932 Desperation Letter**

© FLW FDN.; courtesy the Frank Lloyd Wright Home and Studio Foundation

More than any other document, this letter captures the despair the architect and his wife experienced during what was surely the worst year of their lives. Written on May 19, 1932, by Olgivanna to Maginel, Wright's younger sister, the letter mentions three people who require explanation: the Sechrests were Taliesin employees who had sealed off a portion of the house from the Wrights; the Parsons family owned a nearby meat market and was willing to extend credit to the Wrights; and Mrs. Curran was a potential client. Maginel sent the Wrights $30.

Madisonians out to Taliesin (see Fig. 2.47), where for fifty cents they could see foreign films, inspect his Oriental art treasures, drink coffee, and hobnob with Wright. The plan made Taliesin accessible to many and even generated revenue for the Fellowship.[124]

AN EXHILARATING NEW GROOVE

In 1934 Edward Kaufmann, Jr., a twenty-four-year-old Pittsburgh man, read Wright's *Autobiography* and found that its story "flowed into my mind like the first trickle of irrigation in a desert land." That fall Kaufmann traveled to Taliesin and asked Wright to take him on as an apprentice. Wright admitted the young man, and less than a week later the calculating architect sent a book on his architecture to the young man's father, E. J. Kaufmann, a wealthy Pittsburgh businessman. The son joined the Fellowship in October and in November his parents visited Taliesin to see him and to meet Wright. The senior Kaufmann and Wright hit it off and immediately began talking about big Pittsburgh projects and what Wright called "Broadacre City," a visionary, low-density, automobile-based, exurban community. E.J. was intrigued and asked Wright how much it would cost to make a model of this future city that could tour the country. "$1,000," he replied. "Mr. Wright," said E.J., "you can start tomorrow." The following day the Fellowship began work on a 12-by-12-foot model of the "new city." Wright had a promising new patron and client.[125]

In December Wright met with the senior Kaufmann in Pittsburgh to discuss various downtown projects and examine Bear Run, a rustic two-thousand-acre site about seventy-two miles south of Pittsburgh where the businessman was thinking about building a new weekend house. The two men tramped the hilly wooded area until they came to a ravine with a waterfall. "E.J., where would you like to sit?"

asked Wright. The client pointed to a limestone ledge with a view of the waterfall. Little did either man realize that this ledge was about to become the site of "the most famous house of the twentieth century," as the younger Kaufmann later wrote.[126]

In August 1935 Kaufmann sent Wright a retainer for the weekend house, and a month later the Pittsburgh merchant called Wright from Milwaukee where he was attending a meeting. Could he drive over to Spring Green and see plans for the new house? Without hesitation Wright bellowed, "Come along, E.J." There was just one problem: Wright had prepared nothing, and Spring Green was just two-and-a-half hours from Milwaukee by car. Wright went into his studio and began to draw, plans first, elevations second. An apprentice who watched Wright marveled how the "design just poured out of him." What the apprentices were learning was that Wright almost never put pencil to paper until he had worked out the details in his head. When he was finished, he gave the project a name — as he almost always did — but this one was destined to slip into the American lexicon: Fallingwater. Kaufmann arrived about noon and was enchanted by the architect's poetic explanation of the bold cantilevered shape, site-inspired colors, and breathtaking location *over* the waterfall. When it was completed, the house became famous immediately. Except for the Imperial Hotel, no other building produced so much positive publicity so fast, and it could not have come at a more critical time.[127]

In August 1936, in the midst of producing drawings for Fallingwater, Wright landed a second commission that would give yet another boost to his reputation. This was the famous Johnson Wax Administration Building in Racine. Its famous golf-tee-shaped columns in the main workroom soon became one of the most frequently photographed architectural

Wright and Apprentices at Taliesin

*Chicago Historical Society. HB-04414-W*

Proposed Taliesin Fellowship Complex

*© FLW FDN. 3301.001*

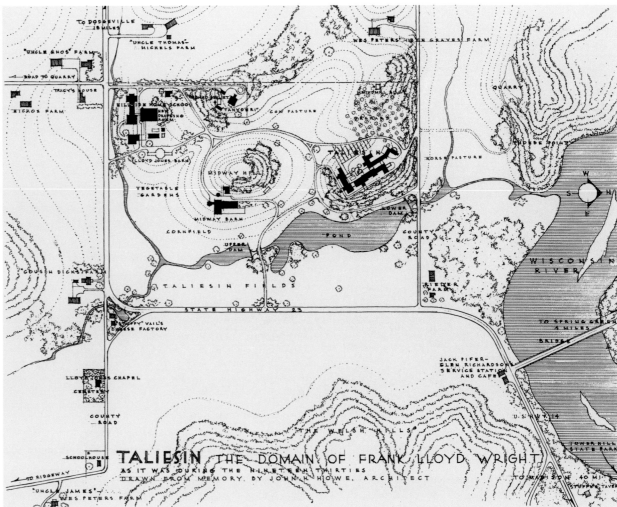

Taliesin and Vicinity

*Northwest Architectural Archives, University of Minnesota Libraries*

## FIGURE 2.44

### Founding the Taliesin Fellowship

Wright's life was the model for the Taliesin Fellowship: he learned the most from working closely with highly skilled professionals, Conover in Madison and Silsbee and Sullivan in Chicago. Thus, when he established the Fellowship in the fall of 1932, he designed the school around the master-apprentice model. This 1937 photo, taken in the Taliesin studio, shows Wright reviewing the work of several apprentices. From left to right are John Lautner (at the table behind Wright), Byron Keeler Mosher, Edgar Tafel, and William Wesley Peters.

The ambitious scale of Wright's new school and its country setting are evident in the color aerial rendering done in 1933. Although it is hard to discern in the rendering, the core building of Wright's new complex was the old Hillside Home School, a progressive country boarding school that his aunts had run from 1887 to 1915. To this central element Wright proposed adding buildings in nearly every direction. The Romeo and Juliet Windmill, a famous Wright design done in 1897, appears on the hilltop in the upper left of the rendering. Only some buildings shown in the rendering were constructed.

The map shows the relationship of Taliesin to other area buildings. Drawn by John Howe, a Wright apprentice, the map shows (from right to left) Taliesin (above the pond), the Midway Barn, and the Hillside Home School, then being refurbished for the Taliesin Fellowship. Unity Chapel (see Fig. 2.16) appears in the lower left corner just above the bend in the road. The bridge across the Wisconsin River still stands, but what Howe showed as a service station and café is now the Frank Lloyd Wright Visitor Center (formerly the Spring Green Restaurant). The road below the three main building complexes is State Hwy. 23.

details in the world. Even before this building was completed, Wright was the beneficiary of still another round of adoring publicity.[128]

What a sudden change in Wright's fortunes! In 1933 the architect was glad to design a small lean-to with windows for a fly-tying "factory," but now, just three years later, he was designing a corporate cathedral. Best of all, he was now able to secure clients with deep pockets who were committed to Wright's designs, clients who could afford huge

cost increases over the architect's estimates. For example, Wright told Kaufmann that Fallingwater would run $20,000 to $30,000, but by the time it was finished, furnished, and its guest house added, the cost had rocketed to $147,000. Similarly, Wright estimated the cost of the Johnson Wax building at $200,000, but when it was completed, the bill stood at $900,000.[129]

The big Johnson Wax project had no sooner begun when Wright received a commission for a much smaller project that forced him to stay within his construction estimate. It was a $5,000 single-family "Usonian" (Wright's acronymic adjective for United States of North America) house for Herb and Katherine Jacobs in Madison (see Fig. 2.48). Compared with Fallingwater and Johnson Wax, the commission may have seemed insignificant to some, but it was one of the more important projects of Wright's career. As Marshall Erdman, one of the architect's protégés, recalled several years later, "One of his greatest ambitions in life ... was ... to build the $5,000 house for the common man.... He saw the affordable house as essential for the survival of democracy." For years the architect had been experimenting with feature-rich houses for people of modest means, but with the Usonian houses Wright gave this goal a powerful push.[130]

Usonian houses, a blend of innovative features and cost-saving construction techniques, included

• Modular design based on standardized grids such as squares, rectangles, triangles, hexagons, or circles

• Concrete slab radiant-floor heating

• A central masonry core containing a fireplace and the house's plumbing

• Variable ceiling heights

• Laminated "sandwich" side walls

• An open-sided carport (Wright argued that cars did not require as much pampering as horses)

• Flat roofs

• Built-in lighting and furniture[131]

When the Jacobses' Usonian house was completed in Madison in 1937, it generated still more kudos for the Spring Green architect. People marveled at the heat coming from the floor, its open plan, efficient layout, and modest cost. And they wanted Wright to design one for them at the same price. Wright would later design more than 170 other Usonian houses, about 140 of which were actually built.[132]

Still other attention-getting projects came to Wright during this period. Using his Fallingwater and Johnson Wax commissions, in late 1937 he bought land outside Scottsdale, Arizona, where he would begin to build Taliesin West in 1938. Also in 1938 he received a commission to prepare a master plan and all the buildings for Florida Southern College in Lakeland, Florida. (The commission was a bitter reminder to Wright that his own alma mater would never give him a crumb of work, yet he could design an entire campus for another university.) And in 1938 Wright started work on the Pew House, dubbed a poor man's Fallingwater (see Fig. 2.49), and a radical residential design based on overlapping circles for Ralph Jester in Palos Verde, California.[133]

Bright as Wright's fortunes appeared in the late 1930s, he was keenly aware that his work was being challenged. In the late 1920s a new group of European architects had developed a fresh new look that emphasized simple geometric shapes, smooth white walls, and almost no ornamentation. By the 1930s examples of this new style were beginning to appear in the United States, including forerunners of the now-common high-rise buildings that resembled

FIGURE 2.46

**Please, Mr. Wright, Pay Your Bill!**

© FLW FDN.; courtesy Richard Frautschi

During the forty-eight years that Wright lived at Taliesin, dozens of Madison-area merchants were stung by Wright's cavalier attitude toward credit. The problem was especially severe during the 1920s, when Taliesin was repossessed by a Madison bank, and in the 1930s, when he was starting his architectural school. During these decades the weekly *Bulletin* of the Madison business organization listed seven judgments against Wright for unpaid bills. In addition, the Wright archives contain dozens of pay-or-else letters from sellers of lumber, paint, clothing, hardware, and other items. Consequently, almost all Madison businesses demanded cash.

The following (edited) correspondence between Irving Frautschi, the owner of a well-known Madison furniture store, and either Wright or his personal secretary, Karl Jensen, shows how exasperating the experience was. This correspondence was triggered by Wright's purchase of more than $400 worth of mattresses for his new Fellowship program in October 1932.

March 16, 1933

Dear Mr. Wright:

You made a very definite promise to me, one-third on December 5th, one-third on January 20th, and one-third on May 10. We have had but one payment of $50.00 on December 5. We would like to hear from you as to the payment you did not make us in January as promised.

Yours very truly,
Irving Frautschi

April 15, 1933

Dear Mr. Jensen:

Several weeks ago I phoned you and it was my understanding that you would have a check sent to us shortly. We must insist upon receiving a payment now or we will have to repossess the goods delivered to you some time ago.

Yours very truly,
Irving Frautschi

April 18, 1933

My dear Mr. Frautschi:

Yes, we are very sorry that the payment you should have had somehow slipped into other channels.... You simply have to see it from our point of view also and to help us out to the best of your ability.... But we will do our best to keep up with your good faith in us and ... [will send] some money within the next 10 days.

Sincerely yours,
Karl Jensen, Secretary

May 16, 1933

Dear Mr. Jensen:

We have your letter of April 18th and wish to state that we did not plan on becoming a partner in your institution. We do expect you to send us a payment of some kind by return mail.

Yours very truly,
Irving Frautschi

June 17, 1933

Dear Mr. Jensen:

We wrote you on April 18th and have had no answer. We have been very much disappointed that Mr. Wright has not kept his promises he made us when he purchased the cots and mattresses. The only payment made was on December 5th and there is $374.00 due us. We will expect a payment now.

Yours very truly,
Irving Frautschi

August 8, 1933

My dear Mr. Frautschi:

Mr. Wright will come in to see you ... the next time he is in Madison — which I expect will be within a week's time.... We can do very little from now to October to pay off accounts as we expect our main income at that time.

Cordially yours,
Karl Jensen

April 10, 1934

Dear Mr. Wright:

I recently had a very interesting visit to Taliesin. I trust that you can make us a payment now on your past due account.

Yours very truly,
Irving Frautschi

August 17, 1935

Dear Mr. Wright:

When I saw you enjoying the circus the other afternoon, I was reminded that you have not made us a payment for a long time. The last payment was on October 17, 1934. We feel that we have been very lenient in allowing this account to run as it has. We would appreciate hearing from you now with a payment.

Yours very truly,
Irving Frautschi

August 1935

My dear Mr. Frautschi:

I know it was wrong to go to the circus when I owed you money, but I thought I owed something to my little daughter too and paid her first. Meanwhile, we are working away for you as best we damn can.

Sincerely,
Frank Lloyd Wright

September 11, 1935

Dear Mr. Wright:

I appreciate you owed your daughter a trip to the circus. I also took my children to the circus, but we are being pushed by our creditors to clean up our bills receivable and I am asking you to send us some kind of payment now.

Yours very truly,
Irving Frautschi

November 20, 1935

Dear Mr. Wright:

As you made no reply to our [last] letter, ... I am arranging with our delivery department to send a truck to Taliesin on November 26th to reclaim the goods sold you on contract.

Yours very truly,
Irving Frautschi

November 21, 1935

Dear Mr. Frautschi:

Mr. Wright is leaving for a lecture tour through Michigan and delivers his last lecture there in Lansing on the evening of November 26th. He returns to Wisconsin on Wednesday — driving — and will stop through Madison with the lecture check in his pocket to make payment "on account."

Sincerely,
Gene Masselink (sec.)

June 16, 1939

Dear Mr. Frautschi:

Mr. Wright has asked me to write you asking you to send us by freight as soon as possible: 6 single beds and mattresses similar to those ordered before and 6 pillows as well.

Sincerely,
Gene Masselink (sec.)

FIGURE 2.47

**Come to Taliesin!**

*Courtesy Taliesin Preservation Commission*

When it came to movies, Madison had plenty of theaters boasting the latest Hollywood films. But if Madisonians wanted to see European art films, they had to travel to large metropolitan areas — Chicago or New York. Or on Sunday afternoons they could drive out to Taliesin and for fifty cents (twenty-five cents for students), the same price of a Hollywood film at a Madison theater, see a classic such as Sergei Eisenstein's *Alexander Nevsky* and an ever-changing menu of art films at Frank Lloyd Wright's Playhouse. To make sure that Madisonians knew about this big-city opportunity, Wright placed a black and white version of this sign in Madison newspapers on the movie page.

The two-hundred-seat Playhouse, a converted gymnasium from the old Hillside Home School, was one of the first construction projects that Wright gave his Fellowship apprentices. That was because he loved the theater and wanted to make drama, instrumental and vocal music, and the best films an integral part of the apprentice experience. Wright also saw the Playhouse as a superb strategy to lure people out to Taliesin, show them models and drawings of the latest architectural projects, and of course make a little money. For an additional dollar Wright or an apprentice would give a tour of Taliesin.

Films changed weekly, were shown on a commercial 35mm theater projector, and were ordered from New York suppliers, including the Museum of Modern Art. Apprentices and their guests would see the films on Saturday night and the general audience would attend on Sunday afternoon.

The Playhouse was a huge success until the University of Wisconsin's new theater in Memorial Union opened in 1939 and began showing art films. Playhouse attendance was further diminished by gas rationing during World War II. The original theater burned in 1952 but was rebuilt and stands today.

FIGURE 2.48

**1936 Jacobs House, the First Usonian**

*Photo by James Dennis*

"We are going into the small house business as a Fellowship next Spring in earnest," Wright wrote to a client in early 1936. Results of that preparation were evident in June 1937 when workers began to build the first Usonian house. The owners, Herb and Katherine Jacobs, naturally wanted the best house, but they had one overriding stipulation: it could not cost more than $5,000. Normally, a house of this price would warrant only ten to fifteen pages of drawings, but for Jacobs I, Wright generated seventy. He did so because it was a prototype for a whole new residential category Wright called "Usonian," his acronymic adjective for United States of North America, and because the house included many features not found in ordinary construction. For example, instead of having unsightly, clanking, space-consuming cast-iron radiators, Wright located loops of pipe in a bed of gravel over which he poured a concrete slab. When hot water was circulated through the pipes, the cement slab radiated heat uniformly and silently. To keep costs low, Wright used cull brick and rubber tile from the Johnson Wax project. To make the fifteen-hundred-square-foot house seem bigger, Wright used floor-to-ceiling glass on rooms facing the backyard. This photo shows the house after an extensive restoration in the 1980s.

glass-walled, steel-fretted blocks. Wright despised everything about this antiseptic style but realized that its leading practitioners were grabbing some of the most coveted academic positions in the country. For example, in early 1937 Walter Gropius, a founder of the famous German Bauhaus, was appointed dean of the School of Architecture at Harvard University, and his colleague, Ludwig Mies van der Rohe, a former director of the Bauhaus, received a similar position at the Illinois Institute of Technology. What galled Wright was that most practitioners of this new school considered him and his "organic" style to be passé. By contrast Wright saw himself as the "most advanced and accomplished *modern* architect in the world" (emphasis added). To this European challenge, Wright threw down the gauntlet: "I intend to be the greatest architect of all time. And I do hereunto affix the red square [the Taliesin logo] and sign my name to this warning." That he was eager to fight this pernicious invasion was evident from his treatment of Gropius and others when they came to Madison to lecture (see Fig. 2.50).[134]

Great credit for Wright's remarkable achievements during the 1930s must go to the Taliesin Fellowship, the enrollment in which had increased to fifty by the fall of 1938 and almost exponentially increased Wright's capacity to turn out architectural work. After several years of working directly with Wright, his extraordinarily talented cadre of young apprentices could take a rough sketch from the master and translate it into beautiful renderings and detailed working drawings. Under Olgivanna's leadership the Fellowship was able to take over almost all responsibility for operating the farm and the household, leaving Wright to concentrate on architecture. To Wright the Fellowship was much more than an aggregation of students and employees. He drew strength from the synergy of the young men and women who surrounded him all

FIGURE 2.49

**1938 Pew House, a Poor Man's Fallingwater**

© FLW FDN. 4012.003

Clarence and Ruth Pew originally hired a Madison architect to design a colonial house for their lot on Lake Mendota in a suburb west of the university. When that proved too expensive, they asked Wright to design one of his modest-priced Usonian houses for them. The couple had seen the extensive publicity about the first Usonian house and hoped the storied architect could produce something they could afford. To keep costs down Wright made extensive use of apprentice labor, cull plate glass, and steel from a demolished building. The architect even appointed Wes Peters, a talented new apprentice, as the contractor and another apprentice, Cary Caraway, as the site supervisor. Even with these money-saving steps, Wright's building came in about 20 percent over the architect's estimates.

But the design, dubbed a "poor man's Fallingwater," shown in this rendering, was a great hit with the Pews and was their home for forty-three years. Like its much more famous Pennsylvania cousin, the Pew House featured a water-oriented wooded lot, cantilevered construction, and large expanses of glass. The exterior of the two-story three-bedroom house was done with native sandstone and wide cypress siding. Drawings for the Pew House were signed September 1938, which meant they were on the drawing boards as Wright was working on Olin Terraces.

day long and they from him. He delighted in their singing, instrumental virtuosity, good humor, and the rollicking times in the big Taliesin living room so reminiscent of the jovial evenings in the parlor of his boyhood home and spirited parties in the Oak Park playroom. And they all called him "Mister Wright." He liked that too.[135]

Throughout 1938 journal and magazine editors sang Wright's praises. Editors of the prestigious professional journal *Architectural Forum* devoted their entire January issue to Wright. In the same month editors of *Time* put Wright on the cover (see Fig. 2.51), which led readers to an applause-filled article inside. In September *Life* ran a feature article on him.[136]

FIGURE 2.50

**Snubbing Walter Gropius**

*Bauhaus Archiv, Berlin*

"Dr. Walter Gropius, an admirer of the work of Frank Lloyd Wright, probably will visit the Taliesin architect during his visit here." That line from a *Wisconsin State Journal* article appeared on November 4, 1937, announcing a lecture by the famous German architect at the University of Wisconsin riled Wright. In fact, Wright had no intention of inviting Gropius to Taliesin or of attending his lecture. What the naive reporter did not realize was that Wright despised the sterile International Style steel-and-glass boxes that Gropius and other European architects were designing. Wright was indignant because he thought these Europeans were stealing ideas from his earlier work and because they considered Wright's work last week's rose. Wright was also exasperated that the Madison Art Association would invite Gropius to spread his aesthetic sedition in Wright's hometown and at his alma mater. Finally, Wright was miffed that Gropius did not have the courtesy to *request* a meeting.

Apparently Wright deliberately encountered Gropius and his entourage at the highly touted Usonian house then being built for the Jacobs family in Madison. As Edgar Tafel reported in *Apprentice to Genius*, Gropius walked up to Wright's car and said, "Mr. Wright, it's a pleasure to meet you. I have always admired your work." Wright retorted, "Herr Gropius, you're a guest of the University and I just want to tell you that they're as snobbish here as they are at Harvard, only they don't have a New England accent." With that putdown, he instructed his driver to pull away.

FIGURE 2.51

**1938 *Time* Cover**

© *1938 Time, Inc.; courtesy FLW FDN. 6005.001*

By 1938 Frank Lloyd Wright was on a roll. The architect had completed Fallingwater (shown in the background of the cover) and was finishing a precedent-shattering corporate headquarters for Johnson Wax (S. C. Johnson and Son) and the first Usonian house, a prototype of an affordable but radically new type of suburban dwelling, for the Jacobs family. For the third time in his tumultuous life, the "greatest architect of the twentieth century" had rebounded from devastating setbacks, said the *Time* writers. That was why the editors put his picture on the cover of the January 17, 1938, issue and gushed his praises in the accompanying article.

*Time* was hardly alone in lauding the controversial architect. *Architectural Forum*, a prestigious professional journal, devoted its entire January 1938 issue to Wright, and *Life* did a feature story on the architect in September.

The stirring crescendo of publicity surrounding Fallingwater, Johnson Wax, the Usonian houses, and others substantially increased the number of cars traveling Highway 14 between Madison and Spring Green (today Highway 14 is the Frank Lloyd Wright Highway). Madisonians flocked to attend Sunday afternoon presentations at the Taliesin Playhouse so they could experience the genius in his famous hilltop lair. Taliesin became a popular destination, and organizations began to schedule tours of the grounds. Prominent Madisonians such as U.W. philosophy professor Max Otto and economics professor Harold Groves eagerly accepted Wright's invitation to give talks to apprentices. Even the Madison press, so recently condescending and critical, began to purr. Betty Cass wove glowing accounts of her visits to Taliesin into her daily column, and beginning in 1934 Madison-area newspapers began to carry a chatty weekly column, "At Taliesin," written by Wright or his apprentices. During this same period Wright and members of the Taliesin Fellowship spent considerable time in Madison shopping, picking up supplies, and attending cultural events.[137]

In just six years Wright had bounced back from his 1932 low and had so many new commissions coming in the door that even the Fellowship-supplemented drafting room could hardly handle them all. Not since the exceptional first decade of the twentieth century and the brief 1923 Imperial Hotel–inspired flurry had Wright's star shown so brightly. The robustly healthy man still rose at 4 A.M., and he amazed apprentices fifty years his junior by climbing to the top of the sixty-foot windmill near Taliesin. By the fall of 1938 the seventy-one-year-old Wright had begun what many consider one of the most creative periods of his life.[138] (For a chronology of the Taliesin years, see Fig. 2.52.)

FIGURE 2.52

# THE EARLY TALIESIN YEARS
# 1911-1938

**1911**
Completes construction of Taliesin and moves there with Mamah by end of the year

Midway Gardens

*Courtesy FLW FDN. 1401.0044*

**1913**
Travels to Japan with Mamah where he negotiates the Imperial Hotel commission

Secures commission for Midway Gardens in Chicago, Illinois, and collaborates with Alphonso Iannelli on ornamental figures (see also Fig. 5.3)

**1914**
Handyman sets Taliesin ablaze killing Mamah, her two children, and four others

Miriam Noel

*Courtesy Phil H. Feddersen*

**1915**
Miriam Noel moves into Taliesin

**1917-22**
Spends extended time in Japan working on the Imperial Hotel

**1922**
Returns from final trip to Japan and obtains divorce from Catherine

Imperial Hotel

*Courtesy FLW FDN. 1509.0698*

**1923**
Establishes architectural office in Los Angeles, California

Designs first of four textile block houses

Imperial Hotel withstands major earthquake in September

Marries Miriam Noel in November

Gordon Strong Automobile Objective Proposal

© FLW FDN. 2505.052

**1924**
Miriam Noel moves out in May and Wright meets Olgivanna Hinzenberg in Chicago

Designs planetarium and a restaurant atop a Maryland mountain for Gordon Strong

**1925**
Olgivanna moves into Taliesin in February

Fire damages Taliesin and destroys some of Wright's original art collection

A daughter, Iovanna, is born to Wright and Olgivanna

**1926**
Wright and Olgivanna arrested near Minneapolis

**1927**
Secures divorce from Miriam Noel

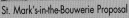

St. Mark's-in-the-Bouwerie Proposal

© FLW FDN. 2905.006

**1928**
Works on Biltmore Hotel in Phoenix and marries Olgivanna in August

**1929**
Major projects including a New York high-rise apartment building (St. Mark's-in-the-Bouwerie) halted by the stock market crash

**1930**
Lectures at Princeton are published in 1931 as *Modern Architecture*

**1932**
Wright's work featured in Museum of Modern Art exhibit

Publishes *An Autobiography* and *Disappearing City*

Establishes Taliesen Fellowship

Johnson Wax Building

*Courtesy S. C. Johnson Wax*

**1934**
Secures commission for Fallingwater near Mill Run, Pennsylvania

**1936**
Designs S. C. Johnson Wax Administration Building in Racine, Wisconsin, and the first (constructed) Usonian house (Jacobs I) in Madison, Wisconsin

Jester House Model

*Courtesy Bruce Severson*

**1938**
Designs circular house for Ralph Jester, Palos Verdes, California

*Life, Time,* and *Architectural Forum* publish feature articles about Wright's work

Begins construction of Taliesin West

Secures commission for Florida Southern campus in Lakeland, Florida

Designs Olin Terraces for Madison, Wisconsin

CHAPTER 3

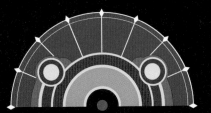

THE DREAM CIVIC CENTER

As a young man Paul Harloff was intrigued by electricity, took courses in electrical engineering at the U.W., and in 1895 opened an electrical contracting business in Madison when he was only twenty-seven. Although much of his business was converting houses from gas to electricity, his firm became sufficiently large and respected to be selected as an electrical contractor for the massive new Wisconsin capitol during its construction from 1906 to 1917.

In the early 1920s Harloff sold his electrical business so he could devote his time to real estate development. He also bought a farm on the south side of Lake Monona with a beautiful view of the city, but getting into town required a long drive around the lake. This time-consuming commute got Harloff to thinking. Why not build a time-saving causeway next to the railroad trestle that cut across the narrow south end of the lake? Why not fill in enough of the lake bed along the city side so that the causeway could be connected to a highway along the isthmus, as proposed by transportation planners in the 1920s? Finally, why not use this filled land along the isthmus as the site for large public buildings such as the city auditorium and the city-county building? This was surely the reasoning that prompted Harloff to get involved in civic affairs and even to approach Frank Lloyd Wright.

Many years later Frank Lloyd Wright claimed that his Monona lakefront project was "a dream I've had ever since I was a little shaver walking the streets of Madison." In fact, the conception of the project was less immaculate and more recent than Wright implied. Two men probably deserve credit for conceiving what is today the Monona Terrace Community and Convention Center: Paul Harloff, a retired electrical contractor, and Wright.[1]

## THE CONCEPTION

One evening in the mid-1930s, both men were at the Park Hotel, a popular hostelry on the south corner of the Capitol Square. Harloff (see Fig. 3.2) was confident that Wright would be interested in doing something big for Madison, and the former contractor had a tantalizing idea for him. As a native Madisonian, Harloff had endured the endless discussions about that most elusive of all public buildings, the auditorium. Now Harloff saw an opportunity to finally build it. He watched trucks dumping rubble into Lake Monona for the future Law Park, and he knew that Mayor James Law was trying to get federal money to build an auditorium-armory, boat harbor, and joint city-county building. The obvious thing to do, Harloff concluded, was to concentrate such facilities on filled land *at the end of Monona Avenue.*[2]

Exactly what Harloff told Wright that night at the Park Hotel is not known, but whatever it was, he persuaded Wright to walk three blocks to Olin Terrace, the small landscaped park at the end of Monona Avenue (see Fig. 3.3). What a night to dream big dreams! A beautiful moon hung in the sky as the two men looked out over Lake Monona. Harloff probably didn't have to say much. As Wright put it, "The possibilities of the site dawned

on me then." In truth, both men were excited. Harloff asked Wright to make a sketch, and Wright said he would — for $1,000. Harloff did not have the money, not then anyway. But sometime in the summer of 1938 — in the middle of the discussions about a joint city-county building — Harloff asked Wright if the offer still stood. Wright said he "was dreadfully busy ... but [he] hated the thought of more office buildings on the Madison streets when that great chance at the foot of Monona [Avenue] lay open." Harloff said he would raise the money from a group of citizens. The deal was strictly verbal.[3]

Wright yearned to do something spectacular for Madison. By 1938 he had already designed fifteen buildings for local clients, but only a few had been built, and none had that big, unambiguous signature quality he craved. Wright had long been exasperated by Madison lakefront buildings that "turned their back on the lake." At the same time, the man whose face adorned the cover of *Time* in January 1938 was angered that Madison's big commercial jobs went to architects he thought were less capable. Wright held a special contempt for the firm of Law, Law and Potter, one of Madison's most prominent and successful architectural offices. Jim Law, the mayor, was a principal in this firm, which virtually assured no love would be lost between Law's firm and Wright. Wright was equally contemptuous of the few national firms that did work in Madison, such as the Chicago firm of Holabird and Root. That so many choice Madison jobs went to these architects made Wright even more eager to do the big Monona lakefront project.[4]

To gain public support for a large public building on filled land at the foot of Monona Avenue, Harloff penned six short, well-written letters to the editors of both newspapers that appeared from July 31 to September 2. In those letters Harloff

FIGURE 3.3

**Olin Terrace,**
**Where Monona Terrace Was Conceived**

*Courtesy City of Madison, photo by Archie Nicolette*

This is Olin Terrace, the half-acre park at the end of Monona Avenue where Frank Lloyd Wright and Paul Harloff conceived what Wright first called "Olin Terraces." The popular street-end park commemorated the incomparable civic leadership of John Olin, who from 1894 to 1909 spearheaded an extraordinary park development program for Madison (see Chapter 1). When the park was completed in 1934, it was an instant hit with Madisonians. The formally landscaped urban oasis offered benches around its perimeter, a small fountain in the center, an inspiring panoramic view of Lake Monona, and, in the opposite direction, a great view of the capitol just three blocks away. Although this photo was taken in the 1980s, the park was virtually the same when Wright and Harloff strolled there in the mid-1930s.

Olin Terrace was not always so picturesque. In the 1860s the land was an undeveloped street end, a rutted, rubbish-strewn hill that sloped abruptly from Wilson Street to Lake Monona. Because the city would not pay to maintain the publicly owned property, neighborhood homeowners won permission to landscape the eyesore and paid the costs.

Olin Terrace and the adjoining elegant Madison Club gave a decidedly patrician view of Madison. According to Frank Custer, a Madison historian, fifty feet below the white linen tablecloths and cut flowers of the Madison Club's dining room was a hobo jungle where mothers forbade their children to go. During the Great Depression men "wearing shabby, worn clothing, dust covered shoes, and battered hats" cooked Mulligan stew "over a fire of twigs and coal dropped from passing steam locomotives."

A totally different Olin Terrace was built in the 1990s to accommodate the Monona Terrace Community and Convention Center. The surface of the new entrance plaza stands about seven feet above the grassy area shown in this photo.

---

urged the city to take the $175,000 it was planning to spend to acquire the site for the city-county building on Monona Avenue (see Fig. 1.36) and use it to fill and develop a big beautiful lakefront park like Milwaukee's Juneau Park. Harloff calculated that a filled lakeshore site also would provide enough space for a six-lane highway, a new civic auditorium, city hall, and county courthouse.[5]

Sometime around the middle of September 1938 Harloff drove out to Taliesin to meet with Wright but was disappointed by the visit. Harloff thought that Wright was much less enthusiastic about the park and building plan than he had been when they had met several years earlier. However, Wright did promise to meet with Bill Evjue, publisher of the *Capital Times*, and Lucien M. Hanks, a prominent banker, just a few days later and to call Harloff after that meeting. Harloff assumed Wright wanted to consult these two prominent business leaders on the political and economic feasibility of the big

project. Wright's first sketches of this building (Fig. 3.4) were almost certainly done before or during this meeting.

Wright never did call Harloff when he said he would, so on September 22 Harloff wrote the architect saying, "Kindly let me know at your earliest convenience just how you feel toward this project ... and weather [*sic*] or not you really are to do any work on it." Harloff had good reason to be concerned. If the federal government approved the $900,000 grant for the city-county building, construction had to begin by December 31, just three months away.[6]

On September 28, six days later, Harloff opened the *Wisconsin State Journal* and learned that Wright had given a truculent talk to the Madison Lions Club at the Loraine Hotel the previous day and that he had described the plan. As Harloff was about to learn, being a client was more a convenient cover for Wright than an obligation to Harloff.[7]

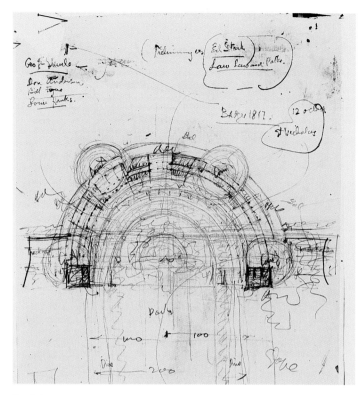

Sketch 1

© FLW FDN. 3909.023

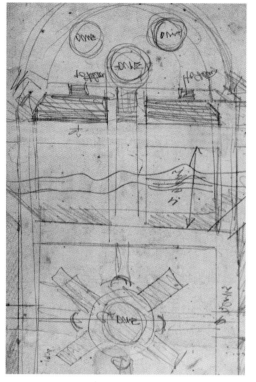

Sketch 2

© FLW FDN. 3909.005

FIGURE 3.4

## 1938 Concept Sketches for Olin Terraces

At first glance sketch 1 looks like a doodle. In fact, it was probably Wright's first concept sketch, done sometime in September 1938. Closer study shows that the concept was already well advanced in Wright's mind. He had established the semicircular shape, its axial relationship with the capitol, the location of a balcony *(bal)* extending around the edge, concentric rings suggesting tiered levels, four symmetrically located circular elements labeled *courts* (presumably for city and county), and the distance separating the entrance drives.

The sketch also captures Wright's lifelong practice of using sketches, plans, blueprints, and renderings as notepads. The name *George Steinle* in the upper lefthand corner was probably mentioned by Paul Harloff, perhaps during one of his visits to Taliesin in the fall of 1938, as one of several Madison businessmen who had agreed to underwrite Wright's initial plans.

*Don Anderson, Bill Evjue,* and *Lucien Hanks* were all men whom Wright told Harloff he would consult about the political realities of the project. Anderson was associate publisher of the *Wisconsin State Journal,* Evjue was the publisher and editor of the *Capital Times,* and Lucien M. Hanks was a Madison banker and former high school classmate of Wright's. The time, *12 o'clock,* and *St. Nicholas,* a popular restaurant just off the Capitol Square, were probably the time and place that Wright was to meet with Anderson, Evjue, and Hanks. *Ed Starck* was an architect with the firm that had produced the official design for the new city-county building. Why Wright wrote the name of the architectural firm Law, Law and Potter on the sketch is not known.

Sketch 2 shows how the concept was evolving in Wright's mind. Beneath its apparent simplicity are great depth, complexity, and originality — indeed, the essence of the project. With just a few strokes of his graphite pencil Wright captured the building's form, its powerful but subordinate relationship to the capitol, and the location of the three domes, the most prominent rooftop design features. Wright's extension onto the top of his building of the two streets flanking the capitol grounds and the avenue between shows his intention to keep the building low relative to the capitol and surrounding buildings. The words *to station* appear under the small darkened rectangular shapes on either side of the central dome, clear evidence that Wright was including a railroad station. Wright later positioned banks of elevators where these rectangles are located.

With stirring gestures and words but no drawings, Wright had announced his "new deal" building. Imagine that you are standing on Monona Avenue looking toward the lake, Wright instructed the Lions. Now imagine a sweeping, flat, circular, parklike terrace extending out from Olin Terrace without cutting off the view. Beneath this expanse would be the new courthouse, the new city hall, and a union depot. (The *Journal*'s story did not mention an auditorium.) Inside this "great civic expression" would be ample parking, and along the lake side of the building would be a parkway for cars. Wright called his new design "something really fine," something truly representing the "America of the future."[8]

Perversely, Wright spent most of his Lions Club talk lambasting Madisonians. He accused Madison of being "a little high-browed community of provincials." For any Lion in the room who wasn't sure what *high-browed* meant, Wright defined it as "a man educated beyond his capacity." He said there wasn't "enough civic spirit in the community to build a new county-city building as it should be built." He called the capitol building a "hangover" marred by "senseless columns" and "idiotic domes." He described the new State Office Building as a monstrosity. He labeled the houses most people lived in as "lousy little boxes." He took a swipe at the University of Wisconsin, saying that "most university graduates will go to their graves without having a single thought." Wright concluded his harangue with one final charge: "You have done nothing for this city that nature did not do for you." As someone in the audience of another Wright lecture would remark, "He was more popular before he spoke than afterwards."[9]

Joe Jackson surely groaned when he read the *Journal* account of Wright's talk. Just when the civic impresario had the city-county building on

Monona Avenue and the auditorium-armory at the Conklin site poised to proceed, Wright had strutted into town and announced a plan that could kill both.

Wright finally responded to Harloff's tell-me-where-the-project-stands letter on October 1. He began by telling Harloff that he had mentioned his name at the Lion's Club but that the reporter left this out. More important, "I am working something up and you will have it soon. So cheer up."[10]

The trail of crumbs left by Wright and Harloff on this project strongly suggests that Harloff drove out to Taliesin again on October 28 or 29 to see Wright's drawings for the project for the first time. Harloff must have been pleased by what he saw. Wright and his staff had completed several new presentation drawings, some of which he evidently gave to Harloff, who brought them back to Madison.[11]

The hour was late. The Dane County Board of Supervisors was scheduled to meet on Wednesday, November 2, and the question that dominated the agenda was whether to go ahead with the joint city-county building that city leaders were promoting (see Fig. 1.36). The federal deadline to start construction was now less than sixty days away.

FIFTEEN MINUTES FOR FRANK LLOYD WRIGHT

Joe Jackson could hardly wait for the county board meeting. As he told readers of his foundation *Bulletin*, there was just "one remaining step yet to be taken" by the county supervisors and that was to "vote acceptance of the PWA [Public Works Administration] award" and approve the county's share of the bonds. He predicted the vote would be "practically unanimous." The *Wisconsin State Journal* called the joint building "seemingly certain." If Jackson and the *Journal* were right, Wright faced the unenviable task of ambushing a well-armed caravan.[12]

November 2, 1938, was an unseasonably warm fall day in Madison. Temperatures inched into the sixties as members of the county board converged on the stately red brick courthouse just one block off the Capitol Square for their regular monthly meeting. By 9:45 A.M. most of the eighty-two supervisors had walked up the broad central stairs to the drab spittoon-equipped second-floor meeting room where they mingled, exchanged greetings, and strategized.[13]

Promptly at ten Dane County chairman Frank A. Stewart banged his gavel and called the meeting to order. Stewart, a merchant from Verona, a small town west of Madison, had been chairman for ten years and ran the board with an iron hand. The supervisors took their assigned seats, simple oak classroom chairs with writing surfaces on the right arm. The room quieted. During the morning session the board dispatched several agenda items and then took a recess until 3 P.M. Everyone understood that this was when the supervisors would debate the big question of the city-county building.

Stewart gaveled the meeting back to order on time and read a letter from Madison mayor Law confirming that the federal grant would pay for the Monona Avenue site for the city-county building. Then Stewart called on Supervisor Paul Robinson of Sun Prairie, a small town just east of Madison, who was a staunch opponent of the joint building. Robinson announced that Frank Lloyd Wright was present and would like to speak "on his plan for building a civic center extending into Lake Monona."[14]

Wright was well known to the board, but because he was not on the agenda the entire board had to approve Robinson's request. Several supervisors thought Wright should not speak because what he had to say might influence the vote on the joint building bonds scheduled for later that afternoon.

Chairman Stewart imperiously ruled that the subject of Wright's talk had nothing to do with this agenda item and that Wright could therefore proceed. Stewart knew better. The day before the board met, Stewart had inspected Wright's plans in Harloff's downtown Madison apartment. Stewart, also a strong opponent of the joint building plan, apparently concluded that Wright's plan would be a tempting red herring and that the internationally famous architect would persuade at least some supervisors to vote against the joint building proposal. (Stewart and Robinson were leading members of the board's rural bloc, which was generally opposed to city initiatives and especially the plan to share a building.) Stewart's ruling to allow Wright to speak was challenged. Thirty-nine voted in favor of allowing him to speak, thirty-nine against. Stewart broke the tie with an aye.[15]

Wright strode to the front of the boardroom, stepped up on the raised platform where the chairman was seated, and positioned his presentation drawings so that supervisors could see them. Before Wright began speaking, Stewart imposed a fifteen-minute limit, and Wright shot back, "Don't you think you're extravagant?"[16]

Wright began, "I came here to represent the people. I have no interest — no ax to grind outside of the fact that I am a native of this region and I am ashamed of the fact that Madison has never done anything for Madison. God did a good deal for this region — plenty, but one has only to look around to see how little cooperation He got from man." Continuing in a more caustic vein, he snarled, "We don't need another office building. Why spend the people's money to build another congested building in a congested site?"[17]

Using the new presentation drawings that appear in Figures 3.1 and 3.5, the jaunty architect began to explain "Olin Terraces," a name he had selected for four reasons: his admiration of John Olin, the visionary civic leader who almost singlehandedly had established Madison's park system; appreciation for Olin's role in securing one of Wright's first commissions after going into private practice (Figs. 2.1 and 2.25, the Madison public boathouses); his calculation that Olin's revered name would help sell the project to city and county leaders; and his desire to create a grand extension to the small street-end park already known as Olin Terrace.

Above all else Olin Terraces was Wright's exuberant, depression-defying prescription for Madison's needs. In addition to the government offices, courts, and jails that city and county officials wanted, Wright told the supervisors — and the city officials who crowded into the back of the room — that they needed a five-thousand-seat, air-conditioned sloped-floor auditorium, a union railroad depot, a marina for five hundred boats, and a parking garage for forty-five hundred cars. Wright touted the features of each component, the wondrous things it would do for the community, and said the complex could be built for just $2.7 million — only $700,000 more than the joint city-county building then under consideration. Wright had their attention.[18]

A few minutes later the board adjourned to inspect the official site along Monona Avenue and to determine once and for all whether it was too congested, as Wright and Harloff argued. Immediately after the tour the supervisors voted the joint building down by a single vote. It was a great victory for Stewart's rural bloc and a conspicuous defeat for joint building backers.

Significantly, Wright remained for the entire afternoon meeting and held court after the supervisors adjourned. As one reporter put it, "No other outsider ... ever drew such an interesting circle around him after a speech." In fact, after the meeting adjourned Wright loosed his heaviest artillery: "When I heard of this monstrous state office building with its back to the lake, I could hardly sit still. But when I heard that you were contemplating another of these things, I didn't sit still.... This project I have planned would put Madison out in the front of progress where it belongs. But maybe Madison can't look ahead 10 years. It is too provincial, backwater, convention[al], highbrow, smug, and satisfied." All this was sweet music to rural supervisors' ears. When Wright was finished, "he cocked on his blue beret and strutted out of the old courthouse," as one reporter noted.[19]

Moments later Wright was walking down Carroll Street near the Park Hotel when two newsboys spotted him. The *Capital Times* already had provided extensive coverage of Olin Terraces with an advance story, and now the *Wisconsin State Journal*, the paper the boys were selling, was carrying a similar big advance story. The newsboys recognized Wright and, as he walked by, one of them said, "That sure is a swell plan y'got here, Mr. Wright. We hope it goes through."[20]

Olin Terraces was terribly exciting to Madisonians — and to Wright. Never before had anyone seen a city hall, county courthouse, union depot, auditorium, parking garage, municipal marina, and lakeshore parkway all in one building. Coming as it did, when the economic landscape was still painted drab depression gray, Olin Terraces was fresh, inspiring, and intriguing. People saw the glint of Wright's gold.

The next day the newspapers dubbed it the "Dream Civic Center" and the name stuck, but it forever changed the local definition of the term *civic center*. Up to this time the term had meant a collection of government buildings in the center of the city. After Wright introduced Olin Terraces, however,

civic center meant a megastructure that contained a mix of government, cultural, recreational, and even transportation facilities. Wright's definition of *auditorium* — a sloped-floor concert hall and not the flat-floor arena that the business community and sports enthusiasts wanted — fueled a long-running controversy.

Newspaper accounts said Wright had played the decisive role in the defeat, and Joe Jackson agreed. In his *Bulletin* report he blamed the defeat of the city-county building on "too many outside forces," a transparent reference to Wright. For the next month Jackson, Law, and all the probuilding forces tried just about everything to get the county to rescind its vote. Charges and countercharges flew. City supervisors infuriated rural representatives by calling them "dirt farmers" and "cornhuskers." Newspapers editorialized about how supervisors representing thirty-eight thousand rural constituents had the same number of votes as supervisors representing seventy-five thousand city residents. Madison leaders demanded the hide of "machine boss" Stewart and even threatened to secede from Dane County.[21]

Then, amid all the name calling came a bizarre development: Mayor Law denounced the joint building. He said building costs would "skyrocket taxes which were already too great for taxpayers."[22]

On November 25, just two days after Law's inexplicable flip-flop, the county board did a flip-flop of its own. The board approved the Monona Avenue site and funding for the joint building with margins of 14 and 10 votes, respectively, But the vote was meaningless; federal officials had already reallocated the $900,000 grant reserved for the $2 million building. Humpty-Dumpty had fallen off the wall and could not be reassembled.[23]

The joint city-county building was not the only casualty tallied in November 1938. On November 16

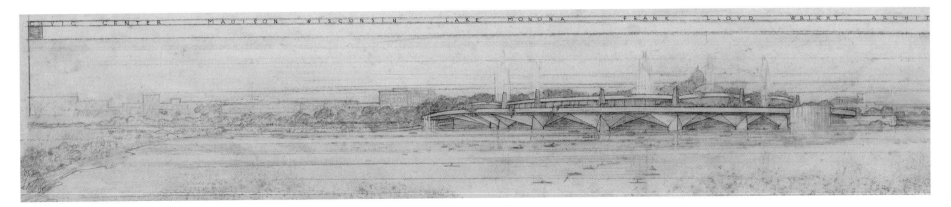

Perspective of Olin Terraces from Lake Monona

© FLW FDN. 3909.004

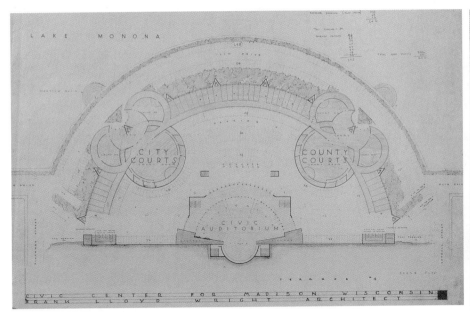

Plan Showing Ring Road, Government Facilities, and Auditorium

© FLW FDN. 3909.021

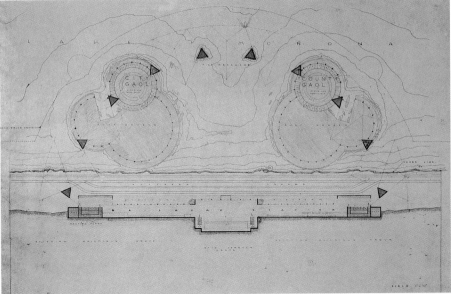

Plan Showing Jail, Boathouses, and Railroad Depot

© FLW FDN. 3909.022

FIGURE 3.5

## 1938 Drawings for Olin Terraces — the Dream Civic Center

### PERSPECTIVE FROM LAKE MONONA

The original 8-by-36-inch colored pencil drawing on tracing paper shows the massive cantilevers but does not fully reveal their scale. Where they enter the water, they are about 125 feet apart. The lower ring is the circumferential lakeshore drive, the upper ring is the edge of the garden level; between them, but only partially revealed, is the three-story glass wall that would surround city and county offices. The rendering also shows the two waterfalls, one in the right foreground and one in the left rear, that carry fountain water back to the lake.

### PLAN OF ROAD, GOVERNMENT FACILITIES, AND AUDITORIUM

This plan shows the four-lane lakeshore drive, the first of three levels of city and county offices around the lake edge of the building, city and county

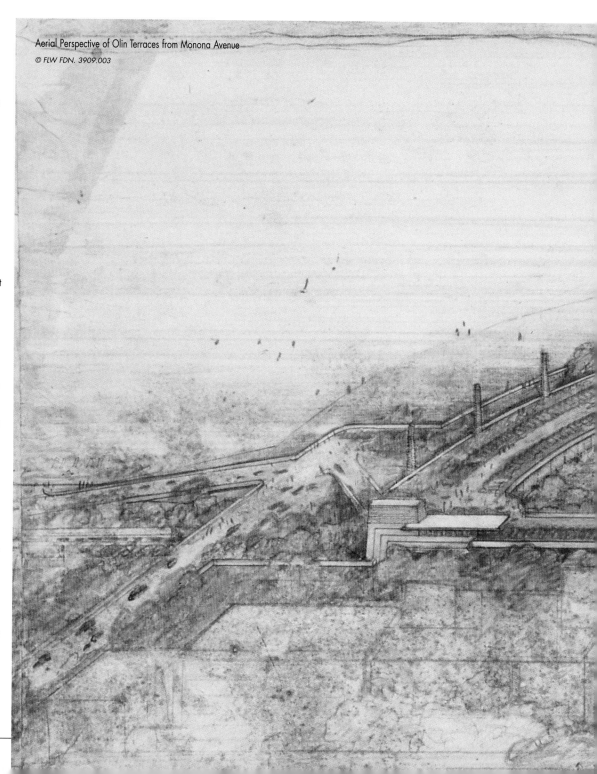

Aerial Perspective of Olin Terraces from Monona Avenue
© FLW FDN. 3909.003

(Fig. 3.5 cont.)

courts, and the five-thousand-seat "civic auditorium." The space between the office facilities and auditorium is parking. The two blue semicircular trays on the outer edge of the lakeshore drive provide a discharge point for the waterfalls.

## PLAN OF JAIL, BOATHOUSES, AND DEPOT

The ten triangles (twenty feet on each side) that extend around the perimeter of Olin Terraces were foundations for the massive cantilevers shown in the aerial perspective. On the lakeward side just above the waterline Wright provided two jails (Wright always preferred the British spelling, *gaol*), one for the city and one for the county, where most prisoners enjoyed lake views. The two overlapping circles on the land side of each jail were marina facilities with storage capacity for five hundred boats. To accommodate the railroad depot, Wright kept the four tracks then running along the lakeshore but added a depot parallel to them. Figure 3.13 shows a cross-section of this 1938 plan.

## PERSPECTIVE FROM MONONA AVENUE

Although the original 17-by-46-inch rendering is stained, torn, and mildewed, it still captures the grandeur of Wright's original vision for Olin Terraces. Measurements from plans show that the semicircular megastructure ran for about one thousand feet along the lakefront and jutted out into the lake about 485 feet from the railing on the lake end of Olin Terrace (see Fig. 3.3). On the heavily landscaped roof Wright provided "civic gardens" where "a thousand tables might be set" for concerts and public events.

Wright's fundamental design premise for Olin Terraces was that it should be deferential and complementary to the capitol. That was why Wright based Olin Terraces on the circle, the shape of the base of the capitol dome, and made the design perfectly symmetrical. That was why the only architectural elements extending above the roof plane were domes, each dutifully echoing the capitol. That was also why the architect kept the roof's surface at fifty-six feet above the lake, the same level as the Wilson Street sidewalk. Wright argued that this level would preserve the lake view from the capitol and allow the roof to function as a huge public extension of its grounds — a design goal in sympathy with what Stout, Olin, and Nolen all had advocated. Technically, Wright was correct in asserting that Olin Terraces would preserve the lake view from the capitol, but that was because its grounds stood about seventy-five feet above the lake. However, for a person standing on the Wilson Street sidewalk looking out over the roof terrace, the lake would not be visible for nearly seven thousand feet.

As anyone who has studied Wright knows, the man had a wonderful, creative, but contrarian streak that seldom failed to delight and surprise. For Olin Terraces the seven large domes shown here exemplify these qualities. With these domes Wright sneaks in the sizzle and shows what fun he can have with an idea. Unlike the heavy, opaque capitol dome, all seven of Wright's domes would be light and transparent, a wispy steel frame filled with glass. Three would lie above the city hall (left), three over the county courthouse (right), and one in the center, about sixty feet in diameter, over the auditorium. Unlike the capitol dome, which was crowned by a gilded figure, all seven of Wright's domes were designed to display large pieces of sculpture inside. Wright designed the domes as skylights for courtrooms below. Unlike the capitol dome, which was illuminated at night from outside, all of Wright's domes would be illuminated from the inside. And if this was not enough, Wright intended all his glass domes as grand fountains. His idea was to pump lake water over them and then through a system of rooftop channels back into the lake in two massive waterfalls, shown in the aerial perspective from Lake Monona.

Pedestrians entered the megastructure through the existing Olin Terrace, shown in the center as a sunken plaza. Motorists would enter the building from roads on the capitol side and from two ramped roads along the new lakeshore drive.

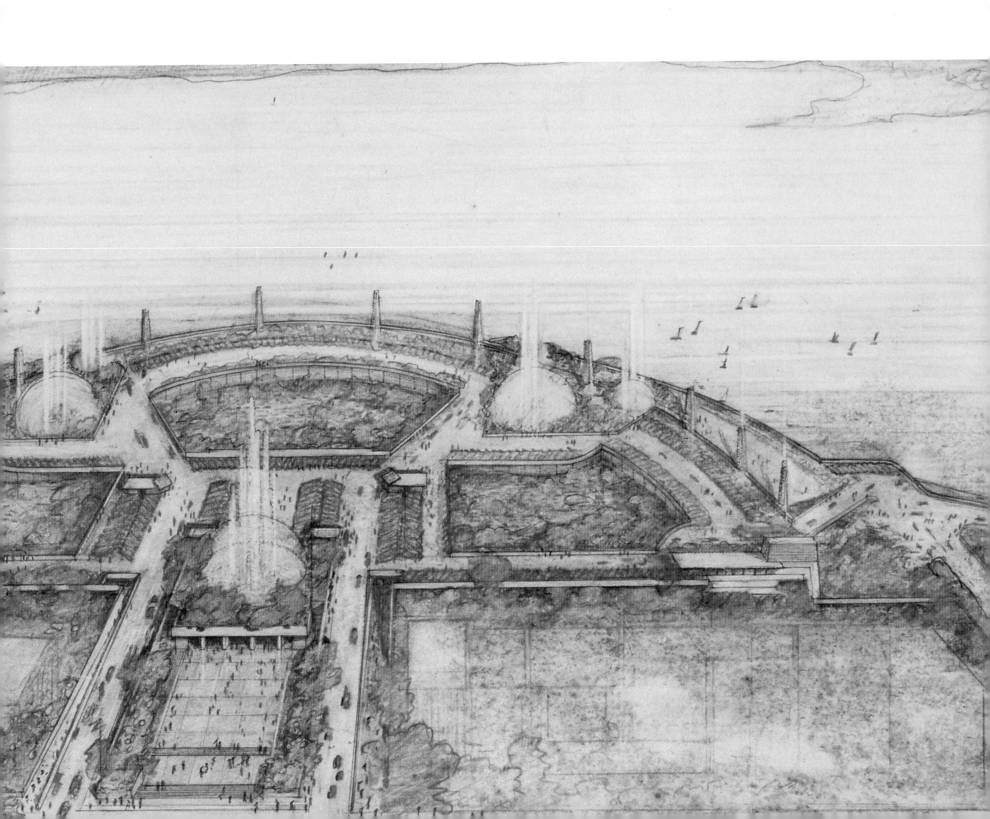

city engineer T. F. Harrington had announced that the Conklins were refusing to give the city permission to build the breakwater in front of their property. This turn of events was particularly frustrating for Jackson because the federal grant for the breakwater had already been approved. Jackson realized this problem had only one solution and that was for the city to buy the Conklin property.[24]

Equally devastating was the rejection in December 1938 of Madison's grant application for construction of the auditorium-armory (see Fig. 1.35). According to the federal agency's lawyers, Wisconsin cities did not have the statutory authority to issue revenue bonds, the form of municipal borrowing that the city was counting on for 55 percent of the project's cost. Jackson rushed into action. Working with the mayor, the Wisconsin League of Municipalities, and other allies, he almost singlehandedly and in less than six months got the legislature to give Wisconsin cities the power to issue revenue bonds. But he was too late; the auditorium-armory would have to wait.[25]

PICKING UP THE PIECES

Wright enjoyed his appearance before the Dane County board. Throwing punches at some of his favorite targets delighted his pugilistic heart, and presenting one of his bold new creations satisfied his artistic soul. Besides, the local newspapers could not have been more generous or more favorable in their coverage of Olin Terraces. He was clearly pleased with his performance in the role of spoiler on the city-county building.

But was it Wright who had scuttled the joint city-county building? Wright thundered against the project as the great drama was nearing its climax, and his criticisms of the joint building played well with the rural wings of the county board. But the

question really is whether Wright's eleventh-hour appearance altered any votes. The record shows that Stewart's rural bloc was solidly united against the joint building. Although some who voted against it may have done so in the hope that they would have a chance to vote for Olin Terraces later, this doesn't seem likely. The rural-urban lines were sharply drawn among supervisors, and Olin Terraces was *not* on their agenda; at best it was an interesting, even meritorious, diversion.

In fact, the joint building failed because it activated the deep-seated rural-urban schism. Rural supervisors had about the same number of votes on the board as their urban counterparts, even though they had 50 percent fewer constituents, and Stewart ran this bloc — many called it a machine — with undeniable skill. Into this situation came the City of Madison, led by Law, and the business elite, led by Jackson. Seldom had the board been subjected to such a well-orchestrated power play, and the rural bloc resented it. Although the county board had acquiesced to the city's joint building initiative, the coalition of the two governments was awkward, fragile, and reluctant. Rural supervisors were convinced that the Monona Avenue site was too small for the big joint building and that they would not find a place to park in its basement. Though seldom voiced, the deciding argument for rural supervisors was their perception that the proposed joint housekeeping arrangement with the city would dilute the county's power, visibility, and prestige. At this point in the history of the Dane County board the very concept, much less a specific version, of a joint building was hard to sell.[26]

Still, the question lingers. Did Olin Terraces ever have a chance of succeeding in 1938? Definitely not. Harloff and Wright tried to do too much, too late, too ineptly. Wright was offering much more

than the city and county were prepared to handle, which alone was sufficient to kill the plan. The city and county had agreed to work together for a joint city-county building but *not* a union railroad depot, marina, auditorium, and forty-five-hundred-car parking facility. The two government units were talking about a 175,000-square-foot office building, and Wright was talking about a megastructure of one million square feet. His proposal also suffered because no one was familiar with it and because drawings were probably not even completed until late October. No more than a handful of county supervisors had seen the plans for Olin Terraces before the meeting. So far as is known, no city official saw the plans until November 2. Even if Wright had completed working drawings by that date, the city, county, and federal governments could not have agreed to proceed in time to start construction before the December 31 deadline.[27]

In summary, the last-minute initiative by Harloff and Wright left no time for reasonable preparation. It required them to act as outsiders and without official sanction. It prevented them from developing effective support groups and champions. Paradoxically, it had the advantage of giving opponents no time to organize, one of the few times in the long history of this project that this was true. In the end, Harloff and Wright had no chance.

Still another factor doomed Olin Terraces: Wright's withering criticism of Madisonians during his Lions Club speech on September 27 and in his remarks to the county board on November 2. The outspoken architect sometimes blamed an imp that resided in his mind, but the real reason is much less sinister. It was undiluted bad judgment.

Why did Wright so thoroughly insult the very people he was asking to build his masterpiece? Clearly, Wright was eager to make a grand architectural statement in his hometown, the capital of his beloved home state. At the same time he was frustrated because he was never asked to do big important jobs in the city. Consequently, Wright had an abundance of free-floating anger toward Madison, and he seemed incapable of presenting Olin Terraces without indulging in a little Madison bashing. But anger was hardly the only emotion that Wright felt about Madison. Behind the anger was an unmistakable love for his hometown. Indeed, it was this combination of opposing feelings that fueled Wright's passion for this project and made him so emotional when he spoke about it.

In analyzing Olin Terraces, one final topic deserves attention: the unusual relationship between Wright and Harloff. Technically, Harloff was the client because he had agreed to raise $1,000 from a group of businessmen in exchange for which Wright agreed to produce plans. Ironically, Wright produced the plans, but Harloff failed to raise the money. In fact, he apparently raised only $250, and Wright's secretary had to send Harloff two letters asking him for the balance. Olin Terraces was not exactly a pro bono project, but it was a close cousin.[28]

That Wright used Harloff to legitimize his passion for the project is clear from a debate that arose immediately after Wright made his county board appearance. Some board members charged that businessmen had paid Wright to go before the board, but in a letter to a Dane County supervisor Wright said it was "silly for anyone to think or say I was paid to come before the Dane county board.... I was asked by Paul Harloff to go — but I went on my own." Later in the same letter Wright said: "I regarded myself as retained by a public spirited group of Madisonians interested in a real development of the Olin [Nolen] plan for a civic center for Madison." (In citing Olin and not Nolen, Wright

was apparently trying to focus attention on the large role that Olin had played in the project.) Wright was naturally eager to deny that he was paid to make the actual board appearance, but his denial belies what may well have been his intent: to have a client to legitimize a project that Wright was eager to do. In the debate about who hired whom for what, Wright forgot that his real client was the Dane County board, and government clients, as the headstrong architect was about to learn, require very different treatment than private clients.[29]

That Harloff was little more than a cover is also buttressed by Wright's awareness that neither Law's nor Jackson's business elites would ever invite Frank Lloyd Wright to do a job in Madison. Wright therefore concluded that the only way to accomplish his goal — designing a great signature project for his hometown — would be to force himself into the process and hope that "the people" would see the superiority of his design. In truth, Harloff was Wright's only ticket to a dance the architect was eager to attend.[30]

Although the Olin Terraces initiative had failed, Wright did not appear to be discouraged. His sparks had fallen on soggy tinder, but the architect was confident the tinder eventually would dry and burst into flame. This was evident from several actions Wright took after the November 2 meeting.

First, Wright prepared for Olin Terraces what may well be the most extraordinary presentation drawing of his career: an 8-by-16-foot color bird's-eye perspective, showing the Olin Terraces project from Monona Avenue. At least two Madisonians saw this unique drawing, Betty Cass, a friend of Wright's and a columnist for the *Wisconsin State Journal*, and P. B. Grove, a member of the Dane County board. Cass described the drawing as a masterpiece in her "Day by Day" column of

November 15, and Grove thought "it was so beautiful and wonderful" that "it should be placed in the rotunda of the Capitol so that people could stand on the balcony and look down on it."[31]

Second, Wright tried to set up a meeting with Jackson to show him the Olin Terraces plans. Wright had almost no chance with Jackson, but he tried. Wright finally tracked him down at the Madison Club, but Jackson told Wright he was not interested in seeing the plans, that he "resented the 11th hour interference," that he was "completely sold on the dual building plan, and that he considered the matter 'closed.'"[32]

Third, Wright accepted an offer from a U.W. professor of landscape architecture to have a student prepare a scale model of Olin Terraces (see Fig. 3.6). Models, Wright well understood, were often an architect's most effective sales tool.[33]

Fourth, Wright sent a set of Olin Terraces plans to James Todd, the contractor for the new Rockefeller Center in New York City. Wright said he wanted Todd to independently estimate the cost of Olin Terraces, but he also wanted him to check the feasibility of the daringly long cantilevered spans Wright had incorporated in his plans. Todd estimated that Olin Terraces would cost about $3 million to build in 1939.[34]

Fifth, Wright tried to encourage members of his hometown church, the First Unitarian Society, to champion Olin Terraces. Wright was confident this group would be a bastion of support and, as it turned out, it did rally behind him — though not as quickly as Wright hoped. The Unitarians offered Wright their pulpit on Sunday, December 4, 1938, and arranged to have the talk simultaneously broadcast on WIBA, a radio station owned by the *Capital Times*. About three hundred people crowded

"Good idea. Go to it." Those were Wright's instructions to Franz Aust, a U.W. professor of landscape design, who had just volunteered a graduate student, Charles Frothingham, to build a detailed model of Olin Terraces. Although Wright's plan had been rejected by the Dane County board, he had no intention of giving up. Indeed, he had just begun to fight, and he well understood that a model would be an outstanding sales tool for a project like this.

Frothingham began work in March 1939 and spent about two hundred hours on it. Wright did not see the model until the Fellowship returned from Arizona in the spring, and he wasn't happy with the result. Frothingham had apparently exaggerated the height of the building so members of the Fellowship had to spend another 220 hours to fix it. The completed table-sized model shown in the photograph was exhibited in a downtown Madison store and on the university campus but never as much as Wright had hoped. What happened to the model is not known.

into the sanctuary that morning and gave Wright prolonged applause at the end. Wright urged his audience to form a citizens' committee to push for Olin Terraces to overcome the paralyzing influence of timorous politicians. However, with the exception of a letter to a high-ranking federal government official, the Unitarian speech produced little.[35] (Significantly, Wright rejoined the society the very Sunday he gave his talk, but he seldom attended weekly services. However, he did maintain a frequent and cordial relationship with its minister, W. Rupert Holloway.)

Clearly, these steps were not taken by a man waving a white flag. They were the undisguised preparations for another battle on another day, a battle that would come more quickly than Wright thought.

## COUNTERATTACK

Sitting in the back of the Dane County supervisors' room while Wright made his impassioned plea for Olin Terraces were two men who probably hoped that Wright would have a fatal heart attack: Joe Jackson and Ladislas Segoe. Segoe was in Madison to do some work on his master plan when Jackson suggested that they go to the courthouse for the big meeting. Of course, Jackson wanted to be there for what he expected would be a major triumph.[36]

Jackson never forgave Wright for his eleventh-hour appearance and spent the rest of his life doing nearly everything he could to thwart the architect's Monona lakefront development. So intense were Jackson's feelings toward Wright that he refused to mention the architect's name in the Madison and Wisconsin Foundation *Bulletin*. Even in private letters to Segoe he would refer to Wright in elliptical terms such as "certain parties." But Jackson's enmity for Wright was hardly limited to what happened on November 2.[37]

Like all Madisonians, Jackson read the stories in the Madison newspapers describing Wright's turbulent and bohemian life, including his 1909 decision to leave his wife and children in Chicago and run off to Europe with Mamah Borthwick Cheney, the wife of a client; the brutal murder of Cheney and her children by a deranged Taliesin employee in 1914; Wright's marital troubles in the 1920s with Miriam Noel, his mentally unbalanced second wife; and his decision to take still another mistress, Olgivanna Hinzenberg, a stunningly beautiful Russian dancer thirty years his junior, whom he later married. For straight-arrow Jackson, Wright's lifestyle was unrelieved moral turpitude.[38]

Wright's leftist leanings were equally well known: the communelike lifestyle at the two Taliesins; the perception that he admired the Soviet system, evidenced by his trip to Moscow in 1937; and his criticism of capitalism. To Jackson — proud veteran of World War I, former army colonel, and unflinching patriot — Wright's politics were beneath contempt.

Wright was also a deadbeat, a quirk with which Jackson was quite familiar. As business manager of the Jackson Clinic, Joe Jackson had to send Wright frequent letters asking for payment of clinic bills for members of his immediate family. Correspondence between Jackson and Wright from 1929 to 1934 suggests that Wright paid most of his clinic bills but never on time. In a letter dated January 24, 1934, Jackson reminded Wright that he had sent him "13 friendly letters" over four years to collect a $25 bill and that Wright had not even given him the courtesy of a reply. Who could blame Jackson for being angry? In fact, as noted in Chapter 2, Jackson's experience was disturbingly common among Madison business owners. Between 1917 and 1935 the *Bulletin* listed seven judgments against Wright in its "business barometer" section. No wonder businesspeople were irritated when they saw Wright driving around town in his fancy cars (see Fig. 3.7).[39]

In addition to all these personal reasons for despising Wright, Jackson was absolutely opposed to the Olin Terraces plan because it would forever destroy the view at the end of Monona Avenue. As Jackson saw it, blocking this unique vista with any building would be a crime against nature and an unforgivable violation of Nolen's splendid plan. Jackson loved this dramatic opening at the end of Madison's shortest axial street — not because it was majestic but because it was so simple, so aesthetically refreshing (see Fig. 3.8).

In 1934 Jackson had had a belief-affirming conversation about this vista with Nolen when the famous planner returned to Madison for the dedication of the University of Wisconsin Arboretum and to address the Association of Commerce. (The creation of an arboretum was one of several recommendations that Nolen included in his 1909 plan.) As Jackson told the story, he and Nolen were standing alone at the end of Monona Avenue, looking out over the lake, when Nolen said: "The greatest mistake Madison or Wisconsin could make would be to permit any building out over the lake beyond the tracks, regardless of who designed it or what its purpose was." Nolen then turned and faced

the capitol and added: "You see, it is the front door to Wisconsin's Capitol, and as such, it belongs to all the people of Wisconsin to remain as it is forever."[40]

Unfortunately, there were no witnesses to corroborate Nolen's words, nor can we be sure that Jackson faithfully reported them, for he sometimes twisted events to his own purposes. The key point is that Jackson passionately believed those were Nolen's exact words, a message from the master. Jackson would tell this story throughout his long crusade against Wright.[41]

Although Jackson despised Wright and his Olin Terraces plan, Jackson was too smart to allow his strong feelings to prevent him from taking Wright seriously. That brief brush with Olin Terraces frightened Jackson. He could see that if Wright's project prevailed, it would kill three of Jackson's high-priority projects: the city-county building on Monona Avenue, the Nolenesque development of Law Park, and the placement of a community center at the Conklin site. Jackson knew he had to do everything in his power to prevent the Wright forces from gaining a beachhead and that the best defense was a good offense. Jackson was reassured to have a national figure like Segoe lead the counterattack.

## THE SEGOE PLAN

When Wright made his brash Olin Terraces presentation to the county board in November 1938, Ladislas Segoe had been working on the new Madison master plan for just six months. With the exception of a brief statement in July 1938 supporting the joint city-county building, Segoe had stayed out of public view. Behind the scenes, however, he was gathering the staggering array of data on Madison for his new plan. This was exactly what Segoe was supposed to do. In fact, he was right on schedule. The problem was that Jackson

FIGURE 3.7

**Another Head-Turning Car**

*Courtesy FLW FDN. 4206.001*

In 1939 Frank Lloyd Wright and several dozen other prominent Americans received an elegantly rendered invitation to buy one of the first Lincoln Continentals, a car that New York's Museum of Modern Art later decreed "one of the finest examples of automotive art." The car, first produced as a convertible sedan known as a cabriolet, featured a V-12 engine and styling that shouted "very important person inside." Wright took delivery of the sixteenth Continental produced by the Ford Motor Company in January 1940.

About two years after Wright bought it, his son-in-law, William Wesley Peters, rolled the car on a gravel road near Taliesin, crushing the convertible top and damaging the windshield. Wright used the opportunity to customize the car, as shown in this 1949 photograph. Changes included lowering the body, chopping the windshield by about five inches, and adding the hardtop over the rear seat. To maximize privacy, Wright eliminated the rear window and added the two half-circle windows on the sides. So distinctive was Wright's customized Continental that even in the 1980s and 1990s older Madisonians could recall seeing the big red car with its famous occupant.

wanted to do everything he could to preempt Wright and his supporters, and he wanted to do it as soon as possible.[42]

Segoe, on the other hand, refused to budge from his professional methodology. According to the contract, Segoe was to systematically analyze various topics and sequentially release his findings in fifteen reports. Jackson was especially eager to have the one called "Report on the Location of and Grouping of Public and Semi-Public Buildings." Here Segoe would disclose what he thought should be done with the Monona frontage, the Conklin site, and city hall. The two men had often discussed

To stand on the capitol esplanade and look down Monona Avenue, as the photographer of this 1940s postcard did, is to see why the territorial legislature picked Madison as the capital and why James Duane Doty ran one of four 132-foot-wide axial streets between the capitol grounds and the lake: the view was dramatic and beautiful. Paradoxically, as buildings were completed along the avenue, they framed the vista and added drama. But it was the shimmering lake at the center of the frame that made people smile with delight. This postcard captures the popular and unique vista as it looked when Wright proposed his Olin Terraces plan and explains why so many, including Joe Jackson, felt so strongly about preserving the view.

Nolen's civic center plan for Monona Avenue, Nolen's esplanade along the city's Lake Monona frontage, and Jackson's plan for the Conklin site. Segoe understood exactly what Jackson wanted. Segoe also understand that Jackson was the man who was responsible for hiring him, finding the money to pay him, and creating the organization whose trustees were officially responsible for the plan. At no point did Segoe ever appear to resist Jackson's ideas on these key issues. Consequently, Jackson knew what Segoe was going to propose at each of these sites, and he was eager to show the superiority of Segoe's recommendations to Wright's Olin Terraces.

So Jackson waited — impatiently. Like a good advance man he used newsletters, press releases,

and speeches to plump up Segoe's credentials with phrases like "the foremost city planner in America," and "selected after a country-wide search." Jackson also used this waiting period to remind Segoe what he wanted. In an April 1939 letter he told Segoe that his "report should state without hesitation that the open, unbuilt-upon front yard is the thing above all that will best set off the beautiful outlook of Lake Monona from the end of the Avenue."[43]

Finally, in May 1939 Segoe gave foundation members a preview of his plan at their annual banquet, and in July Segoe formally released his long-awaited report on public buildings. The city-county building should be located on Monona Avenue across from the post office, exactly where Jackson wanted it.

Law Park should be developed as a "front yard" for the city — the very term Nolen used in his private conversation with Jackson. Segoe suggested building a series of terraces cascading to the lakeshore from Olin Terrace (see Fig. 3.9).[44]

The Conklin site on Lake Mendota, Segoe argued, should be expanded and used as the site for "an auditorium and community building" (see Fig. 3.10). Segoe allowed that many cities place auditoriums in civic centers but said "there is a question whether such a structure, especially if combined with other recreational facilities in a community center, is entirely compatible with a public building group such as proposed for Madison." Significantly, in 1909 Nolen had no reservation about putting an auditorium in his proposal for a civic center on the six blocks bordering Monona Avenue (see Fig. 1.17). In fact, Nolen recommended that "a really fine theater and state opera house" be located in the civic center at the end of Monona Avenue overlooking the lake. Clearly, Segoe was providing the dutiful response that Jackson demanded. Jackson was relieved to have Segoe's Monona and Mendota lakefront plans in public hands. Now Jackson's plans were in play.[45]

Segoe — undoubtedly with encouragement from Jackson — used the release of his public building recommendations to criticize Wright's Olin Terraces plan. Segoe said the Monona shore was "much too good for a glorified garage" and that any architecture "that cannot do better than bury itself in the ground" is a failure. Segoe also blasted Wright's suggestion to put a union railroad depot at the foot of Monona Avenue, saying it would "merely increase congestion." Segoe proposed placing a union station at the county fairgrounds, then outside the city.[46]

Segoe's last and historically most nettlesome criticism of Olin Terraces was that it would block the lake view from Monona Avenue. Segoe noted that Olin

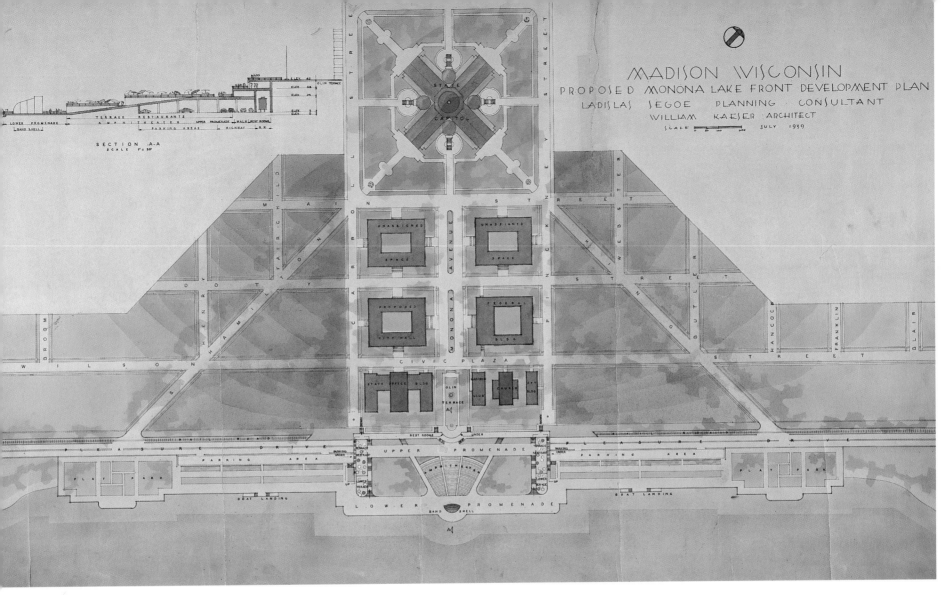

FIGURE 3.9

**1939 Segoe Plan for Lake Monona**

*SHSW. WHi(X)32*

In accordance with Joe Jackson's wishes, Ladislas Segoe's Monona plan was a deliberate update of Nolen's 1909 plan (see Fig. 1.18). Like its predecessor, the Segoe plan designated the six blocks between the capitol and Lake Monona as Madison's civic center. However, by 1939 two government buildings and one block of private buildings were considered fixtures of Nolen's mall. They were the Federal Building (see Fig. 1.21), State Office Building (see Fig. 1.22), and the block fronting the lake to the right of Monona Avenue that contained the Madison Club, Diocese of Madison Chancery, and the Bellevue Apartments. Segoe urged that the three remaining

blocks be used for a city-county building, a public school central administration building, and a museum and art gallery.

Like Nolen, Segoe proposed a series of terraces cascading from the Wilson Street hilltop to the lakeshore. The focal point of the nearly milelong development was to be a large lake-oriented amphitheater with a band shell near the shoreline. On each end of the terraces Segoe proposed restaurants and pavilions for outdoor dining and dancing. Along the lakeshore Segoe suggested children's play fields, a pedestrian promenade, and boat landings.

Segoe saw the Lake Monona frontage as a solution to Madison's acute parking and traffic problem. Accordingly, he proposed a four-lane "Lake Monona Parkway" and parking for six hundred cars. Segoe also reduced the number of railroad tracks from four to one as a part of a comprehensive railroad consolidation and relocation proposal. The plan was drawn by William V. Kaeser, a Madison architect, who worked under Segoe's direction.

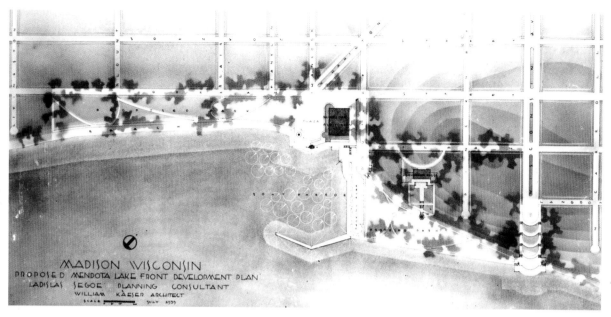

FIGURE 3.10

**1939 Segoe Plan for Lake Mendota**

SHSW. WHi(D48)11850

No one ever accused Joe Jackson of having modest dreams for Madison. One of his boldest visions involved thirty-three hundred feet of prime Lake Mendota shoreline from Wisconsin Avenue on the west (right) to Livingston Street (left) and required filling five and a half acres of lake bed and razing more than fifty houses.

Jackson's vision was embodied in Ladislas Segoe's 1939 plan, shown here. According to Segoe, the site would be dominated by an auditorium and community building (the large building at the center). Segoe boasted that this remarkable building could accommodate concerts, dramatic productions, lectures, commencements, convocations, balls, mass meetings, athletic events, festivals, exhibitions of all types, political and patriotic gatherings, and naval drills. A breakwater and boat storage facility would extend out from the shore and create a harbor for boats.

Although the plan was never realized, the city eventually acquired nearly five blocks of prime Lake Mendota frontage for a park (see Fig. 1.33), now known as James Madison Park, one of the city's great open spaces. Joe Jackson's powerful and persistently presented vision deserves much of the credit. William Kaeser, a local architect who had designed the auditorium-armory in 1938, prepared the plan under Segoe's direction.

the city's intent. However, contemporaneous records do not support Jackson's interpretation; they clearly show that the only reason the city bought this parcel was to create a park.[48]

### THE 1941 AUDITORIUM BOOMLET

From the fall of 1939 until January 1941 the auditorium issue nearly disappeared from the city's agenda because no federal public works money was available. Local officials hoped that Congress would pass another public works bill, but it never did. Auditorium backers saw one surprising ray of hope: city money. Law's unrelenting campaign to reduce bonded indebtedness was succeeding, and for the first time since the depression the city was in a position to play a small but important role in financing an auditorium.[49]

Curiously, the impetus for new auditorium discussions came from a special city committee that urged construction of a large public boathouse at the east end of Law Park. Law leaped on the idea but suggested that the boathouse be combined with an auditorium. Law pointed to a $200,000 boathouse built at Lake Geneva, a city in southeastern Wisconsin that was amortizing its debt with just twelve summer weeks. Combine this with an auditorium, Law said, and the city will have revenue coming in all year, enough to pay for the project. Law even suggested that the city could afford to contribute some property tax revenue for such an important project, although most of the project would have to be covered by revenue bonds. This time it was clear that Law, not Jackson, was driving the auditorium plan. Law was careful not to prescribe a site, but reading between the lines, Law seemed pleased by the prospect of a boathouse-auditorium at the east end of Law Park.[50]

This was great news to frustrated auditorium backers. Hotel owners argued that an auditorium would

Terrace was just forty-five feet above the lake. This meant that "only a three-story structure could be erected without blocking the view." Segoe added, "This would prevent any adequate development of an auditorium or recreation center in addition to the parking space Wright included in his plan."[47]

Moreover, since the abortive 1938 attempt to build an auditorium and armory at the Conklin site, two things had changed in Jackson's favor. First, Jackson had gotten the Wisconsin legislature to

authorize cities to issue revenue bonds, a funding option critically important for any auditorium project. Second, in August 1939, after months of negotiation, Madison finally bought the Conklin site (see Fig. 1.33). Years later Jackson claimed that Mayor Law had asked him to help negotiate the sale with the Conklins because he was a neighbor and longtime friend of the family's. Jackson said that the mayor authorized him "to tell the Conklins the site would be used for an auditorium," and Jackson later used this story to demonstrate catapult Madison from the fifth- to the second-largest convention city in the state, just behind Milwaukee. Auto dealers were delighted to contemplate a first-class venue for their annual show. Lovers of drama, music, and art visualized a dignified setting for an enriched cultural life. Youth advocates looked forward to the possibility of having big-name bands in Madison. Boat owners were eager to have a place to store their boats. Military organizations saw the auditorium as an armory and drill floor. Common council members were sufficiently excited by the prospect to hire an architect to prepare preliminary drawings and schedule a referendum for April 1, 1941. The referendum carried by a margin greater than 2-to-1 and authorized the construction of an auditorium costing up to $750,000 with no more than $200,000 coming from city general obligation bonds (see Fig. 3.11).[51]

The success of the referendum triggered a brief debate — the first of many — about whether to put the auditorium in Law Park, Olin Park, or Olbrich Park, all on Lake Monona (see Fig. 3.12). The exclusive menu of Monona sites provoked Jackson to launch a campaign on behalf of the Conklin site that featured press releases invoking Segoe's recommendations for placing the auditorium there. Jackson stressed the absence of railroad noise and railroad crossings, the availability of sunset views, and included an endorsement from the commodore of the Mendota Yacht Club, who reminded readers that Lake Mendota had more sailboats and motorboats than Lake Monona.[52]

In June 1941 — two months after the referendum — Frank Lloyd Wright realized that the auditorium project was an opportunity to reintroduce Olin Terraces. Since developing the plan in 1938, Wright had made several changes and was eager to explain them. Wright drove to Madison and showed his

FIGURE 3.11

**1941 Auditorium Proposal for Lake Monona**

*Courtesy* Wisconsin State Journal

In February 1941, just after the common council agreed to hold a referendum on whether to build an auditorium, the city hired Madison architect Ferdinand Y. Kronenberg to do preliminary plans and cost estimates so that people could visualize what they were voting on. This elevation for a municipal auditorium and recreation center was published in the *Wisconsin State Journal* on March 30, 1941, just two days before the referendum. Although no site was specified, the understanding was that it would be built somewhere on Lake Monona, probably at the east end of Law Park, the site Mayor Jim Law preferred. Ironically, this was the same site proposed by Frank Lloyd Wright for his 1893 boathouse (see Fig. 2.25).

The design was a typical arena-style auditorium with a relatively large flat floor measuring 98 by 153 feet, a stage at one end, and tiered seating around the sides. The main floor was flat so that it could be used for sporting events and exhibitions or filled with folding chairs for large meetings. Maximum seating capacity was fifty-six hundred. Because the back of the auditorium faced the lake, Kronenberg provided storage for five hundred boats on a lower level and a 34-by-84-foot deck.

plans to A. M. Brayton, the editor of the *Wisconsin State Journal*, and was rewarded with a long glowing story headlined "Once Again Frank Lloyd Wright Plans a Dream City Here." Accompanying the full-page story was a new bird's-eye perspective from Monona Avenue and a cross-section (see Fig. 3.13). Even better than the straight news story was a booming editorial, "Don't Miss the Boat." Brayton wrote that if Wright's project were built, Monona Avenue would become "the most beautiful short street in the world" and Madison would become "the most beautiful small city in the world." The

FIGURE 3.12

**Auditorium Site Wars Begin**

*U.W.–Madison Cartographic Laboratory*

The debate about where to locate the auditorium began in the 1920s and continued in the 1930s with the introduction of Wright's Olin Terraces, but the question did not become serious until 1941 when Madison voters authorized the city to spend up to $750,000 for a municipal auditorium. Although many sites were considered, four lakefront parks were mentioned most often and given the greatest credence. This map shows the four parks: Olin Park, Law Park, Conklin Park, and Olbrich Park.

*Journal* recognized that the price tag for Olin Terraces, then estimated at $3.2 million, far exceeded the $750,000 limit imposed by the referendum, but the paper argued that Madisonians should resist the temptation of "accepting the more expedient and transient things in preference to a long term program." Brayton concluded his editorial by reminding readers that Madison had missed the boat with Nolen, and the city should not miss the boat with Wright.[53]

Encouraged by the *Journal*'s support, Wright announced that he was forming an eighteen-member citizens' committee to back his plan and counteract the "political big shots" — an obvious reference to Jackson and his cronies. But no one stepped forward to chair the committee. As late as October 1941

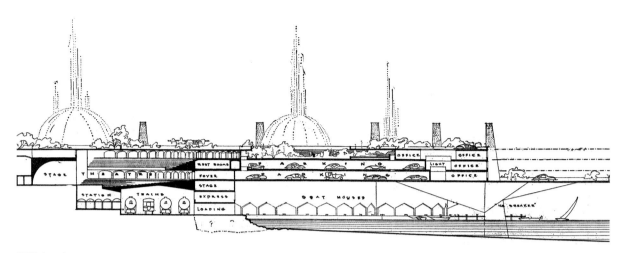

1938 Cross-Section

*Courtesy* The Capital Times

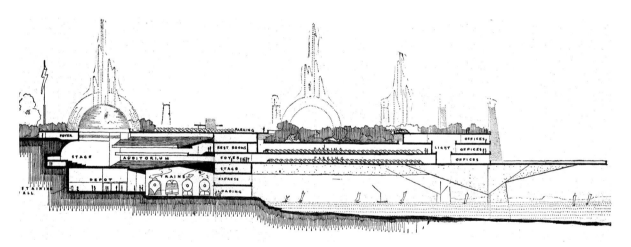

1941 Cross-Section

*Courtesy* Wisconsin State Journal

FIGURE 3.13

**Wright's 1941 Olin Terraces Refinements**

When Wright reintroduced Olin Terraces in 1941 (lower cross-section), he made several significant changes to the 1938 design (upper cross-section). The most dramatic change was the redesign of the sixty-foot-wide dome over the auditorium. In the 1938 version the glass-domed fountain was mounted on the surface of a concrete roof, but in 1941 Wright transformed the steel-framed dome into a skylight for the auditorium. This meant the dome would constantly be drenched with water, creating a fascinating spectacle of light and color on sunny days for people in the auditorium below. On the other hand, this skylight-fountain must rank as one of Wright's most daring creations, especially given the limited abilities of the sealants then available. One can only imagine the effects of a leaking glass dome on a cello or a taffeta dress. Other changes made in the 1941 design included a larger stage, larger depot waiting room, and a reduction of parking spaces from 4,500 to 3,500. Experts said Wright's depot was too small for Madison's needs; even in the 1920s a transportation planner estimated that a union passenger station would require eleven tracks, not the four shown in these cross-sections.

Wright was still trying to gather support for his dream center with a lecture at the University of Wisconsin Memorial Union. Wright failed, but this time his caustic tongue was not the culprit. As a newspaper reporter artfully put it, Wright only "lightly berated Madisonians past and present." No, the real reason Wright wasn't having much luck was that since he had introduced Olin Terraces in 1938, the world had changed.[54]

At the beginning of 1941 Americans hoped that FDR's policy of supplying the Allies with planes, ships, and guns could keep the country out of the European conflagration. However, as the year progressed and U.S. leaders increased production of military supplies, the civilian economy began to feel the pinch. For Madisonians that meant increases in construction costs, which caused many to conclude that this was not the time to build an auditorium. On June 22, just three months after Madisonians approved the auditorium referendum, Hitler stunned the world with his decision to invade Russia. After this, few Madisonians could read headlines in the *Capital Times* and *Wisconsin State Journal* and be hopeful about anything. Then came December 7. Suddenly, the auditorium was irrelevant. The United States was at war.

## THE WAR INTERLUDE

Every day at 4 P.M. the sound of a sweet, deep-toned Asian bell punctuated the country quiet around Taliesin. The bell, hung from a large oak tree on the hilltop just above Wright's sprawling home, was the signal for afternoon tea. From the drafting tables at nearby Hillside, from the fields, and from the adjoining barns, everyone would gather in a shaded courtyard just outside Wright's studio to relax, talk, and drink tea. Beginning in the summer of 1940, one subject dominated Wright's teatime conversations and, as the weeks went by, the Taliesin Fellowship discussions on Saturday and Sunday evenings as well. That subject was the war.[55]

The mere thought that the United States would enter the war made Wright fighting mad. Wright disseminated his views in articles in *The Progressive*, the trusted voice of La Follette liberalism; in *Scribner's Commentator*, an isolationist journal published in Wisconsin, and in *Taliesin Square-Paper*, an occasional journal he published. If these articles reflected his preachments to apprentices at tea, the young men and women were getting a virulent form of isolationism. Wright asserted that the war in Europe represented little more than the collapse of a bankrupt civilization, a plot between "the private money power of London and New York" — and that the United States should have nothing to do with it. "Why throw Nature's gift to us — ISOLATION — away?" he asked. All we need, Wright argued, is a "super air force" and "a true non-war breeding organic internal economy." Wright maintained an abiding faith in democracy and said that if it were truly put into practice, it would somehow vanquish communism and fascism.[56]

But Wright's tirades urging isolationism could not stop the U.S. government. Teatime on October 16, 1940, just one month after Roosevelt signed the Selective Service Act, was a memorable day for Taliesin apprentices. At exactly four o'clock the clerk of Iowa County walked into the drafting room on the Taliesin grounds to register apprentices who had not already signed up in their home areas. When he left, all eligible apprentices were officially part of the Selective Service System. A turbulent period in Taliesin history had begun, a time when nearly everything that happened created grist for Wright's enemies and especially Joe Jackson.[57]

In 1939 and 1940 isolationism enjoyed widespread popularity, but as the months of 1941 rolled by, its chrome turned to rust. Wright nonetheless insisted that isolationism should be the country's response to the war, and some of his closest friends rebuked him for his blindness. For example, Lewis Mumford, the respected architectural critic and urban historian, wrote a stinging letter to Wright in April 1941. Said Mumford: "Unless we have the guts and intelligence to fight [Hitler] now, we will never have the chance to develop an antidote. Are you still in the Neville Chamberlain period? Period politics are as bad as period architecture."[58]

Unfazed by Mumford's rebuke, Wright supported America First, the largest and most outspoken isolationist organization in the country, and put himself in the company of Charles Lindbergh, who, like Wright, had taken engineering courses at the U.W. In 1941 Lindbergh toured the country, making isolationist speeches and reaping a whirlwind of denunciations that ranged from "Nazi" to "peripatetic appeaser." Wright stridently signaled his admiration for Lindbergh's isolationism when he revised his *Autobiography* and added a section praising the aviator's courage to "think straight" and "speak straight."[59]

Wright's politics clearly were influencing his apprentices. On March 28, 1941, twenty-five Wright apprentices fired an antiwar shot heard around Wisconsin and beyond. In a calmly worded two-page manifesto on Taliesin letterhead, the apprentices said they objected to the draft and argued that the highest service they could render to the country would be to remain as an intact unit "working for interior defense." They insisted that their "convictions, educations, and principles" rendered them "unfit for destruction and mass murder called war." They sent their manifesto to

Clarence Dykstra, the president of the University of Wisconsin who in the fall of 1940 had been appointed the first director of the U.S. Selective Service System.[60]

Almost a year went by before the Selective Service began to snare apprentices who refused to heed their country's call. During that year more than half the manifesto signers left Taliesin, some because they disagreed with a new Fellowship income-sharing system established by Wright, some because they were drafted and reluctantly went, and some because they decided to enlist. Of the eleven apprentices who remained at Taliesin in December 1942, at least three were classified as physically or mentally fit, but they had failed to comply with Selective Service directives, such as reporting for physicals or filling out certain forms.[61]

In the glare of front-page coverage in Madison's newspapers the trial of the first apprentice, Marcus Weston, twenty-seven, ran from December 1942 to January 1943 before U.S. District Judge Patrick T. Stone. Significantly, Stone wanted to try Frank Lloyd Wright, not Weston, who had refused to register for the draft. Stone attacked the "seditious character" of the apprentices' manifesto and said, "I think you boys are living under a bad influence with that man Wright. I'm afraid he is poisoning your minds. I think he should be investigated and if he's obstructing the war, he should be indicted. And you can take that back to Mr. Wright. I'm going to ask the FBI to investigate him [see Fig. 3.14], and if there is any evidence, I'll see that it gets before the grand jury. There are too many fine young boys that are being spoiled out there."

Stone sentenced Weston to three years in prison. Two other apprentices, Allen Davison and John Howe, had failed to report for military service and were sentenced to four years in June 1943.[62]

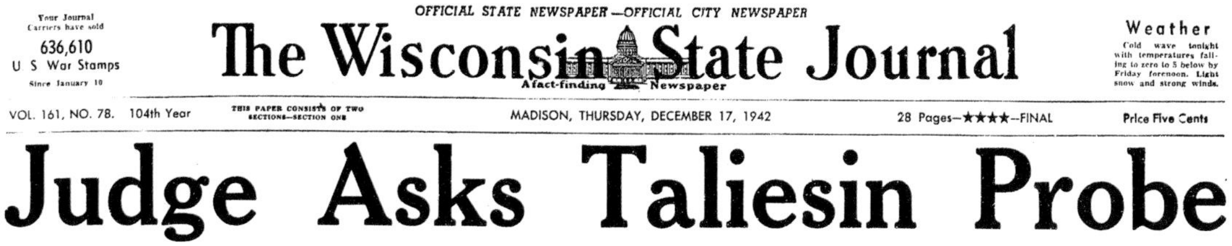
Your Journal Carriers have sold 636,610 U S War Stamps Since January 10

OFFICIAL STATE NEWSPAPER—OFFICIAL CITY NEWSPAPER

The Wisconsin State Journal

A fact-finding Newspaper

Weather
Cold wave tonight with temperatures falling to zero to 5 below by Friday forenoon. Light snow and strong winds.

VOL. 161, NO. 78. 104th Year | THIS PAPER CONSISTS OF TWO SECTIONS—SECTION ONE | MADISON, THURSDAY, DECEMBER 17, 1942 | 28 Pages—★★★★—FINAL | Price Five Cents

Judge Asks Taliesin Probe

FIGURE 3.14

**Madison Judge Demands FBI Probe of Wright**

This headline and its accompanying story appeared in the *Wisconsin State Journal* on December 17, 1942, and was picked up by newspapers all over the country, including two in Washington, D.C. The article quoted federal judge Patrick T. Stone as saying that he was going to demand an FBI investigation of Wright because the outspoken architect was encouraging his apprentices to avoid the draft. Stone's action was triggered by the trial, then underway, of a Wright apprentice who had failed to appear for induction. Someone showed the article to J. Edgar Hoover, who immediately wired his agents in Milwaukee to keep him informed about this case. This and other trials of draft-dodging apprentices provided succulent grist for Wright's enemies, including Joe Jackson, which they later used to argue that the architect should not be allowed to design anything for Madison.

What most Madisonians did not realize was that in April 1942, eight months before Weston's trial, Jackson, a close friend of Judge Stone's, had written FBI director J. Edgar Hoover an indignant letter about Wright's politics. Hoover replied three weeks later, thanking Jackson for his "courtesy and interest" and urging him to communicate directly with a special agent in Milwaukee if he should "come into possession of any further information." FBI correspondence obtained under the Freedom of Information Act shows that Stone formally requested a bureau investigation during the Weston trial but that Hoover learned about Stone's intention from a newspaper account of the Madison trial a week before Stone made his formal request. The diligent Hoover immediately sent a teletype to the Milwaukee bureau office and was no doubt pleased to learn that it had already begun an investigation of Wright's effort to thwart the prosecution of the war.[63]

Meanwhile, nearly all civilian construction projects stopped during the war. However, there was one exception that would later prove essential for Wright's civic vision: the continued filling of the Law Park lakefront (see Fig. 3.15).

## A NOBLE ENTERPRISE FOR A NOBLE PURPOSE

Madisonians celebrated the Allied victories in Europe and Japan by ringing church bells, blowing factory whistles, and forming huge joyous crowds on the Capitol Square. At last the largest and most devastating war in history was over. Everyone was eager for Madison's proud veterans to return home so that life could get back to normal. But for some that was impossible. About three hundred men and women from Madison died in the war, and many others returned with serious injuries. Madisonians sought a way to express their gratitude to those who made the ultimate sacrifice and indeed to all who served in the war. How to properly commemorate their military service was a question that enjoyed the highest priority in postwar Madison.[64]

One embarrassing fact immediately confronted city leaders: Madison had never erected a memorial to the veterans of World War I. By contrast, the University of Wisconsin and the state had built the Memorial Union and Wisconsin General Hospital, respectively. Madison's failure intensified the need to do *something* for its World War II veterans.[65]

As city leaders began to think about it, four war memorial questions required answers: What form should it take? What values should it embody? What process should the city follow? Where should it be located?

Two men provided the most compelling and timely answers. The first was Joe Jackson, who used front-page editorials in his influential Madison and Wisconsin Foundation *Bulletin* to outline his war memorial views. In a moving editorial dated July 7, 1944, Jackson proposed a "great community center" as a war memorial, but what he had in mind went far beyond what he and his business friends had proposed before the war. He began: "Its first objective would be to symbolize and perpetuate the good life of this beautiful Capital and University City — the very thing which its young men and women always went forth to protect and preserve. As far as could be created by man, it would be the heart throb of this community — the living, pulsating, achievement of its educational, recreational, spiritual and cultural life — something noble in itself. The building should be exceptionally well designed and have the finest architectural character — something of great beauty and inspiration — the constant pride of the Capital and University City."[66]

Jackson felt strongly about creating a place that would welcome "all of our people — old and young — including all living veterans of our wars and their families. It would be *theirs* for all time. Within it they would find the better life which Madison offers. Here in the great hall they would gather for symphony concerts, lectures, public forums, theatrical, civic and patriotic meetings. Here would be several smaller rooms for committee meetings and other purposes for which there is a constant need. An Art Gallery would provide suitable environment for exhibits of our ... artists and for the gradual accumulation of art treasures for the education and enjoyment of all. For that greatest of all assets — *our youth* — in which experience has demonstrated is essential to their welfare — *the youth center supreme.*" [67]

Jackson had a clear idea of what he wanted and how to make it quiver with life and promise.

Jackson's emphasis on a youth center owed partly to his awareness of what a large role young people must play in creating a better world, but it also reflected his desire to upgrade and expand a prototype youth center, known as "the Loft," begun in the 1940s at Madison's YMCA. There teenagers could dance, play Ping-Pong, and just hang out.

In 1946 the Loft moved into a larger downtown building, expanded its programs, and became known as the Madison Community Center. At its new facilities the center began to offer dances, euchre parties, and other programs for "older adults" that immediately proved popular. From then on Jackson and other leaders assumed that the Madison Community Center would be a key component of a war memorial. [68]

The second man who provided compelling answers was Porter Butts, the director of the University of Wisconsin Memorial Union (the student center) and an associate professor of social education. Butts, who became involved with the union during its planning phase in the early 1920s when he was still a student, wanted the Wisconsin facility to be a true center for the campus community, a powerful unifying force for the social, educational, and cultural life of students and faculty, a home for the Wisconsin spirit. To achieve this lofty goal architects included an unprecedented array of facilities under a single roof, including several dining rooms; a sumptuous lounge; quiet study rooms; a great hall for dances,

banquets, and large events; an art gallery; bowling alley; billiard room; guest rooms; offices for campus organizations; and more (see Fig. 3.16). The Memorial Union featured the finest architecture and enjoyed a premiere location on Lake Mendota, in the heart of the campus. And as the name implied, it was a memorial, designed to acknowledge the five thousand students and alumni who served in World War I and especially the 122 who died. [69]

By the end of the war Butts had become a nationally recognized expert on the design and operation of multipurpose cultural and social centers. This expertise led Milwaukee leaders to hire Butts in 1945 as a consultant on the design of a war memorial on the shore of Lake Michigan. When Madison leaders heard about Butts's work in Milwaukee, they asked the union director if he would help Madison plan its war memorial. When he enthusiastically accepted, it was yet another instance of Madison's finding a nationally recognized expert in its own backyard. [70]

Both Jackson and Butts, echoing sentiments common after World War I, cautioned against stone shafts, bronze statues, and flag poles, the so-called monumental forms. Better, they said, to build something useful, something that would serve an ongoing community need and thereby be a "living memorial" to those who died. [71]

In an influential guest editorial in the *Wisconsin State Journal* in December 1945, Butts asserted that the United States had fought the war because Americans believe that people should have the right to live together in peaceful communities and be governed by democratic principles. Thus the best way to honor its casualties and veterans would be to create living memorials that embody such values. Unfortunately, Butts noted, the feeling of community so central to democracy had been shattered by the

FIGURE 3.15

**Filling the Lakeshore at Law Park, 1943**

*Courtesy Wisconsin Department of Natural Resources*

One of the few wartime improvements that Madison pursued was the filling of Lake Monona to create Law Park. This photograph, taken from the State Office Building just west of Olin Terrace, shows the operation in 1943 when the fill had been completed almost to Monona Avenue. The formal gardens of Olin Terrace are just visible in the lower lefthand corner of the picture.

Today Law Park contains twenty filled acres. Three acres were filled by the railroads with sand, gravel, and rock, and the remaining seventeen were filled with fly ash and clinkers, old curbs, gutters, and sidewalks, a few slot machines seized by the Madison vice squad, and, at the extreme east end, household garbage. When this picture was taken, the state Department of Conservation (predecessor of the Department of Natural Resources) was located in the State Office Building so that its employees could look out their windows and see what the city was putting in the lake.

FIGURE 3.16

**U.W. Memorial Union: Community Center Model**

*Courtesy University of Wisconsin–Madison Memorial Union, photo by Greg Anderson*

This 1926 rendering shows one of the best-known and most popular buildings on the University of Wisconsin campus: the Memorial Union. Its distinctive architecture, imposing size, and premiere location on Lake Mendota in the heart of the campus have made the building a landmark. But the facilities found within the landmark were what made the building unique. It contained dining facilities, an authentic rathskeller, billiard room, art gallery, guest rooms, meeting rooms, a large room for major events, and plenty of quiet study nooks. When it was completed, no other campus in the country had anything quite like it.

Although primarily designed for students and faculty, it was also popular with Madisonians who went there for art exhibits, lectures, and fine music. In fact, Madison business leaders raised almost 10 percent of the money for its construction. The building opened in October 1928. (A 1939 addition included a state-of-the-art, thirteen-hundred-seat sloped-floor theater, a smaller theater, craft shops, bowling alleys, and extensive boating facilities.)

Frank Lloyd Wright mounted nearly all his Madison exhibits at the Memorial Union and gave most of his Madison lectures there.

After World War II, when the city was planning to build an auditorium, Porter Butts, the union's director, argued that the union constituted a superior template for what the city really needed: a multifaceted community center. This new definition was an almost instant hit with Madison civic leaders and became the dominant model for a civic auditorium from that time forward.

automobile, airplane, radio, and telephone. People still spent leisure time together, he observed, but in a hundred different places. To restore the vitally important sense of community, Madisonians must create a place where people can play, learn, be inspired, and experience democracy.[72]

What Butts wanted was a building that would function as a true community center. The complex should be centrally located, boast inspiring architecture, and accommodate the needs of the performing and visual arts, youth programming, sporting events, political meetings, lectures, courses, and much more. He wanted a flat-floor arena plus a sloped-floor theater for concerts and dramatic performances, as well as an art gallery and youth activities center. This new community center–auditorium model was very different from the type of building the business community had demanded during the 1920s, '30s, and early '40s for conventions, sporting events, and political speeches. Such

buildings almost always had a stage at one end, but it usually was not suitable for dramatic and musical productions. To Madisonians who had endured so many auditorium discussions, Butts's prescription seemed like a shinier, newer version of something very familiar.[73]

Once Jackson and Butts placed their imprimatur on the community center–auditorium concept, almost everyone said, in effect, "Great idea — let's do it." In May 1946 the Madison Plan Commission endorsed the formation of a special citywide committee to study the project and report its findings.[74]

Just a week after the plan commission endorsed the community center–auditorium concept, Wright gave a speech to the Young Republicans of Dane County at the Loraine Hotel. Jackson surely winced when he heard about it. Jackson blamed Wright for killing the joint city-county building project in 1938 and had held his breath when

Wright tried to commandeer public support during the 1941 auditorium referendum. Now in 1946, when just about everyone in Madison seemed eager, in the words of the plan commission's recommendation, to move forward with the "Municipal Auditorium, Community Center, and Boat Harbor," Wright rang Madison's doorbell again.

Wright painted a vivid word picture of his Lake Monona complex for the Young Republicans. Picking up exactly where he had left off in 1941, he extolled its beauty, economy (he thought it could be built for $7 million), and practicality; furthermore, its construction would bring people to Madison from all over the world. The problem, said Wright with his usual chutzpah, was that "it is so simple an idea, so good, so sound, that it would have to get started *by way of youth*" (emphasis added). Wright acknowledged that establishment leaders would never endorse his idea and said that it was up to young people to make it happen.[75]

Jackson need not have worried. Wright's third try in just eight years to find a Madison champion for his dream civic center failed. The Young Republicans — although theoretically more receptive to big new ideas — were not interested in subverting a well-defined process actively promoted by older Republicans such as Joe Jackson. About this time Wright must have realized that getting his project off the ground would require something more than his quixotic lunges.[76]

But if he did, it was not evident even to close observers. Wright's burgeoning postwar practice required a rigorous daily routine (see Fig. 3.17), but the architect still had enough energy to lecture at the University of Wisconsin and elsewhere around the country (see Fig. 3.18).

Formal planning for the war memorial–community center got under way in October 1946 with an elaborate process and structure recommended by Butts. The union director believed that the only way to make people feel they had a stake in the building was to involve everybody — including Madison's suburbanites. They too were interested in the community center and might help finance it if they were involved in its planning. About 500 organizations were invited to participate, and 250 — with a combined membership of 65,000 — accepted. Never before were so many citizens so involved for so long in planning a public building. Butts recommended that Madison leaders create a nonprofit corporation independent of local government to plan and raise money for the war memorial. For that purpose they created the Madison Metropolitan War Memorial Association.[77]

The new association was forced to begin under unfavorable financial circumstances. First, the common council gave the group its blessing but no money. War memorial leaders asked the city to issue $1 million in bonds because this would make raising $500,000 from the private sector much easier. The council refused, saying it could not commit its successors to such a debt. Second, war memorial leaders recognized that their project would have to compete with several city projects with higher priority, such as the city-county building and a major hospital addition. However, everyone assumed that the war memorial association would take several years to complete its work and that the city would have the money by then.[78]

In the fall of 1947 member organizations were asked to prepare a list of facilities they wanted in the war memorial complex. Naturally, every organization asked for everything. One said it wanted a basketball court seating 10,000, an auditorium seating 10,000,

FIGURE 3.17

**Wright's Daily Work Habits**

*Photo by Pedro Guerrero*

This photograph taken at Taliesin West in 1947 caught the eighty-year-old Frank Lloyd Wright in the middle of one of his daily routines: sharpening his lead pencil with a pocket knife. In an era when architects prepare drawings with computers, the photo is a reminder that Wright worked exclusively with wooden pencils and basic drafting tools.

A few years before this photo was taken, Betty Cass, a longtime friend who had spent much time at Taliesin, said, "In all the years I've known you, I've never seen you work. Obviously you MUST work, and hard, but when do you do it? WHEN do you conceive the ideas and do the sketches for the magnificent buildings?"

"Between 4 and 7 o'clock in the morning," he answered. "I go to sleep promptly when I go to bed. Then I wake up around 4 and can't sleep. But my mind's clear, so I get up and work for three or four hours. Then I go to bed for another nap." This allowed Wright to spend regular office hours conferring with his colleagues, handling correspondence, making telephone calls, and holding meetings. On a typical workday at Taliesin he would have tea about 4 P.M. and supper about 7:30. In his later years he added an afternoon nap to his daily regimen.

Cass was impressed that Wright never seemed "hurried or harried." She reported that the architect always moved with "a majestic leisureliness" that was so impressive it was infectious.

Still another remarkable quality about Wright's work habits was his practice of never doing a sketch until he had the entire project worked out in his head. For example, for the Marin County (California) Civic Center, he asked a colleague for a contour map of the site. Several days later Wright sat down at his drafting table, sketched the entire project, and handed it to his associates to prepare more detailed drawings.

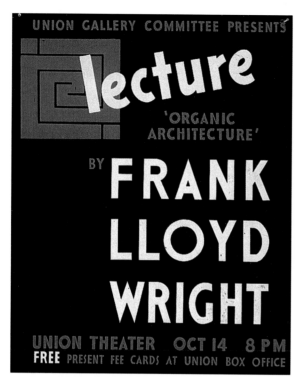

This handsome poster filled the Memorial Union theater with a capacity crowd of thirteen hundred on the evening of October 14, 1948. During his talk Wright defined organic architecture as "the architecture of Democracy — relaxed and in keeping with the site" and as "the natural building" based on studies of a structure's purpose, the nature of materials available, and the type of future occupant. The white-maned architect leavened his lecture with frequent iconoclastic comments, most of which drew vigorous applause. Wright charged that Washington, D.C., was unfit for modern occupation and should be moved to the Midwest's "valley of democracy," that "cities are dated and done," and that University of Wisconsin buildings are "monarchic hangovers" from the dead past. At the end someone in the audience asked the venerable architect, "What do you consider your greatest achievement?" "The fact that I am alive and kicking today," the eighty-one-year-old shot back.

a theater seating 800, a swimming pool, archery range, ice rink, dance pavilion projecting over the water, woodworking rooms, art gallery, arts-and-crafts center, and well-equipped game room. And this was just the list from the Madison Public Schools

Recreation Department. To prioritize the impossibly long list, all the member organizations were polled to see which facilities were most important to them.[79]

Technically, at least in the beginning, no official site was designated. However, the consensus was that the new war memorial should be "located on one of our beautiful Madison lakes." By 1949 war memorial leaders had concluded that the facility "would probably be located on Lake Mendota at the foot of North Hamilton Street," that is, on the Conklin site. No doubt, Joe Jackson was responsible for this decision. Ironically, his failure to get an auditorium built there in 1934–1935, in 1938, and again in 1941 made the Conklin site familiar to nearly everyone. Moreover, by 1946 the city owned 750 feet of Mendota frontage at the Conklin site and had state authorization to build a breakwater there. Jackson used every opportunity to remind community leaders about these two features and that the city had purchased the site for the auditorium, a dubious claim. Thanks to Jackson's tireless cheerleading and his continuing insider role, nearly all city leaders accepted the Conklin site for the war memorial. Jackson had won a major battle.[80]

Finally, in late July 1949, after nearly three years of work, the war memorial association presented its final report to the Madison Common Council. Written largely by Joe Jackson, it called for an auditorium, theater, boat harbor, youth center, and memorial shrine — on the Conklin site (see Figure 3.19). What shocked everyone was the cost. What was once expected to cost $1.5 million had soared to $5.2 million. The timing of the final war memorial report was terrible. Just seven months earlier Madison and Dane County had signed a comprehensive agreement to build a joint city-county building, a project that was expected to cost at least $5 million; council members were keenly

aware that the city had to reserve its bonding capacity for this project.[81]

Days after the war memorial association released its final report, several members of the common council, led by Ted Boyle, a World War II veteran, 1946 mayoral candidate, and lifelong East Sider, launched a relentless attack on the leaders of the war memorial association and their recommendations. Boyle thought the whole war memorial exercise was disgustingly elitist (for years West Siders saw themselves as briefcase-carrying intellectuals and East Siders as lunch-bucket-toting factory workers). Boyle saw Jackson, Butts, and others as big shots who needed a comeuppance. By Boyle's count, the war memorial association's governing body had seventeen West Siders and only three East Siders. Boyle was also angry that four residents of Maple Bluff and Shorewood, wealthy suburban enclaves outside Madison, were allowed to participate in the process. According to Boyle's calculations, the boat facilities, art gallery, and performing arts center comprised 60 percent of the project's costs and would be used by just 1 percent of the people. What the outspoken East Sider wanted was a plain vanilla auditorium that could be paid for with revenue bonds, not tax dollars. Finally, he most emphatically did not want to see the auditorium at the Conklin site. That site, he reminded the council, was purchased for a neighborhood park, not as a site for Joe Jackson's auditorium. Boyle was a hamburger-and-beer kind of guy who enjoyed telling the finger-sandwich and champagne crowd to go jump in the lake.[82]

Boyle refused to say what site he preferred, but on at least one earlier occasion he had expressed interest in Frank Lloyd Wright's dream civic center plan on Lake Monona. Boyle and his allies on the common council prevailed. In May 1950 the council voted unanimously for a no-frills auditorium, rejected the Conklin site, and directed the war memorial association to find other sites. The grand participatory process designed by Butts had failed. What had started out as a "noble enterprise for a noble purpose" ended up "a sorry mess."[83]

Wright failed to secure support for his civic center in attempts both before and after the war, but he did receive a Madison commission that would later prove essential for still another attempt to build his dream civic center: the Unitarians hired him to design a daring new church that broke ground in 1949 (see Fig. 3.20). He also received several major national commissions and international awards for his growing postwar practice (see Fig. 3.21).

Although the effort to build the Madison Metropolitan War Memorial collapsed, it cast long and enduring shadows over future efforts to build an auditorium in Madison. People caught a glimpse of an exciting possibility — a great community center on one of Madison's lakes. People learned that all interested Madison organizations could be involved in the planning and came to think of the community center as a complex for teenagers and for the performing and visual arts — not just a hall for conventions and sporting events. Most important of all, the war memorial crusade produced thousands of people who were convinced that Madison needed a community center — someday, somewhere, somehow. But after an arduous three-year process they were tired and discouraged. They thought they had been given roles in a play that would be performed no later than 1950, but they were wrong. Unwittingly, they had put on a dress rehearsal for still another crusade that would not begin until 1953.

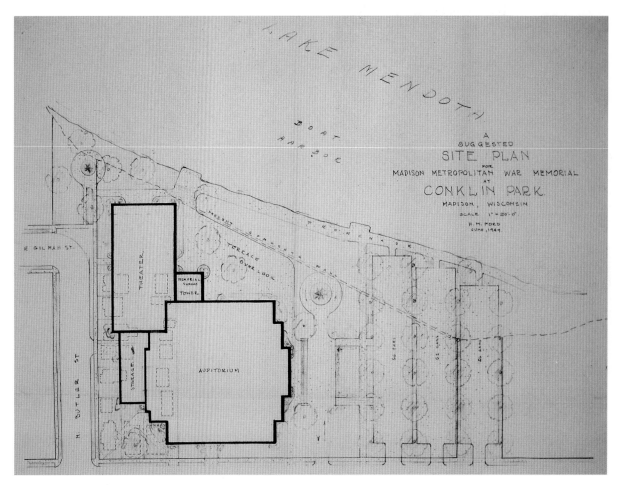

FIGURE 3.19

**1949 War Memorial Auditorium Plan for Conklin Park**

*University of Wisconsin Archives. Gallistel Collection*

Joe Jackson tried but failed to develop the Conklin site for an auditorium and boat harbor in 1935, 1938, and 1941. From 1946 to 1949 he worked with the Metropolitan War Memorial Association to realize the plan shown here, which called for a sloped-floor theater seating fifteen hundred, a flat-floor arena-auditorium seating six thousand, and a twelve-story memorial tower. Also included were a swimming pool in the lower level of the auditorium, an art gallery in the lower level of the theater, and a youth center along the outside walls of the auditorium.

The plan suffered several serious limitations. The association's report said the site should have at least 1,500 parking spaces, but the site plan shows just 184, about 50 of which required filling the lake. Association leaders said that space for the remaining 1,300 spaces could be found by extensively filling the lake, buying lakeshore properties to the east, and building parking ramps on blocks between the site and the Capitol Square. Opponents said the complex would destroy the site as a park and that the traffic it would generate would damage the neighborhood. But the biggest defect of all was its price tag, $5.2 million, more than anyone dreamed and much more than the city thought it could then afford.

1949 Groundbreaking Ceremony

*Courtesy Unitarian Universalist Association*

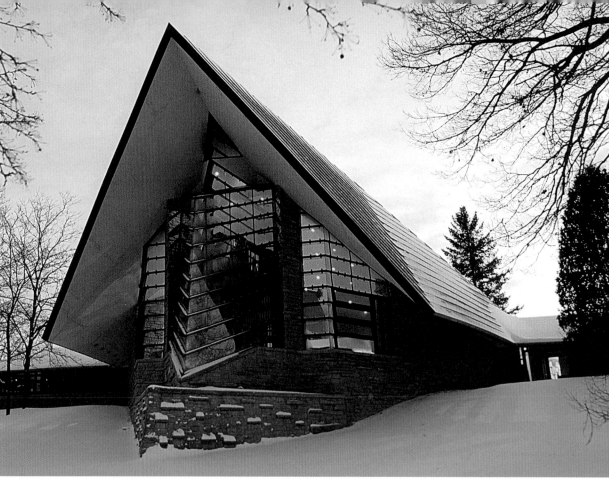

The Completed Church

*Photo by Zane Williams*

FIGURE 3.20

**Unitarian Meeting House**

The groundbreaking for what Wright called his "Country Church for Madison Unitarians" was held at 9:30 A.M. on August 12, 1949. Taking part in the ceremony were (left to right) Marshall Erdman, the contractor, wearing his trademark bow tie; Fred Cairns, pastor of the First Unitarian Society; Kenneth Parson, chairman of the society's board; Frank Lloyd Wright; and Harold Groves, chairman of the building committee, who would later become a proponent of Wright's Monona Terrace.

Even on this festive occasion, the men in this photo were grappling with a serious problem: how to keep construction costs from going beyond what the society could afford. Wright had originally said the building would cost $60,000 but later increased his estimate to $75,000. Just two weeks before groundbreaking, Marshall Erdman upped the figure to $102,000, causing alarm bells to sound.

When church leaders realized the budget was woefully insufficient, they took a page from the American barn-raising tradition. Erdman donated his truck so that members could haul a thousand tons of stone from a quarry thirty miles away, and tradesmen contributed their time. But even after two years of volunteer-supplemented work, the building fund was exhausted and the structure was far from finished. Consequently, another round of creativity was required: Taliesin apprentices spent several weeks landscaping, making furniture, and finishing the interior; Erdman borrowed $6,000 on his life insurance policy to pay for plastering the auditorium ceiling; and Wright gave two fund-raising lectures in the nearly completed meeting house. In the end the young contractor never made a dime and hauling the stone ruined his truck. When the distinctively angular church opened in 1951, its cost had soared to more than $200,000.

The handsomely proportioned building with its unique "prow" steeple quickly became one of Madison's most popular tourist destinations. In 1960 the American Institute of Architects designated it one of the seventeen most important buildings Wright designed. The lovely winter photograph shows why.

FIGURE 3.21

# THE WAR YEARS
# 1939 – 1949

**1939**
Delivers lectures in England; later published as *An Organic Architecture*

**1940**
Museum of Modern Art mounts retrospective of his work

**1941**
Receives the Royal Gold Medal for Architecture from King George VI and gains membership in the Royal Institute of British Architects

Solomon Guggenheim Museum

© FLW FDN. 4305.017

**1943**
Secures commission for the Solomon Guggenheim Museum
Revised edition of *An Autobiography* published

Jacobs II House, Middleton, Wisconsin

*Courtesy Phil Hamilton*

**1944**
Produces design for first solar hemicycle for the Jacobs family

**1945**
Publishes *When Democracy Builds*

Rogers Lacy Hotel
Interior Atrium Proposal

© FLW FDN. 4606.011

**1946**
Secures commission for the Rogers Lacy Hotel in Dallas, perhaps the earliest atrium hotel

Pittsburgh Point Civic Center Proposal

© FLW FDN. 4821.003

**1947**
Prepares first Pittsburgh Point Civic Center proposal for waterfront site

S. C. Johnson Wax
Research Tower

*Photo by Tony Puttnam*

**1948**
Construction of the S. C. Johnson Wax Research Tower finally begins

**1949**
Receives Gold Medal from the American Institute of Architects

FIGURE 4.1

**1955 View of Monona Terrace from Lake Monona**

*© FLW FDN. 5632.002*

This segment from Wright's much larger 1955 rendering captures the powerful horizontal lines of Monona Terrace and Wright's use of domes to respectfully echo the capitol dome (left). The entire sweep of this dramatic drawing can be seen on this book's dust jacket. Shallow arches sweep gracefully between massive support structures that Wright called ice breakers and unify the building. (Wright chose the name because they had to withstand the enormous pressure of winter lake ice.) Tighter, more conventional arches are visible in sunlit shafts on the lakeside surface of the inner building. Wright later used arches with varying radii in other projects, including the famous Marin County (Calif.) Civic Center. Wright said he chose the ice-breakers concept as foundations for the massive building because he did not think the lake should be filled. According to Wright's calculations, this plan would cover about five acres of water. The interior semicircle provides a platform for three large glass domes and a landscaped rooftop Wright called the garden. Surrounding this core is a large, three-level, semicircular structure. The lowest level atop the shallow arches is a cantilevered ring road. Visible above the ring road are two parking levels. The third parking level is located behind the ring road and thus is not visible in the drawing. Wright calculated that this plan would provide parking space for thirty-five hundred cars.

This was one of nine color renderings prepared to introduce the 1955 version of the plan to the public. Two others, a dramatic night scene and a cross-section, appear in Figures 4.14 and 4.15, respectively. For more information about the context of this graphic, see pages 137–39.

**CHAPTER 4**

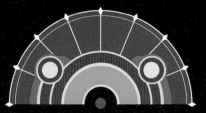

THE CIVIC AUDITORIUM CRUSADE

Ted Boyle was mad. The pugnacious lawyer and four-term former Madison council member wanted to do everything he could in the spring of 1953 to prevent Madison and Dane County from constructing an $8 million joint city hall and county courthouse on one of the most valuable blocks downtown. To Boyle (see Fig. 4.2) the proposed location — an entire city block directly opposite the Federal Building on prestigious Monona Avenue (now Martin Luther King Jr. Boulevard) — made no sense. One third of Madison's property was already off the tax rolls, mostly for government buildings, and the city needed every real estate tax dollar it could get. Boyle argued that taking this prime block for a government office building was irresponsible. He also charged that putting a city-county building there would aggravate the already terrible downtown parking situation by removing and not replacing a much-needed ground-level parking lot.[1]

Almost everyone, including Boyle, agreed that Madison needed a new city hall and that Dane County needed a bigger courthouse. The 1858 City Hall was a grossly undersized firetrap with sagging floors and no elevator. Four citizens had suffered heart attacks climbing stairs to the top story, and one had died. The county had so outgrown the 1886 courthouse that county employees had to use corridors as conference rooms. The first concerted attempt to replace these buildings with a cost-effective joint building had foundered in 1938 (see Chapter 3). Planning resumed in 1944, but progress had been slow until 1952 when local papers ran a rendering of the huge new joint building for the first time. Although some thought its design was only slightly more exciting than a slab of sidewalk, in April 1952 Madisonians had voted 4 to 1 to approve the sale of $3 million in bonds to pay for the city's share of the new building.[2]

Civic leaders agreed that downtown Madison's worst problem was the lack of parking. Since the end of World War II the number of downtown parking spaces had remained constant while the number of cars nearly doubled. Almost all parking was on the street and metered. Unfortunately, downtown employees took most of the spaces and plugged the meters all day, leaving few for shoppers, clients, and patients. By 1953 the cumulative consequences of this problem, the first symptoms of downtown decline in Madison, were evident to all. In the midst of a booming economy merchants reported an 8 percent drop in retail business and blamed it on the lack of parking. In that same year Madison East, the city's first shopping center — "the newest trend in retail business," as the *Capital Times* reported — opened on the edge of town, less than three miles from the Capitol Square. The center featured twelve stores and acres of free parking. Madison's leaders were so desperate to add parking spaces downtown that they were willing to convert Law Park into a parking lot (see Fig. 4.3).[3]

Boyle hoped that because of his reasoned opposition the city and county would abandon the proposed joint building location, but he also knew that the plan enjoyed the support of most common council members, the Madison Chamber of Commerce and Foundation (formerly the Madison and Wisconsin Foundation), and even most residents. Nevertheless, the burly lawyer decided to testify against the project at the joint city-county building committee hearing on May 15, 1953, the last public hearing on the site and the building concept.[4]

Eager to tell people "the truth," Boyle used the public hearing to criticize the proposed location as irresponsible on fiscal and parking grounds, but he did not stop there. He proposed that the new city-county building be built at the end of Monona

Avenue in Law Park. More specifically, Boyle proposed that the city and county build Frank Lloyd Wright's dream civic center and then ticked off its benefits: the site was free and would not require any land to be taken off the tax rolls; it provided much more space than the official site on Monona Avenue; the design included both an auditorium and a new city-county building — and thousands of parking spaces. This was the first time anybody had publicly mentioned the concept since Wright had urged the Young Republicans of Dane County to support his proposal in 1946.[5]

At the hearing Joe Jackson, the former executive director of the Madison and Wisconsin Foundation, and Walter Johnson, Madison's city planner, led a parade of supporters. Although Jackson had retired from the foundation in mid-1952, he remained an active player in civic affairs and was especially eager to make the city-county building a reality. For fifteen years he had fought for the building; he especially wanted to see it on the Monona Avenue site, exactly where his mentor, John Nolen, said government buildings should be. Jackson pooh-poohed Boyle's criticisms, saying that "those who oppose it now will look upon it with pride in the future." Johnson acknowledged that the new building would exacerbate the downtown parking problem but proposed to solve it by constructing a "multi-story parking lot in Law Park with an overhead walkway across the railroad tracks and an escalator to get from [Law] park to the [new] building." At the end of the spirited two-and-a-half-hour hearing, the joint city-county building committee unanimously approved the Monona Avenue site. Most thought it was a done deal and that the city and county would quickly finalize plans and send them out for bids.[6]

Boyle was hardly surprised that the committee ignored his recommendation or that the *Journal*

FIGURE 4.3

**"One of the Best Parking Areas in ... Madison"**

*SHSW. WHi(V4)314*

During the 1950s Madison officials sought almost any place to relieve the intolerable downtown parking shortage. It was for this reason that planners could hardly wait for Law Park to be filled. At a public hearing in May 1953 on the proposed city-county building, then nearing the end of the approval process, Walter Johnson, Madison's chief planner, boasted that when the city-county building was finished, "Law Park will be one of the best parking areas in the City of Madison," as a newspaper account reported. He was right. This 1958 photo shows the lake-edge park transformed into a 630-car asphalt parking lot.

Law Park was not the only lake bed in Madison coveted for parking. In 1953 University of Wisconsin officials whooshed a bill through the legislature that authorized the filling of thirty-four acres of Lake Mendota immediately adjacent to the central campus for a two-thousand-car parking lot. Although the university desperately needed more parking, professors, area residents, and conservationists got the bill repealed in 1955 and forced the university to park cars elsewhere.

did not even mention his reference to Frank Lloyd Wright's grand plan; he understood that he was being punished for being an obstructionist and a member of the "crowbar crew," a group of council members known for their tendency to derail projects. What inflamed Boyle's Irish temper was a sarcastic editorial in the *Journal* depicting his opposition as insincere. Boyle retaliated with an open letter to Roy Matson, the *Journal*'s managing editor, who refused to print it. The rival *Capital Times*, the afternoon paper, was delighted to print Boyle's broadside.[7]

Boyle blasted Matson for failing to tell people the truth: "Why not tell the people that we suggested the construction of this proposed City-County building, and ... a City Auditorium ... to be located at the base of Monona Avenue on the lake shore....

Why not tell them that Frank Lloyd Wright, perhaps one of the greatest architects and planners of all time, suggested this spot years ago and offered to draw the plans for this building as a memorial to what he considered his second home, at no cost to the city?"[8]

For Jackson, Boyle's testimony and his letter to the editor must have been ominously reminiscent of what happened in 1938. That year Jackson had made an all-out effort to get the city and county to erect a city-county building at the same site, but as Jackson saw it, Frank Lloyd Wright had come in at the eleventh hour and persuaded wavering supervisors that the Monona Avenue site was too small. Was Boyle going to use the Wright plan for another hijacking of the city-county building in

1953? Jackson surely tossed and turned at night thinking about that prospect.

Jackson was hardly alone. Nearly all Madison leaders drew their bayonets and surrounded the city-county building proposal with steadfast support. They had spent too much time persuading a reluctant county to cohabit a joint building to allow Boyle to come along with his crowbar and wreck everything. Indeed, Jackson and his cronies had no choice but to take Boyle seriously. In 1949 Boyle had almost singlehandedly killed a carefully crafted, three-year effort by the Metropolitan War Memorial Association to build an auditorium and civic center at Conklin Park. As a result, leaders put the civic auditorium on a back burner and turned their attention to securing a city-county building.

But now in May 1953 the city-county building was about to receive its final approval, and community leaders were once again willing to invest their energy in what had become the most elusive and star-crossed public building in Madison's history, the civic auditorium. F. Edwin Schmitz, the incoming president of the Madison Chamber of Commerce and Foundation, drew loud and prolonged applause on May 13 when he announced at the organization's annual dinner that the civic auditorium would be his main goal. The following day a *Journal* editorial applauded this initiative and urged that the city follow the plans developed by Jackson and his War Memorial Association. This auditorium, the *Journal* intoned, is what Madison "needs and wants and can have" — a flat-floor arena, sloped-floor theater, swimming pool, art gallery, arena, memorial shrine, community center, and boat harbor in Conklin Park. The *Journal* said nothing about the $5.2 million price tag.[9]

## THE CITIZEN CRUSADE

If anyone in the business community doubted the importance of reactivating the War Memorial

FIGURE 4.4

## IVAN NESTINGEN
*MAYORAL CATALYST*

SHSW. WHi(X3)51570

When Ivan A. Nestingen was elected mayor of Madison in 1956 at the age of thirty-four, he was undoubtedly the best-educated person to ever hold that post; in 1949 Nestingen received both a doctorate in history and a law degree from the University of Wisconsin. Had he not served three years as an army engineer in the South Pacific during World War II, he would probably have earned his degrees even earlier.

Nestingen joined a Madison law firm in 1949 and two years later made the fateful decision to enter local politics. Even in his first term on the common council, his competence and extraordinary leadership skills were evident. After he won a second term in 1953, he was appointed chairman of the Auditorium Committee, a post that placed him in the eye of a great political storm for seven years. At first Nestingen opposed Frank Lloyd Wright's Monona Terrace, but he gradually became its most outspoken elected champion.

While serving on the council, the liberal Nestingen became an officer in the statewide Joe Must Go movement, an effort to recall the controversial Wisconsin senator Joe McCarthy. In November 1954 the politically ambitious Nestingen won a seat in the Wisconsin Assembly, a victory that forced him to resign from the Madison council in January 1955 so he had time to earn a living as a lawyer. However, because he had provided such outstanding leadership on the Auditorium Committee, Mayor George Forster asked Nestingen to continue as its chairman but as a citizen. Nestingen agreed.

When a special mayoral election was held in 1956 after Forster resigned, Nestingen ran and won, though by just 1,135 votes. Nestingen concentrated attention on Monona Terrace and in just one year signed the long-stalled Wright contract, secured an additional $1.5 million for a parking ramp for the building, and worked with Wright to refine the design to meet Madison's needs and fit its pocketbook. When the Metzner law (see pp. 152–56) was repealed in 1959, Nestingen worked with Wright to restart the Terrace project, but Wright died that April. Meanwhile,

Nestingen won reelection to a regular two-year term in 1957 by a whopping 3-to-1 margin and in 1959 ran unopposed.

In 1959 Nestingen plunged into national politics, heading the Kennedy for President Club of Wisconsin and in 1960 chaired the Wisconsin delegation at the Democratic National Convention. In January 1961 Kennedy offered Nestingen a job as an assistant secretary in the Department of Health, Education, and Welfare. To accept the federal post, Nestingen had to resign as mayor and leave the Monona Terrace project at a critical time. Nestingen served at HEW until 1965 when he resigned to make way for Lyndon Johnson's appointees. Nestingen stayed in Washington and practiced law until his untimely death at fifty-six in 1978. A year before he had told a *Capital Times* reporter that his only regret in leaving Madison was that had he stayed, he "could have helped just enough to get [Monona Terrace] through."

Association to lead the auditorium crusade, Boyle's demand for Wright's civic complex swept such misgivings from their minds. Business leaders understood that if they failed to provide community leadership, "Crowbar" Boyle and the Wright plan could prevail. The only way to regain control of the auditorium question, they concluded, was to launch a separate, city-controlled process — and do it immediately.

Just five days after Boyle's broadside, an eager young council member introduced a resolution calling for the creation of a city auditorium committee that would determine the type of auditorium that should be built and how it should be financed. The resolution required the committee to work with interested civic groups and to report back to the council "at the earliest practicable date."[10]

Ivan Nestingen, who was just thirty when he was first elected to the common council in 1951, introduced the resolution. During his first term Nestingen had served on the prestigious joint city-county building committee; now, two years later, the articulate liberal had won reelection and continued to demonstrate a flair for leadership (see Fig. 4.4). Although Nestingen had not been a part of the war memorial effort, his decision to introduce the auditorium resolution was undoubtedly an attempt to lead what he anticipated would be a major postwar civic crusade. In June 1953, just two weeks after Nestingen introduced his resolution, Mayor George Forster appointed him to the Auditorium Committee. At the first meeting the members elected him chairman, a position Nestingen would hold for seven tumultuous years.[11]

Nestingen's first two terms on the council came at a happy juncture of city history when low debt and a booming economy allowed city leaders to undertake an unprecedented number of large projects. That was a good thing because pent-up demand from the Great Depression and World War II meant the city needed new schools, roads, downtown parking ramps, an upgraded sewage system, a new city-county building, and the elusive civic auditorium.[12] (Madisonians routinely call a multilevel parking structure a parking "ramp," not a garage, as elsewhere in the country.)

The formation of the Auditorium Committee clearly defined the civic battlefield. Almost all business, political, and civic leaders gathered under the banner of the official city committee headed by Nestingen, and Wright's supporters fell in line behind Boyle. Politically, all the odds were against Boyle, who had no support on the common council and only a handful of backers. But this was just the type of underdog, outsider fight that Boyle relished. Boyle, a shrewd tactician, immediately saw that Wright's support was essential and drove out to Taliesin to see him. Wright was obviously pleased with this rare expression of grassroots support and recognized that this was a now-or-never opportunity. Madison was about to build a city-county building *and* an auditorium, the two major functions in his beloved dream civic center. Miss the boat here, Wright recognized, and there would be no more boats. Wright told Boyle he would help in any way he could. The two men had several other meetings at Taliesin and at Boyle's downtown law office to develop their strategy.[13]

When it came to contempt for the system, Boyle and Wright were temperamental clones. Both had spent most of their public lives criticizing the system, though in different ways. This time, Wright expressed his contempt early in the campaign when he told council members to break the contract with the architectural firm the city had hired to design the city-county building: "It's a pretty poor establishment that can't break a contract that's heading in the wrong direction." But he and Boyle recognized that the council would not vote for the Wright plan and that the duo's only hope was to get the people to support it. As Wright saw it, there was "no known way to prevent mistaken commitments of politicians ... except the referendum." He and Boyle agreed on this strategy, and Boyle said he would try to get enough signatures to require a referendum in the fall of 1953.[14]

The first step, they agreed, was to prepare a fresh set of presentation drawings so that people could understand the exciting but complex project. Wright's good friend, William T. Evjue, editor and publisher of the *Capital Times*, printed the new drawings first, in a four-part series in early July 1953. Because twelve years had passed since any images of Wright's proposal had appeared in the newspapers, many Madisonians were seeing them for the first time. Most people were stunned by its size and by Wright's audacious claims that he had shoehorned into a single building an auditorium seating seventy-five hundred people, a city-county building offering lake views from most offices, a marina for five hundred boats, a union railroad depot, and five thousand parking spaces, enough to increase the downtown supply by 86 percent two blocks from the capitol. And, as Boyle never tired of reminding everyone, the land was free and no valuable downtown land would have to be taken off the tax rolls.[15]

Dazzling adjectives, adverbs, and nouns danced through the *Capital Times* articles like morning sunlight over a breeze-ruffled lake. The building was described as "a seven acre wonderland of trees, fountains and promenades looking down on Lake Monona.... Giant bastions with cantilevered arms would support the structure.... Pumps would bring

EXTENSION AND TERMINAL OF MONONA AVENUE

SEVEN ACRES OF MADE OVER EXISTING RAILROAD TRACKS FOR PARKING.

LAKE WATER THROWN UP INTO MONUMENTAL FOUNTAINS.

CIVIC AUDITORIUM SEATING 10,000, FRONTING OLIN TERRACE.

COUNTY JAIL AND OFFICES, CITY HALL, UNION RAILROAD DEPOT.

MONONA AVE.

COST $17,500,000, RAISE

PINCKNEY ST.

OLIN TERRACE

"THE CITY GOES TO THE LAKE" — SEVEN MONTHS WATERDOMES, FIVE MONTHS EVERGREENS.

(SEE KAUFMANN À LA PITTSBURGH.)

FIGURE 4.5

**1953 Aerial View
from Monona Avenue**

© FLW FDN. 3909.002

This dramatic 1953 rendering, with its distinctive rusty orange background, was a replacement for a similar but torn and tattered drawing Wright had done in 1938 (Fig. 3.5). Wright's eagerness for another opportunity to promote the project was evident in his decision to direct his staff to redo the worn 1938 drawings at no cost to the city and on the basis of a small contingent of Madisonians led by Ted Boyle. For this important job Wright turned to John Howe, one of his longtime associates who specialized in presentation drawings. The original 18-by-41-inch drawing was done on tracing paper with colored pencils and ink.

The ant-sized people in the foreground dramatize the massive size of Wright's plan. The footprint of the megastructure extended for about one thousand feet along the lakeshore and jutted nearly 485 feet out into the lake from the Olin Terrace abutment wall (just in front of the central fountain). The top deck stood about 56 feet above Lake Monona. Wright claimed that the megastructure could be built for $17.5 million, but others thought it would require $37 million.

Wright later said the purpose of his civic center was "to recover the waterfront for urban use and make it as a part of the central avenue tributary to the Capitol Square and the Capitol itself." Punctuating the top of the complex are three glass domes, each echoing the much larger and taller capitol dome just two blocks away. Wright used the domes to symbolize the three major buildings housed in the complex: an auditorium, city hall, and county courthouse. Wright envisioned pumping lake water over these domes into basins where they would be collected in conduits and then discharged at the lakeside edge in two great waterfalls. The building also contained a union railroad depot and a municipal marina for five hundred boats.

up huge quantities of water, to spurt as brilliant fountains on the upper terrace, flow as rivulets down through the three civic gardens ... and would empty as a waterfall back in Monona." The building would jut out into the lake 685 feet from the Wilson Street sidewalk but leave the lake view unobstructed. Wright predicted that his megastructure would attract one million visitors each year, cost only $17.5 million, and be financially "self-liquidating."[16]

During this period the project got a new name. When Wright introduced the plan in 1938, it was known as Olin Terraces, but when he reintroduced it in early 1953, Boyle referred to it simply as "the Wright plan." However, beginning in August and September 1953 Wright, sensing the need for a fresh start, called it the "Monona Terrace Garden plan," the "Monona Terrace Park plan," and the "Monona Terrace Civic Center." By the end of 1953 almost everyone called it Monona Terrace.[17]

The second step was to create an organization to rally public support. In August 1953 Boyle created the City-County Civic Center Committee, the first of many citizen groups to do battle over this building. Under the auspices of the "4Cs committee," as it was commonly known, Boyle and his supporters sponsored six 30-minute radio programs that ran during prime time on Sunday evenings in August and September, began a petition drive, debated opponents, and arranged for the Capitol Square businesses to display the beautiful Wright drawings.[18]

Despite his demanding schedule (among the projects on his drawing board were the Price Tower in Oklahoma and Guggenheim Museum in New York), Wright eagerly participated by appearing on radio and television programs, writing a guest editorial in the *Capital Times*, and testifying before the common council. Although he lavished glowing words on his cherished Monona Terrace, he also

followed his lifelong pattern of trying to embarrass Madisonians into supporting the project. He said that he was ashamed of his hometown because it had "plenty of civic snobbery but no civic pride," that the city was governed by "nickel-pinchers" who thought Madison was a "poverty patch," and that its people had "no vision, no courage, [and] no discontent."[19]

Boyle arranged for Wright to appear before the powerful joint city-county building committee in September 1953. Wright agreed to attend, then refused at the last minute when he learned that he was going to appear before a mere committee and not the entire city council or county board. Fuming committee members sent Wright a scorching letter saying they would never again deal with Boyle on this matter. Wright fired off damage-control letters, saying that "no one has any authority to make appointments for me" and that he had no "sponsors," but by then it was too late. Boyle was deeply embarrassed and from that point forward could not provide effective leadership. Nevertheless, he kept plugging away and did whatever he could behind the scenes.[20]

Meanwhile, Nestingen's Auditorium Committee and his supporters moved to deflate the Boyle boomlet. At the committee's first regular meeting in July 1953, Joe Jackson and Joe Rothschild, the two men who had spearheaded the War Memorial Association effort from 1946 to 1949, urged the committee to consider the comprehensive plans developed by their organization and emphasized that their initiative had absolutely nothing to do with the "monkey wrench" Wright plan. In September the Auditorium Committee issued its first report, which dismissed the Wright plan as "far too costly" and a sure killer of the approved city-county building project. Less than a month later it issued a second report that insisted that

Monona Terrace would cost as much as $37 million, more than twice what Wright had said, that it contained only a third of the office space needed by the city and county, that it could accommodate only a thousand cars, that its construction would aggravate downtown parking and traffic problems, and, finally, that "leaders of the 4C's Committee are not sincere in advocating the Wright plan."[21]

To make sure its voice was heard, the Chamber of Commerce and Foundation issued a press release in late September that disparaged Wright's plan because it encouraged the centralization of functions at a time when nearly all experts agreed that urban salvation lay in decentralization. Further, it provided no bathing beaches, would not make money, and would block the lake view down Monona Avenue. Jackson did not write this report, but his imprint was unmistakable.[22]

Also in September 1953 Wright supporters heard for the first time the stridently critical voice of Carroll Metzner. Like Nestingen, Metzner was a lawyer, a second-term council member, and had served on the joint city-county building committee. Unlike Nestingen, Metzner was a Republican. Although both men were absolutely opposed to any plan that would scuttle the joint building, Nestingen's criticism of the Wright plan was always more muted. Metzner, by contrast, went much further and quickly became the unofficial attack dog of anti-Wright forces.[23]

After four months of public discussion, most critics conceded that Wright's plan was a "glittering, inspiring wonder" but that its cost was far beyond Madison's means. Wright realized that if he did not do something to counter his critics' high cost estimates, no one would take his project seriously. Consequently, he proposed a bold, high-stakes wager. He said he would put up $20,000 to hire independent experts to determine what his complex would cost. If experts said it could not be built for less than $20 million, Wright would lose his money. But if experts showed that it could be built for less than $20 million, the city would be committed to build it. Mayor Forster countered Wright's gutsy move by saying that the city would put up $20,000 to hire experts and if the cost was less than $17.5 million—the amount that Wright had said it would cost—Wright would owe nothing. But if the cost exceeded that amount, Wright would have to pay the $20,000. Neither accepted the other's offer.[24]

It soon became apparent that the Wright-Boyle strategy of appealing directly to residents had been effective. On October 29 Wright appeared before five hundred residents and local elected officials in the auditorium of Madison's Central High School to hear his plan (see Fig. 4.6).

In the audience that evening was Helen Groves (see Fig. 4.7), fifty-three, an active member of the First Unitarian Society who had played a large role in building Wright's distinctive church (Fig. 3.20). Among other things, she had organized the Unitarians to haul one thousand tons of stone to build the church and had coordinated the weaving of a 120-foot custom drapery for the rear of the auditorium.[25]

As Groves listened to Wright describe Monona Terrace, she was struck by the contrast between the stony-faced, disapproving city and county officials and the warm enthusiasm of the audience. She was also thinking about the thousands of tourists who were coming to Madison to see Wright's newly completed church. Something was terribly wrong, she concluded. The city needed a new city hall and an auditorium, and Wright had offered to give the city his glorious design for nothing. Why were city officials so opposed to such a wonderful idea? To Helen Groves, their opposition made no sense.

FIGURE 4.6

**Wright Presents His Plan to Citizens, 1953**

*Courtesy* Wisconsin State Journal

"I'm just an old fool who would like to make a final contribution to my boyhood town." That was how Frank Lloyd Wright, shown here on the stage of the Central High School auditorium on October 29, 1953, justified his decision to revive his "civic center plan."

Technically, Wright had been invited to make a presentation to the joint city-county building committee to show that his plan contained ample accommodations for city and county offices, jails, and courtrooms. But public interest in Wright's proposal was so great that the committee decided to hold the meeting at the high school. Five hundred attended, including 71 members of the 82-person county board and nearly all 20 members of the common council. Wright was coolly received by the joint committee members, who paid little attention to his presentation. "It looks as though I have come here after the obituary has been written," Wright quipped. By contrast, residents greeted Wright's presentation with warm and frequent applause.

Carroll Metzner, then a thirty-four-year-old member of the common council, repeatedly interrupted the eighty-six-year-old Wright with questions from a typed page, according to the *Capital Times.* "Exactly how many square feet does the building contain?" asked Metzner.

"Why do you ask me that?" Wright responded. "Haven't I offered the city of Madison enough for nothing?"

"Do you know how many cubic feet it takes to park a car?" Metzner continued.

"No, but you should know," Wright retorted.

Wright refused to give cost estimates, saying that his role was "to bring an idea to the city," an idea that would "raise Madison from the ranks of mediocrity."

Wright used the presentation drawings arrayed behind him to explain the project. (Several drawings appear in other chapters, including Fig. 3.1, and the large drawing directly behind Wright appears in Fig. 4.5.) Well-known *Capital Times* reporter John Patrick Hunter was seated at a small table in front of the stage. When Wright was finished, he walked off the stage and out the side door. And as he did, Hunter heard the octogenarian say softly, "Good-bye, good-bye, good-bye." It was a vintage performance by the old master.

FIGURE 4.7

# HELEN AND HAROLD GROVES
*STEADFAST CITIZEN LEADERS*

*Courtesy Susan Groves*

"Guess who showed up at my office door this morning?" Harold Groves asked his wife, Helen. "A gentleman wearing a pork-pie hat, a flowing necktie, and knickers." The surprise visitor was none other than Frank Lloyd Wright, who wanted the distinguished professor of economics at the University of Wisconsin to speak at a Sunday meeting of the Fellowship at Taliesin on February 18, 1934. Harold Groves, then just thirty-seven, was completing a two-year term in the Wisconsin Assembly (the first U.W. professor to ever serve in this body) and had already made headlines for his role in securing Wisconsin's unemployment compensation bill, the nation's first. "Bring your wife and plan to spend the day with us," insisted Wright, as Harold Groves recalled in his memoir, *In and Out of the Ivory Tower*. The Groveses agreed, and Harold led a spirited discussion of the close relationship between economic and religious values.

The Groveses' next encounter with Wright came after World War II when the First Unitarian Society sought an architect to build a new church. At the time both were members of the society and voted against hiring Wright, but their side lost. Because Harold Groves was the secretary of the society, it fell to him to ask Wright whether he would be interested in the commission. When Wright agreed, the Groveses threw their support behind the project and worked to make the new church a reality. Working with Wright was a transforming experience for both. They became believers in Wright's organic architecture and the importance of making beauty a prominent feature in the design of all buildings.

The Groveses, shown here as they were about to depart for an evening at Taliesin in the mid-1950s, were endowed with outstanding minds, a commitment to public service, and an abiding belief in ideals. Because of her Quaker upbringing Helen Groves spurned fashion and emphasized functionality. She wore flat-soled shoes, had her hair cut at the barbershop, and did her shopping with a knapsack on her back. Harold Groves derived great satisfaction from hard work, being out of doors, playing baseball, and writing

poetry. Both were impressed with the exemplary civic leadership of John Olin, the father of Madison's park system (see Chapter 1). As Helen Groves put it in a letter to Wright in 1956, "Our prayers each night are that we might emulate John Olin."

When a small group of Madison citizens reintroduced Wright's civic center concept in 1953, Helen Groves, then fifty-three, leaped into the fray. She appeared before the common council and the Dane County board, wrote letters, enlisted friends, and tried to get Madisonians to see the merits of Wright's great vision. But this was anything but work to her. She told a prominent civic leader that she had "set out on a great adventure ... a housewife's holiday," and in a letter she told Wright that she "was having a perfectly wonderful time." The architect appreciated her chatty letters because they kept him informed of what supporters were doing to promote his ambitious plan. Wright's replies would begin, "My dear Sister Groves." In one such letter he expressed his gratitude for her "intelligent pertinacity" and all that she was doing on behalf of the "beneficent idea that has never yet got across to the city."

At first Harold Groves offered only encouragement, but before 1953 ended he had a toe in the water, and by 1954 he was fully immersed in the crusade. From 1955, when he was appointed to the Auditorium Committee, until he was booted from it in 1961 by Mayor Reynolds, Harold Groves played a large, influential role. He appeared before a state legislative committee, debated, gave speeches, wrote position papers, appeared on television, and much more. After Harold Groves became involved, Wright wrote a note thanking the couple for their ability to "persist in a cause in which you have the great faculty to believe."

Helen Groves served as secretary of Citizens for Monona Terrace for many years, and Harold Groves served six years on the Auditorium Committee. When the bids came in in 1961, he spearheaded a drive to raise $1 million and personally pledged $5,000 — more money than any other individual or corporation. To make good on

this pledge he surely used royalties from his *Financing Government*, a popular college textbook that went through seven editions.

Harold Groves died in 1969 in the midst of debate about the Monona Basin plan (a later incarnation of Wright's plan described in Chapter 5). When she learned in the early 1990s that her beloved Monona Terrace might be resurrected, Helen Groves offered to organize support among the residents of her Madison nursing home; she died in 1994, before construction began. In the long history of Monona Terrace this extraordinary couple stands out for their resilience, resourcefulness, selfless commitment, passion, persistence, unquenchable optimism, and inspiring leadership. It is from such rare ore that great cities are fashioned.

She saw the building as a beautifully tailored suit perfectly fitted for Madison's civic needs.[26]

Although Groves had never been active in local politics, she conducted an informal poll of people living in the two blocks surrounding her home. To her astonishment, five families were in favor of the Wright plan, fourteen wanted a referendum to vote on the two plans, and one opposed the Wright plan. That settled it. Helen Groves decided to get involved. She discussed her decision with her husband, Harold (see Fig. 4.7), a distinguished professor of economics at the University of Wisconsin who had given lectures at Taliesin. He had served a term in the Wisconsin Assembly in the 1930s and knew that his wife, a woman with limited political experience, would be much more effective if she teamed up with a seasoned politico. He urged her to contact Mary Lescohier, who was married to another economics professor.[27]

Lescohier, then fifty-two, was the longtime editor of *Land Economics,* a quarterly academic journal headquartered on the U.W. campus. She was also a committed civic activist, devout liberal, brilliant strategic thinker, skilled writer, and articulate representative for the League of Women Voters (see Fig. 4.8). Furthermore, she had enough pluck for a cold-calling sales rep and was a fan of Frank Lloyd Wright's. Mary Lescohier (pronounced les-co-HERE) was the ideal ally and alter ego for Helen Groves. When Groves called, Lescohier said yes. They threw themselves into the crusade for Wright's visionary design and fomented one of the most successful grassroots political campaigns in Wisconsin history. Both papers persisted in referring to Groves and Lescohier as "professors' wives."[28]

December 1953 was a critical month for both sides. By this time thirty-five hundred people had signed the petitions demanding a referendum, and the city and county were scheduled to approve the

preliminary drawings for the city-county building prepared by Holabird, Root, and Burgee, a large Chicago architectural firm. To Monona Terrace supporters, city approval of the Holabird plan was the worst scenario possible. It meant the loss of the $8 million the city and county had earmarked for this project and the loss of a major function that Wright had incorporated in his design. Terrace supporters reasoned that if they got this $8 million *plus* whatever additional amount the city would appropriate for the auditorium, they would have nearly enough money to build Wright's inspiring vision.[29]

It was with this reasoning that Mary Lescohier appeared before the city council and Helen Groves appeared before the county board to try to persuade those bodies to cancel their contract with the Chicago firm and sign a contract with Wright instead. Lescohier told the council that she represented a "movement of the people" and brandished the petitions demanding a referendum. After Nestingen told her that she was "sincere but misled," the council gave unanimous approval to the preliminary plans for the city-county building. The county also approved the Holabird contract but only by a five-vote margin (42–37). Groves and Lescohier had failed; on the other hand, they were fast studies and anything but finished.[30]

In January 1954 Nestingen's Auditorium Committee had almost all the momentum and power. It proposed a referendum for November 2, 1954, a decision everyone accepted, and committee members encouraged Jackson and Rothschild to reactivate their Metropolitan War Memorial Association and lead the public planning effort. However, committee members realized that they also needed expert help. They knew they wanted an auditorium and civic center but little more. The 1949 specifications for a comparable civic complex were now five years

old and the city had grown. To find out what Madison needed in 1954, the committee hired Sprague-Bowman Associates, the first of dozens of consultants that would be commissioned over the next forty years.[31]

While the consultants were gathering data, Groves and Lescohier began a surprisingly vigorous campaign to get people to see the merit of Wright's plan. In March and April they persuaded Bill Evjue to publish eight testimonials by prominent civic leaders in the *Capital Times.* They continued to produce doubt-generating statements about the city-county building, noting, for example, that many costs, such as land acquisition, lost taxes, and landscaping, had been omitted from the estimates, the building would aggravate downtown traffic congestion, it had been secretly downsized, and nobody really knew what it would cost when completed. The two women shrewdly focused nearly all their firepower on the Dane County supervisors, whose collective ardor for the joint building was tepid. These tactics kept Wright's proposal on the front burner and won converts.[32]

Up to this point Evjue had not given the project his full personal or editorial support. He had published Wright's new renderings in July 1953 because of his friendship with the architect (see Fig. 4.9), and he published the Wright plan testimonials because proponents had submitted them. He had three reasons for keeping his distance from the project. First, he detested Boyle—his Republicanism, his notorious obstructionism, and his association with Senator Joe McCarthy. Second, Evjue did not believe that Madisonians would get behind such a "noble and ambitious plan." Third, Evjue refused to be involved in any project that would scuttle the city-county building on Monona Avenue, even Monona Terrace.[33]

FIGURE 4.8

# MARY LESCOHIER
*CRUSADING CHAMPION*

*Courtesy* The Capital Times

One day in October 1953, Mary Lescohier, shown here in a 1956 photo, received a telephone call from Helen Groves. Groves wanted Lescohier to join the fight to build Frank Lloyd Wright's dream civic center. When Lescohier agreed, she did not realize that she was enlisting in a campaign that would continue for more than two decades.

After pursuing a journalism degree at George Washington University, Lescohier did public relations and headed a speakers' bureau for the Community Chest in Atlanta. During the depression she coordinated a relief program in West Virginia sponsored by the American Friends Service Committee. In this latter capacity Lescohier met Eleanor Roosevelt, who persuaded her to join the 1936 Roosevelt campaign. Lescohier, then thirty-five, crisscrossed southern New York State in a motor caravan. She coordinated speakers and even made direct appeals to voters on street corners with a bullhorn. After the campaign she worked in New York as a writer and researcher for New Deal studies of public assistance and met her future husband, Donald. When Lescohier received Groves's recruiting call, she had been editor of a prestigious academic quarterly journal, *Land Economics*, since 1942.

Lescohier threw her heart and soul into the Monona Terrace crusade. She recruited her friends and colleagues, testified at city and county meetings, wrote press releases, spent hours on the telephone, and ran a mimeograph machine. Lescohier was a founder of Citizens for Monona Terrace and for two decades provided spirited leadership. Because of her keen intelligence, sharp tongue, powerful writing, and astute sense of strategy, Lescohier was a formidable proponent of Monona Terrace. She became a trusted Wright confidante, sometimes even ghost-writing articles and letters for his signature. She lobbied the Wisconsin legislature and mobilized opposition to the Metzner bill (see pp. 152–56). Lescohier and her husband also donated thousands of dollars to underwrite various costs of Monona Terrace, including an expensive lawsuit to test the constitutionality of the Metzner law.

Faced with such resourceful and persistent opposition, most citizen volunteers would give up. But Lescohier kept on fighting. She confronted politicians and attended every meeting of any city body that had anything to do with Monona Terrace. Because of her masterful grasp of the complex history of the project and her superb judgment, Wright's Madison attorney frequently sought Lescohier's counsel and even had her dictate letters to his secretary on special topics. In the 1960s and 1970s she continued to play a central role in salvaging the concept of Monona Terrace.

Lescohier died in 1984 believing that her work on behalf of Monona Terrace had been futile. But it was not. Her efforts, along with those of a handful of other civic leaders, kept Monona Terrace on the civic marquee for more than twenty years; in fact, it was this long run that people remembered in the 1980s when Madison's need for a convention center prompted people to suggest adapting Monona Terrace. Had she lived to see her great dream realized, she would have been thrilled but quick to deflect credit to others. In truth, much credit is hers.

But by May 1954 Evjue realized that he had to support Monona Terrace. He was appalled that the "old boys" of the business community were leading Madison down the war memorial path once again. He realized that his constituency needed support against the aggressive opposition from the *Journal.* He was delighted by the new liberal leadership provided by Groves, Lescohier, and others — and that Boyle was no longer leading the charge. He had reread Nolen's 1911 book, *Madison: A Model City*, and had been reinspired by its grand vision and repersuaded by its logic. He had been visited by an unprecedented number of people about the Wright plan and now was convinced that rank-and-file Madisonians would support it. The one obstacle remaining was Wright's insistence that the city-county building be part of Monona Terrace. It was time, Evjue concluded, to have a little talk with his good friend.[34]

As Wright reported the conversation, Evjue began with a question: "Why further divide this old town into sheep and goats? Why not let the officials have their costly office building? Madison needs a damn-sight more than just that! This city needs a ... civic center.... We need a place for conventions. A big auditorium. Yes, a big one and an attractive sports arena. Why must our people go to a stock pavilion if they want to go to a great concert? We have no attractive civic theater either.... Your Monona Terrace is just the thing to satisfy all these public needs and then some."

Wright immediately agreed, recognizing that it was "futile to continue opposing the construction of the city-county building in Madison" and that he should concentrate "on efforts to obtain approval for a new civic center."[35]

This famous Evjue-Wright compromise allowed both projects to go forward — the city-county building *and*

Monona Terrace (minus city and county offices) — and marked the beginning of an era in Madison history when Evjue became the preeminent, outspoken, and crusading champion of Wright's Monona Terrace. Although Wright technically abided by the Evjue compromise, he could seldom resist taking a backhanded swipe at the city-county building. As Wright once put it, "If the bird in the hand is a crow, and if when you let go you are assured to get a pair of pheasants," well then, "which would you rather do, eat crow — or pheasants?"[36]

The Sprague-Bowman report on what facilities Madison needed arrived that June. In the long history of Monona Terrace few documents had such a profound and enduring influence on it. The consultants analyzed several "packages" of facilities they believed Madison should consider, and in early July 1954 the Auditorium Committee concluded that Madison needed a

- Sloped-floor auditorium designed for the performing arts, lectures, and demonstrations, with seating for no fewer than two thousand

- Flat-floor multipurpose exhibit hall suitable for conventions, car shows, large banquets, large public dances, touring entertainment companies, and some sporting events, with temporary seating for thirty-five hundred

- Small theater seating three hundred

- Community center with a game room, dance hall, lounge and snack bar, crafts room, photography rooms, and meeting rooms

- Art gallery

With almost no discussion this array of functions became the template for all future versions of Monona Terrace.[37]

But this mix of functions, Sprague-Bowman emphasized, meant that Madison's civic center would be an exotic hybrid. Most communities were satisfied with an arena, an exhibit hall, and perhaps a theater. But no city in the country, they reported, had put such an unusual mix of cultural, commercial, community, and entertainment facilities in a single complex. Nevertheless, the Auditorium Committee settled on this mix because its members believed it would best serve the most people. Madison was about to attempt something that probably had never been done before.[38]

Sprague-Bowman proposed to call this cluster of functions an "auditorium and civic center." Although the name stuck, it did nothing to clarify what the building would be. In 1910 Nolen and other progressives had defined a *civic center* as a central-city concentration of architecturally similar government buildings artistically arranged around a broad avenue or plaza. Many Madisonians used the phrase in that sense. Wright used civic center to mean a single, large, multipurpose building containing public assembly facilities, including an auditorium, city-county offices, a railroad station, and a marina. Madison's 1949 war memorial planners used *community center* and meant a complex of public facilities, including an arena, swimming pool, and shrine. The problem was, no single term fit Madison's proposal. After the Sprague-Bowman report came out, auditorium and civic center meant a single large building with whatever functions the Auditorium Committee picked.[39]

The Sprague-Bowman report was also the basis for a $4 million estimate for the auditorium and civic center, a figure that proved controversial for many years. The Auditorium Committee picked $4 million because it was a "middle ground" between low and high figures provided by the consultant and

FIGURE 4.9

**Two Close Friends, Evjue and Wright**

*Courtesy* The Capital Times

William T. Evjue, editor and publisher of the *Capital Times*, and Frank Lloyd Wright enjoyed a warm, first-name relationship. The two met in 1914 when Evjue was business manager for the *Wisconsin State Journal*. Wright had just returned from Japan and had stopped in Madison to visit his cousin, Richard Lloyd Jones, then the *Journal's* editor. In the 1920s the paths of Evjue and Wright crossed again when Evjue was a member of the building committee for Madison's Nakoma Country Club, which hired Wright to design a new clubhouse. From these contacts the two men developed a long-term friendship. Evjue and his wife, Zillah, were regular guests at Taliesin events, and Wright would often visit the editor at his downtown *Capital Times* office. The photograph shown here was taken in Wright's study at Taliesin.

Although Evjue did not immediately endorse Monona Terrace when it was reintroduced in 1953, he became its unwavering champion in May 1954 after he persuaded Wright to allow the city and county to move ahead with their planned joint building on Monona Avenue. Although Wright was not happy about removing city and county offices from his civic center plan, he was pleased to have Evjue's support. In June 1954, Wright wrote Evjue, referring to the civic center plan: "There is great chance ahead for something real for the world to remember us by."

because it roughly corresponded to the package the committee thought Madison needed.[40]

About a month after it received the Sprague-Bowman report, the Auditorium Committee recommended that Madisonians be given the opportunity to vote on whether to use Wright as the architect. This thunderously controversial suggestion, which squeaked through the committee by a single vote, came from chairman Nestingen, who had been warming to Wright's Monona Terrace proposal — so long as it did not include city and county offices. Nestingen observed that support had been growing "from all groups, social brackets, and economic levels" and thought that people would resent not being able to vote on the issue.[41]

The *Wisconsin State Journal*, almost all Chamber of Commerce leaders, and the common council, by a vote of 15–3 on July 22, told Nestingen they were adamantly opposed to including Wright's name on the ballot. In effect, the establishment said only one question would go to referendum in November: a $4 million auditorium, yes or no. Evjue pounced on the "peewee City Hall politicians and the Chamber of Commerce" for what he called their "blank check" mentality. These politicians and leaders, Evjue correctly noted, did not want residents to determine the site, the architect, or the design.[42]

The council's refusal to let the people vote on Wright's plan so angered Groves and Lescohier that on August 3, two weeks after the council decision, the two women gathered fifty Terrace supporters at the Unitarian Meeting House for what would later be viewed as a watershed meeting. Up to this point the loose-knit group of supporters had no name, so they decided to call themselves "Citizens for Monona Terrace." That night they voted unanimously to circulate petitions that would compel the city to hold a binding referendum on this question: "Be it

resolved that the City of Madison develop the Monona Terrace site for an auditorium and civic center in accordance with the plan of Frank Lloyd Wright." To succeed they had to gather signatures from sixty-eight hundred voters by September 8, just thirty-six days away. Big job or not, these foot soldiers were in high spirits as they marched out into the warm summer evening. In their heads they had a shimmering vision of a spectacular building designed by Frank Lloyd Wright, a building that would bring incomparable beauty and dignity to their city. In their hands they carried printed petitions, the means by which they hoped to realize their goal.[43]

The petition drive upset conservatives who wanted an auditorium but not one designed by Wright. They predicted that any referendum question with Wright's name in it would "cause bitter debate, deep cleavages, and vast confusion." Worse, as Don Anderson, publisher of the *Wisconsin State Journal*, argued in a telegram to Wright, "The citizenry simply will not vote 'yes' on a multiple question referendum. They never have and all the newspaper editorials in the world will not make them do so." Further, the *Journal* argued, "putting two questions on the same ballot imperils both."[44]

Progress on the petition front was steady, but four days before the deadline the Citizens for Monona Terrace were three thousand signatures short. Edmund Zawacki, a member of the executive committee, said that petition carriers were spending too much time trying to win converts. Forget trying to persuade opponents, said Zawacki; if they won't sign, move on. Using Zawacki's blitz technique, 150 petitioners worked all day on September 8 and at 4:35 P.M., five minutes after the official closing time, Lescohier and Groves delivered to the city clerk a bundle of petitions bearing sixty-nine hundred signatures, one hundred more than they needed.[45]

YES     NO

Shall the City of Madison issue general obligation bonds in the amount of not exceeding $4,000,000 for the erection and equipment of a public building in and for the City of Madison to be used as an auditorium and civic center, in accordance with the initial resolution adopted by the Common Council on July 22, 1954?

YES     NO

Shall the City of Madison employ Frank Lloyd Wright as an architect for designing and planning a municipal auditorium and civic center?

YES     NO

Shall the City of Madison select the Monona Terrace site for a municipal auditorium and civic center?

FIGURE 4.10

**1954 Monona Terrace Referendum Questions**

During the summer of 1954 Don Anderson, the publisher of the *Wisconsin State Journal*, sent Wright a telegram to try to persuade him that the "citizenry simply will not vote 'yes' on a multiple-question referendum." Anderson bluntly told Wright that if he and his supporters persisted with the multiquestion format, they would be committing "auditorium suicide." Neither Wright nor his followers believed Anderson, but many Madison leaders did. As Wright and his backers saw it, voters should have the right to appropriate the money, designate the site, and pick the architect. After a long battle (from June to September 1954), both sides finally agreed on the three questions shown here. Note that although the questions specifically address the site and the architect, they do not mention the design of the auditorium and civic center.

Now two referendum questions were established, the first by council resolution, the second by petition. Or so the petitioners thought. City attorney Harold Hanson, a man who distrusted Wright's ability to deliver on his promises, raised two objections. First, he ruled that the selections of an architect and site were "administrative questions" and therefore would have to be advisory, not binding. Second, he asked, what exactly is meant by "in accordance with the plan of Frank Lloyd Wright"? If petitioners meant that the civic center should include city and county offices, the petition language was illegal — the city council had already approved the city-county building on Monona Avenue. State statutes specifically prohibited the use of referenda to repeal a duly passed law. Suddenly, all the work of the petitioners was in limbo.[46]

After a stormy debate on September 21, council members finally agreed on two new questions to replace the petition-established wording (see Fig. 4.10). Noticeably absent was any reference to Frank Lloyd Wright's Monona Terrace design, heretofore at the center of the debate. Council members were angered by the refusal of Monona Terrace supporters to comply with the Evjue compromise, that is, to exclude city-county offices from the design. Supporters made no secret of their disagreement with this compromise. Their petition-established language was specifically designed to include city and county offices. The night the council hammered out the final referendum language Helen Groves told council members that the people who signed the petitions "wanted the whole works," meaning the city-county offices. Only when faced with the likelihood that the council would completely rewrite her petition language did she concede that the Wright plan could be "cut to size." But the council would have no part of this; mention of the Monona Terrace design was deleted from the

ballot, and the questions on the architect and site were made advisory.[47]

Even after the council's exclusion of Wright's design, his unyielding proponents argued that the ballot questions would permit city-county offices in Monona Terrace. They said that the words *civic center* in the council-approved questions had always meant city and county offices. Historically, they were correct — but not after the Evjue compromise and certainly not after the new referendum questions were established.

Once the three questions were established, the campaign began in earnest. The three questions forced almost everyone into two camps: a coalition that urged citizens to vote yes just once to issue $4 million in bonds for an auditorium and civic center, and a different coalition that urged citizens to vote yes on all three questions.

Campaigning for a single yes vote was a coalition dominated by politically conservative businesspeople who favored a self-financing facility for sporting events and conventions, wanted the facility designated as a war memorial, and preferred that the common council determine the architect, site, and design. Most members of this coalition strongly disliked Wright and did not want any public building designed by him in the city — and certainly not a large building at the foot of Monona Avenue.[48]

Ironically, Madison union members allied with this coalition because they had been angered by a flagrant antiunion remark that Wright had made before the city council in September. In response to a council member's question about the cost overruns on the Unitarian Meeting House, Wright blamed stonemasons who "putter and putter and the money goes away like nobody's business." Union members strenuously denied this and instead

blamed Wright for changes the architect demanded after stone had been laid. Wright's remark provoked a strong editorial in *Union Label News*, the Madison-area union paper representing the building trades, urging members to vote against hiring Wright because he was "consistently anti-union" and hazy on building costs.[49]

Leading this coalition were Mayor Forster and council member Metzner. Backing them up was a new 250-member organization known as the Citizens Committee for Madison City Auditorium. This Chamber of Commerce–spawned organization involved leaders from nearly every mainstream organization who did everything they could to get people to vote yes on the auditorium question and no on the site and architect questions. Their position is evident in their poster, which appears in Figure 4.11. During the campaign they insisted that Monona Terrace would block the view of the lake from Monona Avenue and predicted that Wright would surely die before the job could be finished. They reminded voters that no one had the foggiest notion what Monona Terrace would cost. They explained that the city would never be able to get clear title to the site because the state owned the lake bed under Law Park. (As noted in Chapter 1, this point involved the state dock-line legislation that the city had secured in the 1920s and 1930s.) They predicted that the railroads would never concede the air rights over their tracks so that the project could be built. They pointed out that the Monona Terrace plan included just one of the five facilities required by the Auditorium Committee — the auditorium — and that no one knew whether Wright could fit the remaining four, the art gallery, small theater, community center, and exhibit hall, inside. Monona Terrace, critics were saying, is a very expensive pig in a poke. Shouldn't we peek in the poke before we buy the pig?[50]

# MADISON MUST GROW UP!

## a modern metropolitan city needs a
# CIVIC AUDITORIUM!

We're proud of Madison! Nature has made it one of the world's great communities. But we as citizens have been lax in doing our share to make Madison a "complete" city. Certainly a city of Madison's importance must have an auditorium. So we urge that you

## VOTE [yes] [X]
## for a
## CIVIC AUDITORIUM!

Since " 'way back when" we have all agreed that Madison must have an auditorium. But we never got down to facts. We must not delay any longer — for now we can have a Memorial Auditorium, providing the necessary facilities (based on the comprehensive Sprague-Bowman studies): adequate theatre, exhibition hall, sports facilities, art gallery, community center, all at a cost of $4,000,000 — which adds only one mill to the city's present tax rate.

## The Building With A Thousand Uses!

**CONVENTIONS**—right now — we do not have facilities for an important convention.

**ATHLETICS** — our high school gyms are small, the University's is unavailable.

**ICE SHOWS**—now we have to go to Milwaukee or Chicago to see these spectacles.

**BANQUETS** — no place now for a great civic banquet. We need an adequate banquet room.

**AUTO SHOWS** — now we have to hold such shows under tents.

**ART EXHIBITS**—Madison could well be an art center if we provided proper incentives, such as exhibit halls.

**RECREATIONAL** — a place for our youth to do things in a big way, city-wide, — a youth center.

**CELEBRATIONS** — we need a large place where we stage large dances, demonstrations, exhibits.

**COMMUNITY CENTER** — to properly house all activities now housed on East Doty Street.

**GREAT ARTISTS** — Madison now lacks adequate facilities for artistic and concert presentation.

These are just a few of the countless ways we would put our new auditorium to use. There are so many, many more — political rallies, meetings of professional, labor and business organizations, openhouse for farmers, receptions for important leaders. Needless to say, the auditorium would be the busiest building in town.

**FINANCIALLY** — The new Auditorium will be a great boon to our city. It will bring millions to our city for conventions, cultural events, exhibits, athletic events. It will make Madison a more important community — it will be proof that Madison has grown up.

**THE PRICE TAG** — If your property is assessed at $9,000, it will cost you a maximum of $10.00 per year for no more than twenty years.

## VOTE "YES"
## ON THE AUDITORIUM, NOVEMBER 2ND

**The Referendum Question Will Appear As Follows:**
Shall the City of Madison issue general obligation bonds in the amount of not exceeding $4,000,000 for the erection and equipment of a public building in and for the City of Madison to be used as an auditorium and civic center in accordance with the initial resolution adopted by the Common Council on July 22, 1954?

Authorized, issued and paid for by Citizens' Auditorium Committee, Arnold S. Jackson, Chairman, 1901 Adams Street, Madison, Wis.

---

FIGURE 4.11

**1954 Campaign Poster, Mighty Magnet for Millions**

Like the classic Salad Shooter television commercial (it chops, it dices, it shreds.... and it comes with a free set of knives), Madison's civic auditorium would have "a thousand uses," "make Madison a much more important community," and be a "magnet for millions." Conspicuously missing from the poster shown here was any reference to Frank Lloyd Wright and Monona Terrace. That was deliberate. The poster was produced by the Citizens Auditorium Committee, a group dominated by the Chamber of Commerce that was adamantly opposed to Wright. Its goal was to get voters to approve the $4 million in bonds for the auditorium so that the common council — not the public — could pick the architect, the site, and the design. Monona Terrace supporters thought that giving such a blank check to the common council was unwise and unnecessary. The poster was distributed in October 1954.

---

Monona Terrace opponents were frustrated because all they had to go on were a few beautiful but dimensionless renderings, several floor plans, a cross-section drawing, and what proponents told them. Even Terrace supporters conceded that what Wright was proposing was little more than an idea. Despite this vagueness, Metzner and others attacked wherever they detected a weakness. For example, they leaped on Wright's claim that the facility would provide parking for five thousand cars. Metzner said this was absurd and that something around a thousand was closer to the truth. Proponents, apparently feeling the sting, reduced their claim to twenty-five hundred spaces during the campaign. Then, a week before the election, the *Capital Times* published a signed Wright statement saying that the project contained forty-one hundred spaces — a claim he would later regret.[51]

Campaigning for a triple yes vote were the Citizens for Monona Terrace. Most leaders of this coalition were political and religious liberals, affiliated with the University of Wisconsin, keenly interested in the arts, and unabashed admirers of Frank Lloyd Wright. Most saw the Terrace as an unprecedented opportunity to enhance Madison's civic beauty, sense of community, and reputation as an oasis of antimaterialism. An unusually large number of the project's leaders and members were women.[52]

Although Citizens for Monona Terrace spent an inordinate amount of time discrediting the official city-county building proposal, the group also touted the prestige of having a Wright building in such a prominent location, boasted again that it would be "self-liquidating" (though they didn't say how), and said that it would provide long-needed cultural facilities. Harold Groves said that Madison would be "the laughing stock of the world" if it passed up the Wright plan.[53]

Despite the conservatives' unrelenting attacks, Citizens for Monona Terrace stuck with its game plan, playing the underdog and waging a grassroots campaign (see Fig. 4.12). Although members replied to critics, they mainly hammered away at the good things a Wright-designed auditorium and civic center would deliver for Madison. As proponents saw it, here was a world-famous architect offering a brilliant design to his hometown for free. They lamented that some people felt compelled to kick this gift horse in the teeth. And residents seemed enchanted by the spectacle of two professors' wives fighting establishment churlishness with grassroots grit.

The last week of the campaign got nasty. On October 26 Groves, Lescohier, and Zawacki went to the Dane County board and persuaded supervisors to delay their approval of the appropriation for the city-county building until after the election — a tactic that opponents would soon use against Monona Terrace. On the same day Wright released a signed statement saying that Monona Terrace contained "a city hall and county courthouse with courts for both," an action that can only be interpreted as a willful violation of the Evjue compromise. Clearly, Wright wanted to help his supporters rescue his original idea, but his action infuriated his opponents. Many saw this as nothing less than an attempt to sabotage ten years of work to secure a joint city-county building.[54]

On October 28 Metzner stood on the common council floor and accused Terrace leaders of perpetrating a hoax, and Mayor Forster called their actions "a conspiracy of deception." In response to the proponents' flagrant end-run to the county supervisors, the city council unanimously approved a resolution saying that the referendum had "*nothing* to do with the City-County Building"

(emphasis added). The end-run caused many to see Terrace supporters as fanatics.[55]

During the council meeting Forster held up a pro–Monona Terrace brochure that he said was a "downright deception." The document included a rendering of the comprehensive Wright plan and beside it the words "cost: $4 million will finance." Looking directly at Lescohier, Forster bellowed, "You know and I know it can't be built for anywhere near $4 million. It is high time that someone exposed your group for what they are."[56]

Jackson, the seventy-six-year-old general emeritus of the anti-Wright forces, had the pleasure of firing the last round. Jackson mustered all the old arguments that the Conklin Park site was superior, charged that Wright was not a competent architect or he would have been selected to design at least one University of Wisconsin building, and voiced his outrage that Madison's war memorial would be designed by a man who was so consistently unpatriotic. "The mere thought of a War Memorial ... designed by Frank Lloyd Wright—may the good Lord and our votes forbid it."[57]

Finally, it was election day, November 2, 1954, exactly sixteen years since Wright had unveiled his vision. Seventy-nine percent of voters approved the $4 million bond appropriation, 59 percent voted for the Monona Terrace site, and 52 percent gave Frank Lloyd Wright their vote. Conservatives were stunned. Two women with almost no political experience, completely outside the power structure, armed with little more than an idea, a packet of architect's renderings, and Wright's promise of a building that would create a "greater and more noble Madison," had persuaded hundreds of citizens to enlist in their grassroots army, successfully hijacked a coalition of Madison's most powerful leaders, and elected Wright as the architect. And they did it with campaign expenses totaling $261.51.[58]

FIGURE 4.12

**Professor Zawacki's Capitol Square Campaign**

*Courtesy FLW FDN. 5632.0049*

Edmund Zawacki, a professor of Slavic languages at the University of Wisconsin, demonstrated his strong belief in Wright's Monona Terrace by getting involved in the backer organization early in 1954. In addition to serving on its executive committee and testifying before the city council and Dane County board, Zawacki is remembered for what he did during the days just before the November 1954 election. Using money raised by Citizens for Monona Terrace, Zawacki rented loudspeakers, installed them and a sign atop his 1949 Ford, and drove around Madison's Capitol Square at lunchtime, saying, "Vote right. Vote for the Monona Terrace site. Vote for Frank Lloyd Wright. This is our chance to bring great distinction to Madison." To make sure that his message reached the most people, he would time his trip around the square so that he would hit every red light. Critics laughed at this crude strategy, but it reflected the energetic, low-budget, underdog campaign that proponents were waging and undoubtedly won many votes.

Wright was thrilled (see Fig. 4.13). To him it was a grand "democratic gesture," and "the only one I know of in America where the architect was chosen by the people." Because this was Wright's first elected "office," the question was how Wright would perform with a whole city for a client. Wright was utterly confident. As he told one interviewer, "I have never been in politics before, but since I am in it, I am sure that I can be better than most I have seen." But those who knew the tart-tongued architect and the difficulty of squaring his grand vision with the $4 million budget were not so sure. Meanwhile, there was a honeymoon to enjoy.[59]

FIGURE 4.13

**Frank Lloyd Wright, the People's Choice!**

*Courtesy* The Capital Times

Wright had good reason to beam in this November 19, 1954, photo. Seventeen days earlier Wright was elected project architect for Monona Terrace by the people of Madison. This was the only time this happened in his long lifetime, and he often said that it meant more to him than any other award. Here the exultant architect is arriving at the Madison airport and receiving congratulations from his client and physician, Arnold Jackson (right), and Ivan Nestingen (center), chairman of the Auditorium Committee. Wright had left Madison three weeks earlier to work on major projects in the East. He spent about a week in New York battling city authorities over building code changes needed for his highly unconventional Guggenheim Museum and a second grueling week in Philadelphia where he attended the groundbreaking for a suburban Philadelphia synagogue he had designed, hosted an exhibition of his work, and received an honorary degree from Temple University. This was his first appearance in Madison since the referendum. (For more information about Arnold Jackson, see Fig. 4.32.)

## THE HONEYMOON

Nine days after the referendum Nestingen called Wright in New York to congratulate the eighty-seven-year-old international celebrity on his victory and figure out a convenient time for him to meet with the Auditorium Committee. Finding time was not easy. Wright had received thirty-one new commissions in 1954 and had several major projects under construction. One, the Solomon R. Guggenheim Museum, was demanding so much time that Wright leased a suite at the Plaza Hotel so he could be close to the job site. Wright told Nestingen that he could not schedule a meeting in Madison until November 19, a date Nestingen accepted. In a confirming letter the following day, Nestingen assured Wright that the Auditorium Committee wanted to "expedite completion of the project as quickly as possible."[60]

Nestingen also used his reply to say that he had been elected to the Wisconsin Assembly on November 2 and that he would be resigning from the common council on January 1, 1955. (The resignation was a result of an imminent move from his downtown ward near the U.W. campus to another ward in a Madison suburb, but it also reflected the fact that Nestingen had time for only one political job in addition to his law practice.) Significantly, Nestingen had done such a good job of chairing the Auditorium Committee that Mayor Forster asked the young lawyer to continue in this post but as a private citizen. Nestingen's acceptance was good news for the Terrace's proponents.[61]

"Nothing has touched me so much in my lifetime," said Wright at the beginning of his meeting with the Auditorium Committee. "People of this city have had the courage and guts to tell the politicians what they want." For the next three hours Wright held the floor most of the time, sometimes sitting, sometimes pacing, often "gesticulating with his expressive hands," and periodically making sketches on Nestingen's legal pad. Dressed in a black pinstriped suit with high collar and black foulard tie tucked into a brown vest, Wright was astonished to learn that the city wanted an auditorium with only twenty-five hundred seats. "I thought you wanted a house fit for a convention or almost any kind of gathering... but you want this peanut of an auditorium," he exclaimed. Wright thought the auditorium should hold at least seven thousand and was angered to learn that the city planned only a $4 million complex, not the entire $20 million package he had proposed. "I want to cooperate with you but I'm interested only if the entire plan is understood and accepted and whatever is built will be a part of it," Wright told the committee.

"Can you do it for $4,000,000?" asked Mayor Forster.

"No, but I can do it complete for $20,000,000," Wright responded. "Four million dollars isn't interesting to me at all."

"We can't spend a cent more," Forster said.

"Then the Monona Terrace scheme is out and what do you want me for?" Wright snorted.

"We want you as architect, by vote of the people, for a $4,000,000 auditorium."

"[I] wouldn't turn a hand to take part in a program like that," Wright retorted.

Fortunately, Harold Groves, a trusted friend and loyal Terrace booster, intervened and got the testy architect to agree to do "sketches for $4,000,000 worth of the Terrace plan with the provision that the entire project ... would someday be built."

Wright was mollified but not finished. Still smarting because the city and county offices had been deleted from his original plan, Wright pushed the committee to think of other uses for this space. "There must be other civic needs here — like libraries and museums — to occupy the ... space. What are your pressing civic needs?"

"We need ten or twelve schools and we need them soon," growled Forster. "That's one of the main reasons we have only $4,000,000 for this building."

Wright got the point and began to emphasize that the Monona Terrace plan could be "simplified, modified, contracted and still preserve the integrity of the scheme." He agreed to redesign the Terrace to comply with official city specifications, but to make absolutely sure that he understood what they wanted, city officials sent Wright out the door with a copy of the Sprague-Bowman study, the report containing the approved city auditorium and civic center specifications.[62]

Although Wright's first postreferendum meeting had been productive, it also underlined the ambiguity of the mandate. What exactly had voters approved? The site? The entire Monona Terrace plan, as depicted in proponents' literature? A partial plan?

FIGURE 4.14

**1955 Night Rendering**

© FLW FDN. 5632.001

Wright reserved dramatic nighttime color renderings for a handful of special projects, including Monona Terrace. The rendering captures the dominant visual role Wright intended for the three colored-glass globed fountains that he dubbed the earth (left), moon (above the earth), and sun (on the right). Wright liked to imagine water splashing down over the lighted glass globes. "It will be a wonderful thing for children," he predicted. Defining the edge of the top deck are twelve distinctive light poles. The aerial view highlights the heavily landscaped garden level around the three fountains and the extensive parking surfaces. Olin Drive, a proposed scenic road named after John Olin, extends around the lakeside perimeter. The rendering, dated January 10, 1955, was done by Allen Davison, one of Wright's most talented artists, and first appeared as a program cover for a testimonial banquet on February 10.

FIGURE 4.15

**1955 Cross-Section**

© FLW FDN. 5632.003

This cross-section of the 1955 version shows the evolution of Wright's design. Like the 1938–1941 version, this one contained an auditorium (but cut the number of seats in half, to thirty-five hundred), a railroad station, and storage for five hundred boats but added several new functions: a community center with a library, lounge, game room, and large dance floor; exhibit hall; art gallery; and basketball gymnasium and handball courts.

Note how the auditorium has been moved toward the lake and away from the railroad tracks (the tiny black piano is located on the auditorium stage) and how the railroad station now occupies most of the first level, an attempt to counter earlier criticisms that the depot was too small. Arches appeared for the first time in the 1955 version and continued to be a signature element of the design for the rest of Wright's life. The three huge glass domes that allowed light to stream into the 1941 design have been replaced by large saucer-based fountains, but Wright retained a small skylight at the high point of the auditorium ceiling. These changes are most easily seen by comparing this drawing to the 1938 and 1941 cross-sections shown in Figure 3.13.

Perhaps the most dramatic difference between the 1955 and the 1938–1941 version was Wright's decision to position a three-tier semicircular parking ramp on the lake side of the building. The unfortunate consequence of this decision was to cut off the lake view to anyone inside the auditorium and civic center. The tiny figures in the exhibition hall, the large room on the lake side of the auditorium, illustrate the problem. Instead of enjoying a panoramic lake view, people in the exhibition hall would be forced to look at a parking ramp.

Clearly, Wright thought it was the entire scheme and, as time would show, many voters thought so too.[63]

Three days later the council approved the sale of $4 million in bonds, and in December the bonds were sold, bearing an interest rate of 1.77 percent. In January 1955 the council named three new members to the Auditorium Committee: Harold Groves; Dr. Arnold Jackson (see Fig. 4.13), who was Joe Jackson's brother and for whom Wright was designing a house; and George Elder, an East Side council member who quickly demonstrated his allegiance to Monona Terrace.[64]

Juggling competing demands from a thick portfolio of projects — among them, the Beth Sholom Synagogue outside Philadelphia, additional buildings for Florida Southern College, and a car dealership on New York's Fifth Avenue — Wright spent the next two months doing the first complete redesign of Monona Terrace since the original 1938 plan. On February 7, 1955, about thirty city officials crammed into the tiny council chamber in the temporary city hall to see what Wright had done. (Following the approval of plans for the new city-county building, the council sold the old City Hall and moved into temporary quarters near the Capitol Square.) Using nine elegant new drawings (see Figs. 4.1, 4.14, and 4.15) and a dazzling model nearly as

big as a Ping-Pong table (Fig. 4.16), Wright put on one of his polished performances as salesman extraordinaire. Seldom had Wright been so excited about a project.[65]

Wright had incorporated every function the city said it wanted and three not mentioned: a railroad station, a five-hundred-boat marina, and two ten-story towers for office and/or hotel use. Wright was well aware some city officials thought a railroad depot was not viable and earned points by suggesting that the depot space could be used as a convention hall or even a sports arena. As Table 4.1 shows, Wright met or exceeded every size specification, some by a substantial amount. In fact, using cubic feet as a measure, Wright's 1955 Monona Terrace was twice as large as what Sprague-Bowman had specified and substantially larger than the 1938–1941 version.[66]

TABLE 4.1

**COMPARISON OF CITY REQUIREMENTS AND WRIGHT'S PLANS**

| Required Function | Required Size | What Wright Provided |
|---|---|---|
| Auditorium | 2,000 seats | 3,500 seats |
| Little Theater | 300 seats | 800 seats |
| Community Center | 46,000 sq. ft. | 72,000 sq. ft. |
| Art Gallery | 3,000 sq. ft. | 24,000 sq. ft. |
| Exhibit Hall | 22,500 sq. ft. | 23,000 sq. ft. |
| Parking | 500 spaces | 1,500 spaces (Phase 1) |

Phase 1

*Courtesy* Wisconsin State Journal

Phase 2

*Courtesy* Wisconsin State Journal

FIGURE 4.16

### That Dazzling 1955 Model

Seldom do architects prepare highly detailed phase-revealing models that can be taken apart. Even more rarely would an architect direct staff members to spend thousands of hours preparing such a model before a client had approved a general project concept. But to Frank Lloyd Wright, Monona Terrace was no ordinary project. The model shown here illustrates the extensively redesigned 1955 version.

The upper photo shows phase 1, the central core of the project, consisting of the auditorium and civic center and a parking structure in the rear for fifteen hundred cars. The lower photo shows phase 2, the massive, ring-shaped, three-tier, two-thousand-car parking structure and two office towers. Wright estimated the cost of phase 1 at $4 million and phase 2 at $13 million ($10 million for the larger parking area and $3 million for both office towers). The extraordinary 4-foot-by-8-foot model was built by a team of apprentices who worked around the clock from December 1954 to January 1955 so that it would be ready for Wright's presentation to city officials in early February. Taliesin records show that they spent nine thousand hours building this model.

privilege," he had plaintively written to Nestingen two months earlier. That was why Wright wanted to build Monona Terrace; it would redeem Madison's "default" and brilliantly unite the city's natural and architectural beauty.[68]

The octogenarian's description of the new design was unrestrained. Looking directly at Forster during a council meeting, Wright said, "We've solved your parking problem for you. Once the people see it, they'll want it as fast as they can get it.... It's a dream I have had since I was a little shaver walking the streets of Madison.... The plan is as flexible as nature itself." In fact, added Wright, "This is what the United Nations should have built" instead of that sterile office tower. "It's practical and it's economical and the world has never seen anything like it." A few weeks later in a guest editorial in the *Capital Times*, Wright flatly stated that Monona Terrace was "one of the most coherent expressions of modern beauty in Architecture and civil engineering yet put on record in the world" — surely one of the most breathtaking expressions of self-aggrandizement, even by Wright's panegyric standards.[69]

Wright charmed a tough audience. One longtime Wright hater said he "could not get over Mr. Wright's gentleness and fun and sparkle." In a chatty letter to the Taliesin Fellowship, Helen Groves reported that everyone present "caught the vision and each in his own way responded as though some magic wand had touched him." The presentation and its newspaper coverage made people eager to see the spectacular model; when it went "on tour" at high-traffic downtown locations, thousands flocked to see it.[70]

February 1955 was a wonderful month for Wright. On the seventh he wowed city officials with his dramatically designed Monona Terrace. Three days later he was the guest of honor at a gala testimonial

Wright now asserted that the entire project could be built for $17 million, $3 million less than his estimate in November, and that it could "be built in easy stages, each of which will look good in itself." Trying to compensate for his antiunion gaff during the referendum campaign, Wright emphasized that all cost calculations were based on union labor. Phase 1 would cost just $4 million and would include the auditorium, community center, art gallery, little theater, exhibit hall, marina, fifteen hundred parking spaces, and all architect's fees. Phase 2 would cost $13 million and would include a $10 million, two-

thousand-car parking facility and two office towers at $1.5 million each (see Fig. 4.17). The $4 million cost claim soon became a proverbial tin can tied to Wright's tail.[67]

Wright argued that his new design would make Madison "one of the most inspiring, beautiful, fine cities of America," but he also insisted that Madison had relied too much for too long on its natural beauty and had given too little attention to its designed environment. If only Madisonians could "see the city as it is now. It is a shamefully wasted dinner in Madison where he was lauded by prominent state and national leaders (Fig. 4.18). He even received a warm letter from Forster, who did not attend the event. Said Forster: "We are looking forward to working with you on this project and pledge our full cooperation." Wright responded that he was "looking forward to working with [Forster] with pleasure."[71]

Beginning with the 1955 spring elections, the *Capital Times* limited its local endorsements to candidates who promised to support Monona Terrace. As Evjue put it, Monona Terrace was "the single most vital issue before the people of Madison at the present time." That year Forster and six common council candidates won the *Times*'s nod. The *Times*'s endorsements carried great weight and therefore were an effective way to keep a pro–Monona Terrace majority on the council for many years.[72]

During the 1955 mayoral and common council campaign the Auditorium Committee made rapid progress in completing the details of Wright's contract. Committee members wanted the city to sign the contract quickly because all Wright's work to date had been pro bono. (Wright estimated he had given at least $25,000 of his own time to the project thus far.) Although Wright's fee was always 10 percent of construction costs, the city was accustomed to paying just 6 percent. Once again Wright demonstrated his eagerness to do the job by agreeing to take a 7 percent fee plus $40,000 for engineering services. The city agreed. Other details went quickly and without incident. Wright drew up a contract embodying these details and sent it to Nestingen, saying, "I hope this will be the beginning of an enjoyable fruitful experience for all concerned.... What we have dreamed and planned and built together — you, your comrades and your architect — will be there for centuries to show

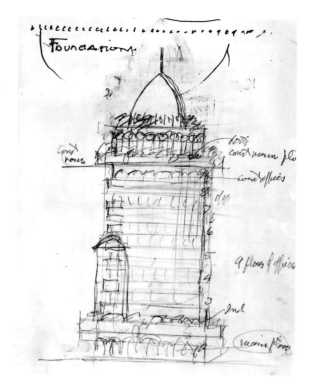

FIGURE 4.17

**Wright's Tower Sketch**

*SHSW. Howe Collection. WHi(X3)50322*

Wright did this tower sketch during December 1954. The architect's penciled notations show that Wright envisioned a ten-story building with a high-ceilinged, domed "courtroom floor" at the top and nine floors of offices below. Proponents hoped the towers would be leased to the state for offices or perhaps to a private corporation as a hotel. The idea was to use them to defray overall project costs. Wright called the towers moneymakers. The sketch shows that Wright wanted to carry the arch motif into circumferential windows on the upper stories — strikingly similar to what Wright had proposed with his 1893 boathouse (see Fig. A.1). Judging from the model made after this sketch, Wright abandoned the domed top for a more conventional flat roof, a globed fountain, and a light pole. Plans show the towers to be about sixty feet in diameter. Wright gave this sketch to Jack Howe, one of his senior designers, who translated the sketch into conventional plans. This sketch is one of many in a little-known collection of materials given to the State Historical Society of Wisconsin by Howe.

what kind of civilization we enjoyed." Wright acknowledged that the contract was probably "too informal" for the city attorney but in his experience "these things are best — simple."[73]

FIGURE 4.18

**The 1955 Testimonial Banquet**

*Courtesy FLW FDN. 6814.0011*

In 1954 the Wisconsin Supreme Court ruled that Wright owed $10,000 in back taxes on Taliesin. For years Wright had insisted that the property was primarily a school and should therefore be tax exempt. The decision made Wright so mad that he threatened to leave Wisconsin, deroof Taliesin buildings, and let them stand as a rebuke to state officials. Happily, Cary Caraway, a former apprentice, had an idea that cooled the architect down. Caraway suggested that Wright's Wisconsin friends express their appreciation by taking up a collection to help him pay his hotly disputed but overdue property tax bill on Taliesin. Mary Lescohier and Helen Groves worked to make the project a success.

In spite of temperatures reaching 15 degrees below zero, 380 Wright supporters gathered on February 10, 1955, in the Great Hall of the U.W. Memorial Union for a warm tribute to the aging architect. Seated at the head table (from left to right) are Wright, Bill Evjue, Ralph Walker (former president of the American Institute of Architects), and Wright's daughter, Iovanna. Also at the head table were Wisconsin governor Walter Kohler and Olgivanna Wright. Speakers praised Wright, and dozens of others, including Illinois governor Adlai Stevenson and Georgia O'Keeffe, sent written tributes. The gala provided a superb marketing opportunity for the brand new Monona Terrace model, visible in front of the head table. Wright was called a genius and a great man. At the end of the program he received a check for $10,000 as a token of Wisconsin's affection.

Also during the campaign the Auditorium Committee began to focus on legal steps the city had to take before starting construction in Law Park. City attorney Hanson told members they had

FIGURE 4.19

**1955 U.W. Honorary Degree**

*Courtesy* The Capital Times

Although he attended the University of Wisconsin for less than a year, getting a degree from his alma mater was secretly one of Wright's cherished goals. However, for most of his life Wright concealed his feelings behind a barrage of anti-U.W. zingers. "About the only thing I gained from my university years was a corn from wearing toothpick shoes," he was fond of saying. As a native son, Wright was nominated for a U.W. honorary degree many times, but his verbal peccadilloes, lifestyle, and financial irresponsibility always caused university officials to reject the suggestion. In 1955 his friend Edmund Zawacki, a professor of Slavic languages, made a fiery speech at a faculty meeting that persuaded his colleagues to endorse the nomination.

When Wright heard about the honor, he wrote U.W. president E. B. Fred to ask whether he could also get his undergraduate degree at the same time. To show that he was serious he enclosed a twelve-page "thesis" entitled "The Eternal Law." Fred had the difficult task of rejecting Wright's request. Wright received his honorary doctor of fine arts degree at Camp Randall Stadium on June 17, 1955. Flanking Wright were professors William Longenecker (left) and Ben Elliot (right).

to secure air rights from the railroads, get state permission to build beyond the dock line (Fig. 1.24), and change a state law that prohibited buildings from being constructed on streets that terminate at a navigable waterway (Lake Monona). Hanson strongly advised against signing any contract with Wright until all these problems could be resolved.[74]

Forster won by a landslide in the April election, and the victory was widely interpreted as a second

mandate for Monona Terrace. Then, on the day he was sworn in for his third term, Forster dropped a bomb. Forster said that if legal problems associated with Monona Terrace could not be resolved within six months, the city should hold a new referendum for a new site. To the Terrace's backers Forster's recommendation was tantamount to betrayal— because everyone agreed that it would take six months to a year to overcome the legal hurdles.[75]

Nearly everyone in Madison could see that the city was in a dilemma. Monona Terrace proponents thought the only way to comply with the voters' mandate was to have Wright move forward with the design while the city was securing the necessary state approvals. This meant signing the contract with Wright. But to Forster, Hanson, and many others, signing a contract that would obligate the city to pay Wright an estimated $300,000 commission for a building that might never be constructed was outrageously irresponsible.

Then, on May 19, when most thought Forster and Hanson would delay the contract, Wright responded with a stunning offer. If "insurmountable legal obstacles" prevented Monona Terrace's construction, Wright would provide his services for free. In the world of architecture this sort of thing just wasn't done — and certainly not by Frank Lloyd Wright. But, as Wright explained to the Auditorium Committee, "This building means more than money to me. I want this building to be something for Madison. The trouble is … you're all afraid…. You don't realize what potentiality this thing has. We're talking about big things, not little sums of money."[76]

To council members Wright's offer was almost too good to be true, and most were inclined to accept. But not Forster. The people demand "an orderly, prudent, systematic process," he insisted. The council, buffaloed by the mayor's growing intransigence, sent

the contract back to the Auditorium Committee to resolve the thorny cluster of site-related problems.[77]

June 1955 was yet another memorable month for Wright. On the eighth he celebrated his eighty-eighth birthday at Taliesin with a larger and more extravagant party than usual. On the seventeenth he received an honorary degree from the University of Wisconsin (Fig. 4.19). Although Wright had received scores of such accolades, this one was different. It was from his alma mater.

From November 1954 to June 1955 Wright had an edifying run in Madison. Never before had his hometown been so hospitable toward him. Alas, the honeymoon was about to end. Wright's enemies were massing their forces, and by that summer the acrid smell of their campfires suffused the air.

## A GAUNTLET OF GENERALS

On the day that Wright received his honorary degree from the U.W., Forster issued a belligerent report to the Auditorium Committee giving twenty-seven reasons not to sign Wright's contract. These included faults with the contract proposed by the Auditorium Committee, demands that the project be certified as technically and economically feasible, and difficulties in getting legal ownership of the site. In hindsight one can read the Forster report as a prudent person's exercise of due diligence. Most points had been raised during the citizen crusade or honeymoon but never together and with such truculence by a single person. In truth, this was Forster's declaration of war on Monona Terrace.[78]

### THE FORSTER FUSILLADE

Three other civic generals enlisted in the war: Metzner, Joe Jackson, and Don Anderson, the publisher of the *Wisconsin State Journal*. Metzner had been unrelenting in his criticism of the Terrace since the fall of 1953 and was the most outspoken opponent on the common council. Jackson bore anti-Wright grudges from the 1930s and '40s and seemed to make the defeat of the Terrace his lifelong goal. Anderson opposed Monona Terrace from the day it was reintroduced in 1953; consequently, *Journal* editorials of that era were laced with ridicule, and reporters complained about having to rewrite their stories two and three times to make them conform to Anderson's disapproving template.[79]

This quartet shared many goals, values, and attitudes. They agreed that the city needed an auditorium and civic center but not at the foot of Monona Avenue and not designed by Wright. They disliked Wright's unconventional lifestyle, were contemptuous of his careless business practices, and believed that his buildings suffered from expensive flaws such as leaking roofs. They were angered by the exaggerated and sometimes dishonest claims made by Monona Terrace's supporters. They believed that frugality, conventionality, and utilitarianism should determine the auditorium's location and design. They thought the city should boost business more than culture and that most Madisonians wanted an arena where they could watch boxing, wrestling, basketball, and ice shows, not a facility for concerts, drama, opera, and art. And when it came to Wright as a person, all thought he was immoral, intemperate, arrogant, and spendthrift. They did, however, differ in the intensity of their feelings. Although Anderson liked to portray himself as a friend of Wright's, he used barrels of ink to berate the architect and the project. Metzner insisted that his opposition was based on the Terrace's faults; Forster said the same thing but relished the opportunity to share his repertoire of derogatory Wright stories. Jackson simply hated Wright. As he put it after Wright's death, "I

thoroughly detested Wright as a man and despised him as an American citizen."[80]

Forster, Metzner, Jackson, and Anderson had been shocked by the ability of Terrace backers to get a majority of citizens to approve Wright and his project. Thus during the honeymoon they had developed a strategy to kill the project. The single most important component of that strategy was to create delays. Time, they quickly realized, was their best weapon. Wright was an old man, and inflation was raging, an average of 6 percent per year. Therefore anything they could do to stall the project would increase the chances that Wright would die and inflation would send the $4 million price tag soaring. Their other strategies included discrediting Wright's ability; arousing discontent, indignation, and even anger about the project; sowing doubts; cramming the contract with difficult if not impossible conditions; and, finally, demanding another referendum. Figure 4.20 summarizes the arguments advanced by both sides.

The generals enjoyed a great advantage in the battle. They knew the approval process for Monona Terrace would be long and difficult even under favorable conditions and that they could use their power, influence, knowledge, and skill to make it even longer, more arduous, and, they hoped, fatal. Unlike ancient tribesmen, who punished the gauntlet runner with sticks, this group of Madison leaders used lawsuits, procedural delays, partisan politics, legislation, the press, and any other weapons they could find along the way.

Challenging the civic generals were the now well-known Helen Groves and Mary Lescohier, who continued to provide inspired and dedicated leadership for Citizens for Monona Terrace. Hundreds had joined the organization during the crusade and honeymoon, and now they were eager to engage the

FIGURE 4.20

**1950s Pro and Con Terrace Arguments**

After voters approved Monona Terrace in November 1954, the project came under greater scrutiny. During this period the following pro and con arguments raged through newspaper articles, debates, and street corner conversations:

**PROPONENTS SAID MONONA TERRACE WOULD**

- Bring fame and prestige to Madison
- Right a great wrong (the failure to build a great Wright building in the capital of his home state)
- Increase Madison's reputation as a great educational and cultural center and strengthen the sense of community
- Enhance the capitol, beautify the lakeshore, and link the lake to the city
- Fulfill the promise of the 1909 Nolen plan for Madison
- Contain all community and cultural facilities that Madison would need for the foreseeable future
- Provide much-needed parking, bring in new convention business, and attract visitors

**OPPONENTS SAID WRIGHT SHOULD NOT BE THE CIVIC CENTER'S ARCHITECT BECAUSE HE WAS**

- Immoral, arrogant, improvident, and a communist
- Unable to stay within a project's budget
- A designer of leaky roofs
- Too high priced
- An architect whose style was ugly

**OPPONENTS ALSO SAID THE CIVIC CENTER SHOULD BE BUILT AT A DIFFERENT SITE BECAUSE**

- The state owned the property at the foot of Monona Avenue.
- Wright's design would block the lake view from Monona Avenue.
- The site was too small.
- Train noise would disrupt performances.
- Squishy subsoil conditions would require prohibitively expensive foundations.
- Filling in Law Park to the dock line would require a $1 million sea wall.
- Famous urban planners had cautioned against putting buildings in Law Park.

**OPPONENTS ALSO COMPLAINED THAT WRIGHT'S CIVIC CENTER**

- Would not satisfy all of Madison's needs
- Could be built elsewhere for less
- Violated the dock-line legislation
- Did not meet building codes
- Was impractical and expensive because of all the circles and curves

enemy. At City Hall Nestingen was the unquestioned Monona Terrace champion even though he was now a member of the Wisconsin legislature; his power came from his continuing role as chairman of the Auditorium Committee. Nestingen was ably backed by Harold Groves, a committee member who was playing an increasingly public role. And Evjue provided unwavering support in the *Capital Times*.

Terrace proponents devised six strategies: keep the shimmering Monona Terrace vision in front of the people; portray themselves as dedicated implementers of the people's mandate; make direct appeals to the people; nurture grassroots support; get supporters elected to the Madison Common Council; maintain a vigilant presence at city government meetings; and seek statewide support.[81]

The core values of the proponents stood in stark contrast to their opposition. Supporters believed that music, drama, and art were essential for human fulfillment and that good architecture added joy, serenity, and beauty to human life. Because they believed in fundamental human equality and democratic government, backers believed that Madison and every city should have a place where all residents could come together to share concerns, experience fellowship, learn, and be inspired. They believed they had a duty to make the world a better place, that the quality of human life is highest when the public interest is emphasized. And, yes, they wanted Monona Terrace because it was designed by world-famous Frank Lloyd Wright.

The pages of the *Wisconsin State Journal* and *Capital Times* became an almost daily battleground. To the editors of the *Journal*, the Terrace was a cancer to be excised from the body politic. The *Journal*'s lexicon for the project ran from *problem* to *stupid* and invoked every word cousin and distant relative in between. The *Journal* used an organ and played dirges. Find a

tiny problem with the Terrace and tomorrow it would be headline news in the *Journal*. Editors treated the story as a tragicomedy whose lead characters were a "small hard core of Wright worshippers."[82]

To the editors of the *Times*, by contrast, Monona Terrace was an unalloyed good. The *Times*'s lexicon for the project relied on scintillating superlatives and compelling comparatives. It blared trumpets and played fanfares. Find a tiny Terrace feature and tomorrow it would appear in a glowing testimonial. Bumbling through *Times* articles and editorials were big, clumsy, vindictive, uncomprehending "gloom peddlers" labeled *Obstructionists*. According to Bill Evjue's field guide, most were members of the Chamber of Commerce, Rotary Club, and Madison Club. Preeminent among this retrograde species of humanity were Joe Jackson and Carroll Metzner.[83]

All too often the great casualty of this adversarial journalism was truth. Most of the time it was forced to hunker down in the no-man's land between the hardened journalistic bunkers, trying to escape the shells each paper lobbed back and forth.

Forster's goal in firing his twenty-seven-point fusillade was to delay and, he hoped, kill the Terrace. Although the project's supporters now enjoyed a clear majority on the council, it was not sufficient to override a Forster veto. This forced the Auditorium Committee to change its strategy. Its original game plan was to have Wright refine the Monona Terrace design in accord with city requirements while nondesign issues were resolved. That was why the committee was pushing to complete Wright's contract. But after Forster's report, design work stopped and attention shifted to the project's feasibility and legality.

The central feasibility question was whether the Terrace could be built at an affordable price. To answer this and related questions, the Auditorium

Committee hired PACE Associates, a well-known Chicago architectural and engineering firm, and directed the company to prepare a detailed budget, determine parking needs and costs, ascertain whether Wright's design was "practicable," analyze subsoil conditions, design the road and rail tunnel through the building, provide an opinion on whether train noises would penetrate the auditorium, and, finally, calculate the added cost of building Monona Terrace in Law Park over the lake. PACE began its comprehensive study in September 1955.[84]

The central legal question was whether Madison could get sufficient title to the Monona Terrace site. That Forster felt strongly about this question was clear from the language of his report and from something he had said in the middle of a shouting match with Nestingen at a common council meeting on June 30. "If you acquire the property," Forster snarled, "I'll sign the contract. If you don't acquire it, I'll never sign it."[85]

As Forster, Nestingen, and most lawyers knew, "acquiring" the site in the usual sense of clear title was out of the question. The fact that the entire Monona Terrace site was a former lake bed created serious questions about whether the city could ever get sufficient title to build anything there. The legal theory was straightforward. Because navigable rivers, lakes, and streams play such a critical role in the nation's commerce, the federal government retained title to these bodies of water in trust for the people. However, to ensure effective administration of this responsibility in such a large country, the federal government transferred title to navigable bodies to the states. This meant that Wisconsin retained title to Lake Monona in trust for the citizens of the state.[86]

The states in turn were empowered to give municipalities and private corporations the right to build

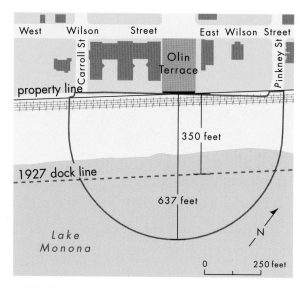

Olin
Terrace

property line

350 feet

1927 dock line

637 feet

N

Lake
Monona

0        250 feet

FIGURE 4.21

**The Dock-Line Controversy**

*U.W.–Madison Cartographic Laboratory*

Tens of thousands have gazed upon Lake Monona, but no one has ever said,
"Oh look, there's the dock line!" A dock line is not a geological formation or
a line of buoys but a legal concept that creates a theoretical vertical plane
along a shoreline beyond which the lake bed cannot be altered. Although
the Madison dock line was established in 1927 by state law, Wright did not
take it into account in his 1938 and 1955 designs. That was why he had to
totally redesign the project in 1956.

This diagram shows key components of the controversy. The 1927 dock line
is shown in red and the footprint of the 1955 plan in olive green. The 1927
dock line was 350 feet into the lake from the Olin Terrace retaining wall; the
1955 plan would have required a new dock line 637 feet into the lake,
which was 287 feet *beyond* the legally established dock line.

piers, bridges, parks, dams, commercial elevators,
railroad tracks, public buildings, and many other
structures in waterways so long as the public interest
was served. What private and public parties could
do within navigable bodies of water under the
public trust doctrine was central to Monona
Terrace. In fact, during the 1950s so much public
trust law surged through local newspapers that
many Madisonians talked about the subject as
easily as they bantered about the fortunes of the
U.W. football team.

In 1927 the state had granted Madison the right
to create a dock line about 350 feet out into Lake
Monona from the original shoreline (see Figs. 1.24
and 4.21). The dock line was the vertical plane that
defined the point beyond which the city could not
alter the lake bed. The original meaning of the term
referred to a point in a waterway beyond which a
dock could not be built, but over the years the
meaning expanded to include filled land on which
one could do only what was authorized by enabling
legislation. In 1931 the state passed a supplemental
law that kept the dock line at the same point but
added language that allowed the city to construct and
maintain within the dock line "parks, playgrounds,
bathing beaches, municipal boat houses, piers,
wharves, *public buildings*, highways, streets, pleasure
drives and boulevards" (emphasis added).[87]

Forster had three legal reservations about the state
dock-line grants. First, he thought they were
unconstitutional because a valid grant of power to
a municipality was limited to actions that enhanced
navigation — hardly the purpose of Monona
Terrace. Second, even if the state dock-line grants
were constitutional, the only title the state could
give the city was revocable. This meant that if the
city built the Terrace, the state could come along and
say, "We think the Terrace obstructs navigation —
remove the building." Third, Monona Terrace was
not the type of building state legislators intended
by the term public buildings.[88] (For an analysis of
legislative intent, see Appendix A.)

Although Nestingen and the Auditorium Committee
members did not share Forster's fears about the
constitutionality of the dock-line grants, they
agreed that all questions related to legal title should
be resolved. The simplest and most direct method
was to get the legislature to pass a bill saying that
Madison owned the site. The second way was to

sue the state for a declaratory ruling, but before the
state could become a defendant in such a suit, the
legislature had to give Madison permission to sue
the state. Ivan Nestingen had introduced bills
authorizing both approaches in May 1955, but
Republicans who dominated the statehouse were not
about to allow a first-term Democrat to look good
to his constituents, so they voted both down.[89]

Meanwhile, Terrace backers were making life
miserable for Forster. From their standpoint,
Forster had betrayed their trust. He had ridden
the Terrace bandwagon into a third mayoral term
and only two months later had issued his anti-
Terrace manifesto. Nestingen accused Forster of
being insincere and refusing to carry out the voters'
mandate. Evjue attacked Forster in *Capital Times*
editorials and accused him of trying to create insurmountable obstacles to prevent Wright from doing
any further work on the project. Citizens for
Monona Terrace distributed ten thousand copies
of Evjue's editorials to Madison residences and
drove the streets in sound cars to exhort people to
pack the council chamber and demand action on
Monona Terrace. Forster fired back, saying that
nobody but "oil barons and wax magnates" could
afford Wright and that Law Park was the most
"expensive building site in the city."[90]

The crescendo of criticism was painful for Forster
and the prospect for a respite was dim. As he
looked into the future, Forster saw an arduous legal
battle over title to the site, bloody skirmishes over
every point in his manifesto, tension-saturated
Auditorium Committee meetings (Nestingen was
still its chairman), stormy council meetings, and a
string of unpopular vetoes to throttle the Terrace
majority on the council. And Forster foresaw that at
the end of his term Ivan Nestingen would run for
his job. The prospect was anything but pleasant, and

so in August 1955, just four months into his third mayoral term, Forster announced his resignation. Although he agreed to continue working until September 15, he refused to have anything to do with the Auditorium Committee. To replace Forster the council decided to hold a special mayoral election in April 1956 and in the interim made the city clerk, A. W. Bareis, acting mayor.[91]

Nestingen used the eight months between Forster's resignation and the special election to resolve the title question. During this period the state Public Service Commission denied that it had jurisdiction, and the Wisconsin Supreme Court refused to hear the case without a circuit court ruling. Finally, Carroll Metzner, who was both a Madison council member and Madison's only Republican representative in the state assembly, introduced a bill that allowed the city to sue the state and get the declaratory ruling on the dock line that it needed. The bill was virtually identical to the one that Nestingen had introduced, but Metzner's party affiliation got it passed. Finally, in mid-January 1956, the city filed its lawsuit in circuit court.[92]

That same month Monona Terrace supporters got some great news: Nestingen announced his candidacy for mayor. The thirty-four-year-old lawyer ran on a well-rounded platform with Monona Terrace as its centerpiece. Nestingen said the project was "Madison's great opportunity of the decade — perhaps of the century."[93]

Critics, most of whom were Republicans, groaned at the thought of Nestingen, a liberal, non-native, McCarthy-fighting Democrat, running for Madison's top political job. Although the election was nonpartisan, everyone knew Nestingen was a Democrat and that he stood a good chance of winning in a profoundly Democratic town. Most council members were Democrats, and every Madison representative in the state legislature except

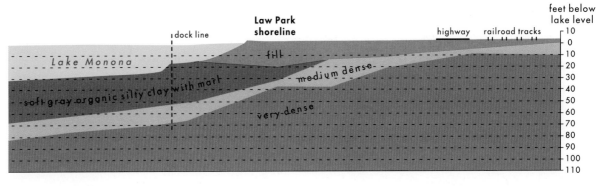

feet below lake level

Law Park shoreline

dock line    highway    railroad tracks

Lake Monona    fill    medium dense

soft gray organic silty clay with marl    very dense

FIGURE 4.22

**The Geological Banana Peel**

*U.W.–Madison Cartographic Laboratory*

Soon after the 1954 referendum, Joe Jackson and others claimed that subsurface conditions at Law Park were unsafe for large buildings. They theorized that the Monona shoreline contained a layer of soft clay and marl and that if Monona Terrace were built upon it, its weight would transform this squishy material into a geological banana peel. Thus, they predicted, Monona Terrace and maybe even the State Office Building would slide into Lake Monona. This became known as the "glacial slide" theory.

To check out this theory, the city in 1956 hired PACE Associates, a highly respected Chicago engineering and architectural consulting company, to do soil borings in Law Park. The PACE experts said the subsoil was not a problem, but this did not satisfy Joe Jackson and his friends. Jackson alleged that the PACE people had failed to hire a "qualified geologist." So the city hired yet another expert, the Madison-based Warzyn Engineering Company, to conduct further tests. Warzyn workers drove large steel I-beam piles into the earth but even with a hundred tons of pressure could only force the piles down by a tenth of an inch. According to this second opinion, subsurface conditions would easily and safely support a large building.

This diagram shows a cross-section of subsoil conditions at the Monona Terrace site. The tan and brown layers represent medium and very dense glacial deposits, which provide outstanding foundations for heavy buildings. The bittersweet layer represents clay and marl, which cannot be used for foundation support. The gray layer represents fill material, also unsuitable for foundations. However, the clay and marl, the basis of Jackson's glacial slide theory, were not a valid concern because Monona Terrace was to be built atop piles driven through this material into the dense glacial deposits below.

Carroll Metzner was a Democrat — facts that made it hard for Republicans to pick an effective opponent. They settled on John Hobbins, the president of a Madison bank. Although he had no experience in city government and was a poor public speaker, he was a loyal Republican, trusted Chamber of Commerce supporter, lifetime Madisonian, and of course a strong Terrace opponent.[94]

Just three weeks before the special election, the PACE consultants announced the results of their comprehensive feasibility study. Terrace supporters could not have asked for a stronger, more credible endorsement at a better time. One by one the prestigious Chicago firm banished the hobgoblins raised by opponents. The consultants said they "were unable to find anything in the design that

can be considered difficult to construct or that should be unreasonable or excessive in cost." The structure, they declared, was "practicable" and contractors "should have no difficulty bidding on it or constructing it." Passing trains would not be heard or felt in the auditorium. The entire site is "underlain by dense sand, silt and gravel" with excellent weight-bearing capacity (see Fig. 4.22). The extra cost for sinking foundations into the lake bed was a mere $50,000. PACE determined that construction of the Terrace would *not* damage abutting properties and that a four-lane highway could easily be accommodated where Wright said it should go; further, Wright's solutions for getting cars in and out of the building were completely satisfactory.[95]

FIGURE 4.23

**Wright and Nestingen Sign the Terrace Contract**

*SHSW. WHi(X3)50803*

This milestone photo of Wright signing his Monona Terrace contract was taken on July 5, 1956 — one year, eight months, and three days after Madison voters approved Monona Terrace. Looking on is the new mayor, Ivan Nestingen, then only thirty-four. Wright had just celebrated his eighty-ninth birthday.

Referring to several onerous clauses in the contract, Wright declared the contract the worst he ever signed and vowed to never "sign one like it again." At the same time, he said, "Nothing has pleased me more than the placing of this confidence in me by the people of Madison.... I think we are going to get along all right."

During the signing ceremony Wright got into a discussion with Nestingen and other members of the Auditorium Committee about the size of the auditorium. Wright urged a seating capacity of thirty-five hundred, but Nestingen countered with the $4 million bond limit. "What is Madison, a blighted area?" snorted Wright. "The people would vote a larger expenditure if necessary." The committee was unmoved. "All right. That settles it. I'll plan for a 2500 [person] auditorium," said Wright.

## NESTINGEN'S GREAT LEAP FORWARD

On April 3, 1956, Madisonians elected Ivan Nestingen by a narrow margin of 1,135 votes, and for the first time Monona Terrace had a real champion in the mayor's office. Wright was so happy that he dispatched a telegram: "U! RAH! RAH! WIS-CON-SIN! Bully boy, Ivan. Virtue is always triumphant if you can live long enough, Affection, FLW." The *Wisconsin State Journal* was not so thrilled. From the paper's point of view the new mayor was "Frank Lloyd Wright's water boy in Madison," a man who promised "frantic obeisance" to Monona Terrace.[96]

Nestingen's first priority was to get Wright back at his drafting table to downsize the 1955 plan. Although this plan contained all the functions Madison needed, its overall size was much bigger than Madison wanted or could afford. Moreover, the 1955 plan projected 287 feet beyond the state-established dock line, and no one thought the Republican-dominated legislature would extend it for Democratic Madison. Happily, Wright understood and said the downsizing was "entirely feasible." This meant that all obstacles to signing the long-delayed contract had been cleared and that the architect could complete the modified design while the title question was being litigated. Backers were betting that the courts would rule in favor of Madison.[97]

During the summer of 1956 Nestingen worked with the council to hammer out a new contract. Metzner and other council opponents insisted that the city retain the bristling array of anti-Wright clauses because they made good business sense. From Wright's point of view, however, the contract was full of ticking noises and flashing red lights. For example, there was Wright's own clause that said he would never get a penny for his work if the city encountered any "insurmountable legal obstacles."

Another clause said Wright would get no money if the city did not approve a referendum authorizing $1.5 million in parking bonds earmarked for Monona Terrace. Yet another clause required Wright to redesign the project indefinitely until its costs were brought in under the $4 million limit and until all city specifications were met. Finally, there was a clause that said the total cost of the project could not exceed $4 million even if some of the money came from state and private sources. But to Wright this was not a business deal; it was a labor of love. Wright signed the contract on July 5, 1956 (see Fig. 4.23).[98]

Nestingen's fast start and early successes emboldened Terrace backers to be more aggressive in wooing state support for the project. Backers were persuaded that the two circular towers Wright had shown in his 1955 plan were an ideal solution to the state's need for more downtown office space and that leasing or buying this conveniently located space made good business sense for the state. Furthermore, this action would bring in money to help pay for the project and secure state support for it. Toward this end Harold Groves appeared before the State Building Commission in September 1956, but none of the commissioners expressed the slightest interest in the concept.[99]

In August 1956 a Dane County Circuit Court judge completely vindicated Madison's position on its declaratory lawsuit. The judge ruled that the 1927 state dock-line law was a constitutional grant of power, that the 1931 dock-line law authorizing public buildings included Monona Terrace, that the city enjoyed concurrent jurisdiction of Law Park with the state, and that the city could build the Terrace under a revocable permit. The judge rejected the lame arguments of Vernon Thomson, the state attorney general who would be elected governor in a few months. According to Thomson, the state had acted improperly in approving dock lines,

dams, and bridges in dozens of Wisconsin cities for many years. If true, Wisconsin was in big trouble. The state appealed the case to the Wisconsin Supreme Court, a step the city supported, because if that court supported Madison's position, the city would have the highest legal authority to proceed with Monona Terrace.[100]

Also in August, just ten days after the circuit judge handed down his Terrace-vindicating decision, Wright submitted a substantially smaller plan, the second complete revision since 1938 (see Fig. 4.24) and the first to respect the state dock line. Wright had the unenviable task of simultaneously reducing the building's cost and satisfying restrictions imposed by the city and state (see Fig. 4.25). However, the plans still contained more space than the city needed or could afford, so Wright had to shrink the project in October and again in December. Finally, after three revisions the council approved the drawings and sent them off to three cost estimators.[101]

While Wright was downsizing his design, Madisonians were preparing to vote in November 1956 in a referendum whose outcome would determine the future of Monona Terrace. The question for voters was whether they wanted to authorize $2.5 million in bonds to pay for new downtown parking ramps (see Fig. 4.26). At this point in Madison's history downtown parking was not a problem—it was a crisis. About 250 feet of prime Capitol Square retail frontage lay vacant, mute testimony to the fact that stores were leaving the square for suburban shopping centers. Part of the bond package was for $1.5 million to pay for an eight-hundred-car garage expressly for Monona Terrace. If the measure passed, the Monona Terrace budget would increase to $5.5 million.

Metzner campaigned against the referendum for two reasons, one public and one private. His public

reason was that proponents had told voters during the November 1954 referendum campaign that the $4 million cost of the project included parking. The private reason was that Wright's contract contained a clause that said Wright would get no fees unless the city "authorized" $1.5 million for parking. To convince voters to reject the parking bonds, Metzner formed the Citizens for a Referendum Committee and came within fifteen hundred signatures of forcing another referendum on limiting total Monona Terrace spending to $4 million. Nonetheless, the parking bond referendum passed by a 4-to-1 margin in November 1956.[102]

In February 1957 the three firms hired to estimate the cost of Monona Terrace announced that Wright's December 1956 plans would cost $6.5 to $7 million—$1 million to $1.5 million more than the amount available. However, because the project still contained more space than called for in the official specifications, Auditorium Committee members asked Wright to make one last downsizing to bring costs down to $5.5 million. This set the stage for one of the stormiest meetings in the history of the project.[103]

Wright was exhausted when he entered the meeting with the Auditorium Committee at 7:30 P.M. on March 18, 1957. The nearly ninety-year-old architect was juggling multimillion dollar projects in New York and California and was about to fly to Baghdad to discuss still another (see Fig. 4.27). That day Wright had been in Chicago fighting to prevent the destruction of one of his most famous designs, the 1908 Robie House, then had endured the long drive to Madison over icy roads. The subject Wright needed to address that evening — cutting the size of his beloved Monona Terrace to fit the budget — was intrinsically unpleasant to the proud architect.[104]

August 1956 Elevation from Lake Monona

© FLW FDN. 5632.013

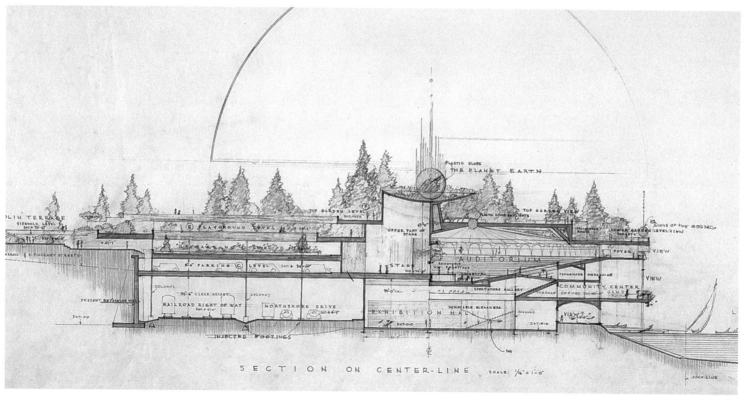

December 1956 Cross-Section

© FLW FDN. 5632.044

## FIGURE 4.24

### 1956 Dock-Line–Respecting Design

Immediately upon signing his contract with the city on July 5, 1956, Wright and his staff went to work on a third major redesign of Monona Terrace. Unlike the original 1938 design and the totally revised 1955 plan, the 1956 plan conformed to the state-established dock line. The *Capital Times* published the rendering showing the new dock-line–respecting design on August 25, 1956.

In this 1956 design Wright first used the distinctive recessed arched windows on the lakeside, a dramatic contrast to the horizontal window lines of the 1955 plan (see Fig. 4.16). Note, too, the appearance of the large Wrightian saucer-shaped fountains with globes. Wright retained both elements in his later revisions, and today they are salient elements of the convention center.

Although Wright's August 1956 design stayed within the dock line, it was still much larger than city specifications required — and thus more expensive than the city could afford. Consequently, Wright had to revise the plans in October and December 1956 and again in March 1957. With these modifications he dramatically reduced the size of the building.

Wright hated to reduce the volume and proportions of the building. Responding to a letter from Nestingen asking the architect to make the building smaller, Wright wrote, "Dear Ivan: What you suggest as an economy is really a destruction of the whole Terrace idea.... The rooms you propose cutting 'are the milk in the coconut.' I don't know whose brain has been masterminding the affair — but if it's typical, I guess we might as well throw up the sponge and avoid the fight." Characteristically, after protesting, he did what the city wanted.

The cross-section shows how Wright reluctantly responded to a demand by local theater managers to increase the height of the stage loft to accommodate road shows. His clever solution, raising the central fountain and tucking the loft beneath it, is evident here.

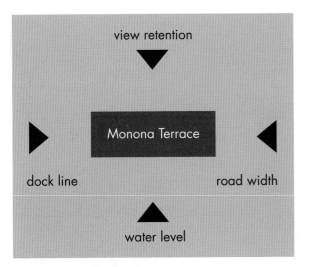

**view retention**

**Monona Terrace**

**dock line**          **road width**

**water level**

FIGURE 4.25

**The Design Vise**

A combination of legal, aesthetic, engineering, and functional requirements added great difficulty to the design of Monona Terrace. On the lake side Wright had to keep the project within the state-established dock line. On the isthmus side Wright had to allow space for four railroad tracks and an expressway. Its lowest level could not be below lake level. And Wright had to keep the building as low as possible to preserve the coveted lake view from Monona Avenue.

These four forces functioned like a cruel vise, constantly squeezing volume from the building and requiring numerous design changes. For example, in 1956 Wright had to move the building fifty feet toward the lake to accommodate a traffic engineer's requirement for a wider road, slice 287 feet off the building that extended beyond the dock line, and increase the height of the building by about ten feet to provide vertical storage space for stage curtains, a decision that further blocked the lake view from Monona Avenue.

In addition to contending with these four viselike pressures on the exterior envelope, Wright had to harmoniously integrate seven very different functions (auditorium, art gallery, little theater, boathouses, exhibit hall, community center, and meeting rooms) — all within curved and even circular walls.

To compensate for the height increase, Wright reduced the level of the lowest floor, the exhibit hall, from four feet above Lake Monona to the average lake level. This was clearly a risky decision because in the spring Lake Monona would often rise nearly two feet above its average level, a circumstance that could have flooded the exhibition hall.

Wright began by acknowledging that he had made a unilateral decision to keep the auditorium size at three thousand seats, five hundred more than called for. He did it, he explained, because "it was foolish to build on yesterday." Then Wright began one of

---

**A CITY SPEAKS**

YES          NO

Shall the City of Madison issue general obligation bonds in the amount of not exceeding $2,500,000 for the purpose of acquiring sites for municipal parking lots and the construction of buildings and other equipment and appurtenances necessary for the operation and maintenance of the same in accordance with the initial resolution adopted by the Common Council on August 9, 1956?

FIGURE 4.26

**1956 Terrace Parking Referendum Question**

Although the language of this referendum question does not say so, $1.5 million of the $2.5 million in bonds that taxpayers were being asked to approve was earmarked for a special parking ramp for Monona Terrace. The referendum passed by a 4–1 margin and significantly increased the money available to build Monona Terrace. The election was held on November 6, 1956.

his harangues. He accused city officials of "unfairly loading" nonbuilding costs, such as feasibility studies, air rights for the railroads, city supervision costs, and his fees onto the building budget. "I thought the city wanted $4 million worth of *building*," he repeated several times. This loading was especially painful to Wright because he had come so close to the city's $5.5 million budget target, even though inflation since 1954 had reduced its buying power by 15 percent, or $825,000. The testy architect told the committee that he "had great confidence in the people" and that if he couldn't reach agreement with the committee, he was going to take Monona Terrace back to the people. "I don't propose to have them sold down the river," he snapped. Disgusted by what he saw as unfair treatment and the presence of opponents who were about to unload on him, Wright donned his porkpie hat and overcoat and walked out into a snowstorm. He caught a taxi and spent the night at a local hotel. The next day the *Journal*'s headline blared "Wright Takes a Walk on Auditorium Committee."[105]

---

Wright's behavior was bad enough to anger some of his staunchest supporters and forced him to send an open letter to the Auditorium Committee. In that letter he apologized for his "caustic criticisms" and thanked Nestingen and his "persistent gallant band" of Madison supporters. Yes, he had walked out on the committee, and, yes, he was angry, but his commitment to the project was unwavering despite what he saw as unfair treatment. Reluctantly, Wright told the committee that he would modify the building yet again.[106]

Three weeks later Nestingen won his first full two-year term as mayor, this time by a 3-to-1 margin. The vote was properly viewed as still another mandate for Monona Terrace and the work of the new young mayor.[107]

A little more than one week after Nestingen's reelection, Wright submitted his downsized plans (Fig. 4.28) but grumbled to Nestingen in a transmittal letter that "this last change knocks the noble Terrace scheme into a peanut but may serve for political purposes." The Auditorium Committee declared that the new plans satisfied the official city specifications. However, Ray Burt, the city building inspector, determined that the latest set of plans would cost $6.1 million, or about $600,000 more than the $5.5 million budget. Still, if the effect of inflation since the 1954 referendum — $825,000 — was taken into account, Wright was under the city budget by nearly $200,000. Members of the Auditorium Committee and a majority of common council members were confident that Wright could wring out the last $600,000 when he prepared final drawings.[108]

Even more good news was about to arrive. In June 1957 the Wisconsin Supreme Court unanimously upheld the circuit court decision; Madison now had

FIGURE 4.27

# THE LATE TALIESIN YEARS
# 1950 – 1959

**1950**
Receives more than forty new commissions

**1951**
Wright exhibition "Sixty Years of Living Architecture," tours Europe

H. C. Price Tower

*Photo by Scot Zimmerman*

**1952**
Secures commission for the H. C. Price Tower in Oklahoma

**1953**
New Yorkers see "Sixty Years" exhibit at the future site of the Guggenheim Museum

Publishes *The Future of Architecture*

Secures Beth Sholom Synagogue commission near Philadelphia

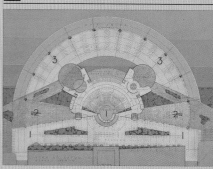

1955 Monona Terrace Footprint Proposal

*© FLW FDN. 5632.008*

**1954**
Works on Guggenheim while ensconced in the Plaza Hotel

**1955**
Unveils new Monona Terrace Civic Center proposal for Madison, Wisconsin

Annunciation Greek Orthodox Church

*Courtesy Phil Hamilton*

**1956**
Guggenheim construction finally begins

Unveils "Mile High" skyscraper for Chicago

Secures Greek Orthodox Church commission near Milwaukee

Marin County Civic Center

*Photo by Tony Puttnam*

**1957**
Secures Marin County Civic Center commission in California

Travels to Baghdad to analyze sites for a major urban project

Crescent Opera House Proposal

*© FLW FDN. 5733.007*

**1958**
Proposals for Baghdad, including plans for the Crescent Opera House, are exhibited at the Iraqi Consulate in New York

Publishes *The Living City*

**1959**
Secures Grady Gammage Auditorium commission in Tempe, Arizona

Dies April 9 in Scottsdale, Arizona

the strongest legal backing it could get to "title" on the Monona Terrace site.[109]

Nestingen had made impressive progress in just fourteen months. By June 1957 nearly all obstacles thrown in the path of Monona Terrace had been removed. One of the best architectural and engineering consulting firms in the country had issued a glowing feasibility study. Wright had redesigned the building to fit behind the city dock line, satisfied all city space requirements, and was so close to the cost target that the Auditorium Committee and most common council members were willing to direct Wright to proceed with construction drawings. The Wisconsin Supreme Court had upheld the circuit court ruling. In addition, the two railroad presidents whose tracks ran through Law Park had agreed to sell Madison the air rights over the tracks for $1, and the Plan Commission had approved the Terrace site.

But instead of throwing confetti and sipping champagne, Terrace backers were a glum lot— and for good reason.[110]

NOT MORE THAN TWENTY FEET

Since 1953 Carroll Metzner had done nearly everything he could think of to stop Monona Terrace. He had embarrassed Wright in public debates, accused proponents of using fraud and dishonesty to win referendum votes, spoken to every civic organization he could, urged other council members to vote against the project, formed the first anti-Terrace citizen group to force a new referendum, encouraged the insertion of onerous clauses in Wright's contract, and tried to torpedo the referendum that allocated additional money for its parking ramp. Unfortunately, nothing had worked. Metzner (see Fig. 4.29) was frustrated but still resolute in his desire to kill the project. The question was how.

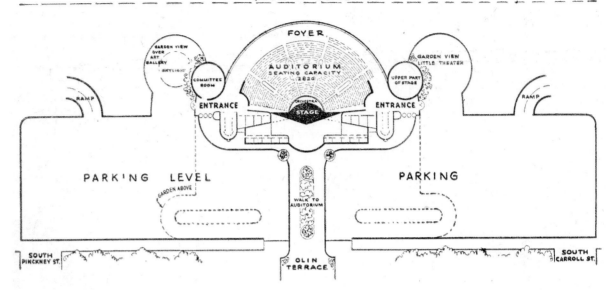

FIGURE 4.28

**The 1957 "Peanut" Auditorium**

*Courtesy* Wisconsin State Journal

This sketch shows the smallest civic center that Wright ever designed for Madison. It appeared in the *Wisconsin State Journal* on March 17, 1957, and was done to bring the project into line with the city's specifications and fixed pocketbook. Although the design satisfied city specifications and could almost be built within the city's budget after post-1954 inflation was taken into account, Wright didn't like it. In a transmittal letter to Mayor Nestingen, Wright said the modification destroyed "the noble proportions" of the building and knocked the whole design "into a peanut," the architect's expression for unacceptably small. On the same day he sent a telegram to Mary Lescohier saying that the changes made were "downright sacrificial." Although Wright's drawings for this iteration were formally conveyed to the city in April 1957, no copies have been found.

Joe Jackson and several of his friends thought they had the solution. Sometime in late 1956 or early 1957 Jackson met with nine other Monona Terrace opponents to devise a Plan B. Because all local efforts had failed, they concentrated on what they could do at the state level, where they thought they had a better chance of succeeding. After all, the governor was a Republican and the party enjoyed majorities in both houses. The idea was for Metzner, an up-and-coming Republican, party activist, and Madison's only Republican in the legislature, to introduce a bill and get it passed on a party vote. They went around the room and each man offered his ideas. Jackson suggested that they

repeal the 1931 dock-line law because it contained the language authorizing the public buildings that supporters thought included Monona Terrace. The problem with Jackson's idea, someone pointed out, was that in repealing the bill, you throw out language authorizing the city to improve Law Park as a lake-front esplanade with a road, boathouses, and other things the men wanted. Better, they concluded, to leave the 1931 law on the books but amend it.[111]

The brainstorming continued, and the men hit upon the diabolically clever idea of placing a height limit on all public buildings. If the height limit were low enough, the lake view from Monona Avenue would

## CARROLL METZNER
### DEDICATED ADVERSARY

To hear Carroll Metzner tell it, his life was a little dull. "I have had just one house, one wife, and one job," he deadpanned in an interview. In truth, his life was anything but dull. In the 1950s and 60s Metzner's name routinely appeared in newspaper headlines for his vigorous and effective opposition to Monona Terrace.

Like many young men. Metzner underwent a political metamorphosis. As an undergraduate at Northwestern University, he voted for the Socialist Party's presidential candidate; as a law student at the University of Wisconsin he became a Democrat; and soon after joining a Madison law firm in 1943, he announced that he was a Republican. In 1951 Metzner, then thirty-two, was elected to the common council, representing Madison's 20th ward, an affluent westside neighborhood known as Nakoma. Upon election he was appointed to the committee that was completing plans for a joint city-county office building on Monona Avenue.

When Wright's civic center plan was reintroduced in 1953 as an alternative city-county building, Metzner immediately became its most outspoken elected opponent. As he later said, "I never had any animosity toward the old bastard. I was always opposed to the cost and the site." To help defeat the project, the articulate and forceful attorney debated all proponents, made countless speeches, became an officer in Citizens for a Realistic Auditorium Association, and adopted the motto "Wright was always wrong." More than forty years later Metzner vividly recalled his 1955 debate with Wright at Madison's Beth Israel Temple. Wright went first, sat down, and Metzner took his turn at the podium. Wright, however, continued to make audible comments about Metzner's remarks, prompting the attorney to turn to Wright and say, "Obviously you haven't finished your speech. Why don't you come back up here and finish it?" Wright never said another word and the next day sent an autographed book to his adversary.

In 1954 Metzner won a seat in the Wisconsin assembly and in February 1957 introduced his controversial bill to limit the height

of all buildings in Law Park to twenty feet. As the sole Republican legislator from Democratic Madison, Metzner was able to get the bill approved by a legislature owned by the Republicans.

The measure cost Metzner his seat in the November 1958 election, and it was repealed a few months later. Neither action stopped Metzner's crusade. In 1966, when Wright supporters were trying to salvage the concept, Metzner filed a taxpayer's suit that stopped the project for nearly a year. When the project resurfaced in the early 1990s as a convention center proposal, Metzner testified against it, wrote critical letters to key officials, and partially underwrote a plan designed to stop any changes to the historic Olin Terrace.

be preserved forever and the Terrace would be dead. Metzner liked the concept but wanted to make absolutely sure that they set the limit so low that Wright could not sneak in one of his ground-hugging buildings. Thus the only remaining question was what the height limit should be. Madison Parks Department officials told them that no building in a city park was taller than twenty feet and that the city needed nothing taller. Metzner thought that sounded low enough.[112]

On February 27, 1957, Metzner introduced his bill amending the dock-line law of 1931. The bill added just seven words, "not more than 20 feet in height," immediately after "public buildings." The bill targeted Monona Terrace in Law Park but also covered all public buildings that could be built along the six-mile dock line. The *Capital Times* blasted the bill the following day for its "frenzied spite." Even the *Wisconsin State Journal* leveled its big guns on the bill, calling it "ill-advised ... dangerous ... poor policy," and "petty, inappropriate, and indefensible." Metzner's assault on home rule — the right of local governments to decide their own affairs — so angered critics of Monona Terrace that they linked arms with supporters to create a new single-purpose organization to oppose the bill. Almost everyone agreed the legislation was conceived in partisan spite and dedicated to the proposition that the state knows best.[113]

Hearings before the assembly and senate committees were highly charged sessions involving hundreds of people, mostly Terrace supporters. Metzner asserted that the bill was *not* a local issue because the state "owned" the land where Madison wanted to construct the huge building. Next, he argued that the state's intention in passing the dock-line laws in 1927 and 1931 was to allow the city to build a park and pleasure drive along the lakefront, not a monstrous public building like Monona Terrace. Having established his arguments regarding state ownership and legislative intent, Metzner accused supporters of using "state property to destroy one of the most beautiful views in the state of Wisconsin." He illustrated his point with a drawing that showed how Wright's building would block the lake view (see Fig. 4.30).[114] (Metzner was right that the lakeshore road was one goal of the 1927 bill, but public documents are silent on the question of how big a public building could be. For a more complete discussion of this point, see Appendix A.)

Metzner shrewdly devoted generous attention to the role played by the *Capital Times*, and especially its editor, Bill Evjue, in the successful November 1954 referendum. Specifically, Metzner accused Evjue of blatantly misrepresenting the project to fool Madisonians into voting for it. To prove his point he submitted copies of Evjue editorials that said voters would be getting an auditorium that would seat seven thousand people and park four thousand cars for just $4 million. To Republican legislators Metzner's harsh criticisms of Evjue were sweet revenge for the editor's years of lampooning Republicans in his newspaper column and during his popular weekly statewide radio broadcast, "Hello Wisconsin." In fact, Metzner was giving his Republican colleagues a welcome opportunity to punish the powerful, stiletto-tongued editor.[115]

Nestingen, Harold Groves, and Madison's Democratic legislators were the principal speakers against the Metzner bill. They said it was a gross violation of Wisconsin's sacrosanct home-rule policy; that the state had made court-tested constitutional grants of authority to the city to build public buildings, including Monona Terrace; that the city relied on these grants to plan the project; and that the view of the lake would be much better from the top of

the building than from the "narrow slot" between the Madison Club and the State Office Building.[116]

In early April 1957 the Metzner bill sailed through the assembly on 59-to-36 vote that was almost strictly party line, but the senate vote promised to be much closer because the Republican majority was smaller there. Moreover, some Republican senators refused to vote for the bill because it meant the state could intervene in their cities. The bill generated more senate mail than any other bill in the 1957 session; lobbying was intense on both sides. Harold Groves talked personally to every senator. Helen Groves toured the state, getting endorsements from mayors and other local leaders. On the other side, Joe Jackson worked the senate anterooms every day and in some cases gave legislators a copy of what he called the "Wright Record," a document that colored the architect red. Once, Jackson thought he had convinced a key senator to vote for the bill, but he later learned otherwise. Jackson was so angry that the following day he stormed into a downtown restaurant where the senator was having breakfast, poked him in the shoulder, and said, "You son-of-bitch. Stand up, I want to punch you in the nose, you dirty liar and bastard." Fortunately, somebody grabbed Jackson, who was then seventy-eight, and separated the two men. In late June the Metzner bill squeaked through the senate by a single vote, 17 to 16. Wright and his Monona Terrace backers were naturally disturbed by passage of the Metzner bill but also by something that happened a few days later: the opening of the new City-County Building (Fig. 4.31), a facility that accommodated the government functions Wright had included in his dream civic center.[117]

Later that summer, but before Governor Thomson signed the bill, Metzner took his family on a three-week California vacation. Although the main

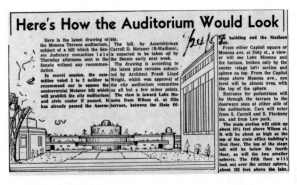

FIGURE 4.30

**Will the Terrace Block the Lake View?**

*Courtesy* Wisconsin State Journal

Carroll Metzner used this type of drawing during the May 1957 legislative hearings on his bill to limit building heights in Law Park. It shows the view of Lake Monona from the intersection of Wilson Street and Monona Avenue. Metzner used the drawing to prove that Wright's building would block the view of Lake Monona from Monona Avenue. According to the *Wisconsin State Journal*, the rectangular-shaped stage house in the center of the drawing would be at the same level as the fourth floor of the State Office Building. Mary Lescohier said it was "an artificially trumped-up so-called view of Monona Avenue." In fact, Metzner was right. After this drawing was introduced, supporters began to argue that the panoramic view from the top of the terrace would be superior to the "slotted" view between the Madison Club and the State Office Building, at left and right, respectively.

reason was to visit friends and see Disneyland, Metzner decided to visit Marin County, a rapidly suburbanizing county just north of San Francisco where Frank Lloyd Wright had just signed a contract to build an $8 million complex featuring county offices, a jail, and a library. Metzner, buoyed by his Madison victory, was eager to try his hand at Wright wrecking in California. While there Metzner met with William Fusselman, the sole opponent of the Wright project on the five-person Marin County board, appeared in a feature story that the local paper ran with his photo, and joined Fusselman for a local Sunday evening radio program. Metzner described his efforts to kill Wright's Madison project and told Marin residents that they "had better have a lot of money" to pay for Wright's plans. The complex went forward despite Metzner, who was immediately skewered by Bill Evjue for "carpet bagging."[118]

Sometime in 1957 Frank Lloyd Wright and Ivan Nestingen were talking on the front plaza of the just-completed $9 million City-County Building (shown here) when George Harb, finance chairman of the Dane County Board of Supervisors, walked up the steps. Harb heard Wright make his initial presentation before the county board in 1938 but had never formally met Wright, so he walked over and Nestingen introduced them. Wright, the master quipster, shook Harb's hand, waved toward the building, and said, "Nice cereal box you have here." Conversation stopped and Harb walked away. Wright's sarcasm was undoubtedly thinly veiled exasperation over big Madison jobs like this, which were going to large firms such as Holabird and whose work Wright regarded as inferior to his own.

Wright's sarcasm aside, few Madisonians knew or cared that Holabird, Root, and Burgee, a large and well-known Chicago architectural firm, had designed the building. Holabird and Root had done two other major buildings in Madison, both for the federal government — the Forest Products Laboratory in the 1930s and the U.S. Veterans Hospital in the late 1940s.

Governor Thomson signed the Metzner bill into law on Saturday, September 21, 1957, thereby assuring the Republican *Journal* of an exclusive story in the Sunday paper. (The *Capital Times* did not print on Sundays.) His statement in support of the bill was a thinly veiled synopsis of a seventy-page "brief" that Metzner had submitted to the governor. To justify the partisan intrusion into local affairs, Thomson was forced to use arguments normally found on the far side of fantasy. Thomson said he was trying to prevent the frightening possibility that Madisonians — if not restrained by the Metzner bill — would use the six-mile state-authorized dock line along

the city side of Lake Monona to build a solid wall of huge public buildings, thereby obliterating "the lake view to the residents along this shore."[119]

Curiously, Metzner and Jackson did not realize that their bill nixed two visionary plans they had trumpeted for Law Park — the 1909 Nolen plan and the 1939 Segoe plan. John Nolen had proposed two large forty-foot-high buildings in Law Park (Fig. 1.17), and Segoe had recommended a thirty-five-foot band shell–amphitheater cascading down to the lake (Fig. 3.9). Both plans proposed structures over the railroad tracks to allow pedestrians to go from the square to the lakeshore, but the minimum clearance required by the railroads was twenty-five feet. Thus any bridge or platform over the railroad tracks would be too high for the Metzner law and too low for the railroads.[120]

Critics of Monona Terrace moved quickly to exploit the new Metzner-designed playing field. Metzner urged Madison to implement the Segoe plan; Jackson got an old friend and longtime city council member to push Conklin Park as the official auditorium site; and the Auditorium Committee directed city planners to identify new auditorium sites. But the most aggressive and sustained initiative came from the *Journal*. Just two days after Thomson signed the bill into law, its editors proposed that Madison build an "arena-type auditorium." "Forget such things as art galleries and little theaters.... Perhaps our auditorium will not be so beautiful as the Wright dream. But there is no reason why it cannot be serviceable without offending the eye." As an insulting sop to what they called "the super-charged Frank Lloyd Wright zealots," the *Journal* suggested that the private sector pony up the money to pay for a Wright-designed art center that "perhaps ... could be built right on Monona Terrace, spread out and under the 20 foot height limit."[121]

Throughout this period the *Journal* exploited the confusion in many voters' minds about what an auditorium really was. As used in connection with Monona Terrace, auditorium always meant a nicely appointed sloped-floor facility with excellent acoustics designed for orchestras, opera, and drama with about twenty-five hundred padded seats. But as the term auditorium was used by Metzner and other Terrace opponents, they meant an arena, a large utilitarian flat-floor facility seating about seven thousand for boxing, wrestling, basketball, ice shows, and other sports events. Whenever Metzner spoke, he accused Monona Terrace backers of omitting the arena and cutting the auditorium seating size from seven thousand to about twenty-five hundred. In fact, Sprague-Bowman Associates, the city's consultant, had specifically told Madison not to build an arena because it was too expensive and because it would compete with university facilities. But to hear Metzner tell it, the public was getting the short end of the stick.[122]

Passage of the Metzner bill stopped Monona Terrace supporters dead in their tracks. In June 1957 they had been poised to have Wright do the final drawings; by that September the building was illegal. Wright must have rued that 1955 day when he became impatient with city contract negotiations and recommended that the city add the "insurmountable legal obstacles" clause.

Although Wright was discouraged by the setback, he was heartened by another Madison development: an open house for the first of a new line of prefabricated houses he had designed for Marshall Erdman (see Fig. 4.32). The event represented still another attempt by Wright to provide affordable housing for the masses.

Insurmountable obstacles or not, Wright needed to get paid. After all, he had received absolutely nothing from the city since signing the contract in July 1956, even though he had completed the preliminary drawings in accord with the contract. In November 1957 Wright asked to be paid for his preliminary drawings, but the city attorney told Wright that the Metzner law was — no surprise here — "an insurmountable legal obstacle." In February 1958 Wright sued the city and state, arguing that the law violated the Wisconsin and U.S. constitutions. Wright's attorneys argued that the law usurped clearly delegated local power, did not uniformly apply to all Wisconsin cities, and deprived the architect of his property (his contract with the city) without due process or compensation. The unfairness of doing thousands of hours of work to satisfy a contract and then not be paid because of a discriminatory state law deeply disturbed the Groveses and the Lescohiers. These two stalwart couples agreed to pay Wright's legal bill, estimated at $3,000 to $5,000.[123]

Although faced with a long, low-odds lawsuit and the strong possibility that he would never get paid, Wright was remarkably philosophical. One Sunday in August 1958, when just about everybody thought Monona Terrace was dead, Wright was having a relaxed discussion with members of the Fellowship at Taliesin on a wide range of topics. An apprentice asked Wright if he would share his thoughts on the seemingly jinxed project. Wright replied: "Well, it is not an altogether discouraging picture, because at least we have had the pleasure and what glory there is ... in doing the project .... Even if it is never built, I shall never regret having put myself into ... the Terrace. And if they don't build it — well, let's see what will happen 10 years from now. It will come about someday."[124]

Just three months after Wright said this, a sea change in Wisconsin politics suggested that the Terrace might be built sooner than its supporters

Wright and Marshall Erdman

*Courtesy FLW FDN. 6820.003, photo by Michael A. Vaccaro*

Cover of Erdman Promotional Brochure

*Courtesy Marshall Erdman & Associates, Inc.*

FIGURE 4.32

### Wright-Erdman Prefab Houses

Although Wright spent much of his early career designing expensive houses for well-heeled clients, he was also keenly interested in designing high-quality houses for people of average means, a goal he thought could best be achieved through prefabrication (Fig. 2.35 describes an earlier effort). Marshall Erdman, the contractor for Wright's Unitarian Meeting House (see Fig. 3.20), was also interested in prefab housing, and after he completed the church project, Erdman worked independently of Wright to develop a line of houses based on this construction system. In 1953 *Life* ran a feature story on Erdman's prefab houses, which may have been why Wright stopped at Erdman's plant sometime in 1954 on his way into Madison.

Wright told the young entrepreneur that his designs were terrible and that he would go broke if he continued to produce them. Erdman asked Wright to design a better one. To Erdman's surprise Wright agreed. Wright's first prefab design, a three-bedroom model known as Prefab I, was completed in 1956 and appeared on the cover of *House and Home* that December. After the story appeared, Erdman received ten thousand inquiries from all over the world. In this photo the two men are standing in the entrance to Prefab I during a 1957 open house. Wright also completed two other prefab designs for Erdman, more than a dozen of which were built around the country. The opportunity to work with Wright on the Unitarian Meeting House and the prefab line profoundly changed Erdman's life. "Everything I have I owe to him," Erdman said in an interview. Erdman's company later specialized in medical buildings and a popular line of cabinetry.

Versions of Prefab I ranged from a basic $22,000 model to the deluxe version, shown here, which appeared on the cover of Erdman's company brochure. This house belonged to Dr. Arnold Jackson, the brother of Joseph Jackson who spent so much of his life trying to kill Wright's Monona Terrace. Arnold Jackson, by contrast, was a member of Madison's Auditorium Committee and favored the Wright project. Known as Skyview because of its panoramic view, the Arnold Jackson House was disassembled in 1985 and moved to Beaver Dam, Wisconsin. Today a large office building known as Landmark Place occupies the hillside below the former site of the Jackson home.

thought. For more than twenty years Republicans had maintained majorities in the assembly and senate and a lock on the governor's office. But then, in November 1958, the Democratic Party made a remarkable surge; for the first time since 1932 voters elected a Democratic governor and Democratic majorities in both houses. The Metzner law — "the ugly duckling of the 1957 legislature" — was not entirely responsible for this change, but its widely perceived unfairness provoked most legislators to campaign against the bill. That it was responsible for Metzner's own defeat is beyond dispute. Suddenly, things looked brighter for Wrightophiles.[125]

Soon after taking office in January 1959 Madison-area legislators introduced a bill to repeal the Metzner law. To expedite passage the two legislative committees to which the bill was referred held a rare joint hearing. The only person testifying against repeal was Joe Jackson, who accused Wright of being "a Communist or a Fellow Traveler." Jackson told legislators that if they knew the "truth about Wright," they would never vote to repeal the Metzner law. To prove his point he eagerly summarized the contents of documents he had collected from the American Legion, the House Un-American Activities Committee, a Madison judge, and possibly the FBI. Jackson thought his "Wright Record" was shocking, but it was little more than a compilation of the architect's consistently antimilitary views and affiliations with leftist organizations. Jackson insisted that he was not smearing Wright because "you can't smear a man with the truth." Nearly all others who testified in favor of the bill said that the Metzner law was "an abuse of legislative power." Gaylord Nelson, the new Democratic governor, signed the repeal into law on March 20, 1959.[126]

The 1959 legislature also passed a special bill making the Monona Terrace site an exception to the state prohibition against building anything at city street ends that terminate at a navigable body of water. This eliminated still another obstacle that opponents hoped would thwart the project.[127]

By the time Nelson signed the Metzner repeal bill, four years and four months had passed since the citizens of Madison had voted for Monona Terrace. Wright was now nearing the end of his ninety-first year, but his interest in Monona Terrace never waned. In fact, sometime in early 1959, before the governor had actually affixed his signature to the repeal, the elderly but still vigorous architect sat down at his Taliesin drawing board to produce still another revision of the beloved project, his eighth since he conceived the project in 1938. Wright did not have any instructions from the Auditorium Committee; he did this on his own. Wright was apparently eager to restore the "nobility" to Monona Terrace that he was forced to remove during his last downsizing in April 1957. Wright initialed this set of Terrace plans on February 15, 1959 (see Fig. 4.33).[128]

Aware that the Metzner law would soon be repealed, Wright submitted his first formal invoice to Nestingen. Wright's cover note on his bill for $122,500, dated March 10, 1959, was brief and moving. "Dear Ivan: Herewith the sorrowful. Probably the most emasculated bill ever presented by an architect for his services. It would be impossible to even outline all of the water that has gone over the dam but I thought it only fitting to mention a modest sum. Hats off to you for your faithful support from beginning to end. Truly yours, Frank Lloyd Wright." Then, at the bottom of the bill, Wright added: "Extra services over and beyond contract — not billed."[129]

It was the last communication that Nestingen ever got from Wright. The distinguished man died in a Phoenix hospital on April 9, 1959, four days after stomach surgery and just two months short of his ninety-second birthday. Associates drove his body back to Taliesin for burial on April 12.

## THE COUNTERCRUSADE

### CHANGING OF THE GUARD

Wright's death triggered the beginning of a new era in the history of Monona Terrace. In his annual address to the council less than two weeks after Wright's death, Mayor Nestingen reminded members that the architect had nearly completed preliminary work for the project and urged the city to have the Frank Lloyd Wright Foundation prepare "working plans and drawings ... as early as possible." A few days later William Wesley Peters, chief architect and vice president of the foundation, sent Nestingen a letter saying the foundation was "ready and able to fulfill all existing contracts." Peters had worked closely with Wright on the project beginning in the 1930s and on several occasions had met with Madison officials when Wright was unavailable. Peters enclosed written preliminary project specifications, which, in conjunction with the plans that Wright had completed on February 15, fulfilled the contract requirement for "preliminary plans and specifications." Now that this requirement was met, Peters asked the city to pay the $122,500 bill that Wright had submitted the month before he died. The council approved the designation of Peters as the foundation architect for the project but not the payment.[130]

### ADVANCING UNDER FIRE

Critics of Monona Terrace experienced Wright's death with a sense of relief and hope; no longer would they have to battle the legendary genius and his powerful mystique. However, opponents also recognized that unless they did something, Wright's

MONONA TERRACE CIVIC CENTER FOR
FRANK LLOYD

LAKE MONONA
SCONSIN
ITECT

FIGURE 4.33

**1959 Rendering, Wright's Last**

© FLW FDN. 5632.10

This rendering, dated February 15, 1959, was completed just seven weeks before Wright died and was part of still another iteration for Monona Terrace, his eighth. The drawing incorporates a design concept that Wright used in several of his last projects: "pendentive architecture." The idea was to design building components so that they appeared to hang like a pendant. For example, note how the arched bottoms of the exterior walls of the great cylinders on either side of the building appear to hang from the building's frame. In the 1955 design, by contrast (Fig. 4.1), the columns supporting these arches were directly below the cylindrical wall. The openings of the parking structure also reveal Wright's use of the pendentive concept, which he introduced in his 1956 iterations but more fully developed here.

death would produce a sentimental surge of support that would sweep the project forward.

In May 1959 Joe Jackson with great pleasure filed a taxpayer's lawsuit charging the city with a "gross abuse of discretion," that is, relying on a revocable state grant of authority to build the Terrace in Law Park. Among other things, Jackson charged that if the Terrace were built, it would slide into Lake Monona on a stratum of slippery clay (see Fig. 4.22). Most issues had been litigated before and the case had a frivolous odor. Even the city attorney thought Jackson's chances of winning were remote but counseled against proceeding until the case was

settled. Jackson used this time to send copies of his "Wright Record" to all new council members; Jackson was absolutely persuaded that once they read the document, they too would demand the architect's banishment from city affairs. Finally, in January 1960 the circuit court ruled against Jackson on every count, but the determined octogenarian didn't care; he had stopped work on the project for another eight months. A *Capital Times* cartoon (see Fig. 4.34) captured the bully-boy tactics.[131]

Once again the common council had a rare green light. In February 1960 the council finally paid the $122,500 bill that Wright had submitted in 1959

and directed Peters to prepare final preliminary plans. Peters took advantage of this process to resolve the cross-cutting demands of groups that would use the facility and to make several significant improvements to the design. For example, Peters hired a Yale University theater expert, who designed an ingenious monorail system for storing stage curtains in rooms on both sides of the stage rather than in a view-blocking stage house above the stage. The Yale professor also helped Peters design a sophisticated sound-radiating flexible curtain that could be dropped in the middle of the large auditorium to transform it into a fifteen-hundred-seat theater. By the summer of 1960 leaders of

FIGURE 4.34

**1960 Stalling Tactics Cartoon**

*Courtesy Ed Hinrichs and The Capital Times*

When this cartoon appeared in the *Capital Times* on July 29, 1960, arch-enemy Joe Jackson was about to appeal his taxpayer's suit to the Wisconsin Supreme Court. In January 1961 the justices ruled unanimously against Jackson, but by then his suit had placed a legal cloud over Monona Terrace for nearly two years.

Madison's theater groups were gushing praise for Peters. They said the theaters were "great," "excellent," and "terrific" and that they contained "unique features which students of the theater will be coming to see." The director of the Madison Community Center said he was "completely satisfied."[132]

One reason Peters got so many rave reviews was an important change in policy. Nestingen and the Auditorium Committee had concluded that after inflation $5.5 million was too little to build an adequate auditorium; quietly and unofficially, they told Peters to make the facility bigger and they would raise the additional money.

Although this decision would later cast a long dark shadow over the project, Peters expanded Wright's February 1959 plans by pushing the rear wall of the auditorium lakeward, a change that increased seating capacity and the size of the exhibit hall below. The Auditorium Committee ratified those changes and directed Peters to increase the size of several other facilities.[133] (The change from 1959 to 1961 appears in Fig. 7.6.)

The decision to have Peters prepare new plans and drawings in February 1960 prompted the *Journal* to begin hammering away at a clever new gotcha strategy. The paper said the auditorium was too small to accommodate six thousand people for "boxing, wrestling, and sports shows" and that the stage house was not tall enough to accommodate the drop curtains needed by road shows. The only solution was to make the auditorium bigger and the stage house taller, but to do either would once again increase the cost, block more of the lake view, and kill the project.[134]

In June 1960 the common council approved the final preliminary plans and directed Peters to prepare final construction documents. However, all elected officials and close observers understood that this bigger, better, and long-delayed building was going to cost more and that another referendum would be needed to determine whether taxpayers would foot the bill. What they did not know was how much more it would cost and when the referendum would be.

## ODDITORIUM OPPONENTS ORGANIZE

The city's decision to direct Peters to prepare final preliminary plans forced opponents to recognize that skillful editorial sniping and even the lawsuits of civic generals could not stop the project. In fact, critics were all coming to the same conclusion: they needed a citizen army to march into the polls and vote the project into oblivion. Toward that end, Jackson sent out postcards to people who opposed the "cut down, cut-up mess" urging them to pack the council chamber on March 10, 1960, and demand a referendum. About 250—the *Capital Times* called them a "jeering mob"—responded to Jackson's call. Taunted Jackson: "Mr. Mayor, are you or your councilmen afraid to let the people of Madison record their judgment of their auditorium?" But the council still had a pro-Terrace majority and voted 13–6 to decline Jackson's invitation to set a referendum.[135]

The council's refusal was the perfect call-to-arms for members of the anti-Terrace citizen army. In early May 1960 Joe Jackson and several of his friends organized the Citizens for a Realistic Auditorium Association. Marshall Browne, a Madison printer and publisher of the weekly *East Side News*, was elected president; Henry Reynolds, owner of a transfer and moving company and a veteran council member, was elected vice president; and Carroll Metzner became secretary. "We are here," announced Browne, "to organize a crusade," a crusade that will produce an "A-U-D-I-T-O-R-I-U-M not an O-D-D-I-T-O-R-I-U-M." Joe Rothschild, the manager of a downtown department store and a leader of the postwar effort to build a war memorial auditorium at Conklin Park, stirred up the seventy-person crowd saying, "Let's do something about [the Terrace]. Let's get mad. It's time for the citizens to stand up and be counted."

William F. Stevens, a retired state architect, drew laughs when he ridiculed Wright's decision to put the floor of the Terrace exhibition hall exactly at lake level. "Everyone knows that Frank Lloyd Wright buildings leaked from the roof. This one is going to leak from the bottom."[136]

Auditorium association leaders left no doubt about their goal: fifty-five hundred signatures on a petition that would force the pro-Terrace council to hold a referendum to "terminate all plans for an auditorium and civic center at the so-called Monona Terrace site at the end of Monona Avenue in Law Park and immediately take steps to select an alternative site." Members began circulating these petitions in August.[137]

Critics tried to arouse arena envy by exploiting the widespread confusion about auditoriums. Using quarter-page newspaper ads, they claimed that other cities had built practical, realistic auditoriums for a fraction of what the Madison project was expected to cost. They compared the twenty-five-hundred-seat auditorium and its expected $6.4 million price tag with twelve-thousand-seat auditoriums that other cities had built for about $5 million. These ads caused many Madisonians to think they were being hornswoggled. What association members did *not* say was that these exemplary auditoriums were really big flat-floored, exposed-truss arenas with attached exhibition halls designed for sporting events, circuses, political rallies, and conventions. Also missing from these big newspaper advertisements was the information that these auditoriums did not include a concert hall, art gallery, community center, small theater, and parking garage.[138]

Recalling that blue-collar voters had played a large role in winning the 1954 referendum, critics went out of their way to woo this group. For example, the *Journal* reminded its readers that there were "those who don't care for string quartets, symphonies, speakers, or looking at pictures in an art gallery" and that the people who want "ice shows, hockey, figure skating, indoor circuses, and arena-type sporting events are losing out." Continued the *Journal*, "They, too, pay taxes and they, too, have a right to find their interests met in the 'civic center.'" Council member Babe Rohr, who was also president of the painters' union, agreed. He said Monona Terrace had become a home for "culture addicts of Madison's suburbs."[139]

Using techniques reminiscent of the proponents' in 1954, Citizens for a Realistic Auditorium Association positioned teams of petition bearers at the Capitol Square and, in a sign of the changing times, at the two new shopping centers. They even organized "flying squads" that delivered petitions to voters' homes for their signatures. By the end of September 1960, Citizens for a Realistic Auditorium Association had gathered almost ten thousand signatures, nearly double what they needed.[140]

Opponents demanded and got a special hearing from the common council on October 11, 1960; because so many were expected, the meeting was held in the auditorium of Central High School (see Fig. 4.35), where supporters had gathered in October 1953 to hear Frank Lloyd Wright explain his project to the public. The meeting began at 7:30 and by midnight forty speakers had given the council a piece of their mind. Most opposed the project and some made outlandish claims. One council member said that the people who would use Monona Terrace were "the intelligentsia and that's what Russia is filled with today."[141]

Two days later the pro–Monona Terrace council voted 13–7 to defer a referendum. The majority claimed to favor a referendum but insisted that the best time to hold it was April 1961 — by that time contractors' bids would be available. "Let's let the people see what they are voting on," said one council member.[142]

Very well, said the leaders of the Citizens for a Realistic Auditorium Association, if you will not respond to the desires of ten thousand voters, we will force you to comply in the courts. Led by Marshall Browne, the association filed suit in circuit court in December 1960 to require the city to hold a referendum. But in February 1961 the court ruled that the city had no obligation to hold a binding referendum. The judge said a referendum could not be used to reverse a council action, would be merely discretionary if held, and would be inappropriate because the city had sold bonds and levied taxes for the project.[143]

STICKER SHOCK

The first four months of 1961 were arguably the most tumultuous, action-packed period in the history of Monona Terrace. In January the state supreme court unanimously upheld the appeal of the circuit court ruling on Jackson's suit, thereby eliminating still another legal challenge. That same month Peters delivered to the city nearly five hundred pages of detailed construction plans and four hundred pages of specifications that contractors needed to bid the job. The council whooshed the complex plans through all approving bodies in just one week, giving its own final approval on January 30, 1961. During this whirlwind week Joe Jackson stood up during an Auditorium Committee meeting and asked whether the plans were the "same as those prepared by Frank Lloyd Wright." Peters answered this first authenticity challenge by saying they were a "logical and legitimate development of Wright's plans."[144]

Also during January Ivan Nestingen filed papers for a fourth mayoral term, but then—because of the

FIGURE 4.35

**Terrace Foes Rally, 1960**

SHSW. WHi(M95)219, photo by Dave Sandell

Seven years made a huge difference in community sentiment about Monona Terrace. On October 29, 1953, about five hundred residents and local government officials had sat in the Central High School auditorium listening to Frank Lloyd Wright give a stirring description of Monona Terrace (see Fig. 4.6). On October 11, 1960, its opponents, Citizens for a Realistic Auditorium Association, demanded a hearing before the city council and got it. Because so many were expected, the hearing was held in the Central High School auditorium. Nine hundred residents jammed the auditorium to register their opposition to the Wright plan. Despite the show of force, Madison council members refused to hold a referendum in November 1960; council members argued that a referendum in April 1961 would be better because bids for the building would be available.

large role he had played in winning Wisconsin for John F. Kennedy (see Fig. 4.36) — the new president offered Nestingen a job as an undersecretary in the U.S. Department of Health, Education, and Welfare under Abraham Ribicoff. Nestingen immediately accepted, and on the night the council approved the final plans for Monona Terrace, the mayor announced that it would be his last meeting. Joe Jackson dashed off a personal letter to Kennedy expressing his deepest gratitude for "removing [Nestingen] from the city."[145]

Nestingen's last-minute decision precipitated a political scramble in the mayor's race. Critics saw Nestingen's departure as a golden opportunity to

FIGURE 4.36

**Nestingen Campaigns for Kennedy, 1960**

SHSW. WHi(X3)51103

As the 1960 presidential primaries neared, almost all the political pundits saw Wisconsin as a bellwether state in John F. Kennedy's campaign. So Kennedy campaign officials gave careful thought as to who should head the statewide citizens committee. They selected Ivan Nestingen because he had chaired the Kennedy for President Club of Wisconsin since early 1959, he had effectively campaigned for Kennedy, and because Patrick J. Lucey, then head of the state Democratic Party, persuaded Kennedy campaign officials that Nestingen would complement the young, articulate, and liberal Kennedy. This picture was taken during the last month of the campaign. In January 1961 Nestingen joined the Kennedy administration.

put their man in the mayor's office and made Monona Terrace the defining issue of still another mayoral campaign. Henry Reynolds resigned his position as vice president of Citizens for a Realistic Auditorium Association and ran on an anti-Terrace platform (see Fig. 4.37), and Bob Nuckles, Nestingen's executive assistant and a former council member, ran as the pro-Terrace candidate. Leaders of both sides used candidates' positions on the project as the litmus test of their political acceptability.[146]

These fast-moving events created several time binds. Terrace backers had planned to hold a referendum at the April election to ask voters for additional money to build the project, but the latest the city

could announce the referendum was early March. Unfortunately, the council could not know what the additional amount would be until the bids had been received — most insiders estimated it would be between $2 and 3 million — and the bidding process for a complex megastructure required at least two months. Because the council had not approved the plans until January 30, members were forced to shorten the bid time from eight to five weeks, three weeks less than needed. The bids would be due on March 7, 1961.[147]

Only two contractors submitted bids, and one was disqualified by a technicality. The winner by default was the Perini Company, a large Boston contractor that had built the City-County Building in the midfifties. Perini's bid was a conversation-stopping $12.1 million, far more than what insiders expected. Peters thought the price was "actually a great bargain. The price is not high for the building you get." Nuckles expressed shock and dismay. Henry Reynolds said, "The people who promoted this unwise and ill-planned project should be ashamed of what they have done."[148]

(Just twelve years earlier Joe Jackson and other conservative business leaders had spearheaded a crusade to build a civic complex at Conklin Park, a project that was supposed to cost $1.5 million but ballooned to $5.2 million. Curiously, no one remembered this.)

At the council meeting two days after the bid opening, critics wore mocking black crepe paper arm bands labeled "Monona Terrace." By a vote of 14–8 the common council rejected the Perini bid and dropped all plans for a supplemental funding referendum in April. Finger pointing began immediately. Terrace backers blamed the delays on the Obstructionists and their insistence that the project's budget include the cost of building a six-lane expressway in Law Park. Opponents blamed the high costs of building on a watery site and on the curvilinear Wright design. Leaders of both sides agreed that five weeks was too little time to get competitive bids and that some project costs were attributable to Cadillac specifications and unique state-of-the-art theater features.[149]

But the question people really wanted answered was who authorized plans for a building that exceeded the budgeted amount by 122 percent. Almost all fingers pointed to the Auditorium Committee, the members of which had been, in the revealing words of a *Capital Times* editorial, "anxious to please" the community and user groups. Looking back at the preliminary planning process, it seems clear that the committee recognized that Monona Terrace could never be built for $5.5 million and that it allowed the demands of user groups and even critics' comments to drive the final design. However, considerable criticism was reserved for Peters, who reportedly failed to give the committee "sufficient information on mounting costs." In fact, in a letter dated September 24, 1960, Peters had told Nestingen that inflation alone would increase building costs by 21 percent and that at the direction of the Auditorium Committee he had made a "sizable and significant increase in size and area" to almost every part of the building. Although he did not say what the magnitude of the total increase was, it is hard to read this letter as anything but a big flashing warning light. The paper trail left by Nestingen suggests that he did not give this letter the attention it deserved. The debate about culpability raged for years but was never resolved.[150]

Citizens for Monona Terrace moved quickly to salvage this devastating turn of events. Two weeks after the bid was announced, a remarkably enthusiastic crowd of 150 gathered at the Unitarian Meeting House, still the epicenter of the movement, to work out a strategy. Harold Groves expressed confidence that "this hurdle will be overcome." He had, he reported, already received a promise of substantial support from Alicia Patterson, the publisher of *Newsday* who was married to Harry Guggenheim, nephew of Solomon (the man who had commissioned Wright to do the museum). This heartening pledge prompted the organization to recommend a supplemental referendum for $4.5 million and a $2 million private fund-raising drive, a combination that would allow the project to go forward at close to the bid level.[151]

Candidate Reynolds was ecstatic. The shockingly high bid had come at the best possible time during the campaign. "Now that the Monona Terrace Civic Center is dead, the way is open to alternate plans," Reynolds announced. The conservative candidate said the solution was to build two buildings, a cultural center in downtown Madison and a full-fledged sports arena in an outlying location, but he refused to say exactly where in either case. However, he did say that "we can put the same facilities ... as are at the Monona Terrace project on any one of four sites" and that "all of this can be done for about $4 million or a little more."[152]

In April 1961, 69 percent of registered voters, in one of the biggest turnouts for a spring election in Madison history, elected Henry Reynolds mayor. For the first time in five years the city had a mayor who was opposed to Monona Terrace. Although pro-Terrace council members still enjoyed a majority on the council, Reynolds possessed the veto, a weapon he promised to use to thwart the project. Whether he would be able to lead the council into the promised land remained to be seen.[153]

Henry Reynolds, shown here in a portrait taken in 1963 when he was fifty-eight, was well known in Madison. In 1928, just five years after he was graduated from high school, he became president of the family business, Reynolds Transfer and Storage Company. From 1943 until 1951 he served discontinuously as a member of the common council and was mayor from 1961 to 1965. His achievements as mayor included a pioneering equal housing ordinance, Madison's first units of subsidized housing, a new library, several new schools, a causeway across Monona Bay, and keeping the tax rate the same for four consecutive years.

The year before he became mayor, Reynolds was elected vice president of the Citizens for a Realistic Auditorium Association, an organization dedicated to killing Monona Terrace and building a much simpler and less expensive building on a "conventional" site. Reynolds thought the attempt to build an auditorium over the lake was an expensive mistake, that the tunnel was stupid, and that the curved Terrace shape wasted space. He maintained that he could erect a building accommodating most of the same functions as Monona Terrace on any one of four other sites for "4 million or a little more." But it was not just his disapproval of the site and the design that brought Reynolds into the anti-Wright crusade; the quiet, conservative man was persuaded that Wright lacked morality and that no public building he designed should ever be allowed in Madison.

Although Reynolds probably had no intention of running for mayor when he became an officer in the association, Nestingen's sudden resignation in 1961 created a fine opportunity. Reynolds reentered Madison politics in 1975 to challenge Paul Soglin, a young radical mayor then completing his first term and who would later play a large role in Monona Terrace. Reynolds died in 1980 at the age of seventy-five.

FOUR MILLION OR A LITTLE MORE

Despite Reynolds' victory at the polls in April 1961, Terrace backers refused to hoist a white flag. Using five-minute television commercials, Citizens for Monona Terrace touted a "realistically reduced" project that could be financed with a supplemental property-tax–based appropriation of just $2.5 million and a $1 million private sector fund-raising drive. However, when members realized that this plan was unrealistic, they endorsed a referendum asking for $5 million more. The pro-Terrace council endorsed a $7.5 million referendum, but Reynolds vetoed the measure.[154]

Proponents reluctantly concluded that so long as Reynolds was mayor, they could do little but practice what they called "watching and waiting," that is, waiting to see what Reynolds produced and how it compared with Monona Terrace. Proponents were confident that no Reynolds-produced auditorium could match Monona Terrace; in fact, Harold Groves calculated that for "$4 million or a little more" the mayor could build only "a warehouse, garage, or manufacturing building."[155]

Reynolds moved quickly to deliver on his campaign promises. Using his new political broom, he swept out all but one Nestingen appointee on the Auditorium Committee and replaced them with his people. Next Reynolds met with leaders of the Dane County board and urged them to build a five- to six-thousand-seat arena at the county fairgrounds, just two miles from the Capitol Square. You build the arena, he said, and we, the city, will build a cultural facility. County officials liked the idea. A few days later Reynolds announced that he wanted to put the cultural complex on Joe Jackson's well-polished site: Conklin Park.[156]

Reynolds then turned to a task he relished: terminating the Wright foundation contract. To no

one's surprise the Auditorium Committee backed the mayor and sent its recommendation to the council, but the council, still dominated by Monona Terrace backers, refused. When a stalemate developed in November 1961, Peters formally notified the city to begin the arbitration process called for in the contract. Peters was persuaded that this was the only way the foundation could collect its substantial unpaid fees. Reynolds refused to arbitrate because he believed the foundation had breached its contract to design a building costing no more than $5.5 million. Therefore, concluded Reynolds, the city owed the foundation nothing; to begin arbitrating would imply the contract was valid. The foundation, by contrast, argued that Peters had done only what he was directed to do by the city and that Peters had therefore fulfilled the contract.[157]

Reynolds got a temporary injunction so that the city could prove that the contract had been breached. However, from the first hearing before Dane Circuit Court Judge Richard Bardwell, Reynolds realized he was in trouble. Bardwell turned to the Alton Heassler, the city attorney, and said, "You aren't really serious, are you, that this is an illegal contract?" The city attorney said he was. Bardwell continued, "You are under contract for six years and you sit by for that time without any legal action and then come in here and raise the point that it is illegal—it shocks me." Bardwell sent the lawyers off to prepare briefs.[158]

By now it was January 1962 and Reynolds had been in office nine months. Although the new mayor was eager to move forward with his auditorium agenda, he was beginning to realize that he would never be able to terminate the contract until he got an anti-Terrace council. Reynolds and his allies were confident they could achieve this end by holding a referendum in April 1962. They had Reynolds in the

mayor's office, ten thousand signatures on petitions, and that jolting $12.1 million price tag — all factors they could exploit to fan anti-Terrace sentiment.

Citizens for Monona Terrace was also eager for a showdown, but this time the battleground favored Reynolds in two ways. First, the mayor had his veto power, and he used it to force the council to adopt referendum wording proposed by the Citizens for a Realistic Auditorium Association during the 1960 petition drive (see Fig. 4.38). This meant that to vote for Monona Terrace, you had to vote no. Second, the ballot also contained a $9.3 million referendum on funding for new city schools, which pitted a nice thing, an auditorium, against a necessary thing, schools.

Once again the city was alive with rallies, speeches, debates, radio commercials, television programs, leaflets, referendum advertisements, and a daily diet of newspaper stories sufficient to numb a Monona Terrace junkie (see Fig. 4.39). When the smoke cleared, the "Terracites," as Marshall Browne called them, had lost. About 54 percent of voters cast their ballots against Monona Terrace, and Reynolds got three new antiproject council members. Since the introduction of Monona Terrace in 1953 its opponents had never enjoyed so much political power. The *Journal* declared Monona Terrace "dead and buried"; the *Capital Times* said the city had missed the boat (see Fig. 4.40).[159]

The election showed how much the city had changed since the 1954 referendum. The suburban surge was at its flood tide (see Fig. 4.41), and many suburbanites were less than enthusiastic about a downtown center. Some thought the removal of the boating facilities and the ice sheet for hockey and ice shows meant that the auditorium had been hijacked by the cultural elite. And for those who were still undecided, there was that price tag,

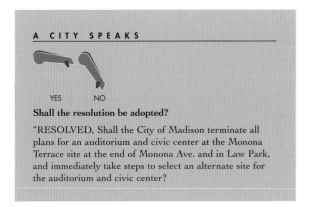

YES    NO

**Shall the resolution be adopted?**

"RESOLVED, Shall the City of Madison terminate all plans for an auditorium and civic center at the Monona Terrace site at the end of Monona Ave. and in Law Park, and immediately take steps to select an alternate site for the auditorium and civic center?"

FIGURE 4.38

**1962 Referendum Question**

The wording of this April 1962 ballot question mirrored the language on petitions circulated by leaders of the Citizens for a Realistic Auditorium Association and, under threat of a Reynolds veto, the pro–Monona Terrace common council was forced to accept it. The wording was also calculated to allow voters who wanted to support a $9.3 million school construction bond issue, also on the ballot, to vote yes twice.

which was big enough to send all but the most resolute into sticker shock.

Although Judge Bardwell had not ruled on the validity of the contract, Reynolds moved quickly to deliver on his campaign promises by getting the council to terminate the contract. Next he agreed to follow Joe Jackson's advice and hire Ladislas Segoe, the urban planner who had done a master plan for Madison in 1938. Reynolds wanted a credible independent consultant to ratify the Conklin Park area as the site for the auditorium and was confident that Segoe would do this, just as he had twenty-four years earlier. Actually, since the election of April 1961 Reynolds had concluded that the half-acre square block across the street from Conklin Park—the site of the old waterworks (see Fig. 1.33)—was the best place for the auditorium. But Segoe refused to select the waterworks block and instead recommended a four-acre site that included one end of Conklin Park and a contiguous residential area to the west. Segoe's decision immediately

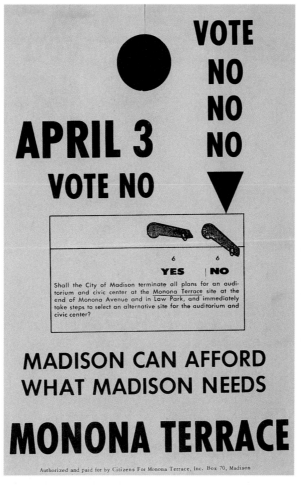

Pro-Terrace Advertisement

SHSW. WHi (X3)51365

Anti-Terrace Advertisement

Courtesy Wisconsin State Journal

FIGURE 4.39

**1962 Referendum Advertisements**

These two political advertisements show the growing power of the anti-Terrace forces. The triple yes advertisement was prepared by the Citizens for a Realistic Auditorium Association, and the triple no advertisement was prepared by Citizens for Monona Terrace. In the past a yes vote had meant support for Monona Terrace, but with Reynolds' threat to veto referendum language he did not like, this referendum was worded to favor opponents. Hence a yes vote favored the "realistic" auditorium. Also on the ballot was a referendum authorizing a large bond issue for new schools. This allowed Monona Terrace opponents to say that for the same price as a Wright auditorium, they could have a realistic auditorium and the new schools.

provoked a vigorous objection from that area's council member and residents of the Conklin Park neighborhood. They argued that the huge new

building would destroy the residential quality of their neighborhood, virtually eliminate a heavily used park, and clog the streets with cars.[160]

Missed the Boat Again

FIGURE 4.40

**1962 "Missed the Boat Again" Cartoon**

*Courtesy Ed Hinrichs and* The Capital Times

Ed Hinrichs, cartoonist for the *Capital Times*, used this wistful image to summarize the results of the 1962 referendum. This cartoon appeared on April 4, 1962, the day after the election.

Although the site question was hardly resolved, Reynolds turned his attention to the type of auditorium he wanted for the waterworks block. Remarkably, the mayor was convinced that the functional specifications developed for Monona Terrace for the large and small theaters, art gallery, and community center were nearly perfect. His goal was to place these facilities in a simple, low-budget building. Once again, the mayor sought credible consultants to ratify his vision. He hired two out-of-town auditorium managers who recommended that Madison build a barnlike flat-floor arena with a temporary stage at one end. They reasoned that such a facility would serve Madison's

diverse needs and even suggested that people attending Beethoven concerts could sit on bleachers.[161]

Reynolds next tried to find an architect who would be willing to design an auditorium for "about $4 million or a little more" on the waterworks site. He spoke first with William Holabird, the senior partner of Holabird, Root, and Burgee, the large Chicago firm that had designed the City-County Building. Holabird toured the site with Reynolds but could not bring himself to recommend such a large building on the tiny waterworks site. Holabird told Reynolds that he should stick with the larger Segoe site, that an auditorium there would cost about $8 million, and that costs there would run about $5 a square foot more than Monona Terrace. That was not exactly what the mayor wanted to hear. The resourceful Reynolds then called in Alfred Shaw, the senior partner of Shaw, Metz, and Associates, the large Chicago firm that had recently designed McCormick Place. Shaw told Reynolds that a splendid auditorium could be built on the waterworks site for about $4 million.[162]

Just when Reynolds had found an architect who agreed to build an auditorium where the mayor wanted it and for the right price, Judge Bardwell dashed everything. In a scathing opinion issued in November 1962, Bardwell said the city's contract with the foundation was "valid and enforceable" and ruled against the city on every count. Reynolds was furious and told Edwin Conrad, the new city attorney, to appeal to the state supreme court, which he did — and lost. Reynolds told Conrad to ask the supreme court to rehear the case, but it refused.[163]

Now it was October 1963 and Reynolds was forced to do something he had vowed he would never do: arbitrate the with the Frank Lloyd Wright Foundation. Nearly two years after the foundation had served legal notice to arbitrate, Reynolds,

Conrad, Peters, and Peters' attorney sat down for a talk. Given the $12 million project, the foundation was entitled to $350,000, but the foundation's lawyer said a settlement of $170,000 would be acceptable. Reynolds dug in, claiming the city owed the foundation nothing, though he did concede that the city had a moral obligation to pay something. Reynolds persuaded the common council to approve $135,000, but the foundation refused this amount, saying that $170,000 was its lowest offer. Although the council was willing to pay the $170,000, Reynolds held out. To him it was a matter of principle.[164]

Angered by the court decisions, the failure of the city attorney to prove that the contract was breached, and his view that Conrad was intimidated by foundation attorneys, Reynolds decided to hire the best legal talent that money could buy to handle the arbitration for the city. Specifically, Reynolds wanted someone who specialized in disputes with architects, someone who was tough, shrewd, and unyielding, someone who could force the foundation to take a token payment for its work.

Reynolds found his man in Philadelphia. Edward Cushman, who counted Bethlehem Steel and Pittsburgh Plate Glass among his clients. Cushman normally charged $1,000 per day, but he did limited work for municipalities for just $350 per day. This amount was substantially more than Madison attorneys were getting, but to the notoriously frugal Reynolds it was money well spent. In February 1964 Cushman appeared before the council and touted his skill, experience, credentials, and client list so much that one council member called him the "Cassius Clay [Mohammad Ali] of the legal profession." From this day forward the *Capital Times* almost always referred to Reynolds' man as "Philadelphia lawyer" Cushman, exploiting the rich pejorative connotations of that term in the Midwest. Bill Evjue got additional mileage by regularly reporting Cushman's rapidly mounting bill.[165]

When Cushman and Reynolds burrowed into the voluminous correspondence between Wright and Peters and the Auditorium Committee, they found discrepancies. In 1957 Wright had calculated that the cost of his recently downsized plans would be $3.3 million. In 1959 Peters predicted that Monona Terrace would cost about $6 million, and then in March 1961 the bids came in at $12.1 million. Something didn't compute. The 1957 and 1959 versions of the complex were virtually identical in size; furthermore, Peters had increased the building's size by only about 38 percent over Wright's 1957-1959 design, and inflation had been less than 2 percent during this twenty-two-month period. (Cushman's experts determined that from 1955 through 1960 building costs had gone up by about 18 percent, substantially less than what Monona Terrace's backers claimed.) Thus the combination of a larger building and inflation since the 1957 plans accounted for about 40 percent of the increase. To be fair, Cushman assumed that a longer bid time and various cost savings could have brought the cost down to $11 million in 1961. Even so, this meant that in less than two years Monona Terrace's costs had rocketed 83 percent over Peters' 1959 estimate, more than double what one would expect. Cushman concluded that Wright's $3.3 million estimate, which he had submitted to the Auditorium Committee in May 1957, was only half what it should have been. Cushman also charged that Peters "juggled the figures" in 1959 and that this was a "willful and deliberate concealment of true construction costs." Cushman and Reynolds were eager to prove these charges in arbitration.[166]

Under the terms of the city-foundation contract, each party picked an arbitrator and the two arbitrators selected the third. This trio then would rule on evidence the city and foundation presented. The two parties selected their arbitrators in the summer of 1964 but could not agree on the third until April 1965, a delay of nine months. The delay was deliberate because Reynolds was not expected to seek a third term.

In December 1964 seven-term county clerk Otto Festge announced his candidacy for mayor. Festge, then forty-three, said he would use his office to expedite the construction of Monona Terrace. After four years of looking into the barrel of Reynolds' veto gun, Monona Terrace's supporters had reason to hope. Festge not only won the primary in March 1965 but, together with other pro-Terrace candidates, managed to get 60 percent of the votes, a back-door mandate for the Terrace.[167]

Festge's good showing in the primary was not just a reflection of his personal popularity; he was the primary beneficiary of a full-page ad that appeared on Sunday, February 14, 1965, in the *Wisconsin State Journal*. The ad was signed by twenty-five downtown merchants, bankers, and property owners who said they wanted a "cultural center" at Monona Terrace based on the Frank Lloyd Wright design. The manifesto carried great weight because it came from prominent business leaders who heretofore had been wallflowers at the Monona Terrace dance. These men were understandably concerned about the rapid decline in downtown retailing resulting from suburbanization and Madison's three shopping malls. In 1960 two-thirds of all retailing was downtown; in 1965 two-thirds was in the suburbs. They saw a Wright-designed cultural center as a powerful and essential remedy for their malaise. Suddenly, obstructionist tactics were on trial.[168]

The merchants' manifesto argued that the cultural center could be built for $6.5 million because the

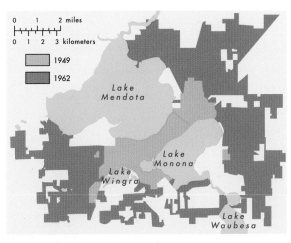

FIGURE 4.41

**Rapid Suburban Growth, 1949–1962**

*U.W.–Madison Cartographic Laboratory*

Like many U.S. cities, Madison experienced rapid suburban growth after World War II. This map shows how the city's area grew from fourteen to forty-two square miles between 1949 (shown in tan) and 1962 (shown in rust). While the city's area more than tripled, its population increased from 96,056 in 1950 to 126,706 in 1960, or 38 percent. Suburbanization left so few young people in the central city that the board of the Madison Community Center voted to close its downtown youth facilities and build new ones on the East and West Sides. Up to this point, Monona Terrace was to include a large downtown community center.

arena function was about to be provided by the Dane County Memorial Coliseum (see Fig. 4.42). Although the merchants did not say so, they also assumed that the Madison Community Center would no longer be part of the downtown complex. In 1961 community center officials decided to build centers in the suburbs rather than downtown.[169]

## A TRUCE WITH HOPE

Festge won the election by 8,000 votes and during the new council's first regular meeting got it to abandon the stalled arbitration process and to form a special committee to mediate a settlement. Festge tried to get Cushman to assist with the negotiations, but he told the new mayor that he was too busy

FIGURE 4.42

**Dane County Memorial Coliseum**

*Photo by James T. Potter, AIA*

The need for an arena to accommodate circuses, sporting events, equipment exhibitions, and conventions was recognized in 1954 by consultants who established the specifications for Monona Terrace. However, these consultants recommended that a full-scale arena *not* be part of Monona Terrace. Instead, they proposed a multipurpose exhibition hall where bleacher seating could accommodate as many as thirty-five hundred spectators for sporting events.

Critics constantly attacked this compromise and caused many voters to think they were being shortchanged. Henry Reynolds correctly insisted that the only enduring solution required two buildings: a cultural complex to be built by Madison and an arena to be built by Dane County. That was why Reynolds met with Dane County officials just days after he was elected in 1961. Bill Evjue immediately attacked Reynolds' initiative because he believed that "if the coliseum is built, the city will never get an auditorium," as he told his *Capital Times* readers.

On March 29, 1965, Dane County officials broke ground for a new coliseum designed by James T. Potter, a principal with the Madison firm of Law, Law, Potter and Nystrom. The seventy-seven-hundred-seat arena, located on the Dane County Fairgrounds just two miles from the Capitol Square, raced from concept to construction in just three years — although no referendum was ever held, no alternate sites were ever seriously discussed, costs soared from $3.5 to $5.5 million, thirty acres of wetland had to be filled, and it required the approval of a ninety-member board, then the largest in the United States. The contrast with the tortuous path of Monona Terrace could hardly be greater.

The building, which is three hundred feet in diameter and one hundred feet tall, was completed in March 1967. It was designated the Dane County Memorial Coliseum, thereby resolving attempts since 1919 to memorialize local veterans with a facility the community would use.

with his "regular appreciative clients." Festge turned to Nathan Feinsinger, a nationally known mediator and professor at the University of Wisconsin Law School. Feinsinger said he would be happy to help settle the dispute.[170]

The marathon session began at 7:30 A.M. on Thursday, June 10, 1965, when members of the city team headed by Festge met for a strategy session. At 9:30 they were joined by Wesley Peters and his attorneys. At first Feinsinger attended as an observer, but as negotiations developed he began to shuttle between the parties during their executive sessions. The negotiation session had a remarkably friendly tone and gave the parties the opportunity to get to know one another. Anticipating a settlement, the council convened at 7:30 that evening but then went into recess as the negotiations continued. From time to time Festge would return to the council chamber to give updates. Finally, just before midnight, the council convened for the third time. Feinsinger explained what had happened during the long day and told the council members that the parties had agreed on $150,000 as "full payment of any claim." When he finished, the council spontaneously applauded and moments later voted unanimously for the settlement.[171]

And so early Friday morning, after nearly fourteen hours of almost nonstop meetings, city officials, foundation representatives, and observers walked out of the council chamber into the warm summer air. Twelve years of almost continuous contention had ended. Remarkably, few felt rancor and some dared to think that something good could be salvaged for Madison.

Peters candidly acknowledged that the settlement was a "tremendous loss" to the foundation. Documents prepared for the arbitration process show that over

a twenty-seven-year period, 1938 to 1965, about forty-five foundation employees logged at least sixty-three thousand hours on Monona Terrace, the equivalent of thirty-one years in a single person's worklife. Foundation records also show that from 1938 to 1960, just before the city made its first payment, the foundation's income from Monona Terrace fees totaled $250, or about 13 cents an hour. Even after the city made its two large payments to the foundation, net hourly income to the foundation was no more than $2.77 an hour. This was at a time when principals billed their services at $8 to $10 per hour.[172]

Few architectural firms—indeed, few businesses of any kind—would be willing to expend so much effort over such a long period of time for so little. But as Peters said after the negotiations, "The foundation has been devoted to this project since Mr. Wright first proposed it, and we are still devoted to it." Peters went further and revealed his motivation for settling: "I do not feel the city should be deprived of this tremendous and beautiful project. If good will and good feeling can enable this project to become a reality, we will certainly be open and happy to talk with the city."[173]

No issue in Madison history polarized the city more completely than Monona Terrace from 1953 to 1965. During these dozen tumultuous years the battle between supporters and opponents created a great political vortex that swept up most citizens in its hot whirling winds.

Proponents were excited by the vision of creating a great civic center; its audacious size and unique shape; beauty; convenient concentration of so many earnestly desired cultural and civic facilities in a single complex; promise to enrich civic life with music, drama and art; potential to deepen the sense of community; and by its pedigree—designed by

Frank Lloyd Wright for his hometown on a unique waterfront site in one of the most beautiful cities in the world. Monona Terrace was one of those big ideas that transformed people into believers and compelled them to become activists on its behalf.

They were attempting something intrinsically difficult: to champion a complex, expensive, and unique new civic center concept by a controversial architect on a problem-laden site. They willingly embraced the challenge of creating something that had never been done before. That they led a grassroots crusade for twelve arduous years with limited political experience, that they did it from outside established power circles, and that they continually made generous financial contributions to the cause showed their extraordinary commitment, resilience, and grit.

By contrast, opponents were motivated by their personal and professional disgust with Wright, his consistent failure to realistically estimate project costs, and their indignation over blocking the lake view from Monona Avenue. Although their cadre of leaders was small, they were savvy, articulate, resourceful, and resolute. Time was their friend and they used it brilliantly to allow inflation to erode what could be built and to consume the remaining years of Wright's life.

No one can survey the roomful of records from this period without concluding that Monona Terrace suffered from inherent problems and champion-generated mistakes. Because the Monona Terrace site was a lake bottom, obtaining legal approval to build there consumed two years. Because they were trying to accommodate so many functions in a single megastructure and simultaneously harmonize conflicting demands to make the building lower, higher, and thinner, Wright and his staff were forced to practice something close to architectural magic. Supporters' early insistence that Monona Terrace

include city and county offices, even though plans were nearly complete for a joint building at another location, alienated almost all civic leaders. Proponents' promises to build all of Wright's huge 1955 project for just $4 million left a sour legacy of mistrust. Uncritical acceptance of the 1954 consultants' cost estimate of $4 million saddled proponents with an anemic budget from the beginning, and the absence of any built-in inflation factor further diminished what could be built. In fact, after 1961 the combination of a hostile mayor, his hand-picked Auditorium Committee, and fewer proponents on the common council gave backers little choice but to abandon the original budget and hope the project hadn't grown too expensive. Finally, the careless cost management of the project after 1960 gave opponents their most potent argument for dumping the Terrace in 1962.

Wright's role in exacerbating the controversy cannot be denied. The sharp contrast between the architect's prescription for Madison's needs and what city officials said they wanted created so many bad feelings that Monona Terrace was nearly dropped. Wright's frequent excoriations of Madisonians for their provincialism, lack of vision, and conservative fiscal policies forced his supporters to go on the defensive. His impatience, even contempt, for government committees created several precarious flash points that nearly killed the project. Still other qualities — his arrogance, cavalier attitude toward money, unconventional lifestyle, and outspoken antiwar views — provided big targets for his enemies. Finally, his flamboyant attire — his unusual hats, cape, and even a cane he used to amplify gestures and tap merchandise — struck many Madisonians as an irritating affectation.

At the same time, everything Wright did during these years revealed his fervent desire to build

Monona Terrace. To make the complex more client responsive, function inclusive, and increasingly sophisticated, Wright redesigned the building six times between 1955 and 1959. During this same period he prepared hundreds of plans and renderings, constructed an incredibly detailed model, attended meetings, participated in debates, wrote countless letters, and received no fees from the city. Clearly, for Wright Monona Terrace was an affair of the heart.

So successful were the critics' delaying tactics that Wright's original concept became obsolete. During the twelve-year civic auditorium crusade the automobile and airplane eliminated the need for a railroad depot. The automobile, the boat trailer, and city-built launch ramps eliminated the need for a marina. Suburbanization made a single centrally located community youth center unnecessary and undesirable. The construction of the Dane County Memorial Coliseum eliminated the need for an arena.

Paradoxically, the elimination of functions infused Monona Terrace with new potential because it allowed the project to become smaller, less costly, and more specialized.

But after fighting for Monona Terrace for twelve years, most of its champions were burned out. Would a new generation endowed with fresh hearts, abundant energy, and inspired commitment continue the crusade? And if a new generation rose to this challenge, could these proponents convince Madisonians, most of whom were tired of watching the Terrace marathon, to once again embrace Wright's civic vision? The question hovered.

William Wesley Peters, chief architect at Taliesin Associated Architects, used the words "great circular drum" to describe this civic auditorium that he designed for the shore of Madison's Lake Monona in 1968. The handsome building shown here in a rendering was sheathed in a warm yellow-brown brick, was more than 80 feet tall (the equivalent of an eight-story building), and about 190 feet in diameter. Peters proposed that the city build the civic auditorium before other buildings in the Monona Basin plan. A map showing its location appears in Figure 5.11.

The large arched windows were designed to give theatergoers a panoramic view of lake and sky from the Grand Foyer on the lake side of the theater. However, construction of the ring-shaped parking structure (see Fig. 5.9) would have seriously degraded this view.

Note that the building lacks a pedestrian walkway on the lake side of the building. Space requirements for a six-lane road forced architects to move the building lakeward, placing it against the dock line, a point beyond which nothing could be built. Thus, if the auditorium had been constructed, it would have prevented people from walking from one end of Law Park to the other.

**CHAPTER 5**

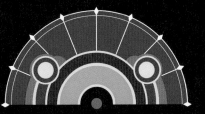

# SALVAGING THE DREAM

FIGURE 5.2

## OTTO FESTGE
*VIOLINIST, MAYOR, CONSENSUS BUILDER*

*Courtesy* Wisconsin State Journal

Otto Festge's musical ability was evident even as he was growing up on a family farm west of Madison. As a high school sophomore he played the violin in the Madison Symphony Orchestra and won a scholarship to the University of Wisconsin School of Music. There he continued his study of the violin and his performances with the Madison symphony. The young musician was appalled that Madison, the proud capital of Wisconsin, had to use the U.W. Stock Pavilion as its concert hall. When his father died in 1940, Festge was forced to quit the music school to help his mother run the family farm.

Festge entered politics in 1944 as a township assessor, and in 1952 — when he was only thirty-one — he was elected Dane County clerk, the top executive position at the time and a post to which he was reelected six times. Festge's integrity, administrative ability, success as a politician, and desire to build a great concert hall — preferably Wright's Monona Terrace — prompted many to urge him to run for mayor in 1965. His four years in that office were difficult. In addition to the challenge of building the auditorium, he was confronted by rioting University of Wisconsin students, a messy urban renewal project, a bus drivers' strike, and a long list of pressing municipal problems. After serving as mayor, Festge became home secretary for U.S. Representative Robert Kastenmeier (D-Wisc.), a post Festge held until his retirement in 1989.

George Forster did it in 1953, Ivan Nestingen in 1956, Henry Reynolds in 1961, and now in June 1965 it was incoming mayor Otto Festge's turn to appoint still another auditorium committee, the fourth of the postwar era. For twelve years the members of these three ill-fated committees had wrestled with the same exasperating questions: where should the auditorium be built, what functions should it contain, who should design it, and what should it cost? Despite the difficulties, each committee had done what it was charged to do, but then a deadly combination of zeal, adamant opposition, inflation, and irreconcilable differences between those for and against Wright produced a flurry of activity but no auditorium.[1]

Remarkably, nearly all Madison leaders and most citizens still believed that Madison needed an auditorium. And if any residents still harbored doubts, they were swept away by a concert on April 23, 1965. That day the famous contralto Marian Anderson appeared in Madison on her national farewell tour, and the biggest facility in town still was the University of Wisconsin Stock Pavilion, facetiously known to Madisonians as the cow barn (see Fig. 1.26). Anderson fans were chagrined that an artist of her stature would have to appear in a building where sawdust failed to conceal the odor of manure, patrons sat on concrete bleachers, radiators hissed during the pianissimo passages, and trains on the track next to the building distracted performers and concertgoers. Indeed, a freight train rumbled by right in the middle of Anderson's moving interpretation of Schubert's *Ave Maria,* but the poised performer kept right on singing.[2]

During the spring campaign Festge (see Fig. 5.2) told everyone that he favored the Monona Terrace project but quickly added that he would entertain other ideas. Indeed, Festge had no choice. As a perceptive observer of Madison, he knew that any effort to reintroduce any of the late 1950s or early 1960s versions of Monona Terrace would be political suicide. Festge concluded that the only way to get anything done was to appoint an auditorium committee that included both opponents and supporters of Monona Terrace—and that was exactly what he did. Opponents included George Forster, the former Madison mayor who had returned after a stint as city manager of a Wisconsin city, and Harold "Babe" Rohr, a council member and head of the painters' union, who wanted the auditorium in Olin Park in his ward. Supporters included Van Potter, a University of Wisconsin cancer researcher who had emerged as the leader of the Monona Terrace forces in the early sixties. Following the example set by his predecessor, Festge chaired the committee.[3]

Festge eagerly sought a viable compromise; he appealed to both sides to "work together so Madison can have the finest facilities possible at a price Madison can afford to pay" and to pick a downtown site that would take advantage of the city's great natural heritage — its lakes. He pleaded with the media to support this fresh start and to "forget past differences so the hopes and aspirations of the past may become a reality."[4]

To dramatize his open-mindedness, Festge changed the Auditorium Committee process. Instead of beginning with a site, a specific design, and the architect, the process used for Monona Terrace, Festge directed his committee to first determine what functions should be included in a civic auditorium, then to decide what sites would most logically serve these functions, and finally to determine how the project should be phased so that it would not exceed the budget. Only after these questions had been answered did Festge want the committee to recommend an architect.[5]

Starting with a fresh functional analysis was not just logical. It was essential. By 1965 three key functions included in the last Monona Terrace plan had found other homes. In March ground had been broken for the Dane County Memorial Coliseum, a seventy-seven-hundred-seat arena designed for sporting events, large concerts, horse shows, and much more. The coliseum, scheduled for completion in 1967, was just two miles from the Capitol Square via the new Monona Bay causeway, a much-needed new entrance to the downtown scheduled for completion in 1967. Leaders of the Madison Community Center had settled into newly remodeled downtown quarters and no longer wanted to be a part of the civic center complex. Finally, in 1963 the Madison Art Center had moved into an abandoned elementary school on the shore of Lake Mendota.[6]

These decisions reflected a trend toward specialized, separate facilities for cultural, community, and entertainment functions. Up to this point most Madison leaders assumed that nearly all such functions would be housed in a single megastructure, Monona Terrace. Although civic buildings serving multiple needs were common across the country, Madison was probably unique in planning to put so many functions in a single building. However, Madison's attempts to design such a facility in the 1950s and early 1960s revealed serious shortcomings in this concept. Multifunction megastructures placed almost impossible design demands upon architects to allocate functions within limited space and to make compromises that were not acceptable to some user groups. Such buildings also required user groups to be ready to move in at the same time, rarely possible, and required cities to make a single huge expenditure rather than several smaller outlays over several years.

Meanwhile, leaders of Madison's growing convention industry were demanding a separate facility to serve their needs. As the state capital, Madison had always been a good convention town, but by the mid-1960s downtown hotels could not accommodate groups larger than eight hundred; anything bigger required a special convention facility. The need was especially acute for the Credit Union National Association (CUNA), a Madison-based national trade organization representing eighteen million credit unionists whose conventions of two thousand delegates could not be conveniently accommodated in Madison. In fact, in 1966 CUNA threatened to leave town if better facilities "within a very short walking distance of business and hotel facilities on the Capitol Square" could not be provided. To accommodate CUNA and other large groups, the Chamber of Commerce said that Madison needed a convention center, then defined as a multipurpose facility that could serve banquets to at least two thousand, exhibit products, and be divided into smaller meeting rooms. These requirements help explain why almost everyone associated with the local convention industry saw a proposed two-thousand-seat civic auditorium as essential and why it had to be located downtown.[7]

Festge's Auditorium Committee went to work in July and by November 1965 had made several critical decisions. Members said Madison should prepare a master plan that would allow the city to build its cultural facilities in phases. During the first phase, they said, Madison should build two facilities under a single roof: an auditorium seating 2,000 to 2,500 and a smaller theater seating 900 to 1,100. The building should cost no more than $4 million, be located in the central city, convenient to transportation, and on a lake or at least have a lake view. Phase 2, the committee suggested, should include convention facilities, including a banquet hall seating twenty-five hundred, and exhibit space, as well as art and recital facilities. On the touchy questions of site and

FIGURE 5.3

**Jackson's Wright-Thwarting Fountain**

*Courtesy Joseph Jackson III*

Joe Jackson loved fountains and did everything he could to build "the world's finest fountain" in Law Park, something comparable to the huge Buckingham Fountain on the Chicago lakefront. Jackson envisioned an oval fountain one hundred feet long and equipped with powerful jets that would shoot streams of water high into the air and thrill passers-by. Jackson said he wanted this grand civic ornament to honor Wisconsin's veterans and urged that it be positioned directly below Olin Terrace. But there was a second reason Jackson was eager to build the fountain: it would kill Wright's Monona Terrace. So Jackson got his friends in the Wisconsin legislature to introduce bills in the 1961, 1963, and 1965 sessions that would give the state control over Law Park and make the fountain its centerpiece.

Jackson contacted leading architects, including Ludwig Mies van der Rohe, to design the fountain and finally found Italian-born sculptor Alfonso Iannelli, who prepared this sketch. Unbeknown to Jackson, Iannelli had been hired by Frank Lloyd Wright in 1913 and 1914 to create sculptured figures for Wright's sprawling Midway Gardens project (see Fig. 2.52), a popular Chicago entertainment complex. If Jackson had known that Iannelli had any association with Wright, he would never have hired him. Similarly, if Iannelli had known that Jackson's fountain project was designed to kill a Wright project, the sculptor would never have provided the design.

architect, the committee fashioned two clever compromises. It said the site should be Law Park, Olin Park, or Conklin Park (see Fig. 3.12) and that the architect should be a Wisconsin resident.[8]

Naturally, not everybody was happy about Festge's new initiatives. Since the repeal of the Metzner law in 1959, Joe Jackson had been eager to replace it with a new state law that would prevent Madison from building anything in Law Park. In May 1965, just a month before Festge appointed his new

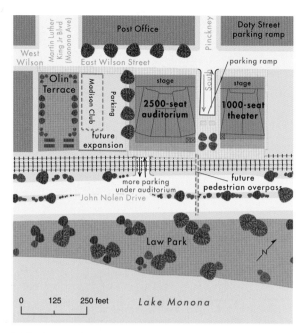

FIGURE 5.4

**1966 Wilson Street Auditorium Proposal**

*U.W.–Madison Cartographic Laboratory*

This proposal developed by the city planning department was a compromise capable of attracting people on both sides of the Monona Terrace controversy. It was located close to but not on the Terrace site, kept Law Park open for development, boasted good transit access, and offered facilities then demanded by user groups. However, it suffered from several serious design problems: it had almost no parking; access to the lake was limited to a scrawny pedestrian bridge; users of the community center (located below the thousand-seat theater) would have looked out at passing trains; and patrons of cultural events who used the lakeside balconies of the auditorium and theater would have received a close view of four railroad tracks and a four-lane highway. The plan never received widespread support and was replaced by the Monona Basin plan.

auditorium committee, Jackson got his friends in the Wisconsin legislature to introduce a bill that would make Law Park a state memorial for Wisconsin veterans, and he even hired a sculptor to design a fountain for it (see Fig. 5.3). Although Jackson was eighty-six and too ill to appear at the hearing, the testimony read by his lawyer made it clear that virulent anti-Wright venom still coursed through Jackson's mind and that he wanted to do everything

in his power to destroy the reputation of the deceased architect. In fact, to persuade senators to vote for the bill, Jackson sent them copies of his frequently distributed Wright dossier, which alleged that the architect was a communist. Although the Wisconsin senate rejected Jackson's bill in October 1965, the aging gentleman continued to testify against any Wright or Taliesin-designed structure in Madison. But by 1965 his vicious attacks on Wright's character had virtually destroyed Jackson's credibility. Wright's old foe died four years later at the age of ninety.[9]

## THE MONONA BASIN PLAN

What happened next caught most auditorium partisans off-guard. In November 1965 the Auditorium Committee directed Kenneth Clark, the director of the city planning department, to evaluate all three parks and make a recommendation. In January 1966 Clark rejected the parks and instead selected a prime city block on East Wilson Street that overlooked Law Park (see Fig. 5.4). It was occupied by the Madison Club, Diocese of Madison Chancery, and Bellevue Apartments, a large 1913 building (see Fig. 1.1). Neither the Madison Club nor the diocese had any interest in moving from their prestigious locations with spectacular views of the lake.

Both the owner and tenants of the Bellevue were initially cool to the idea (the tenants called the proposal extravagant), but the owner, Jacob R. Feldman, later agreed to sell the building to the city if the site was selected. Interestingly, Feldman said Monona Terrace was "the best bet" and even offered to donate $1,000 to the city if that project were built. (Feldman's preference for Monona Terrace is especially ironic because the Bellevue remained in his family; in the 1990s his grandson, Tom Link, strenuously opposed Monona Terrace [see Chapter

6].) Significantly, Clark's concept won two key converts, both of whom were eager to craft a viable compromise: Van Potter endorsed the site because "the Monona Terrace site was gone forever" (by which he meant out of the question), and Festge backed it because it was "an acceptable substitute." Festge even tried to sweeten the pot for entrenched Wrightians by adding to the Wilson Street site about half of Law Park, the original site for Monona Terrace.[10]

However, few others were satisfied with Clark's attempt to craft a quick compromise. Monona Terrace backers were unwilling to exchange the grandeur of Wright's original design and site for Clark's anemic emulation. And in the paranoid atmosphere that prevailed, Monona Terrace opponents feared that Clark's plan was a sneaky way to get Wright's disciples to design another Monona Terrace (see Fig. 5.5). After two marathon sessions in February and another in mid-March exasperated members of the Auditorium Committee responded by rejecting all the sites then under consideration, an action that forced even the hottest heads on the committee to recognize that some kind of compromise was essential. But what?[11]

At its next meeting on April 7 the committee stunned nearly everyone with two decisions. First, it abandoned its own criterion that the auditorium and civic center be located downtown and selected Olin Park as the site. Second, it voted to hire William Wesley Peters as the architect. Anti-Terrace committee members got a site untainted by Wrightian plans, and proponents got Wright's heir apparent as architect.[12]

Although Potter was pleased that the committee had approved his motion to recommend Peters as the architect, he was deeply troubled by problems inherent in the compromise. Exactly where in Olin Park would the cultural complex go, and how

FIGURE 5.5

**A Trio of Wright Opponents**

*SHSW. WHi (M95)219/1966, photo by David Sandell*

When the Auditorium Committee held a public hearing in February 1966 about where to locate the auditorium, the council chamber was jammed with speakers and interested parties. In the audience were three men who had done more than anyone to kill Monona Terrace. In the foreground is Carroll Metzner, then forty-seven, who began opposing the project in 1953 and secured passage of the famous 1957 Metzner bill. Next to him is Marshall Browne, seventy-three, whose opposition escalated in the early 1960s when he was an officer of the Citizens for a Realistic Auditorium Association and publisher of the anti-Terrace *East Side News*, a weekly. At the right is Joe Jackson, then eighty-seven, who had opposed Wright's project since 1938 and who used every tactic he could imagine to achieve his goal.

would its specifications be determined? Where, when, and at what cost would the pressing needs of Madison's stifled convention industry be satisfied? How would the causeway, then under construction, be integrated in the overall design? Finally, how could buildings constructed along this shoreline in

the future be properly coordinated? The more he thought about it, the more Potter realized the compromise was purely political, a mere balancing of power within the committee. What was best for the city, arts community, and convention industry was never considered. Potter realized that he had been an unwitting lieutenant in a Pyrrhic victory.[13]

Just two days after the committee made its decision Potter exchanged his familiar white-coated public persona as a cancer lab director for the bolder image of civic entrepreneur. On Saturday morning, April 9, 1966, Potter (see Fig. 5.6) held a press conference in a large lecture hall at his campus laboratory. Only a few reporters were present and that was by design. Because he saw his initiative as a "preemptive strike," Potter had not informed the mayor or even any other members of the Auditorium Committee what he planned to do.[14]

Reading a prepared statement at the lectern, Potter outlined an audacious proposal. "We can go ahead and build an auditorium and theater at Olin Park," he began. "But that leaves the clutter and ugliness of the Lake Monona shoreline unsolved. We can go farther. We have a unique opportunity in Madison ... to design a comprehensive master plan laid out by one architect which would include harmonious structures on both sides of the lake." He called this graceful arc of land the "Lake Monona basin" and urged that William Wesley Peters be selected as the architect. Then Potter walked to the blackboard behind the lectern, picked up a piece of chalk, and began to sketch the idea. Potter insisted that his plan was not an attempt to get Monona Terrace back into the civic center tent, but he acknowledged that he still thought Law Park would be the best site.[15]

The press conference was anything but a spur-of-the-moment idea. Just two weeks earlier Potter

FIGURE 5.6

## VAN POTTER
### *MONONA BASIN CONCEIVER AND ADVOCATE*

*Courtesy Van Potter*

On October 10, 1960, the auditorium of Madison's Central High School was packed with nine hundred people, most of whom were opposed to Wright's Monona Terrace. Despite this hostile environment, Van Potter stood up and gave a passionate pro–Monona Terrace speech. After the meeting Mary Lescohier invited Potter to join Citizens for Monona Terrace and he accepted. Potter was just the person the besieged group needed. By 1962 he was the foremost spokesperson for Citizens for Monona Terrace and in 1966 conceived the Monona Basin concept, a bold initiative that enjoyed rapid acceptance and placed Potter at the center of the maelstrom for many years.

Potter grew up on a South Dakota farm and received his undergraduate degree from South Dakota State. In 1938 he received a doctorate in biochemistry from the University of Wisconsin and did a postdoctoral stint in Sweden. When he returned to Madison, Potter was hired at the new McArdle Laboratory for Cancer Research by his former major professor, Conrad Elvehjem, later a president of the university. Potter earned national and international acclaim for his work on the biochemical reactions of cancer cells. The indefatigable man retired in 1982 to devote more time to the development of *bioethics*, a term he coined. In *Bioethics* (1971) and its successor, *Global Bioethics* (1988), Potter linked science and philosophy to achieve sustainable development of the earth.

FIGURE 5.7

# WILLIAM WESLEY PETERS
*MONONA BASIN PLANNER*

*Courtesy FLW FDN. 6501.003*

William Wesley Peters was just twenty and an engineering student at the Massachusetts Institute of Technology when he first met Frank Lloyd Wright in June 1932. That spring Peters had read Wright's *Autobiography* and a few months later saw a flyer announcing Wright's new school of architecture. The tall young man was intrigued by the prospect of studying under Wright, so he accompanied his family on a drive from Evansville, Indiana, to Madison to drop his sister off at the University of Wisconsin. Peters took a bus to Spring Green and walked the remaining four miles to Taliesin. Wright enchanted Peters with his grand plans for the Taliesin Fellowship and persuaded Peters to become an apprentice.

Neither man realized what a large role each would play in the other's life. Peters fell in love with Wright's stepdaughter, Svetlana, and married her in 1935. (Svetlana and one of their two children were killed in a tragic automobile accident in 1946.) Peters served as structural engineer for dozens of important Wright buildings, including the Johnson Wax Administration Building and the Guggenheim Museum and was the architect of record for the Annunciation Greek Orthodox Church near Milwaukee. He worked closely with Wright on the Monona Terrace project beginning in 1938 and often represented Wright at meetings with Madison officials. After Wright died in 1959, Peters became chief architect and vice president of Taliesin Associated Architects and was responsible for finishing many Wright buildings then in the late planning stages or under construction and designed 120 others. In 1970 Peters made international headlines when he married Svetlana Alliluyeva, Stallin's daughter, but the marriage did not work out. The two separated in 1972.

A longtime Wright associate recalled Peters' "marvelous imagination" and said that next to Wright, Peters was the "most skilled" conceiver of grand schemes, a trait evident in Peters' Monona Basin plan. Almost all who worked with Wes, as he was widely known, were impressed by his patience, kindness, enthusiasm, selflessness, devotion to projects, and delightful sense of humor. Peters died in July 1991 following a massive stroke.

had given a keynote address to a scientific meeting in Phoenix and used the opportunity to meet with Peters (see Fig. 5.7), then in residence at Taliesin West in nearby Scottsdale. The two men met at the cocktail lounge of the Biltmore Hotel, where Potter explained the basin concept to Peters for the first time. The architect could hardly contain his enthusiasm. "That's what we've got to do," Peters exclaimed and immediately began to visualize "the lights and the fountains" along the causeway and other components. It was at that moment Potter resolved to hold his press conference.[16]

On April 13 the Auditorium Committee formally endorsed Potter's basin concept but with the understanding that all theaters should be at Olin Park and all convention and visual art facilities should be downtown. On April 14, just seven days after Potter's press conference, the Madison Common Council directed city officials to negotiate a contract with Peters. A few days later Mayor Festge spoke for many when he said, "I look upon this proposal as the greatest opportunity for artistic achievement and creative development that has ever been offered to Madison."[17]

Seldom in Madison history had such a big new idea been accepted so quickly. Seldom had a single citizen's initiative galvanized leaders so thoroughly. On the other hand, Potter's concept was a brilliant, splendidly timed political compromise that gave both factions obvious ways to win something important and a superior process by which to achieve it.

More important, it forced every reasonable person to see the compelling advantage of giving a single architect the opportunity to design nearly three miles of prime urban waterfront — something rare in the history of postindustrial cities. With the exception of Doty's original plat, no Madison planner had been given such a panoramic canvas on which to

work. Even John Nolen's 1909 plan was limited to about three thousand feet of prime Lake Monona frontage. Potter's idea prodded Madisonians to remember that the city was blessed with extraordinary potential, which, if properly directed, could culminate in an exemplary new civic form. Ironically, Potter's plan even offered a remedy for Wright's lifelong complaint: that Madison had turned its back on the lakes.[18]

Although people quickly grasped the potential of Potter's vision, it encountered immediate resistance, some predictable, some not. Marshall Browne, a resolute opponent of Monona Terrace, said the plan was a thinly veiled attempt of "Wright worshippers" to "lead this city down some dreary path of waste and controversy." He threatened to reactivate the Citizens for a Realistic Auditorium Association.

Several Madison leaders moved quickly to pressure Peters into putting the large auditorium in Olin Park, but he refused. Peters explained that he had spent twenty-five years of his life helping to design plans for Monona Terrace downtown and that he was completely sold on the merits of locating both the large auditorium and convention facilities there, where the synergy between the two was the greatest. Suddenly, this glorious new basin idea seemed headed for a dusty shelf and the Auditorium Committee for more dithering.[19]

Peters was clearly intrigued by the prospect of doing a comprehensive design for that great arc of lakeshore, but he refused to participate if he could not determine where key facilities should go. After haggling until 2 A.M. on June 24, 1966, the common council agreed to hire Peters to do a master plan for the basin but with the unusual understanding that the auditorium and theater would go at Olin Park unless Peters could persuade the city to the contrary. A council negotiating committee persuaded Peters to go along with the deal. Peters kept his professional integrity, and the council got its architect.[20]

When the thirty-four-page contract was approved by the council in mid-October, Festge applauded the "historic" action, and Peters promised to "give Madison something that will bring it to its rightful place in this country." The contract required Peters to prepare a master plan, locating an art center and gallery, theater, recital hall, large auditorium, and convention and banquet facilities along the three miles from the east end of Law Park to the south end of Olin Park. It even allowed the architect to include more lake frontage if he thought this was desirable. The contract directed Peters to systematically ascertain the needs of user groups and then to prepare a plan in three stages: a schematic master plan, a developed master plan, and construction drawings for buildings the city approved. For this work the Frank Lloyd Wright Foundation was to receive $102,000 and the exclusive right to design anything developed in the basin area for ten years. Peters began work immediately.[21]

Mary Lescohier, the indefatigable field general of Terrace backers, was initially unhappy about abandoning Monona Terrace but soon embraced the basin plan and worked to make it a reality. She met with Festge, attended all relevant meetings, lobbied council members, provided astute and sometimes stern counsel to Peters, and even drafted parts of the basin report.[22]

## METZNER SUES

Twenty-three days after the mayor signed the contract with Peters, Carroll Metzner sued in circuit court. Metzner, the longtime opponent of Monona Terrace, represented ninety property owners who believed that the new contract with Peters was illegal and a "waste of taxpayers' money." Veterans of the auditorium wars rolled their eyes in exasperation at the clear and familiar pattern. Metzner said his clients were "from all walks of life and from all parts of the city," but that was not the whole truth. Most were members of the Republican Party of Dane County, an organization that Metzner then chaired.[23]

According to the suit, the contract was invalid because money from the city's auditorium account could not be spent for a master plan; Taliesin Associated Architects was not licensed to practice in Wisconsin; the 1962 referendum required all planning for the Terrace to stop; the architectural fees were outrageous; the contract contained indefinite provisions; the process embodied in the contract usurped the powers of the city planning commission; one council could not bind another (as required by the ten-year term of the contract); and the contract gave undue "partiality" to William Wesley Peters and the Frank Lloyd Wright Foundation. Whether Metzner thought he could prove that the city had grossly abused its discretion—the legal standard in this case—is not known. At the very least he hoped to prevent a "Peters design anywhere in the city" and to stall for "at least two years." By that time, Metzner reasoned, Madison would have "a new mayor and maybe some new aldermen."[24]

In the past the city had brought all actions involving Monona Terrace to a halt until a suit was settled. This time the city decided to take the risk and proceed. So while the city and Metzner prepared for court, Peters and his associates interviewed user groups.[25]

In early September 1967, after a fireworks-filled nine-day trial in July and August, Dane County Circuit Court Judge Edwin Wilkie rejected all of Metzner's allegations. Wilkie determined that city officials "acted in good faith in what they felt was the best interests of the City of Madison and all of its people and its taxpayers and that they have been diligent ... to represent the interests of the citizens." Festge said he was "extremely delighted" and urged the city to bring "the dream of an auditorium to Madison." Would Metzner appeal? The shrewd attorney refused to say.[26]

## A FOREST OF EASELS

On the morning of Wednesday, December 6, 1967, Peters and his colleagues stood at the front of the common council chamber amid a forest of easels bearing renderings and maps for the Monona Basin plan. For one year Taliesin Associated Architects had been painstakingly gathering data from user groups and making decisions about where cultural, community, and business functions should be located along the three-mile shore. Now Peters was ready to share his long-awaited recommendations with an overflow crowd of city officials and interested residents.[27]

Using a huge aerial rendering (see Fig. 5.8), the architect systematically covered the guiding design principles, the rationale for siting each major building, how the project should be staged, and what it would cost. Of course, the question on everyone's mind was where the large auditorium would go.

Peters said the large civic auditorium and much-needed convention facilities should be built in Law Park (see Fig. 5.9) and the art center and two smaller theaters in Olin Park (see Fig. 5.10). He gave three reasons, the first of which involved money. If the auditorium were placed in Olin Park, its income would be limited to touring companies and large local productions, which would pay for only a fraction of its total operating costs. But if the auditorium were placed in Law Park, both cultural and convention groups would use it and the city

FIGURE 5.8

## 1967 Monona Basin Plan, Aerial View

© 1999 Taliesin™ Architects, Ltd.

"I don't know anywhere in the world which can equal the potential of Madison's lake frontage," said William Wesley Peters, who presented the plan. The former Wright protégé, now chief architect for Taliesin Associated Architects, was referring to the nearly three miles of lakeshore shown here in this bird's-eye drawing from the 1967 Monona Basin plan. An opportunity to develop this much prime waterfront property in a city in the late twentieth century was extremely rare.

Two principles guided Peters' design. First, the entire basin was treated as a single site, which allowed the architect to locate buildings in the best settings possible and to integrate all components into a harmonious whole. One example of this was the esplanade that ran the entire length of the site and allowed pedestrians to experience the water's edge, virgin woods, and spectacular skyline views.

Second, at Turville Point, the large green triangular area on the lefthand page, and Olin Park, the area between Turville and the causeway, Peters said he tried to "maintain the feeling of open country in the midst of the city." That was why he placed few buildings at Turville Point and why he concentrated facilities in Olin Park. From left to right, key components of the Monona Basin plan are

### TURVILLE POINT AND OLIN PARK

The city bought the sixty-seven-acre Turville Point just three months after it released the Monona Basin plan, but its purchase had been in the works for many months. In fact, the prospect of its purchase added great momentum to the basin concept. The circular pond in Olin Park was intended as a boat-launching facility. Once boats are in the water, they are driven through a

canal into the lake. Details of the major buildings that Peters proposed for Olin Park are shown in Figure 5.10. The large circular building to the left of Turville Point is the Dane County Memorial Coliseum.

### THE CAUSEWAY

Peters proposed increasing the amount of parkland on the lake side of the causeway (upper center). He also proposed to add excitement, drama, and beauty to this new land with a series of five fountain jets, each of which would send a plume of water 120 feet in the air and be floodlit at night from under water (see Fig. A.2).

Probably no road in Madison's history was cloaked in more conspiracy theories than the Monona Bay causeway. Although the concept had been

176

SALVAGING THE DREAM

recommended by transportation consultant Harland Bartholomew in 1922, Madison leaders did not act on it until the mid-1950s when the interstate highway system was being planned and downtown streets were clogged with cars. Leaders liked the causeway because it would be a shortcut to the downtown and would make it easier for people to enter the city from the new interstate just east of the city. In 1955 Ivan Nestingen, then a member of the Wisconsin Assembly, introduced a bill that would authorize the filling of Lake Monona for the causeway. However, Bill Evjue immediately attacked the road as a plot by Terrace opponents to make Olin Park more accessible and thus more attractive as an auditorium site. Consequently, during his five years as mayor (1956–1961) Nestingen did nothing to encourage the causeway. Not until Henry Reynolds, a devout Terrace opponent, was elected

mayor in 1961 did the road receive the local political support it required. The controversial causeway was finally opened to traffic in November 1967.

## THE CENTRAL ELEMENT

The centerpiece of the Monona Basin plan was a complex of three buildings — a civic auditorium, convention center, and a state theater — as well as a large semicircular lakeside parking structure. Drawings showing this area in greater detail appear in Figure 5.9.

## THE COMMUNITY CENTER AND MARINA

The small two-story circular building nearly surrounded by water at the east end of Law Park is the community building, a twenty-nine-thousand-square-foot facility

featuring a spiral pedestrian ramp leading to an observation platform on the roof. To the right of the community building is a marina for excursion, rental, and privately owned boats.

Note how Peters continued Wright's use of the circle as a central design element. The community center, civic auditorium, state theater, boat-launching pond in Olin Park, "floating" stage of the amphitheater in Olin Park, and the road in the center of Turville Point are all circular. Note too how the central complex at the end of Monona Avenue, the fountain indentations along the causeway, and path to the lake observation platform at the tip of Turville Point are all semicircular.

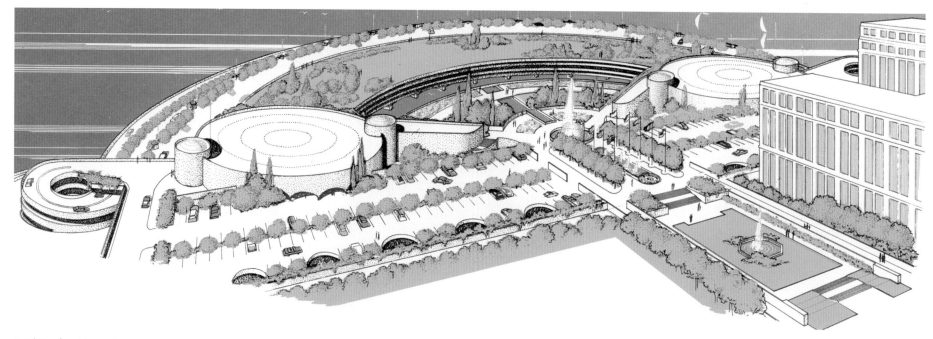

Aerial View from Monona Avenue

© 1999 Taliesin™ Architects, Ltd.

FIGURE 5.9

## Monona Basin Plan, Law Park Components

### AERIAL VIEW FROM MONONA AVENUE

This aerial view reveals several key elements of Peters' design. The large cylinder on the left is the top of the 2,350-seat civic auditorium; the corresponding element on the right is the 1,000-seat "state theater." The large semicircular element extending out into the lake is a three-tier 1,500-car parking structure. The facility echoed Wright's 1955 plan, except that Peters landscaped more of the top surface, a decided improvement. Peters went to great lengths to make sure that his plan did not block the lake view from Monona Avenue, a major criticism of Wright's 1956–1959 designs. This was why Peters located the two theaters on each side of the vista corridor. Note how the fountains and ponds, aligned along the central entrance, extend to the lakeside edge of the building. From that point, about forty feet above Lake Monona, Peters planned a dramatic waterfall, an attempt to recapture one of the most dramatic features of Wright's 1938 and 1941 plans.

### RENDERING FROM LAKE MONONA

This rendering shows the central megastructure as it would have appeared from Lake Monona without the parking structure. Note how Peters' decision to place the lower convention center between the two taller theaters enhanced the lake view from Monona Avenue. Note too how Peters retained many Wrightian touches, including the helixes on each end, the large arched windows in the center, and the cylinders-within-cylinders design.

### CROSS-SECTION

This 1967 cross-section along the Monona Avenue axis shows how substantially Peters changed Wright's design. Instead of using the space for a large auditorium — as Wright did for all three of his basic designs — Peters used it for convention facilities, including an exhibition-banquet room and smaller meeting rooms. This decision produced a much lower building that preserved the view. Note how Peters saved a rectangular block of space above the railroad tracks for an eventual "expressway corridor." The tall element above the car tunnel and exhibit hall is the profile of the civic auditorium.

### PLAN

This plan shows how Peters proposed to accommodate a civic auditorium, convention center, state theater, and parking facility in a megastructure. Linking the three facilities was a truly grand concourse (at bottom). Nearly 80 feet wide and 1,000 feet long, it was supplemented in the center by a semicircular plaza whose diameter was nearly 200 feet.

Probably the most shadowy component of the basin plan was the 1,000-seat state theater, the brainchild of Robert Gard, the director of a Spring Green theater group known as the Wisconsin Idea Theater. Gard believed that every state should have an official theater company and persuaded Wisconsin governor Warren Knowles to back the concept.

Like Wright's 1938 to 1955 plans, Peters' Monona Basin plan extended far beyond the dock line, requiring state legislation to move it farther out into the lake. The plan also shows a serious design fault of the central element: Peters' decision to surround the auditorium, convention center, and state theater with a tiered parking facility reminiscent of Wright's 1955 Monona Terrace plan. For example, people standing in the lakeside foyer of the civic auditorium or on the floor of the exhibition hall would have viewed the lake from *underneath* the parking structure, the bottom of which was about twenty feet above the lake. Depending on the viewer's location in these two rooms, the parking structure would have extended lakeward two hundred to five hundred feet like the brim of a giant hat. The diamond-shaped parking structure foundations (in fact much larger and more elongated than shown in the plan) would have further reduced lake views to narrow slices.

### CONVENTION/BANQUET FACILITIES

When Peters and his colleagues analyzed questionnaires from potential users of the complex, they learned that the lack of a relatively large room for exhibits and banquets was stifling Madison's convention business. Shown here is a Taliesin artist's conception of how the ring-shaped room would look when set for a large banquet. Located in the center of the complex, the room measured twenty thousand square feet and could seat up to two thousand. Conspicuously missing from this drawing is the three-tier parking ramp that Peters planned for the lake side of the complex.

Rendering from Lake Monona

© 1999 Taliesin™ Architects, Ltd.

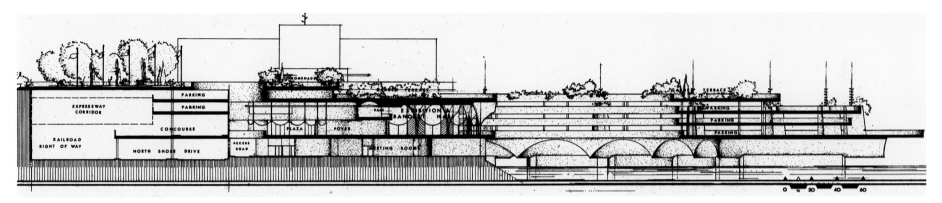

Cross-Section

© 1999 Taliesin™ Architects, Ltd.

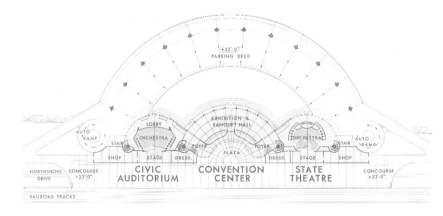

Plan

© 1999 Taliesin™ Architects, Ltd.

Convention/Banquet Facilities

© 1999 Taliesin™ Architects, Ltd.

FIGURE 5.10

**Monona Basin Plan,
Olin Park Components**

Peters recommended that all local theater and art facilities be located in Olin Park because almost all patrons would arrive by car (whereas conventioneers would be staying at downtown hotels and would have to walk to the convention facility), and both cultural facilities would be enhanced by a natural setting. Shown here is the main floor plan for the cultural complex, composed of a 1,000-seat theater (right), the 67,000-square-foot art center (middle), and the 300-seat recital hall (left). This is the one component of the Monona Basin plan in which Peters introduced angular forms. The rendering below shows a crowd using the natural hillside amphitheater and provides a good view of the south side of the cultural building. This site also offered superb views of the Madison skyline.

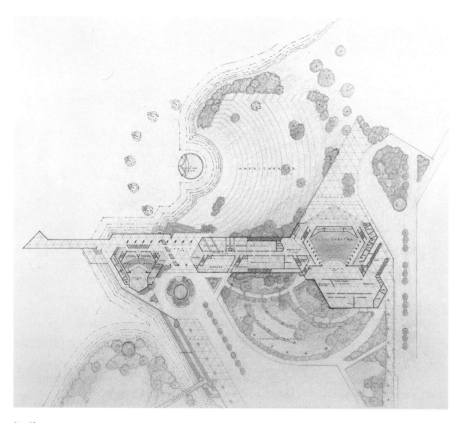

Site Plan

© 1999 Taliesin™ Architects, Ltd.

Outdoor Amphitheater and Floating Stage

© 1999 Taliesin™ Architects, Ltd.

would take in much more money. This was because almost all conventioneers stayed in downtown hotels and strongly preferred that their meeting rooms be within easy walking distance. Second, to put the auditorium and cultural facilities in Olin Park would consume half its acreage, an unacceptable public policy. Third, if Madison was really serious about downtown revitalization, it must concentrate facilities there. Peters argued that the synergy between a convention center and the large auditorium would do more to infuse new economic life in the central business district than any other plan.[28]

With great pride the senior Taliesin architect emphasized that the fundamental design conceived by Frank Lloyd Wright had been "preserved and incorporated in the Monona Basin Plan." Peters estimated that if the entire project were built in 1967, it would cost nearly $25 million, but he recommended that it be approached in phases. For five hours city officials queried Peters about every aspect of the plan, whereupon Mayor Festge thanked Peters and his staff and adjourned the meeting. Peters had given a masterful performance.[29]

Festge was effusive. He said the Monona Basin plan combined all the thinking of "everyone from John Nolen to Frank Lloyd Wright" and put "William Wesley Peters on the same plane with the great Frank Lloyd Wright." He even said that Peters' plan was better than Wright's because it "takes the small area that was once delegated to ... Monona Terrace and spreads it around Lake Monona." Even the normally disapproving *Wisconsin State Journal* editorial writers said the plan was "beautifully done ... and shows flashes of architectural genius." *Architectural Forum* and *Progressive Architecture* were lavish in their praises.[30]

Leaders of the anti-Wright movement were predictably negative. Metzner harrumphed that

Peters had done nothing more than dust off the old Monona Terrace plans, and Babe Rohr said he was amazed that anyone would want to build anything at "that ugly Law Park site." Three former mayors — George Forster, Henry Reynolds, and Harold Hanson — held a press conference to fire a barrage of criticism at the concept. They said the Peters plan would block the lake view from Monona Avenue, create an "intolerable traffic and parking mess in downtown Madison," use public funds to build a "Taj Mahal complex for an art club," and benefit other "small special interest groups." The former mayors urged that the new county coliseum be used for trade shows and conventions, that the city's drama groups use high school auditoriums, and that the Madison Art Association be content with its abandoned elementary school.[31]

William Dawson, director of the University of Wisconsin Memorial Union Theater, argued that Madison was building yesterday's auditorium for tomorrow. Dawson called attention to the steeply rising costs of taking big city orchestras, opera companies, and dramatic groups on tour. In a few years, Dawson predicted, this form of entertainment will be no longer be available. Why, he wondered, would the city build an expensive facility to specifically accommodate these soon-to-be-extinct touring companies?[32]

Other criticisms fell into three categories: siting, phasing, and design. The most substantial criticism of the siting was the recommendation to put the civic auditorium in Law Park instead of Olin Park. The strongest criticism about phasing was the recommendation to build the downtown auditorium before the cultural complex in Olin Park. The most frequent criticism of Peters' design was that people in the convention center would have to look "into the rear of a three-deck parking ramp" (see Fig. 5.9).[33]

Nonetheless, the Monona Basin plan was widely praised and received remarkably rapid approvals from its would-be tenants, the Chamber of Commerce, and the Wisconsin Chapter of the American Institute of Architects. But to basin backers the best news of all was Carroll Metzner's decision in January 1968 not to appeal his suit. Metzner said he was too busy, but he probably recognized that his chances of prevailing at the state supreme court were remote.[34]

These developments accelerated the city's approval process. On February 22, 1968, just ten weeks after Peters' initial presentation, the common council okayed the schematic master plan, including the controversial location of the civic auditorium in Law Park, and in July directed Peters to do schematic drawings for the first building in the plan, the 2,350-seat civic auditorium.[35]

DRUM ON LAKE MONONA

Peters had schematic drawings for the civic auditorium — he called it "a great circular drum" (see Figs. 5.1, and 5.11) — to the city for review by mid-July 1968. The tall architect, then fifty-six, was obviously proud of his state-of-the-art facility and asserted that the auditorium and 750-car parking ramp could be built for $5.3 million. However, it was clear that Peters was deeply concerned about the final cost; he emphasized that $5.3 million would pay for only a "usable but unfinished" building and that some equipment would have to be left out. In September the common council approved more detailed drawings with remarkably little criticism and directed Peters to prepare bid documents.[36]

Meanwhile, the unrelenting demands of office were exacting a cruel toll on Festge. He was working seven days a week, spending no time with his family, and taking fire for raising property taxes. In truth,

he was emotionally and physically spent, and he knew it. On January 1, 1969, he told his family that he would not seek a third term and a short time later made a public announcement. Festge's enemies understood well that if his Monona Basin were going to bear fruit, it had to be before the mayoral elections in April, just three months away. Consequently, when Peters delivered working drawings to the city in January 1969, opponents swarmed over the plans, looking for problems that would prevent Festge from breaking ground before he left office.[37]

Like Wright's Monona Terrace, Peters' Monona Basin auditorium was caught in an exasperating design vise. Traffic engineers' demand for a six-lane highway and an access road through Law Park forced Peters to move the auditorium farther out into the lake and to go beyond the dock line by eight feet. The highway requirement also forced the city to eliminate a nearly essential access road on the city side and a pedestrian walkway on the lake side. This meant the city would have to get the state to extend the dock line.[38]

Peters was caught in a painful budgetary squeeze. Inflation had eroded the buying power of the original appropriations totaling $5.5 million, and several legal and consulting fees had been paid from the account, leaving about $5.2 million. This forced Peters to make cuts, all of which provoked criticism. For example, he reduced the number of parking spaces from 775 to 361, eliminated elevators in the building (which was eighty feet high), deleted landscaping, proposed a temporary pedestrian bridge to the Capitol Square, left many areas unfinished, and made optional a long list of amenities such as the orchestra elevator.[39]

Festge knew that the city had to somehow pump more money into the drum on Lake Monona but

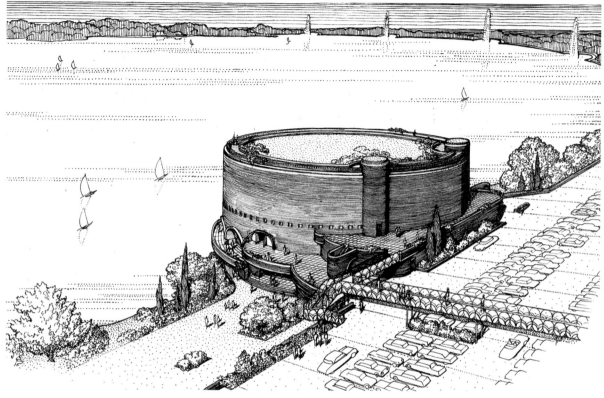

Perspective from the City

© 1999 Taliesin™ Architects, Ltd.

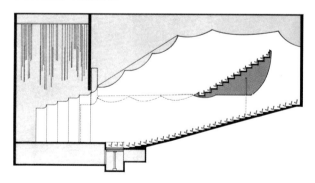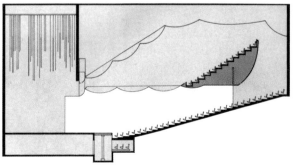

Cross-Sections Showing Flexible Acoustical Ceiling

© 1999 Taliesin™ Architects, Ltd.

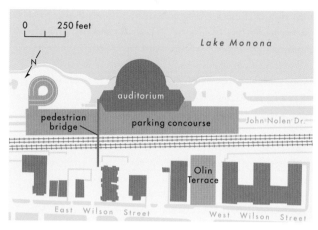

Locational Map

*U.W.–Madison Cartographic Laboratory*

FIGURE 5.11

## Monona Basin Plan, Auditorium Proposal

This distinctive circular auditorium, the first of many buildings scheduled for construction in the sprawling Monona Basin plan, was to be located on the lakeshore just east of Olin Terrace. Until the rest of the central complex was built, Peters proposed a temporary pedestrian bridge, shown in the perspective and on the map. The plan also provided for a parking ramp on the city side of the auditorium. The aerial view shows the circumferential rooftop promenade that Peters proposed for the building, which was to be eighty feet high.

Inside the "great circular drum" was a state-of-the-art theater that would accommodate conventions, touring Broadway plays, musicals, opera, lectures, movies, ballet, concerts, and dramatic productions of all kinds — all, Peters insisted, with perfect acoustics. As the cross-sections show, this remarkable feat was made possible by a sophisticated flexible ceiling that could be raised and lowered. Using these devices, auditorium managers could vary the capacity of the theater from 1,133 to 2,251 people and provide a facility that could accommodate everything from string quartets to grand opera. Peters contended that no other theater in the world had such sophistication.

that the politics of doing this ranged from bad to unthinkable. He chose the best of the bad: trying to persuade the common council to "repay" the interest the city had earned on its invested auditorium funds. When the bonds were issued in 1954, the city had to pay an interest rate of 1.7 percent but quickly found that it could invest the $4 million principal at a significantly higher rate. A city official calculated that if all this "profit" had been put back into the auditorium account and reinvested until 1969, the city auditorium account would have another $1.2 million. Perversely, since 1954 these profits had been deposited in the city's general fund rather than kept in the auditorium fund and compounded. To compensate for this unfortunate policy Festge proposed that the city borrow $560,000 and put it back into the auditorium fund, but the common council refused.[40]

The bidding process for the Monona Basin auditorium was a disaster. The council approved final plans on February 11, 1969, and directed that bids be opened on March 20, too little time for a complex project. A last-minute change required Taliesin to prepare a set of supplemental drawings and forced the city to delay the bid opening until April 1, the same day as local elections. Only two general contractors and one electrician bid the job, hardly a competitive process. Most contractors were persuaded that the building would cost more than the $5.2 million the city still had in the auditorium account and that the city would not appropriate a penny more. Finally, Babe Rohr, Henry Reynolds, and Ray Burt, the city building inspector, apparently used telephone calls, letters, and conversations to discourage contractors from bidding.[41]

For proponents of Peters' golden brick auditorium, April 1, 1969, brought three blasts of bad news. The low bid came in at $6.2 million, about $1 million more than the auditorium account held; William D. Dyke, an articulate conservative, was elected mayor; and a much more conservative group rode Dyke's coattails on to the city council.

During the two weeks remaining in his term, Festge could do little but express frustration. "If we don't build this auditorium soon, we may be the only city in the world which has paid for an auditorium, but never built it," he complained.[42]

On April 14, during the last meeting of the outgoing council, the common council directed Peters to rebid the project. Someone turned to the architect, who was sitting in the back of the room, and asked him if he would be willing to do this. "No," he bellowed. Peters well understood that taking anything more out of the building would leave it a nonfunctional shell. What the project needed was more money.[43]

For auditorium backers the only ray of hope was the Monona Basin Foundation, an organization formed in January 1969 to raise $750,000 from the private sector. Its board glittered with local luminaries and was supplemented by nationally prominent men and women, including Stewart Udall, the former secretary of the interior; the Philip Wrigleys of Chicago; and Sam Johnson, owner of S. C. Johnson Wax. In less than three weeks after the election the foundation raised $110,000 from Madison donors, but then the drive sputtered. Peters' refusal to redraw and rebid the project, Dyke's opposition, the new council's unwillingness to appropriate more money, and the realization that a drive to raise $640,000 was unrealistic all meant just one thing: Peters' great circular drum on Lake Monona's shore was dead. As Festge put it later, "We tried to satisfy too many people's interests ... [and] it drove up the cost."[44]

## METRO SQUARE

Unlike his four immediate predecessors, Dyke refused to participate in an almost hallowed post-election ritual: appointing an auditorium committee. Part of the problem was that the auditorium was not a Dyke priority. The new mayor told everybody that he had seen "too many mayors lose too much blood over this issue," Madison needed a new dump just as much as a new auditorium, and he would not spend a penny more than $5.5 million for an auditorium.[45]

Another reason for Dyke's reluctance was that he had his hands full trying to handle student unrest at the University of Wisconsin. Just one month after he took office, Dyke refused to grant a permit for what had become an annual counterculture celebration of beer, marijuana, and blaring stereos in a student ghetto known as the "People's Republic of Miffland." So the students stood in the middle of Miffin Street—the thoroughfare near the center of the enclave that gave the area its name — and taunted police by guzzling beer, smoking pot, and snake dancing (a drunken conga line). Late in the afternoon of May 3, 1969, riot police moved in and tear-gassed the neighborhood. It took police and sheriff's deputies three days to quell what became known as the Miffland riots. The following March a strike by teaching assistants shut down the campus for three weeks, and in May 1970 Madison's streets once again filled with university students who were angered by the killing of four Kent State University students by the Ohio National Guard (see Fig. 5.12). Then on August 24 student radicals blew up Sterling Hall, the headquarters of the university's physics department and the home of the Army Math Research Center, an agency funded by the U.S. Department of Defense. The explosion killed a brilliant researcher who was working late in his

Few campuses in the United States were more disrupted by Vietnam protests than the University of Wisconsin–Madison. Protests began in 1965 with "teach-ins" and by 1967 escalated to massive demonstrations, including this one in May 1970 by students vehemently opposed to the presence of Dow Chemical Company recruiters on campus. At the time Dow manufactured napalm, a sticky, highly inflammable bomb-delivered jelly that caused hideous burns to anyone who had the misfortune to be near an explosion. As the demonstrations grew in size and frequency, campus police called in their Madison counterparts and eventually the national guard. The protests subsided after a bomb blast on August 24, 1970, killed a brilliant physicist and caused $2 million in damage to Sterling Hall. Although some of the sharpest confrontations occurred on campus, protesters commonly surged up State Street to the capitol, breaking store windows as they went. The protests preoccupied city officials and residents and made building an auditorium seem less important.

lab and made Madison a dateline for newspaper stories around the world.[46]

Not until June 1970, more than one year after he took office, did Dyke finally appoint his auditorium committee. When it met for the first time in July,

Dyke encouraged its members to support "Metro Square," a new concept the city planning department had developed under Dyke's direction for a site two blocks west of the Capitol Square (see Fig. 5.13).[47]

In the long tradition of Madison auditorium plans, Metro Square reaped angry opposition. Paul Soglin, a second-term council member who represented the Miffland area, led the attack. Soglin was just twenty-five and a self-proclaimed radical who had been arrested twice during the riots. But he was remarkably credible on the council floor in opposing Metro Square, arguing that it would trigger a wave of speculation that would cause rents to go so high that his student constituents could not afford to live there. Soglin, then a U.W. law student, worked closely with the anti-Dyke contingent on the council to explore alternatives. It was a warning shot across the bow of Dyke's auditorium ship.[48]

Dyke ignored Soglin's shot and steamed ahead, securing his committee's dutiful endorsement of Metro Square in October 1971. Meanwhile, the anti-Dyke bloc on the council became increasingly frustrated by the mayor's refusal to have any further dealings with Peters and his associates. Why, they wondered, would the city want to build a twelve-hundred-seat auditorium at a retrograde inland site when a similar facility could be built on the lakeshore? This increasingly vocal group wanted Wes Peters to design an auditorium of that size for Law Park.[49]

Dyke, however, stuck with his Metro Square plan and refused to have anything to do with Peters and the Frank Lloyd Wright Foundation. Part of the mayor's intransigence was based on the little-noticed contract provision that gave the Wright foundation the exclusive right to design everything in the Monona basin area for ten years. Festge had inserted the clause in 1966 because he feared that without it the

basin would become a hodgepodge of architectural statements. But the way this clause was written, a city request to do anything at any point during that ten-period would start the clock. If the city had decided to go ahead with the larger auditorium in 1968, the ten-year clock would have run until 1978. Dyke wanted nothing on his watch to start the clock; he hoped the city could regain control of the basin site in 1976.[50]

Finally, in February 1972 Metro Square came before the common council for approval and was rejected on a 15–6 vote. Dyke was furious. "I have no longer any basic commitment to the auditorium project," he announced. Alicia Ashman expressed the frustrations of many other council members when she said, "If we keep going down the path we are on, we may end up with an inflatable bag for an auditorium."[51]

The rejection of Metro Square suddenly cleared the auditorium stage. But the audience, long accustomed to such developments, did not leave its seats. People were confident that another site with a new set of actors would soon wander onto center stage. Their experience had taught them well.

## THE STATE STREET CIVIC CENTER

A year later, on January 11, 1973, the *Wisconsin State Journal* announced that a local business group, the Central Madison Committee (CMC), had secured options to buy the Capitol Theater, a 1928 movie palace, and the vacant Montgomery Ward store next door. The two properties were located on State Street, the eight-block thoroughfare connecting the Capitol Square and the University of Wisconsin. The committee proposed to redevelop the two

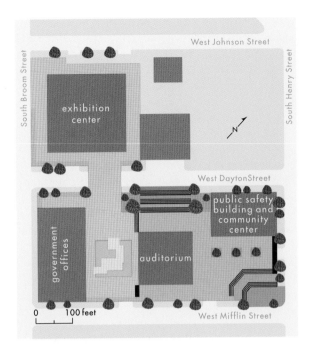

FIGURE 5.13

**1970 Metro Square Auditorium Proposal**

*U.W.–Madison Cartographic Laboratory*

Metro Square was Mayor Bill Dyke's 1970 recommendation for a Madison "civic center." It would have included a twelve-hundred-seat auditorium (half the size of Peters' Law Park concept), an exhibition hall, city offices, and a "public safety and community center." Dyke's city planners spoke glowingly of how Metro Square would revitalize the adjacent student ghetto but couldn't say much more. The site, nearly two square blocks of surface parking, was especially uninspiring. Council member Loren Thorson announced that he would follow the same rule in describing Metro Square that he used for his wife: "You talk about the things you like about her and don't compare her to another woman." When Metro Square failed to win support, its site was used for a new federal courthouse, a $25 million complex of apartments, shops, a senior center, and a parking ramp.

buildings, just two blocks off the square, as a downtown cultural complex.[52]

CMC had been formed a year earlier by business leaders who were concerned about the continuing deterioration downtown and by the fact that the

business community had given more lip service than leadership on this problem. CMC was the first organization to give sustained private-sector attention to downtown's problems. Its board was composed of top executives from financial institutions, newspapers, labor unions, and real estate agencies, as well as representatives from the state of Wisconsin and the U.W. In May 1972 the board hired Michael Duffey, twenty-five, as its first executive director. The handsome young man with a ready smile and conspicuous people skills was fresh from a stint as special assistant to the secretary of the U.S. Department of Housing and Urban Development.[53]

By the early 1970s downtown leaders had many reasons to be concerned, the most obvious of which was the exodus of retailing. The movement had begun in the 1950s and 1960s with the construction of the first shopping centers, but the opening in 1970 and 1971 of two regional shopping malls, East Towne and West Towne, with a total of nearly two million square feet of retail space, instigated the formation of the Central Madison Committee. In fact, downtown's malaise was not limited to retailing. Although financial institutions and professional offices were still there, few thought these functions would grow significantly, and many thought they too would move to the suburbs. By the early 1970s so much suburban development had occurred that many residents no longer needed to go downtown. The exodus left the city's heart with an unprecedented number of boarded-up storefronts and leaders with this big question: What economic functions could revitalize the downtown?[54]

Early CMC leaders believed that conventions and culture offered the greatest promise. A flurry of new hotel construction had increased the city's capacity for conventions and once again pointed to the need for a convention center. But to CMC

officials the highest priority was finding a downtown home for local arts organizations, some of which had become so frustrated by the city's failure to build Monona Terrace, the auditorium in the Monona Basin plan, Metro Square — anything — that they were beginning to plan their own facilities. For example, Madison Theater Guild leaders had started to raise money to build a theater in the suburbs, and their Madison Art Association counterparts had hired an architect to determine whether the newly vacant Montgomery Ward store on State Street could be converted into an art center.[55]

Downtown leaders were also concerned about what would happen when the $4 million in bonds issued in 1954 for the downtown auditorium and civic center were paid off in January 1974. They knew that then the money could be used for any other purpose, including a politically hard-to-resist jolt of property tax relief. As Robert O'Malley, CMC chairman and president of the Madison Bank & Trust, put it in mid-1972, "We've got 18 months to come up with the answers or [we can] forget the whole thing." O'Malley and his colleagues realized the time had come for the business community to act.[56]

They surveyed promising downtown sites and concluded that a square-block parking lot just east of the Capitol Square was ideal for an auditorium. Before they did anything else, they asked leaders of several arts organizations to evaluate the site. Rae Ragatz, the sprightly president of the art association, told CMC officials that instead of trying to build something new on the parking lot, they should buy the Capitol Theater and use it as a concert hall (see Fig. 5.14). Ragatz noted that Pittsburgh's Heinz Hall and several other grand old theaters across the country had been recycled

as state-of-the-art performing arts centers. And if the city bought the Capitol Theater and the Montgomery Ward building next to it, the city would have an outstanding cultural complex, she told CMC.[57]

CMC leaders were so impressed by Ragatz's concept that they hired Ron Bowen, a principal with the Madison architectural firm of Bowen Williamson Kanazawa, to do a feasibility study. Bowen concluded that the Capitol Theater,

Montgomery Ward building, and several adjoining structures could accommodate three theaters and a spacious art center. Best of all, Bowen estimated the complex could be built for $6.1 million. Although this was more than the city had in its auditorium account, CMC officials were confident that the plan could be pared back and that they could spearhead a fund drive to raise the difference.[58]

Heartened that the State Street complex was apparently feasible, CMC had the theater appraised and dispatched George Nelson, its vice chairman and executive vice president of First National Bank, and Mike Duffey to New York to negotiate an option with Matthew Polon, the president of RKO–Stanley Theater–Warner Theater Corporation. Nelson got Polon to give CMC an option for $650,000. The assignment positioned Nelson for a much larger role in 1974, a fact that was then anything but evident to the thirty-four-year-old banker. Meanwhile, CMC negotiated an option with the owners of the Montgomery Ward building.[59]

This aggressive private-sector initiative unfolded in Madison papers between November 1972 and January 1973, just as mayoral candidates were beginning to jockey for position in the spring election. Bill Dyke sought a third two-year term, but his popularity had suffered from his truculent handling of the student unrest and other issues. Opposing Dyke was three-term council member Paul Soglin, now twenty-seven and still regarded as a student radical (see Fig. 5.15).[60]

Soglin's victory in April 1973 stunned Dyke and many Madisonians, who never dreamed that someone so young and radical could be elected mayor. "You can kiss Madison goodbye," said one Dyke supporter. The new mayor, a beneficiary of the 1971 constitutional amendment that allowed eighteen-year-olds to vote, won 90 percent of the

vote in student-dominated downtown wards, more than enough to overcome Dyke's margin in outlying neighborhoods. Because Soglin was regarded as part of a new wave of radical mayors in radical cities such as Madison, his election caught the attention of *Time, The New Yorker, Nation,* and even the *Wall Street Journal.*[61]

In fulfillment of his campaign pledge Soglin worked to build an updated version of the 1969 Peters-designed auditorium in Law Park, but he also said that "if I see that the Law Park site isn't feasible, I'll make a commitment to the State Street site." Updated cost estimates on the Peters-designed auditorium were anything but encouraging. An independent cost estimator said the cost of duplicating Peters' auditorium in 1973 would be $10.5 million, a substantial increase over the 1969 estimate of $6.2 million. Peters blamed the increase on galloping inflation. Nevertheless, Soglin's Auditorium Committee endorsed the Law Park auditorium, but the council approved it only when the new mayor voted to break an 11–11 tie. To make the project more attractive to theater groups that needed a smaller facility, Peters added a rehearsal hall that could double as an intimate theater, but this increased the cost to $12.5 million and failed to satisfy the theater groups. By this time additional fees and costs had further reduced the balance in the auditorium account to $4.8 million, a fact that forced the council to ask for a supplemental appropriation of $7.7 million. To be on the safe side, the council decided to ask voters for $8.5 million. If voters approved, the city could spend as much as $13.3 million on the project.[62]

Meanwhile, CMC officials kept refining the State Street proposal, and Rae Ragatz kept trying to persuade community arts leaders that it was superior to the Law Park plan. CMC and Ragatz made a compelling case. The State Street complex would provide three theaters seating 2,100, 800, and 300, its theaters were tailored to the needs of local groups (which gave the project their strong support), it was much bigger than Peters' complex, and it included an arts center. The clincher was that it was less expensive. By the time the council set the referendum (see Fig. 5.16), CMC officials had determined that the State Street project would cost about $5.7 million and that they could raise $1 million to $1.5 million in a private fund drive, making the net cost to the city $4.2 million to $4.7 million, substantially less than the Law Park alternative.[63]

Encouraged by the logic behind the State Street concept and eager to find a permanent home for the Madison Art Association, the council voted on January 29, 1974, to buy the Montgomery Ward store. To Ragatz and CMC leaders it was a beachhead for the arts complex.[64]

In March 1974 both sides prepared for the referendum battle. Former mayors Henry Reynolds and George Forster and council member Babe Rohr led opponents under the aegis of the 1960s anti–Monona Terrace organization, Citizens for Better Government. Former mayor Otto Festge led the crusade for the Monona Basin auditorium with a new organization, Citizens for a Civic Center. Technically, the referendum was about Peters' Monona Basin auditorium, but in fact the State Street complex was also on the ballot because its backers had successfully positioned it as a bigger, less expensive alternative. During the mercifully brief campaign Madison's extreme left and right took almost identical positions; both argued that the auditorium was a misplaced priority and a bauble for the elite. *The Daily Cardinal*, the student newspaper, called the Peters auditorium "Paul's Palace." Auditorium proponents focused on the

FIGURE 5.15

# PAUL SOGLIN
*RADICAL PRAGMATIST*

*Courtesy Michael Kienitz*

Paul Soglin was only thirty when this photo was taken in 1975, but already he had compiled a remarkable résumé that included undergraduate and law degrees from the U.W., a stint as a cab driver, three arrests during student protests and riots, six years on the Madison common council, two years as mayor, and a discussion with Fidel Castro until three in the morning.

Soglin grew up in Chicago, the son of an activist mother (she once took him to a Hyde Park rally to protest the atom bomb) and a math professor father. As a boy he collected stamps, played baseball, and was captain of the street-crossing patrol. When the time came to select a college, Soglin picked the University of Wisconsin because it was close to Chicago and did not require enrollment in the Reserve Officer Training Corps (ROTC). Soglin held leadership positions in the Student Non-Violent Coordinating Committee and the Committee to End the War in Vietnam, and he fomented a takeover of student government by left-wing radicals. After earning a bachelor's degree with honors in history and political science in 1966, he did graduate work in history but then entered the law school in 1969. During this time Soglin became involved in city politics and won election to the common council in 1968 from a hippie enclave near the U.W. campus. In this capacity he was roughed up, arrested, and gassed by police during student riots and yet earned enough respect to be elected president pro tem of the common council.

In 1973, just a year after receiving his law degree, Soglin was elected mayor of Madison. Although the twenty-seven-year-old won only four of the city's twenty-two wards, his plurality in those four student-dominated wards was so large that it swamped his law-and-order opponent in the other eighteen. His election made the mustachioed young man with droopy eyelids national news. The *Nation* and *New Yorker* dispatched reporters to see what a nice town like Madison was doing in electing this "red mayor." In 1974 *Time* sent a reporter to explain this bewildering anomaly to

its readers. When Soglin was reelected in 1975 the *Wall Street Journal* was so astounded that it did a front-page story.

What national correspondents found was a bright, principled young man eager to enfranchise people his predecessor had excluded, willing to work out pragmatic deals with the business community, and fond of bracing ideological discussions. By this time he owned a three-piece suit but rarely wore it and kept such late hours that callers avoided 9 A.M. appointments if they wanted more than a mayoral yawn.

During his first three 2-year terms as mayor (1973–1979) Soglin converted many doom mongers into believers. He pushed through major downtown revitalization projects, including the $15 million State Street Mall, the $11 million Capitol Concourse project, a major downtown beautification program, and the $7 million civic center on State Street. He also banned the sale of handguns, established the nation's first municipally supported day-care program, hired the first female firefighter, and secured a AAA bond rating for the city, the highest bestowed by the bond-rating agencies.

In 1979 Soglin left public office and practiced law for ten years. He was again elected mayor in 1989, the beginning of another remarkable story (see Chapter 6).

FIGURE 5.16

**1974 Referendum Question**

The wording of this referendum reflected the conflicting forces at work in early
1974. Although the amount was established to cover the costs of building
William Wesley Peters' auditorium in Law Park — the official site selected by
the common council — its wording said nothing about location. This omission
allowed the city to use the money for the State Street complex — or for an
auditorium at any other site. Voters rejected the measure 2–1 in April 1974.

FIGURE 5.17

**Paul "Moneybags" Soglin**

*Courtesy Mike Konopacki and The Capital Times*

When Soglin announced that he had purchased the Capitol Theater for
$650,000, the *Capital Times* ridiculed the move with this cartoon by Mike
Konopacki on July 17, 1974.

superb lakefront site, its new construction, and
superior state-of-the-art design.[65]

When the votes were counted, the Monona Basin
project had taken an old-fashioned drubbing.
Voters rejected the $8.5 million appropriation for
the lakefront auditorium by a 2–1 margin. The mes-
sages were mixed but clear: it was too much money,
not in the right place, and, hey, who needs this elitist indulgence? Even diehard Frank Lloyd Wright
supporters realized the game was over. Monona
Basin, a "beautiful poetic idea," as William Wesley
Peters once described it, was dead.[66]

Conversely, the civic center on State Street, a concept somewhere between the ideal and the possible,
was very much alive. What was remarkable was the
speed with which the council rushed into the State
Street tent. By mid-May the council endorsed the
State Street concept, and a week later Soglin,
Nelson, and Duffey flew to New York to ask Polon
whether the theater was still for sale.

This was the first time that Nelson and Soglin had
worked together, and almost everybody thought they
were an outrageously odd political pair. Here was a
conservative banker, a member of the Chamber of
Commerce board, and a Republican working with
Soglin, freshly minted lawyer, representative of the
city's large counterculture, and a New Left Democrat.
But the match was anything but accidental. When
Soglin beat Dyke in 1973, the chamber's board was
stunned. To most of its board members Soglin was
a bomb-throwing Bolshevik. Nevertheless, he was
now the mayor, and the chamber had to deal with
him. So the business organization made Nelson,
then only thirty-six and among its youngest board
members, the official emissary to the new mayor.
The two quickly developed an extraordinary
working relationship.[67]

When the group got to New York, the RKO president
said the Capitol was still for sale and encouraged
the trio to come back with a hard offer. In June the
council authorized the mayor to pay up to $650,000

for the theater—the same amount negotiated by
CMC officials in December 1972. In July Soglin
and Duffey flew to New York, negotiated the deal
at $650,000, and returned to Madison. To their
great surprise, the two young men were greeted at
the airport by a crowd of sixty cheering, clapping
well-wishers toting signs that read "Welcome
Home," and "Paul, Mike, We Love You."[68]

Not everyone was so thrilled. The *Capital Times*,
long the champion of Wright and the Monona
Basin plan, peevishly refused to support the new
civic center concept. Its editors called the building
"a down-at-the-heels movie house" and said its
purchase was a "series of back alley under-the-table
deals"; its cartoonists ridiculed the price and concept
(see Figs. 5.17 and 5.18). As soon as the deal with
RKO was consummated, two Madison council
members filed suit, both seeking to undo the deal on
technical grounds. Veterans of the now-legendary
auditorium wars wondered whether the new State
Street auditorium, like its predecessors, would
succumb to the depredations of its enemies. But the
city moved quickly to satisfy the complaints of technical improprieties and managed to settle both suits.[69]

With the purchase of the civic center properties
Soglin did something that none of his six predecessors
had been able to do: he dismissed his auditorium
committee and appointed a commission to run the
complex. The new commission interviewed architects
and hired Hardy Holzman Pfeiffer Associates, a
large New York firm that specialized in the restoration
and renovation of old theaters. Hardy Holzman
was known for "aggressively modern, experimental
and even ... playful" design and for "messy vitality
over obvious unity." Significantly, the people who
screamed about Wright's 10 percent fee in the 1950s
were silent in 1974 when the New York firm got
11.5 percent.[70]

Hugh Hardy and his associates began to design the project in April 1975, and in July they presented three alternative plans. The commission and council selected a plan that provided a twenty-one-hundred-seat theater (the restored Capitol), a four-hundred-seat experimental theater, and an art center (in the old Montgomery Ward store). In October the council directed the architects to prepare final construction drawings, a process that would take about a year. Hardy Holzman estimated total construction costs at $5 million, and the city calculated that it had slightly more than $4 million on hand after buying the Montgomery Ward building and paying other expenses. That left the city about $1 million short and posed a huge question: could the private sector raise this amount?[71]

Michael Duffey and Betty Smith, the most outspoken State Street advocate on the common council, answered this question in July 1975 by forming the Greater Madison Foundation for the Arts, a fund-raising arm for the State Street civic center project. Duffey had been expressing his confidence for months. Smith, a widely respected fifty-seven-year-old with boundless energy, a ready smile, and quick wit, said, "I've been trying to raise money for the Republican Party of Dane County," so "this ought to be easy." Council members chuckled because they knew how hard it was to raise money for Republicans in devoutly Democratic Dane County, but they savored the potential power of her position as a liberal and well-connected Republican who knew many potential donors.[72]

Less than three weeks after the creation of the fund-raising foundation, Smith received a telephone call from an executive representing Oscar G. Mayer, the principle stockholder of the famous processed-meat manufacturer whose world headquarters were located on Madison's east side. Mayer was offering

FIGURE 5.18

**Wright Speaks from Taliesin North**

*Courtesy Ed Hinrichs and The Capital Times*

To the editorial board of the *Capital Times*, converting the Capitol Theater into a civic center was a big joke. The newspaper had crusaded for Monona Terrace since 1953 and could not bear the thought of shoving the main function in Wright's grand plan into the fifty-year-old theater on State Street. This delightful cartoon by Ed Hinrichs, who always seemed to find the funny-poignant spin on this civic saga, was published on July 29, 1974, as the Capitol Theater plan was gaining momentum.

$250,000 to kick off the campaign. As Mayer later explained, "We really appreciate this wonderful community. We feel this is the proper thing to do ... for a broadly-based activity such as this." Smith and Duffey were thrilled but not surprised. The Oscar Mayer Company had long been generous to its host community. The gift caused the confidence of community leaders to soar.[73]

The formal fund drive got underway in February 1976 when Walter Frautschi was named the general chairman. Frautschi was chairman of Webcrafters, Inc., a large Madison-based printing company, and a man with a long and impressive record of community service. Because of his stature in the community, he was the ideal person to head the civic center drive; when Frautschi knocked on your door and asked you to contribute, it was usually a question of how much to give, not whether. Under Frautschi's leadership the Greater Madison Foundation for the Arts raised $1.25 million in just five months. Seldom in Madison's history had so much money been raised in such a short period. The successful drive showed that Madison leaders were still committed to the auditorium dream and that they saw the State Street civic center as the last best chance to convert talk to brick.[74]

In December 1976 Hardy Holzman turned over final construction drawings to city officials, who

FIGURE 5.19

**Madison Civic Center and State Street Mall**

*Courtesy Madison Civic Center, photo by Harper Fritsch Studio*

Hardy Holzman Pfeiffer Associates, the New York architectural firm, had a tough assignment: to blend an ornate 1928 movie palace (Fig. 5.14), a utilitarian 1941 Montgomery Ward department store, and a hodgepodge of other buildings into a visually harmonious block. Its solution, shown here, was to retain the Capitol Theater's facade as the centerpiece and replace the remaining storefronts with a new banded brick wall. When it was completed, the complex had 110,000 square feet, including the 2,100-seat Oscar Mayer Theater, the elegantly restored auditorium of the Capitol Theater, the 400-seat thrust-stage Isthmus Playhouse, and the Madison Art Center.

Madison's performing arts center fronts on the State Street Mall, an eight-block thoroughfare that connects the Capitol Square and the University of Wisconsin campus and provides the greatest concentration of downtown shopping. The mall idea was first presented in 1969 but was not completed until 1982.

sent them out for bid. In February 1977 the bids came back at $6 million, $1 million more than the architect's estimate. And this was the good news. A few days later Madisonians learned that the bids covered only the unfinished shell. Said the contractors, in effect, if you want seats, carpeting, and a long list of other "finishing" elements, we will need $7 million—$2 million more than the architects had estimated. The council did the only thing it could: it rejected the bids, pointed fingers, and tried to come up with a politically palatable alternative.[75]

Leaders of the arts community huddled and in an emotion-filled meeting voted to eliminate the smaller theater and several other items, which left the twenty-one-hundred-seat theater, the art center, and lots of unhappy campers. In just five years the civic center had gone from mere concept to detailed architectural drawings, the community had come together to support the State Street location, the city had contributed all its auditorium money, and the private sector had raised an additional $1.25 million. Now the very future of the project was in question. There simply wasn't enough money to do the job the way almost everybody wanted it done. Recriminations flew like dust in a whirlwind. Would everything be for naught? Would this project go the way of Wright's Monona Terrace and Peters' Monona Basin?[76]

If ever there was a time for leadership, this was it. Betty Smith realized that her hour had come. She knew that the only way to get the $2 million the project needed was to amend the already-approved city budget, an act that would require 17 of the 22 council votes. No close observer thought it was possible. As council member Don Murdoch put it, "It's hard to get 17 votes ... to ratify the rising of the sun in the morning." But Smith gritted her teeth and resolved to appeal to her council col-

leagues to amend the budget. Her weapons were a deep understanding of the project, a quick and pragmatic mind, irresistible common sense, confidence-inspiring optimism, and a piquant sense of humor. "We may lose," she said, "but if we do, it's not my fault we didn't try."[77]

Council members agreed to consider the $2 million appropriation and the future of the civic center on June 28, 1977. Debate was long, gut wrenching, almost painful. Everyone had reservations, and many had promised never to spend another penny on the project. A vote at 12:45 A.M. failed by two votes. Then came more debate, caucuses in the back of the council chamber, soul searching, and still more speeches. As one council member put it, "We're in a mess and I see only one way out of it. Appropriate the necessary money and get the goddamn thing built." At nearly 2 A.M. the council took a second vote. Seventeen voted aye and applause erupted. Madison would finally have a civic center.[78]

On February 23, 1980, two and a half years after the momentous council meeting, the Madison Civic Center held its gala grand opening in the elegantly restored auditorium of the Capitol Theater, renamed the Oscar Mayer Theater to honor the company that made the pivotal early gift (see Fig. 5.19). Sitting in the audience that evening were former mayor Paul Soglin and former council member Betty Smith. Although a great political distance separated Soglin, a liberal Democrat, and Smith, a liberal Republican, both possessed a rare blend of leadership, vision, grit, and determination, qualities that had allowed them to forge a remarkable working relationship. Together with Michael Duffey, leaders of the Central Madison Committee, Rae Ragatz, and many others from the arts community, this motley coalition had spearheaded a crusade that few thought would ever succeed.[79]

Mayor Joel Skornicka welcomed everyone with carefully chosen, smile-punctuated words; Martina Arroyo, a Metropolitan Opera soprano, moved the audience with several classics. Following the intermission the Madison Symphony Orchestra played Beethoven's Ninth Symphony with its stirring final movement "Ode to Joy," the victory song of this talented team of leaders who believed that human life could be enriched by a great downtown cultural cathedral. It was a fitting finale for a city that had tried so often and failed so consistently.[80]

"Goodbye, Frank Lloyd Wright, Civic Center Forever Closes Door on His Dream." That was the headline atop an article written by Dave Zweifel, managing editor of the *Capital Times*, just five days before the State Street civic center officially opened. The article wistfully recounted what might have been had Wright's dream been built, but it really was an obituary for Monona Terrace. After all, nearly all the functions Wright proposed during the twenty-one years he worked on the project had either been abandoned or found a home in another building. If there were any citizens who did not consider the Madison Civic Center the last nail in Frank Lloyd Wright's Monona Terrace coffin, they remained silent.

FIGURE 6.1

**1991 View of Monona Terrace
from Lake Monona**

*© City of Madison,
rendering by Anderson Illustration Associates*

This rendering, one of a series
published in "Monona Terrace:
A Public Place By Frank Lloyd
Wright" in 1991 by the Monona
Terrace Commission, shows the
project from the dramatic and
always evocative perspective
from Lake Monona.

CHAPTER 6

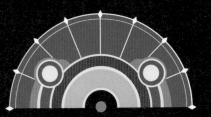

THE CONVENTION CENTER CRUSADE

FIGURE 6.2

**Soglin and Arnold at 1990 Press Conference**

*Courtesy* Wisconsin State Journal, *photo by Joseph W. Jackson III*

This June 27, 1990, photo shows Mayor Paul Soglin in a huge former federal courtroom in the Madison Municipal Building where he is urging about sixty civic leaders to transform Frank Lloyd Wright's 1959 civic center into a convention center. Seated behind the podium is Orville "Bud" Arnold, then the principal of Arnold and O'Sheridan, a large Madison engineering firm. He worked assiduously behind the scenes with others to demonstrate that the conversion was feasible. Soglin's press conference was emblematic of his entrepreneurial leadership style, a rare ability to see opportunities, articulate a compelling vision, and then use his knowledge of the political system to create an effective process to make something happen.

On June 27, 1990, just fourteen months after he had once again been elected mayor, Paul Soglin stood before a bank of microphones in a huge oak-paneled room in the Madison Municipal Building and told sixty community leaders that the city should build Frank Lloyd Wright's Monona Terrace project as a convention center.

"We can with the proper adaptations build a spectacular, internationally recognized convention center," the mayor began (see Fig. 6.2). Soglin estimated the cost at $47 million and promised that no property tax increase would be necessary. Following Soglin at the microphone was Anthony "Tony" Puttnam, a fifty-five-year-old Taliesin architect who had worked with Wright on Monona Terrace

in the 1950s. Using a newly drawn aerial rendering of the project from Lake Monona, Puttnam said that the interior of Wright's 1959 plan could be adapted for a convention center but that the exterior would remain unchanged (see Fig. 4.33). Next came Dane County Executive Richard Phelps, who said he supported the concept but was careful not to commit any money. It was a tightly scripted but exciting press conference.

Most who saw clips of the event on local television that evening and who read the startling announcement in the papers could hardly believe the leaks and rumors they had been hearing were true. Newer residents thought the idea of a convention center on Madison's downtown lakefront had been decisively

defeated in a 1989 referendum. Older residents knew that Law Park was the site of some of the city's longest civic battles and a graveyard for visionary designs: John Nolen's 1909 grand esplanade (Fig. 1.17); Ladislas Segoe's 1939 terraced amphitheater (Fig. 3.9); Jim Law's 1940s park (Fig. 3.15), and Wright's 1938 Olin Terraces "dream civic center" (Fig. 3.5) and his revised 1955 complex (Fig. 4.1); William Wesley Peters' 1967 Monona Basin plan (Fig. 5.8); a linear college campus (1974) and an upscale, tiered shopping mall (1984), both by Kenton Peters (Fig. 6.3); and a 1989 convention center proposal.[1]

Soglin was familiar with these plans; perhaps in his mind's eye he could see a taunting row of gravestones clustered along the shore of Law Park. Why, then, would Soglin launch still another assault on this vision-resistant shoreline? First, he believed what John Nolen had told Madisonians in 1909: this shoreline could be one of the most beautiful urban waterfronts in the world. Second, he deeply admired Wright's architecture. To Soglin, now forty-five, this was the most exciting and important opportunity he would have during his second stint as mayor of Madison. Even so, to urge that Wright's 1959 civic center be transformed into a modern convention center was arguably the gutsiest act of his political career. But Soglin had no doubts; it was a risk worth taking.[2]

Few knew the remarkable story behind the press conference.

### THE CRASH COURSE

Lynn Russell was chagrined. It was 1985 and she had just finished her first year as president of the Greater Madison Convention and Visitors Bureau. Madison was routinely losing conventions to Green

Lake Park Plaza, View from Lake Monona

*Courtesy Kenton Peters*

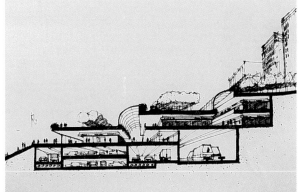

Lake Park Plaza Cross-Section

*Courtesy Kenton Peters*

FIGURE 6.3

**Kenton Peters' Visions for Law Park**

Kenton Peters, a fiercely independent and immensely talented Madison architect, is perhaps best known in southern Wisconsin for his audacious blue federal courthouse just west of the Capitol Square and his swoopy silver University of Wisconsin Foundation headquarters adjacent to the campus. But Peters, a passionate believer in the potential of downtown Madison, also designed two projects for Law Park that deserve to be classified with the grand visions proposed by Nolen, Segoe, and Wright.

When the Madison Area Technical College (MATC) sought to expand its facilities in 1979, Peters designed a bold, $40 million linear campus for Law Park. The four-block campus boasted three levels, 900,000 square feet, and passive solar heating. Unfortunately for Peters, MATC's board had its heart set on a drained-and-filled marsh adjacent to the Madison airport.

Undeterred, in 1984 Peters recycled his college campus as an upscale, five-level, $47 million shopping mall known as Lake Park Plaza, shown here. Peters argued that this project had enough space and glamor to trigger a retailing renaissance in downtown Madison. His plan featured a Nolenesque waterfront esplanade, 500,000 square feet for stores, restaurants, theaters, bars, an amphitheater at the end of Monona Avenue (in the color rendering), fifteen acres of parkland, plus parking for twelve hundred cars. Madison rejected both of Peters' grand civic visions. He is not related to William Wesley Peters.

Bay, of all places. On the surface it didn't make sense. Madison was twice as big, much more beautiful, the capital of the state, and the home of the University of Wisconsin. But Russell knew the reason: Green Bay had just completed a downtown convention complex composed of an all-suites hotel and an attached exhibition hall. To conventiongoers, the Green Bay facility was wonderful. Everything was in one place; nobody had to go outside; and it was both efficient and attractive.[3]

Nor was Green Bay Madison's only competition. Milwaukee had built its convention center in 1974, La Crosse had put one up in 1980, and Oshkosh was scheduled to complete its entry in 1986. Even tiny Wisconsin resort communities such as Oconomowoc

(population 9,909) had built convention centers, and they too were taking convention business from Madison.[4]

The proliferation of convention centers in Wisconsin reflected a national trend. Trade associations were getting larger, fewer could be accommodated in hotel meeting rooms, and meeting planners were demanding more sophisticated facilities. Beginning in the 1960s, U.S. cities began building free-standing convention centers contiguous to relatively large, first-class hotels, which served as headquarters for the conventions. To people in the hospitality industry a "convention center" was a facility that could simultaneously accommodate exhibits, serve banquets, and provide meeting rooms of varying sizes for

"break-out" sessions. Exhibit halls were especially important to meeting planners because exhibitors' fees had become a main way of underwriting convention expenses and because the exhibits provided an efficient and popular way for attendees to get information on the latest developments in their field.[5]

To Russell, Madison's problem was obvious: Madison's convention facilities were increasingly obsolete. Most Madison conventions were handled by downtown hotels equipped with a banquet hall and a few meeting rooms. None had a dedicated exhibit hall, the largest banquet room could accommodate only five hundred people, and the meeting rooms were often inadequate. Madison conventioneers did have access to an exhibit hall, but it was two miles from downtown and owned by Dane County. Either Madison could continue to rely on increasingly obsolete hotel meeting facilities and be content with a declining share of the convention market, or the city could build a competitive new convention center. That was what Russell wanted to do.[6]

Russell, a quiet, articulate thirty-three-year-old workaholic, launched a quiet campaign. Everywhere she went, she hammered away at the need for bigger, better meeting facilities. She urged the city's leaders to act. All listened politely, but many thought she was just lobbying on behalf of her industry. It was as if her message was a stealth bomber that could evade human consciousness. It was an old, old Madison problem. Few knew much about Madison's meeting industry and few seemed to care. Once in a while a community leader would grab peers by the lapels and say, now listen, this industry is important. But most of the time the convention and meeting industry operated inside hotels, out of sight and out of mind.[7]

Madison had been a popular convention city since the turn of the century, and business leaders had been promoting Madison as a convention site since that time. But it was not until the late 1960s and early 1970s that several factors converged to mark the beginning of a new era for the industry. In 1968 Madison became Wisconsin's first city to enact a new state-approved hotel room tax. During the early 1970s the city experienced a small boom in downtown hotel construction, and in 1974 increasingly vocal hotel owners formed the city's first independent convention and visitors bureau. Unfortunately, the city was pouring all revenue from the hotel room tax into its general fund to keep property taxes from rising. Thus, while most other cities used this revenue as a dedicated income source for building convention centers, promoting the hospitality industry, and staffing their visitors' bureau, Madison used the money to mow grass, pick up garbage, and fill potholes. After an acrimonious fight in 1976, Madison gave the bureau a miserly 10 percent of its hotel tax revenues, but that was hardly enough to promote a rapidly growing industry.[8]

The first person to respond to Russell's plea for a convention center was Darrell Wild, the rough-hewn managing partner of Madison's largest downtown hotel, the 378-room Concourse. In January 1985 Wild proposed that the city build a thirty-thousand-square-foot "exhibit hall" on a half-block parking lot across the street from his hotel. His suggestion made sense. The Concourse enjoyed a superior location — one block from the state capitol, Madison Civic Center, and State Street shops and restaurants; three blocks from Lake Mendota; and just seven blocks from the heart of the University of Wisconsin campus. Other downtown hotels offered more than a thousand rooms for visitors. Add an exhibition hall, connect it by skywalks to the Concourse and other nearby buildings, and Madison could once again become an attractive destination for state and regional conventions.[9]

The clang of Wild's concept provoked a strong but behind-the-scenes response from Madison mayor F. Joseph Sensenbrenner and William M. Belden, the executive director of Downtown Madison, Inc. (DMI). Both men saw Wild's idea as a promising downtown revitalization strategy. Sensenbrenner, a thirty-seven-year-old former assistant attorney general, lived downtown with his family and had campaigned to revitalize the central city. Belden's organization was founded in 1972 as the Central Madison Committee and had played a salutary role in creating the Madison Civic Center, launching the popular downtown Farmers' Market, and encouraging the construction of new urban housing. It had restructured itself in 1982 so it could play an even bigger role in promoting the downtown and fostering its development. Members of its board enjoyed a warm relationship with city hall.[10]

DMI leaders were especially eager to find an economic function to replace retailing. By the mid-1980s the only vibrant downtown shopping area was State Street, the eight-block artery connecting the Capitol Square and the University of Wisconsin campus. Nearly all other retailers had joined the massive exodus for suburban shopping malls. Although financial institutions and professional offices were still present downtown, few thought these functions would grow significantly and many thought they would decline. So extensive was suburban development that many people boasted about never having to go downtown.[11]

In January 1986, nearly a year after Wild presented his idea, Sensenbrenner formally urged the Madison Common Council to build an exhibition hall on the half-block opposite the Concourse Hotel. Thus began the crusade to build a modern publicly owned convention center in downtown Madison. At the time the idea seemed so pure, so promising,

so doable, so good for the city. But as Madison leaders were about to learn, the concept would provoke one of the most contentious debates in Madison's history, dominate the next three mayoral elections, and send an incumbent mayor packing.[12]

When Sensenbrenner endorsed Wild's idea, developers naturally interpreted his action as an endorsement of convention centers in general. Within three months the mayor had received three unsolicited proposals from other developers. The proposals required more land, more money, and different sites — all the usual ingredients for a political tempest.

This flurry of proposals forced Sensenbrenner, Belden, Russell, and all other interested parties to recognize that they did not have the answers to basic due diligence questions. Exactly what kind of convention facilities should Madison build on this half-block? How big should the exhibition hall and other facilities be? How much would this complex cost? How much of an operating subsidy would the hall require?

To answer these questions the city and DMI hired consultants and sent civic leaders to other cities to examine their convention centers. This quick foray convinced leaders that Wild's half-block site was much too small and that they had a lot to learn before they did anything. Meanwhile, critics of Wild's idea accused the mayor and his business allies of planning a "welfare for the rich" program. Indignant petition carriers got enough signatures to require a referendum in April 1987 on whether the city should subsidize the construction or operation of a convention center. When the ballots were counted, 3 in 5 voters had said yes, but the referendum was little more than authorization to develop a specific project. During the same election voters awarded Sensenbrenner a third term. One other important

FIGURE 6.4

**The 1989 Nolen Terrace Convention Center Proposal**

*Courtesy Potter Lawson, Inc., Kenton Peters & Associates,
and Loschky, Marquardt & Nesholm, Architects*

Of the five official convention center proposals submitted to the city in June 1988, the only one on the Lake Monona shore was Nolen Terrace. It was the immediate official favorite. "Wow, this would really put us on the map!" said David Wallner, a member of the Madison Common Council. Eve Galanter, also a council member, said it had "sizzle and pizzazz." Mayor Sensenbrenner praised it for finally achieving "the historic link between the downtown and the waterfront." Not everyone was pleased. Ann Fleischli, lawyer and civic activist, said the facility looked like a "concrete burial vault."

In fact, Nolen Terrace had many strengths, including a dramatic southerly exposure on the waterfront and a lushly landscaped rooftop that added two acres of park space to the downtown and provided a platform from which people could watch water-skiing shows on Lake Monona. Cascading stairs on both ends gave pedestrians direct, easy access to Law Park from the Capitol Square, and a generous waterfront esplanade accommodated pedestrians and bicyclists. The entrance, the ramp of glass on the top, was centered on South Pinckney, not on Monona Avenue. Nolen Terrace was a textbook design for accommodating conventions. It met all the city's size requirements, and an all-weather enclosure linked it to a 360-room hotel (the tall building to the left of the capitol dome) and an 850-car parking ramp (not visible here). Its great weakness was its $46 million price tag when the city had only $19 million to spend. The project was rejected by 60 percent of voters in an April 1989 referendum.

Nolen Terrace was proposed by Richard Munz, a Madison real estate developer, and was collaboratively designed by two Madison architectural firms, Potter, Lawson and Pawlowsky and Kenton Peters and Associates, in consultation with a Seattle firm. The hotel was to be developed and operated by Jerry Mullins, a Madison hotelier and real estate developer.

ground rule emerged from this 1987 campaign: the agreement that no convention center would be built in Madison without an affirmative referendum.[13]

The day after the 1987 election, city officials hired Pannell Kerr Forster, a highly regarded convention center consulting firm, to secure reliable answers to key questions about the best site, the size of the downtown hotel market, appropriate convention center specifications, the size of the annual operating subsidy, and the economic impact of such a center.

Pannell Kerr's study revealed that a Madison center would attract 123 events each year but acknowledged that this did not include business generated by the University of Wisconsin — a market many thought to be large. It also provided the first reliable estimates of the annual operating subsidy such a center would require — about $250,000 a year — and the first determination by an expert that a new 250-room convention center hotel would threaten the business of Madison's existing hotels. Pannell Kerr also said the Madison center should have 134,000 square feet, including an exhibit hall of 40,000 square feet, a banquet hall/ballroom of 23,000 square feet, and meeting rooms of 8,000 square feet. These specifications became the yardstick for sizing all subsequent centers and would make the Madison facility second only to Milwaukee's in size.[14]

Armed with Pannell Kerr's specifications, the city solicited proposals from developers and set a deadline of June 1, 1988. Five very different projects came in, but one, "Nolen Terrace," slated for Law Park, was the clear front runner (see Fig. 6.4).[15]

Although Nolen Terrace was the most exciting, its daunting $46 million price tag sobered center backers, who somehow had to find a way to pay for it without using property taxes. During the 1987 referendum campaign Sensenbrenner had emphasized his absolute opposition to using a penny of property tax to pay for the center. Community leaders across the political spectrum responded with a loud amen.[16]

The city had just three cards in its financial hand. Almost everyone agreed that the best way to underwrite a convention center was to use the hotel room tax because it was levied against those mostly likely to benefit from the center. By 1988 the room tax was generating more than $2 million a year — enough to finance a $25 million building — but those figures assumed that all the money was available for this purpose, which it was not. Madison was still using the hotel tax to keep a lid on property taxes.[17]

City officials were torn. They did not want to give up such a wonderful source of property tax relief. But they recognized that continuing to use 90 percent of this money to underwrite city services

was indefensible. Sensenbrenner proposed that the city freeze the amount given to the general fund at the 1987 level and that all additional revenues be directed to a convention center fund. The council agreed, and city accountants estimated that growth in the room tax would generate $11.9 million for Nolen Terrace in fifteen years.[18]

The city's second card was tax incremental financing, known as TIF. Although it sounds complicated, TIF (pronounced *tiff*) is a simple concept. Land occupied by a rundown building generates fewer property tax dollars for a city than the same parcel with a new or substantially rehabilitated building. The State of Wisconsin's TIF mechanism allows cities to keep the difference in real estate taxes — the so-called increment — that property generates after being rehabbed or redeveloped. The state law allows municipalities to keep this increment for as long as twenty-three years and to use this income as collateral to repay bonds. The proceeds of these bonds, less interest costs, could then be used to pay for downtown revitalization projects. Madison officials calculated that TIF could generate about $3.6 million for the project.[19]

The city's third card was parking revenue. The convention center would need a contiguous parking ramp, so the idea was to use revenue from this facility to pay back initial borrowing. City officials estimated that the ramp would generate $3.8 million over fifteen years.[20]

But the numbers didn't add up. The combination of hotel room taxes, TIF, and parking ramp income would generate $19 million and the sticker price was $46 million. That left an embarrassing gap of $27 million, most of which would have to come from the property tax.

These numbers put Sensenbrenner in a terrible position. Here he was, entering a campaign for a

fourth term, committed to a promising but expensive and already controversial convention center with a $27 million funding gap, urged by prominent business leaders to hold a referendum on the same day that his political future would be on the line, saddled with a common council whose commitment to the center lay somewhere between tepid and tentative, and circled by taunting mayoral candidates.

On February 7, 1989, Sensenbrenner made a painful recommendation: hold a referendum on April 4. "I'm putting a lot on the line to make this happen," he began. Sensenbrenner acknowledged that he did not have all the money to pay for the center but explained that if voters approved Nolen Terrace and the $27 million funding package, it would be easier to raise the rest of the money. "The story today is that the citizens are going to have to decide."[21]

And decide they would. Sensenbrenner's opponents smelled blood. Among them was Paul Soglin, who had served as mayor from 1973 to 1979 and had spent the last ten years practicing law before deciding to run for his old office again. "I wish I had the nerve to get up and say we're going to raise $46 million and not say where it's going to come from," Soglin said. Soglin was also in the enviable position of being able to attack Nolen Terrace without providing an alternative.[22]

Uncertainty about its funding was not the only ticking noise coming from the convention center box. By the time Sensenbrenner announced the 1989 referendum, John Q. Hammons, a major Holiday Inn franchisee, had broken ground for a full-fledged convention center attached to a first-class three-hundred-room atrium hotel in Middleton, an independent municipality on Madison's western border. In May 1986 Hammons had asked Sensenbrenner to support his plans to build his hotel–convention center on a suburban Madison site, but the mayor told the hotel developer that he wanted the facility in the central city. Hammons refused and in December 1987 announced that he would build his complex in Middleton. He cunningly positioned his hotel just five feet inside Middleton's boundary to avoid paying room taxes to Madison and then, to twist the knife a little, named his complex "Holiday Inn–Madison West." [23] (In 1997 Hammons sold his hotel, and the complex became known as the Marriott–Madison West.)

Hammons' decision forced the city to secure still another consultant study to determine what the effects of the Middleton facility would be. This study, released in September 1988, was discouraging. It found that Hammons' convention center would cut Madison's convention business by 22 percent and that the city would have to spend about $1 million on advertising to compete. Short of commandeering 100 percent of the hotel room tax revenue — politically out of the question — there was no way the city could generate this amount of money. Critics of the Nolen Terrace plan skillfully exploited these problems. [24]

The 1989 Nolen Terrace campaign was anything but a rerun of the 1987 referendum, which had been little more than a trial balloon. This time voters could consider a specific site, a stratospheric price tag, and what a better-organized opposition had to say. Opponents, who came together under the funky name of the No White Elephant Committee, included a Madison-based leftist group known as the Labor-Farm Party; State Street business owners who thought the center site, Law Park, was too far away to benefit them; the South Central Federation of Labor; and a staunch new voice, that of Ann Fleischli, a lawyer who had been hired by Tom Link, an owner of the Bellevue Apartments (see Figs. 1.1 and 5.4), which would overlook Nolen Terrace.

FIGURE 6.5

**Buy a Cookie, Fight the Center**

*Courtesy Tom Still*

On the day of the 1989 referendum, members of the No White Elephant Committee walked up and down State Street selling these elephant-shaped cookies bearing the word *no* in red frosting. The cost was just 50 cents. It was a low-budget attempt to fight the big-money supporters of the proposed Nolen Terrace Convention Center.

According to Fleischli, Nolen Terrace would surround the Bellevue with high-density development and destroy its viability as a residence. White Elephant's campaign pounded away at the $27 million funding gap, the likelihood that the center would enrich a few hoteliers and real estate developers, creation of yet another subsidy-sucking civic project (the city was already subsidizing the Madison Civic Center), and the exclusion of "the little people" from the development process. To call attention to their cause they sold White Elephant cookies on State Street (see Fig. 6.5). [25]

By contrast, Nolen Terrace supporters, who organized under the Coalition for Madison's Future, had to persuade people to vote for an expensive, controversial project that exceeded Madison's ability to pay by $27 million. They asked people to give Nolen Terrace a vote of confidence with the understanding that no property tax dollars would be used and that the city could raise the rest of the

money later. Exactly where the money would come from remained a mystery. Proponents tried a few rousing refrains celebrating Nolen Terrace's functional design, stunning location, and how it would bring pride to citizens' hearts, visitors to the city, and new life to the Capitol Square. But even when wrapped in the bunting of central city revitalization, Nolen Terrace encountered resistance from voters. Proponents tried to portray the project as a *community* center. After all, its halls and rooms would be splendid for weddings, parties, and proms. That ploy didn't work either. One wag imagined "the guys at Oscar's [Madison's huge headquarters plant for the Oscar Mayer Foods Corporation] are knocking off after a hard day of carving pig bellies and one of them says, 'Hey, I know, let's go to the convention center!' 'Great idea,' says another. 'The kids can come too.'" Convention centers, Nolen Terrace proponents were quickly learning, were hard to sell. [26]

When the votes were counted on April 4, 1989, both Nolen Terrace and incumbent mayor Sensenbrenner had been trounced. Nolen Terrace got 40 percent of the votes, while the mayor received 43 percent. Leaders of the White Elephant coalition were elated. They had taken on Madison's establishment and had won by a whopping 20 percent margin while being outspent 5 to 1. [27]

Opponents thought they had permanently banished a publicly funded convention center from respectable political discourse, but they were wrong. Madison's new mayor, Paul Soglin, had often stated his support for the idea of a convention center. Besides, downtown Madison was still in trouble, something that convention center backers could not forget. By 1989 only a remnant of retailing, one thousand of the city's four thousand hotel rooms, and just 36 percent of the city's office space were still downtown. Meanwhile, downtown financial institutions were continuing to shrink their downtown operations. Vacant buildings and even surface parking lots on prime Capitol Square frontage were insolent reminders that the downtown still desperately needed a powerful infusion of new economic energy. Even more insidious was the prospect of a decline in the huge downtown tax base and a compensatory increase in taxes on all remaining real estate. These bleak conditions forced the city to continue to ask what economic function had the potential to infuse substantial new life into the central city.[28]

Although Nolen Terrace leaders were disappointed by the referendum, their learning curve during the campaign had been nearly vertical. Now they understood that a viable convention center would require at least two city blocks, cost $47 million, and lose money every year. They had learned how important the hotel room tax was for financing a center and understood what a terrible mistake Madison had made when it pumped this revenue into the general fund. They learned that despite this mistake they could cobble together a downpayment of $19.3 million without using the property tax — no mean achievement. They learned that state, county, and private support was essential to cover the $27 million funding gap. They learned that a convention center was one of the most difficult buildings to sell to the public. They learned that educating voters about a complex and controversial issue requires a long campaign and the involvement of more people earlier in the process. They marveled at the excitement generated by the Nolen Terrace lakeshore site and how it kindled the old vision of linking the lake and the city. Finally, they learned that if voters are even going to consider a $46 million building, they have to know where all the money is coming from.

Without realizing it, Madison leaders had enrolled in Convention Centers 101, one of the most rigorous courses in the civic curriculum. They had fought over nine sites, commissioned six consultant studies, and donned battle gear for two referenda. In retrospect the process was desultory, improvisational, and flawed, and the questions were confusing, tough, and unrelenting.[29]

The most important result of this four-year crash course was the emergence of a cadre of civic leaders who could talk hotel vacancy rates, methodologies for measuring market size, state-of-the-art construction specifications, subsidy calculations, and secondary economic benefits. Nolen Terrace was dead; another tombstone for still another grand plan for Madison's downtown lakefront could be erected in Law Park. But in the minds of proponents, the potential of a great convention center to infuse fresh life into one of the most beautiful downtowns in America was alive and well.

## THE QUIET CRESCENDO OF WRIGHT THINKING

It would be tempting to say that the 1987 and 1989 convention center referenda were two more examples of Madison's propensity to spin its wheels without moving forward. But that interpretation would be wrong. In fact, the crusade to build a convention center provoked a small group of people — many operating independent of each other — to assert that the best convention center had been designed long ago by Frank Lloyd Wright. But these comments were made so quietly and so sporadically amid the late 1980s convention center debate that they passed across the Madison stage virtually unnoticed.

Ricardo Gonzalez, a native of Cuba, owner of a popular downtown bar, and council member representing a district just east of the Capitol

Square, had started the buzz. Just two weeks before the 1987 referendum, Gonzalez wrote a letter to the *Capital Times* and asked, "Why is it that the most viable, most beautiful, and unique design and location for a convention center is being ignored by our city fathers?... We have the best design ... right under our noses.... I am referring to the Frank Lloyd Wright Monona Basin project which would include a convention center." Immediately after the referendum Dave Zweifel, editor of the *Capital Times*, wrote a column urging a review of the 1950s Monona Terrace plans to see whether it would "be possible to salvage at least part of the Frank Lloyd Wright concept" for a convention center. In July 1987 the editorial voice of the *Wisconsin State Journal* — the newspaper that for decades had opposed Monona Terrace — said the same thing. By the end of 1987 Madison newspapers had carried at least eight columns or editorials urging a review of Wright's plans. But most leaders were so caught up in the debate that they paid little attention to the papers.[30]

In April 1988 Monona Terrace surfaced again. Geraldine Nestingen, whose husband Ivan had championed Wright's Monona Terrace Civic Center as mayor in the 1950s, wrote a letter to the *Capital Times*. "My heart broke a little yesterday while reading about the plans for the Law Park area," she said. "I hope that does not mean the city will ignore the Frank Lloyd Wright plan." She was referring to newspaper accounts of plans that graduate students from the Harvard School of Design had developed for Law Park. The students had been invited to Madison by the city and DMI to stimulate local thinking on how to develop this urban waterfront. Significantly, three student teams had proposed convention centers for Law Park.[31]

When William Wesley Peters, vice president of Taliesin Architects, Inc. and chairman of the Wright foundation, read Nestingen's letter, he was moved to reply. Peters reassured the widow that he thought it was "eminently possible" to adapt the Monona Terrace design for a convention center. "The Monona Terrace idea is more alive, valid and vital to the best interests of Madison today than it ever has been," he told her. "A great idea never dies!" Attached to Peters' letter in Taliesin files was a "very rough draft" of an "open letter to the people of Madison" — which he apparently never sent, but it showed that Peters retained a keen interest in this project. "If one could close their eyes and at once imagine a vision of architecture — arcs sweeping out from Law Park in a series of ever so graceful curves supporting landscaped terraces hovering just above the softly lapping water below.... Now open your eyes, Madison.... The Monona Terrace project patiently awaits upon the people of Madison."[32]

Apparently spurred by Geraldine Nestingen's letter, Peters called Zweifel on May 9 to say that Taliesin was "very interested in working with Madison officials to revise the old Law Park plans for a convention center" and to ask for a copy of the city's official specifications for a convention center. Sometime in July Peters dispatched a Taliesin architect to sit in on a meeting of Sensenbrenner's Convention Center Criteria Committee. This was the first time in years that anyone from Taliesin had had any contact with Madison on this project.[33]

When the Nolen Terrace plan was unveiled in June 1988, it provoked a second flurry of pro–Monona Terrace letters to the editor. One writer was Betty Scott, a retired Madison schoolteacher who had circulated petitions for the Wright project in 1954. She had just toured Taliesin and had asked Daniel Ruark, the apprentice-guide, whether the Monona Terrace plan could be adapted for a convention center. In late July both newspapers published her letter urging the city to adapt Wright's 1950s civic center for a convention center. Fifteen readers, including the Taliesin public relations director, responded with warm letters of their own. Scott was so encouraged that she called a meeting of all interested parties at her home on August 2. That day the *Capital Times* ran a front-page story headlined "Center Picks Inspire Revival of Interest in Wright Design." That too was encouraging.[34]

Apprentice Ruark was among those who gathered at Scott's home. The next day Peters called Scott to express Taliesin's strong interest in helping with the project. The *Times*'s story about the renewed interest in Wright's plan had included an interview with senior Taliesin architect Charles Montooth. "We're always interested, but a little shy" about updating the Law Park design, Montooth said. "Memories of the old political battles have not died away. But if the public interest was there ... Taliesin Architects would probably welcome the chance to dust off the Monona Terrace plans." No one responded.[35]

Meanwhile, that spring Wisconsin governor Tommy Thompson had appointed Jim Carley, the head of a large Madison-based real estate development company known as the Carley Capital Group, to the Commission on Taliesin. Thompson wanted Carley and the other commission members to prepare a restoration plan for Taliesin, Wright's famous complex. Carley (see Fig. 6.6) had been active in civic affairs since his arrival in Madison in the late 1960s and had followed the city's efforts to build a convention center with great interest. However, Carley thought all five designs submitted in the city in June 1988, including the lake-fronting Nolen Terrace, were dogs. As he drove out to Taliesin for a commission meeting, he mulled the intriguing possibility of adapting Wright's 1959 Monona Terrace plan.[36]

FIGURE 6.6

**James Carley, Project Provocateur**

*Courtesy Wisconsin Public Television, photo by James Gill*

Jim Carley arrived in Madison in 1967 to assist his brother, David, in a growing real estate development business and cut a broad swath from the start. Although many of their developments were outside Wisconsin, the brothers completed several high-visibility projects in Madison, including housing for the elderly, commercial developments, and residential towers; almost all used complex government-financing programs that many developers eschewed. At the same time Carley maintained a relatively large portfolio of civic projects, including his service on the governor's Commission on Taliesin, a body charged with the restoration of Wright's landmark complex forty miles west of Madison. It was in that capacity that Carley first examined a dusty set of Frank Lloyd Wright's plans for Monona Terrace.

At the end of a commission meeting at Taliesin that summer Carley asked Montooth, also a commission member, to lend him a set of old Monona Terrace plans and Montooth agreed. A short time later Montooth returned with a big roll of plans that were based on Wright's 1959 plans but completed by Taliesin Architects in 1960 after Wright's death (see Chapter 4).[37]

Carley hoisted the twenty-pound roll onto his shoulder and walked out to the parking lot, unrolled it on the trunk of his yellow Mercedes roadster, and began to page through the drawings. A few minutes later Marshall Erdman, chairman of the commission, walked by, and Carley explained that he was checking the plans to see if they could be adapted as a convention center for Madison. "It will never work," Erdman said. Back in Madison, Carley used spare time during the next few weeks to compare the plans to the city's latest official convention center specifications. The seasoned developer could see that all the rooms in the official specifications would fit inside the Wright envelope.[38]

In September 1988 the Elvehjem Museum of Art (pronounced EL-vee-em) on the University of Wisconsin campus opened its doors to the "largest, most expensive exhibition" it had ever mounted. The show celebrated the thirty-two buildings that Wright had designed for the Madison area and his eight-decade connection with the city. With a budget of $350,000, including a $230,000 grant from the National Endowment for the Humanities, the show featured fifty original Wright drawings, hundreds of artifacts, and several newly restored and commissioned architectural models. More than fifty thousand people mobbed the show during its two-month run and attended dozens of related events. Local newspapers lavished generous attention on the show.[39]

Most Madisonians had no idea that Wright had designed so many buildings for their city, that they included examples in so many different categories, or that they dated from the first year of his private practice, 1893, to the year of his death, 1959. Wright's designs for Madison, attendees learned, included houses, boathouses, hotels, commercial buildings, a dance studio, fraternity house, country club, church, hospital, and of course the controversial civic center. For almost everyone the show was a revelation. For many its highlight was the newly restored 4-by-8-foot 1955 model of Monona Terrace (see Fig. 6.7). People who saw it for the first time exclaimed, "Why in heaven's name didn't we build that?" Several went home and wrote spirited letters to the newspapers and were almost unanimous in their sentiments: We missed the boat. During this show Carley ran into Soglin, who was then thinking about running for mayor. Carley asked Soglin, "Why don't we dust off the old Monona Terrace plan and use that for the convention center?" Soglin recalled this as the first time he heard about the idea.[40]

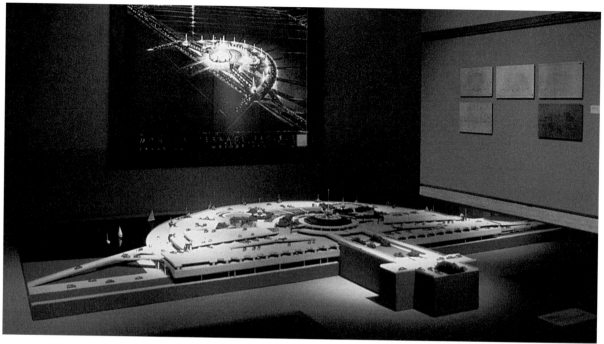

FIGURE 6.7

**1988 Wright Exhibition at the Elvehjem**

*Courtesy Elvehjem Museum of Art*

On September 2, 1988, the Elvehjem Museum of Art, located on the University of Wisconsin campus, opened a new exhibit showcasing the thirty-two buildings that Wright designed for Madison over sixty-six years. Most of the fifty thousand who trekked through the exhibit during its two-month run had no idea that Wright had designed so many buildings for his hometown. The last gallery in the exhibit, shown here, attracted the most attention. It contained the newly restored 1955 model of Monona Terrace built by Wright's Taliesin apprentices (see Fig. 4.16), original renderings not seen since 1938 (see Fig. 3.5), and other artifacts pertaining to this project. The gallery stirred up memories of older Madison residents and provoked younger residents to wonder why the city had rejected such a visionary proposal. The exhibit helped stimulate new interest in the project and prompted several leaders to wonder whether it could be adapted for a convention center.

During the summer of 1991 Madison hosted a second Wright exhibition, "In the Realm of Ideas." The national touring exhibition attracted thousands to the Madison Art Center and heightened interest in Wright and his work. The show's designer was Tony Puttnam.

The Elvehjem show was a part of a remarkable national and even international explosion of interest in Wright and his work since his death in 1959 (see Fig. 6.8). Most Madisonians were aware of their connection to Wright but in a curiously detached way. With Taliesin so close, with so many Wright buildings scattered around the city, and with Wright articles so commonplace in local publications, the architect's great posthumous ascent was like a stop sign along a road you drive every day: you know it's there, but you give it little attention.

Although the Elvehjem exhibit heightened interest in Wright's work and even in Monona Terrace, it failed to divert attention from the official Nolen Terrace Convention Center project. In fact, by the fall of 1988 Nolen Terrace dominated headlines, and its developer was positioning it as the "descendent of Frank Lloyd Wright's lost vision of a lakefront civic center." Betty Scott's group continued to meet for several months, and Phil Ball, the most outspoken opponent of Nolen Terrace, had persuaded Scott's group to join his No White Elephant coalition.

Consequently, for the rest of the campaign the pro-Wright voice was scarcely heard and, when it was, Phil Ball did the talking.[41]

Meanwhile, Carley was quietly pursuing the Monona Terrace concept. Sometime in the fall of 1988 he asked Orville "Bud" Arnold (see Fig. 6.2), the president of Arnold and O'Sheridan, a large midwestern civil engineering company, for his help. Arnold was a friend, a resident of the same downtown luxury condominium complex, and a longtime consultant for Carley's real estate developments. Carley wanted to get Arnold's engineering assessment of the Wright plan. Carley also wanted to get Taliesin architects involved. In November 1988, not long after the Elvehjem exhibit closed, Carley and Arnold met with Montooth and another senior Taliesin architect, Tony Puttnam, to determine whether the Monona Terrace plans could work. The two architects unrolled the big set of plans in Wright's old studio, and the four men began poring over the sheets, measuring distances and comparing them with the recent consultant's recommendations. After several hours they concluded that the 1959 plan could easily accommodate the big exhibit hall, the ballroom–dining room combination, and meeting rooms required of a modern convention center. However, they all realized that having enough gross square footage was but the first of many feasibility tests the building would have to pass. Montooth and Puttnam agreed to do further feasibility work, depending on what voters did in the upcoming April 1989 referendum.[42]

The defeat of Nolen Terrace and the victory of Paul Soglin changed everything. Throughout the campaign Soglin said he was in favor of a convention center but opposed to Nolen Terrace. But what convention center *would* the new mayor support? Eight days after his election Soglin met with the board of Downtown

FIGURE 6.8

## Wright's Posthumous Popularity

Wright enjoyed unprecedented fame while he was alive, but forty years after his death he is arguably better known and more widely appreciated. Five factors explain this phenomenon:

### THE EXTRAORDINARY BREADTH OF HIS WORK

During his sixty-six-year independent practice Wright designed houses, hotels, office buildings, barns, country clubs, civic centers, schools, museums, factories, churches, auditoriums, bridges, and a new type of low-density city. Wright also designed lamps, art glass, furniture, carpeting, posters, textiles, murals, and even sculpture.

### HIS PROLIFIC OUTPUT

Wright archivist Bruce Pfeiffer has documented nearly twelve hundred designs and six hundred published and unpublished manuscripts.

### HIS EXUBERANT CREATIVITY, KEEN EYE FOR BEAUTY, AND ABILITY TO VISUALIZE SPACE

Few human beings have been endowed with such a fertile imagination, respect for nature, and dazzling ability to design buildings in his mind before committing them to paper.

### HIS VISIONARY IDEAS

Early in his career Wright developed his now-famous organic design philosophy, an architectural forerunner of today's ecology movement. Integrate the building with its natural environment was the architect's credo. Wright also demonstrated a lifelong interest in new technologies, in new materials such as steel and concrete, and sought ways to blend them with traditional materials and technologies to create new styles and new solutions. Wright's goal was to improve the human condition by creating beautiful spirit-lifting buildings.

### HIS FASCINATING LIFE AND PERSONALITY

Wright's personality, idiosyncrasies, controversial personal life, resilience from adversity, evolution as a designer, and achievements intrigue a growing number of people.

### EVIDENCE OF WRIGHT'S GROWING POSTHUMOUS FAME IS EVERYWHERE:

- The number of Wright books and articles has sharply increased. Today, readers can buy more than two hundred publications on Wright, including three full-length biographies. Dozens of scholarly articles appear in journals every year.

- A surge in major museum exhibitions throughout the United States, Europe, and Japan has allowed the public to see the architect's drawings and artifacts for the first time.

- Wright buildings are being restored at an unprecedented rate. According to a recent study, 20 percent of Wright's executed designs have been razed. Today, powerful new preservation organizations, such as the Frank Lloyd Wright Building Conservancy, have virtually stopped the destruction of Wright's buildings.

- More Wright buildings are accessible to the public and have become popular tourist destinations. For many years only the Guggenheim and a handful of other public buildings were open to the public. Today dozens are open, including Taliesin and Taliesin West, his Oak Park home and studio, Fallingwater, and Johnson Wax. Hundreds of thousands visit these sites every year.

- Nearly a third of Wright's extant buildings have been placed on the National Register of Historic Places and fourteen have been designated national landmarks.

- Original examples of Wright-designed furniture, art-glass lamps, and other items bring huge prices at private sales, and the market in licensed reproductions is booming.

- Wright was featured on a 1966 U.S. postage stamp, was the subject of a 1973 Simon and Garfunkel song ("So Long Frank Lloyd Wright"), and his early career was the basis for a 1993 opera *(Shining Brow)*.

No wonder the American Institute of Architects in 1991 declared Wright the most important architect of the twentieth century. As people have become more aware of the man and his work, his genius shines more clearly and brightly. Nor does the surge in Wright's popularity appear to be subsiding.

Madison, Inc. and promised to come up with a new convention center site by the end of July. People wondered how he could promise to move so quickly. Soglin didn't know either, but he was eager to try.[43]

Soon after his swearing-in, Soglin had several callers and a postcard that piqued his interest. First came council member Ricardo Gonzalez, whose district included the historic site of Monona Terrace. Gonzalez told Soglin he would be foolish not to build Frank Lloyd Wright's great civic building. The postcard came from Soglin's friend Gary Knowles, an executive with Wisconsin's Division of Tourism. It showed the Sydney Opera House (see Fig. 7.3) and carried this message: "Why don't you build the Frank Lloyd Wright Monona Terrace? It would be recognized around the world by high school students the way anyone can identify the Sydney Opera House." Soglin also heard from two activists from the 1950s crusade — Betty Scott and Geraldine Nestingen. Soglin was intrigued by the diverse constituencies of these new proponents and how they were all operating independently of one another.[44]

Then Carley and Arnold came to call. They told the new mayor that they had studied the 1959 plans, met with Taliesin architects, and that all their calculations showed that Monona Terrace could easily accommodate the rooms required by the city's convention center specifications. Soglin said he was intrigued and that he had long been interested in Frank Lloyd Wright. He explained that he had grown up in Chicago, where everybody was aware of Wright, and that for several years his family had lived in Hyde Park, just a few blocks from the Robie House, one of the architect's most famous designs. Later the Soglins had lived in Highland Park, another suburb with well-known Wright houses. Furthermore, since Soglin's move to

Madison in 1962, Taliesin had been one of his favorite places to take out-of-town guests.

Because Soglin had great confidence in the professional abilities of Carley and Arnold, he encouraged them to quietly proceed with additional feasibility studies. Soglin emphasized that he wanted no public attention drawn to this concept until he was absolutely sure it would work. But, as he later explained, he was already mightily attracted to the concept.

In mid-May 1989 Soglin flew to St. Paul, Minnesota, with a group of prominent civic leaders to study how that city's business community had led a downtown renaissance. On that trip Soglin reconnected with George Nelson. The two men had worked closely together in the 1970s to build the Madison Civic Center (see Chapter 5). While out of office and practicing law, Soglin had maintained a relatively low civic profile. In the intervening decade Nelson had reinvented himself as a television executive and, like Soglin, had been relatively inactive in the civic arena. Ironically, the same year that Soglin was elected mayor, Nelson was elected once again to the Chamber of Commerce board. Its conservative members were persuaded that Soglin would lose the 1989 election. When he won, they once again turned to George Nelson to serve as their emissary because of the special relationship he had established with the mayor in the 1970s. It was just like old times.[45]

As they walked through downtown St. Paul's revitalization projects, Nelson and Soglin talked expansively about opportunities to work together when they returned. Uppermost in their minds was the convention center. Both thought the center should have the highest priority, and both thought Madison should aggressively explore Frank Lloyd Wright's Monona Terrace plan. By the time they landed back in Madison, Soglin and Nelson (see Fig. 6.9) had teamed up once more. First, Soglin

FIGURE 6.9

## GEORGE NELSON
### PROJECT PILOT

Courtesy Wisconsin State Journal

George Nelson was sitting in a meeting room on the top floor of the Inn on the Park in downtown Madison, looking out at the magnificent capitol across the street. "Things have been kind of strange," he said, reflecting on his role as a third-generation Madisonian and the head of the Monona Terrace Commission. "My grandfather did the concrete work on the capitol as an immigrant from Denmark, and my dad for various reasons was against the Frank Lloyd Wright thing.... And here I come along.... Where my grandfather did it with his hands, I did it just by putting things together." With obvious emotion in his voice, Nelson added, "This was the chance of our generation to pay a debt that it owed its greatest son, the greatest architect of the century, and we finally paid that debt."

After getting a business degree from the University of Wisconsin, Nelson went immediately into banking and in 1966, at age twenty-eight, became executive vice president of First Wisconsin National Bank. When the twenty-seven-year-old Soglin was elected Madison mayor in 1973, the Chamber of Commerce board selected Nelson, by virtue of his age, to be their envoy with the liberal new mayor. The two very different men found that they could work together and did so in the development of the Madison downtown cultural center. (That story is told in Chapter 5.) Then for a decade their paths diverged, only to come together again in 1989. By this time Nelson had become a vice president for a communications company that owned television stations and newspapers.

As chairman of the Monona Terrace Commission, Nelson had a large and difficult role and he handled it with a refreshing blend of humor, passion, and equanimity. "The biggest role I played in this whole commission thing," he insisted, "was to get out of the way and let some really great people voice their opinions and then come up with a consensus."

would convene a small convention center task force to define the issues, and then he would appoint a larger, more representative body.[46]

Just two weeks later, on June 1, 1989, Soglin's Convention Center Task Force held its first meeting. Soglin selected fifteen people, including representatives of business, labor, Dane County, and the University of Wisconsin. That he picked Nelson to chair it surprised no one. The new mayor told his appointees that "bringing additional convention and meeting facilities to the downtown is one of my top priorities as Mayor" and that he wanted them to recommend "what actions should be taken to provide appropriate convention facilities." Soglin was not proposing a leisurely stroll; he said he wanted their report by the end of July and suggested that they meet weekly to meet this deadline.[47]

Bud Arnold, meanwhile, planned a secret trip to Taliesin for twelve Madison, Dane County, and state leaders. The group included Soglin; Jim Klauser, a powerful member of Governor Thompson's cabinet; Erdman, the governor's Taliesin commission chairman (and the man who had sacrificed his dump truck to help build Wright's Unitarian church in 1949); Jim Burgess, publisher of the *Wisconsin State Journal*; Zweifel, editor of the *Capital Times*; Clayton Dunn, manager of the Dane County Exposition Center, a complex that included the Memorial Coliseum; George Austin, director of the city Department of Planning and Development; Anne Monks, assistant to Soglin; David Mollenhoff, president of Downtown Madison, Inc.; Carley; Arnold; and George Nelson. The trip had two purposes: to inspect Puttnam's first schematic drawings for adapting the 1959 Monona Terrace plan for a convention center and to determine whether this group of government and private-sector leaders was willing to cooperate to pull it off.[48]

At 2:30 P.M. on July 12, 1989, all these leaders save Carley (who drove out later in the day) rendezvoused in the parking lot of the Hilldale Shopping Center where they boarded a small chartered bus for Taliesin. Going out, nobody talked much. Hopes were high, but so were suspicions and skepticism. Could Madison's two archrival newspapers agree to support a Frank Lloyd Wright project? Except for a fleeting agreement on the concept in 1987, the newspapers had consumed barrels of ink battling each other on this very issue. Would the county help underwrite the project even though it was building a 100,000-square-foot addition to its exhibit hall at the Expo Center, just two miles from the Monona Terrace site? Historically, the thermostat of the city-county relationship hovered around cool. Could some way be found for the state to pay for part of the project without riling legislators from other cities? No one knew. But this much was clear: if the people on this bus were persuaded that adapting Wright's Monona Terrace was the way to go, their collective clout would be formidable.

Puttnam ushered everyone into Wright's spacious light-suffused studio adjoining the residence. Although his desk and office paraphernalia had been removed years earlier, the room retained the serenity and beauty that Wright's guests often mentioned. Outside the studio, flower gardens created a color-splashed foreground for the gentle green hill rising above Taliesin. Except for the gurgle of the courtyard fountain and intermittent warble of songbirds, everything was country quiet. It was a lovely July day.

The delegation sat in a semicircle around three easels. The shy, soft-spoken Puttnam (see Fig. 6.10) showed floor plans as well as a cross-section of how the 1959 plan could be adapted to satisfy the new convention center specifications. He said the first

floor could house the forty-thousand-square-foot exhibit hall, the second floor could provide space for meeting rooms, and the third floor could be the grand ballroom. Using an aerial rendering, Puttnam showed how Wright's roof-garden design would be preserved and how a 650-car parking garage could be built over the railroad tracks. Most important, he said these interior changes could be made without altering the exterior of the building. That, of course, was what the group wanted to hear. They got something else too: Puttnam's calculations in a packet entitled "Tentative Space Allotment," the cover of which bore the distinctive Taliesin red square logo.[49]

Questions followed questions. During the discussion period William Wesley Peters walked through and greeted the group. The years had added a slight stoop to his tall frame, but Peters, now seventy-seven, maintained his proud bearing. Peters had fought by Wright's side for twenty-one years to get Monona Terrace built, and for another seven years in the 1960s and 1970s he tried to get Madison to build the Monona Basin plan. Could this group resurrect Wright's last Monona Terrace design as a convention center? Judging from the quizzical, almost pained look on his face, that question was surely on his mind.

Following a tour of the grounds and a convivial buffet supper at the nearby Wright-designed Spring Green Restaurant (now the Taliesin Visitor Center), the leaders boarded the bus for their trip back to Madison. The mood on the bus back to Madison was totally different from the trip out. Everybody was talking with everybody. There was kidding, joking, enthusiasm. The feeling was, We can do this — now let's go back to Madison and figure out *how*![50]

Nelson's Convention Center Task Force sent its report to Soglin at the end of July, just two weeks after the memorable Taliesin trip. The report was a

## TONY PUTTNAM
### CHIEF ARCHITECT

Courtesy Tony Puttnam

Tony Puttnam, principal-in-charge and design architect of Monona Terrace, arrived at Taliesin in the summer of 1953. He was just nineteen, had finished his freshman year at an Illinois college, and had been invited to the famous residence and architectural school by Wright's daughter, Iovanna. The two met after she and other members of the Taliesin Fellowship gave a presentation in Chicago. To Puttnam seeing the Taliesin complex for the first time was overwhelming. "I was like someone who had never heard music before and then suddenly heard a symphony." After getting Wright's permission, Puttnam spent the summer at the famous school.

When Puttnam's Chicago draft board heard about his Taliesin address, its members threatened to draft the young man for the Korean War. Though blatantly illegal, the threat was rooted in an old grudge: a relative of a draft board member had sold Wright a piano and never got all his money.

Puttnam went back to college in Illinois in the fall of 1953, but in January 1954 he decided to return to Taliesin to become an apprentice. His first job was helping to build the elaborate Monona Terrace model (see Fig. 4.16). Puttnam continued as a Wright apprentice until 1957 when his father, an army brigadier general, insisted that his son withdraw from Taliesin. The general had heard disturbing things about Wright and did not want his son to have any further association with the man or his school. Puttnam's father tried to get the young man into a New York national guard unit. But Puttnam could not pass the eye exam so he stayed in New York City, doing interior design work for an architectural firm.

In 1960 Puttnam heard about the glut of work on Taliesin drawing boards and decided to return, this time permanently. Madison had just approved final preliminary plans for Monona Terrace, and Puttnam was assigned to do construction drawings for the huge project. His initials appear on about a quarter of the architectural plans for the job. From then on Puttnam understood the intricacies of Monona Terrace better than anyone at Taliesin.

In 1989, thirty-five years after he worked on the model as an apprentice and twenty-nine years after he had done working drawings for another version of the project, a small group of Madison civic leaders became intrigued by the possibility of adapting Wright's plans for a convention center. Puttnam got the job of determining whether this transformation was possible. His positive verdict led to his spending most of his time from 1990 to 1997 guiding the massive project through a perilous gauntlet of challenges. Ryc Loope, managing principal at Taliesin Architects, credits Puttnam's quiet credibility and unerring eye for Wright's style for breathing new life into one of the architect's masterpieces.

remarkably accurate template for what would follow, but it had to be read on two levels. The words *Frank Lloyd Wright* and *Monona Terrace* never appeared in the report; instead, the Nelson group urged that a "first class convention center designed to reflect [Madison's] unique geography and history" be built, a facility that would allow the city to "seize this historic opportunity" to create a "destination point facility." But to those who participated in the secret Taliesin trip, the meaning of these phrases was perfectly clear. To everyone else, the report sounded generic and a little high-minded. To make sure that there was plenty of money, the task force said the city should budget $160 per square foot — the upper end of convention center costs. The report recommended that Madison taxpayers contribute $11 million to the center's costs, that the private sector contribute $2.2 million, that the state contribute by building the parking ramp, and that Dane County become "an essential ingredient." To Soglin and Nelson, everything was proceeding according to the plan they had hatched in St. Paul.[51]

In the summer and fall of 1989 Burgess, publisher of the *Journal* and the most outspoken proponent of Nolen Terrace within the business community, formed a new organization of Madison CEOs to push the Wright project — but quietly and behind the scenes. Burgess headed the new organization, and his first priority was to persuade Dane County Executive Rick Phelps to make a financial commitment to the project. This new group reasoned that county support was the logical first step in assembling a center funding package. Between November 1989 and May 1990 the group met with Phelps four times to encourage him to make a financial commitment, but he refused, even after he was reelected by a landslide in April 1990. Phelps feared that anything more than a conceptual approval would provoke many rural and conservative county board members to brand the convention center as a "city" project and line up against it. Consequently, all he would agree to do was support the concept and say that it would not compete with the Expo Center. In May 1990 Burgess's CEO group and Soglin decided they could wait no longer. They would proceed without a financial commitment from the county.[52]

What a remarkable path the convention center concept had taken since 1985. The concept had gripped the community like few others in recent times and involved a remarkable blend of movers and shakers, a small band of poorly organized Wright enthusiasts, and still others who worked independently, often behind the scenes, to secure a modern convention center in downtown Madison. Although they followed different paths through the civic forest, they all emerged in the same clearing. It was a huge, oak-paneled room in the Madison Municipal Building on June 27, 1990. Mayor Paul Soglin was conducting a press conference.

## THE MONONA
## TERRACE COMMISSION

Initial public reaction to the press conference a few weeks later exceeded Soglin's wildest expectations. His mayoral mailbox was jammed with postcards and letters from across the political spectrum, all congratulating him on his bold stand. A few even sent money. Never during his seven years as mayor had Soglin seen anything like this warm outpouring of support. Predictably, some older Madisonians like Carroll Metzner were unhappy. Said Metzner, "I never dreamed that Frankenstein would stick his hand out of the grave."[53]

To the savvy Soglin, all this applause was reassuring. But he also knew the convention center caravan had to cross a whole continent of issues before it reached its destination. Could a redesigned Wright building satisfy discerning convention managers? Could the interior of the building be redesigned without losing the authentic Wright qualities? What would it cost to build and operate? Could Madison afford it? Could the private sector and county and state government be persuaded to make large contributions? Could Madison voters be persuaded to approve a building that was guaranteed to induce sticker shock? Who should run the center? These industrial-strength questions and many more demanded answers.

Soglin was especially eager to avoid the procedural flaws that had marred the Nolen Terrace process: allowing DMI and developers to define the project; not making an aggressive effort to secure funding from the private sector, the county, and the state; not knowing what the operating subsidy would be; not having the total funding package worked out, and several other problems. To Soglin the Nolen Terrace recipe was flawed; he thought he could do better.

At the same time he recognized that building a convention center was one of the most difficult tasks he would ever undertake, analogous to a civic soufflé. To be successful he had to assemble all the right ingredients, mix them together in just the right amounts in a perfectly shaped dish, and bake the mixture at the right temperature for exactly the right time. Open the oven door too early and the delicate air-filled confection would collapse. Insiders began to wonder whether Soglin would succeed in making this disaster-prone recipe on his first try.

To succeed, the mayor concluded that he would have to form a relatively large and representative citizen commission, give it plenty of time to complete rigorous feasibility studies and a relatively large budget for consultants, and make extensive use of the city's talented staff. At the same time the city's leaders would have to make aggressive efforts to get the county, state, and private sector to make large contributions to the center. And, in the end, they still had to persuade a majority of citizens to vote for the center in a referendum. The risk was huge.

The common council authorized the Monona Terrace Commission in August 1990. It would have twenty-eight members, a budget of $100,000, and a mandate to report back to the council in July 1991. The commission was charged with overseeing design and financing questions relating to the adaptation of "Frank Lloyd Wright plans to build a convention center on the Lake Monona Basin."[54]

Picking the right people for the Monona Terrace Commission required exquisite judgment. Naturally, Soglin wanted Nelson to chair it and of course he accepted. The commission members Soglin chose were mostly strong-willed independent thinkers with very different agendas. Some were downright critical of the concept and Frank Lloyd Wright. They came from labor, business, the three levels of government (city, county, and state), and the University of Wisconsin, and included Otto Festge, the former Madison mayor. A complete list of members appears in Appendix B.[55]

Soglin's political sagacity was nowhere more evident than in his decision to create two committees, one for finance and another for physical planning, and to select a liberal and a conservative to co-chair each committee (see Fig. 6.11).

From the first meeting of the commission in September 1990 it was evident that great care had gone into designing the process. Commissioners received a crash course on Madison convention center history, committee structure, and work allocation. At the October meeting city planning

FIGURE 6.11

**Monona Terrace Committee Co-Chairs**

*Courtesy Don Kerkhof*

W. Jerome Frautschi, president of Webcrafters, Inc., a prominent midwestern printing company, and Mary Lou Munts, the former chair of the Wisconsin Public Service Commission and member of the Wisconsin Assembly, seldom worked together on civic projects. That was because Frautschi was a Republican and Munts was a Democrat. Similarly, Don Helfrecht, chairman and CEO of the Madison Gas and Electric Company, and Henry Lufler, associate dean of the U.W.–Madison School of Education and former council member, were also poles apart politically. But the two pairs worked closely for nearly two years to make Monona Terrace a reality. Frautschi and Munts co-chaired the commission's finance committee, and Helfrecht and Lufler chaired the physical planning committee. To have two people at opposite ends of the political spectrum co-chair the same committee was a deliberate strategy of Mayor Paul Soglin's to ensure that the commission product would have the greatest appeal to the most people. The "yoking" concept proved very successful.

director George Austin passed out a detailed diagram showing exactly what had to be done, by whom, and when — for the next four years. The diagram covered commission actions, the complex permitting process, design, and construction. By the November meeting committee co-chairs were giving meaty progress reports on key issues. The momentum was palpable. Decision by decision, the commission passed milestones along its complex itinerary.[56]

## MILESTONES OF TERRACE DESIGN

Don Helfrecht and Henry Lufler led their physical planning committee on a remarkably brisk run through some rigorous terrain that included feasibility, authenticity, development of detailed schematics, maintenance of lake views, what to do about a hotel, the need for a consulting architect, and the nettlesome question of environmental impact.

*Feasibility and authenticity.* The physical planning committee faced two immediate tests: could the 1959 plan be successfully adapted for a modern convention center, and, if so, would it retain its Wrightian authenticity? If the center failed to pass these two tests, the show was over. That was why the commission directed Taliesin architect Puttnam to answer these questions and to report back in December. Although Puttnam had said at the June press conference that the Wright design could be adapted, he emphasized that his preliminary drawings did not take several factors into account: the latest building codes, efficient internal circulation patterns, and structural requirements. However, after taking these factors into account, Puttnam told commissioners at the December meeting with "genuine pleasure and enthusiasm" that the 1959 design will "operate

effectively" as a convention center and "maintain the integrity of ... Wright's concept."[57]

*Schematic plans.* Puttnam's next step was to develop what architects call schematics, that is, floor-by-floor drawings, elevations, cross-sections, mechanical and structural drawings, and preliminary written specifications. These drawings, the most detailed done up to that time, were presented to the commission in July 1991 and functioned as the official center plans until the summer of 1993.

*The size of the building.* Puttnam's drawings for the 1990 press conference showed a building of just 200,000 square feet. By the time he finished his detailed schematic drawings in June 1991, Monona Terrace had grown to 250,000 square feet for three reasons. First, the commission was persuaded that the convention center would eventually need an addition, so it increased the size during the initial design while staying within the dock line and the distinctive Wrightian footprint. Second, modern heating and air-conditioning systems require much more space than they did in Wright's day. Third, convention center managers urged commissioners to provide more space for storage, truck handling, and employee accommodations than the official city specifications called for.[58]

*The view of Lake Monona.* From the time Wright first proposed his Olin Terraces in 1938, critics said the building would block the splendid view of Lake Monona from now Martin Luther King Jr. Boulevard (the name had been changed from Monona Avenue in 1987). Predictably, this objection was raised again by commission members and others (see Fig. 6.12). Two factors legislated against the preservation of the lake view: the minimum ceiling heights required by modern convention centers (thirty feet for exhibit halls and fifteen feet for banquet halls, ballrooms, and meeting rooms); and the height of the thick trusses needed to handle long spans. These two factors meant the building had to be about sixty-eight feet tall, more than enough to block the lake view. Then, a majority of the commissioners directed Puttnam to design an obvious building entrance that would make an "architectural statement" at the end of the avenue. Why have a glorious Frank Lloyd Wright building if you can't even tell it's there, they argued.[59]

*Excluding the hotel.* Almost all meeting planners who schedule conventions in northern states agree that a hotel immediately adjacent to the center is a prerequisite. This posed a cruel dilemma for Monona Terrace planners because studies showed that in Madison's soft downtown hotel market, building a contiguous headquarters hotel would probably put one and perhaps two older hotels out of business. No one wanted to inflict such economic pain. The commission did, however, hire a national hotel consultant to determine when the downtown Madison market might support a new convention center hotel without jeopardizing existing hotels. The answer was that this was unlikely to happen for about three years after the center's completion, which led the commission to recommend that the hotel not be built at the same time as the center.[60]

*A local consulting architect.* Monona Terrace was an unusually complex building; it required more than five hundred large and detailed drawings in a very short period of time. This was more than Taliesin Architects could handle in the time available, so the commission selected Potter Lawson Architects, one of the largest and oldest architectural firms in Madison, to take on this job. Potter Lawson had the extra drafting room horsepower and extensive experience with large projects. The agreement between the two firms was that Taliesin Architects would provide the overall design and detailed interior

FIGURE 6.12

**The Whoops View of Lake Monona**

© City of Madison, rendering by Anderson Illustration Associates

This artist's rendering, "View of Monona Terrace from Wilson Street," was "willfully doctored" to deceive the public into voting for Monona Terrace. That was the charge of Ron Shutvet, a Madison engineer who worked closely with lawyer Ann Fleischli to try to kill the project, in February 1993. Shutvet rented surveying equipment to prove that the sliver of blue water visible over the center roof was nothing but a figment of the artist's imagination. Shutvet alleged that nobody would be able to see Lake Monona from *anywhere* along Wilson Street or Martin Luther King Jr. Boulevard. A few days later city officials conceded that he was correct but denied that it was a deliberate deception. The artist, they explained, had done the drawing before the exact dimensions of the building were known.

The embarrassing admission resurrected a criticism that dogged Monona Terrace from its inception, namely, that it would block the lake view at the end of King Boulevard.

drawings and that Potter would do the detailed exterior drawings. All these agreements and many more were incorporated in the architectural contract signed in March 1991.[61]

*Environmental impact statement.* Wisconsin requires an environmental impact statement (EIS) for state but not for city projects. Thus, the state, which agreed to pick up the tab for the parking ramp, had to prepare an EIS, but the city was not legally obligated to prepare an EIS for the convention center. However, given the high visibility and political volatility of this project, the city asked that the entire project be included in the state-prepared EIS. To make sure that all the right questions were asked, the city even established a "scoping" committee composed of local environmentalists. This group prepared a comprehensive survey of all pertinent

issues and gave it to the independent contractor hired by the state. The draft EIS was not completed until October 1992, just a few weeks before the referendum.[62]

MILEPOSTS OF TERRACE FINANCING

No one envied the job of the finance committee. It included determining actual construction costs, preparing a detailed operating statement, analyzing economic benefits, determining who should pay what share of building costs and where that money would come from, distilling everything into a financing plan for voters, and getting sufficient funding from the private sector and other units of government.

*Building costs.* The first question in everyone's mind was how much Monona Terrace would cost. And everyone wanted this answer as soon as possible.

Curt Hastings, president of J. H. Findorff and Son, Inc., Madison's largest and oldest contractor, delivered the information to the commission in July 1991. Hastings, a widely recognized wizard at projecting accurate construction costs, said the project would run $63.5 million, including site development, railroad right-of-way acquisition, and all fees. The basis for his calculation was the set of schematics prepared by Puttnam in early 1991. For the first time in the history of the Monona Terrace project, realistic construction cost estimates were available at the beginning of the planning process. The finance committee wisely included an inflation factor in all its calculations.[63]

*Operating costs.* One of the most controversial components of the 1989 Nolen Terrace effort was the accuracy and inclusiveness of projected operating costs. Monona Terrace Commissioners therefore went to great lengths to assemble hard, defensible numbers. They concluded that the center would require a subsidy of about $650,000 per year.[64]

*Economic benefits.* What exactly are the economic benefits of a convention center and who gets them? This question was never really answered for Nolen Terrace, but two studies done for the Monona Terrace Commission filled the gap with rigor. Both were done by Kerry Vandell, chairman of the Department of Real Estate and Urban Land Economics at the University of Wisconsin School of Business. Vandell and his associate, James Shilling, showed not only cost-benefit ratios of the project to be exceptionally favorable but exactly who got what benefits and in what amount. For the first time Vandell provided a detailed breakdown showing how quantified benefits flowed to Madison businesses, city, county, and state government, and to the residents of Madison, Dane County, and beyond. Their complex analysis showed how the

center would affect the number and nature of jobs, new downtown real estate development, real estate values, sales and income taxes, and how all these factors would boost the entire local economy. Critics tried to discredit Vandell's work, but his methodology withstood all assaults.

Most important, Vandell's research documented the magnitude of economic ripples emanating from Monona Terrace and gave proponents the compelling data they needed to persuade the state, county, and private sector to contribute. The studies showed that Monona Terrace would generate $20 million in new annual convention business and, given the multiplier effect, would boost the economy by $479 million over a twenty-year period; create seven hundred permanent jobs, most of which would pay more than $25,000 per year; generate "$67.3 million in new construction and property value appreciation," which would actually lower taxes on a typical Madison home by $7 to $12 per year; send 14 percent of new convention-related business into the pockets of county residents and businesses and 32 percent to residents and businesses outside of Dane County; and generate $12 million in new sales and income taxes each year for the state and $15 million in new hotel room taxes for Madison.[65]

*Wooing financial partners.* The most obvious lesson of Nolen Terrace was the inability of Madison to pay for the center alone. By July 1991 the commission had determined that Madison could afford to contribute $30 million to $37 million toward the $63.5 million building and that the rest would have to come from the private sector, Dane County, and the state. A national fund-raising consultant estimated that the private sector would contribute $8 million to $12 million, leaving $14 million to $27 million to be covered by the county and the state. The assumption was that the city would wait until after the referendum to try once more to secure financing from the county.[66]

Center proponents realized that they needed someone to make a big pump-priming commitment to Monona Terrace. Commission chairman Nelson and finance committee co-chairs Frautschi and Munts took on the challenge. They first approached the Evjue Foundation, the charitable arm of the *Capital Times*. Bill Evjue, the paper's longtime editor and publisher, had been a resolute supporter of Monona Terrace in the 1950s and 1960s, and the foundation was one of Madison's largest. As Nelson and Frautschi talked about what to ask for, Frautschi thought that $3 million over ten years was about right, but Nelson thought that was crazy. Nelson, Frautschi, and Puttnam, joined by city planning director Austin and principal planner John Urich, made a special presentation to the Evjue trustees in Wright's Taliesin studio, where the architect and Evjue had often met. On September 27, 1991, the Evjue Foundation announced a stunning $3 million grant, the largest in its twenty-one-year history. Fred Miller, the publisher of the *Capital Times*, explained, "If there was anything Mr. Evjue would want, he would want [Monona Terrace] above everything else."[67]

Just a month later Governor Thompson announced that the state would contribute $21.3 million to the project. The governor explained that he was recommending that the state pick up the tab for the $15.1 million, six-hundred-car parking garage, $3.1 million in improvements for John Nolen Drive, and $3 million for park improvements. Thompson was sold on Monona Terrace. He told reporters that the center would be "a living monument to [Wright's] genius" and "an incredible asset to our state."[68] (The state contribution was later reported as $18.1 million. The $3 million set aside for John Nolen Drive was subtracted because that project was already scheduled.)

Thompson had special reasons for being enthusiastic about Wright's design (see Fig. 6.13). In 1987, just a year after he was elected governor, Thompson led a trade mission to Japan. He was regaling 150 Japanese businesspeople in Tokyo about the glories of Wisconsin cheese and beer, but the eyes of most in the audience were closed. Thompson thought they were asleep, but in fact they were practicing a common Japanese technique for focusing concentration. But then the governor began talking about Frank Lloyd Wright, his famous Imperial Hotel, how it had withstood the 1923 earthquake, and how Wright's home was just forty miles west of Madison. Suddenly, the people in the audience raised their heads, established eye contact, and came alive. It "was the one thing during my speech that had an immediate reaction," recalled the governor. "From that moment on, I realized I had something." Frank Lloyd Wright, the governor quickly learned, was practically a household name in Japan.[69]

Soon after he returned to Wisconsin, Thompson had a unlikely caller. It was card-carrying Democrat Marshall Erdman, whose associations with Wright were well known. Erdman had met with Thompson's four Democratic predecessors to try to persuade them to restore Taliesin. But, as Erdman told the Republican governor, "They all turned me down so I'm sure you will do the same. [But] I wanted to come in and make my pitch." To Erdman's astonishment Thompson said he thought that restoring Taliesin was a good idea. From that day on the two developed what the governor called "a very close relationship." Moreover, the governor and his wife, Sue Ann, became close to members of the Taliesin Fellowship.[70]

George Nelson knew about Thompson's support for the restoration of Taliesin, but he did not know whether the governor would be willing to underwrite a large part of the Terrace costs required by the commission's financing plan. To find out, he scheduled a meeting with Jim Klauser, the governor's closest

associate and alter ego. In preparation for that December 1990 meeting Nelson made a list of twenty-five reasons why the state should support the project. Nelson, accompanied by Soglin and Austin, reminded the powerful official that they were there to explore possibilities for state support of Monona Terrace and was about to launch into his twenty-five reasons when Klauser said, "Oh, yes, we'll provide the parking and as much infrastructure as we can. You know Tommy wants this to happen. We'll put in somewhere around $15 million. You can count on us." Nelson could hardly believe it, but Klauser wasn't finished: "Now people come to Madison to do business with the state and they get lost. But when this new parking ramp is built, they can drive into town, park in the ramp, conduct their business, and have a good feeling about the state." George Nelson, Mr. Salesman, hardly knew what to do next. The deal was closed before he could mention a single reason on his list. "That was when it first hit me that Monona Terrace could really happen," Nelson recalled.[71]

As impressive as the Evjue grant and the state commitment were, more was in the offing. In February 1992 Mary Lou Munts and George Nelson made a presentation to the Madison Community Foundation in which they stressed the project's community-serving functions; the foundation's board of governors responded with a $1 million grant, the largest in its history. Jim Holt, board chairman, explained the action this way: "Our basic mission is to enhance the lives of all citizens of Dane County and we believe the Frank Lloyd Wright–inspired convention center will do just that."[72]

In just five months the governor had promised to pay nearly one-third of the project's costs, and two public-spirited Madison foundations had pledged to

FIGURE 6.13

## TOMMY THOMPSON
### *EARLY PROJECT CATALYST*

*Courtesy* Wisconsin State Journal

If political affinity were the criterion, Governor Tommy Thompson should never have lifted a finger to help Frank Lloyd Wright. After all, Thompson was a Republican, and Wright was to the left of most Democrats. But to Thompson that was not the point. Wright was arguably the most famous person ever born in Wisconsin; his famous home, Taliesin, was listed on the National Register of Historic Places and was even an international tourist destination. To Thompson, Wright was a state treasure, which was why the governor was eager to do so much for the controversial architect. In 1988 Thompson created the Commission on Taliesin to restore the complex, and in 1992 he offered $18 million from state coffers to help build Monona Terrace.

Thompson received his undergraduate and law degrees from the University of Wisconsin in 1963 and 1966, respectively, and was first elected to the Wisconsin Assembly the year he graduated from law school. Thompson won his first term as governor in 1986 and was elected to an unprecedented fourth four-year term in 1998.

FIGURE 6.14

**The Evjue Gardens**

© City of Madison, rendering by Anderson Illustration Associates

One of the most wonderful spaces at Monona Terrace is the dramatic rooftop known as Evjue Gardens, shown in this rendering. The sixty-eight-thousand-square-foot gardens, named to honor the long close relationship between Frank Lloyd Wright and William T. Evjue, founder and publisher of the *Capital Times* (see Fig. 4.9), were made possible by an unprecedented $3 million grant from the Evjue Foundation, the newspaper's charitable arm.

contribute half of the total needed from the private sector. Nelson, Frautschi, and Munts were thrilled. Maybe, more began to say, this project really can be done.

THE COMMISSION'S MARKETING STRATEGIES

The commission had one other important but unofficial function: marketing. Commission planners had four strategies.

*Early community education.* At its first meeting the commission committed itself to an aggressive community marketing program. The initial goal was to create a speakers' bureau and a twenty-minute color video promoting the Monona Terrace concept. The video's soothing music, lyrical narrative, and superb mix of fresh footage and old renderings tugged the heart and nudged the mind. Nelson called the video a "stroke of genius" because it got the story of Frank Lloyd Wright's Monona Terrace out into the community early in

the process, communicated key facts, and conveyed its excitement.[73]

*Emphasis on community use.* Early on, most Madisonians thought that a convention center was an exclusive club for out-of-towners. To allow citizens to take this mistaken opinion into the voting booth would have doomed the project, so commissioners moved to counteract this view. First, citing national usage trends, center backers told residents that families would use the center for weddings, high school proms, and anniversaries and that organizations would use it for fund-drive kickoffs, retirement dinners, and awards banquets. The commission hired consultants to study the amount of local usage and learned that about 20 percent of all meetings held in Madison each year would transfer to Monona Terrace. Second, the commission adopted the phrase "a public place by Frank Lloyd Wright" on most of its marketing documents. Third, the commission officially named

the building the Monona Terrace *Community* and Convention Center. Finally, they directed a well-known illustrator to prepare a set of renderings so that people could more easily visualize the building and its many dramatic spaces, such as the Evjue Gardens (see Fig. 6.14). Other renderings in this series appear in Figures 6.1 and 6.12.[74]

*Emphasis on benefits.* Center boosters understood that voters did not understand what the project would do for Madison and that if they failed to convey these benefits clearly and forcefully, the referendum would fail. That was why the commission secured the Vandell studies noted earlier and why its marketing drums kept beating "benefits, benefits, benefits."

*Use of credible third parties.* Planners recognized that the commission's credibility required that key project data be provided by independent and objective third parties of widely recognized expertise. That was why the authorizing resolution gave the commission $100,000 for consultants. The commission used this budget to validate construction cost estimates, determine economic effects, calculate the amount of money that could be raised from the private sector, and illuminate dark corners of local understanding.[75]

TURNING IN THEIR ASSIGNMENT

When Soglin approached people to serve on the commission, he told them the job would be over in less than a year. He was wrong. When the authorizing resolution expired in August 1991, the commission had made great progress, but its work was far from over. Several critically important finance and usage issues remained. Soglin asked everyone to reenlist and all did. If ever a group of people worked hard and stayed the course, it was the Monona Terrace commissioners. During their two years together they read hundreds of pages of documents, listened to dozens of experts, debated pros and cons, and made thoughtful decisions on a mind-numbing array of topics. Although the commissioners were some of the busiest people in town, all twenty meetings enjoyed a quorum.[76]

Finally, in September 1992 the commission met for the last time and a few days later issued its final report, a thick document summarizing how the center should be financed and operated. The commission had answered all the questions set before it and many more (see Fig. 6.15). Now everything came down to one question: would Madison voters say yes to the Monona Terrace Community and Convention Center?[77]

## MONONA TERRACE FINANCING, A SYNOPSIS

Shown here in summary form from the final report of the Terrace commission are convention center construction costs and sources of financing. All were developed by the Monona Terrace Commission and were included in its final report, released in September 1992. Note that construction cost estimates (shown in 1992 dollars) total $63.5 million but that maximum financing totals $67.1 million. The larger figure allowed for inflation.

### Summary Cost Estimates
(1992 Dollars)

| | |
|---|---|
| Convention center | $39,841,000 |
| Site development and parking ramp | 15,599,000 |
| Other development costs | 8,060,000 |
| Total estimated project cost | $63,500,000 |

### Maximum Sources of Financing

| FUNDING SOURCES | AMOUNT |
|---|---|
| State of Wisconsin | $18,100,000 |
| City TIF | 2,000,000 |
| City room tax | 15,000,000 |
| Private contributions | 8,000,000 |
| City contribution | 12,000,000 |
| County contribution | 12,000,000 |
| Total | $67,100,000 |

## THE 1992 REFERENDUM: YES MEANS BUILD IT!

Tuesday, November 3, 1992, was the day that Madison voters would decide whether Monona Terrace would be built. The challenge was clear: to convince voters who believed their property taxes were already too high to approve an increase to build the most expensive public works project in Madison history, a controversial convention center whose primary beneficiaries were presumed to be out-of-towners. The challenge was daunting even to the most ardent center proponents.

Prospects for a favorable vote were anything but good. Exactly 60 percent of voters had vetoed the Nolen Terrace project when it was submitted to referendum in 1989. And as Marjorie Colson, an opposition leader, put it, "The same voters who KO'd the 1989 convention center proposal are still out there just waiting for the thing to come up on the ballot again."[78]

Officially, the Monona Terrace campaign got underway in the spring of 1992 with the formation of two political action committees: "It's Wright for Wisconsin," urging a yes vote, and "It Ain't Wright," urging a no vote. Both groups were menageries of normally incompatible political species. "It Ain't Wright" included left-leaning political activists, just-say-no conservatives, and open space preservationists. Prominent among its leaders were Ann Fleischli, the leading convention center opponent; members of the Labor-Farm Party, an ultraleft political organization whose name reflected the constituents it sought to serve; and members of a coalition that had recently killed a proposal to build a swimming pool in a city park. Members of "It's Wright for Wisconsin" included Democrats, Republicans, labor leaders, CEOs, environmentalists, and the president

of the Madison chapter of the NAACP. Heading the group were Ken Opin, a Wisconsin Federation of Teachers official, and Mary Lou Munts.[79]

George Nelson understood that the key to victory was finding just the right field general to lead "It's Wright" volunteers into battle. Ideally, Nelson wanted someone who was intimately familiar with Madison's political anatomy, had a track record as a successful campaign strategist, and could work with the organization's diverse leadership. That spring George Nelson had breakfast with someone who fit the profile: Morris Andrews, the former head of the Wisconsin Education Association Council, the largest public employee union in the state. After he retired in April 1992, Andrews had agreed to direct the U.S. Senate campaign of candidate Russell Feingold, but even that responsibility did not fill up the seventy-hour workweek of this human dynamo. Andrews said he'd think it over, then called a few days later to accept.[80]

Andrews, a veteran of hundreds of Wisconsin campaigns, loved politics and was utterly unintimidated by the prospect of getting a majority of Madisonians to vote yes in a $67 million referendum ($63.5 million adjusted for inflation). To this savvy competitor the referendum was just another campaign, except that he was promoting a convention center. His goal was to retain the 40 percent who had voted for Nolen Terrace in 1989 and to persuade 15 percent more of the center's merits.

Andrews was well aware that a victory would require sophisticated preparation, attention to detail, and precise coordination. He was also a great believer in firsthand opinion research. For example, if he was sitting on a stool at the counter of a popular blue-collar diner he'd turn to the fellow sitting next to him and say, "Say, whaddaya think about this convention center anyway?" or "Say, what's the story on this Frank Lloyd Wright guy?" and then listen. By the time he hired Sharon Chamberlain, head of a Madison market research company, to do more sophisticated polling and opinion analysis, Andrews had concluded that people wanted three things before they would vote for the center: an absolutely guaranteed price; compelling assurances that it would not harm the environment; and proof that it would help revitalize downtown.[81]

Andrews ran political campaigns like Vince Lombardi used to coach football. He was blunt, showed no preference for the stars, and expected no one to question what he said. He told his mostly business-suited campaign committee there were "too many suits" and "not enough sneakers" selling the project. He took Nelson off the speaking circuit because he was getting too emotional. After a while everyone got the idea.

Andrews got the campaign rolling months before the election by dispatching the elegant new model of Monona Terrace (see Fig. 6.16) on a nineteen-stop tour of the city. In July, four months before the election, he sent out a you've-got-questions, we've-got-answers flyer. To make sure the campaign was working, Andrews had volunteers call all Madison voters to find out where everybody stood and concentrated the most attention on people on the fence. To win them over Andrews' volunteers sent out a topical and reassuring tract in a hand-addressed envelope. In September he brought in Eric Wright, Frank Lloyd Wright's grandson, a practicing architect and an apprentice who had worked on Monona Terrace in the 1950s, to affirm the authenticity of the convention center design.[82]

Although "It Ain't Wright" could not afford such an elaborate campaign, it compensated with ingenuity. For example, members would appear at public meetings with placards that newspaper pho-

FIGURE 6.16

**1992 Monona Terrace Model**

*Courtesy Wisconsin State Journal, photo by L. Roger Turner*

This detailed and skillfully rendered model of today's Monona Terrace was prepared in 1992 by Madison model maker Bruce Severson. The model was displayed in dozens of locations in and around Madison so that most people could see it. Like earlier models, this one allowed people to understand the complex project more easily than they could from plans and renderings.

tographers and video camera crews found as irresistible as a beer keg at a fraternity party. Fleischli and her colleagues mastered the art of sending doubt-generating zinger letters to the newspapers. For example, in August she sent a letter to the *Wisconsin State Journal*, warning readers that the center budget did not include a tunnel ventilation system and that this would cause "lethal monoxide levels" to "build up in four minutes. Happy commuting, Madison."[83]

Images of Monona Terrace as projected by the two organizations could hardly have been more different (see Figs. 6.17 and 6.18). "It's Wright for Wisconsin" painted a picture of a revitalized downtown, hundreds of new jobs, crowds of people patronizing shops and restaurants, a burst of new center-related construction, and even lower taxes in the suburbs due to increased downtown property values. "It Ain't Wright" portrayed the convention center as a superfluous civic bauble that would increase property taxes and rents, pollute Lake

Monona, poison the city water supply, destroy a beautiful park, require cutbacks in basic city services, benefit the wealthy, and produce a fake Wright building. (For a summary of the arguments advanced by both sides, see Fig. 6.19.)

In October both sides lit the fuses of their campaign finales. Pro and con forces debated the merits of their positions in public forums and traded one-liners that turned up as sound bites on radio talk shows and local news. From October 1 to November 3 the *Journal* published 100 letters to the editor and could not find space for another 450 submissions. Local papers ran pointed cartoons (see Fig. 6.20). Andrews ran a media blitz that included TV commercials featuring "ministers, grandmothers, and students." A few days before the election his phone bank called supporters to remind them of the importance of their vote. And if supporters had not voted by noon, volunteers called them again to urge them to get to the polls. Little was left to chance. Meanwhile, "It Ain't Wright" sent out brochures, targeted

## A $70 Million Convention Center?

## It Ain't Wright!

*Make the right choice for Madison's future...*

*It's up to you.*

Anti-Terrace Brochure

*Courtesy Ann Fleischli*

# WRIGHT
# FOR WISCONSIN

**July 6, 1992**

**Q: Why should we invest in the Frank Lloyd Wright Monona Terrace?**
A: Because it will create jobs and bring thousands of visitors who will spend millions of dollars here. And it will give us beautiful new park and public space we can all use and an international reputation for building perhaps the last and greatest building designed by Frank Lloyd Wright.

*World renowned architect, Wisconsin native, Frank Lloyd Wright.*

movie tickets and popcorn a year. The best estimate is that no more than $12 million in building costs spread over 20 years will be put on the property tax bill — $15 on the owner of the average ($90,700 in 1992) Madison home.

**Q: Will it require a subsidy like the Civic Center?**
A: Probably. And like the bus system and the zoo

Pro-Terrace Tabloid

*Courtesy Mary Lou Munts*

FIGURE 6.17

### Dueling Campaign Literature

From the campaign literature for the 1992 referendum one would never guess that Wright had been dead for thirty-three years. Both sides, "It's Wright for Wisconsin" and "It Ain't Wright," used the architect's picture as if he were a candidate in the middle of a fifteen-stop campaign tour.

"It's Wright for Wisconsin" mailed a four-page, full-color tabloid (see excerpt above) to all Madison households on July 6, 1992, four months before the referendum. Although it was carefully worded, it was also candid. For example, it acknowledged that the center would probably require an ongoing subsidy of about $10 per year from the average homeowner. This tabloid, based on nearly two years of research by the Monona Terrace Commission, addressed the most frequently raised questions and consistently emphasized the benefits Madison would derive from the center.

"It Ain't Wright" handed out this brochure (left) a few days before the election. It framed the referendum as a series of choices. Should Madison hire more police and firefighters or spend "at least $70 million on a show-place for conventioneers"? Should the city clean up its lakes or engage "in a project that may damage the lake and shoreline forever"?

Pro-Terrace Bumper Sticker

*Courtesy Mary Lou Munts*

## DON'T PAVE THE LAKE
### STOP MONONA TERRACE

Anti-Terrace Bumper Sticker

*Courtesy Al Matano*

FIGURE 6.18

### Battling Bumper Stickers

For most Madison political campaigns yard signs, brochures, newspaper advertisements, and sound bites are the workhorses for getting their message across. In their quest for competitive advantage both sides used bumper stickers, shown here. The pro version was distributed by "It's Wright for Wisconsin," while the con version was distributed by the local chapter of the Sierra Club.

---

several neighborhoods for door-to-door work, and did extensive public speaking.[84]

Seventy-four percent of Madison's registered voters cast ballots on two referendum questions (see Fig. 6.21) and stitched together a political crazy quilt. Fifty-three percent approved the Monona Terrace concept, and 51.2 percent voted to issue bonds for the convention center. For the second time, Frank Lloyd Wright was elected architect by Madison voters — this time posthumously. If only 1,137 more people had voted no on the critical bond question, Monona Terrace would have died again.[85]

Madison voters were not the only ones to hold a referendum on Monona Terrace. Because Dane County was being asked to make a substantial contribution, fifty-one of the sixty townships, villages, and cities in Dane County held advisory referenda. Forty-three rejected Monona Terrace. "It Ain't Wright" was fond of combining the city and county ballots to prove that the center really lost by 7,000 votes. They had a point; based on total votes cast, voters said no. The Terrace lost. But only the binding Madison vote counted.[86]

WHY TERRACE PROPONENTS WON — BARELY

The 2.4 percent plurality that Madison voters gave the bond issuance question was the political

equivalent of an unnatural act. Remember that "It Ain't Wright" held the high cards of human nature: the ace of the status quo, king of fiscal frugality, queen of fear and doubt, and jack of who-needs-it. "It's Wright" had to convince voters to make a sweeping change in the status quo, spend a breath-taking amount of money, raise taxes, take a huge risk, and prove that Monona Terrace was essential to the city's future. Anyone who thought "It's Wright" had a great hand just didn't understand this card game. Yet, in spite of these onerous odds, Terrace supporters played their weaker hand against an exceptionally strong hand and won. Eleven factors explain the victory.

FIGURE 6.19

**1992 Pro and Con Arguments**

*Courtesy* Isthmus, *photos by Greg Anderson*

Here are summaries of the most frequently heard arguments put forth by both sides of the Monona Terrace debate.

## PRO

### MORRIS ANDREWS
*CAMPAIGN WIZARD*

1. The convention industry is the only one with enough economic clout to revitalize the central business district.
2. Madison must invest in its economic development. It cannot rely on the growth of government and the University of Wisconsin to create jobs for people.
3. A convention center will expand and diversify the economy.
4. Law Park is Madison's premiere location for a convention center.
5. The center will increase lake access.
6. The center will create a new 1.5-acre rooftop park offering spectacular views of the lake and a place from which to watch water-skiing shows.
7. Conventional bridge-building construction techniques will be used for the center's foundations.
8. The exterior closely conforms to the 1959 Wright design, and the interior was redesigned by a Wright-trained architect.
9. Studies show that about 70,000 conventioneers and spouses will come to Madison each year.
10. The center will have little effect on traffic.
11. A seawall will keep bicyclists dry as they ride along the lakeside path.
12. The center will add $20 million to the economy every year, generate 40 new businesses with 700 new full-time jobs, spur $67 million in new downtown real estate development, and increase downtown's assessed valuation.
13. The city has many consultant studies that have thoroughly assessed the benefits to Madison.
14. The environmental impact statement said that the center would have no significant adverse effects.
15. Most costs of the center will be paid by the state, Dane County, the private sector, hotel room tax, and tax incremental financing.
16. Additional space would be added during construction to accommodate future growth.
17. The city made a terrible mistake by not building the project when Wright was alive. It is time to correct this mistake.
18. Area residents will make extensive use of the center for weddings, proms, bar mitzvahs, and business meetings.
19. Downtown hotels need a convention center to survive.
20. The design is gorgeous.

## CON

### ANN FLEISCHLI
*FORMIDABLE OPPONENT*

1. We don't need a convention center. Things are fine the way they are.
2. A center will divert money from more important, basic government functions. People should come before bricks
3. A center will reduce the quality of life. Libraries will close, the lake clean-up will not continue, and park maintenance will be canceled.
4. Law Park is the wrong place. It will destroy the lakeshore and remove the only remaining natural shoreline in the downtown area.
5. The convention center will reduce access to the lake.
6. The convention center will destroy green space in Law Park.
7. Subsurface conditions are not suitable for a large building.
8. The design is a fake Wright. Wright died in 1959.
9. Nobody will come when it is cold, especially between late October and early April.
10. The center will cause gridlock in the city, and lethal levels of carbon monoxide will accumulate in the tunnel.
11. When the wind is from the south, bicyclists riding along the lakeside bike bath will get splashed.
12. Proponents exaggerate the economic benefits of the center. Almost all jobs generated by the center will pay low wages.
13. We don't have all the facts.
14. The environmental impact statement was a whitewash.
15. Taxes are too high now. With government budgets scarcely able to deliver basic services, spending any money for a convention center is fiscally irresponsible.
16. The building cannot be expanded.
17. We can't afford an expensive Wright building.
18. Fat-cat capitalists will be the primary beneficiaries of the center, but workers will pay the bill. Stop "welfare for the wealthy."
19. A convention center would compete with meeting rooms in Madison-area hotels.
20. The Wright design is an eyesore.

Figure 6.20

**Stop the Lightbulb and the Convention Center**

*Courtesy John Kovalic and* Wisconsin State Journal

Madison has always been a contentious town. Its well-educated citizenry, University of Wisconsin experts on nearly everything, and beauty-driven high standards — coupled with human contrariness and honest disagreement — produced a civic personality that prefers arguing to acting. Nowhere was this more evident than in the 1992 Monona Terrace referendum campaign, captured in this cartoon that appeared in the *Wisconsin State Journal* in late October 1992.

*Unprecedented community leader consensus.* Seldom in Madison's history had so many leaders been so united about anything so controversial. This diversity was apparent in the colorful mosaic of Democrats, Republicans, conservatives, liberals, captains of industry, lieutenants of labor, antisprawl environmentalists, and ethnic minority leaders who served on the board of "It's Wright for Wisconsin." Rarely did these people socialize and seldom did they work together. For example, on the evening of November 3 George Nelson was celebrating with supporters at the Concourse Hotel and, as he looked around the room, he said to himself, "You know, there are only two or three people here that on a normal election night I'd be with." The rare unanimity of Madison's two newspapers was also important. So consistent was their support that a critic called them the *Convention Center Times* and the *Wisconsin State Convention Center Journal.*[87]

*Rectifying a mistake, ratifying a vision.* During the referendum campaign Tony Puttnam was fond of saying that Madison was the only community where a nearly sixty-year-old Wright design could finally be built. Puttnam was referring to the remarkably widespread awareness that Wright had done something great for Madison and the equally widespread understanding that the failure to build it was a great tragedy. It was not just nostalgia; it was a sense that public policy had gone awry. All this sentiment coalesced between 1988 and 1992 and formed a deep broad new current of public opinion. It was banishment seeking a homecoming, a putdown asking for an apology, and an embarrassment looking for pride. Incredibly, Frank Lloyd Wright's Monona Terrace was exciting a whole new generation of Madisonians.

*Awareness of an extraordinary opportunity.* The leaders of "It's Wright" shared a keen realization that 1992 was a time in the city's history that demanded fresh thinking. To have the opportunity to build a Frank Lloyd Wright masterpiece was exciting. To believe that this was the last time history would offer this opportunity was sobering. To acknowledge that the convention industry was probably the only economic force capable of revitalizing Madison's picturesque and beloved Capitol Square was compelling. It was no ordinary time and it required extraordinary action.

*Bold, sustained, new political leadership.* Tommy Thompson and Paul Soglin exemplified the entrepreneurial leadership the project demanded. Both were excited by the prospect of a classic Wright building at the end of Martin Luther King Jr. Boulevard and were willing to brave criticism from all sides to do it. Other political leaders who

shared this view were Dane County board chairmen J. Michael Blaska and R. Richard Wagner. County Executive Phelps also supported the center, but complicated county politics prevented him from offering financial support until late in the game.

*Astute political process.* Bold leadership, a powerful idea, an extraordinary opportunity, and even a coterie of committed leaders were not enough. Success also required a process that allowed these elements to coalesce. Paul Soglin and George Austin were the primary architects of that process. Soglin saw the importance of creating a representative commission to slog through the swamp of feasibility, yoked conservatives with liberals as committee chairs, understood the importance of getting objective experts to answer key questions, insisted on giving the commission plenty of time, a generous budget, and adequate staff, and, finally, understood the importance of making Monona Terrace a project of meaningful partners. George Austin (see Fig. 6.22) blended these elements and many more into an ingenious and ineluctably sequential process, created an extraordinary team spirit among city staffers, state officials and employees, architects and contractors, and wisely insisted upon measurable quality standards at every step along the way.

*Big, early contributions from financial partners.* The $18 million contribution from the state and $4 million from the private sector months before the referendum pushed Monona Terrace from dry dock into the water. These big early contributions from two of the city's financial partners proved that the project would float and let everyone see its rakish look in the water. Without this money, the project would have been much less credible.

*Effective marketing.* Convention centers are among the most difficult public buildings to sell to voters. They cost a bundle, require an ongoing subsidy,

YES    NO

Shall the City of Madison construct the Frank Lloyd Wright Monona Terrace Community and Convention Center at Law Park at a total cost not to exceed $63.5 million in 1992 dollars (as adjusted by the U.S. All Urban Consumer Price Index), provided there will be no significant adverse environmental impact?

YES    NO

INITIAL RESOLUTION authorizing general obligation bonds in an amount not to exceed $12,000,000 for Monona Terrace Community and Convention Center.

BE IT RESOLVED by the Common Council of the City of Madison, Dane County, Wisconsin (the "City"), that there shall be issued general obligation bonds of the City in an amount not to exceed $12,000,000 for the purpose of constructing and equipping a community and convention center to be known as Frank Lloyd Wright Monona Terrace.

Shall the foregoing Initial Resolution of the Common Council providing for the issuance of bonds in the amount of $12,000,000 be approved?

FIGURE 6.21

**1992 Referendum Questions**

Unlike some earlier referenda, in which yes meant no or maybe, the 1992 language was straightforward. Yes meant yes. Mary Lou Munts and Morris Andrews, the principal authors of the referendum, shrewdly incorporated two critically important voter safeguards. They clearly stated that the center would *not* be built if the cost exceeded $63.5 million, adjusted for inflation, or if the center would harm the environment. Similarly, the bond referendum contained a specific upper limit. Voters had to press two levers, one to approve the general terms and conditions, and another to authorize the bonds.

and appear to benefit everybody but taxpayers. Fortunately, Morris Andrews and leaders of "It's Wright for Wisconsin" had the benefit of what must surely rank as one of the most comprehensive and painstakingly assembled basic data kits in the country — the reports and findings of the commission. With great skill Andrews translated these data into

Much credit for Monona Terrace must also go to this talented team of senior city executives who served as staff to the Monona Terrace Commission. Heading the team was George Austin (left), director of Madison's Department of Planning and Development. Austin, known for his quick mind and ready smile, had a profound grasp of city hall politics and a flair for laying out and coordinating complex projects. "I can't say enough positive about George Austin," said George Nelson. "[He] was the glue that held this project together." Nelson also expressed great satisfaction with the work of John Urich (seated), a tall, highly respected principal planner with a distinctive tenor voice who worked with the physical planning committee, and Paul Reilly, city comptroller, who worked with the finance committee. Urich "brought the whole history of the downtown and the passion," Nelson said. Reilly brought "an incredibly thorough grasp of city finance." Reilly used his exhaustive knowledge to keep Madison in the rarefied company of U.S. cities with a AAA bond rating, the highest possible.

a compelling story. He also had superior resources at his command; in fact, he spent about $290,000, compared to just $12,424 for "It Ain't Wright," a ratio of 23 to 1. Andrews' war chest probably ranks as the biggest in a local election in Wisconsin history up to that time.[88]

*Dedicated and committed grassroots supporters.* Hundreds of volunteers worked for the success of Monona Terrace by staffing an information table at the Farmers' Market, distributing literature door to door, making presentations to organizations, testifying at hearings, licking stamps, writing letters to the editor, and myriad other things that grassroots supporters do so well. Not since the citizen crusade of the 1950s had so many worked to realize a great civic vision.

*A revolving door of outstanding cameo performers.* It is impossible to study the Monona Terrace records and not be impressed by the relatively large number of people who walked on stage, gave an invaluable performance, and walked off. They included campaign mastermind Morris Andrews; Ken Opin and Mary Lou Munts, co-chairs of "It's Wright for Wisconsin"; Joe Demorett, Madison's hydrogeologist; Larry Nelson, the city engineer, who guided the project through treacherous and highly technical waters; and Bill Geist, president of the Greater Madison Convention and Visitors Bureau, who made spirited presentations to dozens of groups.

*Availability of a talented and committed staff.* As Austin and his team of fourteen top city executives began to think through the Monona Terrace project, they could see that they were about to traverse "one large piece of complexity none of us had ... experienced before." They realized that the quality of the city staff's work could make or break the project, that everything had to be done right the first time. Consequently, they resolved to conduct the project with an "all one team" approach in accord with the city's customer-oriented philosophy (quality management), complete with a wise and farsighted mission statement. The results of this conscious strategy — a can-do attitude, commitment, outstanding staff work, and exemplary leadership — were evident to commissioners and members of the design and construction teams. Outstanding leader-

ship was also evident at the state level. Secretary of Administration James Klauser handled much of the downfield blocking for the governor, while George Lightbourn, Klauser's executive assistant, and state architect Frederick Wegener worked smoothly with the design and construction teams.[89]

*Learning the lessons of history.* Interviews with Soglin, Austin, and Nelson showed that these three were acutely conscious of mistakes made by their predecessors, and the record shows that they went to great lengths to avoid them. For example, they insisted on getting reliable cost estimates at the beginning of the planning process and excluded the hotel from the referendum package. These astute observers even noticed that the two-year mayoral term had been a factor in killing Monona Terrace on several occasions. It was no accident that Monona Terrace was approved by voters in the middle of the first four-year mayoral term in Madison history.

It is hard to overestimate the importance of these eleven factors. Take away any one, and the razor-thin referendum victory margin could easily have gone to opponents.

## FINAL INGREDIENTS

Exciting as voters' approval of the referendum was to Monona Terrace proponents, they still had four critical tasks to complete before ground could be broken: raising the remaining money, preparing final plans, hiring the construction team, and getting special environmental permits from the State of Wisconsin and the U.S. Army Corps of Engineers. Proponents began work on them immediately, and opponents looked for ways to stop them.

## Twelve Million Dane Dollars

By November 1992 Madison had determined that it could pay $29 million, the state had agreed to contribute $18.1 million, and the commission had established that the private sector would donate $8 million. That left $12 million to collect from Dane County. County Executive Rick Phelps was careful not to commit any money for Monona Terrace at Soglin's June 1990 press conference because he wanted to make sure that doing so would not jeopardize the county's interests. In September 1991 he announced plans to build an $18 million, eighty-thousand-square-foot exhibit hall (see Fig. 6.23) at the Dane County Expo Center, just two miles from Monona Terrace. (The cost of this building increased to $28 million when its size was increased to 100,000 square feet.) Phelps was persuaded that the plushness of Monona Terrace would serve an upscale conference and convention market, whereas the more spartan exhibit hall that the county proposed would serve trade and consumer shows, agricultural programs, and large spectator events. Even so, Phelps was determined to take all reasonable steps to protect his upcoming investment from city competition. Essentially, Phelps was saying to the city, I'll consider giving you the $12 million but only if you can assure me that the operation of the two facilities will be carefully coordinated.[90]

Soglin accepted Phelps's position, and less than a month after the referendum both executives appointed negotiating teams to hammer out a deal. The teams recommended the creation of an independent authority known as the Monona Terrace Board and said it should have twelve members, half from the city, five from the county, and one appointed by the governor. Although the city would have the majority, the county would enjoy a strong voice.[91]

Gaining the county's approval of the proposed operating authority and the $12 million appropriation tied to it was anything but certain. In addition to the new exhibit hall, The county was building a $19 million jail and an $8 million airport expansion and was being pressed to increase its funding of social services. Twenty-one conservative supervisors won seats on the board in the April 1992 local elections, giving conservatives a majority in the thirty-two-member legislative body. This allowed conservatives to elect one of their own, Michael Blaska, as the board's chairman. Most supervisors felt obligated to reflect their constituents' will, as expressed in the advisory referenda on Monona Terrace, which was rejected by county voters in forty-three of the fifty-one jurisdictions that asked their opinion. Furthermore, the schism between rural and urban forces was still a powerful factor in board decisions. One rural supervisor stood up and asked, "So how does building a convention center in Madison get Dane County farmers a better price for their milk?"[92]

That was when Blaska weighed in. Blaska, then forty-two, ran a 260-acre dairy farm in northeastern Dane County that had been started by his grandfather, John M. Blaska. Interestingly, his grandfather had also served on the Dane County board and was vice chairman in 1938 when Frank Lloyd Wright first presented Olin Terraces, the ancestor of Monona Terrace, to that body. Blaska's grandfather voted with the then-strong rural bloc to oppose Madison supervisors, who wanted to build a joint city-county building, a variation of which was Wright's dream civic center (see Chapter 3). Thus Blaska was about to become the second member of his family to vote on the Frank Lloyd Wright project while serving on the county board. A final factor strongly suggesting that Blaska would oppose Monona Terrace was that his constituents had voted against

it. Thus, Michael Blaska had every reason to vote against Monona Terrace.[93]

But he did not. The more he heard about Monona Terrace, the more impressed he became. Blaska (see Fig. 6.23) concluded that this was one of those times that calls for visionary leadership, for the county to transcend the familiar rural-urban and conservative-liberal boxes that confined so many board decisions. At considerable political risk Blaska became a supporter of Monona Terrace and began to lobby his conservative colleagues for their votes. The key to getting county support, Blaska believed, was giving the board a strong voice on an independent managing authority — exactly what city and county negotiators had worked out.[94]

Assisting Blaska was Dick Wagner (see Fig. 6.23), a supervisor since 1989 and the board chairman from 1988 to 1992. Although Wagner was an outspoken liberal, he and Blaska worked together to champion Monona Terrace on the county board and to secure Phelps's support. Like Blaska, Wagner demonstrated political courage by supporting the project because his district, a hotbed of the Labor-Farm Party, had voted 3 to 2 against the project.[95]

When the controversial $12 million appropriation was placed on the county board's agenda for Thursday, March 4, 1993, both sides went into action. Opponents composed of "certified city lefties" and "hard core rural" conservatives forged an uneasy coalition to try to kill the measure. Proponents mobilized their considerable forces, including both Madison newspapers, which urged the county to approve the appropriation. Undecided supervisors fielded telephone calls from earnest aides of the governor, U.S. Representative Scott Klug, and prominent Madison leaders. One supportive supervisor drove twenty-six hours nonstop through rain and snow to make the meeting.[96]

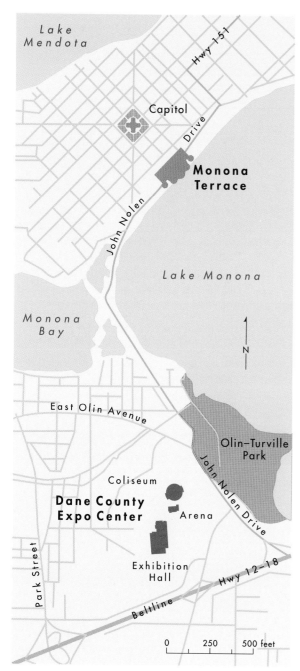

Monona Terrace "Versus" the Expo Center

*U.W.–Madison Cartographic Laboratory*

Exhibition Hall

*Photo by Joe Paskus*

Wagner, Phelps, and Blaska

*Photo by Mary Langenfeld*

FIGURE 6.23

### Dane County Pledges Support for Monona Terrace

While Madison officials were planning the $67 million convention center of 250,000 square feet, Dane County officials were planning this $28 million exhibition hall of 100,000 square feet. Never in Dane County history had so much meeting space been contemplated in such a short period. Although the county facility was designed as a no-frills venue for relatively large consumer and trade shows — a very different market than what Monona Terrace was designed to attract — many county leaders saw the two facilities as competitors. Moreover, as the map shows, the two facilities were just two miles apart. County Executive Rick Phelps feared that if the county broke ground before the city did, many would say "one of these things is enough." Consequently, after nearly all plans for Exhibition Hall had been completed, Phelps slowed the process down to give the city time to do its final planning on the convention center.

Spearheading support for Monona Terrace on the Dane County Board of Supervisors were R. Richard Wagner, board chairman from 1988 to 1992 (left), and Michael Blaska (right), chairman in 1992. Phelps is in the middle.

The boardroom that night crackled with political electricity. Supervisors endured a battery of 56 speakers, and 223 others registered their views with the county clerk. Even Carroll Metzner, the archenemy of Monona Terrace from the 1950s and '60s, came out to express his dismay that this old Frank Lloyd Wright project was still being discussed. "This is like a bad dream," he complained. "We've buried this thing four or five times, but it keeps rising again." The testimony droned on for hours and then came the debate among supervisors. Nearly every argument anybody had ever heard about Monona Terrace was repeated that night from the floor — and one new one. One young woman "begged the board to save Law Park ... because this is where I first kissed my future husband." Finally at 2 A.M. on Friday, March 5, after a draining 6.5-hour debate, the clerk called the roll. The vote was 23–14 — in favor of Monona Terrace.[97]

The city and county promptly appointed their representatives to the Monona Terrace Community and Convention Center Board, which held its first meeting in July 1993. The question on the table was whether the private sector could raise its share of the money. If so, the Monona Terrace funding package would be complete.[98]

Less than two months after the Dane County board approved its financial contribution, a locally commissioned opera on the early life of Frank Lloyd Wright debuted in Madison (see Fig. 6.24). Coming as it did so soon after the final piece of public financing had been secured, many Monona Terrace supporters saw the opera as an occasion to celebrate.

### THE FOUR MILLION DOLLAR MAN

Something extraordinary was going on here. Never in Madison's history had two local foundations contributed $4 million in lead gifts to any campaign.

Even so, that was only half the amount needed from private sources. No one on the commission knew exactly how to raise the remaining $4 million or, more important, who could do it. But as George Nelson and M. Jerome "Jerry" Frautschi (co-chair of the commission's finance committee) thought about it, one person stood out from all others. His name was Paul Berge.[99]

Berge was chairman of the board of M&I Madison Bank and for decades had been a civic activist and proponent for downtown revitalization. He knew just about everybody in corporate and business circles and was highly respected. When Nelson and Frautschi called on Berge just a week after the referendum to ask him to chair the Convention Center Fundraising Task Force, he accepted the daunting job without hesitation. Berge had started with the bank in 1959, the year Wright died, and remembers that the Monona Terrace model was displayed in his bank's lobby during this period. He saw Monona Terrace as a long overdue acknowledgment of Wright's genius and "a unique opportunity [on] ... a unique site ... and an opportunity to showcase not only Madison but the entire state."

Berge assembled a small task force and with its help identified prospects, prepared a strategy, established a new foundation to receive contributions, and personally called on about fifty prospects, stressing the community benefits and financial viability of the project. "He just kept working and working and working," said Nelson. "He was like a bulldog."[100]

Finally, on October 29, 1994, Berge announced that his task force had raised the $4 million from more than one hundred corporations, foundations, and individuals (see Fig. 6.25). Several made large grants. For example, the Frautschi Family Interests contributed $500,000. The following

World Premiere

MADISON
Opera

*Shining Brow*

FIGURE 6.24

### *Shining Brow,* a New American Opera

*Courtesy Madison Opera Inc.*

April 21, 1993, was a gala night at the Madison Civic Center. A powerful floodlight near its entrance swept the night sky as more than two thousand people arrived by foot, in black limousines, and even in yellow school buses. Wearing everything from sequined gowns and tuxedos to sweaters and blue jeans, the festive crowd was about to witness the premiere of *Shining Brow,* a new American opera based on the life of Frank Lloyd Wright. For the Madison Opera Guild to even consider commissioning a new work was plucky. How it happened was remarkable.

In early 1989 the guild's program advisory committee met to decide what operas should be presented the following year. The discussion turned to the success of new operas based on historical figures such as John Adams' *Nixon in China.* Terry Haller, a committee member, urged the group to consider doing an original opera based on the life of Frank Lloyd Wright. He had just finished reading Brendan Gill's new biography, *Many Masks,* and thought the tumultuous architect's life would be a perfect subject for an opera. Committee members were intrigued. Marvin Woerpel, a recently retired university executive and outgoing president of the Madison Opera Guild, said he would enjoy the challenge of planning a new opera. Roland Johnson, music director of the Madison Symphony Orchestra and Madison Opera, was delighted by the prospect. By the fall Ann Stanke, the executive director of the guild, was meeting regularly with interested board members, two of whom offered to underwrite the $50,000 commissioning fee.

Discussions turned to hiring a composer and librettist. Johnson suggested Daron Hagen, thirty, a talented composer who had studied at the Wisconsin Conservatory of Music, Curtis Institute of Music, and Juilliard. Stanke called Hagen at a New Hampshire artists' colony. Hagen was playing billiards when the call came, so he took it at a phone booth just outside. Hagen was so excited by Stanke's offer that he said yes before the guild director could tell him the subject was Frank Lloyd Wright. Stanke asked whether he had a librettist in mind. Just then, Hagen's good friend Paul Muldoon walked by. Hagen opened the door of the phone booth and yelled, "Hey, Paul, how would you like to write an opera with me?" The surprised Muldoon, a highly regarded Irish poet, accepted on the spot.

Hagen and Muldoon limited the opera to the tumultuous period of 1903–1914 when the architect left his wife and six children, ran off to Europe with a client's wife, built Taliesin, and was devastated by a tragedy that killed his lover and her children.

The $500,000 production featuring a rich pool of national and regional talent drew mixed reviews. *New York Times* opera critic James R. Oestreich said the work "exuded intelligence" and was "a daring venture on the part of several bright talents." Nancy Raabe of the *Milwaukee Sentinel* complained of the "dry academism of the work" and its "obscure metaphors." In 1997 the Chicago Opera Theater's presentation of *Shining Brow* drew rave reviews.

donors contributed $250,000: American Family Insurance Group; the CUNA Mutual Insurance Group; Madison jewelers Bob and Irwin Goodman; M&I Madison Bank; Madison Gas and Electric Foundation, Inc.; and Marshall Erdman and Associates, Inc. The six companies that contributed $100,000 or more were Anchor Bank; Firstar Bank Madison; Oscar Mayer Foods Corporation; J. H. Findorff and Son, Inc.; the Lee Foundation/Wisconsin State Journal; and Wisconsin Power and Light.[101]

By Madison as well as national standards, $8 million was a huge sum. Locally, it was more than twice the size of the next-largest capital campaign in Madison's history. Nationally, it was probably the largest private-

sector contribution, expressed as a percentage of total project costs (12 percent), ever contributed for a convention center in the United States.[102]

### FINALIZING THE DESIGN, SELECTING THE CONTRACTOR, AND GUARANTEEING THE PRICE

In October 1990 George Austin proudly hung a new piece of art on his office wall. To many it looked like angular lines of ants posing on a white beach towel. In fact, it was a flow chart for the Monona Terrace project and an itinerary for nearly four years of his professional life. Austin gave copies of the flow chart to all members of the commission at the beginning of their deliberations. He often looked at the complex diagram and wondered whether the project would ever reach the omega point labeled "opening of convention center."[103]

As he studied the flow chart after the November 1992 referendum, Austin could see that to get ready for actual construction in late 1994 he had to bring the center plans to completion, prepare final drawings, hire the construction team, and guarantee the price. Puttnam had completed schematics in July 1991 but had made few changes while the commission and staff worked to complete the financing plan and get the referendum approved. Although no further design work was scheduled for 1993, Austin wanted to use this interlude to make sure that center plans would pass rigorous market tests. He therefore gave Puttnam's schematics to professional meeting planners (the people who book nearly all conventions) and to convention contractors, the companies that design, install, and then take down exhibits for corporate clients.

This final round of review, conducted in the summer of 1993, produced three key changes: adding walls along the lake side of the exhibit hall and the banquet hall so these rooms could be darkened for audio-visual

presentations; making the shape of the exhibit hall and banquet rooms nearly rectangular; and simplifying the floor plan at the ballroom and meeting room level. The last change included a broad new central corridor leading directly to the lake side from the main entrance. Although these changes were made in the summer of 1993, they were not announced until early 1994.[104] (Fig. 6.26 shows the results of these changes.)

The second key task was hiring the construction team, a decision that the city and the state had analyzed in great detail. Almost everyone who had studied the history of Monona Terrace could see that earlier incarnations had failed because the city had used the conventional public works bidding process. That process involved preparing detailed plans, giving them to contractors for competitive bids, and then being told that construction costs far exceeded the money available. That process had killed the project in 1961 and 1974. Consequently, Soglin, Nelson, Austin, and others were eager to find another way.

They selected a much more sophisticated system known as *construction management*. As the term was used for this project, it meant that the contractor was brought in much earlier than normal in the design process, specifically when the architect completed final schematic drawings. The goal was to have the contractor and architect work hand in hand from this point forward to find the best ways to construct the building within the budget. Because the job had two owners (the city was building the convention center and the state was building the parking ramp), it needed a construction manager to coordinate their voices and represent them to the contractor. Because Monona Terrace was full of complex and difficult construction challenges, the owners wanted a construction manager with experience building convention centers. Finally, this job required the construction manager to guarantee the price. Under the terms of the referendum the city had $63.5 million to spend, a figure that could be adjusted only for inflation. That was it. There was no more money. It was for these reasons the city and state decided to hire both a construction manager and a contractor, the combination of which was known as the "construction team." [105]

Although the city and state agreed that this modified construction management system was the only viable plan for Monona Terrace, state law precluded the city from using this system. But the state could, so the city agreed that the state would advertise for the construction team; however, the city would actively participate in the process and was required to concur in every decision.

The state-run advertising process produced six qualified teams. In October 1993 the state hired the team of J. H. Findorff and Son, one of the most respected in the Midwest, and Stein and Company, a Chicago-based real estate developer specializing in construction management. Stein had been part of the team that won the $671 million contract to expand Chicago's McCormick Place Convention Center. [106]

On February 4, 1994, the city and state gave Puttnam official notice to proceed with the last step in the design process, the preparation of final construction drawings, a huge job that required more than five hundred large, detailed drawings and cost nearly $1 million. Furthermore, the city faced a stern deadline imposed by the $15 million state appropriation for the parking garage. The appropriation required construction to begin before December 31, 1994, or the city would lose the money. This meant that project architects had just ten months to do a job that normally would require about fifteen months. [107] (The city had already taken a step toward easing the time crunch by hiring Potter Lawson as

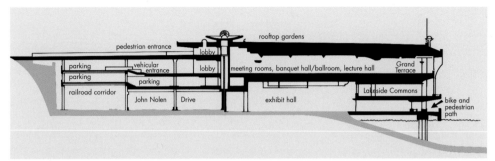

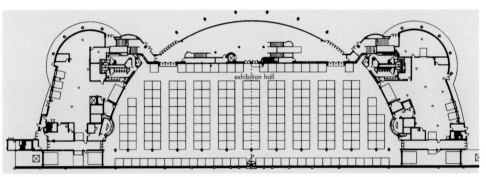

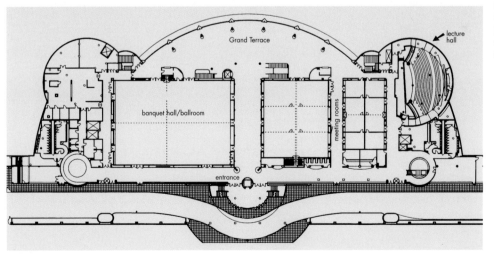

FIGURE 6.26

**Final Monona Terrace Plans**

© 1999 Taliesin™ Architects, Ltd. and City of Madison

Seldom are plans for public buildings scrutinized by so many for so long. Shown here are a 1994 cross-section and two floor plans completed in 1994 by Taliesin architect Tony Puttnam. The result was a state-of-the-art facility with many unique features. The cross-section shows how the lakeside portion of the building was constructed on piles without filling the lake.

The first level contains a 39,000-square-foot exhibit hall; the second level contains a 14,000-square-foot ballroom and banquet facility, 7,000 square feet of meeting rooms, a 300-seat lecture hall (a rare feature in convention centers), and the Grand Terrace. Other levels (not shown) provide space for administration, mechanical equipment, and storage.

consulting architect to assist with the production of construction drawings.)

The second step taken to meet the deadline was the use of state-of-the-art design technology. R. Nicholas Loope, the former managing principal of Taliesin Architects, believes that Monona Terrace was the first project to use "real-time electronic design conferencing," a technical breakthrough requiring high-capacity telephone lines, powerful computers, and sophisticated design software. This system allowed architects at three locations in the United States to simultaneously study the same drawings on twenty-one-inch high-resolution monitors. Architects at all three locations could both talk with one another using speakerphones and see each other in full-motion video in a small inset screen in the upper righthand corner of the monitor. In a typical situation an architect placed a design drawing on the screens and they discussed what needed to be done. Once they agreed, an architect would make the changes on screen and the changes would automatically appear at all three locations. Using this remarkable process, final construction drawings were completed in December 1994, exactly as called for in the contract.[108]

From the time Taliesin Architects received the order to begin work on the construction drawings in February 1994, Findorff-Stein, Taliesin, and George Austin, the representative for the city and state, met almost weekly to work toward the guaranteed maximum price. They did this by painstakingly reviewing every component of the project and blending the owners' expectations, the architect's design, and the contractor's ability to identify alternative ways to achieve the design goal. On each issue this three-element team would identify an optimum solution that would then be embodied in final construction drawings. The team kept a careful

record of cumulative costs. Finally, in October 1994 Findorff-Stein was able to guarantee that the price for Monona Terrace would not exceed $63.5 million adjusted for inflation, or $67.1 million.[109]

By the end of November 1994 Monona Terrace was poised to proceed. All the money was committed, all the environmental permits had been granted, final construction drawings were nearly complete, the common council had given its final approval, and the new center's governing body was planning how to run it. However, these impressive achievements did not mean that the project had clear sailing. Several legal and procedural obstacles were forming on the road ahead.

## THE FLEISCHLI FUSILLADE

While members of the design and construction teams were preparing final construction drawings and Paul Berge was raising money from the private sector, the city and state were seeking the necessary environmental approvals. This included a final environmental impact statement (EIS), a permit from the Wisconsin Department of Natural Resources to allow construction on a landfill (Law Park), and a permit from the Army Corps of Engineers certifying that construction would not pollute Lake Monona.

The release of the final EIS by the Wisconsin Department of Administration on July 12, 1993, provoked an immediate response from project opponents. Fleischli, the lawyer who began opposing convention centers during the Nolen Terrace referendum campaign in 1989, sneered that it "reads like a developer's prospectus" and dismissed its issuance as a "public relations event." Opponents conveyed their contempt for the EIS by peppering the document with 220 oral and written criticisms.[110]

The EIS acknowledged that the center would be built on columns (pilings) that would cover 1.5 acres of the lake, that it would destroy 3.7 acres of green space in Law Park, that landfill under Law Park might contain contaminants that would have to be removed if found, that some lake views would be blocked, and that traffic volumes would be increased by 2 to 4 percent on an average day. But the EIS concluded that construction would not have "a measurable long-term impact" on water quality or fish habitat. In the argot of environmental impact statements, this was as clean as they got.[111]

Fleischli (see Fig. 6.27) charged that the EIS glossed over consequences of long-buried "toxic heavy metals such as arsenic, mercury and petroleum compounds." She argued that such metals could be freed during the construction process when 1,725 steel piles were hammered into the ground for the foundation. In Fleischli's picturesque language the city was creating "a sink with 1,725 drains" that would send toxins "speeding toward" Lake Monona and a bed of limestone about eight hundred feet below the surface — where a city well at the east end of Law Park extracted about 4 percent of the public water supply. The articulate attorney insisted that to proceed with construction would constitute "an environmental disaster of the size that Communist East Germany used to create."[112]

The center's most dedicated opponent was absolutely confident that she had found enough ammunition to demonstrate that the environmental effect on Lake Monona would be "significantly adverse" and that the center could not therefore proceed. The referendum language clearly stated that the project would proceed *only* if there were "no significant adverse environmental impact." Fleischli demanded that the state hold a rehearing of the EIS in October 1993, a process that she said

IGURE 6.27

ANN FLEISCHLI
FORMIDABLE OPPONENT

Courtesy The Capital Times

"A stubborn Norwegian makes a fairly formidable opponent," conceded Ann Fleischli in a 1995 interview with the *Wisconsin State Journal*. Most Madisonians would agree only if *fairly* were deleted. Indeed, her efforts from 1993 to 1995 caused almost everyone to see the intense attorney as the project's leading opponent.

As a girl growing up in Kankakee, Illinois, where her parents were "apolitical insurance agents," Fleischli manifested an early interest in heroes. Characteristically, she read all the biographies in the public library in alphabetical order, looking for "courageous models of behavior." She concluded that she liked Clara Barton best. Beyond the bookshelves, heroes in Kankakee were scarce. She remembers the city as a "corrupt ... one-party town" controlled "by sleazy developers and Republicans." The one real-life hero she found was a man who lived next door, ran for public office each year, and lost. To Fleischli this man was the only person in Kankakee who "had backbone and a public service ethic."

After getting her undergraduate and law degrees from the University of Illinois, Fleischli enlisted in Lyndon Johnson's War on Poverty in South Carolina where she worked as a legal services lawyer. In that capacity she sued the U.S. Department of Housing and Urban Development, provided legal services to minority children, and was accused of being a communist by the "local gentry."

In 1970 Fleischli moved to Madison with her husband, a labor mediator, and the following year bought a small house in an affluent West Side neighborhood. Ironically, she lived near Carroll Metzner, Wright's Monona Terrace nemesis in the 1950s and 1960s. In 1984 and 1986 Fleischli sought a seat on the Madison Metropolitan School Board but was rebuffed by voters both times. During these campaigns she angered former friends in the League of Women Voters by calling them "goo-goo birds" and by asserting that the superintendent of schools had "mush" for brains. Looking

back on her school board tries, Fleischli said, "To this day I'm sorry I didn't sue them. On what grounds I don't know, but I could have come up with something."

Fleischli is one of those people who seldom lacks something to oppose. In 1984 she fought a school district desegregation plan, in 1989 the Nolen Terrace convention center and a plan to build an "aquatic center" in Law Park, and in the early 1990s she took on the director of the Madison Public Library, who wanted to build a few large suburban libraries instead of smaller neighborhood branches.

Fleischli told a Madison reporter that in 1993 she was approached by a group called "It Ain't Wright" whose members asked her to join the fight against Monona Terrace. "At that time I had no suits in court. So I thought, what the heck."

Fleischli contends that people do not understand her. "I've always wondered why people don't understand people like me and [Alexander] Solzhenitsyn," the Russian dissident. "There ought to be more people like us," she told a *Journal* reporter. "...Today most people don't do things for free, and it's sad. My question is, why wouldn't you [oppose Monona Terrace] if you care about parks and our city's aquifers?.... Spending public money is a very serious thing." The confident Fleischli concluded, "It is people like me, who apply the Bill of Rights, who make the system work. Our society's hope is this kind of scrutiny of public behavior.... The alternative is violence. My behavior is better."

could delay the project for as long as five years. The state denied her request.[113]

The intense attorney was not the only one to say that the environmental sky was falling. Al Matano announced that the Four Lakes Group of the Sierra Club was "ready to fight against [Monona Terrace for] however long it takes and [with] whatever legal means are necessary to stop it.... We look forward to fighting you for the next two or three years by which time you will see a $10-million to $30-million cost overrun."[114] (It was during this period that the bumper sticker shown in Fig. 6.18 was produced.)

Fleischli's catastrophic predictions got the attention of Madison's Commission on the Environment, which refused to affix its seal of approval to the center until it could investigate her charges. To determine whether Fleischli's claims were valid, the commission hired Jean M. Bahr, a University of Wisconsin hydrogeologist. Bahr told the commissioners that Law Park groundwater was flowing upward, not downward as Fleischli contended, and that the "good hydraulic connection" between the lake and the landfill that had existed for decades would not be altered by the construction process. On the basis of Bahr's analysis, the commissioners voted 11–1 in November 1993 to approve Monona Terrace. The commission did, however, ask that contractors use several special procedures to minimize adverse environmental effects during construction.[115]

By December 1993 Fleischli had suffered a string of defeats. She had failed to persuade the city to stop the project despite her many appearances before the common council and its boards and commissions. She had failed to persuade a majority of Madison voters to veto the project in the November 1992 referendum. She had failed to persuade the Dane County board to deny funding in March 1993. She had failed to get the voters in her affluent West Side district to elect her to the common council in

April 1993. She had failed to persuade the state to reconsider the EIS in October 1993. And then she had failed to convince Madison's Commission on the Environment to withhold its approval. Faced with so many setbacks and such great odds, many would concede defeat, but not Ann Fleischli. Her defeats only steeled her resolve. In an angry letter to the *Capital Times* on December 1, 1993, she told everyone what she was going to do. "My plan," she declared, "is to kill this project, not just delay it."[116]

On December 10, 1993, just nine days after her angry letter to the *Times*, Fleischli sued the state Department of Administration, citing irregularities in the EIS review process and alleging it had failed to take into account the long-term effect on groundwater supplies of driving 1,725 piles.[117]

Then, in June 1994, she suffered still another setback. The Wisconsin Department of Natural Resources (DNR) approved a permit to allow Madison to build on the landfill. According to a DNR official, "The contaminant levels are so low and the distance they had to travel [was so great], we didn't feel it would be a problem."[118]

These official state approvals infuriated Fleischli. From July to October 1994 she unleashed a legal and procedural attack unprecedented in Madison history for its ferocity. In July she sued the DNR, charging that it had broken its own rules of procedure, had treated certain chemicals inappropriately, departed from the purpose of the 1927 and 1931 dock-line laws, and allowed the scenic beauty of Law Park to be destroyed, contrary to the public trust doctrine. In September she sued DNR a second time, this time charging the department with failing to take into account the effect of toxic chemicals released by the installation of piles. In October she urged the U.S. Environmental Protection Agency (EPA) to nominate Law Park to the Superfund list. Also in October she launched

a referendum campaign to change Madison's charter so that the center could not be built.[119]

In addition to the lawsuits and the attempt to involve the EPA, Fleischli collaborated with Jane Eiseley, a well-known historic preservation consultant, to create a new historic district that included Olin Terrace, the half-acre park at the end of Martin Luther King Jr. Boulevard that was scheduled for a total makeover as the main entrance to the convention center. Fleischli and Eiseley reasoned that if they could get the tiny park on the National Register of Historic Places, they could prevent the city from razing Olin Terrace and then rebuilding it as the primary entrance to Monona Terrace. Toward that end they proposed to create a historic district that would include Olin Terrace, the Madison Club, Diocese of Madison Chancery, and Bellevue Apartments. The Bellevue had made the national register in 1987 as the first large apartment building in Madison. Eiseley submitted her nominations to the Madison Landmarks Commission in August and the State Historical Society of Wisconsin in October.[120]

To people who had lived in Madison since the 1950s, what Fleischli was doing was hauntingly familiar. It evoked the tactics of Metzner and Joe Jackson, who had killed Monona Terrace with lawsuits, legislation, and procedural delays. Jackson had been dead since 1969, but Metzner continued to practice law and to oppose Monona Terrace. But he said he was too busy to actively campaign against the project.[121]

The vehicle for Fleischli's lawsuits was a new corporation known as Shoreline Park Preservation, Inc. In Shoreline's articles of incorporation the attorney described its goals as "the preservation of shoreline parks for free public use." Fleischli saw her constituency as the eight-four thousand people in Madison and Dane County who voted against Monona Terrace in the November 1992 referendum. She also saw her new corporation as

the "successor" to the Madison Park and Pleasure Drive Association, the private organization that had bought, developed, and maintained parkland in and around Madison from 1893 to the 1930s (see Chapter 1). Like Jackson and Metzner, Fleischli sought "to preserve the Madison model city that John Nolen proposed in 1909."[122]

Despite her best efforts, the Army Corps of Engineers granted the special dredge-and-fill permit on October 27, 1994. Under the federal Clean Water Act the corps was responsible for determining whether construction would pollute Lake Monona. Using water quality tests done by DNR and additional tests done by the city, the corps concluded that the center "would not harm the lake or the groundwater under the site." This was the last environmental approval needed to build Monona Terrace. Proponents were jubilant and eager to proceed. As an editorial in the *Wisconsin State Journal* put it, the time had come to "turn some dirt."[123]

To Fleischli the corps' blessing was the final indignity, and she responded with a now-familiar statement: a fourth lawsuit. She accused the corps of violating the federal Environmental Policy Act and the Clean Water Act by issuing its permit for Monona Terrace. This time, however, instead of suing state regulatory agencies in a Dane County Circuit Court, Fleischli sued a federal agency in U.S. District Court, where the burden of proof was much tougher. With her lawsuits against the Wisconsin Department of Administration and the Department of Natural Resources, Fleischli had to prove that an agency had acted "unreasonably." In federal court, by contrast, Fleischli had to prove that the Army Corps had acted "arbitrarily and capriciously."[124]

Meanwhile, she was pursuing still another way to stop the project. Sometime in March 1995 she called officials at Piper Jaffray, the midwestern securities dealer that was handling the sale of

$14.3 million in revenue bonds whose proceeds were earmarked for Monona Terrace. Fleischli's hope was that Piper Jaffray had failed to disclose in its bond prospectus that the site had been designated a potential Superfund site and that four lawsuits had been filed against it. Had Piper Jaffray failed to disclose these facts to bond buyers, the securities company could have been forced to withdraw the bonds from the market.[125]

With the attempt to disrupt the Monona Terrace bond sale the Fleischli fusillade was finally finished. Now the question was whether her artillery shells had hit their targets. The results began to arrive in the summer of 1994. In August Dane County Circuit Court Judge Moria Krueger rejected all of Fleischli's allegations against the Department of Administration, a decision that provoked the angry lawyer to file an appeal.

By December Fleischli had acknowledged that her attempt to change the city charter had failed, a plan she had hoped would pound "a stake through the heart of this project." She had tried to gather ninety-eight hundred signatures on petitions to force a referendum in April 1995 to change the city charter; the change would have prevented the city from building anything costing more than $500,000 on a landfill. For about two months Fleischli sat at a card table on the front lawn of the Bellevue Apartments, the epicenter of Monona Terrace opposition, hoping to get passers-by on this busy downtown street to sign her petition. The local papers reported that she got less than half the signatures she needed.[126] (Sometime after Tom Link hired Fleischli to oppose the Nolen Terrace project, the Bellevue owner provided space in his building for Fleischli. One prominent streetside corner room displayed anti–Monona Terrace messages during the campaign.)

Fleischli appeared to be unfazed. She turned her attention and hope to Al Matano, who as a candidate for Madison mayor was a "walking breathing refer-

endum." If elected, Matano promised to cut off the piles and beautify the park. But in the February 1995 mayoral primary Matano got only 8 percent of the vote, and in the April election, 66 percent of voters returned Soglin to office. He won every ward in the city — hardly a repudiation of his leadership on Monona Terrace.[127]

Also in December 1994 Fleischli learned she and Eiseley had failed to convince the Madison Landmarks Commission and the state historical society to nominate Olin Terrace for the National Register. They rejected the nomination because it failed to satisfy federal criteria. Eiseley appealed to the National Parks Service, but it upheld the local and state actions. Metzner reportedly underwrote part of the cost of the nomination attempt and wrote supportive letters to state officials.[128]

In June 1995 the last of Fleischli's nonlegal challenges to Monona Terrace — the onerous Superfund consideration — was rejected. She had used a provision of federal law that allows citizens to nominate sites, submitting hundreds of pages of documents to the EPA. The EPA conducted additional groundwater tests, took well water samples, and collected samples of the lake sediment in January 1995. On June 29, the agency officially informed Fleischli that Law Park was "not considered a candidate for listing among the most serious toxic waste sites."[129]

June, July, and September 1995 brought uniformly bad news in three of Fleischli's lawsuits. On June 2, Dane County Circuit Court Judge Charles Jones gave an oral opinion rejecting her charges against DNR. On June 26 U.S. District Judge John Shabaz issued a summary judgment rejecting Fleischli's charges against the Army Corps of Engineers and ordered her to pay court costs as well. On July 6 the Wisconsin Court of Appeals unanimously upheld the circuit court in rejecting Fleischli's charges against the Department of Administration.[130]

Finally, in October 1996 Dane County Circuit Court Judge Michael Torphy rejected her fourth suit. He affirmed the propriety of DNR's issuance of the water quality permit for the project.[131]

Although none of Fleischli's legal or procedural challenges stopped the project, they slowed its progress and increased its cost. City and state lawyers estimated that they had charged about $78,000 of their time to defending these cases. Corresponding estimates for Justice Department lawyers were not available, nor were any additional borrowing costs that may be attributable to the delays.[132]

In none of Fleischli's four court cases did she prevail; three circuit court judges and one federal judge ruled against her. Significantly, she did not attack the city or any of its agencies; presumably she believed that her best chances of stopping the Terrace were to demonstrate that state and federal agencies had made administrative errors. Ironically, some of her allegations relating to the public trust doctrine and the dock like had been tried and resolved in *earlier* Monona Terrace battles.[133]

One final point deserves mention: faced with such a fierce legal and procedural attack, many mayors would have frozen the project until these matters were resolved. But Soglin urged the common council to proceed, risking the consequences of Fleischli's lawsuits. The council agreed and on November 1994 voted to authorize the construction of Monona Terrace. In the words of the old Arab aphorism, the dogs barked, but the caravan passed.

## PILE DRIVERS IN THE PARK

One of the most popular events for members of the elegant Madison Club is their annual December holiday brunch. From linen-draped tables laden

FIGURE 6.28

**Building a Landmark**

Photo by Henry Koshollek

Barbara Schneider, a carpenter employed by J. H. Findorff and Son, Inc., Madison's largest and oldest contractor, was one of many women who worked on Monona Terrace.

Photo by L. Roger Turner

Workers install a thick piece of plastic along the lake edge to prevent construction-generated silt from flowing into the lake. This barrier was one of several precautions to prevent pollution of the lake by construction debris.

Photo by L. Roger Turner

This photo, taken from a lakeshore high-rise building looking west, shows the Law Park site in January 1995 at the beginning of the construction process.

Photo by Greg Sweeney

From the boom of this heavy-duty crane hangs a large tube containing a five-hundred-pound hammer for driving more than twelve hundred tubes called "piles" into the earth. Monona Terrace was built atop this network of piles.

Courtesy of UMOJA

William Weaver, Jr., an employee of Ed Kraemer and Sons, worked on the pile-driving crew for Monona Terrace.

Photo by Joseph W. Jackson III

Findorff ironworkers Alvin Powell (left) and Ray Pellicore (center) work with Mark Pertzborn (right), a construction supervisor, to install one of the decorative bowls around the edge of Evjue Gardens. Workers later added clear light domes and twenty-foot light spires to each of the seven bowls.

Photo by Greg Sweeney

Greg Sweeney, a Findorff site engineer, had to arrive before other workers to lay out the complex building every day. On September 1, 1995, he took this photograph of the nearly completed steel framing at sunrise.

Photo by Joseph W. Jackson III

Paul Friedland, a veteran Findorff carpenter, checks the underside of one of the thirty-four-foot concrete saucers that crown the two cylinders at the east and west ends of the lakeside window wall.

Photo by Greg Sweeney

This photograph reveals the intricate, sinuous framing of the Grand Terrace ceiling in January 1996.

Photo by Skot Weidemann

This aerial shot shows the structural steel work nearly completed.

with silver chafing dishes, crystal compotes, and steaming tureens, white-attired chefs serve members traditional holiday favorites. Members then take their china into the dining room, where they listen to a harpist and enjoy the panoramic view of Lake Monona. George Nelson vividly recalls the club brunch on Sunday, December 18, 1994. As he entered the dining room with his wife, he spotted Carroll Metzner. "Is it okay to sit at your table, Carroll?" Nelson asked. "Yeah, yeah, but some people want to spoil the view," replied Metzner, who was well aware of Nelson's role on the Terrace commission. Then he quickly added, "But it will never happen until the fat lady sings." "Carroll," Nelson interjected, "the fat lady just sang because I just signed off on the construction start." Nelson was referring to the issuance of an irrevocable letter that guaranteed the $8 million in private-sector contributions to the city, one of the last steps in completing project financing. Metzner's worst nightmare and Nelson's wildest dream were about to be realized.[134]

Just three days later the city directed Findorff-Stein to begin construction. Site preparation consumed the first few days. Then, in early January 1995, workers positioned two heavy-duty construction cranes on the site. Suspended from the tips of each boom were one-ton piston-shaped hammers that moved up and down within a cylinder. These machines would drive the 1,725 steel piles deep into the earth under Monona Terrace.[135]

The first blow to the first pile came on January 25. A split second before the huge hammers fell, the pile driver would emit an eardrum-piercing *phssst* of super-compressed air, followed by an earth-shaking thunk. Now there could be no doubt that Monona Terrace had at last begun; you could hear it and see it and feel it. Sometimes the first blow would drive a pile twenty feet through the landfill, clay, and

marl. But as the piles were driven deeper, glacier-deposited sand, gravel, and rock offered increasing resistance. When the piles reached depths of 35 to 85 feet, resistance became so great that twenty blows could not move a pile one inch. After nine months the last of the piles was pounded into place, and the relentless phssst-thunk, phssst-thunk, phssst-thunk was heard no more. The Great Monona Terrace Pile Drive was over, and the construction site looked like a freshly cut forest of steel tree stumps. Thick pads of steel-laced concrete then capped the piles, creating the foundation on which Monona Terrace would be built (see Fig. 6.28).

The start of construction also started a parade of national correspondents, who marched to Madison to see for themselves the building of a real Frank Lloyd Wright design, thirty-six years after his death. In February the *New York Times* ran a front-page story in its Sunday edition, followed by the *New Yorker* in March, and *U.S. News and World Report* and *Time* in June. Even the *London Times* dispatched a reporter to Madison. *CBS Sunday Morning* sent a camera crew out to do a feature story. Dozens of articles appeared in architectural, engineering, and construction periodicals. This was big news.[136]

Normally, a groundbreaking ceremony is held at the beginning of the construction process, but January is not a good month for such an event in Madison, where temperatures can plummet to 20 degrees below zero. The city therefore decided to depart from tradition and hold the ceremony on June 8 when the climate, as nineteenth-century brochures used to say, was more salubrious. Besides, this was Frank Lloyd Wright's birthday. In its feature article *Time*, which hit newsstands on June 7, wrote that Governor Thompson would preside over a ceremony for "the most important Wright-designed project never executed in his

lifetime." Hundreds planned to attend, it said. But *Time*'s advance story quickly became an embarrassment.[137]

On Wednesday, June 7, the Findorff-Stein construction team announced that the groundbreaking ceremony would be canceled because of a poor weather forecast. Truth be told, the contractor team was not talking about rain showers but rather a devastating political storm that was developing in the mayor's office. The *Capital Times* broke the story on June 7, just a day before the long-awaited groundbreaking. Soglin had canceled the grand opening — and was threatening to mothball or sell the center. "In two or three hours [the state legislature] did something that Ann Fleischli could not do with all of her lawsuits," the mayor raged.[138]

Soglin was referring to a change in the formula that the state used to share revenue with its cities. Significantly, Soglin's anger was not based on the most recent change but on a steady decline of state aid to Madison. Since 1983 state aid to Madison had fallen from $26 million to $13 million, and each year the city was forced to compensate by increasing its efficiency and its property taxes. What the powerful Joint Finance Committee of the legislature had done was to double the rate, to 10 percent a year, at which this fund would decline for Madison and several other cities. If the full legislature agreed, Madison would receive $1 million less in state aid, money that Soglin and his planners were counting on to pay for the center. The mayor saw this reduction in harsh Watergate terms: What did you know and when did you know it? As Soglin recounted the story, he knew on Memorial Day weekend that the city had lost the critical million dollars. Soglin weighed his options. He could deliver his bleak message at the ceremony, boycott the ceremony, or cancel it.[139]

Soglin's risky ploy got everyone's attention, most important that of the Joint Finance Committee, which a few days later reinstated the old formula (the groundbreaking never was rescheduled). Soglin paid a price for his victory because convention bookings were paralyzed for weeks until the matter was resolved. Supporters expressed disappointment at Soglin's action but not surprise. Somehow it was consistent with the project's rocky history.

Meanwhile, construction proceeded with an almost eerie smoothness, shattering almost everybody's expectations. Monona Terrace should have been a petri dish for Murphy's gremlins. Some of the center had to be built *in* Lake Monona, much of it *atop* a landfill and *across* two railroad tracks, a busy four-lane highway, and a popular bike path. The building had to withstand incredible horizontal pressures from lake ice that some winters was thirty inches thick. The roof had to hold thousands of people, dozens of trees, and could not leak a drop in a deluge. Everything had to be laid out and positioned on radius lines instead of the more familiar right angles. Construction required every type of concrete in the contractor's manual, demanded enough coordination to paralyze a powerful computer, and involved more partners than musicians in a chamber orchestra. Behemoth cranes had to squeeze through tiny openings. Eagle-eyed regulators from the Wisconsin Department of Natural Resources, the Army Corps of Engineers, and other agencies prowled the project looking for code infractions. And everybody who was anybody wanted a special tour every now and then.

The unruffled progress on the job site was no accident. For a full year a team of executives from Taliesin Architects, Inc., J. H. Findorff and Son (see Fig. 6.29), Stein and Company, the City of

Madison, the State of Wisconsin, subcontractors, and consultants had systematically reviewed plans, identified alternative ways to build key parts, and thought through almost every situation conceivable. Before a single pile was pounded into the earth, this talented team had mentally planned the building dozens of times. The product of this extraordinary planning was a billboard-sized flow chart showing exactly when everything would happen during the thirty-month construction period. Few large commercial construction projects were planned as well as Monona Terrace.

Even more remarkable was the team spirit, also no accident. The city held a two-day "partnering retreat" for twenty key players, including the city and state, designers, and the construction manager. Men and women who had primary responsibility for building Monona Terrace got to know one another, determined how they could best work together, and even formulated measurable goals and objectives to confirm that the team concept was working. From this process and early planning sessions came a level of cooperation rare on such large construction projects.[140]

Those who toured the project during construction noticed another unusual quality: the workers' unconcealed pride. They saw Monona Terrace as the last great Frank Lloyd Wright building. They believed they were making history. Workers routinely did things the better but harder way. Supervisors checked out keys to the job site so they could take their families through on weekends. As Larry Thomas, the senior project manager, put it, "Our company always stresses quality, but I have never seen the kind of commitment that this job got from the work force."[141]

Step by step Monona Terrace passed key mileposts. Pile driving was completed in September, the

FIGURE 6.29

**Lynch, Hastings, Thomas, and Brenneman, The Findorff Project Team**

*Photo by Charles McEniry*

These four men had good reason to smile in June 1997: Monona Terrace was coming in on time and within budget — no easy feat considering the size, complexity, and difficulty of the job. The quartet, all veterans of Madison's J. H. Findorff and Son, Inc., are (from left to right) Rich Lynch, project executive; Curtis Hastings, president; Larry Thomas, senior project manager; and Larry Brenneman, superintendent. They are standing on the bike and pedestrian path on the lake side of Monona Terrace.

parking garage in December 1995, the structural steel work in January 1996, and building enclosure in July 1996. One of the last steps in the construction process was the installation of rooftop and entrance plaza tiles, which were part of a popular fund-raising program for the center (see Fig. 6.30).

Ann Fleischli had not gone away. Workers saw her standing on top of the Bellevue Apartment building watching the pile driving. Sometimes she was videotaping the construction process. She told a reporter that she was going to make a movie similar to *Roger and Me*, the low-budget 1989 classic about General Motors' arrogance, insularity, and inhumanity.[142]

FIGURE 6.30

**Lang-Sollinger's Ten Thousand Terrace Tiles**

*Photo by Charles McEniry*

In 1990 Mary Lang-Sollinger, a downtown businesswoman and member of the Monona Terrace Commission, traveled to Seattle with her husband to visit friends. During this trip their friends insisted on taking the Lang-Sollingers downtown to see Pike's Place, the city's historic fish market. Actually, it was not just Pike's Place that the Seattle hosts wanted to show their guests; it was a tile with their name inscribed on it, set in the floor of the landmark building. The sale of this tile and thousands of others had raised money to restore Pike's Place.

Flying home, Mary Lang-Sollinger seized on the idea that custom-inscribed tiles could raise money for the Madison convention center and bring people downtown to see their tile. During the remainder of the flight she completed a concept paper and a preliminary marketing plan. The energetic woman reasoned that the tiles could be sold at affordable prices and set on the dramatic rooftop garden where generations of Madisonians and visitors could enjoy them. The idea was an instant hit with the other commissioners, who encouraged her to proceed. In March 1995 Lang-Sollinger's new organization, Friends of Monona Terrace, began selling square-foot tiles for $50 and two-foot squares for $1,000. Buyers could have their names and other sayings inscribed on the tiles.

By early 1998 the dedicated members of Mary Lang-Sollinger's new organization had sold more than ten thousand tiles, raising $1 million to enhance Monona Terrace. The rooftop tiles were made by the Wausau Tile Company in Wausau, Wisconsin.

Here Mary Lang-Sollinger is holding a tile bearing the name of Mary Lescohier, a leader of the pro–Monona Terrace forces during the 1950s and '60s.

## THE GRAND OPENING

Paul Soglin and George Nelson enjoyed a remarkable but unusual relationship. Soglin, a Chicago native who came to Madison to attend the University of Wisconsin, lived in a hippie ghetto near the campus, drove a cab, got two degrees (one in history and another in law), and at twenty-seven was elected mayor of Madison. Nelson, a Madison native who grew up on the affluent West Side, worked construction jobs in the summer, got a U.W. business degree, and at twenty-nine became executive vice president of Madison's largest bank. Soglin traveled to Havana for an audience with Fidel Castro, whereas Nelson traveled to New York to meet with Wall Street executives.

In the 1970s the two men had collaborated to build the Madison Civic Center. Thus they had been more responsible than anybody else for, as Soglin put, "the final nail in the coffin" of the Wright project. After all, they had taken the money that had originally been approved by voters in 1954 to build Frank Lloyd Wright's Monona Terrace and used it to build a cultural arts facility, the primary purpose for Wright's lakeshore complex. But beginning in 1989 Soglin and Nelson collaborated for a second time, and now, on a hot, humid July day in 1997, they waited with six other dignitaries to open the building they once thought they had killed.[143]

In recent months, as Soglin and Nelson reflected on their eight-year Monona Terrace odyssey, both confessed they had a strong inkling the project would happen even at the beginning of the journey. "It's the opposite of what most people think," explained Soglin, "which is to take [the] project apart piece by piece, then it becomes doable. I was kind of looking at it the other way. Somehow I just knew we were going to do it." For

Nelson this feeling was even more pronounced: "You can sense that things are going to happen and they [are] falling in line." The coincidences were too many and too obvious. There was the fact that he was born in 1938, the same year that Wright proposed the dream civic center. There was his collaboration with Soglin in the 1970s, the fact that both of them had gone their separate ways for ten years, and the fact that a failed convention center referendum suddenly had thrown them back together, working on the greatest public project of their lives. There was that inexplicably tranquil feeling that Nelson had when the architectural contract was signed at Taliesin in March 1991. "That's spiritual," insisted Nelson. "That defies explanation."[144]

Thousands of sweltering people jammed the broad concourse leading to the main entrance of the Monona Terrace Community and Convention Center (see Fig. 6.31). And a fascinating sea of faces it was. In the crowd were the grandsons of Frank Lloyd Wright and his original client, Paul Harloff; Geraldine Nestingen, widow of championing mayor Ivan Nestingen; and at least fifteen Taliesin architects who had worked directly with Wright on the project. Van Potter, head of the Citizens for Monona Terrace, was there and so were former mayor Otto Festge, Betty Scott, and Ricardo Gonzalez. Even recent, steadfast opponents such as Tom Link, owner of the Bellevue Apartments and colleague of Ann Fleischli, showed up. Conspicuously missing were several who would have been supremely delighted to be present, people like Mary Lescohier, Harold and Helen Groves, and Marshall Erdman, who had served on the Terrace commission and became an enthusiastic supporter.[145]

A platform and podium had been set up at the front edge of the low semicircular flat roof that shaded the entrance doors. Workers had wrapped a giant

FIGURE 6.31

**The New Olin Terrace, Main Pedestrian Entrance**

*Photo by Mark Jenson*

This nighttime photograph of the main pedestrian entrance at the end of Martin Luther King Jr. Boulevard shows where thousands of people stood during for the grand opening ceremony. The photograph also shows how Puttnam blended the desires of the Monona Terrace Commission for a "statement" entrance with Wright's 1938 and 1959 plans. From Wright's 1938 plan Puttnam established the plane of the entrance concourse at the same level as the Wilson Street sidewalk (fifty-six feet above the lake), and from the 1959 plan he borrowed its sheltering semicircular entrance.

Just above the main entrance is saucer and globe, thirty-four feet in diameter and a salient feature of Wright's designs beginning in 1938. The architect intended this element to be a grand fountain. Puttnam included the feature in his plan, but the 1994 construction budget was not sufficient to pay for it. However, Pleasant Rowland, founder of Pleasant Company, a Madison-area manufacturer of distinctive dolls, was troubled by the absence of this classic Wrightian feature, especially because it occupied such a central, eye-arresting location atop Monona Terrace. A few days after the grand opening in July

1997, she announced a grant of $500,000 so that visitors could experience the irresistible human fascination of water soaring skyward and the splash of its descent. The fountain was dedicated in August 1998.

red ribbon — Wright's signature color — around the front edge of the roof and tied a huge bow directly behind the speakers' platform. From a distance it resembled one of Wright's drooping cravats. A military band played Sousa marches and patriotic airs as a summer cumulus cloud billowed in the west.[146]

The grand opening was running late, which was somehow appropriate. Someone in the crowd kidded, "Hey, it took six decades to get this far. We can wait for a few more minutes." People smiled knowingly. What a great time, the band director concluded, for "On Wisconsin," the state's official anthem. People tapped their feet and hummed, but it was too hot to sing.

Finally, eight dignitaries marched onto the platform: Sue Bauman, Madison's mayor; Kathleen Falk, Dane County executive; Soglin, Austin, Berge, Phelps, Governor Thompson, and George Nelson. "Oh my god," someone in the crowd said, "you don't suppose they are all going to give a speech do you?" That cumulus cloud was moving closer and getting gray at the bottom.

Nelson welcomed the crowd, gave the first speech, and introduced the others. All the speeches were mercifully brief, attuned to the perspiring crowd, and full of champagne bubbles, warmth, and unconcealed delight. That summer cloud was now a wall of gray rapidly approaching the city.

Then came a spleenful Soglin, who attacked the municipal revenue-sharing policies of the stunned governor. Was this the speech Soglin had intended to give at the aborted groundbreaking two years earlier? Some thought they had mistakenly wandered into a protest rally on state taxes. Coming as it did among so many happy words,

Soglin's speech seemed twice as long as the others. Really, it was the kind of harangue Wright used to give that made the architect less popular after the speech than before.

As the cloud bank darkened and rolled closer, dignitaries wielding a huge pair of scissors cut swatches from the big bow and held them high for eager photographers. Then someone handed Nelson a note, and moments later he walked to podium to report what everyone knew — a storm was moving in. For safety's sake the ceremony would be cut short. Somehow it was appropriate that a building with such a tempestuous history would open with thunder and lightning. Ad-libbing, Nelson said, "Hey guys, the building is open. Come on in."

And so on Friday, July 18, 1997 — 58 years, 8 months, and 16 days after Wright first publicly presented his idea; after thirteen designs and thousands of architectural documents; after five referenda, ten lawsuits, and ten bills in the Wisconsin legislature; after at least four thousand articles in newspapers and periodicals; after being declared dead six times; after Wright was twice elected by the people of Madison (once during his lifetime and once posthumously); after one of the longest and most intensely fought civic battles in American history, the doors of Monona Terrace were finally thrown open.

What a day it was! What a weekend! An estimated fifty thousand thronged nearly nonstop events from Friday to Sunday, sometimes straining the building's capacity. People strolled through the broad halls, examined the wonderful detailing, listened avidly to tour guides, and marveled at the cavernous exhibit hall. Amid the sweeping curves of the Grand Terrace, people sipped wine, nibbled hors d'oeuvres, listened to choirs and string quartets,

and commented on the bright colors in the carpeting. And on the rooftop Evjue Gardens people ate bratwurst, flew kites, searched for tiles inscribed with their names, gathered at the lakeside railing to admire the view, and listened to a gala evening concert (see Fig. 6.32). Mr. Wright would have loved it.

FIGURE 6.32

## Mr. Wright Would Have Loved It

*Photo by Michael Murnan Smith*

On the evening of Sunday, July 20, 1997, eighteen hundred area residents took their seats facing the lake and the orchestra in the Evjue Gardens atop Monona Terrace for the last event of a three-day opening celebration, a concert by the Wisconsin Chamber Orchestra. Behind the orchestra was a panoramic view of Lake Monona. During the first half of the concert, holders of these coveted tickets heard selections from Beethoven and Handel and the world premiere of a new symphony, *Monona Terrace,* composed by the late David Lewis Crosby, the orchestra's artistic director.

The second half featured just one piece: Beethoven's Fifth Symphony. As Crosby lifted his baton to conduct this famous work, darkness had fallen and stage lights illuminated the orchestra. About half-way through the piece a full moon rose above a low cloud bank on the horizon. Then, beginning with the rousing last movement, came the great surprise. The stage lights went out, beams of colored laser lights began to dance above the audience, orange-plumed rockets shot into the sky from hidden launch points on the outer edges of the building, and from a barge anchored six hundred feet out

into the lake fireworks filled the night sky — their thumping reports in perfect synchrony with the Beethoven score. The combination of the surprise, stirring Beethoven crescendo, and spectacular pyrotechnics drew screams of appreciation from the audience. Everyone was a child again.

CHAPTER 7

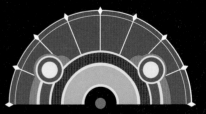

TRIUMPH OF THE VISION

FIGURE 7.2

**Lakeside Curves**

© 1997 Hedrich-Blessing,
photo by Scott McDonald,
courtesy Taliesin™ Architects, Ltd.

This photograph, looking east from the western roof edge of the Evjue Gardens, captures the fascinating interplay of curved forms that Wright wanted for Monona Terrace. The twenty-foot light spires that Wright included in all versions of the project are visible around the edge of the gardens. To see the spires illuminated at night, turn to Figure 7.19. The promenade visible at the bottom of the photo next to the lake was added by Tony Puttnam for pedestrians and bicyclists.

Note how the building overhangs the windows like a swagged valance. This was an example of what Wright called "pendentive architecture," a distinctive approach he developed during the last few years of his life, seeking forms that appear to hang as a pendant around a person's neck. The complex curves of the pendentive window treatment add visual interest and serve as a sun shade for this south-facing elevation. Other other pendentive details can be seen in Figure 7.9.

At long last the great civic megastructure stood complete on the shore of Lake Monona. What had once been a wispy concept contemplated by Frank Lloyd Wright and Paul Harloff as they gazed out upon the lake on a moonlit night in the mid-1930s was now steel, glass, concrete, trees, and a spirit-raising fountain (see Figs. 7.1 and 7.2). To properly understand this transformation requires examination of the sprawling six-decade canvas on which the story was painted. From this more distant and inclusive perspective some of the most important facts, patterns, and explanations emerge: why the project took so long, how the design evolved, whether the design is authentic, the place of Monona Terrace in Wright's lifework, and the power of Wright's vision.

## WHY MONONA TERRACE TOOK SO LONG

How could it be that more than 150 years after Madison was selected as the territorial capital of Wisconsin this premiere downtown Madison public lakefront site was still largely undeveloped? In the nineteenth century the railroads had filled enough lakeshore to hold four sets of tracks. In the 1930s, '40s, and '50s the city filled more lake bed for a four-lane highway, a huge parking lot, and a strip of grass called Law Park. In 1934 the city built the formal street-end park known as Olin Terrace. But if a pedestrian standing in this lovely little park in the 1980s had decided to walk to the lakeshore fifty feet below, doing so meant walking a block, negotiating long steep stairs down the cliff, and crossing four railroad tracks and a busy four-lane highway. The dream of connecting the city with the lake had never been realized. In the words of Ian Nairn, an English landscape architect, this "was a slap across the face with a cold, wet fish, one of the cruelest disappointments in America."[1]

Several factors explain why so little was done with the Olin Terrac–Law Park opportunity and why Monona Terrace stayed on the civic marquee for nearly sixty years.

*The surpassingly beautiful site demanded the highest design standards.* Next to capitol hill, the lake end of Martin Luther King Jr. Boulevard was always considered the sweetest spot of Madison's topography. Doty understood this when he stood atop the hill in 1836, then an open prairie, and looked toward Lake Monona just sixteen hundred feet away. That was why he linked the capitol and the lake with a dramatic, broad boulevard. In 1909 John Nolen affirmed Doty's judgment by selecting this axis for a grand mall and by positioning at its end an eight-thousand-foot esplanade. From then on what later became Law Park was recognized as one of the most beautiful urban waterfronts in the world and one with the greatest potential. Thus it was no accident that this piece of real estate inspired more plans than any other part of the city and that these plans reflected such high standards.

*The state's interests also had to be factored into the design equation.* Deciding what to do with this site would have taken less time if Madison had been the only decision maker, but it was not; state interests had to be incorporated in nearly every plan proposed for this site. As noted in Chapters 1 and 4, the project was sometimes stymied by state officials.

*The site attracted grand civic visions.* Because the site was large, beautiful, and linked to the capitol, it attracted grand civic visions — big, exciting concepts that shimmered in believers' minds and throbbed with promise but also resisted compromise, thwarted incremental implementation, and exceeded the public purse.

*Wright's civic vision conflicted with others'.* None of the Wright plans was ever really alone on the civic stage. There was the incomparable Nolen plan, the copycat Segoe plan, and a cavalcade of others. These plans created debates about whether to favor Lake Mendota or Lake Monona, whether to build a grand esplanade or a megastructure, whether to establish a pleasing vista or an architectural statement, whether it should be fancy or plain, and whether the various elements should be concentrated or dispersed.

*Decades were required to attenuate the Wright animus and recognize his genius.* Wright was one of those people who produce a squall line for some and sunshine for others, and nowhere was this more evident than in his hometown. Madisonians had the unique opportunity to observe and interact with Wright for eighty years, and especially from the time he built Taliesin in 1911. From then on merchants saw Wright driving around the Capitol Square in his ultra-expensive cars and wondered why he wouldn't pay his bills. Citizens seethed over his disdain for conventional morality. Civic leaders resented the torrent of criticisms he hurled at Madison, the state capitol, and the University of Wisconsin. Nevertheless, many Madisonians revered Wright's genius, considered opposition to Monona Terrace petty, and were willing to fight for his vindication. In fact, only after the deeply entrenched animosity was offset by a broad recognition of Wright's genius could a new, ultimately prevailing coalition of champions be assembled.

*Wright's prescriptions for what the patient needed were often at odds with what the patient wanted.* In nearly all cases, the client tells the architect, "Here is what I need. Design something for me." In the case of Monona Terrace, Wright said, "Here is what *I* have determined you need." Wright's insistence on

telling the city and county what they needed was responsible for at least eighteen years of wheel spinning. Not until 1956 did Wright adapt the design to serve *city*-generated specifications.

*Representative government requires time.* Monona Terrace is not a story of Baron George Eugène Haussmann's autocratically inflicting his designs on Paris; it is a story of pro and con forces using persuasion and due process, trading votes, balancing public interests, and making exquisitely difficult decisions, all in free and open debate and with a parade of ever-changing decision makers. Monona Terrace is the story of slow, exasperating, complex representative government in action.

*Decades were required to realize that Monona Terrace was a Wright masterpiece.* When Wright first proposed his project, all were not agog (see Fig. 7.3). Many were incensed by his decision to finish the project with *exposed concrete*, then a material most often associated with utilitarian structures such as parking ramps. Its circular configuration was equally controversial. Only later — many years after Wright's death — did people realize that Monona Terrace was a classic.

*Time was required to develop the necessary financial tools and teamwork to underwrite Terrace costs.* Then there was the sheer expense of the project. Getting Madison, Dane County, the State of Wisconsin, and the private sector to agree to split the cost of the $67.1 million project must rank as one of the most unlikely feats in Wisconsin history. Whether this rare alignment of public and private planets could have happened before the 1990s is doubtful. Earlier in its history few perceived any need to cooperate on such a complex and expensive project, and even if the will had been present, the way was not. Not until the late 1960s and early '70s were two key local financing tools, the hotel room tax

## The Perils of Birthing an Urban Icon

*Courtesy Wisconsin State Journal*
*Courtesy Embassy of Australia*

Whenever a city tries to build a signature building, critics and prophets of doom emerge. Comparing what people said about the Sydney Opera House and Monona Terrace illustrates the syndrome. Comments about the opera house come from *Sydney Opera House, 1973* by Pat Miller.

### MONONA TERRACE

If the Wright project were constructed over the water, it would be a harbor for "dead perch in July and August."

*Joe Rothschild, store manager, December 1955,*
*quoted in the* Capital Times

The [tunnel] will be an attraction for hoodlums at night.

Wisconsin State Journal, *March 28, 1956*

No one is going to use [Monona Terrace] anyway, except a few fanatical women who want to ... build a Wright Memorial.

*Madison council member Harold "Babe" Rohr, February 2, 1960*

Due to the particular geological formation along East Wilson Street, there is a likelihood of all the vibration from driving piles causing a ... slippage of the land along the street towards the lake.

*Philip S. Haberman, retired attorney, August 17, 1992*

If the Center is built, it will ... cover three acres of the lake, possibly raising water levels.

Daily Cardinal, *October 28, 1992*

### SYDNEY OPERA HOUSE

I certainly trust some aeroplane pilot does not mistake it for a new kind of hangar.

*Reader,* Sydney Morning Herald, *February 1957*

This Opera House will be a burden on the people for all time.

*G. Cherry, Hospitals Association of New South Wales, October 1957*

It's not that I'm against culture but that the Opera House has cruelled the fishing.

*A Sydney fisherman, January 1964*

This will probably prove to be the greatest white elephant of the century.

*Norman Ayrton, Sutherland Opera Company, September 1965*

I think it looks like ... a bunch of toenails clipped from some large albino dog.

*Ron Saw,* Daily Mirror *columnist, February 1968*

---

and tax incremental financing, even made available to Wisconsin cities.[2]

Although six decades is a long time for any project to appear on a civic marquee, the delay was not without benefit. Wright was known for his propensity to design things that could not be satisfactorily executed with contemporary construction technology, and Monona Terrace was no exception. For example, Wright's 1959 outline specifications for the rooftop gardens show that he proposed an uninsulated "built-up" roof composed of black rolled roofing sloshed with tar and topped with pea gravel. Although this was the best roofing technology then available, it is decidedly inferior to the insulated rubber membrane system actually used for Monona Terrace. Where Wright specified thin, sprayed-on concrete (gunite) for the curved surfaces, modern construction technology allowed lightweight, insulated, precast concrete panels (see Fig. 7.4). Where Wright specified regular glass, Tony Puttnam used insulated glass that reflects heat and damaging ultraviolet light. Other examples include better sealants, insulation, lighting, and more efficient and quieter heating and air conditioning. Monona Terrace was built better in the 1990s than it could have been during Wright's lifetime.[3]

## EVOLUTION OF WRIGHT'S THREE BASIC DESIGNS

Of the more than seven hundred buildings that Wright designed in his lifetime, few went through a more extensive but less understood evolution than Monona Terrace. Happily, this evolution is less complex than many thought. Wright did three basic designs and five revisions of those designs, eight iterations in all. Those basic designs, their revisions, and the later revisions done by William

FIGURE 7.4

**Cylinders and Shadows**

© 1997 Hedrich-Blessing, photo by Scott McDonald, courtesy Taliesin™ Architects, Ltd.

For Frank Lloyd Wright, Monona Terrace was a study of freestanding, overlapping, and internested cylinders, all arrayed in perfect symmetry. This photograph, taken from the lakeside promenade looking west, shows the edge of the freestanding helix at the left rear, the overlap of large and small cylinders in the middle, and the sweep of the largest partial cylinder, the main building. (See also Figures 7.1 and 7.9.) This early afternoon shot is a reminder that the cylindrical forms create an ever-changing shadow show throughout the day. The larger cylinder contains the lecture hall (see Fig. 7.11), whereas its smaller counterpart conceals a high-capacity stair tower.

To achieve these complex forms two types of high-tech concrete had to be perfectly matched: precast insulated regular concrete for the cylinders and lightweight fiberglass-reinforced precast concrete for the pendentive elements around the windows. Puttnam specified that the color of the concrete should match a blend of five different colors found on the exterior of the Wisconsin capitol.

TABLE 7.1

**MONONA TERRACE DESIGN HISTORY**

| Iteration Number | Iteration Date | Type of Iteration (Basic Design or Revision) | Architect |
|---|---|---|---|
| 1 | 1938 | Basic design | Wright |
| 2 | 1941 | Revision | Wright |
| 3 | 1955 | Basic design | Wright |
| 4 | 1956 (August) | Basic design | Wright |
| 5 | 1956 (October) | Revision | Wright |
| 6 | 1956 (December) | Revision | Wright |
| 7 | 1957 | Revision | Wright |
| 8 | 1959 | Revision | Wright |
| 9 | 1960–61 | Revisions | Wright-Peters |
| 10 | 1989 (July) | Revision | Wright-Puttnam |
| 11 | 1990 (December) | Revision | Wright-Puttnam |
| 12 | 1991 (October) | Revision | Wright-Puttnam |
| 13 | 1993–94 | Revisions | Wright-Puttnam |

Wesley Peters and Tony Puttnam are shown in Table 7.1.

The twenty-one-year evolution of Wright's Monona Terrace designs (1938–1959) can be most clearly summarized by focusing on five qualities of the three basic designs.

*The project began as a prescriptive fantasy but gradually became a practical client-driven facility.* Just thinking about the potential of the Monona Terrace site put Wright in a razzle-dazzle mood. "I will design something great," Wright said in effect. Using Paul Harloff, his client, as a convenient cover and the need for a city-county building as the occasion, Wright heeded the beckoning finger of his artistic muses for a spirit-satisfying splurge. From Wright's deep creative reservoirs came the "dream civic center," an audacious, who-cares-what-it-costs, half cylinder extending out into Lake Monona, a veritable peninsula on an isthmus. The architect filled his great concrete shell with functions he thought Madison needed and embellished its top

surface with trees, fountains, lights, and plants. Ironically, what he produced was not just a dream civic center but a fantasy beyond citizens' wildest dreams. In 1955 Wright once again pulled out all the stops, turned off the cost-accounting meter, and produced a second prescriptive fantasy that was substantially bigger and more function rich than his 1938 design, *his* interpretation of what Madison needed at that time. Not until 1956 did the city demand that Wright satisfy *its* specifications. Wright complied but never did he allow Monona Terrace to leave the special place where he kept it in his mind.

*Functions changed significantly but were always accommodated in a circle-based design.* During the six decades of Monona Terrace so many functions were added and subtracted that they resembled people entering and leaving a building through a revolving door. Those confusing changes are summarized in Table 7.2. In spite of these extensive changes, Wright refused to depart from circle-based symmetry as the central design element. Figure 7.5 shows how Wright ingeniously maintained this design element through all three of his basic designs and how Puttnam continued this tradition.

*From 1938 to 1955 Wright increased the volume and height; from 1956 to 1957 he substantially reduced the volume and added height; and from 1957 to 1959 he slightly increased volume and substantially increased the height.* From 1938 to 1955 Wright increased the size of the building by about 40 percent. However, beginning in 1956, Wright was forced to reduce its size to conform to the city's pocketbook and state-imposed dock line. The downsizing continued until 1957 when Wright produced what he contemptuously called his "peanut" civic center. Just seven weeks before he died, Wright produced his 1959 version and used this opportunity to slightly increase its

TABLE 7.2

**EVOLUTION OF FUNCTIONS
IN MONONA TERRACE**

| 1938–53 | 1955 | 1956–59 | 1994 |
|---|---|---|---|
| Auditorium | Auditorium | Auditorium | |
| | Small theater | Small theater | Lecture hall |
| | Art gallery | Art gallery | |
| | | • Art library | |
| | Community center | Community center | Community center |
| | • Gymnasium | • Gymnasium | |
| | • Handball courts | | |
| | • Dance floor | • Dance floor | |
| | • Snack bar | • Snack bar | |
| | • Game room | | |
| | • Lounge | • Lounge | |
| | • Bowling alleys | | |
| | • Meeting rooms | • Meeting rooms | • Meeting rooms |
| | Exhibition hall | Exhibition hall | Exhibition hall |
| | | | Banquet/ballroom |
| | | Food preparation | Food preparation |
| | Sports arena | | |
| | Office towers | Office towers | |
| Boathouses | Boathouses | Boathouses | |
| City-county govt. | | | |
| • Offices | | | |
| • Courtrooms | | | |
| • Jails | | | |
| Roof garden | Roof garden | Roof garden | Roof garden |
| Parking | Parking | Parking | Parking |
| Road (half-ring) | Road (half-ring) | Road (tunnel) | Road (tunnel) |
| Railroad depot | Railroad depot | | |
| Railroad tunnel | Railroad tunnel | Railroad tunnel | Railroad tunnel |

size, but this design was barely one-third the size of the gigantic 1955 version. During the life of the project the rooftop level rose 32 feet, from 56 feet in 1938 to 88 feet in 1959.[4] (To see how the building's footprint and height changed, see Figs. 7.6 and 7.7.)

*Over the years premiere building space shifted from cars to people.* With the exception of the 1938 version, Wright allocated more space to vehicular movement and storage than to people-oriented functions. That was because the architect was persuaded that the future of cities required generous accommodations for automobiles. Furthermore, Wright earmarked the premiere space on the lake edge of his 1938 and 1955 megastructures for a cantilevered four-lane "scenic drive." In the 1955 plan Wright kept the circumferential scenic drive but added a huge semicircular, three-tier parking garage. Beginning in 1956, however, the city purse and state dock line forced Wright to eliminate the scenic drive and lakeside parking structure and to relocate both on the land side of the building. From this point on, Wright awarded the premiere lakeside space in the building to people.[5]

*Over time Wright replaced angles with arches.* Monona Terrace is one of those rare Wright projects that went on so long that it provided the architectural equivalent of stop-motion photography. A glance at Figure 3.1 shows how Wright's cantilevered construction produced the appearance of a row of gabled roofs. The corresponding rendering from the 1955 version (see Fig. 4.1) shows the introduction of a delicate arched motif spanning angular "ice breakers." The August 1956 elevation (see Fig. 4.24) shows that Wright had selected the arch as the dominant form.

## LIMITATIONS OF WRIGHT'S DESIGNS

Wright's Monona Terrace was audacious, visionary, and exciting, but it was hardly perfect. Had the project been built according to any of Wright's iterations, at least six problems would have been evident.

*The auditorium in the 1938 design was too big.* The seventy-five-hundred-seat theater that Wright

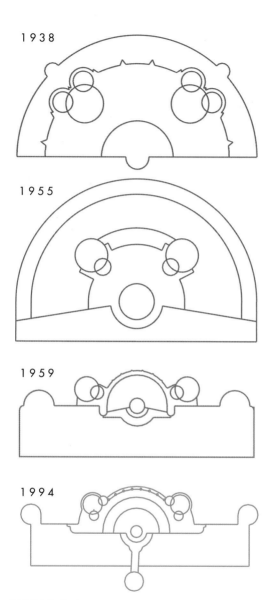

1938

1955

1959

1994

FIGURE 7.5

**The Role of the Circle in the Design of Monona Terrace**

© 1999 Taliesin™ Architects, Ltd. and U.W.–Madison Cartographic Laboratory

Although Wright despised the derivative classical dome of the Wisconsin capitol (he once said it looked like "Kaiser Wilhelm's war helmet"), its circular shape and the symmetrical (Greek cross) shape of the capitol building strongly influenced Wright's decision to make symmetrically organized circles a primary design principle for Monona Terrace. Tony Puttnam's 1994 revision continued this tradition.

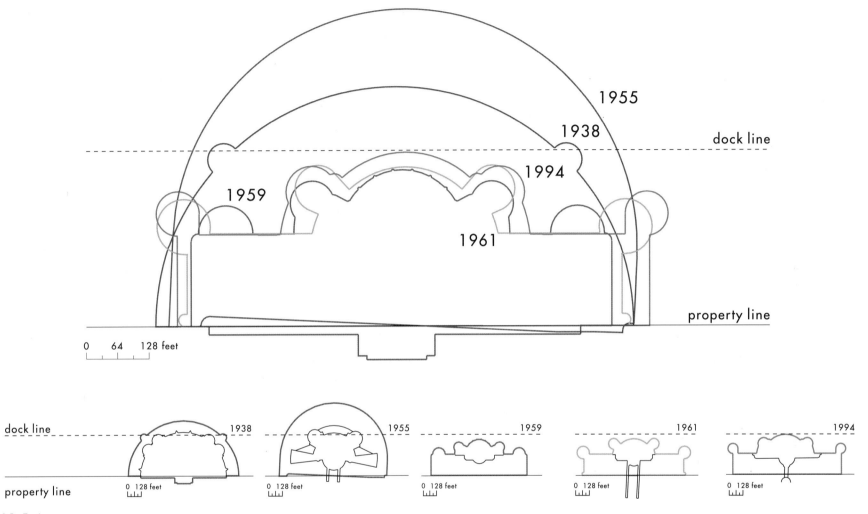

0   64   128 feet

dock line

property line

1955

1938

1994

1959

1961

dock line ............................................. 1938

property line

0 128 feet

1955

0 128 feet

1959

0 128 feet

1961

0 128 feet

1994

0 128 feet

FIGURE 7.6

**The Evolving Footprint**

© 1999 Taliesin™ Architects, Ltd. and U.W.–Madison Cartographic Laboratory

Individual and overlaid footprints reveal some of the most interesting qualities of the Monona Terrace story. The 1938 basic design shown in brown contained more than one million square feet, about the same area as a typical regional shopping center, and it jutted 485 feet out into the lake from the Olin Terrace retaining wall (see Fig. 1.24), 135 feet beyond the dock line. In the smaller diagram of the 1938 plan (lower left) the outer ring denotes the cantilevered half-ring highway, and the inner ring represents the main building. The two half-circle tabs on the outer ring are waterfall "trays," visible in Figure 3.1.

The 1955 basic design shown in olive green was the largest of Wright's eight versions. It contained about 1.5 million square feet, extended 637 feet into the lake from the Olin Terrace retaining wall — 287 feet beyond the dock line.

Because of its size and cost, Wright designed it to be built in two phases. The first phase, the inner core shown in the small drawing, contained all the people functions and a thousand-car parking ramp on the land side. The second phase, the outer ring on the small drawing, was a huge three-tier circumferential parking structure. Significantly, the two large cylinders of the inner core established the eared shape used for all Wright's later designs.

The 1959 iteration shown in blue is the smallest design shown in the diagram, but it was not the smallest plan; the 1957 design that Wright contemptuously called his "peanut plan" holds that distinction. The 1959 design contained about 534,000 square feet, extended 314 feet out into the lake, and was within the dock line by 36 feet.

William Wesley Peters expanded Wright's 1959 iteration in 1960 and 1961. This plan, shown in gold, contained about 679,000 square feet and was inside the dock line by 31 feet.

Puttnam's 1994 adaptation of the 1959 design shown in red contained 603,000 square feet, or 671,000 with the rooftop terrace. It extends 350 feet out from the Olin Terrace retaining wall and is flush with the dock line.

Only the 1955 design assumed that the lakeside private property line was perpendicular to Martin Luther King Jr. Boulevard. All others recognized that the private property line was about four degrees off perpendicular.

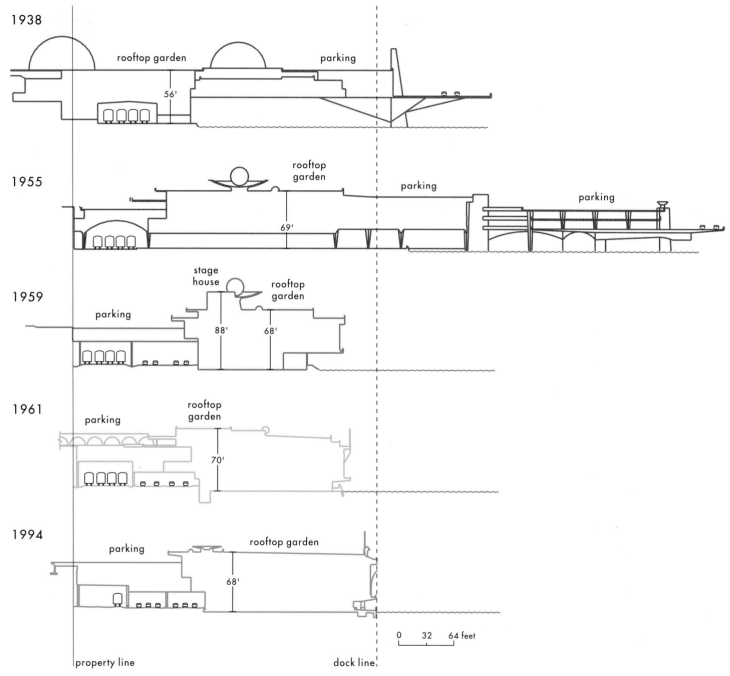

1938

rooftop garden    parking

56'

1955

rooftop
garden

parking

parking

69'

1959

stage
house

rooftop
garden

parking

88'    68'

1961

rooftop
garden

parking

70'

1994

rooftop garden

parking

68'

0    32    64 feet

property line

dock line

FIGURE 7.7

**The Evolving Cross-Section**

© 1999 Taliesin™ Architects, Ltd. and
U.W.–Madison Cartographic Laboratory

Among other things, these cross-sections at the centerline of Martin Luther King Jr. Boulevard chronicle the rise and fall of building height. At 56 feet above the lake, the 1938 design was Wright's lowest. This was the height of the Wilson Street sidewalk, a point Wright selected so that the vista down what was then Monona Avenue would be preserved. However, anyone standing on this sidewalk would have had to look out over a 700-foot plane (Olin Terrace and the garden level of the building) 56 feet above the lake. Consequently, a pedestrian's eyes would not have intersected the lake until nearly 7,000 feet out, leaving little more than a sliver of water.

When Wright increased the height of the rooftop garden to 69 feet in 1955, the lake view for the Wilson Street pedestrian was totally blocked. Beginning with the 1956 plan, Wright added a stage house, a boxy extension on the city side of the building where stage curtains could be stored. As the diagram shows, by 1959 the stage house had grown to 88 feet above the lake, or 32 above the Wilson Street sidewalk. Thus, with the exception of the 1938 design, all of Wright's plans would have eliminated the lake view from the Wilson Street perspective. However, from the lake side of the garden level, all eight of Wright's iterations would have offered spectacular lake views. There pedestrians would have viewed the lake from 7 to 19 feet higher than the old Olin Terrace and from several hundred feet farther out into the lake.

The cross-sections also show why the three-tier parking structure on the 1955 design virtually destroyed the view for people inside Monona Terrace. (For some reason the scale of the 1955 cross-section is different from the footprint shown in Figure 7.6, which causes the cross-section to extend farther into the lake than its footprint counterpart.)

Finally, the cross-sections clearly show how the plans accommodated trains and cars. All except the 1994 plan assumed a railroad tunnel with four tracks. The 1938 and 1955 plans route cars on a cantilevered four-lane highway over the lake, but beginning with the 1956 design, Wright placed cars in a four-lane tunnel; beginning with the Monona Basin plan of the 1970s, six lanes became standard.

proposed would have been about three times bigger than the finest theaters in the world and would have produced complaints about unsatisfactory sight lines, extreme distances to the stage, and the lack of a stage house for dramatic and musical productions.

*Railroad facilities would have been inadequate.* As noted in Chapters 1 and 3, railroad officials and transportation planners correctly noted during Wright's lifetime that a much larger depot and eleven tracks — not four, as the architect proposed — would have been necessary for a workable union depot in Wright's 1938 and 1955 designs.[6]

*Some of Wright's designs meant the lake views from inside the building would have been retrograde.* Wright never tired of saying that his plan would be a long-delayed "marriage of lake and city," but he did not always take best advantage of the visual link for people inside the building. For example, as the cross-section of the 1955 design (see Fig. 4.15) shows, people in the auditorium exhibition hall and community center could not have seen the lake because he surrounded the inner core with a three-tier parking structure. Had it been built, it would have generated jokes about unsurpassed views of hood ornaments and oil stains.[7]

*All the plans would have greatly reduced or blocked the lake view from Martin Luther King Jr. Boulevard.* As Figure 7.7 explains, even the lowest of the eight Wright iterations, the 1938 plan, which was 56 feet high, minimized the lake view for a person standing on the Wilson Street sidewalk, and the later plans eliminated the view. By contrast, the 1909 Nolen plan, the 1939 Segoe plan, the 1979 and 1984 plans by Kenton Peters, and even the 1989 Nolen Terrace Convention Center proposal would have preserved this lake vista.

*Pedestrian access to the lakeshore would have been circuitous.* None of Wright's designs provided direct access to the lakeshore from outside the building, a dramatic contrast with the Nolen, Segoe, and Kenton Peters plans. With Wright's plans pedestrians had to follow a relatively complex path through the inside of the building.

*The 1956–1959 designs suffered from too many functions in too little space.* When Wright was forced to reduce the size of Monona Terrace in 1956 to stay within the state dock line and the city budget, he was also forced to keep nearly all the functions. This meant that the architect had a long trip–small suitcase problem, too much to take along and not enough space to put it in. Through clever packing, Wright was able to get everything in and even close the lid, but this left almost no discretionary space for drama, whimsy, and serenity. If built, the late '50s designs would have been the most complex and exotic mix of functions ever shoehorned into a civic center in the United States. This circumstance would almost surely have caused an embarrassing exodus of functions as they outgrew the tight-fitting shell. Figure 7.8 shows the actual exodus of functions. In fact, it was only *after* most of those functions found homes in other places that Puttnam could inherit a much happier Monona Terrace birthright: a relatively big suitcase and shorter trip, a shell with plenty of space to graciously accommodate a community and convention center.

## BUT IS IT REALLY WRIGHT?

In January 1961, twenty months after Wright died, William Wesley Peters completed a five-hundred-sheet set of plans for Monona Terrace and appeared before the common council to secure its final approval. During the discussion Joe Jackson stood up and asked Peters whether "the plans were the same as those prepared by Frank Lloyd Wright." This was one of the first times someone asked about authenticity but hardly the last.[8]

When Monona Terrace was officially revived in 1990, authenticity became a hot topic. Monona Terrace was called "a tragic compromise of Wright's intentions," "watered down Wright," "McWright," "a fake," "a fraud, not a Frank," "a replica," and "an imitation." These serious charges were not leveled by sidewalk superintendents but by informed opponents, architectural historians, architectural critics, and a Wright biographer. These men and women believed that Tony Puttnam's adaptation of the 1959 iteration violated Wright's design and altered his intentions.[9]

To determine the validity of their criticisms six points deserve consideration. First, there can be little doubt that Wright's singleminded goal during the two decades he worked on Monona Terrace was to leave his bold, unambiguous signature on this unique urban waterfront in his hometown and capital of his native state. He wanted something big, imposing, beautiful, and symmetrical, an inspiring design that was deferential and complementary to the capitol, a building axially aligned with Martin Luther King Jr. Boulevard, and an enduring showcase for his design prowess.[10]

Second, Wright wanted this signature piece *built*, and he did just about everything short of passing out tracts on street corners to make it happen. Indeed, his record of support for the project is almost breathtaking. He testified before official bodies, spoke to Madison organizations, and participated in panels and debates. He wrote dozens of letters, telegrams, guest editorials for local newspapers, pamphlets, and brochure copy. He committed himself and his staff to large amounts of pro bono time. He lowered his fee from 10 to 7 percent. He wined and dined potential

FIGURE 7.8

**The Exodus of Functions**

For his three basic designs noted in Table 7.1, Wright proposed eight functions. As noted in the diagram, seven were either satisfied by other buildings and facilities or, in the case of the union depot, made obsolete by other modes of transportation. This exodus of functions left just one, meetings and exhibits, without a dedicated building. In the decades after Wright's death the need for such facilities, especially for conventions, grew rapidly. One of the great ironies of Monona Terrace was that it was only *after* seven of Wright's original functions had either been satisfied or made obsolete, and *after* the demand for meeting space had burgeoned, that the architect's great megastructure could receive a new functional birthright as a state-of-the-art downtown convention center. There is even the possibility of a future irony: that the union depot Wright proposed in 1938 will become the downtown station for a commuter (light rail) system.

The diagram also shows how three other meeting facilities were constructed to meet the growing and increasingly specialized needs of the market. The Dane County Forum was an early attempt to satisfy the market with an all-purpose facility, while the Dane County Exhibition Hall was designed for large trade shows. The Holiday Inn (now a part of the Marriott chain), a hotel with an attached, relatively small convention facility, is located in Middleton, a municipality contiguous to Madison.

| Government Facilities | Cultural Facilities | Community Center | Marina | Union Railroad Depot | Multi-Purpose Sports Arena | Parking | Meeting and Exhibit Facilities |
|---|---|---|---|---|---|---|---|
| OFFICES, COURTS, JAILS | ART CENTER, THEATERS | YOUTH AND ADULT PROGRAMS | | | | | |
| | | 1946–present A downtown facility whose name and location changed | 1950s–present Public boat ramps on Madison lakes | | | 1950s–1970s Surface parking in Law Park and downtown parking ramps | |
| 1957 City-County Building | 1963 Lincoln School adapted for art center | | | | 1967 Dane County Coliseum | | |
| | | 1972–present Decentralized neighborhood centers | | Made obsolete by automobiles and airplanes | | | 1978 Dane County Forum Building |
| | 1980 Madison Civic Center (art center, small and large theaters) | 1983 Madison Senior Center | | | | | |
| | | | | | | | 1990 Holiday Inn |
| 1994 Public Safety Building | | | | | | | 1995 Dane County Exhibition Hall |
| | | | | 1998 UW Kohl Center | | 1997 Parking ramp in Monona Terrace | 1997 Monona Terrace Community and Convention Center |

supporters at Taliesin. He completed eight iterations, more than for any other project. He worked on the building off and on for twenty-one years, longer than for any other. To do the project he signed what he considered the worst contract of his life and received only $250 in fees during his lifetime for all his work on the building. Wright did all these things because Monona Terrace "was closer to his heart than any other," as Harold Groves once said. Clearly, the architect had deep strong feelings about building this signature piece in his hometown.[11]

Third, Wright was far more interested in maintaining the circle-based shape and proportions of his signature building than in the functions it housed. This is clear from the relative ease with which Wright added and subtracted functions in his three basic designs. With the nonchalance of a person reorganizing a closet, Wright threw out city-county offices, courthouses, jails, and a union railroad depot and then added an art gallery, community center, big exhibit hall, and small theater. Wright's expedient view of interior functions is revealed in a comment he made at a 1954 meeting with city officials. Members of the Auditorium Committee told the architect to reduce the size of his building as a means of cutting its cost, but Wright shot back, "There must be enough other civic functions here — like libraries and museums — to occupy the city and county office space ... in [the] original Monona Terrace plans."[12]

Fourth, only Wright's post-1955 plans for Monona Terrace can be considered a valid point of departure for adaptation as a convention center because these designs are the only ones that place the building *within* the state-established dock line. To go beyond this vertical plane was to propose a political kamikaze mission, an act few Madison leaders were willing to discuss, much less attempt. And of the five post-1955 iterations, the signed plans dated February 15, 1959, are the most valid. They constitute Wright's last will and testament, his eighth and final iteration reflecting twenty-one years of design evolution. That was why Puttnam used the 1959 plans as his template for the Monona Terrace Community and Convention Center.

Fifth, surviving documents of the 1959 redesign — a cluster of sixteen plans, a color rendering (see Figs. 4.33 and 7.9), ten pages of "Synopsis Specifications," and a two-page finish schedule — provide a relatively

clear picture of the exterior, general construction materials, and finishes for various surfaces but, overall, much less information about the inside. To compensate, Puttnam studied the interiors of other large buildings that Wright did near the end of his life, namely, the Marin County Civic Center, the Guggenheim Museum, and the Annunciation Greek Orthodox Church in a Milwaukee suburb.[13]

Sixth, much of what has been published on Monona Terrace (and in aggregate that is very little) contains incorrect, incomplete, or misleading information. At least two factors are responsible for this confusion: most writers have not understood how the design and functions changed over time and have treated the 1955 design as if it were the benchmark.[14]

These six points provide a useful background against which to examine representative challenges to its architectural authenticity.

In an article in the *New Yorker*, Brendan Gill, author of *Many Masks: A Life of Frank Lloyd Wright*, asserted that "the project ... is about half as big as Wright had planned it to be." Although today's Monona Terrace is about half as big as Wright's 1955 design, it is substantially larger than his 1956–1959 iterations. In fact, all of Wright's post-1955 iterations were designed to fit the state's dock line and the city's purse. Thus Puttnam can hardly be accused of diminishing Wright.[15]

In criticizing the height of the building roof, Narciso Menocal, a professor of architectural history at the University of Wisconsin–Madison and a Wright specialist, commented, "It's higher off the street than Wright envisioned." In fact, the top level of the current plan is within six inches of the top level of the 1959 plan. Figure 7.7 shows the relative heights of various versions of the project.[16]

Gill insisted that Wright's original intention "was to create ... a five-deck structure covering seven and one-half acres, which would spread fanwise out over the lake with gardens and fountains on the top deck and, on the decks below, cocktail lounges, restaurants, art galleries, state and county offices, a jail, parking facilities, and a marina." This is a case of iteration confusion where Gill mixes functions from *both* the 1938 and 1955 designs and presents the *combination* as the original recipe. In fact, the 1938 iteration did not contain "cocktail lounges, restaurants, [and] art galleries," nor did the 1955 iteration contain "state and county offices, [or] a jail."[17]

Commenting that "the view of the lake is screened out," Menocal was apparently assuming that Wright's Terrace plans did *not* block the lake view, that Puttnam's convention center did, and that Puttnam's adaptation was therefore a violation of Wright's plans. As noted in Figure 7.7, for a pedestrian standing on the Wilson Street sidewalk at the end of Martin Luther King Jr. Boulevard, the 1938 Wright plan minimized the lake view, and in all seven other iterations Wright eliminated it. Thus it hardly seems fair to say that only Puttnam screened out the lake view.[18]

"The proportions are wrong. [Wright] would not recognize this building as his. It's really sad." This is another of Menocal's criticisms of Puttnam's adaptation. However, a study of the footprints and cross-sections and a comparison of the 1959 rendering and the 1997 completed building (see Figs. 7.6, 7.7, and 7.9) show that Puttnam respected Wright's proportions even as he increased the size.[19]

Referring to Puttnam's conversion of the Terrace to a community and convention center, Gill complained that the new function was "very different than what Wright originally had in mind." What Gill may not have realized was that one of Wright's

FIGURE 7.9

**Comparison of 1959 Rendering and 1997 Building**

© FLW FDN. 5632.10

*Photo by Zane Williams*

One of the best ways to evaluate the authenticity of Monona Terrace is to compare Wright's final lakeside rendering, dated February 15, 1959, with an actual photograph of the completed building. Although an artist's perspective can only approximate a camera's optics, the use of a special panoramic camera allows a meaningful comparison. This photograph, taken with such a camera in December 1997, reveals both similarities and differences.

Monona Terrace is built on the site Wright consistently specified. Tony Puttnam maintained the massing, proportions, and components of the megastructure;

retained in virtually identical form the seven arched lakeside windows; included key Wrightian details such as the three saucer fountains and the drooping mullions on the front window panels; used Wright's choice of concrete for the exterior; and fully incorporated Wright's pendentive concept.

The pendentive concept, explained in Figure 7.2, is perhaps most clearly revealed in the photograph. Wright's goal, to give the building a "lighter ... floating" look, was achieved by employing elements that appear to be suspended in space. For example, the deep recess at the base of the large cylinders makes the outer surface appear to hang from the building.

That Puttnam made changes to the 1959 design is also clear. Federal standards governing minimum highway bridge clearances required that he remove the lowest level of Wright's three-tier parking ramp. State safety codes required Puttnam to truncate the semicircular openings on the sides of the ramp (see Fig. 7.12). He had to add two stair towers, one of which is shown to the left of the large cylinder, to satisfy government codes for emergency exits. To make the towers safer, Puttnam enclosed them in glass. Puttnam also made the entrances to the helixes parallel to the shoreline rather than curved toward John Nolen Drive (see Figs. 4.33 and 7.1). This change allowed cars to

enter and leave the helixes more easily and created an unobstructed staging and loading/unloading area for delivery trucks. To satisfy city demands, Puttnam added a pedestrian and bicycle path along the lakeside of the building. Conversion of the building from a civic to a convention center required Puttnam to lower the floor division point denoted by the canopy on Wright's rendering. Today the thick beams separating the lower and upper levels (see Fig. 6.26) are concealed by a green band of glass across the lakefront facade.

To properly accommodate the convention industry and even allow for growth, Puttnam increased the size of the 1959 building by about 136,000 square feet, which required him to move the front of the building out to the dock line and widen the space behind the large cylinders. This widened space is evident behind the cylinder on the left and can be clearly seen in Fig. 7.6. Finally, Puttnam added the saucers to Wright's light poles around the edge of the Evjue Gardens, changed the mullion pattern on the lakeside windows, and eliminated the two bull's-eye windows on each side of the main window panel.

Additional key facts deserve mention even though they are not evident in the rendering or the photograph. The height of Puttnam's Monona Terrace is within six inches of Wright's 1959 plans and does not contain the hulking stage house on the city side of the building. Wright reluctantly added this feature for vertical storage of stage scenery and curtains and surely would have been delighted by its removal; he thought the stage house destroyed the low profile of the building.

Arguably the most dramatic and inspiring space inside Monona Terrace is the Grand Terrace, the four-hundred-foot south-facing room on the upper level (see Fig. 6.26). Located at the end of the Capitol Promenade, the Grand Terrace and its sweeping arc offer a panoramic lake view and a warm versatile space for receptions, concerts, and large public events. The functional but festive saucer forms selected by Tony Puttnam for this splendid room appear in Wright's work as early as the 1890s.

design goals was to increase Madison's convention business. Beginning in 1955, Wright added a huge flat-floor room that he designated as a "future sports arena, *exhibition hall, or convention hall*" (emphasis added). Similar language appears on plans for the 1956–1959 plan series. Thus to say that Wright did not have conventions in mind for Monona Terrace is wrong. In fact, the exhibit hall in today's convention center occupies the same first-level location chosen by Wright for his post-1955 iterations.[20]

Judy Clowes, a Wisconsin architectural critic, was one of several who criticized changes made to the interior of the building. "The bulk of the interior on all levels has been carved into boxes.... This is a tragic compromise of Wright's intentions....

Wright would also surely have abandoned the project rather than accept the imposition of a trade-show grid. He was much too proud." She is partly right; the football field–sized exhibit hall, the banquet/ballroom, and smaller meeting rooms *are* rectangular. What many do not realize is that meeting planners, the primary clients of convention centers, demand exhibit halls and banquet halls that can be darkened for audiovisual presentations and square display booths that conform to industry standards. From a business standpoint the city would have been foolish to allow the interior to be designed in any form that would have been unattractive to meeting planners. Puttnam's design challenge was to optimize the drama and curves of the lakeside spaces and at the same time satisfy meeting industry standards. Puttnam's decisions to reserve the most

dramatic *curved* lakeside spaces for inviting public concourses and to retain Wright's circular "little theater" as a lecture hall (see Figs. 7.10 and 7.11) are anything but "tragic compromises."[21]

But what about Wright? Would he have abandoned the project rather than comply with meeting industry standards? Probably not. Wright always met or exceeded every specification the city established. Surely he would have met industry standards of the 1990s too. Would Wright have been willing to redesign Monona Terrace as a community and convention center? Given his well-documented desire to build this labor of love, the crusty architect would surely have replied, "Of course, I will redesign it as a community and convention center. What a splendid use for this great building. It will be the best community and convention center in the world!"

This survey shows that most questions about Monona Terrace's authenticity stem from a failure to understand important differences in the various iterations, Wright's overarching interest in erecting a signature building, and the complex history of the project. But this does not mean that Monona Terrace, as built in 1997, is 100 percent authentic. Everyone agrees that the primary function of the building changed from a civic center and auditorium to a community and convention center. The fundamental question is to what extent should Monona Terrace be considered an authentic Wright building? In this context three points should be made:

*The building is located on its original site.* Wright designed almost all his buildings for specific sites, and they cannot be separated from those sites without great loss. No one disputes that Monona Terrace was built on its original site.

*The exterior of the building is very close to Wright's design.* "Identical" would be nice, but contemporary building

**The Lecture Hall**

*© 1997 Hedrich-Blessing, photo by Scott McDonald, courtesy Taliesin™ Architects, Ltd.*

Lecture halls are rarely found in convention centers, and this one has a fascinating history. Occupying the top floor of the large cylinder on the west end of the building, it was earmarked by Wright as a little theater beginning with his 1955 design (see Fig. 4.16). During planning in the 1990s Tony Puttnam learned that University of Wisconsin–related meetings and conventions would represent a relatively large part of the center's overall business and that they would include meetings of international organizations. This prompted the architect to convert Wright's little theater into a lecture hall for the twenty-first century. The three-hundred-seat facility features sophisticated electronic equipment that allows transmission of meetings to satellites, from which they can be "downlinked" to ground-based communications systems around the world. The same equipment allows people in this room to receive satellite signals from almost anywhere. The room also features translation booths for international meetings.

FIGURE 7.12

**Clipped Scallops and a Dreary Tunnel**

*Courtesy* Wisconsin State Journal, *photo by L. Roger Turner*

State codes sometimes thwarted what Wright and Puttnam wanted. This photo captures one such example. The odd opening shapes above the tunnel were supposed to be slices of a perfect circle but had to be truncated because state codes require openings in parking ramps to be no less than 42 inches above the floor. Consequently, safety trumped beauty. Many understandably thought the strange shape was an architectural error. Many also thought Wright would never sanction a purely utilitarian tunnel, but this is not true. In fact, Wright showed the tunnel in all his post-1955 designs, but he never provided instructions for how it should be treated.

codes, materials, and technology make this standard unrealistic (see Fig. 7.12) and even undesirable. Most who compare Wright's 1959 design with the completed building agree that Puttnam followed the plan with sensitivity.

*The redesigned interior has been sympathetically executed with Wrightian grammar, detailing, and colors while accommodating a new primary function, contemporary* building codes, state-of-the-art equipment, and modern materials. *The salmon-tinted beige walls, indirect lighting, and custom-designed furniture, carpeting, and lighting fixtures used in Monona Terrace reflect Wright's approach to interior design (see Fig. 7.13).[22]*

Those who say that constructing Monona Terrace as a community and convention center is an intellectual felony should consider this hypothetical scenario: Suppose that Wright's 1959 version had been built. Would it be adequate today? Almost certainly not. By this time, the size of the exhibit hall, its low ceilings, and inadequate vehicular access would have made it obsolete. Madison Art Center leaders would almost surely have abandoned the gallery in the 1970s because it was too small. The youth (community) center probably would have closed in the 1960s, a casualty of the surge to the suburbs. By the 1980s the voracious space demands of modern heating and cooling systems would have required the conversion of some facilities for mechanical equipment rooms. Thus, after forty years the interior would have required major changes.

Would making these substantial interior changes to the 1959 Monona Terrace be sufficient to drum the building out of the Wright corps? Surely not. Everywhere else in the country, the historic preser-

FIGURE 7.13

**The Effervescent Entrance**

*©1997 Hedrich-Blessing, photo by Scott McDonald, courtesy Taliesin™ Architects, Ltd.*

Among the most interesting architectural features in Monona Terrace is Tony Puttnam's felicitous interplay of arch and shadow just inside the main entrance. The effervescent mix of concentric vertical arches, a sweeping horizontal arc, the shallow curve of saucers and plaster details, light poles, and indirect lighting commonly evokes smiles of pleasure from visitors. The saucers and indirect lighting were Wright trademarks that date to the architect's Oak Park days. Puttnam incorporated the gentle arch shown in this photo along the broad Capitol Promenade that begins between the two saucer-bearing columns and extends to the Grand Terrace. The hallway to the right leads to break-out rooms, lecture hall, and gift shop; the corridor behind the photographer leads to the banquet hall and ballroom.

vation community approvingly calls such changes "adaptive reuse" because the practice gives buildings new functional leases on life. This raises an interesting question: If it is all right to make substantial changes to the interior of a forty-year-old Wright-designed building so that it can serve current civic needs, would this be so different from taking Wright's 1959 plan, building it on the original site, keeping the design integrity of the exterior, and adapting its interior for a community and convention center?

Isn't it better to allow the sun to shine on a Wrightian masterpiece and allow people to experience its beauty than to require the building to remain encapsulated in a great roll of dusty plans? Monona Terrace is a compelling case in point. If a new mix of functions had not been found for the Terrace, its plans would still be languishing in the Taliesin Archives. The Terrace also shows that at least some of Wright's unexecuted designs can be responsibly and successfully adapted for these new uses. This type of life-giving adaptive reuse should be encouraged even though the new functions were not envisioned by Wright or his clients.

Wright would have been the last person to insist on absolute adherence to any of his plans. He could hardly go through a room in either Taliesin complex without swinging his cane at a wall and decreeing to his entourage, "Boys, I want you to move that wall out eleven feet and add more glass." He seldom passed an associate's drafting table without penciling in changes. And he routinely told contractors to make changes in the middle of construction.

On the question of who Wright would have wanted to do the final Monona Terrace design, there can be little doubt that he would have strongly preferred a Taliesin-trained associate. A remarkable but little understood quality of the Taliesin design studio was Wright's extraordinary success in developing architects who could function as "pencils in his hand."

This cadre of architects became so proficient at working in his idiom that all Wright had to do was prepare a rough sketch and his associates could take it from there. So Wright surely would have been pleased to have Puttnam adapt Monona Terrace. As a young apprentice in 1954–1955 Puttnam worked on the model for Monona Terrace. As a young drafter in 1960, he did about a quarter of all the architectural drawings that contractors used to bid the project in early 1961. And during the years he worked directly with Wright and later with the successor firm, Puttnam developed unusual skill in doing plans and designs in the Wright idiom.[23]

In summary, to describe Monona Terrace as a "tragic compromise of Wright's intentions" or, indeed, in any of the other terms used by the critics quoted earlier, is to grossly misunderstand the history of this building and Frank Lloyd Wright's regard for it. Monona Terrace is a brilliant reuse of one of his masterpieces and a vindication of his apprentice system. As William Wesley Peters told Joe Jackson in 1961 when he asked if Peters' revision was "really Wright's plans," "They are a logical and legitimate development of his plans."

## THE PLACE OF MONONA TERRACE IN WRIGHT'S LIFEWORK

"Your difficulties with Frank Lloyd Wright seem to be interminable," commiserated Ladislas Segoe in a 1958 letter to Joe Jackson. "It is a pity that people of his stature so often do not realize that they have outlived their usefulness professionally or otherwise — and conduct themselves accordingly. Singers and other musicians most often make this mistake and so do some so called 'elder statesmen.'... I think it is deplorable and also sad."[24]

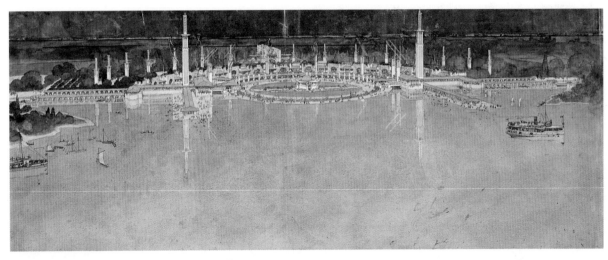

FIGURE 7.14

**Wolf Lake Amusement Park**

© FLW FDN. 9510.001

Forty years before Wright conceived Monona Terrace, he designed this recreational complex on Wolf Lake, southeast of Chicago, where people could drink, dine, gamble, swim, listen to music, and shop. Like its Madison counterpart, this unrealized, turn-of-the-century proposal was symmetrical, semicircular, and extended into the water. A close study of the plans shows that Wright even included parking spaces for automobiles — then owned only by the wealthy.

Happily, Wright did not realize that he had outlived his usefulness when at seventy-one he dashed off his first pencil sketches of Monona Terrace. Happily, Wright did not think of his condition as "deplorable and sad" when at ninety-one he signed his eighth and last set of plans for his late-life passion. Now that the building stands, it demands its place in the Wright oeuvre. So where, exactly, does it belong?

*Assorted superlatives.* Of all Wright's designs, Monona Terrace, with its 603,000 square feet and $67 million price tag, is the largest and most expensive yet to be constructed. With a cumulative total of at least four thousand sheets of sketches, plans, and renderings, and about one thousand pages of specifications, Monona Terrace is Wright's most extensively documented building. Wright's eight designs for it make Monona Terrace his most frequently designed building. And surely his twenty-one years of work make it his longest-

running project. The personal effort he devoted to Monona Terrace is not exceeded by any other project. More than four thousand newspaper clippings testify that no building in Wright's corpus generated more controversy than Monona Terrace. And then there's the distinction that most delighted Wright: Monona Terrace was the only building for which he was ever elected architect.[25]

*Circle-based designs.* For Monona Terrace the circle and its evolved cousins — the cylinder, saucer, sphere, and dome — constituted the primary forms in its design and decorative details. The circle commonly appeared in Wright's murals, light screens, and terra cotta ornaments, and the architect had used its three-dimensional forms as the basis of entire buildings since the 1890s. One of the best but least known early examples is the cylindrical 1893 Lake Monona boathouse (see Fig. A.1). By the mid-1930s circle-based buildings had

**The Guggenheim Museum**

*Ezra Stoller © Esto*

The Guggenheim shared several qualities with Monona Terrace. Next to the Terrace, on which Wright worked on and off for twenty-one years, the Guggenheim was the architect's second-longest-running project. Wright signed his first contract to design the museum in 1943, but it did not open until October 1959, six months after Wright died. During those sixteen tumultuous years the original client died, the site was expanded, and costs soared. Wright had to redesign the building six times, invert the ziggurat shape, and battle New York building codes and a new, unsympathetic museum director. As in the case of Monona Terrace, Wright's decision to finish the Guggenheim with concrete provoked sustained criticism. Another similarity with Monona Terrace is the museum's circle-based design and use of the helix. Finally, contrary to his usual build-in-the-country imperative, Wright had to integrate the Guggenheim and Monona Terrace into difficult urban settings.

become more common and remained so for the rest of his career.[26]

*A rare example of symmetry.* Axial symmetry represented a rare but persistent pattern in Wright's work and most often appeared in public buildings such as Monona Terrace, Midway Gardens, the Imperial Hotel, and Wolf Lake Amusement Park (see Fig. 7.14).[27]

*A challenging urban waterfront site.* Wright spent most of his life railing against cities and cramped urban sites and counseling clients to seek larger suburban and rural sites. Monona Terrace, however, could not be exported to the country; Wright's only choice was to make it blend with its natural and created environment. In many other urban settings Wright designed fortress-like buildings that denied their ugly surroundings and boasted beautiful skylighted interiors. But the site for Monona Terrace was anything but dreary. It stood on a narrow isthmus two blocks from the capitol on a thirty-four-hundred-acre lake. Though beautiful, the site bristled with challenges. To build there Wright had to thrust the structure out from a cliff, cross four busy railroad tracks, and anchor its foundation in a soggy lake bottom. Wright relished this stimulating mix of engineering and aesthetic problems. Elsewhere, challenging sites such as cliffs, ravines, craggy mountain tops, and water frontages (see Fig. 7.14) evoked some of Wright's boldest and most visionary designs. That clearly happened with Monona Terrace.[28]

*Fascination with concrete.* Although concrete became a common structural element in the early twentieth century, most architects preferred traditional finish materials such as brick or stone. To Wright this practice was unforgivably stodgy. Concrete is a magnificent material that can be molded into almost any shape, tinted and textured, and strengthened with steel to defy gravity; it also has a clean, modern look. Consequently, throughout his career Wright used concrete to achieve some of his boldest designs for churches, museums, and banks as well as houses. That was why Wright specified concrete for Monona Terrace. Among his other famous concrete structures are the Unity Temple (see Fig. 2.29), Annunciation Greek Orthodox Church (see Fig. 4.27), and the Guggenheim (see Fig. 7.15).[29]

*One of several multifunction megastructures.* Monona Terrace was one of several large multipurpose buildings by Wright. Perhaps the best known is a 1947 fantasy designed for the confluence of the Ohio, Allegheny, and Monongahela Rivers in downtown Pittsburgh known as Pittsburgh Point. The project covered thirty-six acres and would have cost about $400 million in 1947 (see Fig. 7.16).[30]

*Emphasis on automobile accommodations.* Monona Terrace embodied Wright's deep belief that buildings and cities had to be redesigned to accommodate the automobile. As early as the turn of the century, when cars were little more than toys of the rich, Wright began to include parking facilities in his projects, such as Wolf Lake (see Fig. 7.14). In the early 1930s he designed a utopian automobile-based community known as Broadacre City. When he designed a church in Kansas City in 1940, he began with the footprint of the parking garage and put the church on top. But Wright was not just interested in providing a convenient place to park cars; he also wanted to enhance the pleasure of driving, and he found many ways to do this. In 1924, for example, Wright prepared a plan to build a great spiral road around a sugar loaf–shaped Maryland mountain with a planetarium inside and a restaurant on top. To Wright the destination was important, but getting there, going up and down the mountain on this great ziggurat road, was half the fun. Similarly,

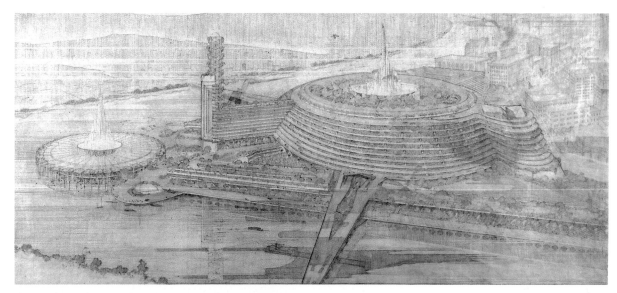

FIGURE 7.16

**Pittsburgh Point Civic Center**

© FLW FDN. 4821.003

Wright's fifteen-level complex for Pittsburgh contained parking, a planetarium, cinemas, art galleries, concert halls, an opera house, convention facilities, and a glass-covered sports stadium. Like the architect's design for Monona Terrace, Pittsburgh Point was circle based and featured a rooftop garden and water dome. The multifunction complex far exceeded what Pittsburgh could afford and was never built.

Wright's dramatic cantilevered roads in the 1938 Olin Terraces and the 1955 Monona Terrace plans were designed to delight motorists as they swooped out over Lake Monona.[31]

*Transformation of traditional forms.* One expression of Wright's genius was his ability to offer fresh variations on traditional forms. When the governor of Arizona insisted that the new capitol building have a dome, Wright proposed a huge copper-clad concrete hexagon whose interior space offered soaring beauty and people-friendly spaces, the antithesis of the traditional symbol of government authority (see Fig. 7.17). Similarly, Wright had no interest in duplicating the classical dome of the Wisconsin capitol, yet he found ways to create visual echoes of this form in his Monona Terrace designs. Instead of a single heavy stone dome, Wright proposed

three lightweight transparent counterparts of steel and glass and placed them over the auditorium and courtrooms to serve as primary light sources. Then, instead of positioning a sculptured figure on top of a dome, Wright advocated placing figures inside them. As a further transforming element, he proposed pumping water over the glass domes. Wright and whimsy were good friends.[32]

*Substitution of alternative designs for officially approved ones.* "Permit me," Wright would sometimes seem to say, "to substitute a superior alternative for your pedestrian design." That was what happened with the official Arizona capitol proposal that Wright ridiculed as a "telephone pole with a derby hat and two wastebaskets for the legislature." That was also what happened in Madison. The proposal to construct a large, yawningly ordinary city-county building on a conventional site made Wright so mad that he intervened. The more undistinguished the architect and mundane the design, the more Wright was likely to offer his own solution. In these situations Wright would sometimes abandon his usual fee for the sake of righting a great wrong. He took on the Madison project merely hoping for some remuneration or, in the case of the Arizona project, with no hope at all, or, as he called it, his "Pro Bono Publico."[33]

*A rare government commission.* Wright rarely received government commissions and of these only three were built: the hill-bridging Marin County Civic Center (see Fig. 4.27), a two-room school near Spring Green, and Monona Terrace. The dearth is explained by the controversy that swirled around Wright so much of his life — his consistent antiwar stands, tendency to try new and untested designs and technologies, the costliness of his designs, and his impatience in dealing with government committees. All these factors were hallmarks of Monona Terrace.

*Recycling designs.* Monona Terrace offers manifold examples of Wright's lifelong tendency to refine, revise, and recycle architectural details from one project to another. For example, the saucers that appeared in Olin Terraces as great fountains actually had been appearing in Wright's work since the 1890s as planters; the festive light poles that surrounded the lake edge of the Monona Terrace roof first appeared in his 1914 Midway Gardens project; and the huge "water domes," those fanciful fountains in the 1938 design, first appeared several months earlier in a plan for the campus of Florida Southern College. By the same token, some features of Olin Terraces later appeared in other buildings (see Fig. 7.18).[34]

*Bold signature statements for his primary places of residence.* During the last decade of his career Wright designed major buildings for each of the cities in which he spent

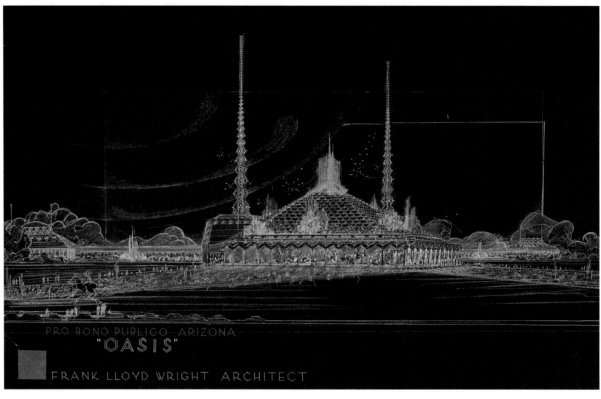

FIGURE 7.17

**Arizona Capitol**

© FLW FDN. 5732.004

Dismayed by the prospect of a downtown high-rise addition to Arizona's capitol, Wright intervened in 1957 with what he thought was a better idea: put the building in a suburban park, give it a fresh, nontraditional hexagonal shape, and adorn it with native materials such as onyx, copper, and turquoise. Wright's proposal spawned a dedicated support group that pushed for its consideration in a statewide referendum.

the most time: Madison, Chicago, and Phoenix. For Madison he did Monona Terrace, for Chicago the mind-boggling 528-story "Mile High" office building for 100,000 people and 15,000 cars, and for Phoenix the bold design for a new state capitol (see Fig. 7.17).[35]

## THE POWER OF WRIGHT'S VISION

What if Paul Harloff, the retired electrical contractor, had not button-holed Wright at the Park Hotel

one night in the mid-1930s and inveigled him with an irresistibly big idea? What if Madison had not been Wright's hometown? What if Ted Boyle, a maverick Madison council member, had not tried to use Wright's dream civic center to derail a plan to build a city-county building in 1953? What if Helen Groves and Mary Lescohier, the two "professors' wives," had not pulled off a referendum that almost everybody said was impossible? What if Ivan Nestingen, the young lawyer, had not championed Monona Terrace from the mayor's

Many who walk down these dramatic multistoried corridors of the famous 1957 Marin County Civic Center think this was the first building in which Wright incorporated the graduated (V-shaped) light well that allowed daylight to illuminate offices at the lowest level. Actually, Wright introduced this detail in plans for his 1938 Olin Terraces. The earlier light well, shown in Figure 3.13 (note the word *light* in that cross-section on the left of the three-story space marked *offices*), is just one of many instances in which Wright recycled design concepts.

This shot, taken while the western sky was still painted in dusky hues, is reminiscent of the familiar 1955 night rendering (see Fig. 4.14). Light poles surround the Evjue Gardens like a tiara, spotlights illuminate the relief of the recessed windows, and bollards mark the lakeside promenade. Visible at the top of the arched windows is the Grand Terrace; below the dark band is a popular room called Lakeside Commons; and below the canopy is the lobby outside the exhibition hall.

office in the late 1950s? What if Wright had refused to sign the "worst architectural contract in his life"? What if Van Potter, the U.W. cancer researcher, had not proposed treating Madison's three-mile urban waterfront as a single site for cultural facilities? What if William Wesley Peters, the head of Wright's successor architectural practice,

had not kept the flame burning with his Monona Basin plan? What if Paul Soglin, the radical young mayor, had not tried to build a Wright auditorium on Madison's lakeshore in 1974? What if George Nelson, a prominent Republican businessman, had not developed a strong working relationship with Soglin while working on the Madison Civic

Center? What if Governor Tommy Thompson had not had his eyes opened to Wright's international fame during a Tokyo trade mission in 1987? What if Jim Carley, a prominent real estate developer, had not taken home a set of Monona Terrace plans while attending a meeting at Taliesin in 1988? What if Soglin and Nelson had not conspired to reintroduce

FIGURE 7.20

**The Long View**

*Photo by Zane Williams*

Almost everyone who goes to Monona Terrace gravitates to the highest point closest to the lake — where this couple is standing — to take in the panoramic view of Lake Monona and the gentle hills of southern Wisconsin beyond. It is a view that inspires big thoughts. In the mid-1930s Frank Lloyd Wright and Paul Harloff stood at the railing of Olin Terrace, a similar promontory 350 feet behind this couple. There the two men conceived the vision of a great civic building linking the city to the lake, but the idea triggered one of the most contentious civic battles in American history, a battle that Wright finally won posthumously. The couple at the railing appear to be enjoying Wright's vision.

Monona Terrace as a convention center in 1990? What if Dick Wagner and Mike Blaska, two former Dane County board chairs, had lacked the courage to oppose their constituents' will in the 1992 referendum?

This list of questions could be continued for pages; if it were, it would only show how wildly improbable Monona Terrace is. But it *did* get built, despite the overwhelming odds, and the credit must go to Wright and a handful of dedicated champions who kept thwarting the statisticians with their seemingly quixotic behavior.

Something special was going on here or this story would have ended with one of Wright's gidd lunges for the brass ring. Whatever it was persisted through three different Wright designs and propelled three different coalitions of champions during three different decades.

Although many hoped that Wright's big-shouldered building would boost business, what propelled this project for nearly six decades went beyond money. What inspired people over time was that Wright's plan was not just an idea; it was an *ideal.* Monona Terrace champions pushed for its construction because it would contribute brilliantly to Madison's destiny as a great city and the capital of a proud commonwealth, because it would be a place where citizens would experience true human community, and because its beauty would inspire and enrich its users (see Figs. 7.19 and 7.20).

These transcendent values were what excited most Monona Terrace champions most of the time, what allowed them to endure for so long and through so many defeats, what motivated their reluctance to compromise for something ordinary, and, in the end, what allowed this great vision to triumph over such great odds. John Nolen well understood the connection between transcendent values and great achievement. As he said at the 1934 dedication of the University of Wisconsin arboretum, "Ideals are popularly regarded as visionary, but nothing could be more erroneous. History shows that achievements in art, architecture or engineering were ideals before they were realities." No building shows this more clearly than Monona Terrace. If it had not been forged with ideals and cast as a great vision, it would never have been built.

In 1953, before construction of the Guggenheim began, an elaborate exhibit of Wright's work was staged in a temporary structure erected on the museum site. While in New York overseeing preparations for the exhibit, Wright bought two large granite lions from an art dealer and had them shipped to the Fifth Avenue site. A few minutes after they were delivered, Wright arrived by taxi and told John Rattenbury, an apprentice, "John, go tell the foreman to assemble a crew and have them move these figures to the entrance of the model house," a major part of the exhibit. The crew arrived, and Rattenbury told the foreman where Wright wanted the lions. Six burly workers bent over and tried to pick up the half-ton stone felines. They struggled and struggled, but nothing worked. The workmen told Rattenbury that they would have to use a forklift. When Wright heard this, he turned to Rattenbury and said, "John, go get the boys from Taliesin over here." He was referring to a group of apprentices he had brought to New York to help set up the exhibit. When the "boys" arrived, Wright walked over to the first lion, tapped it on the head with his cane, and said, "Okay, boys, I want you to pick up this lion and follow me." With that, Wright whirled around and walked to where he wanted the lion. Moments later, Wright, his apprentices, and the lions passed the foreman and his laborers. The foreman could not believe what he was seeing and gasped, "That's not possible!" What the foreman did not understand was that, to Wright, anything was possible.[36]

Even Monona Terrace.

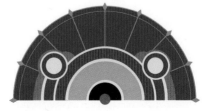

# AFTERWORD: FUTURE SYNERGY

Few cities have a more potent Frank Lloyd Wright legacy to share with the world than Madison, Wisconsin. The architect is arguably the most famous person ever born in Wisconsin, and Madison is his hometown. Many buildings that were important to Wright as a young man still stand and can be appreciated (see Fig. 2.4). Madison's famous son designed thirty-two buildings for his hometown, and they span nearly every category undertaken during the sixty-six years of his independent architectural practice, 1893 to 1959. Counting Monona Terrace, twelve were built and nine still stand, including the world-famous Unitarian Meeting House.[1]

Surely the time has come to more effectively realize this powerful Wright legacy. At the very least, government agencies or historical organizations could erect markers denoting the locations of Wright's unexecuted designs. A mix of private and public funds could be pooled to construct several of those designs on their original sites and for their original purposes. These include the 1893 boathouse on Lake Mendota (see Fig. 2.25), the 1893 boathouse on Lake Monona just a thousand feet east of Monona Terrace (see Fig. A.1), and the 1905 boathouse designed for a Yahara River site (see Fig. 2.27). Several structures designed by William Wesley Peters for the 1967 Monona Basin Plan also could be constructed, including the dramatic lake fountains along the causeway (see Fig. A.2) and a center for performing arts in Olin Park (see Fig. 5.10). Still another opportunity for Madison to enhance its hometown link with Wright would be to establish a museum featuring a thoughtfully constructed permanent exhibit and touring shows. Finally, one of the world's great architectural treasures, Taliesin, lies just forty miles west of Madison. The tourism synergy of these opportunities could be extraordinary.

FIGURE A.1

**1893 Lake Monona Boathouse Rendering**

*Courtesy Anderson Illustration Associates*

On Saturday, April 22, 1989, just three weeks after the defeat of the Nolen Terrace Convention Center referendum, the front page of the *Capital Times* carried this full-color artist's rendering of Frank Lloyd Wright's 1893 boathouse. As Chapter 2 and Figure 2.25 note, Wright designed the building when he was just twenty-six and in his first year in private practice. The boathouse was in the news because it had just been awarded a $1 million grant from the Evjue Foundation, the charitable arm of the *Capital Times*, to allow the building to be constructed close to its original site and in accordance with Wright's plans.

The grant was a response to a mid-1980s effort of the city parks department to create an additional public lakefront open space and recreational opportunities on the east end of Law Park. The "aquatic facility" required that four and a half acres of the lakeshore be filled and included the construction of a marina and a building at the foot of King Street, roughly in the center of the park. What the planners did not realize was that this was where Wright had proposed to build his splendid boathouse in 1893.

The rendering clearly shows that Wright wanted to use the building as an architectural punctuation point at the end of King Street, the street leading to the capitol. Unfortunately, the city later vacated the King Street right-of-way between Wilson Street and the lake so that a private building could be constructed, thereby blocking the view of the capitol from the boathouse and vice versa. The Shingle Style building includes Sullivanesque features such as the broad arched door and early Prairie features such as banded windows, broad roof overhangs, and low-angled hipped roofs (visible in the corner rooms).

Although the $4.5 million project was supported by most neighborhood residents, the state Department of Natural Resources, and the Army Corps of Engineers, it was attacked by environmentalists, several council members, and others because it required filling part of the lake. Immediately after his election Mayor Paul Soglin supported the construction of the boathouse but put it on the back burner after he introduced Monona Terrace.

The unique 1893 building could still be built within just a few feet of its original site (pushed lakeward by John Nolen Drive) and used exactly as it was intended — as a public boathouse for nonmotorized watercraft. The Monona boathouse is probably the first cylindrical building that Wright ever designed and a rare example of a nonresidential structure from Wright's early career. To have two Wright buildings within a thousand feet of each other, one designed during his first year of private practice and the other during his last (1959), would be a rare distinction.

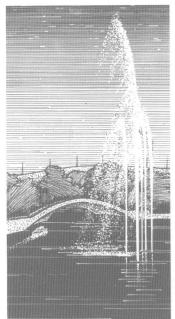

Drawing of Causeway Fountain

© 1999 Taliesin™ Architects, Ltd.

Plan Showing Fountain Locations

© 1999 Taliesin™ Architects, Ltd.

FIGURE A.2

**Monona Basin
Causeway Fountains**

One of the most dramatic features of William Wesley Peters' Monona Basin plan was his proposal for a series of fountain jets around the edge of the causeway. Peters suggested that they be located in semicircular bays, shown on the color plan, and equipped with pumps capable of shooting water high into the air from a point just slightly below the surface of the lake.

APPENDICES

NOTES

BIBLIOGRAPHICAL ESSAY

INDEX

ANALYSIS OF LEGISLATIVE INTENT FOR 1927 AND 1931 DOCK-LINE LAWS

Why did Madison ask the state legislature to pass dock-line bills in 1927 and 1931? The question was raised and answered by opponents of Monona Terrace during the the 1950s auditorium crusade. Their goal was to prove that the legislature never intended to allow a large building such as Monona Terrace to be built on the new filled land authorized by these bills. However, our research failed to find any evidence that the city or the state had any interest in regulating the size of a public building in what would become Law Park.

We could find just one contemporaneous document that addressed the question of intent for the 1927 law (Laws of 1927, Chapter 485). It was a letter from Edwin Witte, chief of the Legislative Reference Library, to Madison city attorney Frank Jenks, dated March 21, 1927. Witte asked Jenks, the bill's author, for instructions on how to proceed with Jenks's bill "relating to the establishment of the city of Madison of dock lines and the construction of a road across

Lake Monona." However, from discussions at the time it seems clear that city leaders also sought to remove illegal privately owned boathouses from the Monona shore and to at least partially implement the 1909 Nolen plan.

Sometime after the 1927 dock-line bill was passed, someone discovered that the law suffered from two serious problems: it failed to specify the purposes for which the city could fill the lake, and it did not give the city the power it needed to remove the dilapidated boathouses along the Lake Monona shoreline. Both problems were corrected with the 1931 bill that authorized "parks, playgrounds, bathing beaches, municipal boat houses, piers, wharves, *public buildings* [emphasis added], highways, streets, pleasure drives and boulevards." The bill specifically authorized the city to "bring any action to restrain, enjoin or abate any nuisance or purpresture" (boathouses) in the area created by the dock line.

The 1931 bill (which became Laws of 1931, Chapter 301)

was introduced by the Committee on Corporations and Taxation on April 10, 1931. State records show that the bill was written by Ted Lewis, the Madison city attorney, and brought to the committee by state senator Glen D. Roberts. The bill was referred to the assembly's committee on State and Local Government Affairs, which held a hearing on May 26, 1931, at which Lewis spoke in favor of the bill and no one spoke against it. A second hearing before the Senate Committee on Corporations and Taxation was held on May 6, 1931, at which Roberts and Lewis spoke in favor and Judge George Kroncke (a boathouse owner) spoke against. The state senate passed the bill unanimously on May 15, and the assembly followed suit on June 12, 1931.

A single newspaper account of a legislative hearing specifies the purpose for which the 1931 bill was passed. A *Capital Times* article dated May 7, 1931, says the bill was designed "to clean up the Lake Monona shore line of its old shacks near the railroad tracks." The article

suggests that once the shacks were removed, the city could use the area for any of the purposes outlined in the bill.

Lewis' inclusion of eleven functions in his bill strongly suggests that city officials wanted to authorize the broadest possible range of desirable uses for this filled land. The absence of any language limiting building size shows that the city was not then interested in this subject.

These points notwithstanding, opponents of Wright's Monona Terrace were eager to prove that the 1931 bill was intended to preclude a *large* public building, but the arguments for this position are hardly convincing. In his "brief" submitted in support of his 1957 bill to limit the height of buildings within the dock line to twenty feet (Summary of Facts in Support of Bill 300A), Carroll Metzner argued that no 1931 bill–related document shows "one scintilla of evidence that the city contemplated a large public building" at the end of Monona Avenue. Neither is there a scintilla of

evidence that the legislature wanted to limit the size of public buildings.

In a letter dated August 28, 1958, Joe Jackson fallaciously argued to Ladislas Segoe that "since the Nolen Plan was the *only* [emphasis added] plan in existence when the City of Madison requested the Legislature in 1927 and 1931 for permission to fill in along the Monona shore line in order to *create a park and driveway* [Jackson's emphasis]," the city and legislature were using the dock-line bills to implement the 1909 Nolen plan. Jackson goes on to say that he and other opponents of the Terrace prepared a 42-by-102-inch enlargement of the Nolen plan and used it at legislative hearings to prove that this was the plan Madison sought to implement with the 1927 and 1931 bills.

This was a classic attempt by Jackson to revise history. There can be no doubt that Nolen was Jackson's hero and that Jackson zealously sought to implement the 1909 Nolen plan.

Nevertheless, by 1927 Madison had *two* plans: the 1909 Nolen plan and the 1922 Bartholomew plan, and the latter specifically proposed a road around Lake Monona *in the same location* as the 1927 dock line. Both plans were given great play by the newspapers of the time and were seriously considered by civic leaders. Moreover, if the Nolen plan had been the only goal of city leaders in 1927, the city would have had to seek permission from the legislature to fill in much more of the shoreline. The 1927 bill allowed the city to fill out about 350 feet from the Olin Terrace retaining wall, whereas the Nolen plan required fill to about 600 feet. It is true that Madison officials thought that filling the lakeshore was desirable and that *one* of their long-term goals was to imple-ment the Nolen plan. Indeed, as the 1927 dock-line bill was working its way through the legislature, city leaders were making long-term plans that included Nolen's plan. For example, in June 1927 the common council officially designated the six blocks on

either side of Nolen's mall as the official city "civic center." However, from none of these circumstances can we say that city leaders were interested in 1931 in limiting the size of public buildings that might be built on the new filled land. Ironically, Nolen himself had proposed two very large public buildings in his plan (see Figs. 1.17 and 1.18), but Jackson chose not to acknowledge this fact.

# APPENDIX B

MEMBERS OF THE MONONA TERRACE COMMISSION, 1990 TO 1992

George A. Nelson, Chair

FINANCE
COMMITTEE

W. Jerome Frautschi, co-chair
Mary Lou Munts, co-chair

Wayne Bigelow
Deborah Carter-Lawson
Betty Franklin-Hammonds
Ann Kovich
Darold Lowe
Huey L. Mays
Sue Rohan
William Sayles
Scott Truehl
Linda Weimer
Robert Zache
Richard Zillman

PHYSICAL PLANNING
COMMITTEE

Donald Helfrecht, co-chair
Henry Lufler, co-chair

Judy Bowser
Jim Cavanaugh
Robert Dye
Marshall Erdman
Otto Festge
Ricardo Gonzalez
Mary Lang-Sollinger
Kelly McDowell
Wayne McGown
Thomas Miron
Frederic Mohs
George A. Nelson

# NOTES

## FREQUENTLY USED ABBREVIATIONS

Madison's primary business organization, which put out a regular newsletter called the *Bulletin*, changed its name several times over the years. Until 1937 its newsletter was known as the *Association of Commerce Bulletin*. From 1937 to 1952 it was called the *Madison and Wisconsin Foundation Bulletin*; from 1952 to 1957 it was the *Madison Chamber of Commerce and Foundation Bulletin*; from 1957 to 1972 it was the *Madison Chamber of Commerce Bulletin*. All citations within the notes are simply to the *Bulletin*.

**BUC**
Butts Unprocessed Collection

**CMM**
City of Madison Microfiche Collection (old council records, etc.), City Records Center

**CMU**
City of Madison Unprocessed Collections (old mayoral files, etc.)

**CT**
*Capital Times*

**DCBP**
*Dane County Board Proceedings*

**DCD**
*Dane County Deeds*

**FLWA**
Frank Lloyd Wright Archives

**LUC**
Lescohier Unprocessed Collection

**MCCP**
*Madison Common Council Proceedings*

**MMRS**
Madison Municipal Reference Service, Madison Public Library

**SHSW**
State Historical Society of Wisconsin

**TAA**
Taliesin Architects Archives

**UUA**
Unitarian Universalist Archives

**UWA**
University of Wisconsin Archives

**WSJ**
*Wisconsin State Journal*

## CHAPTER 1

### A STAGE FOR THE DRAMA

1. For excellent firsthand accounts see the *Madison Democrat* and the *Wisconsin State Journal (WSJ)* for February 27, 1904, and for several days thereafter. For a more scholarly view of the fire see Stan Cravens' article, "Capitals and Capitols in Early Wisconsin," *Wisconsin Blue Book, 1983–84* (Madison: Wisconsin Legislature, 1983), pp. 163–65.

2. For details on the competition see Capitol Improvement Commission, *Program for Architects' Competition for Wisconsin State Capitol*, April 1904. The commission was established by Laws of 1903, Chapter 399, which took effect May 27. Extensive information on the capitol construction, including the *Program*, is available in State of Wisconsin Capitol Commission, general files, 1903–27, series 833 and 138, State Historical Society of Wisconsin (SHSW). (The commission was known as the Capitol Improvement Commission until the 1904 fire, after which it became the Wisconsin State Capitol Commission.)

3. "Report of the Capitol Improvement Commission," *Senate Journal*, January 30, 1905. The other entrants were H. C. Koch and Company and Ferry and Clas, both of Milwaukee. For a helpful general account of the process, see Henry-Russell Hitchcock and William Seale, *Temples of Democracy: The State Capitols of the USA* (New York: Harcourt Brace Jovanovich, 1976), pp. 240–42. To get a flavor of the debate surrounding the Gilbert proposal, see "Objections to the Selection of Gilbert Plans," 1905, a booklet privately published by opponents and presented to the Joint Committee on Capitol Grounds (Government Documents Division, SHSW). Significantly, Gilbert put the main entrance on Monona Avenue. Consequently, he oriented the building along Main Street, and its wings nearly touched the sidewalks along Carroll and Pinckney Streets.

4. David Mollenhoff, *Madison: A History of the Formative Years* (Dubuque, Iowa: Kendall-Hunt, 1982), pp. 295–96.

5. For background on this fascinating period in Wisconsin's history, see Bernard Weisberger, *The La Follettes of Wisconsin: Love and Politics in Progressive America* (Madison: University of Wisconsin Press, 1993); Robert C. Nesbit, *Wisconsin: A History* (Madison: University of Wisconsin Press, 1973), p. 429; Robert S. Maxwell, *La Follette and the Rise of the Progressives in Wisconsin* (Madison: State Historical Society of Wisconsin, 1956), pp. 100, 195; Wisconsin Library Association, *Wisconsin: A Guide to the Badger State* (New York: Duell, Sloan, and Pearce, 1941), pp. 62, 84–85, 100; William Francis Raney, *Wisconsin: A Story of Progress* (Englewood Cliffs, N.J.: Prentice-Hall, 1940), pp. 386, 389; and David P. Thelen, *The New Citizenship: Origins of Progressivism in Wisconsin, 1885–1990* (Columbia: University of Missouri Press, 1972).

6. The capitol fire required the legislature to modify its instruction to the commission, which it did with Laws of 1905, Chapter 516. Davidson's message to the legislature on October 1, 1907, was reprinted in the *Senate Journal*, p. 63. The commission issued a booklet, called "Program," describing the rules for the new architectural competition on March 10, 1906; it can be found in series 833, box 1, folder 2, Wisconsin Capitol Commission files.

7. For background on the remarkable Daniel Burnham, see Thomas Hines, *Burnham of Chicago: Architect and Planner* (New York: Oxford University Press, 1974). The other entrants

were Ferry and Clas, Milwaukee; H. C. Koch and Company, Milwaukee; Peabody and Stearns, Boston; and Shipley Rutan and Coolidge, Boston. Burnham's handwritten "Report of D. H. Burnham on Competitive Plans to the Wisconsin Capitol Commission" is dated July 11, 1906, Wisconsin Capital Commission files, series 833.

8. See *WSJ* and *Madison Democrat* for February 27, 1907, and several days thereafter.

9. See Dwight Agnew, *James Huff Stout: Maker of Models* (Menomonie: University of Wisconsin–Stout, 1990), and Fred L. Holmes, *Badger Saints and Sinners* (Milwaukee, Wisc.: E. M. Hale, 1939), pp. 427–41. One Menomonie project that bore a similarity to Madison's was the reclamation of Lake Menomin, once a holding pond for effluent from the mill, as a public recreation area. A second Stout-guided project was the improvement of the western approach to the downtown area from the Omaha Depot. For information on these two projects, see Agnew, *James Huff Stout*, pp. 60–62.

10. Holmes, *Badger Saints and Sinners*, pp. 427–28. The senator with whom Stout was speaking

was J. J. McGillivray of Black River Falls.

11. S579, calling for the purchase of the six blocks, was introduced on May 8, 1907, and tabled on June 28, 1907. Joint resolution 60S was introduced on June 22, 1907, but failed when the assembly failed to concur on July 9, 1907.

12. Mollenhoff, *Madison*, p. 47.

13. Ibid., p. 230.

14. Ibid., p. 231.

15. See William H. Wilson, *The City Beautiful Movement* (Baltimore, Md.: Johns Hopkins University Press, 1989).

16. Mollenhoff, *Madison*, pp. 231, 324–38.

17. Ibid., p. 329.

18. Ibid., pp. 324–38.

19. *WSJ*, June 5, 1907. Olin and Stout knew each other and almost surely collaborated on the passage of this bill and, indeed, other matters. Their relationship was based on two factors. First, Olin's father-in-law was related by marriage to the Tainter family of Menomonie, Wisconsin, one of four wealthy families associated with Stout's lumber company. Second, to implement a major lakeshore improvement project in

Menomonie, Stout used what was widely known as the Olin Law, which permitted the state to undertake improvement projects, to acquire and develop project land. The Olin Law, enacted while Stout was in the state senate, probably created another opportunity for the two men to collaborate. We are indebted to John Holzhueter, a senior staff member at the SHSW, for information on the Olin-Stout relationship.

20. Mollenhoff, *Madison*, p. 124.

21. Ibid., p. 267.

22. Ibid., p. 189.

23. Ibid., pp. 341–45. With Olin's help Nolen secured many Wisconsin commissions. That story is best told in Barbara Jo Long's unpublished master's thesis, "John Nolen: The Wisconsin Activities of an American Landscape Architectural and Planning Pioneer, 1908 to 1937," Department of Landscape Architecture, University of Wisconsin, 1978.

24. Mollenhoff, *Madison*, p. 344. For more information about the development of city planning, see John W. Reps, *The Making of Urban America: A History of Urban Planning in the United States* (Princeton, N.J.: Princeton

University Press, 1965); Mel Scott, *American City Planning Since 1890* (Berkeley: University of California Press, 1969); and M. Christine Boyer, *Dreaming the Rational City: The Myth of American City Planning* (Cambridge, Mass.: MIT Press, 1983).

Selling Nolen and city planning to the common council, as Madison's city council is known, was especially difficult. In addition to persuading council members that they needed something most had never heard of, Olin had to convince them to take all the money they had used for a full-time resident parks superintendent and give it to a high-priced Boston consultant. However, as noted in Mollenhoff, *Madison*, p. 344, the council agreed.

25. Mollenhoff, *Madison*, p. 345.

26. *WSJ*, January 27, 1909.

27. For an account of the meeting see the *WSJ*, April 28, 1909. Olin's caveat appeared in the 1909 *Annual Report* of the Madison Park and Pleasure Drive Association, p. 75.

28. *WSJ*, April 28, 1909.

29. Ibid.

30. *WSJ*, April 27, 1909. Nolen's "new standard" comes from his introduction to *Madison: A Model City* (Boston: n.p., 1911).

31. See joint resolution 68S.

32. Stout's joint resolution 68S was laid over by the senate on May 8, 1909, and never reconsidered. On May 20 the assembly voted 53–36 to not concur, and attempts to get the matter reconsidered failed. For details on the approval of the Nolen final report, see Mollenhoff, *Madison*, p. 349. Stout's death on December 8, 1910, was widely reported in Wisconsin papers.

33. For additional discussion of why the Nolen plan failed, see Mollenhoff, *Madison*, pp. 349–50.

34. See Lew Porter to French, March 28, 1914, Capitol Commission files series 833, box 4; telegram from James Otis Post to Lew Porter, June 24, 1914, and a letter from James O. Post to Porter, June 23, 1914 (both in series 833, box 9). See also Stanley H. Cravens, "The Lady on the Top of the Dome," *Madison Magazine*, October 1981, pp. 9–12, and *WSJ*, June 30–July 20, 1914.

35. The effort to secure a new post office for Madison actually began in 1912, but the assumption was that a new structure would be built on the old site at the corner of Wisconsin Avenue and East Mifflin Street. But as the city

grew, postal officials concluded the old site would be too small, which sparked a battle about where the new building should go. World War I delayed progress and triggered a high rate of inflation immediately afterward; this caused construction costs to soar and required supplemental appropriations. See also *Bulletin*, February 8, 1929, and "Madison Post Office to Be Handsome Structure," *Master Builder* (Appleton, Wisc.), February 1927, p. 16.

36. Madison mayor A. G. Schmedeman created the Future Development Committee in January 1927, and the committee met for the next six months. The *WSJ* serialized the Nolen plan in February, and in March the paper serialized a five-year-old plan by Harland Bartholomew, a St. Louis city planner hired by Madison in 1920 to do a transportation and zoning plan, which was released in 1922 as *Madison, Wisconsin: Report on Major Streets, Transportation, and Zoning*, published by Bartholomew in St. Louis, 1922 (a copy can be found at the Madison Municipal Reference Service [MMRS], Madison Public Library). The document clearly demonstrated Bartholomew's ability to move cars and trains through the city. To achieve these ends he recommended destruction of the only park in an East Side neighborhood, use of ugly elevated concrete structures to move trains through the isthmus, and filling in about three miles of

Lake Monona shoreline for a highway. And at the end of Monona Avenue, that sweet spot of Madison's anatomy where Nolen had proposed a grand fountain and a quiet esplanade, Bartholomew proposed eleven railroad tracks and a four-lane highway. If Nolen's recommendations had the disadvantage of being expensive, Bartholomew's were expensive and ugly.

The common council approved the civic center recommendation on June 11, 1927. City officials had been thinking seriously about replacing the 1858 City Hall since the 1890s, but the concept did not become a staple of local official wish lists until the second and third decades of the twentieth century. Thus it was only natural that city leaders would have viewed Nolen's mall as a logical and appropriate site for a new city hall. The county also began to talk about replacing the 1886 county courthouse in the teens and twenties. Probably the first instance of the city and county's coordinating new or expanded facilities came in 1923 when the city was considering a new city hall on a downtown site. In this context the two local governments agreed to explore the desirability of a new joint heating plant (see the *Dane County Board Proceedings [DCBP]*, November 1923, p. 96). One of the first mentions of a joint building was in 1928. See *DCBP*, January sess., 1928, p. 396.

37. Inclusion of the auditorium in inaugural addresses to the organizational meetings of common councils can be found each year in mid-April in the *Madison Common Council Proceedings (MCCP)*. For a rare history of municipal auditoriums in the United States, see F. Stuart Fitzpatrick, "Municipal Auditoriums: A Report Compiled by the Chamber of Commerce of the United States," unpublished and dated August 1928, in the Joseph W. Jackson Papers (hereafter, Jackson Papers), box 16, folder 14, SHSW.

38. Mollenhoff, *Madison*, pp. 407–8.

39. Ibid. Interestingly, smaller, more homogeneous cities such as Richland Center, Wisconsin, enjoyed greater success in building community centers than cities like Madison, especially if the project had a benefactor. Stout, for example, provided such a facility for Menomonie.

40. The assembly room innovation is described in Thomas D. Brock, "Randall School at Ninety Years," *Journal of Historic Madison, Inc.* 8 (1996): 33. Ward's book, *The Social Center* (New York: D. Appleton, 1913), created great national interest when it appeared. According to William T. Evjue's autobiography, *Fighting Editor* (Madison, Wisc.: Wells Printing, 1968), pp. 183–84, Wilson assured conventioneers that civic centers would create true democracy: "People are

separated by tastes. They are separated by racial and religious and political and prejudicial differences. They cannot work for an ideal government, one which will voice the desire of the entire community, until they come to understand each and to give way, each a little bit, until the harmonious whole is formed. And this the social center will do."

41. "Liberty Buildings as Victory Monuments," *American City* 19, no. 6 (December 1918): 471–73. Other *American City* articles during this period covered the design, promotion, funding, and maintenance of liberty buildings; see the issues dated January, February, May, July, and August 1919.

42. *MCCP*, February 4 and 25, and March 7, 1919.

43. *Bulletin*, October 23, 1926, p. 3. Among Wisconsin cities that built town halls were Eau Claire, Racine, and Milwaukee. Atlantic City, Baltimore, San Francisco, Seattle, and dozens of others also built town halls.

44. Mollenhoff, *Madison*, pp. 167 and 428.

45. Nolen, *Madison: A Model City*, pp. 85–86.

46. See Edward Koblitz, "Concerning a Concert Season" and "From Modest Beginnings — Tonight Is Possible," two undated historical surveys of the Madison Student Union Concert Series that are in the University of

Wisconsin Archives (UWA) and appear to have been written about 1939 or 1940; and E. David Cronon and John W. Jenkins, *The University of Wisconsin: A History*. Vol. 3: *1925–1945 — Politics, Depression, and War* (Madison: University of Wisconsin Press, 1994), pp. 589–90.

47. Cronon and Jenkins, *University of Wisconsin*, 3:589–90.

48. Two examples of the anti–cow barn sentiments appear in Betty Cass, *Madison Day by Day* (Madison: Wisconsin State Journal, 1932), p. 15, and William T. Evjue, "Are We Ever Going to Get Out of the Cow Barn Era?" *Capital Times (CT)*, March 3, 1961. The best single source for information about campus buildings is Jim Feldman, *The Buildings of the University of Wisconsin* (Madison: University of Wisconsin–Madison Archives, 1997).

49. Mollenhoff, *Madison*, pp. 257–64, 286.

50. Ibid., p. 286.

51. *WSJ*, December 8, 1905; Mollenhoff, *Madison*, p. 286.

52. Mollenhoff, *Madison*, pp. 257–64, 286. When it was formed in 1913, the organization was known as the Board of Commerce, but in 1917 it merged with several other commercial organizations and changed its name to the Association of Commerce. To

avoid confusion we use the Association of Commerce.

Remarkably little has been written about the national convention industry. One excellent exception is Margie Markarian's article, "Turning Back the Clock: The History of Convention and Visitor Bureaus," *Meeting News*, August 1989, pp. 30–42.

53. For examples of association convention-boosting pamphlets see the SHSW pamphlet collection 57-2274. The *Bulletin* from 1917 through the 1930s is replete with convention-boosting squibs. A summary of association convention and tourism pamphlets is found in the *Bulletin*, June 25, 1927.

54. See the "liberty building" articles cited in note 41 from *American City*. For background on the association's transformation of the concept, see the *Bulletin*, December 28, 1918, and January 4, February 22, and March 1, 16, and 22, 1919. The association's report, "Information for the Common Council–City of Madison on Auditorium and City Halls," dated 1919, is available at the MMRS. The council failed to muster the necessary 17 votes on March 7, 1919.

55. *MCCP*, January 1 and February 10, 1922. Use of the warehouse of Union Transfer and Storage was reported in the *Bulletin* on January 4, 1919.

56. Kittleson's proposal first appeared in the *MCCP* on April 21, 1925. Judging from what

happened later, council member Thomas J. Ross appears to have been the source for Kittleson's auditorium-boathouse plan. The Ross plan was detailed in the *WSJ*, April 26, 1925. The plan also reflected the need to accommodate a relatively rapid increase in private boat ownership and do so aesthetically. Everyone was eager to eliminate the dozens of privately owned shantylike boathouses that lined the Monona shore and recognized that the only viable alternative was to build large public facilities. The auditorium-boathouse was hardly the first suggestion for a building at the end of Monona Avenue. Past suggestions included building a platform out over the tracks with a bandstand on top. See *Bulletin*, January 22, 1921. The common council authorized the Auditorium Committee on June 12, 1925. The *CT*, July 7, 1925, reported that the lakeshore site was the "front runner" for the auditorium-boathouse.

57. Articles documenting association support can be found in the *WSJ*, October 18, 1925; *CT*, September 5 and December 11, 1925; and *Bulletin*, February 11 and September 4, 1926. The best articles documenting the downtown parking problems can be found in the *Bulletin* beginning in about 1924. For selected references to the Loraine Hotel, see the *Bulletin*, June 7, 1924, and *WSJ*, February 19, 1923, and January 6, 1924. For the

Belmont Hotel see the *Bulletin*, August 16, 1924; *CT*, September 19, 1924; and the Madison Landmarks Nomination form prepared by Les Vollmert and Katherine Rankin and dated March 4, 1993. For references to hotel capacity see the *Bulletin*, July 25, 1925. The Loraine and the Belmont were the first fireproof (poured concrete) hotels in Madison. For a critical summary of hotel conditions before these new hotels were built, see the *WSJ* editorial, March 6, 1912.

58. The association's point man on the lakefront proposal was F. G. Oetking, who was also a member of the mayor's auditorium committee. For newspaper coverage of his role see the *CT*, September 5 and December 11, 1925, and *WSJ*, October 18, 1925.

59. Efforts by the association to circumvent state-imposed bond limitations are described in the *CT*, May 26, 1927. That the Madison Civic Music Association strongly supported and aggressively promoted the one-mill plan is evident from a document dated October 13, 1927, in the Jackson Papers, box 16, folder 14, and from the *CT* of the same day.

60. The third auditorium committee was authorized by the common council on January 13, 1928, was staffed on February 10, 1928, and made a report to the common council on March 22, 1929. James Law's letter to

Arthur Peabody, March 15, 1929, appears on city microfiche E.G. 94-04, City of Madison Microfiche (CMM). The marshland site was announced in an undated subcommittee report found on city microfiche E.G. 94-04. The association's strong preference for a lake site appeared in the *Bulletin*, February 4, 1928.

61. This proposal appears in a letter of August 10, 1929, to then-mayor A. G. Schmedeman from the Beecroft Building Corporation. See microfiche E.G. 94-04, CMM.

62. Association of Commerce annual statistical report, *Bulletin*, January 31, 1936. The *MCCP* provides the figures for tax for all years in this period except 1933, which can only be estimated. Signs of the recovery are reported in the *Bulletin*, January 31, 1936.

63. *Bulletin*, April 26, 1935.

64. *MCCP*, April 16, 1935. See also a letter from Jim Law, January 24, 1935, in Madison (Wisc.) Mayor, correspondence and subject file, 1921–65, Dane series 5, box 28, SHSW.

65. *CT*, February 7, 1935. The city submitted its list to the state, which collated it with other cities' projects, and forwarded them to the federal government. For general background on the Works Progress Administration, see Arthur Schlesinger, Jr., "The New Deal" in John M. Blum, Bruce Catton, Edmund S.

Morgan, Arthur M. Schlesinger, Jr., Kenneth Stampp, and C. Van Woodward, *The National Experience* (San Diego, Calif.: Harcourt Brace Jovanovich, 1985).

66. Despite the depression, Madison's convention business stayed remarkably strong. *Bulletin*s during this period are filled with articles trumpeting the industry's vitality — and the need for an auditorium to fully realize its potential. For background on the armory see J. B. Arnold, lieutenant commander, USNR, to James R. Law, July 9, 1934, Dane series, box 28, folder 4-5. See the *WSJ*, May 9, 1934, for business leaders' opinion of the auditorium as a necessity.

67. *WSJ*, April 19 and June 2, 1934.

68. The impressive story of Jackson and the arboretum is told in Cronon and Jenkins, *University of Wisconsin*, 3:703–6. Jackson's roles included persuading reluctant owners to sell, raising money, and providing spirited leadership. In the *Bulletin* of April 25, 1935, Jackson portrayed the prosperity campaign as "the most constructive undertaking launched in Madison since the World War." Jackson's role in the centennial was acknowledged in the *WSJ*, January 30, 1936. Jackson's talent was sufficient to secure his election in 1931 to a one-year term as a director of Rotary International (for more information see John W. Jenkins, *A History*

*of the Rotary Club of Madison* [Madison, Wisc.: Rotary Club of Madison, 1990], pp. 77, 210).

69. The *Bulletin* of June 21, 1935, describes why the pier committee was created. The committee's report appears in the *Bulletin*, June 28, 1935. Its official recommendation was in accord with what the mayor's advisory committee had announced just two months earlier (see *CT*, April 10, 1935) — that the city should build a convention hall or auditorium because tourism and conventions were a huge source of business.

70. Both steps were apparently taken with the full approval of Mayor Law. See *Bulletin*, June 28 and September 6 and 27, 1935; the state authorization is found in Laws of 1935, Chapter 509.

71. Jackson's description appeared in a letter to Nolen, September 22, 1936; see Jackson Papers, box 8, folder 11. The *Bulletin* of December 31, 1937, outlined the role of the committee.

72. Membership figures appear in the *Bulletin*, April 28, 1928, and May 20, 1938. The absence of a comprehensive and compelling program is clear from the thirty-two-page document, the "Madison and Wisconsin Foundation Program Statement," that was serialized to members in the *Bulletin* from December 31, 1937, to March 11, 1938. The association's budget decline is documented in the *Bulletin*, March 11, 1938. The association's pro forma interest in

higher priority proposals is assailed in an editorial, *WSJ*, August 25, 1935.

73. Jackson's hopes for the new organization appear in the *Bulletin*, May 5, 1939. Jackson wrote fifty foundations and community trusts, the U.S. Chamber of Commerce, and the American City Bureau to gather information about community organizations, but none had the hybrid he was contemplating.

74. After Jackson became executive director of the Madison and Wisconsin Foundation, he made dozens of references to Nolen's book in the weekly *Bulletin;* his 1937 organization program, a densely argued thirty-two-page goals statement, extolled Nolen's work. Jackson's well-worn copy of Nolen's book is preserved in box 8 of his collection.

75. Jackson's letter to Nolen is dated June 5, 1934, and appears in the Jackson Papers, box 8, folder 11.

76. Jackson to Nolen, August 12, 1936, Jackson Papers, box 8, folder 11.

77. Nolen to Jackson, August 23, 1936, Jackson Papers, box 3, folder 18. For a copy of an article on community foundations that Nolen submitted to the *Atlantic Monthly*, see Nolen to Jackson, September 14, 1936, Jackson Papers, box 8, folder 11.

78. This perspective on Jackson's life appears in Halsey Kraege's

testimonial address, delivered at Jackson's retirement banquet on June 10, 1952, and contained in File 1952 June 12, SHSW Archives.

79. See Nolen to Jackson, September 4 and 14, October 9, and November 10, 1936, and Jackson to Nolen, September 22, 1936, Jackson Papers, box 8, folder 11.

80. Jackson's salary reduction and unique qualifications for the job are described in "Mr. X," in the *WSJ*, February 25, 1952 (upon his retirement), and *Bulletin*, February 5, 1937 (when he was considered for the position).

81. Although Jackson wrote the program statement, at least one of his special committee members made significant contributions. In the *Bulletin*'s obituary for Paul E. Stark, the founder of one of Madison's largest real estate companies, Jackson acknowledged that Stark, a former president of the Association of Commerce, was the primary "originator" of the thirty-one-point program. See *Bulletin*, December 21, 1945.

82. Jackson to Nolen, February 13, 1937, Jackson Papers, box 8, folder 11.

83. Jackson Papers, box 3, folder 18.

84. For background on Dykstra, see the *WSJ*, February 1 and March 18, 1937, and Cronon and Jenkins, *University of Wisconsin*, 3:337–402.

85. The Segoe-Dykstra connection is noted in an unpublished paper, "The Development of the Practitioner's Art: Ladislas Segoe," by David Allor, Elizabeth D. Byrne, and Robin Corathers, delivered at the First National Conference of American City Planning History, March 13–15, 1986, Columbus, Ohio. Dykstra's high regard for Segoe was reflected in his introduction of Segoe to the Rotary Club of Madison on July 11, 1937. In that introduction Dykstra referred to the excellent work Segoe had done as the head planner for Cincinnati in the 1920s and as the technical director for the National Resources Board from 1935 to 1937 (*Rotary News* [July 18, 1937]). Dykstra's high regard was also evident in a letter dated April 29, 1939, to the president of Occidental College. In that letter Dykstra said: "I think you could not find a better man than Segoe." See Chancellor and Presidents Record Group, Dykstra, Clarence A., series 4/15 (hereafter, Dykstra Files), UWA.

86. *Rotary News*, July 6 and 13, 1937; *Bulletin*, July 9, 1937.

87. Jackson's correspondence with Segoe shows that Jackson surely ascertained Segoe's fees during Segoe's 1937 visit to Madison. Immediately after he returned to Cincinnati, Segoe provided a rationale for a "Comprehensive Master Plan" at Jackson's request. Segoe's detailed outline of his comprehensive plan

and his initial official estimate of $19,550 appear in the minutes of the Madison Planning Trust, a copy of which is in the Business Administration Record Group, Gallistel, Albert F., series 26 (hereafter, Gallistel Papers), Madison Planning Trust, UWA.

88. A copy of the draft resolution dated January 18, 1938, to transfer the assets from the Wisconsin Centennial, Inc., is attached to a letter to Dykstra dated February 1, 1938, Gallistel Papers. The transfer of the money is reflected in the *MCCP*, November 26, 1937.

89. Serving on the trust's board were Martin Torkelson, the director of the state planning board, named by Governor Philip La Follette; Clarence Dykstra, named by the university's regents; John St. John, named by the Madison Business Association; Mayor Law, named by the common council; and Emerson Ela, named by the Madison and Wisconsin Foundation. See *CT* and *WSJ*, February 24, 1938.

90. Minutes of Trustees of the Madison Planning Trust, March 5 and 7, 1938, Gallistel Papers, and *CT*, May 10, 1938. Jackson's boast appears in the *Bulletin*, May 13, 1938.

91. See *MCCP*, August 12, 1938; *Bulletin*, August 5, 12, and 19, 1938; and "Report of Naval Armory-Civic Building and Boat Harbor Project Committee," July 21, 1938, in the William T.

Evjue Papers (hereafter, Evjue Papers), box 98, folder 17, SHSW.

92. The *WSJ* on November 4 and 15, 1938, detailed the following shortcomings of the county courthouse: hallways had been commandeered for offices, a tiny elevator forced supervisors to walk up stairs, the parking lot was too small for supervisors' cars, the jail had been condemned, and the building was anything but fireproof. For discussion of an annex see the *DCBP*, November 18, 1935. Attempts to build a city-county building can be traced to 1923 when the county board proposed a joint heating plant to serve a then-planned addition to the courthouse and a new city hall on the other end of the courthouse block. See *DCBP*, November 1923, p. 96. In 1928 a supervisor had proposed that a committee be established to investigate a full-fledged city-county building, but that motion was defeated. See *DCBP*, January 1928, p. 305.

93. See *DCBP* for November 19, 29, and 30, 1937, and February 11, 1938; *CT*, February 18 and 29, 1938. On June 20, 1938, the federal government notified the county that its grant had been approved. About three years later Hubert A. Schneider, an architect involved in the dual building, provided Evjue with a behind-the-scenes account of actions never reported in the local papers. See Schneider to Evjue, March 8, 1941, Evjue

Papers, box 70, folder 2. For newspaper reaction to the county grant announcement, see the *WSJ*, January 30, 1936, and *CT*, September 8, 1937.

94. *MCCP*, July 5, 1938; *DCBP*, July 7, 1938. Just in case the city failed to get its grant, the supervisors formally accepted the grant for the annex.

95. See the *MCCP*, September 23, 1938, for referendum results. During the planning for the joint building supervisors learned that Wisconsin statutes made no provision for a true joint building. In other words, the city and county buildings could be contiguous, but ownership and operation of both land and buildings had to be legally separate, like two townhouses sharing a common wall. This was why almost everybody called it the "dual" building. See *DCBP*, July sess., 1938.

96. Federal approval of a $56,000 Conklin site breakwater was reported in the *CT*, October 23, 1938. The breakwater was projected to be 950 feet long with an illuminated walk on the top. For the county approval see the *DCBP*, September 27, 1938.

97. For Law's role in developing the park, see the *CT*, May 26, 1934. The *MCCP*, September 10, 1937, notes that the railroads had ceded their riparian rights. An article in the *WSJ*, August 31, 1934, reported that the boathouses "were being removed," and Henry Noll, a *WSJ* columnist, reported on

March 7, 1937, that "all the boat shacks ... have been eliminated."

98. Jackson's remarkable behind-the-scenes power was evident when he wrote a strong editorial advocating a dual building and the *WSJ* printed it on October 25, 1938, with few changes. Jackson's original draft and transmittal letter are in the Jackson Papers.

CHAPTER 2
**AN OLD MADISON BOY**

1. For William Wright's tenure at the Weymouth church see Gilbert Nash, *Sketch of Weymouth* (Weymouth, Mass.: Weymouth Historical Society, 1885), p. 122; John H. Butterson, "Weymouth Music and Musicians," in Howard H. Joy, ed., *History of Weymouth, Massachusetts*, vol. 2 (Weymouth, Mass.: Weymouth Historical Society, 1923), pp. 864–65; and Frank B. Cressy, *Semi-Centennial, 1854–1904, Baptist Church* (Weymouth, Mass., n.p., 1904), pp. 15–16, 27. See also Meryle Secrest, *Frank Lloyd Wright* (New York: Knopf, 1992), pp. 55–56; and Robert Twombly, *Frank Lloyd Wright: His Life and His Architecture* (New York: Wiley, 1979), pp. 7–9. For Elizabeth's residence with family, see Elizabeth Wright Heller, "The Story of My Life," typescript, pp. 44–45, Iowa Historical Society Archives, Iowa City.

2. William and Permelia Holcomb Wright's children included Charles William (1856–1931), George Irving (1858–1934), and Elizabeth Amelia (1860–1950). For accounts of the Lloyd Jones family's history in Wisconsin, see Chester Lloyd Jones, *The Youngest Son* (Madison, Wisc.: Democrat Printing, 1938).

3. Concerning William's education, see *Madison* (now Colgate) *University Catalogue* (1848–49), pp. 20–21; Elmer W. Smith, ed.,

*Colgate University General Catalogue Number*, vol.1 (Hamilton, N.Y.: Colgate University, 1937), p. 94 for William and p. 48 for his brother Thomas; and Twombly, *Frank Lloyd Wright*, pp. 6–9. William Wright wrote three books: *Piano Forte Manual* (1854), *The Golden Monitor* (1890), and *Golden Precepts for Vocal Art* (1895), as well as articles in musical journals. His last article, "A Point in Five-Finger Practice," *Étude* 22, no. 9 (September 1904): 361, was published posthumously.

4. For the family's multiple moves and William's pastoral affiliations, see Twombly, *Frank Lloyd Wright*, pp. 4–7. See Secrest, *Frank Lloyd Wright*, p. 55, for the family's residence in Central Falls, Rhode Island, where William served his first year in the ministry.

5. Quotes are from William Wright to Grindall Reynolds, secretary of the American Unitarian Association, November 14, 1881, Letter-Books of the American Unitarian Association, Unitarian Universalist Archives (hereafter, UUA), Boston. See Twombly, *Frank Lloyd Wright*, p. 9; and Secrest, *Frank Lloyd Wright*, pp. 19–34, for background; for Unitarian connection to Wright and his Lloyd Jones forebears, see Max Gaebler, "Unitarianism in the Life and Work of Frank Lloyd Wright," pamphlet published by the First Unitarian Society, Madison, Wisc., 1997; Merle E. Curti, "Our

Golden Age," pamphlet, First Unitarian Society, 1954; and First Unitarian Society, Madison, Records: 1878–1976 (hereafter, Unitarian Records), State Historical Society of Wisconsin (SHSW).

6. For Jenkin Lloyd Jones's Unitarian affiliations, see C. H. Lyttle, *Freedom Moves West: A History of the Western Unitarian Conference, 1852–1952* (Boston: Beacon, 1952); Thomas Graham, "Jenkin Lloyd Jones and the Gospel of the Farm," *Wisconsin Magazine of History* 67 (Winter 1983–84): 121–48; and Richard Thomas, "Jenkin Lloyd Jones: Lincoln's Soldier of Civic Righteousness," Ph.D. diss., Rutgers University, New Brunswick, N.J., 1967. For the family's arrival in Wisconsin and settlement in Madison, see Twombly, *Frank Lloyd Wright*, p. 9; and April 21 and December 18, 1878, entries in the Enos Lloyd Jones Diaries (1873–87), SHSW Archives.

7. See chap. 1 for a more thorough discussion.

8. The Wisconsin conference convened November 12, 1878; a group of prospective Madison members, presided over by William Wright and Hiram Giles, met in January and received fourteen pledges and a donation of $1,200 from the national Unitarian organization.

An August 29, 1950, letter from one of William Wright's descendants to another, copy in possession of

the authors, describes a second family residence in the Mansion Hill area across the street from an elegant home occupied in the 1870s by the Thorpe family and later by Wisconsin governors. The Tax Rolls, City of Madison, 1879, Dane series 89, microfilm, SHSW Archives, show that the Wrights also lived somewhere in block 54, a less affluent area of the city. Because the family did not own either property, it is not possible to determine where the Wrights lived during the first year. Madison directories from the 1880s identify individuals offering musical instruction.

9. On October 25, 1879, the Wrights purchased lots 1 and 2 of block 139 and sold the second in 1882. For real estate transactions, see *Dane County Deeds (DCD)* vol. 113, p. 264; vol. 93, p. 102; releases, vol. 93, p. 102; and miscellaneous records, vol. 116, p. 143. Contemporary city directories describe the Wright house at 804 Gorham. Houses were later renumbered, and the location is now 802 East Gorham. See Timothy F. Heggland and Hillary Anne Frost-Kumpf, "The Old Market Place Neighborhood: A Walking Tour," pamphlet, Madison Landmarks Commission and the Old Market Place Neighborhood Association, 1991.

10. For Frank Lloyd Wright's descriptions of the family's Gorham Street house, see Frank Lloyd Wright, *An Autobiography*, vol. 2, p. 126, of Bruce Brooks

Pfeiffer, ed., *Frank Lloyd Wright Collected Writings*, 5 vols. (New York: Rizzoli, Frank Lloyd Wright Foundation, 1992–95); for his sister's recollections see Maginel Wright Barney, *The Valley of the Almighty Joneses* (New York: Appleton-Century, 1965), pp. 58–61.

11. Wright, *Autobiography*, p. 126; Barney, *The Valley*, pp. 73–75.

12. See Wright, *Autobiography*, pp. 127–28. The Madison Free Public Library was located in City Hall on the Capitol Square, less than a block from Wright's high school and not far from Allan Conover's office. An 1877 catalogue lists several authors and books mentioned in Wright's autobiography, including *The Arabian Nights' Entertainments*. See Janet S. Ela, *Free and Public: One Hundred Years with Madison Public Library* (Madison, Wisc.: Friends of Madison Public Library, 1975).

13. Wright told of being called Shaggy in *Autobiography*, p. 130. The cream brick school that presently occupies the site is described in Heggland and Frost-Kumpf, "The Old Marketplace Neighborhood."

14. As a child, Robert M. Lamp (1866–1916) lived in the 700 block of Johnson Street, only a block from the Wrights and the Second Ward School. See Wright, *Autobiography*, pp. 125, 126, and John O. Holzhueter, "Frank Lloyd Wright's Designs

for Robert Lamp," *Wisconsin Magazine of History* 72 (Winter 1988–89): 83–125.

15. Wright, *Autobiography*, pp. 127, 129; also see note 12.

16. Moses R. Doyon (1845–1933) was one of three founders of the Capitol City Bank. His son, Charles, was several years younger than Wright and Lamp. For Wright's youthful printing adventures see *Autobiography*, p. 129.

17. Ibid., pp. 128, 137.

18. For William Wright's work for the Unitarians, see William and Jenkin Lloyd Jones to Grindall Reynolds, including a letter dated June 11, 1881, from Jones in which he notes that William's work required him to travel seventy to eighty miles every Sunday and that "his compensation is scarcely more than enough to meet his traveling expenses." Jones asks the national office to send $200 to help defray William's travel expenses, UUA. For Anna's Unitarian activities, see Unitarian Records, box 23. The Unitarian Sunday School program established by Jones included the study of the Old and New Testaments, the Apocrypha, Confucius, Zoroaster, Buddha, Moses, Socrates, Mohammed, and Jesus and culminated with a study called "The Flowering of Christianity into Universal Religion" — not a curriculum young Wright would have encountered in the Baptist churches that once employed his

father. See Richard W. F. Seebode, "Jenkin Lloyd Jones: A Free Catholic," Ph.D. diss., Meadville Theological Seminary, Chicago, September 1929, pp. 92–99.

19. During the summers he spent with his maternal relatives in the Wyoming Valley, Wright stayed with Uncle James Lloyd Jones, an enterprising young farmer who served as town treasurer, town chairman, and later as a University of Wisconsin regent (representing the state's agricultural interests) until his death in a freak farm accident in 1907. For a discussion of Wright's other maternal relatives see Secrest, *Frank Lloyd Wright*, pp. 36–48.

20. Wright, *Autobiography*, p. 138.

21. See Thomas S. Hines, Jr., "Frank Lloyd Wright — The Madison Years: Records Versus Recollections," *Wisconsin Magazine of History* 50 (Winter 1967): 109–19, the first article to correct Wright's birth date, college record, and his parents' divorce. On the divorce see *William C. Wright v. Anna L. Wright*, Dane County Circuit Court, in the Frank Lloyd Wright documents deposited by Hines in the University of Wisconsin Archives (UWA). See also *DCD*, vol. 122, pp. 474–75, for the transfer of the Gorham Street house to Anna. See also Wright, *Autobiography*, pp. 139–49; Hines, "Frank Lloyd Wright,"

pp. 111–12; and Enos Lloyd Jones Diaries, December 13, 1884, and January 20, 1885.

22. For examples of Anna Wright's mental and physical abuse toward her step-daughter, see Elizabeth Wright Heller, "The Story of My Life," pp. 5–6, 9–10, 15, 16–17; for plans for her wedding in Madison in November 1881, see pp. 78–79 and 83–84.

23. Ibid., p. 111. According to Heller, her father was able to afford the trip because the railroads were in the midst of a price war, offering round-trip tickets for just $1.

24. For Wright's version of the job see his *Autobiography*, p. 140. In 1885 Conover's downtown office was at 7–9 S. Pinckney and William Wright's conservatory was at 23 N. Pinckney.

25. For the new Dane County Courthouse designed by Henry C. Koch and supervised by Allan Conover, see the *WSJ*, November 8, 1886. Conover had a recent engineering student, Lew Porter (who later became Conover's partner), oversee the day-to-day work on the job site. On April 7, 1885, the legislature approved the allocation of $190,000 (Laws of 1885, Chapter 332) to cover the cost of four new buildings on the U.W. campus (Science Hall, heating plant, machine shop and chemical lab). By the time bids came in for Science Hall, the regents had authorized $61,000 for the other three and so had no choice but to reject the bids for Science Hall (which ranged from $179,000 to $229,000); they hired Conover to serve as the contractor as well as supervising architect. See Jim Feldman, *The Buildings of the University of Wisconsin* (Madison: University of Wisconsin Archives, 1997), pp. 52–62.

26. The Madison directory for 1885 lists Wright as a draftsman for Conover, but Conover's testimony at the Science Hall hearing in 1887 suggests otherwise. When asked about his expenses and employees, Conover responded, "I had to keep an office and pay my office rent. I had to keep an office man [presumably Wright], [and] a draftsman [named elsewhere in his testimony], and pay all the incidental expenses which come with an office" (Conover testimony, p. 156, Wisconsin Legislature, Investigations, 1837–1945, series 173, box 7, SHSW). Office man was an entry-level position, somewhat akin to a gofer. Wright may have been given some drafting to do, but it would not have involved major responsibilities. For the capitol collapse, see Stanley H. Cravens, "Capitals and Capitols in Early Wisconsin," *1983–84 Blue Book* (Madison: Wisconsin Legislature, 1983), pp. 99–168 (esp. pp. 150–154); "Collapse of the Wisconsin State Capitol," *Sanitary Engineer* 8, no. 26 (November 1883): 608–11; *Inland Architect* 2, no. 5 (December 1883): 141; and Wright, *Autobiography*, pp. 142–43. On the original Science Hall see Feldman, *Buildings of the University*, pp. 49–50. The *WSJ*, on December 2, 1884, and a few days thereafter, ran accounts of the fire that destroyed the newest and most expensive building on campus, a four-story, wood-frame, sandstone-faced Italianate structure completed in 1877 at a cost of nearly $100,000. The costly experience prompted regents to demand that potentially flammable components (shops and boilers) be housed in separate buildings rather than in the new Science Hall.

27. See Feldman, *Buildings of the University*, pp. 482–85, for materials tests confirming the use of steel in Science Hall. For a general history of its construction, see Clarence Olmstead, *Science Hall: The First Century* (Madison: Department of Geography, University of Wisconsin, 1987). In his *Autobiography* Wright overstated his supervisory role in the construction of Science Hall. Olmstead notes on p. 3 that Wright's name does not appear on any list and state records show no payment to him, indicating that he was paid directly by Conover. Albert Parman, one of Conover's recent engineering graduates, served as assistant superintendent of construction and spent two months in Pittsburgh, beginning in February 1886, testing the steel beams produced by the Carnegie plant for Science Hall. See Conover testimony, pp. 21 and 329–32. For Wright's dangerous climb, see his *Autobiography*, p. 144.

28. For general background on Wright's first self-appointed commission, Unity Chapel, see the Spring Green *Weekly Home News*, August 20, 1885. Wright's efforts to secure his first commission are detailed in William Channing Gannett, "Christening a Country Church," *Unity* 17 (August 28, 1886): 356.

29. For the U.W. engineering curriculum, see multiple references in Merle Curti and Vernon Carstensen, *The University of Wisconsin: A History, 1848–1925*, 2 vols. (Madison: University of Wisconsin Press, 1948); Frederic A. Pike, *A Student at Wisconsin* (Madison, Wisc.: Democrat Printing, 1935), p. 183; and Storm Bull, "Technical Education at the University of Wisconsin," *Wisconsin Engineer* 3 (January 1899): 1–17. For cost figures see *University of Wisconsin, Catalogue* (1885–86), pp. 27 and 94, and Pike, *A Student*, pp. 204–6. The winter term of the 1885–86 academic year, which was the first that university records show Wright as an enrolled student, started January 6 and ended March 31, 1886. He registered again for the fall term of the 1886–87 school year that began September 8 and ended December 22, 1886.

30. By 1886 the engineering teaching staff had expanded to four university faculty members: Allan D. Conover, Storm Bull, Charles I. King, and Leonard Hoskins. See Reuben Gold Thwaites, *University of Wisconsin, 1836–1900: Its History and Its Alumni, with Historical and Descriptive Sketches of Madison* (Madison, Wisc.: Purcell, 1900), pp. 318 and 709; and Conover's obituary and a tribute, *WSJ*, May 24 and 25, 1929.

31. For information about college life and Wright's social activities at the U.W., see his class yearbook, *Trochos* (1887). For Wright's view of campus activities and clothing see his *Autobiography*, p. 143. Wright's fraternity met every Saturday night, the engineering association on Friday evenings, the Contemporary Club every other Wednesday, and the Unitarian Channing Club (for college-age members) every Sunday evening.

32. For the freshman party see Wright, *Autobiography*, pp. 141–42, and the student newspaper, the *Aegis*, for February 8, 1886, p. 4.

33. On Turner see Ray Allen Billington, *Frederick Jackson Turner: Historian, Scholar, Teacher* (New York: Oxford University Press, 1973), pp. 50–51.

34. Wright was not the first or the last family member to alter his given name. His mother, uncle, and nephew all spent their adult lives with names other than those given them as children. See Secrest, *Frank Lloyd Wright*, pp. 79–81.

35. See Hines, "Frank Lloyd Wright and Madison," pp. 109–11,

on Wright's date of birth; Barney recounts Anna's instructions to the children regarding the divorce in *The Valley*, p. 72, and Anna identified herself as a widow on the deeds for the Madison and Oak Park properties. Wright claimed his mother was born in 1842, but 1838 is the date that appears in the Bible of the family matriarch, Mallie Thomas Lloyd Jones, and in "Lloyd Letters and Memorial Book," p. 66, reprinted for the family's 1886–1986 centennial.

36. In the fall of 1886 Wisconsin newspapers reported that the U.W. regents had spent the $190,000 appropriated by the legislature in 1885, the $41,000 insurance settlement, as well as $30,000 more lent by a Madison bank, yet Science Hall stood roofless, and no money was available to finish and furnish the building or pay several outstanding bills for labor and materials. Conover, who was owed $800, was taking a lot of criticism, as were building committee members. In January 1887 a bill seeking $200,000 to complete and furnish Science Hall was introduced in the legislature and triggered a resolution calling for an investigation.

37. Madison directories from the 1880s describe Benjamin F. Perry's "second hand goods store" at 107 King Street. For Wright's explanation of his departure for Chicago, see Wright, *Autobiography*, p. 146. Secrest, *Frank Lloyd Wright*, pp. 83–84, offers one version of Wright's departure for Chicago

and Joseph Siry another in his "Frank Lloyd Wright's Unity Temple and Architecture for Liberal Religion in Chicago, 1885–1909," *Art Bulletin* 73, no. 2 (June 1991): 260.

38. We want to thank Frank Custer for calling our attention to the June 10, 1889, article in the *WSJ*, eleven lines buried on the back page under "Local Matters," a column of social and personal announcements.

39. The editor was Levi Alden, who was affiliated with the First Unitarian Society.

40. For Joseph L. Silsbee see his obituary in the *Chicago Tribune*, February 1, 1913; a review of his work by Susan Karr Sorell, "Silsbee: The Evolution of a Personal Style," *Prairie School Review* 7, no. 4 (Fourth Quarter 1970): 5–13; and for his interest in Japanese art, Kevin Nute, *Frank Lloyd Wright and Japan* (New York: Van Nostrand Reinhold, 1994), pp. 22–24.

41. Corwin established an independent practice in 1890 and beginning in 1893 shared office space with Wright in the Schiller Building. See Wright, *Autobiography*, pp. 152–53, 190–91.

42. On Paul Mueller, see Edgar Kaufmann, Jr., *Nine Commentaries on Frank Lloyd Wright* (Cambridge, Mass.: MIT Press, 1989), pp. 42–62.

43. For primary materials on the Hillside Home School, see the

Ellen and Jane Lloyd Jones Papers, SHSW Archives, for a nearly complete run of the yearly promotional booklets. For published photographs of the earlier and later Hillside buildings, see Grant Manson, *Frank Lloyd Wright to 1910: The First Golden Age* (New York: Van Nostrand Reinhold, 1958), pp. 18–20, 130–33.

44. For Louis H. Sullivan (1856–1924), see Robert Twombly, *Louis Sullivan: His Life and Work* (New York: Viking, 1986).

45. Catherine Lee Clark Tobin (1871–1959) and her family lived in the Kenwood area of Chicago and attended Jenkin Lloyd Jones's church. The costume party at which she met Wright was the culminating event for the Monday night Novel Club's study of *Les Misérables*. (After finishing a book, the club planned some type of special event — a play, pageant, tableau, or in this case a costume party.) She died about two weeks before Wright did.

46. For Wright's version of his courtship and marriage to Catherine Tobin, see *Autobiography*, pp. 155–63, 176–77; also Secrest, *Frank Lloyd Wright*, pp. 96–102.

47. A quitclaim turning the Madison house over to Anna was drawn up on December 13, 1884, but not recorded until May 2, 1885, as part of the final divorce settlement. A warranty deed transferring the house to Adolph H. Kayser was dated October 15 and recorded October 22, 1889.

48. Wright, *Autobiography*, p. 172.

49. On May 5, 1889, the Wrights paid $2,875 for the north and west portions of Lot 20, located at the corner of Forest and Chicago Avenues, an area then on the outer edge of the developed portion of Oak Park. The warranty deed for the parcel was not filed until August 20, the same day the title deed was assigned to Louis Sullivan, who had lent Wright $5,000 to cover the purchase of the lot and the construction of his new house. One day later, August 21, Anna Wright secured the east portion of the large lot; the filing of that transaction was delayed until September 12, 1889. We wish to thank Frances Steiner for sharing these details with us. For drawings of the additions, changes to the house, historical photos, and information about these, see *Plan for Restoration and Adaptive Reuse of the Frank Lloyd Wright Home and Studio* (Chicago: University of Chicago Press, 1978).

Author Vincent Scully first called attention to the similarity of Wright's Oak Park home to those designed by Bruce Price (1843–1903) for Tuxedo Park, New York, a six-thousand-acre wooded retreat developed by Pierre Lorillard IV for residents with "vintage money, congenial habits, and impeccable social antecedents" that opened in June 1886. (At the first Autumn Ball held there that October the founder's son supposedly introduced the first tuxedo. Price's

daughter was Emily Post.) See Scully, *Frank Lloyd Wright* (New York: Braziller, 1960), pp. 33–34.

50. Wright's six children were Frank Lloyd Wright, Jr. (1890–1977), John Kenneth (1892–1972), Catherine (1894–1979), David (1895–1997), Frances (1898–1959), and Robert (1903–1986). The quote about luxuries and necessities is from Wright, *Autobiography*, pp. 177–81.

51. Wright's early "bootleg" houses are generally identified as six designed and constructed in the Chicago area between 1890 and 1893: the Harlan House (1891–92), the Emmond House (1892), the Warren McArthur House (1892), the Blossom House (1892), the Thomas H. Gale House (1892), and the Robert Parker House (1892). The Walter Gale House (1893), long considered a bootleg residence, has been shown to be one of Wright's earliest independent commissions. For publication of Wright's plans under Corwin's name and contemporary precedents, see Patrick Pinnell, "Academic Tradition and the Individual Talent" in Robert McCarter, ed., *Frank Lloyd Wright: A Primer of Architectural Principles* (New York: Princeton Architectural Press, 1991), pp. 18–58 (esp. pp. 30–34). The pencil quote appears in Wright, *Autobiography*, p. 176.

52. For the large theater in the Auditorium Building, see Dankmar Adler, "The Theater,"

*Prairie School Review* 2, no. 2 (Second Quarter 1965): 21–27. For the theater's influence on Wright, see Freda Estes Bridgeman, "The Development of a Theatre Concept as Reflected in the Theatrical Architecture of Frank Lloyd Wright," Ph.D. diss., University of Wisconsin–Madison, 1971, pp. 28–33.

53. On the Schiller Building, see Paul E. Sprague, "Adler and Sullivan's Schiller Building," *Prairie School Review* 2, no. 2 (Second Quarter 1965): 5–20. For Wright's description of space he shared with Cecil Corwin, see Wright, *Autobiography*, pp. 185–86.

54. On the Madison Improvement Association, see Secretary of State, Corporation Division, File #M683, series 2/4/2, SHSW; for list of contributors and boathouse expenses, see the *WSJ*, October 22, 1895; and for history of both boathouses, see John O. Holzhueter, "The Lakes Mendota and Monona Boathouses," in Paul Sprague, ed., *Frank Lloyd Wright and Madison: Eight Decades of Artistic and Social Interaction* (Madison, Wisc.: Elvehjem Museum of Art, 1990), pp. 29–34.

55. For the executive committee's role in selecting the competition winner, see article in the U.W. student paper *Daily Cardinal*, May 12, 1893, p. 4; for the official boathouse opening, see the *WSJ*, April 25 and 27, 1894. Lucien S. Hanks was president of the State Bank, the building in which

Conover had his office in 1885; Wright mentions Hanks's son, Lucien, a childhood friend, in chap. 3 of Wright, *Autobiography*, p. 143.

56. The Milwaukee competition was announced in mid-September; the entries were due November 15, 1893; and the winner, the Milwaukee firm of Ferry and Clas, was announced January 4, 1894. The construction budget of $500,000 would have been attractive to Wright — and so would the competition's prizes: $25,000 for the winner and $500 to the next four runners-up. For Wright's description of the meeting with Daniel Burnham and Edward Waller in the latter's home, see Wright, *Autobiography*, pp. 187–89. For an early study of Wright's classical tendencies, see Henry-Russell Hitchcock, "Frank Lloyd Wright and the 'Academic Tradition' of the Eighteen-Nineties," *Journal of the Warburg and Courthauld Institutes* 7 (January–June 1944): 46–63. For historical precedents for Wright's Milwaukee design and his grasp of classical principles, see Neil Levine, *The Architecture of Frank Lloyd Wright* (Princeton, N.J.: Princeton University Press, 1996), pp. 6–8; and Robert McArthur, *Frank Lloyd Wright* (London: Phaidon Press, 1997), pp. 21–25.

57. Wright's interest in creating an indigenous American architecture was sparked by his mentor, Louis Sullivan, whose influence on

other young architects is evident in Robert C. Spencer, Jr., "The Work of Frank Lloyd Wright," *Architectural Review* (June 1900): 61–73.

58. For overview of this period in Wright's career see Levine, *Architecture of Frank Lloyd Wright*, pp. 13–30.

59. On the Larkin building see Jack Quinan, *Frank Lloyd Wright's Larkin Building: Myth and Fact* (Cambridge, Mass.: MIT Press, 1987); on the (Rogers Lacy) hotel in Dallas, see McArthur, *Frank Lloyd Wright*, pp. 197–98.

60. On the Lamp House see John O. Holzhueter, "Wright's Designs for Robert Lamp," in Sprague, *Frank Lloyd Wright and Madison*, pp. 13–27.

61. On the Unity Temple see Siry, "Frank Lloyd Wright's Unity Temple."

62. See John O. Holzhueter, "The Yahara River Boathouse," in Sprague, *Frank Lloyd Wright and Madison*, pp. 37–44.

63. The points noted here are discussed more thoroughly in H. Allen Brooks, *Frank Lloyd Wright and the Prairie School* (New York: Braziller, 1984), pp. 9–28.

64. *Prairie School* is a relatively new term, in use since the 1960s, for what had earlier been called the *Chicago School, New School of the Middle West*, or other terms. These are described, along with

work by other architects and designers who shared Wright's interests, in various articles in the issue of *Museum Studies* [21, no. 2 (1995)] devoted to *The Prairie School: Design Vision for the Midwest* and published by the Art Institute of Chicago.

65. The most comprehensive treatment of Prairie practitioners in addition to Wright is still H. Allen Brooks, *The Prairie School* (New York: Norton, 1972). For Madison architect Louis Claude (1868–1951), see Gordon Orr, "The Collaboration of Claude and Starck with Chicago Architectural Firms," *Prairie School Review* 5, no. 25 (November 1975): 5–12; on the Robie House see Donald Hoffmann, *Frank Lloyd Wright's Robie House* (New York: Dover, 1984); on the Gilmore House see Tim Heggland, "The Gilmore House," in Sprague, *Frank Lloyd Wright and Madison*, pp. 45–53.

66. By 1901 Oak Park — Wright's base of operations — had eighteen new or remodeled buildings designed by Wright; earlier, All Souls Church had provided clients such as the Bagleys, the McArthurs, and the Byes; several couples, like the Wrights, had moved to Oak Park and joined the Universalist congregation, which provided residential commissions and selected Wright to design a replacement church. Charles Roberts, a wealthy Welsh inventor and longtime church trustee, had two sisters who married future

Wright clients: Harley Bradley of Kankakee and Warren Hickox. Wright and a son of the owner of Browne's Bookstore joined the Caxton Club the same year that Wright designed a house for one of the club's charter members, George Millard; Browne's board included Wright's earlier client, Avery Coonley. Still other clients, William Winslow and the Luxfer Prism Company, maintained offices in the Rookery Building, which was managed by Wright's client-patron Edward C. Waller.

67. William Martin lived in the Chicago area, where Wright designed a house and a factory for the family's EZ Polish Company and a large house for his brother Darwin in Buffalo, plus still others for Larkin company officials.

68. For comparisons of several early Wright clients and those of another Chicago architect, Howard van Doran Shaw, see Leonard K. Eaton, *Two Chicago Architects and Their Clients* (Cambridge, Mass.: MIT Press, 1969).

69. On Wright's collection of Japanese prints see Julia Meech-Pekarik, "Frank Lloyd Wright's Other Passion," in Nelson C. Bolon and Linda Seidel, eds., *The Nature of Frank Lloyd Wright* (Chicago: University of Chicago Press, 1988), pp. 125–53.

70. For Wright's dealings with the Wasmuth Publishing Company and its Wright publications, see Anthony Alofsin, *Frank Lloyd Wright: The Lost Years, 1910–22*

(Chicago: University of Chicago Press, 1993), pp. 54–55, 88–92.

71. Wright, *Autobiography*, p. 219.

72. Ibid., pp. 178, 219.

73. Alofsin, *Frank Lloyd Wright*, pp. 23–28.

74. Ibid., chap. 2, for trip to Europe and Wright's and Mamah Cheney's activities.

75. Ibid., chaps. 1 and 2, on Catherine and Mamah Borthwick Cheney.

76. Ibid.; for choice of Fiesole, a quaint hill town overlooking Florence, see Levine, *Architecture of Frank Lloyd Wright*, pp. 66–67. For analysis of who produced various drawings for the portfolio, see H. Allen Brooks, "Frank Lloyd Wright and the Wasmuth Drawings," *Art Bulletin* 48 (1966): 193–202.

77. See Alofsin, *Frank Lloyd Wright*, chap. 3.

78. Wright, *Autobiography*, p. 223.

79. For Taliesin background see Levine, *Architecture of Frank Lloyd Wright*, chap. 4.

80. See articles in *Chicago Examiner*, September 8, 1911, and *Chicago Tribune*, December 24, 1911. For obituaries see the *WSJ*, January 13, 1941 (Chester Lloyd Jones); *CT*, September 3, 1931 (Thomas Lloyd Jones), and *Tulsa Tribune*, December 5, 1963 (Richard Lloyd Jones). The parents' decision to withdraw

children from Hillside could not have come at a worse time. Wright's aunts had been forced to declare bankruptcy in 1909 and were desperately trying to keep the school open in 1911 when their nephew and his mistress moved in. Years earlier the aunts often had helped their brother James by cosigning loans when he purchased many area farms, but his death in an accident in 1907 and the cessation of his loan payments caused bankers to attach the assets of the aunts. (According to Secrest, *Frank Lloyd Wright*, p. 197, James owed about $65,000 when he died.)

81. See *WSJ*, December 26 and 30, 1911, and *Chicago Tribune*, December 26 and 28–30, 1911.

82. See *Chicago Herald*, December 31, 1911, *Weekly Home News*, Spring Green, December 28, 1911; and Richard Lloyd Jones to Wright, December 28, 1911, FLWA.

83. Information about Wright's commissions is based on a list provided in McArthur, *Frank Lloyd Wright*, pp. 347–48. Arthur L. Richards (1877–1958), the Milwaukee businessman for whom Wright designed the Madison Hotel, had also commissioned a Chinese restaurant, an office building and shop, the Lake Geneva Hotel, and the American System-Built houses. See Mary Jane Hamilton, "The Madison Hotel" and "The Kehl Dance Academy" in Sprague, *Frank

Lloyd Wright and Madison*, pp. 57–63, 65–68.

84. On Midway Gardens see Paul Kruty, *Frank Lloyd Wright and Midway Gardens* (Champaign: University of Illinois Press, 1998). See also Joseph Griggs, "Alfonso Iannelli: The Prairie Spirit in Sculpture," *Prairie School Review* 2, no. 4 (1965): 5–23.

85. See coverage in Brendan Gill, *Many Masks: A Life of Frank Lloyd Wright* (New York: Putnam, 1987), pp. 229–33; in Secrest, *Frank Lloyd Wright*, pp. 216–22; and *Weekly Home News*, Spring Green, August 20, 1914. See also Ann Van Zanten, *John Lloyd Wright: Architecture and Design* (Chicago: Chicago Historical Society, 1982), pp. 43–71; *CT*, November 1, 1926.

86. On Maud Miriam (Hicks) Noel (1869–1930) see Secrest, *Frank Lloyd Wright*, pp. 237–48; Levine, *Architecture of Frank Lloyd Wright*, pp. 193–94, 446; Wright, *Autobiography*, pp. 239–40. Shortly after Wright's autobiography was published in 1932, a serialized autobiography by Miriam Noel appeared in the Sunday magazine section of the *Milwaukee Journal*, May 8, 1932, p. 1; May 15, p. 3; May 22, p. 6; May 29, p. 2, and June 5, p. 9.

87. See Frederick Gookin to Wright, October 16, 1911, FLWA; *The Imperial: The First Hundred Years* (Tokyo: Imperial Hotel, 1990); Kathryn Smith, "Frank Lloyd Wright and the

Imperial Hotel: A Postscript," *Art Bulletin* 67 (June 1985): 296–310; and Levine, *Architecture of Frank Lloyd Wright*, pp. 144–55. Secrest, *Frank Lloyd Wright*, p. 214, provides different figures for the hotel's cost and Wright's commission.

88. See Shirley du Fresne McArthur, *Frank Lloyd Wright American System-Built Homes in Milwaukee* (Milwaukee, Wisc.: North Point Historical Society, 1983). One of Wright's major clients during this period was Aline Barnsdall, who provided him with forty-five commissions, only four of which were realized. See Kathryn Smith, *Frank Lloyd Wright: Hollyhock House and Olive Hill* (New York: Rizzoli, 1992), for a detailed account of their often stormy relationship.

89. See Smith, "Frank Lloyd Wright and the Imperial Hotel," and Meech-Pekarik, "Frank Lloyd Wright's Other Passion."

90. For critical response to Wright's hotel see Louis Mulgardt, "A Building That Is Wrong," *Architect and Engineer* 71 (November 1922): 81–89. For positive response see Louis Sullivan, "Concerning the Imperial Hotel, Tokyo," *Architectural Record* 53 (April 1923): 335–52.

91. For Wright's textile block houses see Robert Sweeney, *Frank Lloyd Wright in Hollywood: Visions of a New Architecture* (Cambridge, Mass.: MIT Press, 1994); David De Long, ed., *Frank Lloyd Wright: Designs for an American Landscape* (New York:

Abrams, 1996); and A. N. Rebori, "Frank Lloyd Wright's Textile-Block Slab Construction," *Architectural Record* 62 (December 1927): 448–56.

92. *The Imperial*, pp. 130–36; *San Francisco Chronicle*, September 2, 3, and 22, 1923; Baron Okura to Wright, September 13, 1923, FLWA. The *Who's Who* tale is from Smith, "Frank Lloyd Wright and the Imperial Hotel," p. 310.

93. See William T. Evjue, *A Fighting Editor* (Madison, Wisc.: Wells Printing, 1968); *CT*, October 18, 1923, and David Mollenhoff, *Madison: A History of the Formative Years* (Dubuque, Iowa: Kendall-Hunt, 1982), pp. 299–302.

94. See four decades of Evjue-Wright correspondence, FLWA; also invitations, holiday cards, and letters to and from Olgivanna Wright and other members of the Taliesin Fellowship in William T. Evjue Papers (hereafter, Evjue Papers), box 155, SHSW.

95. See Mary Jane Hamilton, "The Nakoma Country Club," in Sprague, *Frank Lloyd Wright and Madison*, pp. 77–82, and Nakoma Country Club materials in the Charles E. Brown Papers, box 13, SHSW. During the summer of 1923 Wright had begun work on a large resort project for Lake Tahoe for which he also provided tepee-like forms. Both are discussed in De Long, *Frank Lloyd Wright: Designs*, pp. 47–66. See Mary Jane Hamilton, "The Phi Gamma Delta House," in

Sprague, *Frank Lloyd Wright and Madison*, pp. 69–76; and Sweeney, *Frank Lloyd Wright in Hollywood*, pp. 114–15.

96. For Miriam's strange behavior and divorce see Secrest, *Frank Lloyd Wright*, pp. 280–84.

97. On Mary Bingham Hurlbut Costello, see Leon Herold, interview by August Derleth, Zona Gale Collection, box 5, SHSW; and Dione Neutra, ed., *Richard Neutra: Promise and Fulfillment, 1919–32* (Carbondale: Southern Illinois University Press, 1986), pp. 135–46. Hurlbut earned a bachelor's degree in 1925 and a master's in 1929. See related editions of the *Badger*. On Zona Gale see August Derleth, *Still Small Voice: The Biography of Zona Gale* (New York: Appleton-Century, 1940); and *Autobiography* (Book 5), vol. 4, Pfeiffer, *Collected Writings* (New York: Rizzoli, 1994), p. 203.

98. For introduction to Olgivanna Wright (1898–1985), see Wright, *Autobiography* (Book 5), pp. 204–7; Secrest, *Frank Lloyd Wright*, pp. 303–21. The *Chicago Tribune*, November 23, 1924, sec. 8, pp. 1, 2, and 8, describes an American orchestral group and thirty Russian dancers and ballet numbers on the program, including Thamar Karsavina, described as "the Great Russian Dancer" from Petrograd, who would be appearing in Thursday and Sunday matinee performances the following week at the Eighth Street Theater.

99. See *CT*, April 21, 1925, for second major fire at Taliesin.

100. Secrest, *Frank Lloyd Wright*, pp. 280–84.

101. Wright offers his recollections of these dramatic events in his *Autobiography*, pp. 309–18. See also Gill, *Many Masks*, pp. 292–97; Secrest, *Frank Lloyd Wright*, pp. 327–32; and Twombly, *Frank Lloyd Wright*, pp. 188–90.

102. In 1926 Wright lost not only the country club and the fraternity jobs but also his only public building in Madison, the 1893 Lake Mendota boathouse, which was demolished in February. See the one-column article in the *CT*, February 16, 1926. At a meeting held October 16, 1926, the Phi Gamma Delta alumni board voted to dismiss Wright and to hire the firm of Law, Law and Potter; the Nakoma Country Club later hired a Madison architect, Philip M. Homer, to design its clubhouse.

103. An inventory dated October 1, 1926 (copy in Island Woolen Mills Records, SHSW), of the items Wright turned over to the Bank of Wisconsin in 1926 shows fifteen boxes and a pearl-inlaid chest containing 5,016 Japanese prints. For the auction of still other Wright prints at the Anderson Gallery in New York on January 6 and 7, 1927, see Secrest, *Frank Lloyd Wright*, pp. 335–36. For still another fire at Taliesin, see *Baraboo* (Wisconsin) *Weekly News*, February 24, 1927.

104. Frank Lloyd Wright, Inc., was formed in January but not registered with the Wisconsin secretary of state until August 6, 1927. On the corporation and its contributors, see Secrest, *Frank Lloyd Wright*, pp. 332, 337.

105. For a detailed account of these transactions see Secrest, *Frank Lloyd Wright*, pp. 339–43. Part of the settlement appears to have been the sale of the prints by the Bank of Wisconsin to U.W. mathematics professor Edward Van Vleck for $4,000. He began selling them that fall, recouped his investment within a few months, and by 1940 had sold 2,162 of them, nearly tripling his investment. Many of his unsold Wright prints were in the collection given to the Elvehjem Museum of Art in Madison by Van Vleck's son in 1980. See *The Edward Burr Van Vleck Collection of Japanese Prints* (Madison, Wisc.: Elvehjem Museum of Art, 1990), p. v.

106. Wright's Biltmore client-collaborator, Albert McArthur (1881–1951), was the son of Warren McArthur, whom Wright had met at Uncle Jenkin's All Souls Church soon after Wright arrived in Chicago. Wright also had designed an early bootleg house for McArthur in 1892. The younger McArthur, who had worked in Wright's studio around 1908 or 1909, moved to Arizona in 1925 and designed many houses and hotels there.

107. In May 1928 Wright and Olgivanna left Arizona for California where Wright continued work on San Marcos drawings. The couple were married at Rancho Santa Fe on August 28, 1928.

108. The first draft of the prospectus for the Hillside Home School of the Allied Arts was written in 1928 but not published until 1931. Multiple drafts and replies from several individuals who reviewed them are at FLWA.

109. On Glenn Frank, see Lawrence H. Larsen, *The President Wore Spats* (Madison: State Historical Society of Wisconsin, 1965), pp. 50–147; and "An Educational Center for Creative Art," December 13, 1929, a memorandum in the Glenn Frank Presidential Papers, series 4/13/1, box 55 (1928–29), UWA. For Wright's correspondence, see Franz Aust to Wright, December 7, 1928; Wright to Werner Moser, July 25, 1929; Wright to Glenn Frank, December 17, 1929, all at FLWA.

110. For the 110-room hotel for Dr. Alexander Chandler, a veterinarian-turned-real-estate-developer, and Ocatilla, see Levine, *Architecture of Frank Lloyd Wright*, chap. 7.

111. *New York Times*, October 18, 1929, p. 22, and October 19, 1929, p. 24, describe the intended New York city site and $400,000 price tag. William Gutherie, St. Mark's minister, to Wright, March 4, 1930, mentions $700,000, FLWA.

112. See Donald Young, ed., *In Politics: The Memoirs of Philip La Follette* (New York: Holt, Rinehart and Winston, 1970), p. 172.

113. On the Richard Lloyd Jones House, see De Long, *Frank Lloyd Wright: Designs*, pp. 114–16, and Sweeney, *Frank Lloyd Wright in Hollywood*, pp. 181–99, 212, 229.

114. Wright could not afford to maintain an office in Chicago, so he worked out an arrangement with Charles Morgan, a 1914 University of Illinois architectural graduate who often prepared renderings for other architects, to meet prospective Chicago clients in Morgan's office on the thirty-third floor of 333 North Michigan Ave., a new 1920s Holabird and Root high-rise that was a high-status address.

115. For information about Arthur Peabody (1858–1942), see the biographical file at UWA; his obituary, *WSJ*, September 3, 1942; and Gordon Orr, *Perspectives of a University* (Madison: Department of Planning and Construction, University of Wisconsin, 1978). In 1905 Peabody was appointed University of Wisconsin architect and from 1915 to 1939 served as the state architect. As a result of his long tenure in these powerful positions, approximately seventy buildings around the state were developed under his direction. His name appears as project architect on many drawings, even though the work was often done by others. For the selection

of Holabird and Root for the Forest Products Laboratory, see *Chicago Tribune*, August 23, 1931, and for the completed building, see "The U.S. Forest Products Laboratory," *Wisconsin Alumnus* 59, no. 5 (November 1957): 16–21.

116. The sale of the Gilmore House was announced in an article in the *WSJ*, March 9, 1930, which identified the original architect as "Harold" Lloyd Wright. It is not at all surprising that the new owners, Nell and Howard Weiss, selected Law, Law and Potter over Wright. The Law brothers both lived in University Heights and were responsible for about thirty recent new houses or remodelings there. They also had designed large houses for several wealthy executives, chapter houses for more than a dozen U.W.–Madison fraternities and sororities, a large new high school and major bank, and collaborated on a major department store for the Capitol Square. See Wright to James Law, July 12, 1930, concerning the Gilmore House and a November 25, 1938, letter to Law concerning the proposed city-county facility, FLWA.

117. The Kahn Lectures at Princeton took place May 6 through 12, 1930, and the exhibition sponsored by the New York Architecture League ran from May 29 to June 12. Midwestern venues included Chicago (September 25–October 12), Madison (October 15–22), and Milwaukee (November 20–December 7).

The show then traveled to Europe, opening May 9, 1931, in Amsterdam and thereafter went to Berlin, Stuttgart, Antwerp, and Brussels. Wright's first Madison exhibit was displayed for one week in 1930 in the fourth-floor gallery at SHSW. For Wright's October 1930 lectures and exhibit, see the U.W. *Daily Cardinal*, October 15–18, 1930, and articles in the *WSJ* on the same dates. Wright presented other campus lectures in 1932, 1941, 1948, 1952, 1955, and 1957. Except for a weeklong exhibition in June 1935 at SHSW, subsequent exhibitions in 1932, 1938, 1948, and 1955 were held at the U.W. Memorial Union Gallery.

118. For Charles Morgan's role in paying for Wright's Cord, see Morgan to Wright, June 19, 1930, and July 17, 1946, and Wright to Morgan, January 19, 1932; for retaining an expensive grand piano, Wright to Lucien M. Hanks, March 17, 1932, all in FLWA. The book story is described in Herbert Fritz, "At Taliesin," *Uplands Reader*, April 1979. For the broken nose story see the *WSJ*, November 1, 1932; for the response against Sechrest by apprentices, see *Daily Cardinal*, November 5, 1932, and see the account and photo in Gill, *Many Masks*, pp. 330–32.

119. For a revealing passage on Wright's desperate condition see Secrest, *Frank Lloyd Wright*, pp. 397–98.

120. For samples of national coverage suggesting Wright's lingering industrial arts emphasis for the new school, see "Taliesin," *Art Digest* (September 1, 1932): 2, and "Wisconsin Architect Defies the Depression," *Milwaukee Journal*, September 4, 1932, p. 3. Initial announcements in 1932 mention seventy, but the size of the group was soon decreased and the per-person cost increased. Many apprentices paid less in return for doing more chores. The Taliesin Fellowship also drew from other sources, including Olgivanna's experience with Georgi Gurdjieff's institute, the new Bauhaus in Germany, and Cranbrook Academy in Bloomfield Hills, Michigan, as well as the original Hillside Home School.

121. See accounts by early apprentices Robert Bishop, John Howe, Yen Liang, Bryon Mosher, and William Wesley Peters in Edgar Tafel, *About Wright* (New York: Wiley, 1993), pp. 105–15, 123–26, 127–32, 146–55, 156–71, and Tafel's Taliesin experience in his *Years with Frank Lloyd Wright* (New York: Dover, 1985), pp. 10–16, 140–62. Howe attended Evanston High School, where Morgan presented one of his promotional talks.

122. Wright describes this process in *Autobiography* (Book 5), vol. 4 of Pfeiffer, *Collected Writings*, pp. 136–45.

123. That Wright was able to rehabilitate the old Hillside

school plant and provide for the physical needs of new apprentices owed in large measure to materials and services he secured from Madison firms. These included a new typewriter (Stemp), printed materials (Straus Printing), cots and mattresses (Frautschi), seeds for food (Olds Seeds), miscellaneous items (Hills Dept. Store), plus paint/stains, hardware and custom glass, and milled lumber (Mautz, Wolf Kubly, and Findorff firms). See related correspondence to and from these and other Madison companies in FLWA.

124. An article in the *CT*, November 1, 1933, announced the opening that evening of the $30,000 Taliesin Playhouse; in his column "Good Afternoon Everybody" (*CT*, December 13, 1933), William T. Evjue offered a contemporary account and even plugged the current show, a Russian film by Sergei Eisenstein. Wright secured historical films and modern classics from the Museum of Modern Art's circulating collection as well as Russian films from Artkino Pictures, a choice that attracted the attention of the FBI (see the agency's BuFile 100-240585, obtained under the Freedom of Information Act). For a partial list of films shown at the playhouse, see Randolph Henning, ed., *"At Taliesin": Newspaper Columns by Frank Lloyd Wright and the Taliesin Fellowship, 1934–37* (Carbondale: Southern Illinois University Press, 1992), pp. 321–22.

125. See Donald Hoffmann, *Frank Lloyd Wright's Fallingwater: The House and Its History* (New York: Dover, 1978), pp. 11–12 (Kaufmann is quoted on p. 11 — Hoffman identifies his source as "Twenty-five Years of the House and the Waterfall," *L'architectettura–cronache e storia* 82 [August 1962]: 39); Tafel, *Years with FLW*, pp. 1–2.

126. Hoffmann, *Frank Lloyd Wright's Fallingwater*, p. 12, and Tafel, *Years with FLW*, p. 3.

127. For September 1935 drawings that Wright dashed off for Kaufmann, see Hoffmann, *Frank Lloyd Wright's Fallingwater*, pp. 15–17, and Tafel, *Years with FLW*, pp. 3–9.

128. See Jonathan Lipman, *Frank Lloyd Wright and the Johnson Wax Buildings* (New York: Rizzoli, 1986); and McArthur, *Frank Lloyd Wright*, pp. 277–89. Johnson officials first met with Wright in July 1936; the completed building was opened to the public in April 1939. Wright encountered opposition on multiple fronts: from Racine architects because he had taken the commission away from one of their colleagues and Wright did not then hold a valid license to practice in Wisconsin, and from the state industrial commission because he had failed to submit plans before beginning construction.

129. See Mary Jane Hamilton, "The Fly Craft Studio," in Sprague, *Frank Lloyd Wright and Madison*, pp. 169–71. The projected budget for that roofing-paper-

covered structure was $1,500. The Johnson Wax cost figures come from Lipman, *Frank Lloyd Wright and the Johnson Wax Buildings*, p. 75, and those for Fallingwater from Hoffmann, *Frank Lloyd Wright's Fallingwater*, p. 52.

130. For the Jacobs I, see Herbert and Katherine Jacobs, *Building with Frank Lloyd Wright: An Illustrated Memoir* (Carbondale: Southern Illinois University Press, 1978), and Donald Kalec, "The Jacobs House I" in Sprague, *Frank Lloyd Wright and Madison*, pp. 91–100.

131. For general information about Wright's Usonian houses, see John Sergeant, *Frank Lloyd Wright's Usonian Houses: The Case for Organic Architecture* (New York: Watson-Guptill, 1976); and McArthur, *Frank Lloyd Wright*, pp. 249–57; for information about specific houses, see Susan Dandes, ed., *Affordable Dreams: The Goetsch-Winkler House and Frank Lloyd Wright* (East Lansing: Kresge Museum and Michigan State University, 1991).

132. Many who toured the Jacobs I after it was featured in *Architectural Forum* in 1938 were surprised by its small kitchen (Wright called the 7-by-8-foot area with just twenty square feet of floor space a "workspace" instead of a kitchen) and often were disappointed to find that Wright could not provide them with designs that could be built for $5,000. One cost-saving difference was that cull bricks

and rubber tile from the Johnson Wax building held down the construction costs of Jacobs I.

133. When Wright came down with pneumonia in December 1936, his doctor advised him to find a warmer place to spend the winters. Wright had been looking for land in Arizona for some time, and in December 1937 he purchased half a section in Paradise Valley near Phoenix. In January 1938 the Fellowship set up a makeshift camp and began work on the first permanent structure. Thereafter Wright and the apprentices spent the winter months in Arizona, Wright expanded his holdings, and the construction process continued through the 1950s. See Levine, *Architecture of Frank Lloyd Wright*, pp. 256–97, and for Florida Southern see pp. 308–10, and McArthur, *Frank Lloyd Wright*, pp. 291–97. Wright's eighty-foot water dome for the Florida campus predates those for Olin Terraces. The Jester House, an oceanfront commission, came in during July 1938, and work on the Pew House was underway while Wright and his staff were preparing the Olin Terraces drawings in late summer and fall 1938. See Paul Sprague and Diane Filipowicz, "The Pew House," in Sprague, *Frank Lloyd Wright and Madison*, pp. 109–13.

134. For more on Gropius's visit, see the *WSJ*, November 4 and 9, 1937; *CT*, November 9, 1937; Charles Samson, "At Taliesin," in Henning, *"At Taliesin,"* pp. 274–76;

Tafel, *Years with FLW*, pp. 66–68; Wright to Franz Aust, November 5, 1937, and Aust to Wright, November 20, 1937, FLWA. For Wright's response to the International Style and red square quote see Levine, *Architecture of Frank Lloyd Wright*, pp. 218–19.

135. For an informative description of work assignments in the Taliesin drafting room, see Curtis Besinger, *Working with Mr. Wright: What It Was Like* (Cambridge: Cambridge University Press, 1995), pp. 27–30, 88–92.

136. The *Architectural Forum* article ran for 102 pages and included photographs and drawings of Wright's work during the 1920s and 1930s, including Fallingwater and the Johnson Wax Administration Building. Robert L. Sweeney, *Frank Lloyd Wright: An Annotated Bibliography*, Art and Architecture Bibliographies, no. 5 (Los Angeles: Hennessey & Ingalls, 1978), identifies at least seventeen other articles on Wright that were published that year; Pfeiffer, *Collected Writings*, vol. 3, includes many of the published and unpublished contemporary texts by Wright.

137. For examples of the 285 columns written by Wright and apprentices between 1934 and 1937, see Henning, *"At Taliesin"*; still others appear in Tafel, *About Wright*, pp. 265–90. During this period the *Daily Cardinal*, *Wisconsin State Journal*, and *Capital Times* ran Wright's columns, which are

easily identified by the distinctive Taliesin logo. For Max Otto see files on him at UWA and Max Otto Papers, SHSW. See Harold M. Groves, *In and Out of the Ivory Tower* (Madison, Wisc.: n.p., 1969), pp. 160–61, for descriptions of his Sunday visit and lecture at Taliesin. Betty Cass wrote about six thousand pieces for her "Madison Day by Day" column, which first appeared in 1928 and continued for twenty years. See tributes in the *CT*, October 22, and *WSJ*, October 26, 1977.

138. For an account of Wright's prowess by a former apprentice, see Tafel, *About Wright*, p. 184, where Marcus Weston describes Wright's inspection of his resurfacing of the sixty-foot Romeo and Juliet Windmill tower. This required the architect to climb the internal ladder to the balcony level: "It [the ladder] was straight up with the pump rod in the middle of it and not easy to climb."

1. The quotation appears in the *Wisconsin State Journal* (*WSJ*), February 5, 1955. For information on Harloff see *Madison Past and Present* (Madison: Wisconsin State Journal, 1902), p. 234, and his obituary in the *WSJ* and *Capital Times* (*CT*), June 27, 1947.

2. Harloff's knowledge of these matters is reflected in his letters to the editor, dated July 31, August 5, 12, 19, and 26, and September 2, 1938. The concept of a combination city-county building and auditorium did not originate with Wright or even Harloff. The concept was proposed on the floor of the Dane County Board of Supervisors in January 1928 (see *Dane County Board Proceedings* [*DCBP*], pp. 304–5) and again in January 1936 (*DCBP*, p. 216). Both proposals were voted down. These county board initiatives may have been the source of what Wright's dream civic center later embodied, a building that embraced many functions.

3. The most contemporary and therefore reliable accounts of the project's conception are Wright to P. B. Grove, member of the Dane County board, November 14, 1938; Harloff's interviews with reporters, carried in the *WSJ* and *CT* on November 2, 1938; and letters exchanged by Harloff and Wright in September and October 1938, all in the

Frank Lloyd Wright Archives (FLWA). Wright's comment on "the possibilities" appears in his letter to Grove. Just how many citizens joined Harloff to come up with Wright's $1,000 fee for sketches is not clear. Wright understood that Harloff, George Steinle (a Madison businessman), and five others (seven in all) had agreed to raise the money. See Wright to Grove. Steinle, an inventor and factory head, owned land on Monona Avenue contemplated as the site for the city-county building.

4. For detailed accounts of Wright's fifteen Madison commissions to date, see Paul Sprague, ed., *Frank Lloyd Wright and Madison* (Madison, Wisc.: Elvehjem Museum of Art, 1990). For Wright's desire to do something big, see the *WSJ* and *CT*, November 2, 1938.

5. *CT*, August 7, 1938. Harloff also urged the city to abandon its plan to fill in the lakefront with rubbish. He said this process would take forever and that a sand dredge would be faster and better. See *CT*, August 28, 1938, and *WSJ*, August 27, 1938. For Juneau Park see Landscape Research, *Built in Milwaukee: An Architectural View of the City* (Milwaukee: City of Milwaukee. 1980), pp. 118–19.

6. See Harloff to Wright, September 22, 1938, FLWA. Wright may have waited to answer Harloff's letter until he knew the results of the special election in September when Madison voters authorized the issuance of bonds for a joint city-county building.

7. *WSJ*, September 28, 1938. In a letter dated August 17, 1938, Albert Michelson, the Lions' program chairman, invited Wright to speak on "any subject that you might choose" — so he chose to talk about Olin Terraces. On September 30, 1938, Michelson wrote to thank Wright for his "inspiring talk." These letters are in the FLWA.

8. *WSJ*, September 28, 1938.

9. Ibid. The "more popular" comment was made by a student after Wright lectured at the Memorial Union on October 6, 1957. See Social Education, Butts, Porter, general files, series 26/11, University of Wisconsin Archives (UWA) (hereafter, Butts-UWA).

10. Wright to Harloff, October 1, 1938, FLWA.

11. Gene Masselink, Wright's secretary, to Harloff, October 18, 1938, FLWA. This letter said the plans for the Madison project were ready but that Wright had to leave for a lecture tour and could not see Harloff until October 28 or 29 to show him the drawings. According to newspaper accounts, Harloff showed the drawings to Frank Stewart, chairman of the county board, on November 1, 1938.

See *WSJ*, November 2, 1938.

12. *Bulletin*, October 14, 1938; *WSJ*, October 14, 1938.

13. According to the *WSJ*, November 3, 1938, the temperature eventually reached 74 degrees and set a new record.

14. *DCBP*, 1938, pp. 123–24.

15. *WSJ*, November 2, 1938. The *WSJ* and *CT* accounts of this and subsequent meetings make it clear that Stewart was strongly opposed to the joint building concept.

16. *CT*, November 3, 1938.

17. Ibid.

18. See accounts in the *WSJ* and *CT*, November 3, 1938.

19. Ibid.

20. Betty Cass, "Day by Day," *WSJ*, November 15, 1938.

21. For accounts of Wright's role in the defeat, see the *CT* and *WSJ*, November 3, 1938. Jackson's comments appear in the *Bulletin*, November 11, 1938. This turbulent period is described in the *WSJ*, November 4, 11, 12, and 15, 1938, and *CT*, November 4, 6, 12–14, 17, 18, and 26, 1938.

22. *CT*, November 24, 1938. Although his flip-flop may have represented nothing more than the realization that with the sweet federal money came an unacceptably large tax increase, Law may have had other reasons. It is hard to understand how such a well-informed man who understood the fiscal side of this transaction could wait so long to do his homework or announce his real feelings.

23. See *CT* and *WSJ*, November 26, 1938. Federal officials withdrew the Madison and Dane County grants on November 18, 1938, after receiving a letter from Law saying the county board had failed to approve the building. Copies of correspondence from federal officials appear in the William T. Evjue Papers (hereafter, Evjue Papers), box 70, folder 2, State Historical Society of Wisconsin (SHSW).

24. *WSJ*, November 16, 1938.

25. Jackson to Law, December 12, 1938, Madison Mayor, correspondence and subject file, 1921–65, Dane series, box 1, SHSW. Jackson's correspondence with federal officials includes Jackson to Joseph Guandolo, regional counsel to the federal Public Works Administration (PWA), December 8, 1938; Jackson to PWA regional director D. R. Kennecott, February 9, 1939; and Guandolo to Jackson, February 15, 1939. All this official correspondence appears in the Joseph W. Jackson Papers (hereafter, Jackson Papers), box 16, SHSW. In the same box see also Jackson to Heggie Brandenburg, July 7, 1939. Brandenburg was the owner of a Madison printing company, and Jackson wanted his help in blasting Jackson's bill out of a state legislative committee.

Brandenburg, a former newspaper publisher, still carried a lot of weight with the political elite. The new law authorizing cities to issue revenue bonds was passed as Laws of 1939, Chapter 395.

26. Evidence for the rural bloc's resentment toward the city and its business elite is found in Harloff's letter to the editor, *CT*, November 13, 1938. George Harb, a member of the Dane County board when Wright made his presentation, confirmed the political situation (George Harb, interview by authors, May 9, 1996).

27. The square footage of the city-county building is included in the *DCBP*, July sess., 1938. The square footage for Olin Terraces is noted in MT box 54, FLWA.

28. See Masselink to Harloff, February 15 and April 26, 1939, FLWA.

29. Wright to Grove, November 14, 1938.

30. On several other occasions, such as the Arizona capitol project in 1957, Wright bullied his way onto the public stage without a client.

31. See *WSJ*, November 15, 1938. Grove represented Shorewood Hills, a wealthy Madison suburb just west of the University of Wisconsin along Lake Mendota. This huge drawing was never included in any public presentations of Olin Terraces or Monona Terrace, nor does

it appear in the FLWA. What happened to the drawing is not known. It was probably not a single drawing but a composite of panels that had been enlarged and then attached to a backing. The man who did the original from which the enlargements were made was Charles Leonard Morgan, an exceptionally talented rendering specialist who did considerable work for Wright and other midwestern architects. From letters from Masselink to Charles Morgan, February 10, 1939; Morgan to Wright, January 21, 1939; and Wright to Morgan dated January 25, 1939 (all in FLWA), we can surmise that the rendering probably was thrown away. In the January 25 letter, Wright is talking about the 8-by-16-foot drawing when he tells Morgan, "Anyway, it was out of perspective and I couldn't use it as intended. I worked it over as best I could before I let anyone see it. You can see what I did for your self [sic]. We started laying out a new one right away but had to drop it as unimportant at the moment." In the next sentence Wright refers to the county board's rejection of the dual office building, then adds, "I don't know whether it would have done any good if I did have the drawing I needed, the whole matter is a dead issue for the time being."

32. *CT*, December 5, 1938.

33. The professor, Franz Aust, offered the services of Charles Frothingham, one of his students,

in a letter to Wright dated February 4, 1939. Wright gleefully accepted with a return letter of February 10, 1939. Aust and Wright worked out the details in subsequent letters of February 16 and April 10, 1939, all in FLWA. For Aust, see Susan O. Haswell and Arnold R. Alanen, "Colonizing the Cutover: Wisconsin's Progressive Era Experiments in Rural Planning," *Landscape Journal* 14 (Fall 1995): 171–87.

34. Todd's cost estimates were among the last things that he did before he died on January 5, 1939. For information on James Todd see *The National Cyclopedia of American Biography*, vol. 29 (New York: James T. White, 1941), p. 170.

35. The *CT* account of Wright's speech appeared on December 5, 1938. Holloway wrote to Harold Ickes, Roosevelt's secretary of the interior, urging him to support the project (December 8, 1938, FLWA). Wright's name appears on p. 38 of the Unitarian Society membership registry and is dated (Friday) November 4, 1938 (see First Unitarian Society, Madison, Records: 1878–1976, microfilm roll P82-4845 [1903–1958], SHSW; hereafter Unitarian Records). In a letter of November 2, 1938, FLWA, Holloway offers the pulpit to Wright to speak on "organic religion" at an unspecified time.

36. References to Segoe's visit to Madison are found in Segoe to Jackson, October 28, 1938, in

Dane series 228, general correspondence, box 1, and in Segoe to Jackson, June 14, 1941.

37. For an example of Jackson's manner of referring to Wright, see Jackson to Segoe, April 24, 1939, Dane series 228, general correspondence, box 1.

38. See *WSJ*, August 15, 1914, on the fire and murders; *CT*, November 30, 1925, on his relationship with Miriam Noel and their divorce; and *WSJ*, October 21, 1926, on his tumultuous relationship with Olgivanna Hinzenberg.

39. See Jackson letters of July 17 and 20, 1929, October 9, 1931, and January 24, 1934, FLWA. Wright's name appeared in the *Bulletin* on May 19, 1917, October 9, 1921, June 4, 1927, September 1, 1928, November 22, 1929, October 5, 1934, and November 29, 1935.

40. Jackson mentions this incident to Segoe in a letter dated April 25, 1957 (Jackson Papers). Carroll Metzner, a Madison council member who became a staunch opponent of Monona Terrace, later included the incident on page 13 of his "Summary of Facts in Support of Bill 300A," a brief supporting a law limiting building height in Law Park to twenty feet, also in the Jackson Papers.

41. Sometimes Jackson changed key facts to strengthen his case. For example, the funding package for the 1938 Conklin site auditorium-armory-marina included a federal

grant covering 45 percent of project costs. The balance had to be covered with revenue bonds issued by Madison. This meant that the city would sell bonds to investors whose sole recourse for payment would be revenue generated by the auditorium complex. Jackson clearly understood how this worked and explained it to his readers in frequent newsletter articles. However, two years later he switched to a different story. On November 29, 1940, Jackson told his newsletter readers that *all* the money (for the auditorium project) was available from the federal government. This was not true and never was. A second example was Jackson's misrepresentation of the process used to hire Ladislas Segoe. These and other instances require one to treat Jackson's explanations with some skepticism.

42. See the *CT*, July 17, 1938, for Segoe's statement on the city-county building.

43. *Bulletin*, April 28 and May 12, 1939. Jackson to Segoe, April 24, 1939, Dane series 228, general correspondence, box 1.

44. Documents relating to the May 9, 1939, presentation include a copy of Segoe's speech notes and a transcript of a radio address that Segoe gave on May 10, 1939, in the Ladislas Segoe Papers, Blegen Library, University of Cincinnati; *WSJ*, May 10, 1939; and *CT*, May 10, 1939. See page 4 of the radio transcript and

Segoe's notes for his talk to the Madison and Wisconsin Foundation on May 9, 1939.

45. Ladislas Segoe, *Comprehensive Plan of Madison, Wisconsin, and Environs*, 2 vols. (Madison, Wisc.: Trustees of Madison Planning Trust, n.d.), vol. 2, chap. 12, pp. 21–22; John Nolen, *Madison: A Model City* (Boston: n.p., 1911), p. 40.

46. *CT*, May 10 and July 30, 1939.

47. *CT*, July 30, 1939.

48. Jackson's recollection of his conversations with the Conklins and Law on this matter is included in a handwritten copy of a speech Jackson gave on October 30, 1957, to the city Auditorium Committee, Jackson Papers, box 16, folder 11. Park Commission minutes dated May and August 1939 refer only to buying the land "for park purposes." *Madison Common Council Proceedings (MCCP)*, August 11, 1939, also say that the land was to be purchased for a park. Other articles that speak to the intent include the *WSJ* for June 28, 1937, and May 1 and 10, 1939.

49. Law announced the improvement in the city's financial position to members of the Madison Common Council in February 1941. See *CT*, February 19, 1941.

50. *CT*, January 17 and February 19, 1941; *WSJ*, January 17 and February 16, 1941.

51. For descriptions of the auditorium see the *CT*, February 19, 1941; *MCCP*, February 4, 1941. See also *WSJ*, May 7 and 8 and June 1, 1941.

52. See *CT*, January 17 and February 15, 1941, and H. K. Harley to Law, May 26, 1941, Jackson Papers, box 16, folder 16.

53. Brayton's editorial appeared in the *WSJ*, June 4, 1941. Brayton even arranged for Wright to meet with Daniel Mead, a nationally known engineer, and got Mead to give the *Journal* an objective engineering analysis of Olin Terraces. Mead concluded that Wright was an architect of "great artistic ability, extended experience, and great originality" and that his plans were "worthy of the most careful and detailed consideration." A copy of Mead's paper was provided by Howard Mead, his grandson. The *WSJ* article based on Daniel Mead's analysis was published on July 18, 1941.

54. Wright tried to get his Madison high school pal and prominent Madison banker Lucien M. Hanks to chair the committee, but Hanks declined because he had just agreed to head the Red Cross drive and had urged the city to buy the Conklin icehouse property for a community center. Hanks's declination letter to Wright is dated June 5, 1941, FLWA. For a report on Wright's lecture at the Memorial Union, see the *WSJ*, October 15, 1941. The lecture was sponsored by the

Madison Art Association. After his lecture Wright's presentation drawings were placed on display in glass-fronted cases outside the Union Theater.

55. Curtis Besinger, *Working with Mr. Wright, What It Was Like* (New York: Cambridge University Press, 1995), pp. 95–96.

56. *Progressive*, July 27, 1940, p. 5; *Scribner's Commentator*, Lake Geneva, Wisconsin, October 1941, pp. 35–37. Sixteen issues of *A Taliesin Square-Paper: A Nonpolitical Voice from Our Democratic Minority* were published from 1941 to 1954; of the six issued during 1941, five treated war-related issues.

57. Besinger, *Working with Mr. Wright*, pp. 95–96. According to the Spring Green *Weekly Home News* of October 10, 1940, October 16 was *the* day set aside for all men to register.

58. Lewis Mumford to Wright, April 20, 1941, FLWA.

59. Brendan Gill, *Many Masks: A Life of Frank Lloyd Wright* (New York: Putnam, 1987), p. 404. The *CT* on March 19, 1941, reported that Wright and several other prominent Americans had endorsed Lindbergh's recent "Letter to America." For reactions to Lindbergh's 1941 tour, see Wayne S. Cole, *American First: The Battle Against Intervention, 1940–41* (Madison: University of Wisconsin Press, 1953), pp. 142–43.

60. A copy of the manifesto is in the Jackson Papers, box 3, folder

22. See also Besinger, *Working with Mr. Wright*, p. 113; E. David Cronon and John W. Jenkins, *The University of Wisconsin: A History*. Vol. 3: *1925–1945 — Politics, Depression, and War* (Madison: University of Wisconsin Press, 1994), pp. 400–403.

61. Besinger, *Working with Mr. Wright*, pp. 139–40, 142, 148.

62. *WSJ* and *CT*, December 17, 1942. Weston's bail of $1,000 was provided by William T. Evjue, the publisher of the *Capital Times*. See District Court to Evjue, acknowledging $1,000 refund of bail for Weston, January 14, 1942, Evjue Papers, box 146, folder 16.

Wright got further front-page treatment in the Madison papers when he denied Stone's allegations. See *CT*, December 17 and 20, 1942, and January 14, 1943. Evjue also attacked Stone during the publisher's popular WIBA radio talk show. See Evjue to Masselink, January 7, 1943, Evjue Papers, box 155, folder 25. For the sentencing of Davison and Howe see the *CT* for June 6, 1943.

63. Hoover's reply to Jackson, dated May 13, 1942, is in the Jackson Papers, box 3, folder 10. Jackson's letter of April 23, 1942, is specifically mentioned in Hoover's letter but is missing from the Jackson Papers. The following documents from Wright's FBI file, 25-133757, obtained under the Freedom of Information Act, reflect this story: teletype from Hoover to

Milwaukee, December 17, 1942; memorandum from R. H. Cunningham of the Washington, D.C., bureau office, to Mr. Ladd, December 21, 1942; note from the Milwaukee office to Hoover, December 31; memorandum from Hoover to Assistant Attorney General Wendell Beege, January 5, 1943; and a letter from H. T. O'Connor to Hoover, February 9, 1943. Weston and Howe were sent to the federal prison at Sandstone, Minnesota, where Wright visited them. Two other apprentices, Curtis Besinger and Howard Tenbrink, went to conscientious objector camps.

64. See *CT*, December 14, 1945, and *WSJ*, November 28, 1945, and February 20, 1946.

65. See "Recent Background of the Madison Metropolitan War Memorial Project," June 15, 1946, Butts Unprocessed Collection (BUC).

66. *Bulletin*, January 11, 1946; see also July 7, 1944.

67. Ibid.

68. For Madison Community Center see the *CT*, January 26, 1946, and June 18, 1967, and *WSJ*, February 7, 1966.

69. Cronon and Jenkins, *University of Wisconsin*, 3:589–606.

70. Butts's Milwaukee consultancy is documented in a series of letters in the archives of the Milwaukee Art Museum (MAM). They

include Butts to Max Friedman, a Milwaukee merchant, June 16, 1945; Butts to Leroy Riegel, a New Jersey architect then serving as executive secretary of the Milwaukee War Memorial, September 22, 1945; and Butts to Riegel, October 24, 1946. Butts's Madison experience is summarized in a letter to Jerry Bartell, prominent Madison arts advocate, September 27, 1973, BUC. Butts's large role in Madison was partly the result of his chairmanship of the Social Planning Committee of the Madison Recreational Council, a large umbrella group that acted as a sounding board for the community on the war memorial movement. As chairman of this organization Butts wrote the influential report entitled "Madison and the War Memorial" in November 1945. A copy can be found in BUC.

71. For examples of Butts's and Jackson's advocacy of living memorials, see the *WSJ*, December 16, 1946, and *Bulletin*, July 7, 1944, and January 11, 1946.

72. Butts's editorial ran in the *WSJ*, December 16, 1945.

73. Butts recognized that the community center he was proposing would cost more to build and would require an ongoing subsidy from property taxes. One reason that the arena-auditorium had such great appeal to the business community was the widespread understanding

that its revenues would pay for the building.

74. *WSJ*, November 28, 1945, and December 14, 1945. See the Plan Commission report in the *MCCP*, May 24, 1946.

75. *CT*, May 31, 1946.

76. *WSJ*, May 28, 1946.

77. Butts based his recommendations on a national survey he had just completed; he outlined his views on process in his November 1945 fact-finding report (see note 70). See the *WSJ*, July 3, 1946, and September 25, 1946, and *CT*, July 12, October 4, and October 16, 1946, for the work done by the organizations. Joseph Rothschild, the manager of Baron's Department Store, was elected president of the corporation.

78. *WSJ*, May 29, 1947; *CT*, May 29, 1947.

79. *WSJ*, August 24, 1947.

80. Halsey Kraege, who succeeded Law as mayor of Madison, urged a lakefront location in his inaugural address to the common council, (*MCCP*, April 16, 1946). The war memorial association's remark about the site comes from "Report and Recommendations of the Madison Metropolitan War Memorial Association," July 1, 1949, p. 5. To make sure that the war memorial project could proceed, Jackson got the legislature to pass a law that allowed the city to fill in more of Lake Mendota. Laws of 1949, Chapter 414,

increased the submerged lands that could be used for the project to one thousand feet; the measure was approved July 6, 1949.

81. "Report and Recommendations." Joe Rothschild, war memorial chairman, originally put the auditorium's cost at $1.5 million, but by 1947 its cost had risen to about $2 million (*CT*, February 9, 1947, and *WSJ*, May 23, 1947). Even Jackson was sobered. In a confidential letter to Segoe dated July 8, 1949, Jackson says, "This is considerably more than we anticipated." See Jackson Papers, box 3, folder 18.

82. Boyle's criticisms appeared in several articles over several months. See *WSJ*, October 15 and November 22, 1949; *CT*, May 24, 1949, and December 28, 1950.

83. Jackson to Butts, May 9, 1946, BUC; *WSJ* editorial, April 26, 1950. For an example of Boyle's reaction to the project, see the *WSJ*, November 22, 1949. The common council vote was reported in the *CT* and *WSJ*, May 24, 1950.

## CHAPTER 4

## THE CIVIC AUDITORIUM CRUSADE

1. *WSJ*, May 16, 19, and 23, 1953; *CT*, May 16, 1953.

2. The inadequacies of the two buildings are documented in chap. 3. The heart attack story is found in the *WSJ*, June 11, 1952, and the bulging corridor comment is found in the *WSJ*, May 15, 1953. The rendering, done by the Madison firm of Law, Law, Potter and Nystrom and by John Messmer, a Milwaukee architect, appeared in the *WSJ*, February 17, 1952. For earlier renderings by the same firm see the *CT*, December 4, 1947. Referendum results were reported in the *CT*, April 2, 1952. Later the Chicago firm of Holabird, Root, and Burgee became the lead architects for the project. Key Dane County developments can be found in *Dane County Board Proceedings (DCBP)*, June, August, and September 1944; December 1947; July, November, and December 1948; and December 1949. Key Madison developments can be found in *Madison Common Council Proceedings (MCCP)*, May 10 and 24, June 28, and July 16, 1951, and March 13, June 12, August 14, and October 23, 1952. The Holabird, Root, and Burgee plan appeared in the *CT*, November 19, 1953.

3. According to Traffic Engineering Department, "An Overall Parking Plan for Madison, Wisconsin,"

June 1956, Madison had 18,902 cars in 1945 and 38,631 in 1955, a 104 percent increase. This information appeared in an article entitled "Parking in Downtown Madison" that appeared in the *WSJ* in the mid-1950s (probably 1955 or '56). According to the *WSJ*, November 7, 1954, downtown Madison had 7,000 parking spaces in 1939 and 6,600 in 1954, a drop of 8 percent. See the *CT*, September 30, 1953, for the quote about retail trends. Helen Groves told Wright in a letter March 24, 1954, Frank Lloyd Wright Archives (FLWA), that in her conversations with downtown businesspeople she detected "signs of panic" about the damage the parking problem was doing to their businesses.

4. The Madison and Wisconsin Foundation was renamed the Chamber of Commerce and Foundation in 1952 after the retirement of Joe Jackson. The business community felt that the model developed by Jackson in 1937 was out of step with the modern chamber movement.

5. See *WSJ* and *CT*, May 16, 1953, and Boyle's letter to the editor, *CT*, May 23, 1953.

6. *WSJ*, May 16, 1953. See the *WSJ*, April 16 and June 2, 1946, for early stories about creating a parking lot in Law Park.

7. A subsequent *WSJ* editorial (September 15, 1953) said, "[The] No. 1 spokesman has a long record as an obstructionist

in Madison public life. He has stood against everything looking toward public improvement here for years." The *WSJ* editorial that angered Boyle appeared on May 19, 1953, headlined "Fun's Done on C-C Building." The editorial said that Boyle and other critics had presented their point of view many times but that the council had not supported them. The editorial continued: "All right, let's get on with the city-county building. Please, boys, fun is fun, but you've had it."

8. Boyle, letter to the editor, *CT*, May 23, 1953. Boyle was also angered by the hypocrisy of Joe Jackson's and Walter Johnson's support for a parking lot in Law Park. Boyle said that several years earlier he had proposed the same thing, but Jackson and Johnson had "violently opposed" the idea, claiming it was "too costly, not practicable, and that it would destroy the beauty of the sunrise over Lake Monona." Clearly, the prospect of a parking lot in Law Park was unpleasant for Jackson because it violated Nolen's great vision for the park. Nevertheless, he was willing to allow the parking lot to get his much desired city-county building (see *WSJ*, May 23, 1953).

9. *CT* and *WSJ*, May 14, 1953. The *WSJ* editorial anointing the Conklin Park plans appeared on May 15, 1953.

10. *MCCP*, May 28, 1953.

11. *MCCP*, June 25, 1953.

Biographical information about Nestingen can be gleaned from the Ivan Arnold Nestingen Papers (hereafter, Nestingen Papers) and the William T. Evjue Papers (hereafter, Evjue Papers) at the State Historical Society of Wisconsin (SHSW).

12. The first Auditorium Committee report, dated September 10, 1953 (City of Madison Unprocessed Collections [CMU]), addresses the city's remarkable financial capacity. The report notes that city officials assured committee members that the Madison debt limit "will not be threatened" by an ambitious capital expenditure program, including "schools, street improvements, Fire Department improvements, City-County building, Park Department improvement, storm sewers ... diversion of sewerage effluent" and a "municipal auditorium and civic center."

13. Boyle's colleagues included Lou Wagner, the owner of the Washington Hotel; Joe Silverberg, a University of Wisconsin law student; and Richard Lent, Boyle's law partner. Lent described the 1953 Boyle-Wright meetings to Mary Jane Hamilton in a telephone conversation on April 19, 1997. Lent recalled that he and Boyle drove out to Taliesin for Sunday morning chats and that Wright came into town to meet with them at their downtown law offices. The Boyle-Wright meetings were also described by Boyle in

the *CT*, June 9, 1956. According to Boyle, he met "several times" with Wright in 1953–54, and Wright was "most cooperative."

14. Wright proposed breaking the architect's contract in the *WSJ*, August 24, 1953. Wright called the referendum "a life-saving clause ... of our Democracy" in a spirited *CT* guest editorial, "Wright Is Now Ashamed of His Home Town," August 25, 1953.

15. Wright appears to have paid all costs of preparing these new drawings, which were published by the *CT*, July 7–10, 1953.

16. Ibid. All quotations come from this *CT* series. Wright made his comment about self-liquidation in a guest editorial in the *CT*, August 25, 1953.

17. Wright's first use of *Monona Terrace* appeared in his guest editorial for the *CT*, "Wright Is Now Ashamed." See also Wright's article in the *CT*, September 21, 1953.

18. For articles describing activities of the 4C committee, see the *CT*, July 31, and August 5, 25, and 31, 1953, and *WSJ*, September 14, 1953. The drawings were also displayed at a home show held at Marshall Erdman's University Avenue plant where he was manufacturing prefab homes. See *CT*, September 8, 1953.

19. *CT*, August 25, 1953.

20. This incident is described in the *WSJ*, September 21, 1953, and *CT*, September 22, 1953. In

a letter to Wright of December 21, 1953, FLWA, Helen Groves reports that "Mr. Boyle is treated as an untouchable." One example of Boyle's behind-the-scenes leadership and his tactical skill was his suggestion, in the spring of 1955, that Wright plan supporters identify and vote for common council candidates who favored Monona Terrace. See Groves to Wright, December 4, 1954, FLWA.

21. For the September report see the *WSJ*, September 11, 1953, and "Report of the Municipal Auditorium and Civic Center Committee to the Common Council," October 1, 1953, CMU.

22. See the Chamber of Commerce press release dated September 30, 1953, in the Lescohier Unprocessed Collection (LUC), FLWA. Serving on this committee were George Hall, Halsey Kraege, Leon Smith, Harrison Garner, and Larry Larson.

23. As reported by the *WSJ*, September 11, 1953, Metzner first criticized the Wright plan as unworkable, too small to include a city-county building or a railroad station, and beyond serious consideration. For an account of the Metzner-Boyle radio debate, see the *WSJ*, September 14, 1953. Metzner and other members of the joint city-county committee gathered some early ammunition from a meeting with Ellis Potter and Ed Law, principals in the firm of Law, Law, Potter and

Nystrom, who disliked Wright. See *WSJ*, September 19, 1953.

24. The "glittering" comment appeared in the *WSJ*, September 15, 1953. See also *WSJ*, September 17, 1953.

25. See *CT*, October 15 and 20, 1953, and Mary Jane Hamilton, *The Meeting House: Heritage and Vision* (Madison, Wisc.: Friends of the Meeting House, 1991), pp. 8–10.

26. Transcript of Diane Kostecke's 1987 interview for public TV station WHA of Helen Groves, SHSW.

27. Ibid.

28. For Lescohier see the *CT*, June 29, 1981.

29. The *WSJ* reported the petition results on December 18, 1953. For a drawing of the proposed city-county building at this stage, see the *CT*, November 19, 1953.

30. See *WSJ*, December 14 and 19, 1953.

31. The Auditorium Committee voted to hire Sprague-Bowman at its meeting on March 4, 1954, to "determine the most desirable size and type of building" (*WSJ*, March 5, 1954). Helen Groves appeared before the common council on February 23, 1954, when the council appropriated the $10,000 for this study, to urge that this money be used instead to estimate the cost of Monona Terrace. Auditorium Committee members rejected her request in part because they

were convinced that Groves included the city and county offices in her definition of a civic center. A copy of her remarks, dated February 23, 1954, is in the Harold Groves Papers (hereafter, Groves Papers), SHSW.

32. The testimonials ran in the *CT* on March 4, 11, 13, 19, 25, and 31, and April 11 and 23, 1954.

33. Wright was keenly aware that Monona Terrace was hostage to Evjue's hatred for Boyle. As Wright put it in a letter to Helen Groves dated February 23, 1954, "Too bad Bill [Evjue] hates Boyle more than he loves me, or Madison" (Groves Papers, box 8, folder 5, SHSW). Evjue's "noble and ambitious" comment appears in the *CT*, August 24, 1953.

34. Evjue's comment about the number of people who spoke to him regarding the Wright plan appears in Groves to Wright, January 30, 1955, FLWA. Evjue's reading of the Nolen book is mentioned in Groves to Wright, March 24, 1955, FLWA.

35. *CT*, May 25 and 27, 1954. Although Wright agreed to stop insisting that city-county offices be included in Monona Terrace, he refused to stop criticizing the design of the Holabird, Root, and Burgee building. As Wright saw it, this was another mediocre office building. Don't Madisonians want to "leave a greater, more noble Madison to their children?" he wondered. The quote about futility comes from the *CT*, May 27, 1954.

Ironically, Helen Groves proved more difficult to subdue than Wright. Said Groves in a letter to Evjue on June 11, 1954, "The best and most economical answer still remains." She was referring to the inclusion of the city-county building in Monona Terrace (Evjue Papers).

36. *CT*, October 4, 1954.

37. Sprague-Bowman Associates, "Analysis of Madison Auditorium and Civic Center Requirements," June 1, 1954 (CMU). Sprague-Bowman analyzed earlier documents from Madison's auditorium crusades and relied heavily on material provided by the Chamber of Commerce and Foundation.

38. A well-known national theater expert who later examined plans based on the Sprague-Bowman template said that he knew of "no project in this country or elsewhere that is as inclusive as this one" (*WSJ*, March 29, 1962). The theater expert was George Izenour, a Yale University professor, whom William Wesley Peters later hired as a consultant to the Monona Terrace project.

39. Porter Butts suggested the term *city center in* a letter to Ivan Nestingen dated July 15, 1954 (in Butts's private collection), but but it never caught on.

40. "Report of the Municipal Auditorium Committee," July 8, 1954. Costs for the proposed 1954 complex were based on updated 1949 war memorial costs. The *WSJ*

(November 6, 1953) quoted Ray Burt, the city building superintendent, as saying that the cost of the war memorial project in 1953 would be $6.6 million, a 28 percent increase over the 1949 price. Although the war memorial complex included an arena, it provides the most comparable costs of any Madison project.

41. *CT*, July 21, 1954.

42. *MCCP*, July 22, 1954. Evjue's editorial ran in the *CT*, July 21, 1954.

43. Minutes of this meeting and a copy of the original petition are available in the Groves Papers, box 23, folder 6, SHSW. For an explanation of the petition process, see the *CT*, August 4, 1954.

44. The "bitter debate" and the "imperils both" comments appeared in a *WSJ* editorial on August 11, 1954; the Anderson telegram to Wright was printed in the *WSJ* on July 16, 1954.

45. The signature shortfall was reported in the *CT*, September 4, 1954. The Zawacki technique was explained in Harold Groves, *In and Out of the Ivory Tower* (Madison: n.p., 1969), p. 166. Delivery of the petitions to the city clerk's office was described in the *CT*, September 9, 1954.

46. *WSJ* and *CT*, September 10, 1954. Carroll Metzner, interview by authors, April 22, 1997; Robert Nuckles, interview by authors, May 9, 1997. Nuckles served on the Auditorium Committee, as an

assistant to Nestingen, and later ran for mayor; both he and Metzner mentioned Hanson's skepticism about Wright.

47. The *CT*, September 17, 1954, describes the strategy the Citizens for Monona Terrace (CMT) adopted in response to these developments. Accounts about how the final language was worked out ran in the *CT* and *WSJ*, September 22, 1954.

48. See Dr. Arnold Jackson to members of the Citizens' Auditorium Committee, October 4, 1954 (CMU). The letter accompanied the poster shown in Fig. 4.11.

49. *Union Label News*, November 1954; *CT*, October 24, 1954.

50. Information about the Citizens Committee for Madison City Auditorium can be found in the *CT*, September 3, 1954. Examples can be found in the *CT*, June 3, September 3, and October 16, 1954, and *WSJ*, September 10, 1954.

51. Harold Groves, in an op-ed piece lauding Monona Terrace that ran in the *CT*, August 11, 1954, said, "Mr. Wright's design was mainly an idea and the preliminary sketches included no dimensions that could serve as the basis for an objective and independent appraisal." The lack of parking spaces was mentioned in city Auditorium Committee reports in 1953 and was a favorite of critics. For an example of Metzner's attack on the lack of parking spaces, see

the *WSJ* and *CT*, October 30, 1953. Wright's handwritten specifications saying that Monona Terrace would have forty-one hundred spaces appeared in the *CT*, October 26, 1954.

52. Lists of leaders of Citizens for Monona Terrace included religious liberals — Max Gaebler, minister at the First Unitarian Society; Alfred W. Swan, minister at First Congregational Church; and Manfred Swarsensky, rabbi at Temple Beth El. Political liberals included Don Lescohier, Harold Groves, and Edmund Zawacki. For an example of obvious anti-materialism as well as political liberalism, see the pro–Monona Terrace essay written by Max Otto, U.W. professor of philosophy, printed in the *CT*, November 1, 1954. See the *CT* editorial that appeared on November 4, 1954, for architecture's power to add beauty; see also the leaflet touting Monona Terrace: "Now we can MAKE MADISON MORE BEAUTIFUL." The preponderance of women leaders and members among the proponents is noted in Harold Groves's memoirs, *In and Out*, p. 166.

53. Wright used the self-liquidating phrase several times. Groves was quoted in the *WSJ*, September 10, 1954.

54. *CT*, October 27, 1954. Wright's statement appears in the *CT*, October 26, 1954.

55. The *WSJ*, October 29, 1954, has the common council's reaction.

56. *CT*, October 29, 1954. Wright's own estimators said it would cost $10 million to $20 million, and the leaders of Citizens for Monona Terrace knew this. Wright got his estimate from Roger H. Corbetta, the president of a large New York City construction firm, Corbetta Construction. See Corbetta to Wright, June 18, 1954, Groves Papers, box 8, SHSW.

57. *WSJ*, October 29, 1954.

58. See the *CT*, November 3, 1954, for election returns. A copy of the CMT campaign expense statement is found in the Groves Papers, box 23, folder 4, SHSW. The "greater and more noble" quote comes from an article that Wright wrote for the *CT*, May 27, 1954.

59. Wright's elation was recorded by the *CT*, November 20, 1954, and in taped conversation with the Taliesin Fellowship on August 17, 1958 (tape 216, FLWA). On November 4, 1954, Evjue commented editorially about the difficulty of getting Wright to conform to the $4 million budget.

60. Although the Guggenheim was then not under construction, Wright was battling New York authorities on building code questions. See Nestingen to Wright, November 12, 1954, MT box 61, FLWA.

61. Ibid.

62. For revealing newspaper accounts of the meeting see the *CT* and *WSJ*, November 20, 1954.

63. On December 4, 1955, Wright wrote Nestingen a long letter in which he tried to account for his "impatience" and "disappointment" at the meeting. As Wright explained it, he "expected, as I am sure most all voters did, that they had approved the [entire] Monona Terrace Plan which they had seen and they were voting to build the center of it as shown calling it a 'civic center and auditorium.' Concerning this I found only confusion at the official meeting as you will remember" (MT box 61, FLWA).

64. The council approved the sale of the bonds on November 22, 1954. The *CT*, December 17, 1954, noted the interest rate. The expanded membership of the Auditorium Committee was approved by the council on January 13, 1955.

65. The meeting was not open to the public because officials expected to talk about Wright's contract. However, they did allow reporters to attend with the understanding that they would have to leave if the contract came up. See *CT* and *WSJ*, February 8, 1955. For this presentation Wright used three new renderings (the dazzling night aerial view, the cross-section, and the view from the lake) and six floor plans.

66. The Sprague-Bowman calculations were reported in the *CT*

and the size of the facility was carried by the *WSJ*, March 14, 1955.

67. *WSJ* and *CT*, February 8, 1955.

68. Wright to Nestingen, December 4, 1954, FLWA.

69. These quotations come from the *CT* and *WSJ*, February 8, 1955, and *CT*, April 21, 1955.

70. Groves to Taliesin Fellowship, February 8, 1955, FLWA. The model went first to the Madison Bank and Trust Company for two weeks, then to the First National Bank for two weeks, and finally to the capitol. The reference to the traffic count appeared in the *CT*, February 18, 1955.

71. Forster's testimonial letter was printed in the *CT*, April 26, 1955. That Forster was angling for the support of Monona Terrace backers was evident from a letter from Lescohier to Forster dated January 14, 1955, in which she thanks the mayor for "the opportunity to circulate your nomination papers." She asks Forster to give her and other proponents his assurance that he will give the project the "courageous leadership" the project requires (Lescohier papers). Curiously, Forster's opponent came out against the referendum mandate; thus proponents would have construed as positive anything Forster did this side of neutrality. Wright's warm comments about Forster appeared in a letter to Ivan Nestingen, April 9, 1955, MT box 61, FLWA.

72. The first *CT* endorsements of common council candidates based on their position on Monona Terrace and Evjue's explanation ran March 30, 1955.

73. As early as February 1955, Nestingen had written Wright to express the committee's desire to secure "a working arrangement ... in the very near future." The correspondence between them, which constitutes early contract negotiations, appears in MT box 61, FLWA: Nestingen to Wright, February 18, 1955, and Wright to Nestingen, February 22, 1955. Nestingen conveyed the committee-approved terms in a letter to Wright of March 4, 1955; Wright's optimistic expectations appeared in his letter to Nestingen of March 12, 1955, FLWA. Wright also agreed to do the parking ramp for a 4 percent commission.

74. Hanson's cautions were reported in the *CT* and *WSJ*, March 18, 1955.

75. See *WSJ*, April 20, 1955, and *CT* on April 19, 1955.

76. *CT*, May 20, 1955.

77. *CT*, May 19 and 27, June 1, 3, and 7, 1955.

78. "Report to the Municipal Auditorium Committee, June 17, 1955, CMU. Contract shortcomings included Forster's refusal to pay Wright a 7 percent commission instead of the usual 6 percent and reluctance to sign a contract with the Frank Lloyd Wright Foundation rather than Frank

Lloyd Wright as an individual. Forster wanted the contract to be with Wright personally so that when he died, the city would have no further obligation. The idea of contracting with Wright and not the foundation apparently came from Metzner. According to a memo from Harold Hanson, May 27, 1955, CMU, Metzner and Hanson met the previous day to discuss this point. In his memo Hanson provides specific language to satisfy Metzner's request. Other points in Hanson's memo appear to have come from the city attorney. Forster's feasibility and legal title questions are treated elsewhere in this chapter.

79. That *Wisconsin State Journal* reporters had to rewrite stories comes from the authors' interview of Nuckles.

80. Anderson revealed his personal feelings about Wright and Monona Terrace in a letter to Wright, July 1, 1954, FLWA. Anderson wrote, "You know I'd like very much to have you do the Madison civic center-auditorium" and "when the proper time comes I'll work as hard as I can to bring it about." For Anderson that time never came; Forster's enjoyment in telling anti-Wright stories comes from the *CT*, June 17, 1966. Metzner summarized his view of Wright in a 1981 interview, *CT*, June 29, 1981. Jackson's comment about Wright comes from Jackson to John F. Kennedy, July 20, 1961. Jackson's views on Wright's

morals was straightforward: "He didn't have any, so they can't be discussed." See Joseph W. Jackson Papers (hereafter, Jackson Papers), box 3, folder 22, SHSW.

81. A typical CMT grassroots strategy was to organize "ward clubs," described in the *CT*, July 22, 1955. Efforts to elect Monona Terrace supporters to the council included a questionnaire sent to all candidates requesting written responses. One question: "If you are elected, will you back every effort to start construction without delay on the Monona Terrace Auditorium and Civic Center?" (MT box 59, FLWA). The best collection of CMT documents can be found in the Groves Papers, box 23, SHSW.

82. *WSJ*, May 28, 1959, and March 19, 1956.

83. *CT*, July 11, 1956, and April 5, 1960.

84. The common council approved the study on September 8, 1955. For background on the PACE study, see the *CT*, August 4 and 18, 1955.

85. *CT*, July 1, 1955.

86. The history and legal theory of dock lines in the United States can be found in John Dillon, *Commentary on the Law of Municipal Corporations*, vol. 1 (Boston: Little, Brown, 1911), pp. 501–4. For outstanding explanations of the public trust doctrine in Wisconsin see *Muench v. Public Service Commission*, 261

Wis. 492–99 (1952), and Joseph L. Sax's article, "The Public Trust Doctrine in Natural Resource Law: Effective Judicial Intervention," 68 *Mich. L. Rev.* 471, 509–23 (1970). For a short, readable summary of public trust doctrine in Wisconsin, see a booklet by Katie Kazan, "Champions of the Public Trust: A History of Water Use in Wisconsin," published by the state Department of Natural Resources, Madison, 1994. We wish to thank Steve Schur, retired attorney for the Public Service Commission and widely recognized authority on the public trust doctrine, for sharing his expertise.

87. See Laws of 1927, Chapter 485, and Laws of 1931, Chapter 301.

88. The constitutional question was apparently raised by William Aberg, a senior member of Metzner's law firm, in connection with the 1955 repeal of a 1953 law giving the University of Wisconsin permission to fill in a large part of Lake Mendota at the foot of Park Street for campus parking. Aberg, who also chaired the State Conservation Commission, predecessor of the Department of Natural Resources, argued that the legislature had no authority to give the lake bed to the university and that this act was unconstitutional. Aberg's testimony was reported in the *CT* and *WSJ*, February 4, 1955.

Forster argued in his report that the city had good reason to distrust the state and cited the Lake Wingra

case then underway. Here the city had received approval from the Public Service Commission to fill in the edge of the lake in Vilas Park for a swimming beach, but the state attorney general challenged the order. This matter was being adjudicated as Forster wrote his report. The attorney general stepped in because he believed that this action eroded the public trust doctrine.

89. Nestingen's two bills were introduced on May 18, 1955, and then either recalled or indefinitely postponed on June 22, 1955. The first, Bill A770, authorized the state to convey the Monona Terrace site to Madison; the second, Bill A771, permitted the city to seek a declaratory ruling on the constitutionality of the 1927 dock-line law. Because Nestingen was a Democrat and Republicans enjoyed majorities in both houses, the bills did not become law; both were rejected on a 53–35 vote on June 22, 1955.

90. The *CT* editorial appeared on June 28, 1955. CMT actions were described in the *CT*, July 13, 1955. Forster's comments appeared in the *CT*, August 19, 1955. Forster was referring to Harold C. Price, a wealthy oil man who commissioned Wright to build Price Tower in Bartlesville, Oklahoma, and Herbert F. Johnson, president of the S. C. Johnson Wax Company, who commissioned Wright to do a complex of corporate buildings in Racine, Wisconsin.

91. Forster's resignation was announced in the *WSJ*, August 18, 1955, and took effect October 15. Rather than continue to serve until October 15, Forster went on vacation on September 15. Just before he resigned, Forster was appointed city manager of Janesville, Wisconsin. According to the *WSJ*, March 15, 1956, Forster was hounded out of town by "Wright zealots."

92. The city's application to the Public Service Commission was filed on August 4, 1955, two weeks before Forster resigned. On November 25, 1955, the PSC ruled that it did not have jurisdiction. The city attorney filed his pleadings with the state supreme court on January 12, 1956, and the appellate court rejected the case on January 16. On September 22, 1955, Nestingen had gotten the common council to pass a resolution asking the state for permission to bring a friendly lawsuit. The Metzner bill made its way through the legislature and was approved on October 28, 1955, as Laws of 1955, Chapter 629.

During this interim period Nestingen also worked with PACE consultants to expedite the feasibility study. See *CT*, September 28, 1955; the Auditorium Committee report dated January 12, 1956; and *MCCP*, January 25, 1956.

93. *CT*, February 25, 1956.

94. For information on Hobbins see the *WSJ*, March 3, 15, 16, 19, and 30, 1956. For detailed

information on issues and candidates during this period, see election analyses prepared by the League of Women Voters at the Madison Public Library.

95. PACE Associates, "A Report Relative to Monona Terrace, Madison, Wisconsin," March 9, 1956, Chicago (Madison Municipal Reference Service [MMRS]). Roger Kirchoff, the architect who was a member of Henry Reynolds' Auditorium Committee, said in a letter of August 5, 1961, CMU, to committee member Frank Ross that the PACE report was soft on Monona Terrace because PACE wanted work from Wright.

96. For election results see the *CT* and *WSJ*, April 4, 1956. Wright's telegram is preserved in the FLWA.

97. Wright's willingness to build within the dock line is chronicled in the *CT*, May 17, 1956.

98. The *CT*'s account of the contract signing appeared on July 6, 1956. The actual contract is preserved in CMU auditorium files. With respect to the total project costs, the contrast between the contract language and what Forster was quoted as saying in the *CT* on November 4, 1954, was striking. Said Forster: "The referendum established that the city cannot issue more than $4 million in obligation bonds to finance the project, but it doesn't mean that the total cost couldn't run to $6 or $7 million if revenues

can be obtained from other sources including revenue bonds and public subscription."

99. See *CT*, April 28, September 26, and October 12, 1956. To secure state support, Citizens for Monona Terrace mailed information packets to people who had signed the visitor book at the Wright-designed Unitarian Meeting House since its opening in 1951 and asked all to urge their legislators to support Monona Terrace. Similarly, they mailed information packets to all legislature candidates and asked for their help.

100. *CT*, August 15 and 16, 1956.

101. For newspaper stories about the modified plans, see the *CT*, August 25, 1956; the series beginning on August 29, 1956; and individual articles dated October 26, December 11, and December 28, 1956. Under the terms of the contract, one cost estimator was Ray Burt, the city building inspector; a second could be picked by the city and a third by Wright. The city chose PACE Associates, and Wright chose Haskell Culwell, the Oklahoma contractor who had built Price Tower.

102. For details of Metzner's organization, see the *CT*, September 1, 1956. Metzner's opposition to the bond issue so vital for downtown was more than the *Journal* could stand. One day before the election, the paper withdrew its endorsement and gave it to William Gorham

Rice, a liberal Democrat. See *WSJ* editorial, November 5, 1956.

103. *CT* and *WSJ*, February 23, 1957.

104. *CT*, March 19, 1957.

105. *WSJ*, March 19, 1957.

106. *CT*, March 25, 1957.

107. See *CT* and *WSJ*, April 3, 1957. Nestingen's opponent was Madison businessman Anthony Fiore.

108. Wright to Nestingen, April 15, 1957, MT box 61, FLWA. Burt's calculations were reported in the *WSJ*, May 3, 1957; he said that Wright had removed more than 500,000 cubic feet of space and saved another $640,000, compared to the December 1956 design. This meant that even with all the nonbuilding costs left *in* the budget, and using an average cost established by the three estimators, Wright was only $632,000 over the $5.5 million budget. In February 1957 the average cost developed by the three estimators was $6.78 million. Subtracting Burt's estimated savings of $640,000 from this amount leaves $6.14 million, or $640,000 more than the city's budget. At the same time, however, inflation had reduced the buying power of the $5.5 million by 15 percent, or $825,000.

109. *Madison v. State*, 1 Wis. 2d 252 (1957).

110. The *CT* of December 1, 1956, reported preliminary approval

from the state industrial commission and the railroads' action on air rights on May 3 and May 21, 1956.

111. Details of this strategy session appear in Jackson to Gaylord Nelson, January 23, 1958 (Jackson Papers, box 16, folder 7). Metzner's desire to prevent Wright from designing a Prairie Style building is described in Metzner's 1987 interview by Kostecke.

According to Jackson, three of the men at the pivotal strategy session were lawyers. Other lawyer friends of Jackson's who might have been present were Walter Ela, Jackson's lawyer, who later filed a suit against Monona Terrace on Jackson's behalf; and Halsey Kraege, a former mayor. Whether Metzner was present at this meeting is not known. Another lawyer who may have attended was Aberg, Metzner's law partner and chairman of the powerful State Conservation Commission.

112. Jackson to Nelson, January 23, 1958. Jackson also related the history of the twenty-foot height limit in a letter to Segoe, July 26, 1958 (Jackson Papers, boxes 3 and 16).

113. *WSJ*, March 13, 1957. The new organization's clever name was CIVICA, Committee of Indignant Volunteers Against Interference in Civic Affairs. See Nestingen Papers and *CT*, April 16, 19, and 26, 1957.

114. The assembly hearing was held March 14, 1957, and the

senate hearing on May 1, 1957. Jackson also testified and told senators that the lake view at the end of Monona Avenue was a "priceless heritage" they were obligated to preserve, that famous urban planners such as John Nolen and Ladislas Segoe had specifically pleaded against placing any view-blocking building in Law Park, and that the bill would preserve the view for "the people of Wisconsin forever." For newspaper coverage of the state senate hearing see the *CT*, May 2, 1957.

115. The misrepresentation that Metzner almost always cited in this situation ran in the *CT* on October 26, 1954. There on the front page in Wright's own hand was a photograph of a paper that says the city would get parking for forty-one hundred cars and an auditorium seating seventy-eight hundred. Metzner would then hold up a copy of the CMT brochure that contained a tiny picture of the entire 1953 Wright plan and the words "4 million will finance" next to the picture. For evidence of Evjue's reputation, see the *WSJ* editorials, February 25, 1955, and June 27, 1957; the Metzner interview by authors and a *WSJ* editorial of June 27, 1957, make it clear that Evjue was not beloved among legislators. Evjue's radio program was broadcast throughout the state on twenty stations at noon on Sunday. The program lasted fifteen minutes and was based on his "Hello Wisconsin" column.

116. For examples of statements by Citizens for Monona Terrace, see the press release dated May 25, 1957, and a moving address given to the Junior Chamber of Commerce by Harold Groves on May 21, 1957, MT box 62, FLWA.

117. Results of a committee vote were reported in the *WSJ*, March 28, 1957. Groves's lobbying activities were reported in Lescohier to Wright, April 11, 1957, FLWA. Helen Groves's trip around the state is described in Harold Groves's memoirs, *In and Out*, p. 167. Metzner described the Jackson confrontation in his interview by authors. The senator Jackson nearly assaulted was Allen Busby. The Metzner bill passed the assembly on April 3, 1957, and the senate on June 26, 1957.

118. For *CT* stories about this incident, see August 31 and September 3, 1957. Even the *WSJ* questioned Metzner's motives in an editorial, September 4, 1957. For other excellent background and detail see Evelyn Morris Radford, "The Genius and the County Building: How Frank Lloyd Wright Came to Marin County, California, and Glorified San Rafael," Ph.D. diss., University of Hawaii, August 1972, pp. 127–37.

On July 31, 1957, a month before Metzner visited Marin County, a large contingent of American Legion members in medal-bedecked overseas caps attended a meeting of the Marin County Board of Supervisors

and through their spokesperson demanded to read a seven-page statement detailing Wright's supposedly extensive support of communist activities during World War II. Upon hearing this, an obviously agitated Wright said, "There's no substance in that. I'm a loyal American! Look at the record," and walked out. This material was so similar to Jackson's "Wright Record" that the *CT* later charged in an editorial dated March 21, 1962, that Jackson was the source. Interestingly, the *CT* ran a story announcing the Marin County job and mentioning Fusselman's name on June 27, 1957, more than a month before the legionnaires appeared at the Marin meeting. Although we found nothing in the Jackson Papers to prove that Jackson did this, we did find one intriguing entry on his "to do" lists dated October 6, 1956: "Get California people at San Rafael to bring it out [the Wright record]."

119. The governor's statement was printed in full in the *WSJ*, September 22, 1957. Metzner's brief was entitled "A Summary of Facts in Support of Bill 300A" and was found in the Jackson Papers, box 16, folder 19. A *CT* editorial containing the six-mile reference appeared on September 23, 1957. The *WSJ* also did an editorial on September 23, 1957; it portrayed Thomson's signature as a "mercy killing" and the law as "impossible to repeal."

120. Heights of buildings in the Nolen rendering were estimated by a rendering specialist. PACE consultants determined that the minimum heights demanded by the railroads ranged from twenty-three to twenty-five feet.

121. *WSJ*, September 23, 1957. The "zealot" quote comes from a *Journal* editorial, April 3, 1957. To make sure that readers got the arena idea, the *Journal* ran a high-profile series from October through November 1957 describing what other cities had done. Most examples in the series featured buildings that resembled Quonset huts, barns, and factories.

122. A good example of Metzner's claim that CMT was omitting important facts was his debate with Nestingen before the Rotary Club of Madison on September 5, 1956. According to *Rotary News*, September 8, 1956, Metzner said, "The arena need for sports facilities was left out." This increasingly common claim prompted Wright to write an strongly worded letter to Nestingen on September 6, 1956. Said Wright: "Now it appears a more or less sporty audience a third larger than the cultured auditorium audience was sneaking in that requirement." Wright protested that such a facility was clearly outside his mandate. If the city really wants a "junior stadium," it should put it "just outside the city on some Madison freeway: the right place for a sports crowd" (Groves Papers, box 8, folder 5, SHSW).

123. For newspaper accounts of the lawsuit, see the *CT*, November 27, November 29, and December 21, 1957, and February 26, March 4, and March 18, 1958. The lawsuit was filed as *Frank Lloyd Wright Foundation v. City of Madison and Stewart G. Honeck, Individually and as Attorney General of the State of Wisconsin*, Dane County Circuit Court No. 102-110. Members of the Citizens for Monona Terrace launched a campaign to raise a legal fund for Wright and reduce the financial liability on the Groveses and Lescohiers (LUC). Still another instance in which the Groveses provided financial assistance was during the summer of 1958 when they bought a special Lloyds of London insurance policy to cover any damage done to the Monona Terrace model while it was displayed in Olin Terrace. Proponents were so confident that the balance of power in the statehouse would shift from Republicans to Democrats that they decided to start a fresh campaign to acquaint people with the project. One method they selected was to display the Monona Terrace model in a Wright-designed pavilion. Although city officials gave permission to erect the pavilion at Olin Terrace, they refused to insure the model against damage. This was where the Groveses stepped in.

124. Tape 216, August 17, 1958, FLWA.

125. For an excellent discussion of Wisconsin politics during this remarkable period, see William F. Thompson, "The Democratic Years, 1957–64," *The History of Wisconsin: Continuity and Change, 1940–65* (Madison: State Historical Society of Wisconsin, 1988), chap. 13. Madison mayor Otto Festge, in an interview published by *Isthmus*, a Madison weekly, on May 18, 1984, said that the Metzner bill "finished off the Republicans" at the state level. "The act turned off a lot of Republicans too — not just in Madison but around the state — who just felt that it was an abusive use of legislative authority. I've personally felt that what Metzner and the legislature did cost Vernon Thomson the governorship and elected Gaylord Nelson." A *CT* editorial of February 12, 1959, said that "a clear majority of legislators campaigned" to repeal the Metzner bill.

126. The best account of this hearing is found in the *CT*, February 12, 1959. Wright began collecting the documents in 1956 after Nestingen signed the contract with Wright. All the documents in what Jackson called his "Wright Record" purported to show that Wright embraced communism and/or organizations formed to advance communism. To acquire the documents Jackson wrote directly to Joseph McCarthy, the American Legion, U.S. Rep. Glenn R. Davis (R-Wisc.), and old military friends. For example, one charge Jackson leveled against Wright was that he was a member of the

Russian war relief effort. What Jackson didn't realize or chose to ignore was that Roy Matson, managing editor of the *Wisconsin State Journal*; Marvin Rosenberry, former chief justice of the Wisconsin Supreme Court (and close personal friend of Jackson's); and many other prominent, unquestionably loyal Madisonians were also members. A copy of the "Wright Record" is preserved in the Jackson Papers, box 2. The repeal law was passed as Laws of 1959, Chapter 9. The FBI source is suggested by the similarity of many entries in bureau files and those in Jackson's "Wright Record."

127. This bill was passed as Laws of 1959, Chapter 8. Jackson spoke movingly and with great emotion against the bill. According to his testimony, entitled "Presentation to the Legislature Joint Hearing on Bills 40S and 29A," preserved in the Groves Papers, box 23, SHSW, the old gentleman said Monona Terrace would "transform one of Wisconsin's most magnificent panoramic views out over beautiful Lake Monona into an *eyesore*" (the emphasis is Jackson's). The very idea of Monona Terrace was "preposterous, senseless, and downright wicked," Jackson said.

128. Regarding the impetus for the February 1959 version, Wright's senior staff may have been responsible for initiating this design. After all, they knew the Metzner bill was going to be repealed and that the success of the project required Wright's *signed*

plans. These two assumptions, coupled with a keen awareness of the architect's advanced age, may have prompted someone in the inner circle to make sure that this project got done.

129. Wright's cover note and bill are found in MT box 61, FLWA. The bill was calculated on the basis of 2.5 percent of $4 million ($100,000) and 1.5 percent of $1.5 million for the parking structure.

130. The Nestingen annual address is available in City of Madison Microfiche Collection (CMM) file #4270-2. The *WSJ* and *CT*, April 28, 1959, reported the contents of the letter from the foundation. Payment of the $122,500 bill also required that the foundation drop a suit challenging the constitutionality of the Metzner law and naming the city as a party. The foundation officially dropped the case in mid-May 1959. See *WSJ*, May 14, 1959.

131. For the city attorney's position and his advice, see the *CT*, May 29, 1959. *Jackson v. City of Madison* was filed on May 27, 1959. The case was heard by Dane County Circuit Court Judge Norris E. Maloney, who rendered an opinion so strongly supportive of the city that city officials were confident they would prevail if Jackson appealed the case to the Wisconsin Supreme Court. Indeed, that was exactly what happened. In September 1960 Jackson appealed but in January 1961 the Supreme Court unanimously upheld the

city's position (*Jackson v. City of Madison*, 12 Wis.2d 359 [1961]). Jackson's circulation of his "Wright Record" is described in the *CT*, August 29, 1959.

132. For the belated payment of the bill from Taliesin for $122,500, see the *CT*, February 24, 1960. Yale expert George Izenour was hired by the foundation in April 1960. With his help Peters designed the "monorail scene-shifting system" to keep the height of the stage house as low as possible. When he was assisting Peters, Izenour was serving as a technical consultant to the Lincoln Center for the Performing Arts in New York. For newspaper reports of the rave reviews, see the *WSJ*, June 19, 1960, and *CT*, May 26 and June 21 and 23, 1960.

133. For descriptions of Peters' new plans see the *WSJ* and *CT*, April 5, 1960. Size increases were reported in the *CT*, April 28, 1960. Among the cost-increasing changes requested by the committee was the addition of theater workshops and rehearsal space.

134. For a good example of this gotcha strategy see the *WSJ*, March 7, 1960.

135. *CT*, March 11, 1960.

136. *CT*, May 25, 1960.

137. *CT*, August 9, 1960.

138. For an example of how critics exploited this confusion, see the full-page ad that appeared in the *WSJ*, July 22, 1960. The

*CT*'s rebuttal appeared on August 1, 1960.

139. *WSJ*, July 5, 1960; *CT*, March 22, 1960. To counter this attack, the *CT* published an eight-page black-and-white brochure written by Herb Jacobs that featured the latest Taliesin renderings.

140. *WSJ* and *CT* coverage of this campaign began August 9, 1960, and ran through early November.

141. *WSJ* and *CT*, October 12, 1960. When the council refused to hold a referendum in response to the ten thousand signatures, the *East Side News* ran its familiar "In Memoriam" logo over a front-page mock obit for the "Right of Referendum" in its October 12, 1960, issue.

142. *CT* and *WSJ*, October 14, 1960.

143. *Miller v. Nestingen* was filed in Dane County Circuit Court on December 19, 1960, by B. E. Miller, Marshall Browne, and William F. Stevens. Technically, it was a petition for a writ of mandamus directing the city to hold a referendum, but at the hearing the judge issued a summary judgment that upheld the council's actions.

144. *Jackson v. Madison*. For accounts of Peters' plans and council approval, see the *CT*, January 17, 23, and 30, 1961. Jackson's authenticity question

was quoted in the *CT*, January 24, 1961.

145. Nestingen's large role in the Kennedy campaign is acknowledged in Theodore H. White, *The Making of the President, 1960* (New York: Atheneum, 1961), pp. 93–96. Jackson's letter of July 20, 1961, appears in his papers. For articles on Nestingen's circulation of nomination papers, see the *CT*, January 13, 1961, and for his appointment, see the *WSJ*, January 28, 1961, and *CT*, January 10, 1961.

146. For an example of efforts by Citizens for a Realistic Auditorium Association (CRAA) to use common council candidates' position on Monona Terrace as a litmus test, see the *CT*, February 13, 1961. Clarence Bylsma, the executive director of Citizens for Monona Terrace, was eliminated in the mayoral primary. For general information on Reynolds, see "Know Your Madisonian," *WSJ*, February 10, 1957; March 3, 1961, on his family company; April 19, 1965, on his accomplishments; and November 3, 1980, for his obituary.

147. Although the council approved the final plans on January 30, 1961, one month was required to determine which contractors met the bonding requirements. That left just five weeks. See *CT*, February 25 and 28, 1961. As noted in the *CT*, February 15, 1961, mayoral candidate Nuckles

expected the project's cost to increase by $3 million.

148. *WSJ*, March 8 and 9, 1961. Before the dust settled at the $12.1 level, both local papers indulged in some predictable ideological horn-blowing. For example, the *WSJ* said the bids came in at $13 million, while the *CT* said the cost was just $9.6 million. No wonder many were confused.

149. *WSJ*, March 13, 1961. The debate about causes went on for several weeks in the newspapers. One fact is clear from examination of bid documents and correspondence: almost everything was included in the bid, including many categories that are rarely considered in such bids — china, kitchen pots and pans, office equipment, mops, usher caps, and flags.

150. The bid, $12.2 million, exceeded the $5.5 million budget by $6.7 million, an increase of 122 percent over the base. The *CT* editorial ran on March 9, 1961. A clear acknowledgment of the committee's culpability was made by Richard Kopp, a pro–Monona Terrace council member and member of the committee, who was quoted in the *WSJ*, April 27, 1961, as saying that in searching for a scapegoat, "this committee will have to point to itself." However, Kopp also complained that Peters had failed to give the committee "sufficient information on mounting costs." Peters countered by saying that he had kept the city fully informed. Peters was

almost surely referring to a four-page letter he sent Nestingen on September 24, 1960 (MT box 61, FLWA), alerting Nestingen that inflation alone had increased the cost of the building "at least 21 percent" and that other increases were likely because Peters was continuing to incorporate in construction documents (then being prepared) changes the Auditorium Committee directed him to make. Referring to those changes, Peters says he has made "a sizable and significant increase in size and area in almost every individual function and facility over the provisions of the program outlined in the original contract." Peters does not say what the total is, but the clear implication is that the cumulative total is large. This clearly was not the first time that Peters alerted Nestingen to inflationary increases because he also writes, "We have previously submitted to you a detailed list outlining increased overall construction costs in this area due to a lapse of time from March 1955 to March 1960."

Harold Groves in "Testimony of Harold M. Groves" (Groves Papers, box 23, folder 11, SHSW) states that he was present during two meetings in which Peters told Nestingen that costs were substantially exceeding the contract level. At those meetings Groves said that Nestingen told Peters "that it was not politic at the moment to revise the contract; that the architects should go ahead anyhow and not worry; that they could depend upon it that at the proper time the City would make an all-out effort to raise the additional money. This vague arrangement was accepted by the architect under protest and with the gravest of reservations."

Sometime after he took office, Reynolds and his aides went through all the correspondence from Peters to Nestingen, looking for evidence that Peters had kept the mayor informed. On September 6, 1961, Reynolds sent Peters a stinging letter saying that the mayor had gone through the "voluminous file" on this matter and that "the only writing that bears upon your statement" (to keep the city fully informed about cost increases) was Peters' letter dated September 24, 1960. Reynolds conceded that Peters' letter alerted Nestingen to cost increases, but at no point did Peters say that he "expected costs to run two and one-half times the maximum limitations specified in the contract" (MT box 61, FLWA). Nestingen then was spending considerable time working on the Kennedy campaign.

151. See *CT*, March 23, 1961. Groves's contact with Patterson was reported in the *CT*, March 16, 1961.

152. *WSJ*, March 13, 1961, and *CT*, March 16, 1961.

153. The turnout was reported by the *WSJ*, April 5, 1961. To help ensure Reynolds' election and to

elect anti–Monona Terrace council members, critics formed Citizens for Better Government. According to its literature, the quality of the common council had declined, meaning that supporters still enjoyed a majority. See the collection of critics' electioneering items (Wisconsin Political Vertical File), SHSW Archives.

154. The $7.5 million CMT plan assumed that construction costs would remain at $12.2 million but that $2.5 million would be covered by revenue bonds, $1.2 million could be saved through alternative construction techniques, and a fund-raising effort would bring in $1 million from private sources. The plan was described in the *CT*, July 12, 1961. The CMT television commercials were described in the *WSJ*, July 9, 1961. For background on the referendum on $5 million and Reynolds' veto of it, see the *CT*, October 11, 1961, and *WSJ*, October 22, 1961.

155. See *WSJ*, April 4, 1962; *CT*, October 6, 1961, and August 18, 1962.

156. Reynolds' new auditorium appointees were noted in the *CT*, April 18, 1961; his meeting with Dane County officials in the *CT*, May 16, 1961; and his preference for Conklin Park in the *CT*, May 20, 1961.

157. The Auditorium Committee voted to terminate the contract on June 14, 1961, but the council refused on November 9, 1961. See *CT*, June 15 and November 10,

1961. For the *CT* account of the formal notification of the arbitration process, see November 15, 1961. Examination of foundation records (MT box 57, FLWA) shows that it was anything but eager to settle the dispute. In a revealing letter of December 29, 1962, Randolph Connors, the foundation's Madison attorney, tells Orme Lewis, the foundation's Phoenix attorney, "If we settled with the City it would give the mayor (a) free hand to proceed with the Conklin site and might assure his reelection."

158. See *CT*, January 15, 1962. Heassler died soon after becoming city attorney and was replaced by Edwin Conrad.

159. For a vivid account of the stormy meeting on referendum wording, see the *CT*, February 23, 1962. For evidence of the intense debate, see both papers from March through early April 1962. The full-page school-or-auditorium ad appeared in both papers on April 2, 1962. Referendum results appeared in the *CT*, April 4, 1962.

Groves quotes the *Journal* editorial in *In and Out*, p. 169. The *CT* of April 5, 1962, noted that the three most conservative wards in Madison, the 10th, 19th, and 20th, "cast the largest vote in the election and provided the margin by which the project won the election." Browne's references to "Terracites" comes from the *East Side News*, March 29, 1962.

160. Jackson first urged the hiring of Segoe in a letter to the editor of

the *WSJ* that ran on July 6, 1960. Then in March 1962 Jackson began writing to Segoe to urge him to return to Madison as a special consultant to Mayor Reynolds. Those letters are found in the Jackson Papers, box 16, folder 11. The revealing meeting of the Auditorium Committee at which it hired Segoe is described in the *CT*, May 17, 1962. Segoe's inspection tour is described in the *CT*, July 5, 1962; Segoe's decision got front-page coverage in the *WSJ*, August 3, 1962. For articles on Reynolds' preference for the waterworks site, see the *WSJ*, August 18, 23, and 31, 1962.

161. Reynolds' satisfaction with the Monona Terrace specifications is noted in the *CT*, August 31, 1962. For articles describing the auditorium consultants' recommendations, see the *WSJ*, July 6, 1962.

162. *CT*, October 4 and 15, 1962. In an angry letter printed in the *CT*, April 28, 1966, former mayor Reynolds recalled how in 1963 the council came within just one vote of hiring Alfred Shaw. Reynolds had a tendency to underestimate project costs. He thought the causeway would cost $1 million, but it ran $2 million. He said he thought the Dane County coliseum could be built for $1 million, but it came in at $5.5 million.

163. For newspaper coverage see the *CT*, November 15 and 24, 1962, June 28, 1963. For the

ruling see *Madison v. Frank Lloyd Wright Foundation*, 20 Wis.2d 361 (1963).

164. See *CT*, November 26, 1963, and January 19, 24, 28, and 31, and February 10, 1964.

165. Reynolds got Cushman's name from the American Institute of Architects. Key clients were listed in the *Martindale-Hubbell Law Directory, 1963*. According to the *WSJ* of March 27, 1964, council member Richard Kopp made the Cassius Clay comment. For other articles on the early Cushman episode, see the *CT*, February 27, March 18, and March 27, 1964.

166. Cushman based his conclusion on work done by several specialists, including an architect and a contractor who independently and quite precisely calculated the area and volume of the 1959 and 1961 versions. These calculations showed that Wright's 1957 and 1959 plans contained 202,000 square feet and that Peters increased the project to 278,000 square feet in 1961, an increase of 38 percent. Cushman's specialists also determined that inflation during 1959 and 1960 had been 1.6 percent and 0.3 percent respectively. Cushman then examined Wright's letter to Nestingen of May 11, 1957, in which Wright said that the project should run about $3.3 million and concluded that the cost could not have increased from $3.3 million in 1957 to $12.2 million in 1961. Cushman even assumed

that if a longer time were allowed for bids and if various cost savings were taken, the project could probably have been built for $11 million. Even so, a $5 million increase over Peters' $6 million estimate represented an 83 percent increase. This conclusion appears in Cushman's letters to Henry Reynolds of July 28, 1964, and September 24, 1964. Detailed estimates of inflation from 1954 through 1960 appear in Roger G. Kirchoff to Frank A. Ross, July 17, 1961. Reynolds had appointed the two men to the Auditorium Committee. Kirchoff, the former state architect, did extensive behind-the-scenes research for Reynolds and Cushman. This correspondence is preserved in CMU.

There is one intriguing explanation for Wright's low estimates versus the high final bids: gunite, Wright's construction system for Monona Terrace. Gunite was a construction technique whereby concrete was blown into a frame of wire mesh, an ideal system for achieving the complex curves of the Wright's design. There can be no doubt that this system would have been much less expensive than pouring concrete in specially made forms, but exactly how much it could have saved will never be known. What we do know is that Wright assumed he would realize substantial savings from gunite and that Peters' decision to use poured concrete significantly increased construction costs.

167. Festge's candidacy was announced in the *WSJ*, December 18, 1964. For primary results, see the *CT*, March 10, 1965. Backers had good reason to believe that Festge would revive Monona Terrace. He secretly met with Peters at Lescohier's house. Peters later wrote Festge a four-page letter saying that the cultural center idea was entirely feasible (MT box 61, FLWA). Evidence that the delay was deliberate comes from a letter from Randolph Connors to Orme Lewis, February 9, 1965, in which Connors says, "I had a meeting with Stafford and Lescohier and decided that, if possible, we stall until after the election on April 6" (MT box 61, FLWA). Stafford was a Madison lawyer and adviser to the foundation.

168. *WSJ*, February 14, 1965. The shift in retailing was reported in the *WSJ*, October 24, 1965. The first suburban mall, Madison East Shopping Center, opened in 1953, followed by Westgate in 1960 and Hilldale in 1962. For articles describing the openings of these centers, see the *CT*, October 29, 1953; *WSJ*, March 25, 1960; and the October 25, 1962.

169. On September 5, 1961, the Madison School Board voted to locate community centers in schools and not in Monona Terrace. According to the *WSJ* of September 24, 1961, the school board thought these centers could

meet needs more cost effectively than new single-purpose facilities.

170. Festge ran against George C. Hall, the owner of a large Madison electrical contracting company and former campaign chairman for Henry Reynolds. See the *WSJ*, April 23, 1965, for Festge's move to negotiate a settlement and the *CT*, May 25, 1965, for Cushman's retort. Feinsinger's role is mentioned in the *WSJ*, June 11 and 12, 1965. Feinsinger enjoyed a glowing national reputation for settling dozens of major labor disputes, including the 1966 New York subway strike.

171. *WSJ*, June 11, 1965.

172. Peters' acknowledgment appeared in the *WSJ*, June 11, 1965. In preparation for what the foundation expected to be tough negotiations, Peters directed employees to assemble a detailed summary of hours logged on Monona Terrace. Foundation employees had to reconstruct their hours from personal calendars, which suggests that the foundation had no project accounting system. Even after they had completed and tallied their collective estimates, large gaps remained. This suggests that project time estimates were significantly underreported. The foundation's research is summarized in a March 26, 1965 document, "A Chronological History and Summary of Time Devoted to Project by Architect, His Associates, and Employees" (MT box 54, FLWA). According

to this document, from 1938 to March 1965 the foundation logged 63,511 hours; at the rate of two thousand hours per year (a forty-hour workweek for fifty weeks) this is the equivalent of one person's working for more than thirty-one years.

We found just four instances in which the foundation received payment for architectural services for Monona Terrace: 1938, when it received $250 from Paul Harloff as partial payment for the original concept drawings; $2,000 as a "birthday gift" from Monona Terrace supporters in 1954; $122,500 from the city in 1960; and the final settlement of $150,000 in 1965. Together they total $274,750.

From the 1965 negotiations we know that the foundation had legal and consulting bills totaling at least $98,704, leaving a "net" for the entire project of $176,046. In fact, the foundation incurred other expenses before 1960, but we could find no summary. Dividing $176,046 by 63,511 hours yields the project average of $2.77 per hour. Other foundation records reveal that in the 1950s architects and engineers were paid at the rate of $8 to $10 per hour and that from 1938 to 1965 forty-five foundation employees worked on Monona Terrace.

173. *WSJ*, June 11, 1965.

1. Members of the Auditorium Committees are identified in *Madison Common Council Proceedings* (*MCCP*) soon after the elections of the mayors identified here. Other people were named to the committee at various points, either to replace members who resigned or members who had sat on the common council but had failed to win reelection.

2. Sources for this incident include the *CT*, March 5, March 25, and November 7, 1965, and Otto Festge, interview by authors, August 26, 1997. Anderson also performed in the cow barn for her first Madison appearance in 1938.

3. Festge so feared the reaction of critics that he did not publicly acknowledge his preference for the project until eleven days before the election; in fact, the *Capital Times* withheld its endorsement until after Festge announced his preference. Mary Lescohier comments on Festge's fear in a letter to attorney John Frank dated April 3, 1967, MB, box 219, FLWA. However, Festge did contact Peters and asked him for information on Monona Terrace. Peters replied in a long letter dated February 11, 1965, a copy of which is in the same collection.

4. *WSJ* and *CT*, July 13, 1965.

5. *WSJ*, June 23, 1965.

6. See the *CT*, September 30, 1965, for details of the community center. The new use of the school was an early example of recycling, a concept then becoming popular.

7. The CUNA threat to move was reported in the *WSJ*, February 15, 1966. Although CUNA never left, its threat forced business leaders to give convention facilities sustained attention. National credit-union membership statistics are available in Carroll Moody and Gilbert C. Fite, *The Credit Union Movement: Origins and Development, 1850–1970* (Lincoln: University of Nebraska Press, 1970), p. 359. A revealing article in the *WSJ* of April 24, 1966, provides specifications for a convention center. See the *MCCP*, April 14, 1966, for the resolution for the Monona Basin concept, which specifically provided for "general convention facilities, and other such multi-purpose accommodations as necessary."

8. See also Madison City Planning Department, "A Report on an Auditorium Site Study," November 1965, and a memo from Ken Clark to James G. Marshall, "Review of Auditorium Sites," December 28, 1965, both in Parks Department files. For stories explaining the site and architect, see the *CT*, November 4, 1965, and *WSJ*, October 14 and November 4, 1965.

9. The story of the state senate's rejection of Jackson's 1965 bill, SJR 63, on October 11 ran in the *CT*, October 12, 1965. To no one's surprise, Metzner and Forster testified in favor of Jackson's bill. For other background on this bill, see the *CT*, April 21 and June 15, 1965. In his statement Jackson said, "It is inconceivable that any loyal, red blooded American man or woman of Madison or Wisconsin who knows the truth about Frank Lloyd Wright would want him or his Wright Foundation to have any part whatever in designing its War Memorial Auditorium or to select a site for it that is owned by the state."

10. Clark had presented the East Wilson Street concept to the Auditorium Committee in November 1965 but only in a schematic form. Clark's report was distributed to Auditorium Committee members on January 28, 1966, and reported by both papers that day. For an analysis of its merits see the *WSJ*, March 7, 1966. For reaction of the tenants and owner of the Bellevue see the *CT* and *WSJ*, January 29, 1966; *WSJ*, March 7 and April 8, 1966; and Figure 5.4. For endorsements from Festge and Potter, see the *WSJ*, February 16, 1966, and *CT*, March 14 and April 5, 1966. Festge's expansion of the Wilson Street land to mollify backers of Monona Terrace is described in the *CT*, April 7, 1966.

11. See *WSJ* and *CT*, March 16, 1966. For an example of Marshall Browne's views see the *CT*, April 5, 1966.

12. See *WSJ*, April 8, 1966.

13. Van Potter, interview by authors, August 25, 1997.

14. *WSJ*, April 10, 1966, and Potter interview. The press conference was held at the McArdle Laboratory for Cancer Research.

15. *WSJ*, April 10, 1966. The concept of a coordinated master plan for both Olin and Law Parks was first mentioned by Van Potter in the context of Reynolds' attempt to hire a Chicago architect to design an "auditorium" at the city waterworks site. In reaction to this location, council member William Evans, whose ward contained both Conklin Park and the waterworks, began to work with council member Harold Rohr, whose ward contained Olin Park, to locate the auditorium at Olin Park. Both said they would be interested in having the Wright Foundation as architect for an Olin Park facility. This Evans-Rohr compromise, as it was then called, prompted Potter to propose another compromise during the week of December 10, 1962. According to the full text of Potter's remarks, printed in the *CT* on December 15, 1962, Potter urged "the planned development on both sides of Lake Monona" that would "follow a consistent overall plan for architecture." Potter criticized Reynolds for not "planning harmonious structures on both sides of Lake Monona" and envisioned "an overall plan" that would include "a compromise Monona Terrace Civic Center and Auditorium, an Olin Park Arena, and a Monona Bay Bridge as an interconnected facility with the coordinated type of architecture that the Taliesin group knows how to design so well."

16. Potter interview; Potter, personal communication with Mary Jane Hamilton, January 23, 1997.

17. For details of the history-making committee meeting see the *WSJ* and *CT*, April 14, 1966. See the *CT*, April 15, 1966, for the account of council authorization for negotiations with Peters. Festge's quotation is found in the *WSJ*, April 20, 1966.

18. Potter interview.

19. Browne's views were reported in the *WSJ*, April 23, 1966, and Peters' views in the *WSJ*, June 11 and June 15, 1966. Peters, apparently following Wright's tendency to scold Madison leaders, said, "This city has failed to realize [its] potential more shamefully than any city I know of. I frankly could not participate in a program that seems to have been developed by political expediency." See *WSJ*, June 11, 1966.

20. *WSJ*, June 24, 1966. The final terms of the deal were hammered out on June 28, 1966, and reported in the *CT* of this date.

21. Comments about the contract signing were reported in the *WSJ* and *CT*, October 14, 1966. The final contract, "An Agreement for a Master Plan and Architectural Services for the Monona Basin Auditorium and Civic Center and Related Parking Facilities," was dated November 7, 1966, and is available from the city clerk's office. The contract directed the foundation to include facilities for an art center and gallery with 10,000 square feet, a drama theater seating 800 to 1,000, a recital hall seating 300, an auditorium seating 2,000 to 2,500, and convention facilities that would include exhibit space and a banquet room seating 2,000 to 3,000. See *CT*, November 7, 1966.

22. In his 1997 interview by the authors Festge credited Lescohier with having suggested that Nathan Feinsinger sit in on the negotiations. Further evidence of her influence with Wes Peters is evident from her letters in the files of the Taliesin Architects Archives (TAA) from 1967 to 1972. For an example of a particularly stern piece of Lescohier advice, see note 27. But the highest accolade to Mary Lescohier came in a letter dated April 22, 1974, from Helen Groves to Wes Peters in the TAA files. Said Groves: "Well, Madison still has Mary Lescohier. Think of what she did alone these past 10 years."

23. See *WSJ*, November 30, 1966. That most plaintiffs were Republicans comes from *CT* editorials dated November 8 and November 30, 1966.

24. See *Jane C. Braun v. City of Madison*, Dane County Circuit Court, November 30, 1966;

*WSJ*, November 30, 1966; and *CT*, October 14, 1966, and May 10, 1967.

25. Because the mayor and common council were named in the suit, the city appropriated $25,000 so the named city officials could hire lawyers. See *WSJ*, January 4, 1967.

26. Judge Wilkie's forty-three-page opinion was dated September 12, 1967; the quotes appear on page 39. Both local papers gave extensive coverage to the trial, which ran July 24–28 and August 22–24. For Metzner's reaction to the opinion, see the *CT*, September 13, 1967. Judge Edwin Wilkie was a brother of Horace Wilkie, the Wisconsin state senator who introduced the measure repealing the Metzner bill in 1958. Metzner was aware of this relationship and raised no objection.

Interestingly, the event might have become the first civil trial ever covered by live television, but Judge Wilkie rejected the proposal by WHA-TV, the University of Wisconsin station. Professor Lee Sherman Dreyfus, then an associate station director (elected Wisconsin governor in November 1978), proposed that the trial be covered without commentary. For the proposed TV coverage, see the *WSJ*, February 15 and 16, March 7 and 26, and May 9, 10, and 16, 1967, and corresponding coverage in the *CT*. Festge's comment about being delighted appeared

in the *CT*, September 12, 1967. Several letters in the FLWA also outline the views of basin backers. For example, see the letter dated April 3, 1967, from Mary Lescohier to attorney John Frank.

27. In September Peters had given the Auditorium Committee a preview of his December recommendations so there were few surprises. Interestingly, Peters' September presentation appears to have been heavily influenced by stern counsel he received from Mary Lescohier. In a letter to Peters dated May 1, 1967, FLWA, she told the architect to quit telling the committee he was gathering data. "You must take command. You must tell the City what you have found out and how you interpret your findings; and what you recommend and why. I repeat: you were hired as a professional architect and consultant…. This is your job: read the contract." Continuing her lecture, Lescohier implored Peters to not "come in with any piece-meal, first-stage ideas or statement or data until you have the framework for the Master Plan Program." This was characteristically tough talk from a tough and astute woman. See *CT*, December 6, 1967.

28. *WSJ*, December 8, 1967

29. *WSJ*, December 8, 1967. Assisting in Peters' presentation were his Taliesin colleagues John Rattenbury and Tom Casey.

30. *CT*, December 6, 1967; *WSJ*, December 7, 1967. "Milestone in Madison," *Architectural Forum* 127 (November 1967): 30–31; "Wright's Madison Plan Comes to Life," *Progressive Architecture* 49 (May 1968): 66–67. When Peters completed the design for the circular auditorium, another article, "The New Madison Civic Center," appeared in *Progressive Architecture* 49 (December 1968): 48.

31. Metzner's and Rohr's comments were quoted in the *WSJ*, December 7, 1967. Comments made by the three former mayors come from the *WSJ*, January 19, 1968, and *CT*, January 18, 1968. At least one effort was made to kill the basin concept with state legislation. According to the *CT*, October 27, 1967, Assemblyman Bryan Wackett introduced an amendment to the budget bill that authorized the state to acquire Law Park as a site for a state office building. The bill was defeated.

32. *WSJ*, January 24 and 30, 1968. A copy of Dawson's original statement, presented on WMTV on January 24, 1968, is available in the TAA files.

33. *WSJ*, December 7, 1967, and January 22, 1968. Representatives of theater organizations feared that if the downtown facility were built first, there would be no money for the cultural complex in Olin Park.

34. Would-be tenants that approved of the plan included the Madison Theater Guild (see

*WSJ* and *CT*, December 28, 1967), the Madison Civic Music Association (*CT*, January 4, 1968), and the Madison Arts Council (*CT* and *WSJ*, January 10, 1968). The state AIA chapter announced its support in the *CT*, March 1, 1968. The chamber announced its support in the *CT*, January 23, 1968. Metzner's decision was reported in the *CT*, January 10, 1968.

35. The common council voted 15–4 to approve the plan on February 22, 1968 (see *WSJ* and *CT*, February 23, 1968). Peters presented schematic drawings for the auditorium on July 17, 1968.

36. *WSJ*, July 18 and August 7, 1968, and September 10 and 13, 1968.

37. Festge interview. The criticisms of a property tax increase were particularly hard for Festge because his predecessor, Henry Reynolds, boasted that he never raised the local millage rate during his four years in office; however, he did this in many cases by deferring expenditures. When Festge took over, many expenditures could no longer be delayed, and the new mayor had the unpopular task of raising the tax rate. In fact, by the beginning of this fourth year he had raised the millage rate to such an extent that his enemies were calling him "eleven mill Otto." The millage was the number of dollars a property owner had to pay for each $1,000 of assessed valuation.

38. For articles on the simmering dock-line dispute see the *WSJ*, January 24 and February 11, 1969, and *CT*, January 31, 1969. For information on the dock-line extension, see the *CT*, November 1, 1969. In a letter to Festge dated January 27, 1969, Peters said the balcony extended eight feet over the dock line, but in a report dated January 24, 1969, John Bunch, the city traffic engineer, said the original plans exceeded the dock line by thirty-eight feet (see *WSJ*, February 11, 1969). The new dock-line law (Laws of 1969, Chapter 188) allowed for the overage. See the *CT*, November 1, 1969, for the new dock-line legislation.

39. *WSJ*, January 16, 21, 23, and 28, and February 13, 1969.

40. For articles on this fascinating episode see the *CT*, January 29 and 31 and April 2, 14, and 15, 1969, and *WSJ*, January 29 and April 5 and 11, 1969. See the *WSJ* and *CT*, February 12, 1969, for accounts of council approval process.

41. The *WSJ* reported the council's approval of the plan on February 12, 1969. The supplemental drawings were necessitated by the city's failure to work out an agreement with the state to secure steam from its nearby plant to heat the auditorium. Preparation of drawings for a self-contained boiler took more than three weeks, a snafu described in the *WSJ*, February 12 and March 12, 1969. The two contractors were the

Corbetta Construction Company of Chicago and Kraemer Brothers of Plain, Wisconsin. It is clear that the contractors thought the city's $5.5 million appropriation was too little and that the city was unlikely to set aside more money. A few days after the bids were received, the city's Board of Public Works approved a resolution that said, "It is apparent that the lack of city funds was a substantial factor in the lack of competition among many of the bidders" (*CT*, April 15, 1969). Reports of bid sabotage first surfaced in the *CT*, April 4, 1969, when the paper described Peters' attack on "completely false reports" that were "passed on to bidders" by "several longtime auditorium foes" who allegedly urged prospective contractors "not to submit bids because it would be a waste of time and money." On March 21, 1974, in a story in advance of the latest referendum, the *CT* identified Rohr as having used "letters" to convey discouraging information to interested contractors. In his 1997 interview Festge said that he thought Reynolds and Burt were also involved in the sabotage effort.

42. For nearly two weeks after the bids were opened, people argued about how much the bids exceeded the budget. Estimates ranged from $877,000 to $1.5 million. For articles on this, see the *WSJ*, April 5 and 11, 1969, and *CT*, April 4, 1969.

43. See *WSJ*, April 15 and 20, 1969.

44. For background on the foundation, see the *CT*, January 20 and April 14, 1969, and *WSJ*, February 21 and April 14, 1969. Organizers included Gerry Bartell, Reed Coleman, Marshall Erdman, Morgan Manchester, Dorothy Knowles, Jesse Hyman, and Al Goldstein. Although the largest pledge came from the Evjue Foundation ($25,000), some of the most remarkable came from people of much smaller means. Mary Lescohier pledged $12,000; the Groveses $5,000; Elsa Fauerbach, a social worker, $1,000; and Alfred Swan, Congregational minister, $1,000. Festge's comment appeared in *Isthmus*, May 18, 1984.

45. *CT* and *WSJ*, July 17, 1969. Dyke did meet with Peters on June 24, 1969, but they apparently agreed on nothing (*CT* and *WSJ*, June 24, 1969).

46. Arthur Hove, *The University of Wisconsin: A Pictorial History* (Madison: University of Wisconsin Press, 1991), pp. 245–48; Tom Bates, *RADS: The 1970 Bombing of the Army Math Research Center at the University of Wisconsin and Its Aftermath* (New York: Harper Collins, 1992), pp. 115–21; and Therese R. Loose, "Public Relations Policies and Directions During Major Campus Disturbances at the University of Wisconsin–Madison from the October 1967 Anti-Dow Demonstration to the August 1970 Sterling Hall Bombing," honors thesis, School of Journalism, University of Wisconsin, May 1973.

47. The Metro Square site had been suggested for an auditorium as early as 1962 by William Bradford Smith, the council member from the 19th Ward, as a compromise to the Conklin Park site. See *WSJ*, October 20, 1962.

48. For an early article on Metro Square, see the *WSJ*, January 14, 1970. Metro Square was included in an elegant full-color report prepared by the city planning department entitled "Downtown: Proposals for Central Madison," released in April 1970. The unusual report contained a number of farsighted proposals that were later implemented, including the creation of the State Street Mall and the city landmarks commission. Dyke's first meeting with his Auditorium Committee on July 21, 1970, was reported in the *WSJ* and *CT* the following day. Soglin's opposition is noted in the *CT*, September 30 and October 7, 1970, and in *WSJ*, December 8, 1971.

49. *CT*, October 22, 1971, and *WSJ*, October 15 and 18, 1971.

50. The ten-year clause appears on page 30 of the contract dated November 7, 1966. Festge explained why he wanted the clause in his 1997 interview. When the effects of this clause became widely known, council members chafed at its restrictions. In 1972, for example, as noted in the *WSJ*, September 8, 1972, the council denied a request to build a bike path through Law Park because this would have given Taliesin

another ten years of exclusive design opportunities. Conrad's opinion on this matter appeared in a memo dated September 6, 1972, to council member John Healy and is available in the Parks Department files. The contract with the Frank Lloyd Wright Foundation was finally voided in 1979. See also note 66.

51. For the council's action see the *WSJ*, February 2 and 3, 1972; for Ashman's comment, see the *WSJ*, January 26, 1972. The council vote was no surprise.

52. *WSJ*, January 11, 1973.

53. Leaders of the CMC included Bob O'Malley, then president of the Madison Bank & Trust Company, and Donald Hovde, a real estate broker and developer who specialized in downtown properties.

54. *WSJ*, October 14, 1970, and October 13, 1971. For information on earlier shopping center development, see note 168 in chap. 4.

55. *WSJ*, June 18 and October 10, 1978. Both Robert O'Malley, chairman of CMC, and Richard Depper, executive director of the Chamber of Commerce, believed that the sudden increase in the number of new and proposed hotels would have positioned Madison to become a premiere convention venue except for the lack of a convention center that could "feed and water" about a thousand people. Such a facility would allow Madison to bid for much larger conventions.

56. *WSJ*, June 18, 1972.

57. This story was pieced together from a newspaper account (*WSJ*, September 10, 1978) and telephone interviews with Rae Ragatz on August 30, 1997, and Mike Duffey on September 14, 1997. The square block selected by the CMC was bounded by East Washington Avenue, South Webster, East Main, and South Butler. The idea for the State Street civic center may have come from Gordon Harman, a common council candidate from Madison's 2d Ward. The *WSJ* reported on February 10, 1972, that Harman had formally proposed at a candidates' meeting that the city buy the Capitol Theater and Montgomery Ward as a "multi-purpose civic center."

58. Although Bowen Williamson Kanazawa was the lead architect, the firm collaborated with two other Madison architectural firms, Peters and Martinsons and John J. Flad and Associates. Their undated study, in Mollenhoff's personal files, was entitled "Cultural-Urban Center Project, Madison, Wisconsin." The study envisioned a two-stage process. The first phase would include acquisition and remodeling of the Capitol Theater, Montgomery Ward, and several adjoining properties to provide theaters seating 2,100, 800, and 300, and the art center. The second phase involved buying Yost's Department Store and several other properties and converting them to a museum,

a small convention center, and commercial facility. The architects estimated the second phase would cost $5.9 million. This study was described in the *WSJ* on November 15, 1972. Details of the appraisal process come from CMC minutes dated October 12, 1972, in the personal files of Mollenhoff.

59. This account is based on a telephone interview of George Nelson in September 1997 and contemporary newspapers accounts, including the *CT*, February 3, 1975, which reported that the appraisal came in at $780,000, a figure that caused Nelson and Frederick E. Mohs, a prominent lawyer and civic activist, to offer Polon $600,000 to $625,000. The owner of the Montgomery Ward building was the Wisconsin Alumni Research Foundation, an arm of the University of Wisconsin.

60. See Soglin folders at the Municipal Reference Service, Madison Public Library.

61. See *WSJ*, April 4, 1973. The Twenty-sixth Amendment was ratified on June 25, 1971. See the *Nation*, June 25, 1973; *New Yorker*, December 3, 1973; *Time*, July 1, 1974; and *Wall Street Journal*, March 24, 1975.

62. For Soglin's support for the State Street site, see the *WSJ*, July 4, 1973. For Auditorium Committee and common council actions, see the *WSJ*, November 27 and December 5, 1973. For the cost of the expanded auditorium, see the *WSJ*, February 14, 1974.

For coverage of the vote on the referendum language, see the *WSJ*, January 3, 1974.

63. For an excellent summary of State Street's advantages, see the minority report of the Auditorium Committee dated November 28, 1973, and the *WSJ*, December 4 and 11, 1973. Ragatz encountered considerable resistance from art community leaders who balked at becoming part of the State Street plan. Many were so disillusioned by so many city failures to build a civic center that they decided to plan and build their own facilities.

64. The common council approved a resolution committing the city to the full transaction on April 23, 1974.

65. For the formation of pro and con organizations, see the *CT*, March 21, 1974, and *WSJ*, March 22 and 24, 1974. For an example of leftist opposition, see "Vote NO on $8.5 Million Auditorium Bond Issue," prepared by Central City People for a NO Vote and contained in scrapbooks (*History of the Civic Center, Scrapbook, 1946–81*; hereafter, Smith scrapbooks) donated by Betty Smith to the State Historical Society of Wisconsin (SHSW). They are available on microfilm, reels P82-4846–48.

66. The vote, reported in the *WSJ*, April 3, 1974, was 29,421–15,410. See the *CT*, January 28, 1972, for Peters' comment. Significantly, the work done in 1974 by Peters and his associates started the ten-year clock in the foundation contract;

this meant that the foundation had the exclusive right to design anything in the Monona Basin area until 1984. In fact, the exclusive design agreement, and indeed the entire basin contract, was terminated by mutual agreement between the parties in March 1979. By this time the State Street civic center was nearing completion. The resolution was approved by the common council on March 21, 1979.

67. Paul Soglin, interview by authors, April 8, 1997, and George Nelson, interview by authors, February 5, 1997.

68. See the *WSJ*, May 15, 1974, for concept approval; the *CT*, June 26, 1974, for sale authorization; and the *WSJ*, July 12, 1974, for an account of the warm reception. Michael Duffey said that the airport reception was orchestrated by Rae Ragatz (interview by Mollenhoff, September 14, 1997).

69. For examples of critical comments see the *CT*, August 30, 1974, and January 30, 1975. Thomas George, an earthy, cigar-smoking, opera-loving attorney, filed a taxpayers' suit charging that auditorium bonds could be used only for new construction. The suit was made moot when the council voted to use another account to buy the theater. For accounts of how George's suit was settled, see the *WSJ*, July 27, 1974, and *CT*, August 2, 1974. No sooner was George's suit resolved than council member

Eugene Parks sued the city. Parks charged that the city followed an inappropriate procedure in buying the theater and that the transaction was therefore invalid. Like George, Parks used legal technicalities to correct what he saw as a policy mistake. For accounts of Parks's lawsuit, see the *CT*, January 23, 24, and 28, 1975.

70. For articles on the selection of Hardy Holzman, see the *CT*, April 3, 1975; for source of firm's design philosophy, see the *CT*, July 14, 1975; and for information on architect's contract, see the *WSJ*, May 7, 1975. As noted in a letter dated March 24, 1974, to Paul Soglin and signed by most Madison architects, the decision to interview nonlocal architects was extremely unpopular (Smith scrapbooks). In her interview by the authors on August 29, 1997, and in unpublished reminiscences dated August 20, 1997, given to the authors, Smith said that out-of-town architects made better presentations and had more experience than Madison architects interviewed by the commission.

71. See *WSJ*, July 17 and September 14, 1975; *CT*, July 17, 1975; the Hardy Holzman Pfeiffer Associates estimate dated August 20, 1975; and a summary of Madison's auditorium account dated August 15, 1975, in the Smith scrapbooks.

72. *CT*, July 19, 1975, and *WSJ*, May 15, 1974. Smith served on

the common council from 1973 to 1979.

73. Smith interview; *CT*, August 6, 1975; *WSJ*, September 19, 1975. Harry Backer was the Oscar Mayer executive who telephoned Smith on behalf of Mayer.

74. *CT*, February 24, 1976. Frautschi had a long association with Madison's United Way organizations and their predecessors, the University of Wisconsin, State Historical Society of Wisconsin, and Rotary Club of Madison. For newspaper accounts of the fund drive, see the *CT*, April 28, May 13, July 29, and October 26, 1976, A foundation financial report dated November 22, 1976, in the microfilm copy of the Smith scrapbooks, shows pledges totaling $1,351,029. The primary drive ran from March to July 1976. Frautschi died on December 2, 1997.

75. *CT* and *WSJ*, February 10, 1977; *WSJ*, February 15, 1977. The city would have had plenty of money to pay for a civic center — even with the $2 million overrun — if it had plowed the interest earned on the $4 million bond issue back into the auditorium account. A memo from city comptroller Paul Reilly, dated March 3, 1974, in the Smith scrapbooks, shows that from 1965 to 1977 the city received nearly $3 million in interest, $2 million of which the city transferred to its general fund.

In October 1977 the council ordered an investigation into the causes of this cost overrun. The report prepared by Reilly attributed the overrun to faulty calculations by the architect, extras added along the way, and inflation. For information on this investigation, see the *WSJ* and *CT*, March 7, 1978, and Reilly's report of March 3, 1978, in the Smith scrapbooks.

76. *CT*, March 8, 1977.

77. *CT*, June 17, 1977, and *WSJ*, June 27, 1977.

78. *CT*, June 17 and 29, 1977, and *WSJ*, June 27, 28, 29, and 30, 1977. Wavering council members probably supported the center because they knew that the same appropriation could be made the following year with only twelve votes and that delays in a rapid-inflation environment would only cost taxpayers more. (Council rules require seventeen votes to amend a budget but only twelve votes to include a project in the next year's budget.)

79. "The New Madison Civic Center by Hardy Holzman Pfeiffer Associates," *Architectural Record* (July 1980): 77–86, praised the design.

80. See the dedication program in the Smith scrapbooks.

CHAPTER 6

### THE CONVENTION CENTER CRUSADE

1. Not a word about Soglin's plans surfaced in local media until June 23, 1990, four days before the press conference, when a *WSJ* reporter got word of the project from the ever-widening circle of insiders. For the next four days both dailies printed stories reporting the rumors but never got the full story before the official announcement.

2. Paul Soglin, interview by authors, April 8, 1997.

3. Lynn Russell Holley, interview by Mollenhoff, December 16, 1996.

4. See survey of Wisconsin convention centers, *WSJ*, March 30–April 2, 1986.

5. David C. Peterson, *Convention Centers, Stadiums, and Arenas* (Washington, D.C.: Urban Land Institute, 1989), p. 7. Peterson is a managing director of Laventhol and Horwath, a nationally recognized accounting firm specializing in the financial analysis of public assembly buildings. One of the few histories of the hospitality industry is Margie Hazerjian's "Turning Back the Clock: The History of C&VB's," *Meeting News*, August 1989.

6. Lynn Russell Holley interview.

7. Ibid.; *WSJ*, January 2, 1986.

8. This section is based on extensive research done by Mollenhoff on the early history of the Madison Convention and Visitors Bureau (CVB) that included examination of its minutes, newsletters, and promotional materials.

9. Wild was first quoted in *Isthmus* on January 10, 1985, but he may have suggested the idea to others earlier.

10. The 1982 reorganization of the Central Madison Council created an umbrella organization known as Downtown Madison, Inc., with several subsidiaries, including a nonprofit real estate development corporation known as Downtown Madison Partners, Inc. and a retail promotion arm known as Central Madison Merchants Council.

11. In 1982 the State Street Mall was completed and, contrary to many gloomy predictions, retailing flourished. Although State Street served the large U.W. student population, it also enjoyed the patronage of many outside the university community. For information on shopping center development, see note 168, chap. 4, and note 54, chap. 5.

12. *WSJ*, January 2, 1986; John Urich, interview by authors, March 11, 1997; Joe Sensenbrenner, interview by authors, March 19, 1997.

13. *WSJ*, April 8, 1987.

14. The $45,000 Pannell Kerr Forster study was entitled "Report of Potential Market Demand Statement of Estimated Annual Operating Results and Economic Impact for a Proposed Convention Center Facility to be Located in Madison, Wisconsin" and was released to the public in July 1987.

15. The proposals follow.

• A hotel and convention center, an office building on an adjoining downtown block, and an underground parking facility under Martin Luther King Jr. Boulevard, submitted by Warren Barberg, who had parted company earlier in the year with Madison hotelier Jerry Mullins. It was grand, sketchy, and estimated to cost $105 million.

• A $37 million vanilla version of the hotel and convention center for the south side of the Capitol Square that Jerry Mullins had submitted in 1987.

• A handsome $68 million complex requiring the other half of the Concourse block, submitted by Darrell Wild.

• Two proposals from Richard Munz, a well-known Madison real estate developer: Lake Terrace and Nolen Terrace. For both schemes Munz placed his hotel on the bluff on East Wilson Street over-looking Lake Monona. Under the Lake Terrace scheme the convention center would occupy the East Wilson Street bluff just west of the hotel; under the Nolen Terrace scheme the convention center was positioned in Law Park. The $46 million Nolen Terrace garnered almost all the positive adjectives and was officially declared the winner of the sweepstakes in August 1988.

For accounts of these proposals see the *CT*, June 2, 1988; *WSJ*, June 10, 1988; and *Isthmus*, July 8, 1988.

16. Sensenbrenner promised not to use property taxes in the *WSJ*, January 2, 1987.

17. *Isthmus*, February 17, 1989. The analysis was conducted by Paul Reilly, city comptroller.

18. Paul R. Reilly, "Nolen Terrace, Summary of Public Construction Costs and Financing," unpublished working paper dated September 22, 1988. Sensenbrenner's recommendation created a fund that later proved invaluable. Normally, city staff members would have to go back to the council for an authorization at every key step along the way. The availability of this funded account reduced the number of times staff had to go back to the council for approval.

19. Reilly, "Nolen Terrace." The city created a tax incremental district for this purpose on September 29, 1987. TIF funds paid for infrastructure, including the improvement of Martin Luther King Jr. Boulevard and the refurbishing of Olin Terrace as a new entrance for the center. Reilly also calculated that $900,000 was

available from other downtown Madison TIF districts.

20. Reilly, "Nolen Terrace."

21. *WSJ*, February 8, 1989. Two weeks later the common council ratified the mayor's recommendation and referendum language.

22. *Isthmus*, February 10, 1989.

23. The Holiday Inn specifications called for a 48,000-square-foot exhibit hall and a 1,700-person banquet hall. Nolen Terrace, by contrast, called for a 40,000-square-foot exhibit hall and a 1,000-person banquet hall. For Hammons' announcement, see the *WSJ*, December 21, 1987.

24. "Market Evaluation and Economic Impact Assessment for a Proposed Convention Center in Downtown Madison," September 1988, was done by Laventhol and Horwath at a cost of $50,000.

25. The full name of the committee was "No White Elephant Committee Opposed to the Munz-Mullins Convention Center." Principal opponent Phil Ball's initial opposition was made in the *WSJ*, August 23, 1988. Ball was a former assistant to Soglin at City Hall. Fleischli's initial opposition appeared in *Isthmus*, July 8, 1988, and *WSJ*, August 24, 1988. Her letter to the Convention Center Criteria Committee of July 28, 1988, is filed with city records (Madison Municipal Reference Service [MMRS]). The *CT* of March 22, 1989, quoted labor leader James

Cavanaugh as saying that he opposed the center because it would not pay "a living wage." For examples of articles emphasizing campaign themes, see the *CT*, March 27, 1989; *WSJ*, April 4 and August 23 and 24, 1988; and *Isthmus*, September 2, 1988.

26. See press release from Coalition for Madison's Future, March 8, 1989, authors' files. For the Oscar Mayer story see *Isthmus*, September 2, 1988.

27. Official campaign expense reports dated January 31, April 3, and July 10, 1989, show that No White Elephant spent $7,932. Corresponding reports filed by the Coalition for Madison's Future, dated February 1, March 28, June 30, July 1, and December 19, 1989, show expenditures of $40,737.

28. See the *WSJ*, September 12, 1989, for number of hotel rooms. Percentage of downtown office space comes from Michelson Investments, "Office Vacancy Survey," Madison, Wisconsin, June 1989, authors' files.

29. The sites were (1) the half-block opposite the Concourse Hotel, originally proposed by Darrell Wild (block 82); (2) the full block opposite the Concourse Hotel proposed by Glen Hovde (block 82); (3) the South Square site (blocks 88 and 89); (4) the Civic Center site originally proposed by George Icke (block 66); (5) the full block occupied by the Concourse Hotel (block 83); (6) the Lake Terrace site (blocks 87

and 106); (7) the Nolen Terrace site (blocks 106 and Law Park); (8) the West Towne Shopping Center site proposed by John Hammons; (9) the Middleton site proposed by John Hammons. (The block numbers correspond to those on the original plat of the city.)

30. See the *CT*, March 23, 1987, for Gonzalez's letter; Zweifel's column ran April 27, 1987; and the *WSJ*'s editorial appeared on July 1, 1987. Other letters urging consideration of the Wright plan were published in *Isthmus*, March 27, 1987, and *CT*, March 31, May 8, 11, and 19, 1987.

31. The city and DMI paid the Harvard School of Design $20,000 to cover students' expenses. The students flew to Madison in February for a briefing and then returned to Cambridge. Professor Jonathan Lane presented the results to DMI members at their annual banquet on April 7, 1988. The publicity surrounding this presentation triggered Geraldine Nestingen's letter to the editor of the *CT*, April 27, 1988.

32. William Wesley Peters to Geraldine Nestingen, May 10, 1988, Peters file, TAA.

33. Peters' comment comes from a Zweifel column dated May 16, 1988. Peters says in his May 10 letter to Nestingen that he called Zweifel on May 9. The reference to dispatching the architect to monitor the city committee comes from the *CT*, August 2, 1988.

34. Scott's articles appeared in the *WSJ*, July 18, 1988, and *CT*, July 20, 1988. These and the authors' conversations with Scott were supplemented by a personal communication, March 25, 1997, from Daniel Ruark to Mary Jane Hamilton. Other letter writers included Geraldine Nestingen and Helen Groves. Groves, a leading proponent of Monona Terrace in the 1950s, offered to organize residents of her nursing home; she died on August 17, 1994, in the midst of Ann Fleischli's legal barrage to stop Monona Terrace. The Taliesin public relations director was Dixie Legler. Additional letters to the editor were sent by Agnes Blair, a relative of Paul Harloff's.

35. Betty Scott, interview by authors, February 13, 1997; *CT*, August 2, 1988.

36. This behind-the-scenes account is based on the authors' interviews with Bud Arnold, January 27, 1997; Jim Burgess, February 5 and 6, 1997; Jim Carley, February 4, 1997; Tony Puttnam, January 29 and March 13, 1997; and Paul Soglin, April 8, 1997, as well as newspaper articles and personal correspondence with Puttnam and Arnold. However, the principals' recollections of what happened do not always agree. This account is the authors' assessment of what probably occurred.

37. Carley interview. Carley chaired the Taliesin commission's

Physical Preservation Committee, and Montooth was a member of that committee.

38. Carley interview.

39. See *CT*, August 20, 1988; *WSJ* series, August 21–27, 1988; and *Isthmus*, August 26, 1988; and Paul Sprague, ed., *Frank Lloyd Wright and Madison: Eight Decades of Artistic and Social Interaction* (Madison, Wisc.: Elvehjem Museum of Art, 1990), a book based on the show.

40. For general articles on the Elvehjem show, see the *CT*, October 3 and 11, 1988. For editorial reference to "missed the boat," see the *WSJ*, July 1, 1990. See also Soglin interview.

41. Nolen Terrace developer Richard Munz was quoted on Nolen Terrace's pedigree in the *WSJ*, July 13, 1988. Examples of this perspective on Nolen Terrace include *Isthmus*, July 8 and August 26, 1988; *CT*, August 2, 8, and 31, September 2 and 4, and October 3 and 11, 1988; Scott interview; *WSJ*, August 24, 1988.

42. Arnold and Carley interviews.

43. *WSJ*, April 13, 1989; Soglin interview. The day he met with the DMI board, Soglin heard for the first time about a Frank Lloyd Wright project that the organization had quietly undertaken nearly a year earlier — a plan to build Wright's 1893 Lake Monona boathouse on the east end of Law Park (see chap. 3). Soglin immediately wrote a letter of support to the

Evjue Foundation, which was considering giving DMI a grant. DMI had applied to the foundation five months earlier for $1 million to build the boathouse according to the original plans. For additional background on this project, see Figure A1.

44. Soglin interview.

45. George Nelson, interview by authors, February 5, 1997.

46. Soglin and Nelson interviews.

47. Charge letter from Soglin to Convention Center Task Force, June 1, 1989, in authors' files. Soglin's charge to the task force repeated the goal of restoring downtown Madison as a regional tourist and convention destination, as stated in "Downtown 2000," a report released in draft form a few days later by the Planning Unit of the Madison Department of Planning and Development.

48. During the two months before the July 12 trip, Puttnam, Arnold, and DMI staff members met and discussed how the 1959 plans could best be revised, taking the recent Nolen Terrace proposal into account.

49. Puttnam based his schematics on the 1987 Pannell Kerr Forster specifications. The full title of Puttnam's undated handout was "Tentative Space Allotment Schedule, Monona Project." At this point Puttnam had access to several sheets from Wright's plans, dated February 15, 1959, and the entire set of drawings

that were done in 1960–61 but based on the 1959 plans. Puttnam's initials appear on about 25 percent of the architectural drawings in this set.

50. Burgess, Soglin, and Nelson interviews.

51. "Report of the Convention Center Task Force," July 31, 1989.

52. Rick Phelps, interview by Mollenhoff, November 24, 1997; Nelson and Burgess interviews. Those present also included George Nelson; Bob Brennan, president of the Chamber of Commerce; and Don Helfrecht, chairman of Madison Gas and Electric. The meetings with Phelps were sponsored by Future Madison, a new organization created by Burgess as a replacement for Downtown Madison Partners, Inc. (DMPI). The newspaper executive envisioned Future Madison as a SWAT team of top CEOs who could focus their attention on projects anywhere in the city; he did not wish to be limited to downtown projects, as required by the DMPI charter.

53. On the warm outpouring, see the *CT*, July 2, 1990. The *WSJ* quoted Metzner on July 1, 1990.

54. Substitute Resolution 46,995, approved on August 7, 1990.

55. Technically, Soglin appointed everyone, but Nelson said he wanted four individuals on the commission because they were well-known and essential consensus builders: Jerry Frautschi, a

prominent businessman whose family had been active in civic affairs for four generations; Don Helfrecht, then the chairman of the board of Madison Gas and Electric Company and a dedicated supporter of the downtown; Fred Mohs, a prominent lawyer who lived in a refurbished mansion just two blocks from the capitol and who had worked tirelessly for three decades to revitalize the central city; and Marshall Erdman, former protégé of Frank Lloyd Wright's and former chairman of the Commission on Taliesin. Outspoken critics included Mohs, who said he thought the idea of a Frank Lloyd Wright convention center was terrible (*WSJ*, September 2, 1990). The December 17, 1990, minutes of the Architectural Contract Subcommittee note that Mohs thought that Taliesin Associated Architects was a cult.

56. George Austin, "The Frank Lloyd Wright Monona Terrace Convention Center Project Schedule."

57. The description of the design refinement is based on a telephone conversation between Puttnam and Mollenhoff on February 12, 1997. Puttnam's conclusions are from his "Feasibility and Predesign Analysis Report," December 12, 1990. The importance of authenticity is evident in the committee's interim report, delivered to the common council on January 8, 1991.

58. Minutes of the physical planning committee, June 18, 1991; Puttnam interviews.

59. For background on the lake view question, see minutes of the physical planning committee, January 15 and March 19, 1991, and the minutes of the full commission dated February 12 and November 20, 1991.

60. See commission minutes, June 11, 1991, and the *CT*, June 12, 1991, for recommendations of Brian Py of the Py Development Group. According to John Urich (interview by authors, December 31, 1996), a second reason that the hotel was deleted was its cost. In the Nolen Terrace proposal it accounted for nearly $20 million. To add this amount to the Monona Terrace cost would be tantamount to killing the entire project. Some local experts, such as Bill Geist, president of the Greater Madison Convention and Visitors Bureau, said that his research showed that a contiguous hotel was not essential (see *CT*, May 14, 1991).

61. Nelson and Puttnam interviews. See also the architectural contract dated March 21, 1991.

62. The *CT*, July 7, 1992, identified members of the scoping committee as Caryl Terrell, a lobbyist for the Sierra Club; Pam Porter, a former head of the Audubon Society; Jim Cobb, chairman of the city transportation commission; Jerri Linn Phillips, a member

of the city commission on the environment; Steve Carpenter, a U.W. lakes expert; Grant Cottam, professor emeritus of the U.W. Institute for Landscape Architecture; and Erhard Joeres, a U.W. professor of civil and environmental engineering.

63. See commission minutes, July 9, 1991, and Ellerbe Becket, consultant, "Review of Cost Proposal, August, 1991."

64. The most detailed and definitive statement of Monona Terrace financing is found in Monona Terrace Commission, "Financing and Operations Report of the Frank Lloyd Wright Monona Terrace Commission," a thirty-nine-page document published in September 1992.

65. See Kerry D. Vandell and James D. Shilling, "Financing the Frank Lloyd Wright Monona Terrace: Issues of Equity and Economic Efficiency," May 1991, and Vandell and Shilling, "Monona Terrace: An Analysis of Job Creation and Property Tax Impacts," July 1992. The first study was commissioned by Future Madison, the second by the Monona Terrace Commission. Excellent summaries of reports focusing on economic benefits are found in two other reports published by the commission, "The Report of the Frank Lloyd Wright Monona Terrace Commission," October 1991, and "Financing and Operations Report."

66. The national consulting firm Sophia Counsel made its report to the commission in August 1991.

67. George Austin, interview by authors, February 18, 1997, and Nelson interview provided details about preparation for the Evjue meeting. The announcement of the grant was in the *CT*, September 27, 1991. For foundation history see a brochure entitled "The Story Behind the Evjue Foundation, Inc.," 1996, available from the foundation. Austin recalled that city staff had placed on a corner easel an enlargement of the well-known photograph of Wright and Evjue in Wright's studio (see Fig. 4.9), where the foundation was meeting. When the trustees entered the room and saw the photo, several exclaimed, "Oh, look, there's Uncle Bill."

68. *CT*, October 25, 1991. The state contribution was later reported as $18.1 million. The $3 million set aside for John Nolen Drive was subtracted because that project was already scheduled.

69. Tommy Thompson, interview by authors, March 31, 1997. This incident was confirmed in a telephone conversation with Bob Brennan on February 7, 1997. Brennan was a member of the governor's 1987 Japan trade mission and was present.

70. Thompson interview.

71. Jim Klauser, interview by authors, March 12, 1997, and interviews with Nelson and

Thompson. Thompson said that he and Klauser came up with the idea of contributing to Monona Terrace over a cup of coffee. Klauser's own interest in Wright dates from a lecture he heard Wright give in the Memorial Union theater when he was a freshman at the U.W. See also Soglin to Klauser, December 21, 1990, in the authors' files.

72. Nelson interview. Office of the Mayor press release, February 12, 1992.

73. Commission minutes dated September 11 and October 9, 1990, and January 8 and February 12, 1991; Nelson interview. The video was prepared by MPI Film and Video of Madison. The executive producer was Roberta Gassman, executive assistant to Mayor Paul Soglin; Margaret McBride of MPI was producer-writer; and Jon Aleckson was the director-editor.

74. For one example of how the commission reached out for community support, see the "Instructions to Monona Terrace Speakers Bureau," March 1991. For the addition of *Community*, see *Madison Common Council Proceedings (MCCP)*, March 30, 1993. George Austin explained that the city had to get permission from the Frank Lloyd Wright Foundation to use the phrase "a public place by Frank Lloyd Wright" (Austin interview).

75. These studies are listed in the two commission reports noted earlier.

76. Nelson interview. The unanimous vote occurred on August 27, 1991, when the commissioners were issuing what they thought was their "final" report; it was published October 15 as "Monona Terrace: A Public Place by Frank Lloyd Wright."

77. The final report of the Monona Terrace Commission, "Financing and Operations Report," was published on September 15, 1992.

78. Marjorie Colson, letter to the editor, *Isthmus*, February 28, 1992.

79. For official campaign kickoff descriptions, see the *WSJ*, April 28 and May 20, 1992. For Monona Terrace supporters' opinions on the project and urban sprawl, see the *WSJ*, October 27, 1992. Supporters saw the project as encouraging development downtown, which they believed would curb sprawl.

What happened in the swimming pool referendum in April 1992 cast a long shadow over Monona Terrace. Residents had been pressuring the city for years to build a public swimming pool as an alternative to city beaches; in 1991 the head of a major company made a large lead gift, which brought total private donations to nearly $1 million. Pool construction had been estimated at $2.7 million. However, pool opponents were angered by what they perceived as an attempt by private donors to

force nearby residents to accept the pool, which was slated for Olin Park. In fact, the common council had approved the pool on a 16–4 vote on June 18, 1991, after deciding that Madison's south side needed the pool most and Olin Park was the best place to put it. About this time convention center opponents began to see the April pool referendum as a preview for the November referendum on the convention center, indeed as an opportunity to develop opposition to it. Consequently, the two groups worked to secure fourteen thousand signatures to force a vote on a question to permanently change Madison's charter to require that all projects in lakefront parks with costs in excess of $500,000 be submitted to binding referendum. Coalition leaders argued that the pool was extravagant, an expression of political and corporate arrogance, and that it would cause a "now quiet natural area" to "be filled with noise from hundreds of people swimming and playing." At the April 1992 election 61 percent of Madison's voters vetoed the swimming pool at Olin Park; they also endorsed the requirement for a referendum for any lakeshore project costing more than $500,000. For more on this episode see the *CT*, February 8, 1991, and March 30, 1992; *WSJ*, September 10, 1992; and *Isthmus*, April 10, 1992.

80. Morris Andrews, interview by authors, March 12, 1997; Nelson interview; and Chuck Knowles,

"The Intimidator," *Madison*, February 1993, pp. 21–24.

81. Andrews interview.

82. The model's tour was described in *Isthmus*, September 18, 1992. The *CT*, September 16, 1992, describes the Eric Wright visit.

83. Ann Fleischli, letter to the editor, *WSJ*, August 7, 1992.

84. The *WSJ*'s editors discussed the heavy mail load in a sidebar that ran November 4, 1992. For details of the campaign, see Knowles, "Intimidator," and Nelson and Andrews interviews. For details of the opposition's campaign, see the *WSJ*, October 4, 1992.

85. The election results defy simple explanation. All of Madison's East Side districts voted against the convention center, while all but three West Side districts voted for it. At the same time, 62 percent of Madison's voters cast ballots for Democrat Bill Clinton; 53 percent voted to reelect Scott Klug, a Republican member of Congress; and 74 percent voted for Russell Feingold, a first-time Democratic candidate for the U.S. Senate. Madison has twenty districts, each of which is divided into several wards. Wards are therefore the smallest unit of electoral analysis and thus the most revealing. Some West Side wards gave Monona Terrace pluralities as high as 68 percent, whereas some East Side wards turned in anti-Terrace pluralities

as high as 64 percent. The authors are indebted to John Bauman of the Department of Planning and Development for detailed electoral data, including a colored map analyzing the 1992 vote by ward. Three weeks after the referendum the common council adopted the convention center financing plan and authorized negotiations with Dane County.

86. The eight jurisdictions that approved funding the center were the townships of Blue Mounds, Madison, Middleton, and Montrose; the villages of Maple Bluff and Shorewood Hills; and the cities of Fitchburg and Monona. Outside Madison, 30,357 residents voted for the center and 39,529 voted against it. Thus the total vote for the center was 77,486; 84,405 voted against it. The question before suburban and rural voters was worded differently than the question before Madison voters. County voters were asked: "Shall the Dane County board financially support the Monona Terrace Convention Center in the city of Madison?" Because the non-Madison vote was not binding on the county board, the county clerk did not collect statistics; we reconstructed the results from newspaper reports. The vote on the board itself reflected its refusal to approve a countywide referendum. Center proponents, led by Blaska and Wagner, convinced their pro-center colleagues to reject a formal countywide referendum

because it would provoke yet another urban-rural skirmish. However, this action angered several rural supervisors, including Betsy Schulte, who worked through the Dane County Towns Association to get 51 of 60 communities to add the nonbinding referendum to their ballots. See *CT*, September 22, 1992, and *WSJ*, September 23, 1992, and letters from the Dane County Towns Association, dated February 26, 1992, August 25, and September 22 to all town, village, and city officials. The authors thank Pat Ampe of the Dane County Towns Association for copies of these letters.

87. See *Isthmus*, November 6, 1992; Nelson interview.

88. *Isthmus*, January 29, 1993. According to campaign finance reports filed with the city clerk's office, "It's Wright for Wisconsin" raised $290,000, while "It Ain't Wright" raised $12,424. The reports are dated January 6 and February 2, 1993, respectively. No agency monitors local election costs, but the Wisconsin State Elections Board monitors expenditures for *all* political action committees that spend more than $25 in any election, including local referenda. A review of volume 2 of the *1993–94 Statistical Report* published by the state elections board revealed no local referenda that even came close to attracting such heavy spending. Moreover, Kevin J. Kennedy, the executive

director of the state elections board, said he knew of no recent local election as expensive as the referendum on Monona Terrace (Kennedy, telephone interview by Mollenhoff, August 15, 1997).

89. These efforts are detailed in George Austin's "Frank Lloyd Wright's Monona Terrace: Profile in Quality," *Total Quality Review* (November–December 1995): 15–19. The mission statement of the city team read:

"The partners [city staff team] will work together to make Monona Terrace a world-class convention and community center recognized by its customers as an excellent facility, and to provide a Frank Lloyd Wright-inspired civic building for future generations. We will use a team-oriented approach to design and build Monona Terrace, always knowledgeable of our future customers' needs, and delivering the complete facility within the budget, on time, and consistent with Frank Lloyd Wright's 1958 design."

(At the time the staff did not realize that the project was based on Wright's 1959 design.)

90. In August 1990, just a month before Madison created the Monona Terrace Commission, Phelps got the Dane County board to create the Dane County Convention Center Task Force to ensure that the design and operation of the new Dane County exhibit hall and the new city convention center would be

complementary. In its final report, released in September 1991, the county group proposed several management models that later became part of city-county negotiations. The county task force concluded that the two facilities would serve different markets. Significantly, Phelps's first offer to help the convention center was to consolidate overlapping city and county services — such as parks and police — and for the city to use whatever savings it would realize from this as the county's contribution. Phelps conveyed this idea to Soglin in a letter dated April 22, 1991.

91. The county board approved its team on December 3, 1992, Resolution 239, 1992–93; the city appointed its team on November 24, 1992. For terms of agreement see the *CT*, February 18, 1993.

92. Factors that made county participation unlikely were given in the *WSJ*, April 9, 1992. Nearly all villages and cities contiguous to Madison approved the ballot question (see note 86; *CT*, November 11 and December 4, 1992). The *WSJ*, March 3, 1993, quotes the rural supervisor.

93. Michael Blaska, personal communication with Mollenhoff, April 21, 1997.

94. *CT*, February 18, 1993, and *WSJ*, February 19, 1993. Blaska said that the "largely rural and suburban supervisors who had elected me chair felt that I had

betrayed them to some degree" (personal communication).

95. Dane County Clerk, printout of 1992 election results.

96. *CT* and *WSJ*, March 5, 6, and 7, 1993. Terese Berceau was the supervisor who made the daylong drive to be present at the meeting.

97. *Dane County Board Proceedings*, vol. 79, Sub. 1 to Resolution 313, 1992–93, March 4, 1993. See also newspaper accounts of this meeting, *CT* and *WSJ*, March 5–7, 1993.

98. *CT*, May 3, 1993; *WSJ*, May 5 and June 18, 1993.

99. Nelson interview.

100. Ibid.; Paul Berge, interview by Mollenhoff, April 1, 1997. Other members of Berge's task force were Bob Brennan, Jim Burgess, Jim Carley, Jane Coleman, Jerry Frautschi, Richard Hansen, Don Helfrecht, Robert Koch, Ann Kovich, Tod Linstroth, George Nelson, Robert Schlicht, Jay Smith, Bjorn Thompson, and Robert Walton. Working as staff to Berge's task force were Ann Kovich and Barbara Brummer, M&I Madison Bank executives.

101. *WSJ*, October 29, 1994, and M&I Madison Bank press release, October 29, 1994, authors' files.

102. According to Jodi Bender, director of capital funds for the

Capital Fundraising Committee, the largest previous campaign raised $3.5 million to improve the Olbrich Botanical Gardens (telephone interview by Mollenhoff, February 18, 1997). David C. Peterson, managing director of Price Waterhouse and one of the most knowledgeable convention center consultants in the country, said that he could "not recall any other private sector contributions as large as the 12 percent share your center received" (personal communication with Mollenhoff, March 31, 1997).

103. Austin interview. A simplified version of Austin's flow chart appears on pp. 66–67 of the October 1991 Monona Terrace Commission report.

104. *WSJ*, March 23, 1994; *CT*, March 24 and 25, 1994; Austin interview. Some meeting experts participated in focus groups arranged by Bill Geist. Another expert on convention center design, Bill Cunningham, was hired under separate contract.

105. Nelson and Austin interviews.

106. *WSJ*, October 12, 1993; Austin interview. The common council concurred on December 14, 1993.

107. *Terrace View* (contractor's newsletter), November 1994, p. 2; Puttnam interview.

108. R. Nicholas Loope, interview by authors, April 15, 1996; *Terrace View*, Spring 1996.

109. Rich Lynch and Larry Thomas, interviews by authors, February 25, 1997.

110. See Wisconsin Department of Administration, "Summary of Written Comments of the Monona Terrace Convention Center, Final Environmental Impact Statement," and "Summary of Oral Comments on the Monona Terrace Convention Center Final Environmental Impact Statement," July 1993. Fleischli's comments are in the *WSJ*, October 26, 1993, and *CT*, October 19, 1993. The *WSJ*, August 24, 1993, quoted other critics: Gary Gates said the EIS was sloppy, and Marjorie Colson said it was nothing but "hyped advertising bytes [sic]."

111. Woodward-Clyde Consultants, "Final Environmental Impact Statement for the Monona Terrace Convention Center Project," Middleton, Wisconsin, July 1993.

112. The first Fleischli quote is from the *CT*, October 19, 1993. She spoke of the "sink with 1,725 drains" in the *WSJ*, April 13, 1995, and of toxins "speeding toward" the lake in the *CT*, March 21, 1995. The *CT*, October 19, 1993, reported her reference to East Germany; Fleischli expanded on her views in a *CT* guest column, October 26, 1993.

113. Fleischli leveled several other charges against the center. For example, the *CT*, August 23, 1993, quoted her as saying that

the center could not be built because it created a public project on public land (a filled lake bed) that would produce profits for private industry. Jackson and Metzner had used this argument many years earlier, but a series of court cases rejected it. Fleischli was also quoted in *Isthmus*, August 20, 1993, as saying that Law Park contained methane gas that would turn the center into a "bomb of some size" if it were not dealt with. Fleischli's petition for a rehearing is dated October 26, 1993, and the state Department of Administration's denial is dated November 12, 1993. See also *CT*, October 27, 1993.

114. Matano was quoted in a *WSJ* editorial, September 17, 1993. Matano said he made the remark on March 16, 1993, at the common council (telephone interview by Hamilton, March 8, 1997).

115. *WSJ*, November 16, 1993. Bahr provided her opinion in a letter of November 10, 1993, to the Commission on the Environment.

116. City records show that Fleischli lost to Sue Bauman by a 2–1 margin. See the *CT*, December 1, 1993, for the quote about Fleischli's plan.

117. *Shoreline Park Preservation, Inc. v. Wisconsin Department of Administration*, December 10, 1993, Dane County Circuit Court, assigned to Judge Moria Krueger.

118. *WSJ*, June 29, 1994.

119. According to John

Rothschild, former assistant city attorney, no city project had attracted so much litigation in twenty years (Rothschild, interview by authors, May 22, 1996).

120. Eiseley's application is dated July 15, 1994. The Madison Landmarks Commission discussed the nomination on September 12, 1994, and the State Historic Preservation Review Board discussed it on October 21, 1994. See also Eiseley, telephone interview by Hamilton, October 28, 1997.

121. Carroll Metzner, interview by authors, April 22, 1997.

122. The articles of incorporation are dated December 2, 1993, and are signed by Ron Shutvet, Marjorie Colson, and Ann Fleischli. Although Fleischli claimed that 90,000 voted against Monona Terrace in the 1992 referendum (see *CT*, July 28, 1994), fewer than 85,000 did so — 44,876 voted against it in the city and 39,529 in the county for a total of 84,405. For details of how Fleischli saw her new organization, see her press release dated December 10, 1993.

123. The corps' conclusion was in the *WSJ*, October 28, 1994. See the *WSJ*, November 1, 1994, for editorial "Turn Some Dirt."

124. *Shoreline Park Preservation, Inc. v. U.S. Army Corps of Engineers*, No. 95-C-164-S. Judge John Shabaz of the Western District of Wisconsin set a hearing for April 12, 1995, on Fleischli's request for

a temporary injunction against the project. A copy of the opinion may be obtained at the Federal Records Center in Chicago.

125. See Ann Fleischli, letter to the editor, *CT*, March 21, 1995; Piper Jaffray prospectus dated November 21, 1994; and the addendum dated December 12, 1994 (the latter two documents are in the authors' files). Fleischli declined to be interviewed for this book.

126. See the *CT*, October 15, 1994, the stake quote. For information on Fleischli's efforts to win passage of the charter ordinance, see the *CT*, October 19, 1994; *WSJ*, November 12, 1994; *Isthmus*, November 4, 1994, and January 6, 1995; and *WSJ*, January 31, 1995. See the *WSJ*, June 25, 1995, for a photo of Fleischli in the corner room of the Bellevue.

127. *WSJ*, February 2 and 15, April 5, 1995.

128. The Madison Landmarks Commission unanimously rejected the application on September 12, 1994; the State Historic Preservation Review Board rejected the nomination on October 21, 1994, by a vote of 6–4. Eiseley's appeal to the National Parks Service is dated November 1, 1994; the rejection by the parks service is dated December 22, 1994. See also *CT*, September 9, 13, and 29, and December 25, 1994, and *Isthmus*, November 4, 1994. However, Fleischli did wring a modest

victory from this exercise. After complaining to the city that the driving of test piles in Law Park could damage the Bellevue Apartments, a local and national landmark, she got the city to stop the work for a month. The city directed the contractor to resume driving test piles on October 27, 1994, when the Army Corps of Engineers issued the permit. Metzner confirmed his role as a funding underwriter in an interview by the authors, April 22, 1997. His supportive letter to Jeffrey Dean, then head of historic preservation, is dated July 8, 1994, and is in the SHSW files.

129. *WSJ*, April 8, May 11, June 30, November 14, 15, 20, and 21, 1995; *CT*, April 8, May 10, June 29, and November 14 and 16, 1995. See also Donald Bruce, chief of the EPA Emergency Response Section, to Fleischli, June 29, 1995, MMRS.

130. Judge P. Charles Jones, Dane County Circuit Court, Branch 3, ruled on June 2, 1995 (case 94-CV-2371); see also Judge John Shabaz's memorandum and order in *Shoreline Park Preservation*, June 26, 1995; and *Shoreline Park Preservation, Inc. v. Wisconsin Department of Administration*, 537 N.W.2d 388 (1995).

131. Torphy's opinion in *Shoreline Park Preservation, Inc. v. Wisconsin Department of Natural Resources*, 94-CV-2788, is dated October 10, 1996.

132. Estimates of the costs of Fleischli's litigation appeared in the *CT*, April 26, 1995.

133. The only case in which the city intervened was the federal case against the Army Corps of Engineers (see note 124 for cite). State interests in the Fleischli cases were defended by assistant attorneys general Steve Wickland and Daniel Farwell. As Assistant City Attorney John Rothschild explained to the authors, Fleischli may have decided not to sue the city because the city had anticipated legal challenges and prepared for them (Rothschild interview). For example, to head off the charge of environmental irresponsibility, the city set up the rigorous but completely voluntary scoping committee to produce a thorough, tough-minded environmental agenda for the contractor who was preparing the EIS. The city also had its Commission on the Environment review and approve the project (Rothschild interview).

134. Nelson interview.

135. *Terrace View*, January 1995, pp. 2–3; Thomas and Lynch interviews; personal communication from Thomas to Mollenhoff, March 17, 1997. On the day the contractor moved onto the site, Fleischli pitched a tent and videotaped contractor activities. She left quietly later in the day.

136. See Ron McCrea, "Wright's Hometown Finally Sees Its Future,"

*New York Times*, February 23, 1995, p. 1; Brendan Gill, "Wright Again — Sort Of," *New Yorker*, March 13, 1995, pp. 36–37; Betsy Wagner, "Frank Lloyd Wright's Dream Lives Again," *U.S. News and World Report*, June 5, 1995, p. 12; John Elson, "The Wrong Wright," *Time*, June 12, 1995, p. 70; and James Bone, "Last Wrights," *London Times*, June 24, 1995, pp. 30, 31, 33, 35.

137. Elson, "The Wrong Wright," p. 70.

138. *CT*, June 7, 1995.

139. Soglin interview. The following newspaper accounts reported on the change in state aid: *CT*, June 7 and 9, 1995; *WSJ*, June 6, 8, 9, 11, 15, and 26, 1995.

140. Austin, "Frank Lloyd Wright's Monona Terrace: Profile in Quality."

141. Thomas and Lynch interviews.

142. Thomas and Lynch detailed the construction mileposts in their interviews with the authors. Fleischli's continued opposition was given in the *CT*, December 20, 1993, and September 2, 1995.

143. Soglin interview.

144. Soglin and Nelson interviews.

145. Wright-trained architects and designers included John Rattenbury, Thomas Casey, Charles Montooth, Edgar Tafel, James Pfefferkorn, Joe Fabris,

David Dodge, Cornelia Brierly, Herbert Fritz, Aubrey Banks, Louis Wiehle, Arnold Roy, Stephen Nemtin, Thomas Olson, and Bill Calvert.

146. The *CT* and *WSJ* devoted extensive coverage to this event in their editions of July 19, 1997.

CHAPTER 7

TRIUMPH OF THE VISION

1. Ian Nairn, *The American Landscape: A Critical View* (New York: Random House, 1965), p. 65.

2. Legislation for the hotel room tax was passed in 1967 (Laws of 1967, Chapter 209); tax incremental financing was passed in 1975 (Laws of 1975, Chapters 105, 199, and 311).

3. The sophisticated roof system is explained in "Monona Terrace," *Roofing Specifier* 1, no. 4 (November 1997): 8–13.

4. Making comparative statements about the sizes of Wright's iterations is not without hazards. In some cases detailed breakdowns of space (square footage) by function are provided by Wright, but over the twenty-one years of this project this information is seldom provided in precise apples-to-apples terms. Short of very time-consuming and expensive takeoffs of multiple iterations, it is not possible to determine exact areas of every iteration or even the three major designs. Consequently, size comparisons used in this book can be given only in general terms. For the most detailed size breakdown of the 1938 project, see MT box 54, FLWA; it shows total area for the project to be 1.06 million square feet. A similar breakdown for the 1955 project, but only for the people function areas, can be found in "Outline, Areas, Uses, and Locations of Various Parts of the Proposed

Monona Terrace Development, Frank Lloyd Wright Architect," dated February 13, 1955, in MT materials at FLWA; it shows people functions totaling 347,126 square feet but does not include the rooftop gardens or parking. A reasonable estimate of rooftop size is 70,000 square feet and a reasonable estimate for parking 3,500 cars is 1.1 million square feet. Reliable size estimates for the 1957 "peanut" version are not available. According to FLWA, the 1959 project contained about 534,000 square feet and the 1961 version contained about 679,000 square feet. The 1994 design contains 603,000 square feet (including the helixes) and 671,000 square feet with the rooftop terrace.

5. According to Taliesin records, space allocated to parking and moving cars averaged 60 percent in Wright's designs.

6. Harland Bartholomew's 1922 plan, discussed in chap. 1, was the most detailed critique. As noted in chap. 3, Segoe, another experienced railroad depot planner, thought Wright's depot plans were unworkable.

7. The two sources for the quote about marriage are the pamphlet "Greater Madison: The Monona Terrace Project," put out by Taliesin in 1955, and a paper prepared to persuade legislators to support Monona Terrace: Citizens for Monona Terrace, "A Challenge to State Officials, Legislative Candidates, and All

Wisconsin Citizens to Act Aggressively to Beautify Our Capital City," Groves Papers, box 23, folder 6, no date, SHSW.

8. *CT,* January 24, 1961.

9. Sources of the more general charges were Judy Clowes ("a tragic compromise"), a Wisconsin architecture critic who writes for *Isthmus,* July 11, 1997; historian and Wright biographer Robert Twombly ("watered down"), quoted in *Isthmus,* July 20, 1990; Monona Terrace critic Ann Fleischli ("McWright," "a fake," and "a fraud"), quoted in James Bone's "Last Wrights," *London Times,* June 24, 1995, pp. 30–33, 45, and *CT,* November 29, 1994; Robert Campbell ("a replica"), architecture critic for the *Boston Globe,* quoted in the *WSJ,* October 25, 1992; Narciso Menocal ("an imitation"), University of Wisconsin architectural historian, *WSJ,* October 25, 1992.

10. Clowes, writing in *Isthmus,* July 11, 1997, said that one of her most "serious disappointments" in regard to Monona Terrace was that it was "canted slightly" out of axial alignment with Martin Luther King Jr. Boulevard. What she did not realize is that Wright *designed* all but his 1955 plan to be aligned with the slightly angled property line and not with King Boulevard. This is explained in Figure 7.6.

11. Harold Groves, statement to the Auditorium Committee, MT box 62, FLWA. Although the

statement is undated, it is clear that it was delivered during the 1959 Auditorium Committee meeting right after Wright's death.

12. *WSJ,* November 20, 1954.

13. Sets of the sixteen 1959 plans are available at SHSW and FLWA. Interior information on the 1959 building comes primarily from "Synopsis Specifications" and "Schedule of Finishes," both dated April 24, 1959 — fifteen days after Wright died. What is not known is whether these specifications were completed (in whole or in part) before he died or whether they were done entirely or partly by William Wesley Peters. Tony Puttnam examined these documents and is confident that they were prepared by Wright himself. However, even if we assume that they were the sole creation of Wright, the documents (MT box 63, FLWA) provide sketchy information. An inventory of plans prepared by Taliesin Associated Architects in connection with a lawsuit and found in MT box 57, FLWA, shows that at least ten additional plans were done for the 1959 project. According to that document, the 1959 plans were comprised of "6 sheets dated 2-15-59, 6 sheets of #4 and #8 are marked 'revised,' 8 sheets all marked 'revised,' and 6 sheets in 1 role and 8 in another marked with FLLW sig. (color)."

14. For example, when the project was featured in the March 1998 issue of *Architectural Record*, the

cover carried the famous 1955 night rendering (Fig. 4.14), the same image used in nearly every article and book in which the project appeared. With the exception of the author's chapter in Paul E. Sprague's *Frank Lloyd Wright and Madison: Eight Decades of Artistic and Social Interaction* (Madison, Wisc.: Elvehjem Museum of Art, 1990) no post-1955 drawings have appeared in a major publication. Another source of confusion comes from the FLWA's classification system, which groups all Terrace drawings and correspondence in two categories, 3909 and 5632. The system was based on the assumption that Wright did just two designs for this project, one in 1939 and another in 1956, not eight as currently known.

15. Gill, "Wright Again — Sort Of," *New Yorker,* March 13, 1995, pp. 36–37. See also *Many Masks: A Life of Frank Lloyd Wright* (New York: Putnam, 1987), pp. 475–76. Relative size data appear in note 4.

16. Menocal is quoted in the *Milwaukee Journal-Sentinel,* July 21, 1997.

17. Gill, "Wright Again," p. 36.

18. *Milwaukee Journal-Sentinel,* July 21, 1997.

19. Ibid.

20. Gill, "Wright Again," p. 36. The words *convention hall* appear on Wright's drawing 5632.039, FLWA. Wright added these words (and functions) to the

1955 plan when he removed the railroad depot.

21. Clowes, *Isthmus,* July 11, 1997.

22. *CT,* April 4, 1995.

23. John Rattenbury and Arnold Roy, former Taliesin apprentices, interviews by authors, November 5, 1996.

24. Segoe to Jackson, July 30, 1958, Joseph W. Jackson Papers, box 16, SHSW.

25. For inventory of Monona Terrace–related drawings see MT box 57, FLWA. For size calculations see note 4.

26. The same circle and square configuration is also found in the Music Pavilion and Bathhouse of Wright's Cheltenham Beach near Chicago (1899) and in the Music Pavilion for Wolf Lake, an amusement park near Chicago that was also never built.

27. See Paul Laseau and James Rice, *Frank Lloyd Wright: Between Form and Principle* (New York: Van Nostrand Reinhold, 1992), pp. 22 and 154.

28. See David De Long, ed., *Frank Lloyd Wright: Designs for an American Landscape, 1922–32* (New York: Abrams, 1996), for representative examples of Wright's designs for challenging sites.

29. Frank Lloyd Wright, "In the Cause of Architecture VII: The Meaning of Materials — Concrete," *Architectural Record* 64 (August 1928): 98–104.

30. Richard Cleary, "Edgar J. Kaufmann, Frank Lloyd Wright, and 'Pittsburgh Park Coney Island in Automobile Scale,'" *Journal of the Society of Architectural Historians* 52 (June 1993): 139–58.

31. For the Community Church in Kansas City, see Curtis Besinger, *Working with Mr. Wright: What It Was Like* (New York: Cambridge University Press, 1995), pp. 88–94 and 114–21. See Mark Reinberger, "The Sugarloaf Mountain Project and Frank Lloyd Wright's Vision of a New World," *Journal of the Society of Architectural Historians* 43 (March 1984): 38–52.

32. For background on the Phoenix project, see Bruce Brooks Pfeiffer and Yukio Futagawa, eds., *Frank Lloyd Wright Monograph*, vol. 8 (Tokyo: A.D.A. EDITA, 1988), pp. 302–3.

33. Ibid. Wright's hat quote comes from an article in the *Arizona Republic*.

34. The Wyoming Valley School was built just a short distance from Taliesin. Wright's tendency to recycle was hardly limited to building features; it included entire buildings. For example, his 1920s New York City high-rise apartment complex, St. Mark's-in-the-Bouwerie, was resurrected several times; its lineal descendent was finally built in Bartlesville, Oklahoma, as the Price Tower. Among other features that migrated from Florida Southern College were diamond-shaped concrete supports for covered walkways that Wright called "ice breakers" in Olin Terraces.

35. For background on the Chicago project, see Pfeiffer and Futagawa, *Monograph*, vol. 8, pp. 268–69.

36. Rattenbury interview.

AFTERWORD
**FUTURE SYNERGY**

1. The thirty-two buildings designed for Madison are identified in Paul E. Sprague, ed., *Frank Lloyd Wright and Madison: Eight Decades of Artistic and Social Interaction* (Madison, Wisc.: Elvehjem Museum of Art, 1990).

# BIBLIOGRAPHICAL ESSAY

SUMMARIZED BY CATEGORY HERE ARE THE SOURCES WE USED TO RESEARCH THIS BOOK. OUR GOAL IS NOT TO BE EXHAUSTIVE BUT TO IDENTIFY THE RICHEST CONCENTRATIONS OF DOCUMENTS AND SOME OF THE BEST SOURCES IN EACH CATEGORY. ABBREVIATIONS USED TO DENOTE EXTENSIVELY CITED SOURCES ARE LISTED ALPHABETICALLY AT THE BEGINNING OF THE NOTES.

## ARCHITECTURAL DRAWINGS

The most extensive collection of original Wright drawings is housed at the Frank Lloyd Wright Archives (FLWA), Taliesin West, Scottsdale, Arizona. Drawings for Olin Terraces are identified as project #3909 and those for the later Monona Terrace as #5632. Drawings produced after Wright's death in 1959 and those for the Monona Basin project are housed at Taliesin Architects Archives (TAA), a facility affiliated with the William Wesley Peters Library, also located at Taliesin West. The most comprehensive source of published drawings from the FLWA collection is Bruce Brooks Pfeiffer and Yukio Futagawa, eds., Frank Lloyd Wright Monograph, vols. 1–8; Preliminary Studies, vols. 9–11; In His Renderings, vol. 12 (Tokyo: A.D.A. EDITA, 1984–88).

Wright's 1955 concept sketch for the Monona Terrace tower and numerous blueline prints, including a set dated February 15, 1959, are housed at the Visual and Sound Archives of the State Historical Society of Wisconsin in Madison.

Sets of the five-hundred-sheet bid documents from 1961 and comparably sized 1994 documents are preserved but not yet available in a public repository.

## CORRESPONDENCE AND PAPERS

The Frank Lloyd Wright Archives is the repository for thousands of letters to and from Wright and his staff, including correspondence with Paul Harloff, Charles Morgan, Helen and Harold Groves, William Evjue, Mary Lescohier, Ivan Nestingen, and many others noted in the text. All such letters are usually indexed by author, addressee, date, and building project in Anthony Alofsin, ed., *Frank Lloyd Wright: An Index to the Taliesin Correspondence*, 5 vols. (New York and London: Garland, 1988). In the course of our research at FLWA we found unindexed correspondence, identified in the notes by MT (Monona Terrace) and the corresponding box number.

Three unprocessed collections proved especially valuable. The

extensive Monona Terrace–related materials of Mary Lescohier, referenced in the notes as the Lescohier Unprocessed Collection (LUC), are housed in the Frank Lloyd Wright Archives. A collection of project-related papers of Madison mayors from the 1950s and 1960s is listed in the notes as the City of Madison Unprocessed Collections. The papers of Porter Butts related to his effort to build a war memorial civic auditorium and community center are referenced in notes as the Butts Unprocessed Collection (BUC) to distinguish them from another major cache of Butts's papers described under the University of Wisconsin Archives; they are in the custody of the City of Madison. Unfortunately, none of these unprocessed collections is yet available to scholars.

The State Historical Society of Wisconsin Archives (SHSW) houses the papers of Franz Aust, William Evjue, Harold Groves, Joseph Jackson, Ellen and Jane Lloyd Jones, Ivan Nestingen, John Olin, and the First Unitarian Society. The society's microfilm collection includes a copy of Betty Smith's Madison

Civic Center files, referenced in the notes as the Smith scrapbooks.

The University of Wisconsin Archives (UWA) in Madison is the repository for the papers of many university presidents, officials, professors, the former Memorial Union director (Porter Butts), and other individuals, including a rich file of primary materials on Frank Lloyd Wright. When Butts documents from the archives are cited in notes, we designate them Butts-UWA to distinguish them from the unprocessed Butts collection. For additional information about UWA holdings, see the heading Local, State, and University History.

Most recent city records are on microfiche and are identified in the notes as CMM (City of Madison Microfiche) and are available at the City Records Center; a collection of project-related mayoral correspondence, beginning with George Forster's, has been preserved on paper but is not yet catalogued. This unprocessed collection is identified in the notes as CMU (City of Madison Unprocessed Collections).

## PERSONAL INTERVIEWS

We conducted more than fifty interviews with key individuals, including city, county, and state officials; proponents and opponents of Monona Terrace; consultants; civic leaders; and former Wright apprentices. All the interviews were conducted in Madison, Wisconsin, or Scottsdale, Arizona (Taliesin West), during 1996 and 1997. We regret that Ann Fleischli, one of the primary project opponents during the 1990s, declined to be interviewed. We also made extensive use of transcripts from videotaped interviews conducted during 1988 by Diane Kostecke, the producer of a public television documentary prepared in conjunction with the Wright exhibition mounted at the Elvehjem Museum. Transcriptions of her interviews are available at the SHSW Archives.

## THESES AND DISSERTATIONS

Three theses and one dissertation by students at the University of Wisconsin–Madison offered valuable perspectives that often differed from those of participants or the local press. These documents are identified in the notes to chapters 2, 3, and 4.

## LEGAL DOCUMENTS

Opinions in all state supreme court cases are available at the University of Wisconsin Law Library. Most opinions handed down in Dane County Circuit Court are available on microfilm at the City-County Building. See the notes for specific citations.

## PRIVATE ORGANIZATIONS

The weekly *Bulletin* for members of the Association of Commerce and its successor organizations (the Madison and Wisconsin Foundation, Chamber of Commerce and Foundation, and Chamber of Commerce) proved to be one of the most useful sources for assessing the business community's responses to Wright's

proposal; all are available on microfilm at SHSW; see the Notes for additional information about the *Bulletin*.

For biographical information on local candidates and pro/con analyses of referenda positions, we found the materials prepared by the League of Women Voters especially useful. Copies of these items are available at the Madison Public Library.

Copies of old minutes, correspondence, and sample mailings from pro and con groups are available at several locations. Items generated by Citizens for Monona Terrace can be found in the Harold Groves Papers, SHSW, and the Mary Lescohier papers (unprocessed), FLWA. Personal notes, correspondence, and promotional materials produced by the Citizens for a Realistic Auditorium Association are included in several boxes of the Joseph Jackson Papers, SHSW.

## CITY, COUNTY, AND STATE RECORDS

City and county records are available at several Madison locations. Bound copies of the *Madison Common Council Proceedings* *(MCCP)* and *Dane County Board Proceedings (DCBP)* are available in the Government Documents Division of the SHSW as well as from the Madison Municipal Reference Service (MMRS), located in the Madison Public Library. Unless otherwise noted, copies of reports prepared by city staff, outside consultants, and private organizations, including environmental impact statements, are available at MMRS. Election results and copies of architectural contracts are housed in the city clerk's office in the City-County Building. Madison Parks Department records are retained by the Parks Department, whereas Madison landmark nominations are available at the Madison Department of Planning and Development; both agencies are located in the Madison Municipal Building. The SHSW Archives houses an extensive collection that includes 1930s mayoral correspondence, efforts to

secure depression-era federal funds, activities of the Madison Planning Trust, and the work done by Ladislas Segoe.

The SHSW is the major repository for state records. The Government Documents Division of its library maintains a collection of legislative journals, bills introduced in both houses, and state statutes; its archives house the files for the Capitol Commission, state agencies, defunct corporations, and architectural licenses (registrations), including Wright's in 1937. National Register nominations and related documentation are available at the Historic Preservation Division.

The state's Legislative Reference Library in Madison contains records relating to the history of bills and public reaction to controversial legislation, such as the Metzner bill in 1957.

## NEWSPAPERS

The differing editorial perspectives of Madison's two daily papers, the *Wisconsin State Journal* and the *Capital Times*, proved invaluable.

Microfilm copies of both papers are available at the SHSW and Madison Public Library. The public library also has clip files for major figures in the Monona Terrace story and an historical file on the civic auditorium. *Isthmus*, a weekly newspaper established in 1976, carried many provocative articles about Monona Terrace, and its letters to the editor page also provided a forum for supporters and opponents.

University of Wisconsin–Madison newspapers provided a useful perspective on campus life while Wright attended in the 1880s. Beginning in the late 1960s, campus papers reflected student reaction to his proposal for Madison. The two papers cited most extensively in the notes are the *Aegis* and the *Daily Cardinal*.

We found the *Home News*, the weekly newspaper serving the Spring Green, Wisconsin, area, an informative source on Wright, his family, and the Taliesin Fellowship from the 1870s through the present. Finally, we found the most consistently useful statewide perspective on Monona Terrace to be the *Milwaukee Journal*. Its outsider viewpoint on issues like home rule was especially illuminating when the legislature was considering the Metzner bill in 1957 and again during its repeal in 1959.

## LOCAL, STATE, AND UNIVERSITY HISTORY

The most comprehensive treatment of the city through 1920 is David V. Mollenhoff, *Madison: A History of the Formative Years* (Dubuque, Iowa: Kendall-Hunt, 1982). Since 1975 *Historic Madison: A Journal of the Four Lakes Region*, the official publication of Historic Madison, Inc., has offered articles on a variety of Madison-related topics.

The most comprehensive treatment of Wisconsin is the six-volume series *History of Wisconsin*, edited by Paul Hass and Jack Holzhueter (Madison: State Historical Society of Wisconsin, 1973–98). Other books that treat specific individuals and special topics are identified in the notes. The *Wisconsin Magazine of History*, the official publication of the SHSW, has featured a number of important articles on Wright.

The most comprehensive history of the University of Wisconsin is Merle Curti and Vernon Carstensen, *The University of Wisconsin: A History, 1848–1925*, 2 vols. (Madison: University of Wisconsin Press, 1949), and by E. David Cronon and John W. Jenkins, *The University of Wisconsin: A History*. Vol. 3: *1925–1945 — Politics, Depression, and War* (Madison: University of Wisconsin Press, 1994). Arthur Hove, *The University of Wisconsin: A Pictorial History* (Madison: University of Wisconsin Press, 1991), provides a good overview of the institution and a wealth of historical photos; Frederic Pike, *A Student at Wisconsin Fifty Years Ago* (Madison: Democrat Printing, 1935), offers a view of campus life during the period that Wright attended; and the yearbooks, *Trochos* and *Badger*, document student interests and activities. The UWA maintains files on university buildings, regents' meetings, honorary degree selections, and events and exhibits held at the Memorial Union, including several by Wright. The UWA's Wright file includes his parents' divorce papers and the twelve-page document he submitted in 1955 as his undergraduate thesis. For information on extant as well as demolished campus buildings, we found Jim Feldman, *The Buildings of the University of Wisconsin* (Madison: University of Wisconsin Archives, 1997), especially informative.

## PUBLICATIONS BY WRIGHT

The most comprehensive source for Wright's published and unpublished writings is Bruce Brooks Pfeiffer, ed., *Frank Lloyd Wright Collected Writings*, 5 vols. (New York: Rizzoli, Frank Lloyd Wright Foundation, 1992–95). All references to Wright's *An Autobiography* in the notes are taken from the version reprinted in volumes 2 and 4 of *Collected Writings*.

## PUBLICATIONS ABOUT WRIGHT

Some of the most informative sources on Wright's Wisconsin designs are Paul E. Sprague, ed., *Frank Lloyd Wright and Madison: Eight Decades of Artistic and Social Interaction* (Madison, Wisc.: Elvehjem Museum of Art, 1990); Herbert and Katherine Jacobs, *Building with Frank Lloyd Wright: An Illustrated Memoir* (Carbondale and Edwardsville: Southern Illinois University Press, 1978); and Jonathan Lipman, *Frank Lloyd Wright and the Johnson Wax Buildings* (New York: Rizzoli, 1986).

Among the many biographies of Wright, two efforts stand out. Robert C. Twombly, *Frank Lloyd Wright: His Life and His Architecture* (New York: Wiley, 1979), made extensive use of contemporary newspaper accounts; Meryle Secrest, *Frank Lloyd Wright* (New York: Knopf, 1992), was the first to rely on correspondence in the FLWA. Brendan Gill, *Many Masks: A Life of Frank Lloyd Wright* (New York: Putnam, 1987), is colorfully written and provides numerous anecdotes in an entertaining but less scholarly volume.

We found useful perspectives on Wright, his work, and the Taliesin Fellowship in several books. For the most extensively documented treatment of Wright's work to date, see Neil Levine, *The Architecture of Frank Lloyd Wright* (Princeton, N.J.: Princeton University Press, 1996); for lavish photographs of Wright's buildings, see Robert McCarter, *Frank Lloyd Wright* (London: Phaidon Press, 1997). We also recommend two highly regarded classics: Henry-Russell Hitchcock, *In the Nature of Materials, 1887–1941: The Buildings of Frank Lloyd Wright* (New York: Duell, Sloan, and Pearce, 1942); and Grant Carpenter Manson, *Frank Lloyd Wright to 1910: The First Golden Age* (New York: Van Nostrand Reinhold, 1958). For contrasting accounts of their experiences as Taliesin apprentices, see Edgar Tafel, *Years with Frank Lloyd Wright: Apprentice to Genius* (New York: Dover, 1985), and Curtis Besinger, *Working with Mr. Wright: What It Was Like* (Cambridge: Cambridge University Press, 1995).

Several research guides are crucial for any scholarly foray. For the most complete bibliography of publications by or about Wright through 1977, see Robert L. Sweeney, *Frank Lloyd Wright: An Annotated Bibliography*, Art and Architecture Bibliographies, no. 5 (Los Angeles: Hennessey & Ingalls, 1978); for the thousands of letters in the FLWA see Alofsin, *Frank Lloyd Wright*; and for photographs and floor plans of all extant as well as demolished Wright buildings, see William Allin Storrer, *The Frank Lloyd Wright Companion* (Chicago: University of Chicago Press, 1993).

Images are identified in **BOLD FACE**; legends and tables, in *ITALICS*.

Although Wright's civic vision went through multiple iterations from 1938 to 1994, just four categories are used in the index. They are (1) Olin Terraces (1938–46), (2) Monona Terrace (1953–65), (3) Monona Basin (1966–74), and (4) Monona Terrace Community and Convention Center (1989–97). The four categories are abbreviated as OT, MT, MB, and MTCCC respectively.

# COLOPHON

## FRANK LLOYD WRIGHT'S MONONA TERRACE

**DESIGNED**

Kathy Schoenick, Hyperion Studios, Inc., Madison, Wisconsin

**SCANNED AND COMPOSED**

Hyperion Studios, Inc., Madison, Wisconsin

**PRINTED**

Straus Printing Company, Madison, Wisconsin

**BOUND**

Reindl Bindery, Glendale, Wisconsin

The University of Wisconsin Press